Strategies for
African Development

Strategies for African Development

Edited by
Robert J. Berg
Jennifer Seymour Whitaker

A Study for the
Committee on African
Development Strategies

Sponsored by the
Council on Foreign Relations and the
Overseas Development Council

UNIVERSITY OF CALIFORNIA PRESS
Berkeley · *Los Angeles* · *London*

University of California Press
Berkeley and Los Angeles, California

University of California Press, Ltd.
London, England

2   3   4   5   6   7   8   9

LIBRARY OF CONGRESS CATALOGING-IN-PUBLICATION DATA

Main entry under title:

Strategies for African development.

Includes index.
1. Africa—Economic policy—Addresses, essays,
lectures. I. Berg, Robert J. II. Whitaker, Jennifer
Seymour, 1938–   . III. Committee on African
Development Strategies (U.S.). IV. Council on Foreign
Relations. V. Overseas Development Council.
HC800.S76   1986   338.96   85-23304
ISBN 0-520-05784-8 (alk. paper)
ISBN 0-520-05782-1 (pbk. : alk. paper)

Contents

Foreword

The work of the Committee on African Development Strategies came to fruition first in its report and recommendations, "Compact for African Development," released in December 1985. In pursuing its work, the Committee commissioned a set of studies, of which most are published in this volume.

Authors were asked to suggest policy and sectoral strategy guidance not only for Africans, but for their economic development collaborators. Most of the papers were discussed in full meetings of the Committee. In each case a dialogue of African and American experts was involved in these discussions.

The authors and a large number of other experts we consulted found a variety of internal and external factors requiring serious attention by African states and the major states interacting with Africa. In fact African authorities are actively re-examining their development options and this creates an almost unparalleled opportunity to enter into discussions on broad, fundamental issues as well as specific internal and external changes necessary for improved development performance.

Both African and external development experts agreed on the need for internal reforms supported by long-term, larger and qualitatively better external aid. The critical issues are the content of the reforms, their timing and whether sufficient political and social sense is brought to the process. Moreover, once better policies are adopted, and indeed much is changing in Africa along recommended lines, there are still major questions of sectoral strategy on which too little discussion has taken place. It is here where many of the authors of this volume were asked to make their main contributions.

There is some hope now that African economies can recover from the famine and economic depression of these past years in a way which can enable a range of sectoral strategies to be pursued. The reforms now taking place in a large number of countries are showing positive effects. Continuing external problems such as market access and relatively high interest rates may prove difficult to systemically correct, even if they are the culprits causing some of Africa's problems. National economic policy and institutional performance are the ingredients in their destiny Africans ought to be best able to affect.

The stark crisis in Africa—the starvation and displacement of peoples—has elicited an impressive nationwide response in America. Yet those who want to help must be concerned not only with ending the current crisis, but with preventing future crises. The challenge is to find a way of translating their concerns and questions into significant future action. We believe a way can be found to help create self-sustaining, prospering societies in Africa, but it will take deep commitment—particularly from Africa, but also from its friends.

Just as African development needs qualitative improvement, so must donors improve the quality and quantity of their aid if the prospects for Africa's development are to be greatly improved. Too often donor aid has served narrow political and commercial ends rather than being rigorously tied to development performance. The effectiveness of aid to Africa also is undercut by poor coordination among the donors and, in this time of rehabilitation of economies, by its being tied to new purchases rather than to fostering existing investments. Given its key position among donors and the influence of its policies in world aid, debt and trade discussions, we see an especially pivotal role for the United States in helping Africa to help itself. Stronger U.S. leadership is required even during this time of domestic budgetary stringency.

The Committee we chair represents a wide spectrum of backgrounds and viewpoints. Its members come from business, universities, media, voluntary organizations and political life. We are grateful for their active participation and informed advice. When we began this inquiry, the members of the Committee saw these issues as important; today, leaders across America are recognizing them as urgent and must also speak out to help effect the changes discussed in this volume.

We are also grateful to the Council on Foreign Relations and the

Overseas Development Council for suggesting the creation of this Committee and for supporting its work, and to Senior Fellows Bob Berg of the Overseas Development Council and Jennifer Seymour Whitaker of the Council on Foreign Relations for their able direction of the Committee.

We particularly appreciate the financial support of the Carnegie Corporation of New York, the Ford Foundation, the Ford Motor Company, the W.K. Kellogg Foundation, the Rockefeller Brothers Fund, and the Rockefeller Foundation. Most of their support was given prior to the general awareness of the crises in Africa, demonstrating the critical and farsighted roles so often played by private foundations.

In the course of our work, we have benefited from the thoughts of officials from African countries, the United States, and the international institutions who served in an ex-officio capacity during the discussion phase of the Committee's work.

The Committee on African Development Strategies neither proposes nor expects panaceas. Our recommendations, appended in this volume, are a set of actions the U.S. and other donors need to take in concert with African actions. The Committee proposed a considerable amount of additional aid because it felt the basis of a compact for African development existed: improved performance in Africa supported by enhanced levels of aid. The costs may seem high now, but the financial, political and human costs of not facing issues squarely will be incalculably greater.

This Committee is aware that setting out its recommendations for public consideration has only initiated the broader, longer term review of Africa's dilemmas and U.S. policy that we see as necessary. It will take hard work by Africans and their friends in the United States and other donor countries to bring about the long-term changes recommended. For our part the Committee will be working with public and private leadership groups across the United States to increase awareness of the need for action on the issues discussed in this volume. Efforts to become better informed on these issues cannot but help. And acting on these issues may well be the key to a more secure Africa and relationships between Africa and the United States built on the confidence of peoples living with dignity and progress.

Lawrence S. Eagleburger
Co-Chairman

Donald F. McHenry
Co-Chairman

January 1986

Acknowledgments

To the many colleagues who generously shared with us ideas and counsel we offer warm thanks. We wish particularly to express our appreciation to Wayne Fredericks, who played a major role in the inception of this project and in bringing the Council on Foreign Relations and the Overseas Development Council together to carry it through; to David Hamburg, whose insights inspired us along the way; and to John Sewell and Paul Kreisberg, who supported and guided our efforts within our two Councils. Val Kallab skillfully guided the Compact to publication. This book itself owes much to Margaret Novicki. It would have taken twice as long to produce—and to read—had it not been for her knowledgeable and adroit editing. The ingenious and thorough coordination and copy-editing of Meg Hardon and the keyboard wizardry of Terry Calway and Alice McLoughlin were also invaluable. Finally, David Kellogg's creative and unstinting marshalling of all our forces was central to producing this book.

R.J.B. and J.S.W.

The Policy Setting: Crisis and Consensus

Jennifer Seymour Whitaker

Over the past several years, Africa's economic crisis has generated a growing body of analysis and prescription on what has gone wrong and what should be done. This rethinking of African development policies has proceeded on parallel tracks in primary donor countries and the World Bank. It has sometimes converged, and sometimes clashed, with the anxious stock-taking of African officials and scholars. As usual, the Westerners are drawing sweeping conclusions about *what Africa ought to do*. And, as usual, the Africans have neither the flexibility nor the wherewithal to either reject the advice totally or follow through on it fully. But the heightened concern and intellectual energy focused on the crisis, both within and outside of Africa, provide at least the initial condition for change.

The Committee on African Development Strategies was created to study what makes sense for Africa's longer-term development, and how U.S. policy can best support that development. The present volume of papers commissioned by the Committee represents a concerted effort by experts on African systems to seek remedies for obviously grave dilemmas. As it evolved, we realized how far a number of our conclusions fit into a kind of consensus that has grown among Western donors and the World Bank since the extremity of Africa's problems became clear early in this decade. From this recognition springs both hope and wariness. Viewed most positively, general agreement brings hope for concerted action. On the other side of the coin, orthodoxy can inhibit our own best efforts and those of Africans. Therefore, we need to consider both the utility of the consensus and its limits.

The outlines of Africa's current economic crisis are well known. While recognizing the perils of generalizing about an area as vast and diverse as sub-Saharan Africa, this analysis will focus on the widely visible problems and patterns of causality that have given rise to current conclusions on policy.

Africa's problems did not start with the oil price hikes of 1973 and 1979. At independence, African governments inherited gerry-built institutions staffed by a thin layer of trained personnel. During the preceding decade, high commodity prices financed accelerated expansion of education and health care systems and creation of infrastructure, easing the transition from colonialism and raising expectations about upward mobility.

During the 1960s, Africa's average per capita growth was steady though modest (at about 1.5%, it lagged behind most of the developing world). But with the oil shocks and the deepening international recession, international terms of trade in Africa's main commodities fluctuated widely and eventually fell decisively; the prices of African minerals and agricultural commodities deteriorated while oil prices rose sevenfold, grain rose fivefold and manufactures rose proportionately to Western inflation. In addition, in the early seventies and then in the eighties, drought desiccated first the Sahel regions of Western and Central Africa and then an arc of countries from West Africa to the Horn of Africa and into southern Africa. Burgeoning population growth, a result of successful development programs, further strained land resources while increasing urban food needs.

The 1973 jump in oil prices created a series of external and environmental shocks that, in combination with poor domestic economic management, brought stagnation or decline in the growth of per capita national income—particularly in agricultural productivity—in many African countries. Political instability also exacerbated weaknesses in economic institutions.

From 1970 onward, per capita agricultural production for the continent as a whole fell about one percent a year. African shares in the international trade of many agricultural and mineral exports—affecting more than half of Africa's main commodities exports—declined. At the same time, food imports rose from previously low levels to a point where one in three Africans is dependent on imported food. The cumulative effect of rising import costs and falling export revenues led to growing balance of payments deficits, amounting to $7.9 billion in 1984.

Unable or unwilling for both political and economic reasons to cut expenditures as fast as revenues were falling, governments resorted to deficit financing. In these circumstances, it is not surprising that Africa's debt increased by an average 22 percent a year from 1973 to 1983, greatly exceeding the growth of output or exports. As total debt rose, the level of net capital inflows to low-income Africa, from public and private sources, dropped sharply—by 45 percent between 1980 and 1983. By the end of 1986, payments required to service African debts are projected to equal two-thirds of all aid receipts.

In addition to the rising debt service ratios, Africa's gross foreign exchange reserves have fallen overall to the equivalent of only four to five weeks of imports, and many countries are in arrears on current obligations. In countries that cannot pay their bills, current productive capacity is being wasted and continues to deteriorate.

Since the late 1970s, policymakers and scholars have been debating the relative importance of external and internal causes of Africa's problems, notably in the World Bank's *Accelerated Development in Sub-Saharan Africa*[1] (produced by a team led by Elliot Berg and popularly known as the "Berg Report"), with its focus on shortcomings of African economic policies, and the Organization of African Unity's *Lagos Plan of Action*,[2] with its emphasis on the adverse effects of international trends on African development. The debate cannot be entirely resolved; the skeins of causality are, finally, impossible to clearly disentangle. On one hand, it seems clear that the macroeconomic policies of African governments, which discouraged exports, were a primary cause of Africa's declining trade shares. On the other hand, government policies responded to crises engendered by adverse external trends. In addition, declining maintenance of infrastructures and cutbacks in essential government services—at least in part the result of the foreign exchange shortfalls—eroded effective implementation of policy. All of these unremittingly negative indicators accelerated the flight of capital from Africa.

In this volume, Stephen Lewis enters the debate most directly. He points (in Chapter 17) to evidence on both sides of the debate, asserting that economic performance in Africa could have been better—by a couple of percentage points a year—if either the external environment had been more helpful or African governments had implemented better policies. Most of the authors in this book, however,

focus on internal performance—both policy and institutional effectiveness. Within this context, data showing the positive effects of
specific policies—particularly on exchange rates and import-export
balances[3]—offer modest grounds for optimism. National economic
policy and institutional performance are ingredients in their economic destiny that Africans ought to be best able to affect.

WHAT WENT WRONG

As noted above, Africa sustained major external shocks in the
1970s and early 1980s. However, it is also clear that African economic
and political behavior played a major role in the continent's economic
decline. As Crawford Young argues in Chapter 1, in many instances
African leaders inherited an authoritarian state model, with a tradition of strong government control over the economy. As popular
expectations of modern economic life rose and governments had to
draw on state resources to secure political control, demands on state
economic resources burgeoned.

From the time of independence, government policies in many
countries eroded incentives for economic growth, and particularly for
agricultural production. With declining per capita growth in agriculture, after two-and-a-half decades much of Africa still relies almost
entirely on agriculture for its export income, and four-fifths of its
people depend on farming for their livelihood. For Africa's increasingly dependent economies, the most promising area for import substitution now is in food crops. Yet, on average, governments have
invested a meager five percent of annual expenditures in agriculture,
have held down agricultural prices and distorted markets to the disadvantage of farmers. Moreover, as Jane Guyer explains in Chapter
14, government extension, credit, and technical assistance programs
have largely bypassed the women farmers who grow some 70 percent
of the continent's food.

Both Africa's loss of trade share and the dramatic fall in rates of
return on investment within most African countries—to about half of
that in developing countries as a whole—point to poor economic
management. African governments have pursued a wide variety of
policies, but some generally counterproductive patterns have become discernible. Low prices to farmers—to raise government revenues on export crops and keep down food prices to urban consumers;
severely overvalued exchange rates; and cumbersome trade regimes

favoring import substitution and luxury consumption were the main culprits.

These policies—exchange rates, tariff and tax structures, import control systems and macroeconomic policies affecting the balance of payments—are integrally related to international trade. And for Africa's small, open economies they create the context for domestic productivity.

Too often exchange rates, tariff structures and credit allocations have favored import substituting industrialization over agriculture, and urban over rural well-being. Low food prices and artificially high values of national currencies favored imports of components for manufacturing, as well as food and even luxury goods. Perhaps most fundamental, inexperienced and sometimes venal leadership lacked the ability to analyze and change policies, and few African governments succeeded in maintaining balances between resource inflows and expenditures from fat times to lean ones.

POLITICAL INSTABILITY

In many countries, political instability has also severely inhibited economic development. Expressing the relationship between political and economic development in terms of its least common denominator, political stability is a necessary—though not sufficient—condition for economic progress. On the most basic level, insecurity about the future inhibits investment in African economies—both by citizens and foreigners. Looking at the African countries which have done comparatively well at building relatively more solid bases for growth—including Ivory Coast, Cameroon, Botswana, Malawi, and Kenya—they have almost without exception enjoyed strong continuous leadership, sometimes incorporating peaceful transfers of power.

Striking negative examples, on the other hand, include Ghana and Uganda, where, in countries blessed by rich human and material resources, continuous political upheaval has left infrastructures in ruins and caused increasing numbers of people to take refuge in the subsistence and "informal" sectors, largely outside government regulation. Again, the countries waging long continuing conflicts with their neighbors or with internal insurgents—including Chad, Ethiopia, Sudan, Somalia, Angola and Mozambique[4]—have heavily mortgaged their economic growth and in almost every case are among the chief victims of devastating famine. Nigeria's civil war also left a legacy of high societal costs. Obviously, expenditures on arms and armies drain scarce resources and war destroys infrastructures basic to production, marketing, and distribution.

Most African countries today are not fighting with their neighbors or with organized insurgent movements, but have been prey, since independence, to abrupt regime changes, usually via military coup. Only twelve countries in sub-Saharan Africa have not succumbed to military coups and at least half the countries of Africa today live under military rule. The consequences of military rule for development have been often, and inconclusively, debated.[5] In fact, the civil servants who run the economy under a military government are usually the same people who would do so in a civilian government. Moreover, the same economic and political motives—for growth, on the one hand; and for personal gain, patronage, urban order, revenue extraction, on the other, appear to drive military and civilian leaders alike. Ultimately, therefore, it has proved difficult to measure differences in performance. What has declined under the repressive regimes often characteristic of military rule is the ability to offer alternatives, to debate the necessity for change in policies.

In fact, regime weakness and its corollary—the use of state economic resources to bolster incumbent governments—have profoundly affected economic performance in most African countries.[6] Rational calculations about economic policy are often based on political rather than economic goals.[7] The more extensive the state's involvement in the economy, the more emoluments will be available to insure loyalty and reward constituents. Apart from draining national resources, constituency building through patronage fosters a variety of economic distortions.

Job creation through expanding bureaucracies is the most obvious distortion. This action has proven highly costly. First of all, the burgeoning state payrolls themselves drain resources: in the 1980s, government consumption has taken a higher percent of GDP in contemporary Africa than in all other developing regions save the Middle East and North Africa. African governments, moreover, spend an unusually large portion of recurrent costs simply covering wages and salaries of their employees: about thirty percent in the 1974–80 period, compared to roughly twenty percent in the Latin American/

Caribbean Region and about fifteen percent in Asia and the Middle East.[8]

Second, state-run corporations often have tended to regard profit as secondary to other non-economic goals—including employment creation—and their balance sheets have reflected this. Further, the channelling of virtually all larger investments through government, and complex licensing and allocation of foreign exchange often create rewards for loyal allies and windfalls for the government officials who administer them. Regulating international commerce and investment becomes a major source of revenue for individual bureaucrats as well as for the state itself.

ETHNICITY

Ethnicity also profoundly affects economic performance. Clearly, ethnic ties often constitute a major element in constituency-building and patronage relationships in national politics. But ethnic support networks starting at the village level also fundamentally shape economic decision making. As Goran Hyden argues in Chapter 2, ethnic and community links, often strongly held between rural and urban areas, lead to investment patterns aimed at diversifying and sharing risks, often by solidifying group ties.[9] What this means is: (1) profits and savings are often invested in enterprises aimed at securing ethnic links and security but unlikely to earn a *monetary* profit, such as village real estate, education and sustenance of kinfolk, installation of group members in high places, cultivation of "big men"; (2) whatever the stated aim of African businessmen, their enterprises are likely to respond first of all to communal pressures—principally job creation—and only secondarily to profits and growth.

Most important, ethnic ties supersede national allegiance for many, perhaps most, Africans. Thus the state's resources are not seen primarily as the common property of all citizens, but rather as fair game for ethnic groups building their own bases of support. The state is, in fact, regarded as the primary source of available resources. In these circumstances, public attitudes about government officials' accountability for national monies become somewhat ambivalent. Insofar as they think of themselves as citizens of a nation-state, everyone is opposed to corruption, but on the deeper level where they identify with particular groups, they do not question the legitimacy of taking their share. Rather than worrying about how the state has encroached on the private sector, one African scholar declared ironically that the state *is* often, in fact, a private fiefdom whose resources belong to a few powerful individuals rather than the citizenry as a whole.[10]

In sum, meager resources, scarce qualified manpower, weak governance and confused institutional goals have left African governments peculiarly unprepared to run command economies where virtually all decisions and allocations are made by government officials. Most African states have been living beyond their means, both in failing to push the exports necessary to finance growth, and in building state structures whose size has grown in inverse proportion to their effectiveness in fostering economic productivity.

THE ROLE OF DONORS

Looking at the record of donor aid over the last several decades, it is clear that development assistance has both helped and hindered African development. Donor programs have made important contributions in infrastructure, but as Timberlake and Guyer show (and Berg summarizes more comprehensively) donors have often been insensitive to fundamental environmental and social questions. Fluctuating fashions in aid levels and rationales—from "take-off," through integrated rural development, through basic human needs, to privatization—have sent conflicting signals from donors to recipients and increased problems in carrying out effective development. Complex donor interventions, in societies where the effects of external actions are not well understood, have often proved burdensome to weak African institutions.

Non-developmental objectives have all too often dominated donor priorities, with security and political interests skewing U.S. resource allocations in particular. Turf battles among donors and the tying of aid to exports also worked to distort assistance programs. Coordination among donors, or by African governments, has been poor. In its absence, proliferating and overlapping projects have drained the administrative energies of African officials and raised recurrent costs. Aid has in fact sometimes provided a negative model for African governments in emphasizing planning and building, without maintenance and follow-through. For the United States, the year-by-year

Congressional appropriations process has exacerbated endemic difficulties with longer-term planning.

THE CONSENSUS

The broad outlines of this analysis, accepted almost without exception by the contributors to this volume, lead to a set of conclusions on policy reform, which are also widely shared, both within this volume and among Western policymakers and scholars. The following, in summary, express the consensus:

First, agriculture is central: as the main present base for productivity in all African countries except the mineral exporters, and the main source of income for most people in all countries, it must receive priority attention and investment from both African governments and donors.

Second, policy changes within Africa are key to building African agriculture and diversifying Africa's productive base. Specifically, African governments should eliminate the bias toward import dependence inherent in past strategies of import substituting industrialization.

Third, effective African utilization of scarce available resources will be fostered by the reduction of excessive state controls which discourage private economic initiatives, and the streamlining of government bureaucracies.

Finally, donors should use the leverage inherent in development assistance to work with African recipients toward the achievement of appropriate reforms. This means, paradoxically, that donors must now use increasing African dependence to press African governments to take more responsibility—to become more accountable for both aid and national resources. Non-project aid, involving more direct transfers of financial resources and fewer schemes for complex new systems or institutions requiring ongoing maintenance expenditures, can provide needed leverage and avoid additional burdens on weak African governments.

Anyone familiar with the history of development assistance over the past 20 years must regard the emergence of a new consensus with some skepticism. How did the analysis evolve and who disagrees? How enduring is the strategy likely to be? Will the present reaction against strongly state-centered economic investment be followed by an equally strong swing back in the other direction? How can those who support the basic policy avoid the overcorrection that will produce its own reaction?

DEBATE ON POLICY

The first major component of the current consensus came in 1981 with the Berg Report. Commissioned at the request of the World Bank's African Directors, the study generated considerable debate, both within Africa and among Africanists. Elliott Berg laid out therein the now standard critique of African policy, emphasizing that the primary cause of Africa's malaise lay in African countries' failure to provide incentives for the agricultural exports which bring in the bulk of their earnings. He also asserted the need for loosening government controls and fostering a greater role for the African private sector.

The Report's critics took issue with Berg and the Bank on a number of issues. Some, like Gerald Helleiner, argued the importance of external shocks to Africa's plight and sought to demonstrate that the crucial variable in adjustment was maintaining imports.[11] Others, including, notably, a group of scholars at the University of Sussex's Institute of Development Studies (IDS), questioned the feasibility of Berg's prescriptions. Generally known for their advocacy of a strong state role in the economy, the Sussex scholars questioned particularly the importance of market forces or "getting the prices right" for agricultural products. They also pointed out that increasing output could further erode commodity prices. For their part, African commentators criticized the report's assumption that African countries should continue their excessive reliance on an export-led strategy. They also seized on the report's neglect of food production in the face of Africa's increasing dependence on imported food.

Three years later, the subsequent World Bank report on Africa: *Toward Sustained Development: A Joint Program of Action For Sub-Saharan Africa*[12] reiterated the need for policy reform but also took account of the reactions to Berg. It laid out a more nuanced strategy, with due regard for the difficulties involved in implementation and a more downbeat view of African prospects.

From the early 1980s, U.S. AID was also beginning to advocate "policy dialogue." This was, in effect, both a push for reform and an assertion of donor leverage over recipients' use of resources. After the Americans had been reiterating this theme for several years, the European Community more timidly initiated its own negotiation on the relationship between aid and performance, in its third five-year agreement on aid and trade with African, Pacific and Caribbean countries, at Lomé. While the Americans and Europeans put varying emphases on the need to strengthen the African private sector, they agreed on the importance of macroeconomic policy in stimulating productivity.

Significantly, many of the Berg Report's critics agree on the need for "structural adjustment" of African economies and other elements of the World Bank/U.S. prescription. At the same time, however, they take issue with aspects of the "privatization" analysis which they see as sweeping and inaccurate. In an important compilation of European views published in the fall of 1985, leading IDS scholars and others continued to point out the hazards in applying macroeconomic panaceas in Africa.[13] Here and elsewhere[14] they expressed continuing concern about the effects of increasing competition on the welfare of weaker members of society and of open markets in increasing the dependency of economies already highly vulnerable to forces beyond their control. They generally declined to defend the state's role in African economic development with any zeal, however, and in many instances agreed on the need for policy reform.

The main African counterpart to these Western intellectual trends, the Lagos Plan, was published a year before the Berg Report. In the Plan, African leaders proposed a development strategy emphasizing national self-reliance to be fostered through regional linkages. While acknowledging economic mismanagement, they placed most of the onus for declining African performance on the hostile external environment. Reiterating the need for industrialization, they also emphasized the importance of agriculture but principally in terms of food self-sufficiency.

Five years later, African and Western views appear somewhat closer. The ambitious goals of the Lagos Plan have been deeply shadowed by harsh present prospects. At the 1985 OAU summit, Africa's leaders declared that agriculture is the major economic problem facing the continent today, and that burgeoning populations and environmental deterioration threaten all development gains. They also acknowledged that solving Africa's economic problems largely depends upon African performance. At least on the level of ideas, many Africans are considering reforms that would run counter to the centralized economic controls they inherited at independence and have worked to expand. More than 15 African countries have instituted stabilization programs geared to IMF and donor recommendations. In the crisis, African leaders are casting about—often Westward—for new solutions.

IMPLEMENTING POLICY REFORM

In implementation, the current consensus is no more likely to provide easily applied answers than previous attempts to design wholesale solutions. Nonetheless, the converging analyses of what has happened in Africa since the early sixties and what resources may realistically be available to re-start African economies are likely to provide a strong continuing impetus for policy reform.

Without reiterating the analysis, it is clear that government policies—especially on agriculture—offer much room for improvement. But policy dialogue means different things to different people, and the great variations in African policy suggest the need for quite different prescriptions to be undertaken by African governments within their various contexts. Not surprisingly, advocates of conditionality vary widely in their approaches.

Until recently the IMF based its remedies for African debt on fairly strict application of neo-classical nostrums—particularly devaluation and elimination of consumption subsidies. On privatization, some analysts, including influential officials within the current U.S. Administration, advocate divestiture of government-run enterprises (widely known as parastatals) to private purchasers. Others, including Benno Ndulu and David Leonard in this volume, support early devolution of the economic activities which may be best handled privately—including transport and marketing—so that the state can perform its essential tasks more efficiently. Still others advocate a cautious approach to the largely inchoate African private sector (composed mostly of subsistence farmers and mini-enterprises), but push for macroeconomic policies favoring exports. Stephen Lewis, while strongly advocating price and exchange rate adjustment to correspond to international levels, carefully qualifies his call for liberalized trade, pointing out that some protection is necessary if African aims of diversifying production and exports are to be achieved. Jane Guyer cautions that decontrol of some agricultural prices could cut production if cheap imports are not restricted.

On agriculture, most of the contributors to this volume join a broad consensus advocating support for smallholder farming as Africa's only viable agricultural basepoint for development. Bruce Johnston and others concur on the need to shift the bias in exchange and interest rate policies as well as investment—where these favor import-substituting industry (and capital-intensive farming)—to benefit small farmers. Jane Guyer points out that decontrol of markets will not help small farmers unless institutionalized discrimination against them, affecting, for example, market access, market taxes, police controls, vehicle taxation, is addressed.

David Leonard argues that agriculture in Africa is at a crossroad as land limits are being reached in a number of countries, while sharp population growth is predicted everywhere. In his view, this will necessitate transformation from extensive production to a more intensive system and far more attention to rural institutions capable of stimulating and servicing science-based agriculture. Given the weaknesses of central government management, this leads him to support the transfer of many of these services into private or governmentally decentralized hands.

Discussing potential industrial development, on the other hand, Helmboldt et al. (in Chapter 12), Liedholm and Mead (in Chapter 11), and Hawkins (in Chapter 10) also emphasize that industry must build on agricultural expansion. Helmboldt, et al., argue as well that both African and foreign private investors can accommodate regulations in an environment in which regulations are fairly and predictably enforced. Reviewing the trade policies of a number of states, Hawkins analyzes the drawbacks of industrialization based on import substitution, but like the other authors, recognizes that some infant industry protection will be necessary for the export- and resource-led industrialization which is Africa's best bet for development of manufacturing. Liedholm and Mead point to the vitality of enterprises within the "informal, non-agricultural sector," which lies largely outside government purview, and show how it has been systematically discriminated against in access to credit and foreign exchange. They endorse more equal treatment and generally advocate reduced government regulation as a sine qua non for the emergence of entrepreneurship.

EXTERNAL TRENDS

In all its variations, the drive for policy reform is likely to endure because, simply speaking, there are few credible alternatives in view.

In the short and medium term, Africa's crisis is unlikely to be ameliorated by a significant improvement in external factors. Terms of trade for the continent's main commodities are not projected to change for the better during this decade. And although improved patterns of rainfall obviously will increase crop production in many instances, burgeoning populations and the associated continuing deterioration of the natural resource base will continue to increase pressures on arable land. Further, while concerted international efforts to relieve Africa's debt burden will release resources needed for development, without significant changes in present trends aid levels cannot be expected to rise sufficiently to maintain external resource inflows at the level of the seventies. For the past decade AID has financed about 40 percent of Africa's imports and nearly half its gross domestic investment. However, from 1980–84 external aid to Africa declined in absolute terms from $8.5 to $6.7 billion. In all these areas, then, it is evident that the rehabilitation and regeneration of African economies cannot depend upon improvements in the international environment.

HOW DURABLE THE CONSENSUS

This conclusion has been very little disputed. Its corollary, that economic progress in Africa must be based on far-reaching internal reforms and much more cost-effective use of resources by both Africans and donors, is more controversial. Nonetheless, it is difficult to evade the recognition that policy reform and institutional change constitute the main factors within human control to foster growth in Africa. Looking at institutions, it is particularly risky for donors to draw up blueprints for systems that Africans must build and run. Yet, it is clear enough that whatever the balance between state and private control, enterprises charged with productive use of African resources must emphasize the bottom line: they simply do not have the wherewithal to ignore profit and loss calculations.

Surveying African countries individually, it is apparent that those which have supported smallholder agriculture, like Zimbabwe, Malawi, Kenya and the Ivory Coast, and tried to keep imports generally in line with export revenues have done better than others. Minerals exporters such as Botswana and Cameroon have adjusted particularly well to external shocks by adroit fiscal management, prudently husbanding export revenues to compensate for shortfalls in diamond and oil prices as well as recurrent drought. Moreover, reforms now being undertaken in a number of countries have shown some positive results.

Looking at the effect of policy changes on overall performance, some proponents of privatization argue, at least tentatively, that separating economic institutions from the state could mitigate some negative effects inherent in weak government accountability. First of all, occasions for corruption would be reduced as state controls over allocation of economic opportunities diminished. And second, the profit motive might give concern for efficiency some edge over patronage in the management of enterprises.

Turning to donor policies, the environment of international and African resource scarcity also creates a context powerfully supportive of policy reform. For reasons of domestic politics as well as development objectives, donors must use assistance as effectively as possible to support improvements in African economic performance. This is not a new idea. But the current emphasis on "conditionality," on linking aid and policy reforms, represents a marked difference in the degree if not the kind of donor commitment to reform and results. In the African context, the importance of conditionality for donors is not likely to disappear with next year's aid program. Whether it involves policy reform, institutional management, high standards of accountability and policing of corruption, getting the desired effect from "policy dialogue" between donors and recipients will be a long-term process. But the present and enhanced commitment can only be justified if donor countries feel that their aid has helped spur successful African performance.

REALISM ABOUT POLICY REFORM

Because it will take a long time, realism about what is involved in implementing policy reform is imperative. In itself, the consensus on policy reform and dialogue can take us only so far. For the immediate and longer-term period, several central problems must also be faced. First, the squeeze on African imports and capital investment will decrease the flexibility of African governments. As Chandra Hardy shows clearly in Chapter 16, Africa's debt, increasing at 24 per cent per annum between 1973 and 1984, threatens to siphon off a major share of export revenues and mortgage all future investable resources. While the debt grew (by $21 billion between 1979 and 1983), the level of net inflows to Africa increased by only $1 billion, and between 1980 and 1983 net capital inflows to Africa declined markedly—with commitments from private sources falling from $1.5 billion to $137 million and official commitments dropping by 31 percent. Although, as Carl Eicher argues (in Chapter 9), African economies have often failed to absorb aid flows productively, it is also evident, as Helleiner posits, that the African countries most successful in adjusting to international economic crises have been those with sufficient resources to maintain needed levels of imports. During a transitional period, significant debt relief will be required to get African economies moving again.

Secondly, African countries must strengthen their physical, technical, institutional and human infrastructures significantly before their efforts to increase productivity can be expected to bear abundant fruit. As Eicher points out, Africa lags far behind Asia and Latin America in trained scientific and managerial manpower. Although some experts see Africa's technical lag as a failure to use existing technologies, Eicher and Dunstan Spencer (in Chapter 8) argue that the existing technical stock cannot provide the basis for the needed surge in agricultural productivity. Eicher estimates that it will take about fifteen to twenty years to develop technical inputs needed to accelerate agricultural productivity. Spencer underlines the need to strengthen the systems that provide farming technologies within African countries. At the same time, deteriorating and inadequate roads as well as marketing and storage facilities must be improved to increase the security of African farmers who will be taking risks on new technologies, and to facilitate the entry of private entrepreneurs into the marketing and transport business.

Third, many of our authors emphasize what is probably the most serious ongoing problem threatening Africa's future economic viability: population growth. As Fred Sai shows in Chapter 5, the size of Africa's population threatens to double within ten years. In many countries this means that traditional methods of expanding agriculture through the cultivation of surplus lands are no longer possible. Thus, the exploding populations place significant pressures on Africa's ecology, leading to deterioration and erosion of fragile soils and the denuding of forest areas.

In addition, continued urbanization has outpaced the capacity of governments to provide a bare minimum of social services in the cities. Moreover, as David Court and Kabiru Kinyanjui show in

Chapter 13, education systems energetically built up since independence are increasingly overloaded, with already evident declines in quality, and probable decreases in overall proportions of educated manpower. As Kenneth King argues in Chapter 15, policy issues affecting manpower and training urgently need to be reformulated. Specific and concerted attention to both education and health are needed, not only to build the African work force but to create a base for dealing with fundamental ecological problems. In their turn, population and environment will profoundly affect policy and institutional reforms.

Both Lloyd Timberlake's analysis of environmental problems (in Chapter 4) and Fred Sai's on population bring home again the need for African governments to plan with donors for the long term. Results of environmental programs are unlikely to be visible in three-to-five year time frames, and indeed in many instances unlikely to materialize at all unless effort is sustained for a much longer period of time.

In addition, progress particularly on population but also on environmental problems seems to entail an emphasis on equity and local participation which figures infrequently in current policy dialogues.[15] Beyond the generally observed demographic effects of improvements in social welfare, dealing with both population and environmental problems requires people at the village level be able to see how their own interests are served by family planning and conservation of natural resources. It also requires that they help to shape programs affecting them.

Fourth, donors must assess the feasibility of specific policy reforms with African governments within the political contexts of their countries. Because the consolidation of power often depends on direct government control of economic benefits, austerity and structural adjustment programs that threaten the emoluments of elites or the cost of living of city dwellers may seriously undermine regimes. Liberia's 1979 rice riots, which led eventually to the overthrow of the Tolbert regime, and the 1985 coup in the Sudan were triggered by highly resented government attempts to "get the prices right." In seeking reforms, then, the IMF, the World Bank, and bilateral donors must proceed with a sensitive concern for the political realities affecting the African governments involved.

Further, as David Leonard suggests in Chapter 7, both donors and African governments should seek alternative economic payoffs for

African constituents that will not obstruct productivity as subsidies and patronage have done. For example, Leonard proposes that road and infrastructure building projects employing seasonal labor represent a form of distributable economic goods that avoids the permanent drain on government revenues inherent in expanding employment in government bureaucracies.

Fifth, policy reform will impinge on current methods of taxation and thus on revenues available to finance government payrolls and programs. Cutting duties and lowering government's share of agricultural prices may seriously deplete domestically generated government resources in the absence of income or sales tax systems. When government salaries fall in real terms, incentives for job performance also drop and incentives for corruption increase. Thus donors, with African governments, will have to take account of financial trade-offs involved in reforms.

Sixth, African efforts to increase trade and decrease dependence will ultimately hinge, in great part, on the development of intra-African trade links and, eventually, a continental market. In the past, donors have been tempted to move ahead of Africans in promoting regionalism, and experiments with regional economic institutions within Africa have shown little success. Reducing interstate barriers will require vision and political courage on the part of African leaders that will probably remain in short supply while the economic crisis continues. Although the economic viability of the continent over the long term demands regional efforts, heavy national agendas will come first.

Donors have taken little interest in regional schemes since the demise of the East African community. They can now, however, encourage intra-African links, by aid to communications and transport infrastructures. As Stephen Lewis suggests, they can also provide credits to assist with financing African exports to other parts of the continent and support currency clearing arrangements.

In sum, the road to African development cannot be seen as a straightforward drive to policy reform. The map will inevitably be much more complicated: African governments (supported by donors) must enable their people to better plan family size, arrest the corresponding erosion of the environment, and strengthen the productive sinews of their societies while simultaneously instituting more rational macroeconomic policies. Only with due attention to the other problems may the macroeconomic policies be expected to work.

Correspondingly, only with workable macroeconomic policies can African states expect to generate revenues to sustain domestic investment in the needed infrastructures and improve the quality of people's lives. Finally, only by strengthening regional links will Africa begin to experience the stimulus to productivity of a large continental market.

IMPLICATIONS FOR DEVELOPMENT ASSISTANCE

The Committee on African Development Strategies' Report (Appendix II) reiterates the need to incorporate longer term development objectives into the immediate focus on survival and then on rehabilitation. Given the need to move forward on several fronts simultaneously, the transition to self-reliant growth in Africa will take a considerable amount of time, leadership, and resources. If amassing the technical inputs necessary to spur African agriculture will take at least 15 years, a generation will be needed to educate the scientists, technicians, and managers who must staff modernizing African economies. At best, the most difficult transition—changing attitudes about fertility, including the relationship between childbearing and economic well-being—will take at least that long.

During this time, pushing through these changes will require an unparalleled order of effort and commitment from both African government leaders and donors, and both African and Western private sectors. It is likely that while some African countries will produce the leader or leaders able to mobilize the polity in an all-out effort, others will not. Thus, the performance of African countries will be increasingly differentiated according to the human resources at the top and in other levels of society.

For their part, donors must stand ready to adjust their course in response to perceived results within Africa, adopting what Robert J. Berg, in Chapter 18, calls the "learning model approach." This implies a highly flexible form of conditionality, involving an attentive policy dialogue and a willingness to commit aid on the basis of development performance. As the process continues, donors will have to differentiate in order to encourage success, measured variously in: upping productivity, building infrastructure, curbing population growth, fostering private initiatives.

What does all this imply for donor planning, regarding levels of resources and kinds of assistance? In the view of the Committee, immediate relief requirements—regarding debt and food aid increases in response to population growth—will place significant demands on Western coffers over the next one to two decades. If African states are to rehabilitate and build their infrastructures, significant new monies must also be available. For the Committee, this implies a need for a doubling of total bilateral and multilateral aid to Africa to a level of $16 to $20 billion a year over the rest of this century, including a tripling of U.S. aid to Africa. Building and maintaining support for aid at these levels is, realistically, a very tall order, calling for reallocations within existing programs and raising of new resources. However, attaining the desired results without it is not a realistic prospect.

Well-nigh universal agreement exists on the need to minimize distortions caused by aid, and particularly to counteract the debilitating effects of dependency. Both for this reason and because of Africa's acute balance-of-payments crisis, most of our authors concur on the desirability of non-project aid financing, in some cases involving balance-of-payments support and in others direct aid to particular sectors. In his analysis of aid programs over the past several decades (in Chapter 18), Berg agrees on the current imperative for direct resource transfers, but argues that project aid is particularly required for the transfer of technical and managerial knowledge and for larger capital project activities needed to lay a base for long term growth. And for this a variety of reforms are necessary to improve the quality of their programs.

Other authors also differ on the question of recurrent costs, with Eicher vehemently disparaging support for ongoing costs while others, led by Berg, defend the assumption of costs generated by assistance programs. Surely a symptom of dependence, donor responsibility for some recurrent costs is justified in the current crisis as the only way of protecting expensive—and necessary—investment. On the other hand, cutting way back on separate projects and initiating them in coordination with African governments should reduce problems of maintenance and recurrent costs.

Again, in all of this, the aim will be to reduce distortions generated by donor interventions, and support African institution building that donors see as potentially productive. Direct financial assistance conditioned on policy or institutional goals now seems to offer the most leverage and thus the most promise.

However, certain donor interventions appear essential for the growth of African technical capabilities. For the time being, research on plant varieties and farming systems within Africa require a great many Western scientists. Almost inevitably, a heavy research effort will involve a number of quasi-Western enclaves within African systems. Eventually, these must and will be staffed by Africans, but the research effort cannot wait until they are. With skill, the progressive integration into African systems that Dunstan Spencer calls for in Chapter 8 will enable the technical inputs to be integrated into African farming.

Each of these factors clearly will affect the record on policy reform in Africa. With the need to work on so many fronts simultaneously, the going will not be easy. If the commitment to policy reform falters, however, good alternatives may be hard to find. As has been argued, in a time of resource scarcity this set of policies offers the best hope and leverage for better use of those resources. Moreover, within Western countries, it is difficult to visualize alternative strategies which might be embraced *with enthusiasm* by publics being called upon for significant development assistance allocations. The release of private initiative offers an ideal that is congruent with the major donors' ideologies. Aid aimed at improving central government control over African economies—or at direct donor social engineering—does not. Thus it is to be hoped that African governments and donors will be able to stay—and skillfully tack—along the course now being set. The specifics may sound quite different ten and twenty years hence, but an unwavering commitment by both Africans and donors to effective investment of available resources will continue to be the sine qua non for a productive African future.

NOTES

1. World Bank, *Accelerated Development in Sub-Saharan Africa: An Agenda for Action* (Washington, D.C.: The World Bank, 1981).

2. Organization of African Unity, *Lagos Plan of Action for the Economic Development of Africa, 1980–2000* (Addis Ababa: OAU, 1980).

3. David Wheeler, "Sources of Stagnation in Sub-Saharan Africa," *World Development* 12 (1): 1–23 (1984).

4. Like the rest of South Africa's neighbors, Angola and Mozambique will be vulnerable to Pretoria's attempts to destabilize their governments and interdict ANC activity until the end of the apartheid system.

5. See Henry Bienen, *Armies and Parties in Africa* (New York: Africana

Publishing, 1978); also R. D. McKinlay and A. S. Cohan, "A Comparative Analysis of Political and Economic Performance of Military and Civilian Regimes," *Comparative Politics* 8 (1) (October 1975).

6. For a classic account of African styles of governance, see Robert H. Jackson and Carl G. Rosberg, *Personal Rule in Black Africa: Prince, Autocrat, Prophet, Tyrant* (Berkeley: University of California Press, 1982).

7. For an impressively full account of the interplay between political and economic decision making, see Robert H. Bates, *Markets and States in Tropical Africa: The Political Basis of Agricultural Policies* (Berkeley: University of California Press, 1981).

8. David Abernethy, "Bureaucratic Growth and Economic Stagnation in Sub-Saharan Africa." Paper presented at the American Political Science Association meetings, September 1984.

9. For an excellent account of how ethnic and family relationships among a group of Nigerian Yorubas affect economic choices, see Sara S. Berry, *Fathers Work for Their Sons* (Berkeley: University of California Press, 1985).

10. Ali Mazrui at the October 23, 1984 meeting of the Committee on African Development Strategies, Washington, D.C.

11. G.K. Helleiner, "Outward Orientation, Import Instability and African Economic Growth: An Empirical Investigation." Paper prepared for the Paul Streeten Festschrift, to be edited by Sanjaya Lall and Frances Stewart, April 1984.

12. World Bank, *Toward Sustained Development in Sub-Saharan Africa: A Joint Program of Action* (Washington, D.C.: 1984).

13. The World Bank, Tore Rose, ed., *Crisis and Recovery in Sub-Saharan Africa* (Paris: OECD, 1985).

14. See, for example, Manfred Beinefield, "The Lessons of Africa's Industrial 'Failure'," *IDS Bulletin* 16 (3) (1985): 69–87 (Sussex: Institute of Development Studies).

15. Edward Green, "U.S. Population Policies, Development and The Rural Poor of Africa," *Journal of Modern African Studies* 20 (1) (1982), p. 55.

PART I

MANAGING AFRICAN ECONOMIES

CHAPTER ONE

Africa's Colonial Legacy

Crawford Young

Impasse, crisis, decline—a grim vocabulary has come to dominate discourse on African development. From the hope and optimism that prevailed in the 1960s to the unease and apprehension of the late 1970s, the mood in the 1980s has shifted to acute anxieties and forebodings. The annual reviews of African affairs published by *Foreign Affairs* have captured this shift—an optimistic tone still pervades the 1980 summary, written by Andrew Young, but by 1982, John de St. Jorre speaks of a "loss of confidence," and in 1983, Jennifer Whitaker writes of a struggle for survival.[1]

The impasse in the development process evident today is inextricably linked to a crisis of the state. A state in disarray cannot perform the firm tutelary role which was central to the major developmental success stories of the late 1970s—the newly industrializing countries (NICs)—a category notably missing in Africa. In turn, deteriorating economies deny states the resources to carry out such missions, intensifying pressures toward further decline.

On the developmental side, the dismal litany is sufficiently familiar to require little elaboration. However, it is striking that much of the debate in developmental circles assumes that Africa's crisis has shallow historical roots, using the 1970s as the chronological baseline. A deeper historical perspective is indispensable for grasping both the political and economic dimensions of the present crisis.

The character of the contemporary African state has been determined by its colonial origins. The colonial state legacy in turn has been altered in crucial and often negative ways since political independence was achieved. While all trends in contemporary Africa cannot be simply laid at the door of the former colonizers, neither has the development crisis arisen simply from flaws in the post-colonial African ruling class. Rather, some patterns of state behavior and structure that arose out of the character of the colonial state and the ways in which the post-colonial state adapted its colonial legacy contribute toward an understanding of the dimensions of the present crisis.

DEFINITION OF THE STATE

Classical political theory defines the state[2] in terms of territoriality, sovereignty, institutions of rule, nationality, and law. Contemporary schools of analysis view the state in terms of the forces and interests it is presumed to serve: For liberal pluralists, these are competing interest groups; for Marxists, the ruling class; and for dependency theorists, the "international capitalist system." In this analysis, the state is viewed as an autonomous actor in the political and economic realms, and the prime determinants of state behavior can be summarized as hegemony, security, autonomy, legitimation, and revenue. Whereas these different imperatives often push the state in contradictory directions, they can help illuminate patterns of state behavior over time.

Hegemony, the first imperative of a state, reflects the need to establish the supremacy of government's laws and its authority over its territory and civil society. The full force of state power will descend upon individuals and groups who openly flout its authority. Security is a second state imperative, often taking priority in state revenue allocation, with the agencies that enforce internal security and external defense at its core.

Autonomy is a third imperative. The doctrine of sovereignty asserts that independence is a fundamental norm of true statehood, undaunted by the impossibility of its full realization. Internally, states assert their autonomy from particular interest groups through the claim to serve a broad "national" or "public" interest.

Legitimation, the fourth imperative, is a fundamental need in accumulation of power and effective exercise of authority. Civil society will usually offer voluntary compliance to authority which is perceived as legitimate in origin and behavior. Fear and force are sometimes used, but in the absence of legitimacy, recourse to such tactics can be costly. Lastly, the quest for revenue is a constant imperative of statecraft. As the resources necessary to satisfy the other imperatives must, in the last analysis, be derived from civil society, the state's revenue drive is a source of ceaseless tension with its citizenry.[3]

Before tracing the evolution of the African colonial state, some of its special characteristics must be outlined. Sovereignty was held by the occupying power and its prerogatives were delegated to the colonial administration. For the most part, colonial administrations held untrammelled authority to rule and to dispose of land, resources, and subjugated peoples—rights derived in conquest. Colonial territories were invariably endowed with a financial and legal personality separate from that of the metropole.

Although the colonial administration was designated by and hierarchically responsible to the metropolitan state, in practice, it enjoyed wide latitude in the exercise of its rule. Its personnel enjoyed a scope of arbitrary authority and could assume a social distance from their subjects unimaginable at home. A distinctive code and culture of rule emerged, carried out by an official class professionally specializing in colonial service. The colony was a state-like entity, though with special characteristics—alien to the core, erected upon a command relationship, and shaped by its vocation of domination.

CONSTRUCTION OF THE COLONIAL STATE

For simplicity of analysis, the African colonial state will be viewed in three epochs: construction, institutionalization, and decolonization. In the first stage, extending from the late 19th century partition until World War I, the most salient imperatives governing colonial state building were hegemony and revenue. The need to establish hegemony was particularly pressing because of the intensely competitive nature of the African partition and the determination of metropolitan finance ministries to force self-sufficiency upon the newly conquered domains.

With few exceptions, the use of European armies for conquest was far too expensive, as the Algerian experience had amply demonstrated. Cost-effective techniques were developed in India in the 18th century, based upon the organization of indigenous peoples under European officers, weapons, doctrine, and discipline. Particularly with the availability of the Maxim gun from 1889, such armies could defeat much more numerous resisting forces with relatively small losses.

While military superiority was a necessary condition for establishing hegemony, it had to be secured through institutionalization—by identifying and enlisting networks of collaborating indigenous intermediaries. Doctrines justifying their role differed, reflecting divergences in the state doctrines of various European powers, the strategic thinking of particular proconsuls, and local circumstances. The fledgling colonial state thereby acquired a rough-hewn apparatus of control, permitting the sparse band of soldier-administrators to claim that a framework of rule existed.

Mechanisms for economic intermediation were also required. For its own sustenance, the colonial state needed to gain leverage over the indigenous economy and acquire instrumentalities for its redirection. Many different groups took on these functions: long-established mercantile communities in coastal West Africa;[4] Zanzibari and Swahili planters in coastal East Africa;[5] and Mediterranean and other Indian sub-continent immigrants in a number of areas. At the upper end of the hierarchies of economic intermediation were large metropolitan trading houses, and, in some countries, settlers, plantation enterprises, and mining ventures entered the scene. Generally, the new colonial economy required destruction of intra-African trading systems which were not Europe-oriented and the capture of their resources.

Efforts toward gaining legitimation of the colonial state were directed at the metropolitan governments and societies and the European concert of states. In European parliaments, segments of the official community, and portions of the public up until the 1890s, there was substantial opposition to colonial conquest. Advocates of empire were forced to justify their actions by citing the benefits of colonialism in terms of strategic advantages, markets, and religious missions. The crucial bargain struck with critics of imperial conquest, however, was the pledge by all save the Italians that the metropolitan treasury would be guaranteed against any but temporary colonial expenditures. This pact of legitimation, therefore, imposed fiscal self-sufficiency upon the new colonial states.

Squeezed between the hegemony and revenue imperatives, the colonial state faced excruciating dilemmas. The harsh reality in much of the continent was that no revenue source was available, or at least nothing comparable to land in India, the highly valued exports of the

Dutch East Indies, the sugar of Caribbean slave plantation colonies, or the precious metals of Peru or Mexico. In Africa, the few exceptions were Islamic northern Nigeria, with a developed fiscal base that needed only to be directed to colonial purposes; coastal West Africa with some taxable external trade; and the southern African colonies after gold and diamond discoveries.

But much of the continent offered no evident fiscal resources, a fact that had often inhibited pre-colonial state-building as well. Therefore, the revenue imperative directed colonial states to their sole exploitable resource, African labor. Capitalization of African human resources was accomplished in several ways: direct taxation, labor conscription for infrastructure construction and transport services, and service on plantations and mines whose output could be subjected to state rents. Lastly, labor was compulsorily directed into crops such as cotton which were taxable on export.

The basic character and daily operation of the colonial state was thus profoundly shaped by its response to the twin exigencies of hegemony and revenue. Much of its early law hinged upon these requirements, as an ample arsenal of arbitrary ordinances empowered state agents to dominate and extract. By World War I, the basic framework of the colonial state was in place, but the infrastructure of military, political, economic, and cultural hegemony was far from complete, as the classic non-confrontational tactics of evasion, dissimulation, passive resistance, and private ridicule provided Africans with opportunities to preserve zones of autonomy, as Hyden has eloquently argued.[6] However, the scope of domination achieved by the colonial state was sufficient for its own ends and its agents acquired the conviction that their hegemony was entrenched for as far as one could peer into the future.

INSTITUTIONALIZATION OF THE COLONIAL STATE

Institutionalization, the second phase of the colonial state, covered the years between the first and second world wars. Whereas the 1920s were years of global prosperity, the depression and the following decade brought about severe pressures for revenues, with the head tax and labor service in kind again becoming crucial to state consumption after customs taxation had shown signs of providing an adequate fiscal base in the 1920s. Overall, the colonial state sought to consolidate its resources for the long haul.

In this second phase, the constant use of brute force was no longer required, as hegemony had been routinized. The skills and knowledge of the agents of the colonial state were upgraded through professionalization of the career service, raising entry requirements, and providing specialized training. Ad hoc strategies of domination were replaced by elaborate doctrines of colonial rule. Literacy and competence, along with ancestry and obedience to colonial authority, became criteria for the employment of African intermediaries.

The framework of the colonial state underwent significant change, as "development," "trusteeship," and "good government" entered colonial vocabulary. Albert Sarraut, French colonial minister from 1920–24, tirelessly propagated the notion of "mise en valeur" as a duty of the international community. Britain, newly conscious of the strategic asset the "undeveloped colonial estates" represented, symbolically offered a similar statement through the 1929 Colonial Development and Welfare Act, although this remained a largely unfunded metaphor until World War II.

Colonial state ideology allowed for the prudent management of the colonial realm by professionalized cadres who applied scientific methods. As trustees for a civil society lacking the capacity to articulate its own desires, colonial officialdom claimed to supply impartial adjudication of conflict and economical governance in the "paramount interest" of the subjugated.

However, static colonial revenue flows did not permit very extensive implementation of these new state doctrines. In rare cases, such as the Gold Coast, exceptionally favorable revenues from rising cocoa export taxes, along with an energetic governor personally committed to these concepts, did provide some momentum to welfare development. But much of the welfare responsibility remained with ancillary private agencies of the colonial domain—mission societies and, occasionally, corporations. During the depression, shrinking revenues restricted state operations to the reproduction of entrenched structures of hegemony.[7]

DECOLONIZATION

In the final stage of the colonial state, decolonization, dating from the close of World War II, the determinants of state behavior were altered significantly. Hegemony and legitimation took on new meaning; autonomy and security became important; and, for a period, revenue became an invitation to state expansion rather than a constraint. At the outset, no one foresaw how short the timetables of transition would be, nor the real nature of their outcome. Gradually, weakening colonial hegemony in most instances contributed to its own demise. The seeming inevitability of power transfer fostered by failed colonial military campaigns in Vietnam, Indonesia, Algeria, and later the Portuguese territories weighed heavily in the calculus of the withdrawing powers.

The imperative of hegemony was totally changed by the unfolding perspective of power transfer. The colonial state had to remain intact, yet both colonizer and nationalist wanted its internal structures of hegemony to be gradually Africanized. But Africanization of the colonial state was not enough, as formal recognition of the civil society was required. Some compact had to be devised whereby subjects were to become citizens. Here the constitutionalist ideology of the metropolitan state had a crucial impact. Withdrawal, it was said, had to be carried out with honor, which required replication of the metropolitan state organization as the exemplary model of the ideal polity.

For the nationalist political class, the metropolitan state was seen as an acceptable model, partly because of the prestige the metropolitan institutions commanded. For the nationalist forces, its representative and constitutional structures were also vehicles by which they could challenge colonial domination and accelerate its demise.

The constitutional blueprint for the post-colonial state was in profound contradiction to the entire colonial state heritage. Deeply embedded in the autocratic legacy of the colonial system was a concept of the state as the institutionalization of an alien command, reflected in its laws, routines, and mentality. The chasm that separated these two models of state was much wider than was appreciated at the time.

Undeterred by such gloomy thoughts, the colonial state set about unveiling the secrets of hegemony and encouraging the emergence of an array of associations—unions, cooperatives, and local government councils. In this new pedagogical role, the colonial official class and metropolitan state continued to assume ongoing proprietary rights. Decolonization was not to be a rupture of relationships, but rather a redefinition that would guarantee senior partner status to the metropole and its interests. The withdrawing colonizer frequently retained the capacity to orchestrate the decolonization process sufficiently to exclude from power its most intransigent adversaries.

As an African political class gained ascendancy within the institutions of power transfer, autonomy became a major preoccupation. The new leaders sought to sharpen the territorial personality of their own state, emphasizing differences with contiguous political units and redefining anti-colonial African nationalism into an exaltation of nationhood. Diversifying external links to escape the encompassing shadow of the metropole began to be discreetly supported.

Doctrines of legitimation required complete redefinition. Common ground was found between the colonial official class and the nationalist leadership around the themes of development and welfare. The promise to deliver rapid and tangible improvement in material conditions became crucial to the ability of the colonial state to retain tutelage over the decolonization process and to control its timetable. Nationalists were required to promise rapid delivery of material benefits to the rank and file in order to activate a mass clientele who could gain control over representative institutions and bring pressure for acceleration of power transfer.

This conjunction of the legitimation drives by the colonial official class and the nationalist elite gave dramatic impetus to state expansion. The construction of a developmental welfare state proceeded with remarkable speed. On the colonial side, from a skeletal pre-war base, large technical and specialized services were created, a veritable "second colonial occupation."

Although nationalists denounced the belated and insufficient efforts of the terminal colonial state to become preoccupied with subject welfare, there can be no doubt as to the efficacy of its welfare and developmentalist thrust in the final years. In the Belgian Congo, what had been a rudimentary educational system until the last colonial phase became a huge network enrolling 70 percent of school-age children by independence. In the 1920s, no real medical service for Africans existed; by 1960, the Belgians could boast that their health service was "without doubt the best in the whole tropical world."[8] Economies flourished in the 1950s, an era of rising real wages and prosperity in which the rural populations also shared. Although not noted at the time, the 1950s became a retrospective golden age and later came to serve as the yardstick for the performance of the post-colonial state.

The surge in welfare and development expenditures was remarkable. In the Belgian Congo, state outlays rose eleven-fold between

1939 and 1950, then tripled in the final colonial decade. In the last decade of British rule in the Gold Coast, public expenditures multiplied ten-fold; in the preceding 35 years, they had merely doubled. These patterns were characteristic.

This swift rise in state consumption was made possible by an exceptionally fortunate conjuncture on the revenue front. The prolonged commodity boom, extending through the Korean War, brought windfall gains to the colonial state. The state's capture of the profits from the price boom was facilitated in many instances by new public institutions created for wartime purposes that controlled marketing and export of agricultural crops. At the same time, driven by the new legitimation requirements, the metropolitan state for the first time was willing to undertake substantial public investment in the colonial territories. Rising levels of economic prosperity, in part fostered by expanding state investment and activity, further enlarged the fiscal potential.

In the field of revenue generation, colonial state behavior exhibited a striking continuity with its earlier forms. Rural taxation was heavily utilized, though the patterns of extraction had changed. In its first phase, the colonial state financed hegemony and conquest by rudimentary methods of transforming African labor into state cash flow. Now the revenue devices were far more subtle: taxation through export commodity price regulation; export taxation levied particularly upon African crops; marketing board monopolies whose surpluses were in effect transferred into the state capital account; discriminatory schedules of rail freight charges; and differential customs duties on imports mainly consumed by Europeans and those destined for African markets.

The older head tax became much less significant, though in many territories it remained an important revenue source well into the second phase of colonial state development. Data from Uganda in the 1950s demonstrated that real taxation rates for peasant households were well over 50 percent, vastly higher than fiscal rates affecting wealthier strata, immigrant or African.[9]

Overall, the African colonial state differed in significant ways from its analogues in other regions.[10] Although there were harsh periods, plundering episodes, and disruptive intrusions in other areas of the world, the colonial state elsewhere was much less dependent upon subjugated civil societies. Although its period of rule was brief compared to Asia and Latin America, the African colonial state was implanted in a highly competitive environment where consolidation of its rule was an immediate requirement.

The European state from which doctrines of rule were derived was a much more sophisticated and elaborated structure than in early phases of imperial expansion into Asia and the Americas. The colonial class had a more profound conviction of its cultural, biological, and technological superiority, and a more systematically negative view of its subject population than was the case elsewhere. The subjugation and exclusion of civil society was particularly thorough. The difficulties of adapting this state to the new circumstances of political sovereignty were bound to be enormous.

NATURE OF THE POST-COLONIAL STATE

The post-colonial state operated within a profoundly different framework, as entirely new threats to hegemony appeared. The legitimacy born out of the process of power transfer proved evanescent, and more enduring doctrines were as necessary as they were elusive. Autonomy and security as driving forces in state behavior became much more important. The revenue-fed momentum of state expansion of the 1950s continued, but was progressively undermined by a growing disequilibrium between state consumption and its resource base. By the late 1970s, a revenue crisis was at hand.

But in the triumphant mood of the early 1960s, these patterns were much less visible than the seeming success of the colonial state in organizing its own metamorphosis, with the important exception of the revolutionary cases. The keys of the kingdom were handed over in a veritable orgy of self-celebration, but the institutional synthesis upon which decolonization was founded proved exceedingly short-lived.

In its last years, the colonial state had institutionalized open political competition and a constitutionalized state-civil society relationship. While this formula provided adequate legitimation for the power transfer process itself, it swiftly decomposed in the post-independence environment. It soon ran afoul of the more enduring autocratic and hegemonic impulses of the colonial state. Only in Botswana and Mauritius can it be said that the power transfer pact in its original form still exists.

SECURING POWER

The issues of competition and alternation did not arise in the colonial state, as the ultimate arbiter and repository of sovereignty was the metropole. Governors might come and go, but the colonial state was a permanent structure and its agents, in large measure, interchangeable parts. But decolonization placed political agents in command of the state who had a different perspective, animated by the innate incumbent propensity to perpetuate their hold on power.

More was involved than a primal lust for power or the monarchical germ within every ruler's breast. Many of the nationalist generation regarded themselves—with some justification—as bearers of an unique historical mission of liberation and uplift. Sanctioned by a special mandate as founders of new polities, they viewed their task as requiring an enduring tenure to secure the fledgling state against its innumerable potential enemies, foreign and domestic.

Radical nationalist movements, such as the Parti Democratique de Guinee (PDG) or the Convention People's Party (CPP) of Ghana, regarded themselves as having earned permanent entitlement to rule through their aggressive and confrontational posture toward colonial authority and the enthusiasm which their aggregation of grievances and expectations had engendered. In some instances, this conviction was reinforced by their belief that they were launching an ideological project of socialist construction, which required assurance of protection against reversal or subversion by the menacing forces of international capitalism.

The insulation against threats from outside the colonial framework provided by the metropolitan security organizations was removed, and new states were at once subjected to the competitive environment of the Cold War. The Central Intelligence Agency, the KGB, and kindred agencies seeking a foothold in Africa recruited local clients, activities which by no means passed unnoticed.

Particularly in the early years of independence, the former metropole sought to preserve bastions of influence within the post-colonial state and to exclude the new intruders. These global rivals, each pursuing its own manichean security imperatives and entitled position in the newly sovereign domains of Africa, stalked each other through the corridors of power. The new rulers endeavored as best they could to avail themselves of services that could be extracted from external actors, while at the same time becoming acutely conscious of their vulnerability to penetration and the disposition of global powers to impose solutions favorable to their own strategic concerns.

Internal enemies soon became apparent to new rulers, often rendered all the more deadly—and illegitimate—by their potential access to external support. Additionally, open political competition in the terminal colonial epoch had amply demonstrated its potential for politicizing cultural cleavages within civil society. During the anticolonial struggle, nationalist movements had propagated the concept of subjugated civil society as a "nation-in-the-making"—an historically ordained collectivity in which ethnicity was a dangerous and reactionary force. The swiftening pace of decolonization had triggered new apprehensions among many about the perceived risk of domination by particular groups and the ethnic allocation of postcolonial resources.

The politically ambitious had discovered that crystallizing ethnic consciousness was the swiftest and surest way to attract a political clientele. The unfamiliarity of the electoral process itself reinforced the intensity of ethnic politics, escalating fears and insecurities, and lending an apocalyptic aura to competitive balloting. Set against the demon of politicized cultural pluralism, national integration was represented as the consummate good, not only by ruling elites but by expert opinion of all stripes, not least in the earnest prescriptions of the social science literature of the day. By this logic, restraint of political competition was both morally imperative and a convenient pretext for political monopoly.

Added to these factors propelling rulers toward restoration of the autocratic hegemony of the colonial state was a more curious belief that collective public energies were an inherently limited good which was distributed in zero-sum fashion. Whatever effort was dedicated to political competition was subtracted from the available quantum of developmental energies. Thus political competition was inherently wasteful and a luxury that could not be afforded.

Finally, beyond impulses to power innate in humans as political animals, more sordid attractions swiftly became apparent. In his deft critique of political monopoly two decades ago, Arthur Lewis encapsulates this dimension: "Personifying the state, ministers dress themselves up in uniforms, build themselves palaces, bring all other traffic to a standstill when they drive, hold fancy parades and generally demand to be treated like Egyptian pharaohs. . . .There are also vast opportunities for pickings in bribes, state contracts, diversion of public funds to private uses, and commissions of various sorts. To be a minister is to have a lifetime's chance to make a fortune."[11]

SINGLE-PARTY STATE

From the moment of independence, these pressures combined to yield a new form of political monopoly that reproduced the autocratic heritage of the colonial state—the single-party state. Only thrice in post-colonial African history has a change of incumbents come about through the electoral processes—Somalia, by parliamentary vote in 1967, Mauritius in 1982, and—ambiguously, with military interregnum—Sierra Leone in 1967–68. After independence, through coercion and cooptation, de jure or de facto one-party regimes spread throughout the continent.

When it became apparent that political monopolies guaranteeing incumbents indefinite prolongation of their mandates were becoming the rule, disaffection flowed into new channels, particularly the military. Although initially not perceived as such, the trend of the military coup as a vehicle for ruler displacement began in Egypt in 1952, moved to Sudan (1956), occurred half-heartedly in Zaire (1960), Benin (1963), and Togo (1963), and then became an institutionalized pattern with a rapid-fire sequence of putsches in 1965–66 (Algeria, Zaire, Nigeria, Ghana, Central African Republic, Benin). While displacement of incumbents to remedy their abuses served as entry legitimation for military regimes, longer-term power retention required other justifications. Military regimes themselves—with Egypt again as pioneer—adopted single-party ideologies and constructed monopolistic institutions for permanent legitimation of rule.

The single party has tended to combine populist rhetoric with exclusionary practices. Considerable energy and resources are devoted to the ritualization of legitimacy through ceremony, spectacle, and periodic plebiscitary elections. Within the single-party framework, some interesting experiments pioneered by Tanzania have been undertaken to improve the credibility and responsiveness of the party through competitive elections for legislative representatives, but not for the ruler. But the basic fact of political monopoly remains.

Political monopoly, however, solved only part of the problems facing rulers, merely offering a pre-emptive hegemony. There remained the challenge of assuring ruler ascendancy over the state

apparatus and preventing hostile combinations from forming within
it. The colonial official class was disciplined and controlled through
the formal hierarchy, administrative regulation, and deontological
code. Whereas informal clans founded on religious, ideological, or
linguistic orientation might be found, especially in the French and
Belgian cases, overall the colonial state bent to the will of its over-
layer.

PATRIMONIAL RULE

Abstract bureaucratic jurisprudence no longer sufficed after independence. Hostile cliques and conspiracies had to be pre-empted by
ensuring placement of personnel at critical points in the state apparatus whose fidelity to the ruler was not simply formal, but immediate and personal. Thus rulers constructed an inner layer of control—
key political operatives, top elements in the security forces, top
technocrats in the financial institutions—whose fidelity was guaranteed by personal fealty as well as by hierarchical subordination. The
surest basis for such fidelity is affinity of community or kinship. Close
scrutiny of the inner security core of the state will usually disclose
such connections in states as diverse as Toure's Guinea, Nyerere's
Tanzania, or Mobutu's Zaire.

Beyond and often in addition to affinity, personal interest is the
most reliable collateral for loyalty. Accordingly, rulers must reward
generously and impose severe sanctions for any weakening of zeal.
Thus public resources become a pool of benefits and prebends, while
dismissal from office, confiscation of goods, and prosecution face
those who show slackness in their personal fidelity. Holders of high
office individually tend to become clients of the ruler and collectively
a service class. This process of patrimonialization of the state has been
elegantly characterized as "personal rule" by Jackson and Rosberg,
"a system of relations linking rulers not with the 'public' or even with
the ruled (at least not directly), but with the patrons, associates,
clients, supporters, and rivals who constitute the 'system.'"[12]

LEGITIMACY

The post-colonial state required new doctrines of legitimation, as
the older colonial themes of trusteeship and good government were
no longer serviceable. However, the terminal colonial ideology of

development and welfare could be retained, joined to a populist discourse and nationalist vocabulary which promised an acceleration of momentum and a reinterpretation of its content. State-directed change would be rapid, Africa-centered, and mass-directed.

The new state began the era of independence with a substantial capital of legitimacy. In many countries, the nationalist platform generated vast enthusiasm, particularly among the young. Despite its vulnerability to the nationalist assault, the colonial state also had some elements of legitimacy which it bequeathed to its successor—an image of competence in execution of its mandate, some degree of trust as arbiter of conflicts, and the indisputable material accomplishments of its final decade.

Over time, the reservoir of legitimacy dissipated, due in part to performance. Disappointment came quickly, even though retrospectively in the 1960s, economic progress was generally respectable. But extravagant promises had been made and hopes unleashed which could not be met. As economies stagnated in the 1970s and decayed in the 1980s, the public mood turned skeptical. As governments' populist discourse lost its credibility, their exclusionary character became more resented.

Political succession through coups resulted in the long-term delegitimation of the state; each new regime sought entry legitimacy by erecting a veritable "black legend" around its predecessor. The venality of the previous rulers was exposed to public view and a catalogue of nefarious misdeeds compiled: extravagance, incompetence, ethnic favoritism, subservience to foreign interests, even treason. Cumulatively, the "black legend" came to encompass past, present, and future leadership.

AUTONOMY

The autonomy imperative has been a source of deepening frustration for the post-colonial state, as the developmental impasse has made its realization ever more remote. The colonial state had pursued a contradictory policy of, on the one hand, promoting privileged economic links with the metropole in which the latter's interests were naturally paramount, and, on the other, forcing autonomy on the colonies to avoid metropolitan subsidies. At independence, major enterprises were invariably owned by metropolitan capital, and trading relations were dominated by the colonizer. The lack of autonomy was greatest in the former French colonies that remained subordinated to the franc zone and relied upon undeniably efficient French security services, not only through defense pacts, but also through more informal intelligence support.

Today, the autonomy imperative is articulated in a commitment to non-alignment, formation of an African bloc in international agencies, and involvement in the network of Third World groupings, including the Group of 77 and the non-aligned, which have sought a "new international economic order" since 1973, though with little success. The emphasis on self-reliance and internally directed development in the OAU's conceptual response to the economic crisis— the creation of the 1980 Lagos Plan of Action—resonates with the autonomy imperative.

For the weaker states in an international system dominated by the strong, diversification of external linkages is one means of protection. In the economic realm, most states have sought to terminate the proprietary claims of the erstwhile colonizer. This has been particularly apparent in nationalization or indigenization measures which peaked in the early 1970s. These were invariably directed at colonial corporations or Mediterranean and Asian economic intermediaries who fashioned their niche under the protection of the colonial state.

Success was by no means certain in autonomy-driven assaults on colonial economic interests. In all but liquidating French interests save for one bauxite enterprise, Guinea brought about a prolonged decline in almost all spheres except bauxite mining because of its inability to successfully manage a large socialized sector. The state found itself singularly dependent upon this single source of external revenue and the French, American, and Soviet mining enterprises. Zaire, whose epic struggle with the arrogant colonial giant, Union Miniere du Haut-Katanga, seemed to end in triumph in 1967, wound up paying a very high price in management fees, compensation, and, arguably, global market shares.

THE SECURITY IMPERATIVE

By the 1980s, the growing costs upon the post-colonial state which the security imperative had slowly imposed had become substantial. In the colonial era, after the initial period of conquest, security demands weighed lightly on the state, save for the sacrifices resulting from involvement in the two world wars and for those colonial situations which degenerated into revolutionary liberation wars. Colonial constabularies, designed solely for internal security, were composed of small and lightly armed infantry units.

A number of factors brought security and defense preoccupations to the forefront during the independence era. Since 1966, 40 to 50 percent of the regimes in the continent have been military in origin, and in states not under military rule, intervention by the security forces remains a tangible threat. The armed forces have therefore become a potent corporate interest in the struggle for state resources.

The intensely competitive international environment plays its part, with major powers' ceaseless quest for allies and clients on the one hand, and African states' search for external patrons and protectors on the other. The provision of weapons, necessitating continuing supply of logistics, training, and spare parts, is particularly useful for the external state. Commercial motivations are also significant for a number of suppliers; France, the Soviet Union, Israel, and Brazil in particular depend heavily on the foreign exchange generated by weapons sales. The very competitive nature of these relationships, both political and mercantile, tends to drive African states to higher levels of armament.

A seemingly inexorable rise in levels of conflict in Africa set in after independence, gaining momentum in the 1970s. Several regional theaters of tension emerged—the Horn, the Middle East, the Western Sahara, Chad, and southern Africa—each setting in motion an arms race within its zone of impact. By the 1980s, it had become clear that liberation or dissident movements which succeed in building an internal zone of support and some access to external supply could sustain themselves virtually indefinitely, forcing the states involved to devote the greater part of their available resources to security (e.g., Angola, Morocco, Ethiopia).

The consequence is that security-driven state consumption is rapidly increasing. The minor role of security imperatives in the final phases of the colonial state meant that outlays for the armed forces were remarkably modest. From 1960 to 1980, however, for the developing world as a whole, there was a 117-fold increase in defense expenditures.[13] Research now in progress by Robert West demonstrates that in recent years for African states, real military expenditures as a percentage of government expenditure have been increasing faster than in any other group of countries, substantially exceeding economic growth rates. For small, low-income countries, military expenditures today constitute a higher effective burden than the security costs of the major world powers.[14]

OTHER STATE CONSUMPTION PRESSURES

Security has been far from the only factor exerting pressure on state consumption. Social expenditures driven by the legitimation imperative have also risen rapidly, a carry-over from terminal colonial patterns and external donor philosophy in the 1970s. The claims of the educational sector were especially powerful, as the perceived link between educational opportunity and social mobility became anchored in the popular consciousness. Even if they were so inclined, states find it difficult to arrest such expenditures.

More significant, efforts to match quantitative enlargement with qualititative performance or transmission of technical and vocational skills have fallen far short of the most modest expectations. The correlation between provision of education and economic growth has been axiomatic in developmental theory and appears validated in such exemplary success stories as Japan, South Korea, and Taiwan. In Africa, however, the relationship is much less clear; the more immediate results of education seem to have been increasing pressures for public employment and rural exodus.

Another potent factor in the growth of state consumption has been the trend to vest the accumulation function in parastatal agencies, a tendency visible across the ideological spectrum. For socialist states, the construction of a sprawling state sector corresponded to a blueprint of non-capitalist development; in the Tanzanian case, Reginald Green, economic adviser and partisan of the socialist strategy, was able to boast that by the mid-1970s, in the pursuit of state socialism, 80 percent of medium and large-scale economic activity was located in the public sector, a figure which exceeded that of Soviet bloc states at a comparable time period.[15] But parastalization of the economy did not require the stimulus of socialist doctrine; in Ivory Coast, the exemplary center of African capitalism, the number of parastatals grew from six in 1960 to 84 in 1977 (since somewhat trimmed back). Of the 54.6 percent of the industrial sector in Ivorian hands in 1977, 90 percent was held by the state.[16]

As economic entities, parastatal organizations are not necessarily inefficient; one recent study provides evidence that Brazilian public sector enterprises have played a major part in national growth.[17]

Singapore has a number of big public corporations that have contributed to its remarkable growth. Egypt generates $1 billion yearly from its parastatal Suez Canal Corporation. But overall, state enterprise performance in Africa has been dismal; one finds only a few contrary examples. All too characteristic is the Ghanaian Cocoa Marketing Board, which in the early 1980s employed 105,000 persons to export a crop half the size as that handled more efficiently by 50,000 employees in 1965. The ultimate necessity for the state to make good parastatal deficits and to resupply operating capital is a major factor contributing to swollen state consumption.

An important factor behind rising state expenditures has been increasing public sector employment. In Kenya, public sector employment rose from 188,000 in 1965 to 390,000 in 1978; the civil service alone expanded from 14,000 in 1945 to 45,000 in 1955 and 170,000 by 1980. In Senegal, those employed by the government swelled from 10,000 on the eve of independence to 61,000 in 1973.[18] In Congo (Brazzaville), the state agricultural extension service multiplied by 10 from 1960 to 1972, reaching a level where salaries exceeded the total cash income of the nation's 600,000 peasants; worse, this expansion was accompanied by a decline in output of most crops they endeavored to service.[19] In 1967, state consumption as a percentage of GDP was less than 15 percent for Africa as a whole, and often well below 10 percent in the 1950s. By the 1980s, it exceeded 40 percent for many countries.

African state revenues tend to be tightly bound to returns from price-volatile primary commodity exports. The post-colonial state has exhibited a formidable capacity to instantly transform a momentary revenue windfall into recurrent expenditure obligations, especially salaries. Nigeria, for example, converted virtually all of its oil revenues in 1973 and 1979 into state consumption. Government outlays ballooned from N997.4 million in 1971, to N17,513.1 in 1980.[20] Indeed, the trend toward state pre-emption of societal resources may be greater than official figures suggest. For most African states, most of the budget goes for wage and salary payments and the purchase of goods for state use; "government" thus enters national income accounts at factor cost, irrespective of its "product."

SOURCES OF REVENUE

The revenue imperative thus weighed heavily in state behavioral choices. Three basic strategies had emerged, which by the 1980s had proved harmful. Firmly established from the beginning of the colonial state, the pattern of relentless fiscal pressure upon the peasant sector was maintained and reinforced, producing demoralization, disaffection, and disengagement by the countryside. Second, the state sought to enlarge its rents from the former colonial sectors through diverse formulas of parastalization. There were some successes here, particularly in the mineral sphere; in the short run, for example, both Zaire and Zambia greatly increased their fiscal cut in copper proceeds. Over time, however, this strategy has been progressively undermined by the dispiriting performance of the state sector. Finally, states sought revenue relief from external sources. Initially, this seemed deceptively effective, as during the honeymoon years, foreign aid both from the former metropole and from the new entrants—United States, Soviet Union, Israel, China, Scandinavia—rose rapidly and was often on a grant basis. As Robert Berg points out, per capita official aid was higher to Africa than to any other region.[21]

However, very soon state consumption increases ceased to be matched by expansion in external aid. In the early 1970s, a new phase of external resource acquisition—borrowing—emerged. The period 1970–75 was extraordinarily propitious for public and private external borrowing. The major international financial institutions had large liquidities, and industrial world lending was relatively unpromising. Lending to less developed countries seemed attractive, as interest premiums could be charged. African debt burdens were then small, and, in practice, Western governments and the International Monetary Fund (IMF) were viewed as collectors of the last resort guaranteeing the loans. For African states, borrowed funds seemed an appealing and painless mechanism for overcoming short-term foreign exchange pressures. Further, real interests rates were at record lows, at times even negative, and the borrowed funds seemed a bargain.

By the late 1970s, all three of these avenues for revenue expansion were not only blocked, but had clogged channels of fiscal access. Rural populations turned to smuggling their crops or redirected their efforts to farming, artisanal, or commercial activities outside the reach of the public realm. Rather than replenishing public coffers, the deficitary parastatal sector put new pressures on the treasury. By the late 1970s, external lenders had become extremely wary of African exposure and instead concentrated their efforts on collection. The foreign exchange bind intensified by debt service burdens forced recourse to the IMF, with its battery of standard remedies, their inevitable political costs in delegitimation, and distant and speculative returns.

WEAKNESS IN ECONOMIC MANAGEMENT

The debt crisis has especially highlighted basic infirmities in state economic management. The permeability, weakness, and often venality of the state apparatus rendered it peculiarly vulnerable to colossal misestimates of project viability. In particularly pathological cases, such as Zaire, external borrowing patterns seem to closely approximate Issawi's calculations for the debts accumulated by Egypt, Tunisia, Morocco, and the Ottoman Empire in the late 19th century (leading in the first three cases to loss of sovereignty). In the Ottoman instance, no more than 5 percent of the funds obtained were placed in ventures that could be amortized.[22]

Looseness of control within a swelling state sector fragmented by the proliferation of parastatals was one factor. In countries as diverse in management reputation as Ivory Coast and Zaire, there was an identical pattern in the phase of debt run-up, wherein parastatal agencies engaging the credit of the state made substantial commitments without central bank knowledge. Thus, when consciousness of a debt problem suddenly dawned, neither state financial officials nor the external lenders initially had clear knowledge of what the debt was.

A recurrent pattern in the interaction between the state and external capital finds state agents and external interests with a common interest in structuring the arrangements so that each can secure a profit on the transaction. External capital offers turnkey projects, management services on contract, and technology, but avoids equity commitments. The entire risk is borne by the state and must ultimately be extracted from civil society. Examples are the $1 billion Ivory Coast sugar disaster and the equally costly Zaire Inga-Shaba power line. Within the state apparatus, the very nature of the project review process and its structural irrationalities leave the state prone to highly risky choices.

Out of these patterns of state behavior over the post-independence years has come a perplexing and difficult state-civil society relationship, which itself troubles and probably obstructs the development process. There may be both powerful continuities with the colonial state and new aspects flowing from characteristics of the post-colonial state of contemporary origin. The developmental impasse is reflected in the state-civil society nexus as both cause and effect.

The relationship between civil society and the post-colonial state is profoundly contradictory. The state remains deeply marked by the hegemonial pretensions and authoritarian legacy of the colonial state. In innumerable ways, the peremptory, prefectoral command style of the colonial state remains embedded in its successor. The citizenry lack empowerment, whether the ideology of the state is Leninist or capitalist. Civil society remains an aggregate of subjects confronted with the state.

Yet there is a crucial difference in the operation of the post-colonial state. The colonial state, in its second and third stages, had aggregated its authority and built reservoirs of institutional competence to a point where it had the capacity to accomplish a number of its goals at considerable cost to its subjects, upon whose shoulders the colonial state was able to place the entire burden of its hegemony. The appearance of "hardness" inherited from the mentalities and routines of the colonial state was sapped from within by the inner "softness" inherent in the process of patrimonial and clientelistic politics, by which civil society was able to penetrate the state, deflect its authoritarian strictures, and ultimately transform its despotic surface into a hollow shell.

As Hyden concludes: "The mechanisms of the soft state are the antithesis of the type of economic efficiency that is necessary for growth and development. The 'soft' state phenomenon is particularly harmful in Africa because of the wide scope of the public sector. The state apparatus is not limited to the provision of basic public services, levying taxes, maintaining law and order, but extends its tentacles to embrace broad economic activities with often catastrophic consequences."[23]

In his lament concerning the infirmities of the socialist orientation, Iliffe adds that African states have demonstrated their ability to block capitalism, but have not exhibited a capacity to find an alternative formula for releasing the social energies of their populace.[24]

A little noted but important field in which this shrinkage of institutional capacity has occurred is at the local government level. In many countries, the structures of intermediation, which the colonial state had carefully nurtured, have been corroded by a self-defeating compulsion of the central institutions to extend their own hegemony to the local level and the attendant suspicion of them as chiefly instruments of colonial control. Local government bodies have lost their revenue base, the effective support of regional state authorities, and their standing with the citizenry.[25] A survey of three Nigerian universities concerning attitudes about public servant integrity showed an overwhelming percentage of respondents (90 per cent) believed that relatively few civil servants in most African countries are capable of putting national interests ahead of their own interests.[26]

POLICY IMPLICATIONS

What then is to be done? Eight prescriptive reflections are put forward with a hesitancy borne of the conviction that the current African development impasse is not only far-reaching, but historically rooted. No handful of facile formulas can overcome Africa's travail. No single observer is likely to have sufficient breadth of perspective or vision to propound a definitive charter for future resurrection, nor are the thoughts that follow translatable into immediate operational directives.

• If not arrested, the present trends in African development and the nature of the post-colonial state condemn Africa to long-term marginalization and pauperization. There might be solace in the thought that only 15 years ago, African prospects still seemed encouraging, while Asia represented the crisis region of the world.[27] The Asian developmental configuration has changed beyond recognition, but the NIC pathway thorough which a number of Asian states have emerged as stellar-performance political economies requires a highly efficacious state. The contemporary African state is absolutely incapable of producing a NIC.

• If there are any grounds for subdued optimism at the present time, they are to be found in the growing recognition within and without Africa of the dimensions of the problem and the willingness to contemplate a reconsideration of the state which would have been unthinkable five years ago. Emblematic of courageous and forthright new patterns of state thought is the excellent contribution in this volume by a leading Tanzanian economist, Benno J. Ndulu, who notes the urgency of dismantling state controls and the need to reconstruct state institutions embued with greater accountability and competence.[28]

The 1982 Ndegwa Committee Report undertaken for the Kenyan

government is equally remarkable for its candor and the scope of its prescriptions. The scale of the adjustments that African states are called upon to make go far beyond the selective rollback of the "welfare state" which is occurring in a number of advanced Western industrialized states. Only state authorities' recognition that elemental survival overrides the other imperatives of state behavior which led to the present impasse can rally the "official mind" behind remedies as far-reaching and, in the short run, risky.

• The present impasse is far more than economic in nature. Thus, it will not readily yield to purely economic prescriptions. Herein lies the major difficulty with reform programs promoted by international financial institutions. Their mandate is essentially limited to the economic realm, and thus their remedies are incomplete. Directly political conditionality is doubtless unfeasible. However, "structural adjustment" programs need to include acknowledgement of their implications for the state: whether, given the nature of the state, they are realistically sustainable and whether they contribute toward the reorientation from control to service and from exclusion to accountability.[29]

• The basic texture of the state-civil society relationship is antithetical to development and requires restructuring. Efforts in this direction must be founded upon a realistic grasp of the nature of civil society and its divisions. The post-colonial state cannot sustain either the "hardness" of the bequeathed style of colonial state hegemony, nor the "softness" that undermines its efficacy. The empowerment of civil society in order to impose higher levels of accountability upon the state requires acceptance of spheres of autonomous operation for such diverse bodies as unions, cooperatives, churches, and local governments. Enlargement of the scope of private markets is another path to reinforcing civil society in its interaction with the state. In the longer run, a stronger civil society is not antithetical to a restructured and stronger state, better able to fulfill its role of guidance and orientation of the development venture.

• The legitimation imperative can no longer be met by ideological formulas, or by "mobilization" from above, be it Leninist or personalist. Self-celebratory state ritual and ceremony has lost all semblance of credibility. Performance is the key to recapturing the confidence of the populace. This standard cannot be met by the hypertrophic, over-extended contemporary state.

- Levels of state consumption far exceed resource possibilities and now constitute a veritable engine of underdevelopment. At present consumption levels, the revenue imperative drives the state into a confrontation with the rural sector that it is too weak to win. The state is also driven into debilitating recourse to external sources. Survival and self-reliance dictate load-shedding, particularly of the deficit-ridden parastatal sector.

- Consideration of the disabilities of the contemporary African state must incorporate international system factors. In innumerable ways in the pursuit of short-term advantage, public and private external actors have contributed to the African developmental impasse. Great power competition and arms sales have played a part in inflating military outlays. An honest inquest into the poor performance of external donor agencies is only beginning; organizational self-protection impulses obstruct. Full and public self-criticism by the external partners is a necessary accompaniment to the internal African process of rethinking the state.

- A major, long-term commitment to external assistance must accompany African efforts at overcoming present weaknesses of the state. Recent trends are in the opposite direction. Even more ominous is the possibility that stagnating levels of available aid resources are committed to security-driven objectives of external actors and the growing number of disaster relief and refugee crises which present trends in demography, climate, conflict, and economic decline make likely.

The reconsideration of the state now in progress and its adaptation to the reality of parallel economies and peasant disengagement involve a momentous process. The great challenge to developmental statecraft is to find creative and positive means to transcend the present impasse. No one can contemplate a mere perpetuation of present patterns far into the future. Existing trends evoke chilling visions of Africa's rendezvous with the 21st century.

NOTES

1. Andrew Young, "The United States and Africa: Victory for Diplomacy," *Foreign Affairs* LVIX, (3)(1981): 648–66; John de St. Jorre, "Africa: Crisis of Confidence," *Foreign Affairs* LXI, (3)(1983): 675–91; Jennifer Whitaker, "Africa Beset," *Foreign Affairs* LXII, (3)(1984): 746–76.

2. The term has been employed in innumerable ways; one author identified no less than 145 different meanings of the concept. A more elaborate explanation of our approach will be found in the introductory chapter to Crawford Young and Thomas Turner, *The Rise and Decline of the Zairian State* (Madison: University of Wisconsin Press, 1985).

3. The centrality of this factor is given powerful demonstration in the influential study by Robert H. Bates, *Markets and States in Tropical Africa* (Berkeley: University of California Press, 1981).

4. The importance of this petty mercantile class is well documented by A.G. Hopkins, *An Economic History of West Africa* (New York: Columbia University Press, 1973).

5. Frederick Cooper, *From Slaves to Squatters: Plantation Labor and Agriculture in Zanzibar and Coastal Kenya 1890–1925* (New Haven: Yale University Press, 1980).

6. Goran Hyden, *Beyond Ujamaa in Tanzania* (Berkeley: University of California Press, 1980).

7. In the welfare realm, state action was most visible in the public health field. Here the stimulus was not simply trusteeship obligations, but also more elemental revenue-imperative calculus. In many areas, the conviction grew that African populations were declining, endangering the fiscal base of the colonial state.

8. Jean Stengers, "La Belgique et le Congo," *Histoire de la Belgique Contemporaine* (Brussels: La Renaissance du Livre, 1974).

9. The calculations were made for Bwaamba, but we believe they are applicable to many, if not most, areas; E.H. Winter, *Bwaamba Economy* (Kampala: East African Institute of Social Research, 1958), pp. 34–35. Vali Jamal, "Taxation and Inequality in Uganda, 1900–1964," *Journal of Economic History* XVIII, (2)(June 1978): 418–38, shows the pervasive discrimination in import and excise taxes against rural households.

10. This argument is developed at greater length in Crawford Young, "The Colonial State and its Connection to Current Political Crises in Africa," Colloquium paper, Woodrow Wilson International Center for Scholars, Washington, May 1984.

11. W. Arthur Lewis, *Politics in West Africa* (New York: Oxford University Press, 1965), pp. 31–32.

12. Robert H. Jackson and Carl G. Rosberg, *Personal Rule in Black Africa* (Berkeley: University of California Press, 1982), p. 19.

13. Ruth Leger Sivard, *World Military and Social Expenditures 1982* (Leesburg, Va: World Priorities, 1982), p. 26.

14. Robert C. West, "National Security Provision in African Countries: Military Expenditures in the 1970s," typescript, 1984.

15. Bismarck Mwansasu and Cranford Pratt, eds., *Towards Socialism in Tanzania* (Toronto: Univeristy of Toronto Press, 1979), pp. 19–45.

16. Sheridan Johns, "Reform of State Enterprises in the Ivory Coast: Reform and Redirection," annual meetings, African Studies Association, Washington, D. C., November 1982.

17. Thomas J. Trebat, *Brazil's State-Owned Enterprises: A Case Study of the State as Entrepreneur* (New York: Cambridge University Press, 1983).

18. David B. Abernethy, "Bureaucratic Growth and Economic Decline in sub-Saharan Africa," paper presented to Annual Meetings, African Studies Association, Boston, December 1983.

19. Hugues Bertrand, *Le Congo* (Paris: François Maspero, 1975), p. 188, p. 256.

20. Sayre P. Schatz, "The Inert Economy of Nigeria," *Journal of Modern African Studies* XXII, (1)(1984): 19; Pauline H. Baker, *The Economics of Nigerian Federalism* (Washington, D.C.: Battelle Memorial Institute, 1984); Richard A. Joseph, "Affluence and Underdevelopment: The Nigerian Experience," *Journal of Modern African Studies* XVI, (2)(1978), pp. 221–40.

21. Robert J. Berg, "Foreign Aid in Africa: Here's the Answer, Is It Relevant to the Question?" paper for Committee on African Development Strategies, September 1984.

22. Charles Issawi, *An Economic History of the Middle East and North Africa* (New York: Columbia University Press, 1982), p. 63.

23. Goran Hyden, *No Shortcuts to Progress* (Berkeley: University of California Press, 1983), p. 63. The "soft state" concept was originated by Gunnar Myrdal, *Asian Drama* (New York: Pantheon, 1968), I, p. 66.

24. John Iliffe, *The Emergence of African Capitalism* (Minneapolis: University of Minnesota Press, 1984).

25. This topic deserves closer attention than it has received. For a careful inquest into the demise of local government in Ghana, see Anthony A. Edoh, *Decentralization and Local Government Reform in Ghana*, doctoral dissertation, University of Wisconsin—Madison, 1979. His findings are applicable to many countries.

26. Paul Beckett and James O'Connell, *Education and Power in Nigeria* (London: Hodder and Stoughton, 1977), p. 148.

27. Donald K. Emmerson, "Pacific Optimism," University Fieldstaff International, Fieldstaff Reports, 1982.

28. Benno J. Ndulu, "Economic Management in Sub-Saharan Africa: Key Issues, Experiences, and Prospects," paper for Committee on African Development Strategies, April 1985.

29. David K. Leonard, "Developing Africa's Agricultural Institutions: Putting the Farmer in Control," paper for Committee on African Development Strategies, January 1985.

CHAPTER TWO

African Social Structure and Economic Development

Goran Hyden

Independent Africa was born into a world characterized by its strong faith in progress. Captivated by scientific and technological advances, the post-war generation in both East and West dismissed all references to man's natural limitations as unfounded pessimism. In the West, as Albert Hirschman reminds us,[1] development economics spearheaded the effort to bring about an emancipation from backwardness. Coming to power in this intellectual climate, African leaders shared the spirit, if not the methodology of this positivist philosophy. From their no less ahistorical perspective, they viewed the attainment of political independence as merely a prologue to other victories.

Whether inspired by the "modernization" or "social transformation" paradigms, post-independence development strategies called on Africa to adopt contemporary models with historically alien antecedents. Consequently, pet notions from both East and West—many not fully understood even in their country of origin—were applied in Africa in order to bring it into the mainstream of international development. As Carl Eicher points out, development theorists drew heavily not only on Europe and North America, but on Asia and Latin America—particularly China and India—for their assumptions about agrarian institutions, economic behavior, and empirical evidence about the development process.[2]

As a result, the last 25 years have been a period of endless and sometimes shameless experimentation in Africa. In this atmosphere, governments and donors alike have ignored the narrow margins of survival that characterize African countries at all levels. Above all, they have failed to adequately look for African solutions to African problems.

African public institutions have run on imported energy rather than on domestically available resources. As Hart argues,[3] "development" in Africa is a process in which words and numbers bear little relationship to the material and social realities of the continent. Africa has been brought to adulthood with little respect for its own dynamics and abilities. No wonder, therefore, that it has taken so little time to bring it to its knees.

At long last, Africa is beginning to realize the shortcomings of past development strategies. Without suggesting that the continent can manage without foreign assistance, a growing number of policy-makers and intellectuals concede that it has been a waste, as a senior Kenyan official puts it, "to apply half-baked theories, which find favor in their countries of origin, to countries where economic and social structures are completely different."[4]

It is high time, therefore, that the present crisis in Africa is recognized to a very large extent as the product of human arrogance and impatience in years past. Africa's problems are not primarily its backwardness and poverty, but rather the unwillingness of those concerned to accept that the continent is caught in its own historical process of development. Such an awareness requires patience, humility, and respect for those institutions that already serve the continent's peoples. Provided on conventional terms, money and expertise from abroad will not solve Africa's problems.

Rather, the entire agenda of the debate about African development must be recast and intellectual horizons must be broadened. Existing schools of thought and paradigms are unlikely to be very useful guides for that exercise. This chapter is an attempt to take stock of those features peculiar to Africa's political economy and to suggest actions for governments and donors in order to render their interventions more attuned to local needs, capacities, and processes.

AFRICA'S HISTORICAL SPECIFICITY

As the dust of the debates on development that raged in the 1960s and 1970s finally settles, it is possible to identify those factors that differentiate Africa from other continents.

THE ABSENCE OF INTERMEDIATE TECHNOLOGY

Unlike in other continents, there was no indigenous tradition of land alienation and concentration in Africa. Only in colonial times did such tendencies emerge, becoming prominent primarily in those territories with a considerable number of European settlers, such as Kenya and Rhodesia. Nowhere in Africa did truly feudal societies develop, nor the highly regimented small-scale agriculture that permitted the rise of the great civilizations of Asia. Precolonial agriculture in various parts of the continent remained technologically simple, characterized by limited scope for surplus extraction. Although colonial authorities turned the majority of African peasants into commodity producers, causing considerable changes in farming systems, agriculture remained largely controlled by peasants with access to their own land at the time of independence.

To be sure, both in precolonial and colonial days, social differentiation led to apparent differences in wealth, but this process was very feeble. A major reason for the virtual absence of land alienation and concentration in sub-Saharan Africa is that societies did not acquire the technological means to realize it. As Jack Goody has argued, in the absence of wheel, plow, and other "intermediate technology" for agricultural development, sub-Saharan Africa was unable to match the improvements in skill and productivity and hence changes in specialization and stratification that marked agrarian societies in medieval Europe or the Far East.[5]

Africa's failure to acquire technological advances cannot be explained by the denial of such innovations by other powers, because in those days Africa had a number of empires and kingdoms. But its rulers sustained their regimes not by advancing agriculture but by appropriating surpluses from long distance trade.[6] As a result, African societies south of the Sahara never developed the institutional mechanisms that tied rulers to a system based on the exploitation of land. Being almost exclusively dependent on long distance trade, their fortunes and power waned with its decline.

While African farmers today are engaged in commodity production, usually for world markets, their systems and modes of production remain precapitalist in nature, characterized by low productivity levels per unit of land. Unlike capitalist production units, activities are not differentiated according to a strategy of specialized production, nor is labor specialized; hence money wages are still a marginal phenomenon in Africa's rural economies.

The low productivity of peasant agriculture is manifested in the discrepancy between rates of output on the continent and those achieved elsewhere. While world output of cereals averages about 2000 kg per hectare, Africa's average is only half that figure and the gap is widening.[7] These discrepancies reflect at least in part the lag in productivity-increasing agricultural research, particularly with regard to local varieties and conditions that Eicher has pointed out.[8]

Compared with Asia, African agriculture remains extensive. As a result, economic behavior tends to differ from that assumed in conventional household economics which postulates that as the size of farm-households increases, net farm production surpluses shrink. To the contrary, where land is not an immediate constraint and extensive cultivation is still possible, as in many parts of Africa, farm-households with larger labor forces tend to produce greater crop surpluses. Moreover, micro-economic studies of rural Africa indicate that peasant farmers have been quite quick to adopt agricultural innovations under certain circumstances, although attempts by public authorities to increase per hectare productivity have been largely unsuccessful.[9] In other words, productivity gains are not necessarily translated into a greater willingness to engage in surplus agricultural production. Instead, labor savings on the land have normally led to a reallocation of household labor to off-farm activities.

THE RELATIVE AUTONOMY OF THE PEASANT PRODUCER

Compared to peasant producers in other parts of the world, most African farmers enjoy a relatively high degree of autonomy from other groups and institutions in society. The main reason for this is the prevalence of rudimentary production technologies, in spite of many innovations. Because there is virtually no product specialization, there is a very limited exchange of goods between various units of production and no structural interdependence that brings them into reciprocal relations. Consequently, the scope for a refinement of the means of production is quite small. The limited product variety of households means that members are primarily engaged in socially necessary labor. In addition to tilling the land, rural labor forces do a great many other things both during the farming seasons and after it.

The fragmentation and autonomy at each level of production is reinforced by the absence of independently systemized knowledge to underpin prevailing modes of production. The necessary knowledge is in the producer's head and is normally transmitted from one generation to another through apprenticeship rather than formal training.

One significant illustration of structural autonomy is the method by which the surplus output is appropriated. Under feudalism and capitalism, for example, such appropriations are made in the context of either the landed estate or the factory. In such systems, the state is functionally and structurally linked to the productive demands of the economy and can be used by the rulers to run and control society. The submerged classes have no recourse but to respond to the dictates of the system at large. Where independent producers prevail, however, this relationship is qualitatively different.[10] Appropriations by those in control of the state have to be made in the form of taxation and as such are simple deductions from an already produced stock of values.[11]

To the independent peasant producer, the state is structurally superfluous and most public policy actions aimed at improving agriculture are viewed as having little or no value beyond any possible immediate gains to the producer himself. Because the peasant so extensively controls his own production, he is able to escape government policy demands to an extent that is certainly denied a tenant under feudal rule or a worker under capitalism. There is growing evidence that peasants in Africa use this "exit" option, particularly when policies are viewed as a threat or as devoid of any apparent benefits.[12]

What emerges from this analysis is that African governments are structurally less well-placed to influence agricultural development than governments in Asia or Latin America. Access to the peasant producer is limited and often must be accepted on the latter's terms. The notion that agricultural productivity can be markedly enhanced by "fine-tuning" the organizational instruments of government or by evolving new approaches to training the farmer is a costly illusion in most parts of Africa today. The African peasant producer is structurally less integrated in the wider economic system than his counterparts in Asia or Latin America, making him a particularly unpredictable actor. It also explains why so many policies based on official perceptions of "farmers' needs" have failed on the continent.

NO AGRICULTURAL SURPLUS LABOR

Another unique aspect of African history is that urbanization and industrialization have occurred without a concomitant "freeing up" of agricultural surplus labor in the rural areas. Between 1960 and 1980, Africa's rural-urban migration rate was the world's highest. From less than 20 percent in 1960, Africa was nearly 30 percent urbanized in 1980—an annual growth rate of about 5 percent or almost double the growth rate of total population.[13] Urban migrants almost invariably claim that they plan to retire in their home villages, consequently remitting considerable amounts of money not only to sustain the family members left on the land but also to invest in agricultural expansion and improvement.[14]

Because towns are only a place to live, but not home, the social and political orientation of most of Africa's urban residents has remained rural. Thus, Elkan's observation in 1960 that it is wrong to equate the growth of Africa's towns with the emergence of an urban proletariat seems equally valid today.[15] Certainly, when compared to the colonial days, Africa's urban centers have become increasingly ruralized in the process of accepting an accelerating influx of immigrants from the countryside. Hence, the distinction between rural and urban life has become less clear. Modes of interaction and of conducting business have increasingly taken on indigenous and rural characteristics.

The influx into the urban areas of both rich and poor who, through ownership and access to land, maintain a rural orientation, and the absence of a firmly established ruling class and thus an elite culture, give an inevitably populist character to African society. Strong informal ties and linkages between town and village exist that are rarely found in societies where productivity gains in agriculture have rendered a growing proportion of the labor force on the land superfluous. Because these ties are largely invisible—they do not show up in official statistics—and thus difficult to quantify, they tend to be ignored by economic analysts and policy-makers.

THE ECONOMY OF AFFECTION

The cellular character of agricultural systems and the rudimentary means of production, together with the extension of rural households to the urban areas, provide the African political economy with its historical peculiarity. The internal dynamics of the household and the relations they give rise to[16] constitute economic systems of their own within which members protect and promote their own interests, often at the expense of the larger system.

The economy of affection denotes networks of support, communications, and interaction among structurally defined groups connected by blood, kin, community, or other affinities such as religion. In this system, a variety of discrete economic and social units which in other respects are autonomous are linked together. The economy of affection is the articulation of principles associated with "peasant" or "household" economics as developed since the days of Chayanov, the intellectual forerunner of this school.[17] Chayanov argued that a peasant household would apply its own labor to farming in accordance with its internal equilibrium, determined by equating family demands and needs with the time required to meet them, not in terms of maximizing monetary profit. In this scheme, returns to family activities could not be broken down into components of wages and other factor payments. Rather, non-market aspects of both production and consumption were stressed and household decisions were based on use values rather than exchange values.

Chayanov recognized that the consumer/worker ratio within each household would vary according to its own development cycle, that is, as children grew older and could participate in production, the ratio improved and permitted greater consumption. He also accepted that within the household was the possibility of developing various forms of cooperation to enhance production efficiency. He also assumed, however, that the amount of land available to any household was given, in line with land tenure laws that prevailed in pre-revolutionary Russia. Thus, as its members increased, households had to make more intensive use of their time in order to meet consumption needs. These latter assumptions do not seem immediately applicable to Africa where land use is still extensive. Nor did Chayanov consider the possibility of members of rural households migrating to the towns and making their contribution to the household from an urban-based occupation. These two factors, however, have tended to enhance the autonomy of households vis-à-vis the "system," thus making household economics particularly relevant and influential.

The economy of affection is premised on the presence of structural opportunities for development through horizontal expansion, both economically and socially, within known and acceptable networks.

Although urban-rural remittances are generally less extensive in Latin America than in Africa, studies from that continent show how the economy of affection provides the basis for survival strategies of the poorer segments of the population.[18] With the exception of remittances by overseas workers, such transfers are also less important in the economies of Asia. But as in Latin America, they do form a regular part of the income of many poorer households.[19]

The single best contemporary example of both the strengths and weaknesses of the economy of affection is Lebanon, where economic prosperity was based on the institutionalization of economic and social forms of organization within each religious and ethnic community. Thus, business was typically conducted through family associations, and the political framework that was created permitted the spin-off effects of their activities to bolster the development of the country as a whole. Although the constitutional setup began to crack in the mid-1970s with the fragmentation of the political base, its affective components, because of their strong internal solidarity, survived and continued to provide the economic means to sustain military imperatives.

The Lebanese example shows that societies organized along the lines of an economy of affection can achieve quite impressive economic results but that their social and political fabrics tend to be fragile and, if torn, hostility among groups is likely to be both strong and difficult to overcome. In spite of Lebanon's current grave predicament, the country is one of the best examples outside of Africa of how an economy of affection can be made to work. Of particular relevance is the evolution of indigenous modes of economic organization and cooperation and their integration into a national economy that was able to attract large quantities of foreign capital, making it a show-case for the rest of the Middle East.

The motto of the economy of affection may be summarized in the words: "Diversification pays!" Whether applied by the household unit or the budding business firm, the strategy is the same. This inclination to spread the risks or maximize the opportunities for gains best summarizes the prevailing philosophy among Africans. The ability of the household to practice the economy of affection is a major reason why official development strategies have been contradicted or have failed altogether at the implementation stage.

In Africa, where the urban migrant usually does not lose his right to land, the introduction and adoption of improved technology may not arrest the movement from on-farm to off-farm employment but rather reinforce it, as Low has demonstrated with reference to southern Africa.[20] From an agronomic and development theorist point of view, more labor-intensive husbandry is a necessary corollary to the adoption of yield-increasing technologies. Yet, this is not happening on the average peasant farm in Africa. Instead, the acceptance of new technologies is accompanied by the use of less intensive cropping methods. In other words, rather than being the victims of the practices that pave the way for a more intensified capitalist penetration, the rural households manipulate the official innovations to their own advantage. The household can produce more food for itself using less time while still retaining the benefit of supplementary off-farm income to meet its cash needs.

To some extent, this discrepancy may be particularly acute in southern Africa because of the relatively low prices at which staple foods are available on the open market. Yet, it is also evident elsewhere if for no other reason than that urban wages have often been kept so high that male heads of rural households find it economically more rational to go off to the towns in search of additional income. It is no coincidence that the problem of an urban influx is less serious in Malawi because it is one of the few countries on the continent that has kept urban wages at a relatively low level.

The economy of affection does not disappear with increasing social differentiation. Organizations based on lineage and extended family connections have been significant in helping local entrepreneurs succeed in both West and Central Africa.[21] The age grade system has often served as a valuable substitute in East Africa.[22] Accumulation and social differentiation tend to be contained within the economy of affection and, as Sara Berry has shown in a study of Nigeria,[23] they run contrary to a strategy of economic development still predominant on the African continent which is based on centralizing investment decisions.

As Africa's answer to the attempt to impose other economic systems on the continent, the economy of affection reflects the self-help and harambee traditions so closely associated with the continent's peoples. Although not fought in those terms, the anti-colonial struggle was very much an expression of the sustenance of the principles of affection underlying African economics. The ability of leaders to mobilize the relations of affection for political purposes made a difference in the long run in the struggle against colonialism. As Hodgkin[24] and later Skinner[25] showed, urban-based welfare associations in West Africa were not only created to cope with the social and economic problems facing urban migrants, but developed into political tools used to fight the colonial presence.

Cliffe's review[26] of the emergence of anti-colonial movements in rural Tanzania also stresses the importance of mobilizing support through the unofficial channels of the economy of affection. These and other examples show that, under stress, the scope of this type of economy can be extended to incorporate relations that may not be considered under normal circumstances. Criteria of affinity are redefined and in a battle against an external enemy, a person from a very different community is accepted as "brother."

The ability of the economy of affection to open its doors to assist persons in stress makes it a very convenient weapon in political struggles and in self-defense against natural calamities. A foremost case in point is the armed independence struggle which was facilitated or in some instances made possible only due to the fighters' ability to make use of their relations of affection, thereby not only enhancing military effectiveness, but also popular support. The economy of affection served as their hinterland base for attacks on the colonial fortress.

Paradoxically, in post-independence Africa, the values and principles for which much of the anti-colonial struggle was fought run contrary to those underpinning the operations of the state machinery. Because the economy of affection does not presuppose appropriation of a surplus outside the context of given relationships, it is by definition hostile to formal bureaucratic principles common to Western societies. Relations of affection are constantly used to divert public funds for other purposes more in accordance with the ethos of the economy of affection. As a result, the state in Africa has increasingly lost its efficiency and effectiveness.[27] In much of Africa today, a "silent" guerrilla war has developed against those who in the name of "efficiency" or "socialist revolution" have tried to extend an impersonal bureaucratized state control over society. Using the peculiar structural safeguards of the economy of affection, these silent fighters are likely to outlast those in control of a sinking state.

Rights and obligations are still defined primarily in relation to the precapitalist structures associated with a system of smallholder production. The state is generally regarded as an arena to make gains if possible to enhance the relations of affection. It is the prevalence of this orientation that gives African politics its peculiar character. Politics of affection—or "clan politics" as Cruise O'Brien terms it[28]—continue where social differentiation has not yet crystallized into a distinct division between those who own the means of production and those who serve as workers. At present, Africa is witnessing only the early vibrations of its social transformation, tending to remain encapsulated in the communal relations sustained by the economy of affection.

Unlike their counterparts elsewhere, African leaders are not effectively in charge of a "system" in which policy instruments can be used to realize their private and public interests. Peasants can escape their demands and, therefore, they must be induced to serve the interests of government. As Sara Berry has noted,[29] accumulation strategies in Africa tend to be directed toward exerting power over resources rather than increasing their productivity. Whether the country is capitalist or socialist, property rights are politicized rather than privatized and used by the budding bourgeoisie to safeguard its own position.

The result is that the politics of affection is characterized by investments in patronage relations at all levels. The head of the household invests in the purchase of land for his wives and offspring even if this means ownership of many small plots operated at low productivity. If new land is unavailable, existing plots are subdivided or off-farm employment is sought to achieve the same end. Similarly, in order to safeguard his own position and respond to the affective pressures of his home community, the business entrepreneur tends to invest in many small enterprises which absorb labor at low levels of productivity rather than in the improvement of productivity within one or two operations.[30]

While the manager of a public enterprise may be bound more tightly by official regulations, he is not free from the pressures of affection, responding by steering investments to his home area and hiring people to whom he has an obligation. Even the civil servant finds it difficult to escape these pulls, particularly if he has to serve a politician whose legitimacy is almost wholly dependent on bolstering relations of affection.

With the investment of considerable sums of public money in "political maintenance," it is no surprise that public finances are in disorder. Problems of financial management on the continent are not due to lack of talent and experience, but rather originate in the emphasis of the politics of affection on channeling public funds to local constituencies, irrespective of considerations of efficiency and effectiveness. In the absence of countervailing pressures, efforts to improve the management of public finance in African countries are likely to prove futile.

SHORTCOMINGS OF EXISTING
DEVELOPMENT STRATEGIES

The peculiarity of the contemporary African political economy stems from low levels of technology in the peasant agricultural sector, giving rise to individual household strategies aimed at diversifying and maximizing economic gains within known social networks. While such a system has its own development potential, strategies adopted by governments and donors to date have failed to transform it or enable it to develop on its own terms.

Post-independence efforts in most African countries have separated state and society rather than bringing the two closer. Today the state sits suspended in mid-air above society, unable to break up existing networks and incapable of providing individuals with a means of transcending the narrow and often parochial confines of the economy of affection. Development strategies have failed to have an impact in most African countries because they have been formulated using criteria applicable to more technologically advanced systems.

The development strategies that have been adopted in the past have several major shortcomings. First, the inclination to tie strategies to specific target groups, notably the poorer segments of the population, overlooks the question of how to create self-sustaining development at the national level in economies that are still dependent on peasant producers using rudimentary technologies. The target group approach erroneously presupposes that systematic linkages exist for the transfer of resources to the poorer groups in society. In Africa, these linkages are either weak or non-existent, particularly where the official economy has more or less collapsed. Where the majority of rural producers enjoy an unusually high degree of autonomy from other groups in society, programs targeted on the rural poor are likely to have few systematic benefits. Thus, development aid has been placed in the proverbial cart without sufficient recognition that in order to move forward, it must be tied to a strong and healthy horse. Only in countries where the peasantry is increasingly "captured" (i.e., dependent on the macro-economic system for its own reproduction) will programs targeted on the poor begin to have an impact.

Second, there has been a tendency to develop programs and projects that bear little relationship to available management capacity. The Integrated Rural Development Program, so avidly endorsed by the World Bank and many bilateral donors, is one example. In addition to failing to benefit the poor, these programs have not succeeded in changing prevailing administrative practices and orientations, as a recent study of the IRDP in Sri Lanka shows.[31] In Africa, the IRDP has typically become a loose assemblage of individual projects run by single government departments. Attempts to add a planning structure to achieve integration have generally produced few results. Rather, these programs have limited government's operational flexibility and exacerbated red tape.

Third, the pressure on donors to spend large sums of money has resulted in projects that are overly complex in design and expensive to implement. In the case of urban housing, for example, the constraints of a time schedule and donor-approved standards that must be met make the completed schemes far too expensive for the average urban resident and thus wholly inadequate in dealing with urban housing needs. A recent survey completed in Nairobi indicates that there are three formal housing projects addressing the needs of the "low-income" residents, but at the same time there are least 20 squatter camps expanding much faster.[32]

Fourth, there is the notion that development problems can be solved if resources are concentrated in the most critical sector. Given the plausibility of the notion that the poverty and hunger of the rural poor can be best tackled if their agricultural yields are increased, it is not surprising that agriculture as the priority sector is embraced by all members of the donor community, including the international financial institutions. But in a situation where the peasant producer is not yet effectively captured by the official economic system, there is no assurance that he will respond in the expected manner. Furthermore, agricultural policy cannot be isolated from measures affecting job opportunities and wage levels in the urban areas. Sector-specific outlooks that have been so characteristic of the development debate in Africa have made the pendulum swing too far in either direction, overlooking the inevitable links between urban and rural development and agriculture and industry.

Although donors play a prominent role in determining African development strategies, it would be wrong to absolve the recipient governments, which have reinforced the above shortcomings and contributed their own. One is the notion that economies can be developed like armies under a single command. Relatively autonomous institutions like cooperatives and elected district councils have been subsumed under central government control. Kenya, Zambia, and Tanzania are only a few of the countries to have applied this notion, but as the Tanzanian experience suggests, mobilization and management of scarce economic resources requires a different approach.

A second shortcoming of African governments has been their tendency to view development as a collection of things to produce. They have almost totally ignored the fact that development is a do-it-yourself process, as all of today's highly developed economies were once backward. The prevailing illusion in Africa and in many other places (e.g., Iran under the Shah) is that development can be bought with revenue from oil or with aid. One of Africa's particular problems is the absence of an indigenous artisanal tradition from which to develop technology. The result is limited indigenous capacity for such key tasks as research, development, repair, and maintenance, creating the embarrassing paradox that industries begun only a few years ago remain inoperative or operate only at minimal capacity levels, while African governments continue to press for investments in new ventures.

Closely related to this orientation has been the belief that the continent's backwardness can be reversed by ready-made schemes for predetermined choices of products developed with assistance from the industrialized countries. Rather than encouraging trade within Africa, governments continue to pay primary attention to the dead-end trade with the more advanced economies. Instead of developing linkages between the cities and their rural hinterlands, the strategy pursued so far has left African countries as supply regions for the industrial world. Import-substituting schemes have been priced out of international markets and unlike efforts of a similar kind in Southeast and East Asia, imported industries have failed to break out of their limited domestic market.

The diversification of the economies of Kenya and Zimbabwe due to the presence of settler minorities made those countries structurally better equipped to make progress on their own. The same point is more applicable to South Africa, whose economic strength and growing role as a regional power is not only the result of exploiting cheap black labor or its position as a supply source for the industrialized countries.

A LOOK TO THE FUTURE

Because so many mistakes have been committed in the past two decades, it is easy to conclude that the outlook for Africa is a gloomy one. Gloom, however, is not necessary if governments and donors agree that conditions in Africa are different. It is easy to argue that pricing policies are wrong, that subsidies should be abandoned, or that excessive protection for local manufacturing is harmful to economic development. In Asia, for example, correcting failures in these areas produced positive results. Economies in Africa, however, are still such that they must be made better equipped to take on the challenge. Development is not merely a matter of choosing between a market of a planned economy. The conditions for the pursuit of these policies have yet to be created out of what remains a precapitalist base. African policy-makers are caught in structures and processes that place definite limits on what they can realistically accomplish, yet recognition of this point is absent in virtually all documents produced for consideration by African governments. Neither the Lagos Plan of Action nor recent World Bank reports on African development acknowledge it.

To develop a more balanced and realistic perspective on African development, it is necessary to accept what exists on the ground in African countries, starting from the premise that the fragile state of the African political economy creates pressures on leaders to centralize control and rule society through expensive gestures of state patronage. The preference for state control and direction cannot be explained by reference to African leaders' socialist inclinations. The prime rationale for such an approach is that it provides a better means of social control in a fluid political setup than does a market economy. The validity of this point is demonstrated in countries like Mozambique and Tanzania where socialist policies have not created socialism, but have only reinforced precapitalist forms of social and economic organization.

This statist orientation has also delayed or prevented the growth of an indigenous manufacturing and merchant class with power to act independently and demand policies that serve their interests. Even in West Africa where a merchant tradition has been kept alive, development policies have generally ignored the role of indigenous traders and in several cases treated them as pariahs. While a market economy approach seems more appropriate in contemporary Africa than one based on central planning, the legacy of the past cannot be ignored: Africa lacks the principal carriers of such an approach; the state is controlled by the volatile politics of affection; and rural producers remain constrained by rudimentary technologies, labor shortages, and a philosophy that puts higher premium on diversifying investments than intensifying agricultural production.

But if there are no shortcuts to progress, what are the ingredients of a development strategy more in tune with Africa's own social and material realities? In attempting to answer that question, consideration should be given to four principal propositions, each relating to choices of emphasis that will have to be made between elite and masses; town and village; government and non-governmental organizations; and direction and spontaneity.

STRENGTHEN AFRICA'S BOURGEOISIE

Africa's greatest shortcoming is its shortage of people with the creative capacity and power to set long-term development processes in motion. The bureaucratic bourgeoisie—politicians, administrators, and professionals in public institutions—may have the nation's interests at heart, but their efforts are hampered by cumbersome rules and regulations. African managers recruited by multinational companies, on the other hand, may possess the economic know-how and achievement orientation associated with entrepreneurship, but their impact is constrained by considerations of rates of return and other corporate principles guiding business ventures.

The historical artificiality of Marxism-Leninism in the contemporary African context is increasingly obvious even to leaders of states which continue to be categorized as such—far too simplistically—in Western media. Pressures to generate a bourgeoisie may in fact be strongest in those countries where the contradiction between political rhetoric and material reality is particularly striking. If these leaders find it difficult to retreat from a strategy of state control, it is less because of their belief in Marxist philosophy than their fear of political disunity caused by the economy of affection. Consequently, even in capitalist Kenya, for example, pressures toward political centralization and state control are also evident.

Africa's primary challenge is how to break out of its precapitalist cocoon. History suggests that the most probable strategy is to strengthen the bourgeoisie by encouraging the establishment of indigenous manufacturers and merchants. Liberals and socialists ought to have no difficulty in agreeing on such an approach, for only a strong bourgeoisie will overcome the constraints inherent in current primitive accumulation approaches and thus facilitate a sustained domestic capital formation. Without creative and productive talent of that kind, the African bourgeoisie will remain unable to protect and defend the continent against efforts by others to determine its course. Only a wholesome bourgeoisie will be able to create economic and political structures that eliminate the uncertainties associated with an economy of affection and without it, the evolution of durable socialist forms and relations on the African continent is likely to remain a faint possibility.

What is being proposed here has nothing to do with the assertion made in neo-liberal economic circles that capitalism is superior to socialism. Rather, the rationale behind a greater scope for capitalist principles in Africa today is their role in paving the way for a necessary transformation of prevailing precapitalist structures. In other words, capitalism must create the conditions under which it may prove its competitiveness with socialism in Africa.

What should African governments and donors do? Clearly, strategies must extend beyond the notion that multinational or state investments in agricultural and industrial development are the keys to progress. Incentives and support must be provided for the development of an indigenous corporate class. For example, special incentives could be provided for public servants to facilitate their move into private business without resorting to dishonest means to accumulate capital for such a purpose. Multinational companies could assist local managers in setting up their own businesses. By sponsoring local manufacturers in sub-contracting roles, foreign corporations could contribute to an improved business climate in Africa.

Another approach is based on the sister-industry concept, whereby small-scale manufacturers in Europe or the United States assist African entrepreneurs to set up similar businesses and provide them with access to export markets. Governments and donors should pay more attention to the local support structures required to facilitate entrepreneurship, such as credit institutions, technical assistance, and management training programs. Private capital must be allowed to work under conditions that facilitate rather than preempt local development.

DEVELOP A COMPREHENSIVE STRATEGY
BASED ON THE CITY

History shows that cities, not national governments, are the power-houses of economic development. The development of constructive relations between the urban centers and the hinterlands is at the heart of successful national economies. Compared with other continents, Africa lacks a tradition of city development. While cities existed in precolonial Africa, they were not productively linked to their rural hinterlands, flourishing instead on long-distance trade. Colonial rulers did little to change the situation, creating cities as intermediary links between Europe's financial and commodity markets and primary producers in Africa. The artificiality of African cities was further reinforced by economic subsidies provided by the colonial authorities as a means of attracting a permanent indigenous workforce to the newly built towns.

In the post-independence period, Africa's economic development efforts started with the double handicap of lacking cities integrated with their local countryside and citizens able to tap the full potential of urban centers. The growth of a bureaucratic bourgeoisie lacking the ability to develop new linkages between the towns and villages has only reinforced this handicap in recent years. Given the present crisis in the agricultural sector, efforts to improve rural productivity are legitimate but, as Jane Jacobs reminds us,[33] evidence from other parts of the world shows that sustained improvements in rural productivity have been possible only when cities have begun to replace imports with cheaper domestic innovations. Evidence tends to confirm Jacobs' thesis that both rural welfare and national wealth are proportionate to the economic vitality of cities. Urban residents' remittances to their home villages in the context of the economy of affection are significant contributions to rural development.[34] Private investments in agriculture by urban residents are particularly important where the prospects for agricultural improvement are good.

The differences between Kenya and Tanzania's economic performances since independence are less likely to be the result of their ideological approaches to development than the ability of the former to develop creative linkages between town and countryside.[35] Kenya's

sustained economic growth has been in part due to its encouragement of the urban-based Asian minority to redirect its merchant capital into productive investments, thus gradually replacing imports
and facilitating African capital's entry into commerce and industry.
Tanzania, on the other hand, discouraged private capital from establishing more productive linkages between town and countryside,
leaving the task to inefficient state enterprises.

Governments and donors must accept that any future development strategy requires a more systematic focus on the role of cities in
rural development. Although it may sound paradoxical, the roots of
Africa's present crisis are urban rather than rural. African cities lack
the local manufacturers and merchants with ambition and ability to
improvise and innovate. Urban consumers are subsidized at unrealistic prices and urban wages render local goods uncompetitive with
imports. Because productivity-increasing innovations in African agriculture are unlikely to curb the influx to towns and may indeed encourage it, governments and donors have little choice but to pay
closer attention to urban issues, in particular how town and countryside can be linked more productively.

As part of encouraging the growth of local entrepreneurs, the bureaucratic bourgeoisie should be cut to size through various privatization measures, including incentives for public servants to start private business, as suggested earlier. Other interventions should aim at
reducing the privileged and protected status of African cities. Lowering real wage income for urban residents is necessary to make local
products more competitive, to limit the scope of the economy of
affection, and to make income differentials between urban and rural
areas less apparent.

Many economists would argue that the urban-rural equation cannot be satisfactorily resolved unless measures are taken to enhance
rural productivity. While in the long run such an approach makes
sense, it is unlikely that prime attention to rural productivity—at the
expense of urban issues—will yield any developmental benefits.
While peasant farmers may respond to better prices by producing
more of a particular crop, they may not be able to enhance productivity due to labor and other physical constraints. Nor is increased support for research likely to have immediate payoffs in Africa's locale-
specific and rainfed agricultural system. A green revolution is
impossible as long as developing Africa's agriculture is a more risky
strategy than diversification into various off-farm activities.

The backbone of the economy of affection needs to be broken, and the only groups strong enough to perform this painful function are businessmen and manufacturers who from a city base can articulate their demands for policies that enhance productivity or efficiency both at micro and macro levels. It is these people rather than government officials or development workers in the rural areas who are best placed to foster progress. For instance, much of the well-intended ingenuity that goes into developing "appropriate technology" is a waste of time. These solutions should be developed in conjunction with urban-based technicians and businessmen, as they are best placed to assess the marketability of the innovation. If the product proves successful initially, these marketing agents will ensure that the word of its success spreads into even the remotest village.

Town and village must also be considered together when setting food prices. As Low has shown in reference to southern Africa,[36] food price policies aimed at stimulating domestic production must take into account not only retail prices, but the implications of altering the availability and prices of imported foodstuffs. Raising retail food prices and reducing food aid and commercial imports in order to stimulate domestic production measures involve political risks. Such measures reduce the real income of net consuming households, adversely affecting the nutritional status of poorer households. So far, low-income households have remained unaffected by macro-economic measures because they have had access to the economy of affection as a safety valve. If on the other hand, policies are to be more than welfare measures, instead designed to enhance the capacity of African economies to stand on their own feet, the conflict between production and welfare goals will be intensified in the future. Well-developed cities, with productive linkages to their rural hinterlands, are a precondition to affording subsidies and other welfare programs.

DIVERSIFY INSTITUTIONAL RESPONSIBILITIES

Without a creative bourgeoisie in the driver's seat and productive cities as the powerful engine, Africa will become a perpetual "welfare" case. The rest of the world will have to pump endless amounts of money into the continent to stem misery and death. If the two propositions suggested above are taken seriously, there is at least a chance that the problem of human and social welfare on the continent will prove manageable. This strategy would provide options with a potential to make a difference.

Social development in post-independence Africa has lacked consideration of its long-term economic and political implications. For example, education has expanded without limit because it has proved popular and there is nothing wrong with providing new knowledge to people. Whereas basic health facilities have not been in as great demand as education, their provision has been a prominent part of Africa's development strategies to date, viewed as a "basic need" by donors. Both education and health projects are popular with politicians because they make for good political patronage. Even when these facilities have involved an element of self-help, they have been far less controversial with the local people than projects involving improvements in agricultural practices.

Thus, it is no coincidence that self-help efforts organized by political leaders have tended to focus on the social rather than economic aspects of life.[37] Whereas the provision of a school or health center makes a politician look responsible and concerned, insistence on agricultural improvements makes him a colonial taskmaster in the eyes of the local people. The result is that African countries today are saddled with a social welfare sector that the state is unable to handle. Unless something drastic is done, education, health, and other social sectors will decline, making African societies unmanageable entities.

In order to salvage the situation, African governments have little choice but to diversify institutional responsibilities by encouraging local communities, elected local councils, and voluntary agencies to play a greater part in running the country. Thus far, policy has been outright hostile toward these bodies with the result that people have lost the interest and motivation to participate in development programs and have been left with no venue to express their views. As long as a volatile economy of affection sets the stage for politics, there will be resistance to any change away from this pattern.

There is evidence, however, that its limits are increasingly being realized. Even those who do not necessarily favor the emergence of institutions independent of the state are ready to accept that government cannot do everything and that non-governmental organizations (NGOs) are needed to help carry out public responsibilities.

Although the door is being opened to the private and voluntary sectors, there has been little thought of what their contributions to development should be. Policy questions requiring attention at this stage include to what extent responsibility for primary education, basic health, and local water supply can be transferred to local authorities and voluntary or private agencies. Delegating responsibility for such tasks would be a meaningful step toward the establishment of more democratic forms of government, particularly if the responsibility is located at the community or village level rather than the district.

The district councils set up by the colonial powers were justified on the grounds of economy of scale. They operated in a satisfactory manner as long as they were under the tutelage of colonial officials, however, after independence they quickly fell into disrepute because they lacked accountability to the local communities and thus became arenas for indiscriminate dispensation of patronage by individual councilors. Any future local government system should be built from below, involving viable local communities in tasks meaningful to their own development.

Africa also lacks strong indigenous voluntary agencies, despite a deeply ingrained spirit of self-help. Most voluntary groups on the continent remain small-scale and unofficial and thus invisible to policy-makers and donors. A challenge therefore is how to mobilize the voluntarist spirit toward broader development goals. Best placed to perform this role are the many intermediary, often church-based organizations, which have become increasingly concerned with development issues in recent years. They are in close contact with local people, enjoy their confidence, and can usually rely on their voluntary contributions. Although they often lack management capacity, they are more likely to achieve results than heavy-footed public bureaucracies.

What then can African governments and donors do? In many countries, a first step would be to investigate the policy issues involved in a broader delegation of responsibilities to local governments and NGOs. Their role in domestic resource mobilization should be fully assessed in the context of national development strategies. Donors must increase their funding flexibility, no longer taking refuge behind avowals that they can only give funds to governments. Agreements must be reached with African governments to allow the flow of direct aid to NGOs.

Donors and African governments should pay greater attention to private and voluntary organizations because they demonstrate that development can be promoted more efficiently and effectively than through official channels. Investments to improve them are more likely to have tangible benefits than similar efforts in public bureaucracies. Second, governments will not be able to deal adequately with poverty alleviation in Africa for the foreseeable future. The only way to avoid a catastrophe is to engage the NGOs more directly in this task, as they have the flexibility and the contact with poverty groups that governments lack. They can develop and incorporate into their programs non-conventional solutions to poverty remediation issues.

In other parts of the world, poverty alleviation was handled almost exclusively by non-governmental agencies. The successful institutionalization of these measures subsequently paved the way for government to take over these functions once its revenue base permitted. It has been a tragedy that in Africa, governments and donors have continued to see poverty remediation as a state responsibility, particularly since government machineries are so ill-equipped to handle the task. Poverty remediation issues in Africa should not continue to be seen in contemporary Western terms.

Third, NGOs deserve increased support because, by becoming stronger, they will facilitate implementation of government programs and hold public officials more accountable for their actions. At present, many government programs achieve very little because there are no developed structures into which government agencies can plug their own operations. By strengthening these organizations, donors can indirectly help improve public management and promote democratic forms of governance. Because NGOs tend to cut across the narrow bonds of the economy of affection, they are important mechanisms for overcoming its often parochial outlook.

ADOPT A "GREENHOUSE" APPROACH

Given the positivist spirit that rapidly evolved in post-independence Africa, it is not surprising that policy-makers espoused a strong faith in planning and proper project designs and in their ability to contribute to the development process. Themselves captive of the positivist era, donors were only too eager to endorse this approach. To enable the state to perform its developmental role, it was necessary to enhance planning capacity at various levels and through the assistance of technical advisers, to ensure that individual projects were adequately prepared on the drawing board, with or without prior testing.

While careful programming and design may be of utmost importance in technical projects where variables can be manipulated at will, such an approach is inherently limited when applied to development efforts that depend on human resolution and will. For many years, Africans and donors alike attributed the inability to reach anticipated development objectives to insufficient planning skills, faulty programming methods, or inadequate project preparation, proposing more training, better programming, and fuller preparation as remedies.

This "blueprint" approach has an appealing sense of order because of its concentration on clearly defined activities with discrete and visible outcomes.[38] It also elevates the professional to a superordinate role in the development process. However, it presupposes a stable and predictable environment in which variables can be satisfactorily controlled and manipulated. For infrastructural projects, for example, tasks are defined, outcomes terminal, the environment stable, and costs consequently predictable. In Africa's predominantly rural environment, however, the situation is the opposite. Policymakers do not have control of their environment. In the typical rural setting, it is the peasant rather than the government officer who makes the ultimate decision on how factors of production like land, water, labor, technology, and capital are being utilized. The notion of the uncaptured peasant is particularly applicable to Africa where his marginal incorporation into a market economy and continued dependence on a simple technology leave officials with few strings to pull in order to influence his behavior.

The frustration of failing to control peasant production has caused many governments to resort to capital-intensive, large-scale farming or complex settlement schemes in which producers are treated as tenants. Direct government involvement in development projects of this kind, however, has generally proved no more successful, as even in these production settings, and the "autonomous" peasant has prevailed.[39]

The almost blind application of the blueprint approach has decreased confidence in public institutions' abilities to bring about progress. Today, citizens show great reluctance to participate in new government schemes, and scarce human resources are being wasted. For this reason, African governments and donors must consider alternatives that can restore human motivation to contribute to national development.

An appropriate alternative, the "greenhouse" approach is based on the assumption that people will organize and accomplish tasks of common concern if provided with the stimuli and incentives. Rather than organizing people for purposes beyond their comprehension and interest, the greenhouse approach focuses on factors that help local efforts grow on their own. True to its name, it provides a hospitable climate for growth even in otherwise adverse circumstances. For example, rather than implanting organizational models in the cooperative sector, the greenhouse approach starts with what already exists and encourages organizational development from below or within. It tries to accelerate progress on the basis of what society already offers.

Local savings efforts are cases in point. Studies show that "informal" credit and savings efforts are widespread in Africa and recent efforts in Kenya and Zimbabwe to recognize their role in rural development are beginning to pay off in increased income generation. The greenhouse approach would help strengthen local efforts by facilitating expansion beyond the parochial boundaries of small communities. While this approach recognizes that fostering progress in Africa involves much more than the application of capitalist principles, the latter are an integral part because only through an "open economy" policy will it be possible to accelerate a transformation of the continent's still predominantly precapitalist economies. Governments and donors will have to recognize and support institutions that address the issue of how the poor in the urban and rural informal sectors can become respected and meaningful participants in development.

A corollary of such a strategy would be to encourage alternatives to government involvement in economic activities. More scope must be given to improvised solutions such as the development of extension services organized by private, voluntary, or cooperative institutions. A plan must be devised for the reduction and reallocation of official manpower resources to NGOs. If such institutions do not already exist, policies that encourage their creation and growth must be adopted.

In short, the greenhouse approach enables governments and donors to discover how Africa's own wheels of progress can move faster and ultimately replace the foreign wheels which, because of their size and inappropriate construction, inevitably destroy the African terrain.

CONCLUSIONS

In 1973, the All-Africa Conference of Churches' call for an aid moratorium, based on its view that the spirit of self-reliance in Africa was undermined by ill-conceived aid projects that often preempted rather than facilitated local development, was not taken seriously. With the number of aid programs that have ground to a halt, it is tempting to agree with the AACC.

However, the prospects for African development have deteriorated considerably over the last decade and ceasing aid at this point is a much more controversial proposition. What is required is a retreat from the notion that Africa can be treated like any other Third World region because its historical circumstances are different. Even a market economy approach, which is favored in this chapter as the most effective way of transforming the precapitalist economy of affection, cannot harvest any easy victories in Africa, and is rather justified to prepare the ground for future productivity gains and social progress.

Africa needs to develop on its own terms. Its current crisis cannot be blamed simply on factors such as corruption and inefficiency because, thus far, African countries have been forced to progress on terms foreign to their own material and social realities. They deserve the benefit of a home game. African leaders, though very slowly, are gradually getting ready for such a game. Are the donors ready to adjust their strategies?

NOTES

1. Albert Hirschman, "The Rise and Decline of Development Economics," in *Essays in Trespassing: Economics to Politics and Beyond.* New York: Cambridge University Press, 1981, pp. 1–24.

2. Carl Eicher, "West Africa's Agrarian Crisis," paper presented to the Fifth Bi-Annual Conference of the West African Association of Agricultural Economics, Abidjan, Ivory Coast, December 7–11, 1983, pp. 19–26.

3. Keith Hart, *The Political Economy of West African Agriculture.* London: Cambridge University Press, 1982, p. 105.

4. J. G. Karuga, Permanent Secretary in the Ministry of Energy and Regional Development, quoted by *The Standard* (Nairobi), 7 July 1984.

5. Jack Goody, *Technology, Tradition and The State in Africa.* Oxford: Oxford University Press, 1971, p. 71.

6. See, for instance, Robin Law, *The Oyo Empire c. 1600–c. 1836: A West African Imperialism in the Era of the Atlantic Slave Trade.* Oxford: Clarendon

Press 1977; Richard Roberts, "Long Distance Trade and Production: Sinsani in the Ninetheenth Century," *Journal of African History* 21(2) (1980).

7. Economic Commission for Africa, *ECA and Africa's Development 1983– 2008: A Preliminary Perspective Study*. Addis Ababa: Economic Commission for Africa, April 1983, p.9.

8. Eicher, op. cit., p. 10.

9. Particularly extensive and interesting materials are provided by Allan Low, *Agricultural Development in Southern Africa*. London: James Curry Publishers, 1985, especially Chapters 11–13.

10. In my own writings, I usually refer to existing pre-capitalist modes of production in Africa under the common label of the "peasant" mode, the reason being that those who appropriate the surplus are themselves dependent on the peasant producers and lack the means of effectively enforcing their own will on these producers. The dominant culture, therefore, also tends to reflect peasant values rather than forming a distinct "high culture" that is associated with more deeply stratified class societies.

11. This point is further elaborated by Barry Hindess and Paul O. Hirst, *Pre-Capitalist Modes of Production*. London: Routledge & Kegan Paul, 1975.

12. Evidence is provided by Sara S. Berry, "Agrarian Crisis in Africa? A Review and an Interpretation," paper presented for the Joint African Studies Committee of the Social Science Research Council and the American Council of Learned Societies, September 1983, p. 4.

13. Economic Commission for Africa, op. cit., p. 7.

14. Compare, for example, John O. Caldwell, *African Rural-Urban Migration: The Movement to Ghana's Towns*. New York: Columbia University Press, 1969; John C. Mitchell, ed., *Social Networks in Urban Situations*. Manchester: Manchester University Press, 1969; Joyce Moock, "The Content and Maintenance of Social Ties Between Urban Migrants and Their Home-Based Support Groups: The Maragoli Case," *African Urban Notes* 3 (Winter 1978–79); Thomas Weisner, "The Structure of Sociability: Urban Migration and Urban Ties in Kenya," *Urban Anthropology*, 5 (1976); and Richard Sandbrook, *The Politics of Basic Needs: Urban Aspects of Assaulting Poverty in Africa*. London: Heinemann, 1982.

15. Walter Elkan, *Migrants and Proletarians: Urban Labour in the Economic Development of Uganda*. Oxford: Oxford University Press, 1960.

16. For a useful overview of intra-household processes and the place of households in the context of community structures, see Jane I. Guyer, "Household and Community in African Studies," *African Studies Review* 24(273) (1981): 87–138.

17. A. V. Chayanov, *The Theory of Peasant Economy*. Homewood, Ill.: Richard D. Irwin for the American Economics Association, 1966.

18. See, for example, Dani Kaufmann, "Social Interactions as a Strategy of Survival Among the Urban Poor: A Theory and Some Evidence," Ph.D. dissertation, Harvard University, 1981.

19. See Mary Hollnsteiner, "Reciprocity in the Lowland Philippines," in F. Lynch and A. Gusman, eds., *Four Readings on Philippine Culture*. Manila: Ateneo de Manila University Press, 1973.

20. Low, op. cit., Ch. 11.

21. See, for example, Polly Hill, *Migrant Cocoa Farmers in Southern Ghana*. Cambridge: Cambridge University Press, 1963; John M. Janzen, "The Cooperative in Lower Congo Economic Development," in David Brokensha and Marion Pearsall, eds., *The Anthropology of Development in Sub-Saharan Africa*. Lexington, Ky.: Society for Applied Anthropology, 1969, Monograph 10, pp. 70–76; William Ogionwo, *Innovative Behavior and Personal Attitudes: A Case of Social Change in Nigeria*. Boston: G. K. Hall & Company, 1978.

22. Peter Marris and Anthony Somerset, *The African Entrepreneur: A Study of Entrepreneurship and Development in Kenya*. New York: African Publishing Corporation, 1972; Kenneth King, *The African Artisan: Education and the Informal Sector in Kenya*. London: Heinemann, 1977.

23. Sara S. Berry, "Oil and the Disappearing Peasantry: Accumulation Differentiation and Underdevelopment in Western Nigeria," unpublished manuscript, Boston University, 1984.

24. Thomas Hodgkin, *Nationalism in Colonial Africa*. London: Frederick Muller, 1956.

25. Elliot P. Skinner, "Voluntary Associations in Ouagadougou: A Reappraisal of the Function of Voluntary Associations in African Urban Centers," *African Urban Notes*, Series B, No. 1 (Winter 1974/75).

26. Lionel Cliffe, "Nationalism and the Reaction to Enforced Agricultural Change in Tanganyika during the Colonial Period," paper presented to the East African Institute of Social Research Conference, Makerere University, Kampala, December 1964.

27. The concept of the "soft" state was first coined by Gunnar Myrdal in his *Asian Drama: An Inquiry into the Poverty of Nations*. New York: Twentieth Century Fund and Pantheon Books, 1968.

28. Donal B. Cruise O'Brien, *Saints and Politicians: Essays in the Organization of a Senegalese Peasant Society*. Cambridge: Cambridge University Press, 1975.

29. Berry, "Agrarian Crisis in Africa?, op. cit., p. 67.

30. See, for example, ibid, and Glen Norcliffe, "Operating Characteristics of Rural Non-Farm Enterprises in Central Province, Kenya," *World Development* II (11) (1983).

31. Report on the Integrated Rural Development Programme in Sri Lanka, quoted in *Kenya Times* (Nairobi) 14 June 1984.

32. Graham Adler, advisor to National Cooperative Housing Union in Kenya, personal communication, July 3, 1984.

33. Jane Jacobs, *Cities and the Wealth of Nations: Principles of Economic Life*. New York: Random House, 1984, pp. 151–53.

34. Paul Collier and Dipak Lal, "Poverty and Growth in Kenya," Staff Paper No. 389, Washington, D.C.: The World Bank, 1980, p. 35.

35. It should be pointed out that within Tanzania, the situation of Dar es Salaam stands in contrast to the northern town of Arusha which has quite successfully developed a productive relationship with its rural hinterland and as a consequence has been prospering in spite of the country's general economic decline.

36. Low, op. cit., pp. 312–18.

37. For a discussion of this issue, see Frank Holmquist, "Class Structure,

Peasant Participation and Rural Self-Help" in Joel D. Barkan and John J. Okumu, eds., *Politics and Public Policy in Kenya and Tanzania*. New York: Praeger, 1979, pp. 129–53.

38. This approach is reviewed and analyzed by David Korten, "Community Organization and Rural Development: A Learning Process Approach," *Public Administration Review* 40(5) (1980): 481–511.

39. Robert Chambers, *Settlement Schemes in Tropical Africa: A Study of Organizations and Development*. London: Routledge & Kegan Paul, 1969.

CHAPTER THREE

Governance and Economic Management

Benno J. Ndulu

Whereas the magnitude of the economic crisis that has afflicted Africa over the last decade has varied from country to country, a consensus has developed concerning both the external factors and internal policies that have contributed to the current stagnation. Domestic economic management policies are increasingly drawing the attention not only of donors and international institutions, but also of African governments themselves.[1] Pan-African organizations have also begun to reassess economic policies and institutional structures in order to address the current crisis.[2] This new introspection has stemmed from a realization that the impact of external shocks can be minimized by sound economic management and that economic structures can be strengthened by a more efficient use of development resources.

THE POLITICAL-ECONOMIC CONTEXT

Development planning and economic management in Africa involve a careful balancing of different and often conflicting interests. The assumption implicit in liberal economic theory–that the state is a "neutral" and even benevolent arbiter whose role is to further the national interest in economic growth, efficiency, and social welfare–is not borne out in practice (Sandbrook, 1982, p. 77).

In most African political systems, whether civilian or military, the majority of the population is politically impotent, the power of the government is implicitly acknowledged, and elites cater to some of the demands of their "clients," while assuring that these demands do not reach levels requiring severe structural reforms. As a result, policies reflect in part the interests of the national elites, and in part, those of the population at large (Cleaves, 1980, p. 25). In the absence of more open political systems, in which organized interest groups can thrash out their differences, the state's involvement in resource allocation is more pronounced and often used as a means of balancing different interest groups and maintaining patron-client networks.

Another dominant characteristic of African regimes is the close link between the state bureaucracy and the private sector, both foreign and indigenous. Elites use state power either independently or in conjunction with private entrepreneurs to enter into the business sphere,[3] tending to create a strong symmetry of interests between the private sector and the state bureaucracy. As some price distortions, such as lowered tariffs for imports and subsidized capital, have benefited private and public sector interests at the expense of an overall efficient allocation of resources, they represent among the more formidable constraints to the implementation of lasting reforms.

Although the above characterization of African political structures seems to be generally applicable, there are important distinctions between the various regimes that are relevant to the analysis of macro-economic management. On one end of the spectrum are regimes with liberal open economies, in which foreign private sector interests dominate and national elites are weak, such as Ivory Coast, and on the other, states with strong "nationalistic" interests, such as Tanzania. Between these extremes, there are wide variations in the extents to which the state intervenes and to which non-economic goals are pursued.

It is in terms of the link between state-society power relationships and macro-economic management policies pursued that three regime typologies can be broadly defined.[4] The first, liberal economies, are characterized by an open door foreign investment policy and by a national elite and state machinery which play a secondary role in resource allocation. Such regimes allow for relatively free inflows and outflows of resources. State intervention in the markets for goods and resources is minimal. Development strategies aim at achieving maximum growth rates, while income distribution and equity are secondary concerns. The state's primary economic function is to maintain adequate infrastructure and a stable and attractive environment for foreign private capital. State intervention is confined for the most part to the domestic food markets where foreign private capital interests are not strong. While Ivory Coast is the best example of this regime typology, others might include Senegal, Niger, Chad, and Malawi.

Whereas development planning in these countries is indicative of the economic direction the country is pursuing, it is neither binding nor specific in allocation of resources. Over time, however, pressures have grown in these countries for indigenization of both the management and ownership of foreign capital. As a result, the public sector has expanded via equity state participation or new investments wholly owned by the state. The indigenous private sector has also grown, as has its involvement in large-scale agriculture.

The second typology includes those countries such as Nigeria, Ghana, Zambia, Botswana, and Kenya with strong "nationalistic" regimes, where the interests of the national elites take precedence over foreign private capital. National interest groups are strongly represented and have some influence on the state machinery and bureaucracy. In this type of regime, sometimes referred to as "state capitalist," the state plays a key role in allocating resources and controlling the development process. State participation in and control over directly productive sectors, either through wholly owned enterprises or partnerships with private capital, are consistent with the goals of economic nationalism and with public officials' own sense of identity with the state (Bienen and Diejomaoh, 1980, p. 138).

Economic growth is a key objective, but structural adjustment strategies and the indigenization of economic activities are also national priorities. Consequently, partial nationalization of foreign interests, expanded state investments, and encouragement of domestic private investment are part of the accumulation process. Not only are foreign capital inflows channeled through and controlled by the state, but resources are allocated either directly through the state budget or indirectly through commodity and price controls. Price distortions, however, are more severe than in the liberal economies because of the controls, while at least at the rhetorical level, distributional and equity issues are addressed in development planning.

The third typology, the "national-collectivist" system, includes those countries aspiring to socialism such as Tanzania, Mozambique, Angola, and Ethiopia. Rather than focusing on economic growth, these regimes make serious efforts to tackle issues of distribution and equity. While many features of the second typology apply here, the extent of government intervention in investment and marketing is greater. Public spending on social programs as a percentage of available resources is higher than in the other typologies. Although the use of price controls is more prevalent, the private sector's contribution to national output is nonetheless strong.

These distinctions between regimes are useful to our analysis because the extent to which the state intervenes and non-economic issues are considered in policy formulation has a bearing on the constraints to economic adjustment and stabilization measures. In the second and third typologies, more cautious approaches to such policy reforms will have to be adopted because of the more active involvement of domestic interest groups in the political arena and of the state in resource allocation.[5] By contrast, regimes in the first category face less political risk in implementing economic reforms. Given fewer controls and thus distortions in these economies, the political and financial costs associated with shifting resources are negligible. The sheer size of foreign private capital interests constitutes a formidable "voting" bloc that most often favors reforms, as "weak" national elites cannot ignore the threat of foreign sector withdrawal.

KEY ISSUES IN ECONOMIC MANAGEMENT: PROBLEMS AND PROSPECTS FOR REFORMS

The key issues in African economic management are the role and size of the public sector, the level of state intervention in resource allocation, and the use of counter-cyclical economic policies. While each of these issues will be addressed, it is necessary first to outline the climate in which reforms in these areas will take place, as it will have a bearing on the degree to which they are accepted and implemented by concerned governments.

Despite the political constraints on economic adjustment outlined here, recent developments have decreased the risk of implementing reform. The growth of parallel markets and corruption has, in effect, given impetus to some adjustments, eroding state control over markets. The black markets in foreign exchange and imports have indirectly increased domestic prices of scarce commodities and have undermined government subsidies on foodstuffs. When shortages occur, goods obtained at official subsidized prices are resold in parallel markets. In effect, this erosion of state control has significantly altered the political calculus of economic adjustment.

Reducing or eliminating food subsidies at a time when consumers are already purchasing more than 70 percent of their supplies from parallel markets at prices often more than double the official rate may be more acceptable than prior to the existence of such markets, when subsidized prices were maintained by using food imports to make up for shortages. Similarly, requiring that the costs for public services that were previously free be shared should be politically easier in a period when both the quantity and quality of free services are declining.

A more favorable attitude toward economic reform in sub-Saharan Africa has resulted not only from external economic pressures, but also from perceptions of the growing costs of ineffective state control over the economy and of the detrimental effects of economic deterioration on various interest groups. These elements have a bearing on the extent to which a government can politically and economically accommodate the burdens of adjustment.

It is still too early to judge whether the current willingness on the part of African governments to undertake reform can be sustained once economic conditions improve, or whether it is a temporary phenomenon. More detailed studies on the impact of economic retrenchment on interest groups and on state-society relationships will be required. It would appear, however, that sustainable reform will hinge upon the strengthening of institutional structures capable of defending the resultant changes. Further, it must be recognized that the causes of the current economic deterioration are long term, and that structural adjustment rather than short-term stabilization is the central issue. Therefore, this chapter will focus on the institutional aspects of reform which constitute the focal point of sustained change.

THE SIZE OF THE PUBLIC SECTOR
RELATIVE TO EFFECTIVE MANAGERIAL
CAPACITY

Over the past two decades, the public sector in sub-Saharan Africa has grown very rapidly. Governmental activities have expanded into the productive and commercial spheres through commercial enterprises, and the governmental sector itself (public administration) has also grown. The public sector now accounts for an average of over 50 percent of total wage employment, growing faster than the private sector partly because of changes in ownership, through nationalizations and majority equity participation, and partly because of an absolute rise in public sector activities. Other indicators, such as the growing share of public sector expenditures in the national accounts, corroborate this observation.

The expansion and diversification of activities of the public sector have seriously overtaxed management capacities. In addition to macro-economic management, the public sector is also responsible for the supply of economic and social infrastructure and management of commercial enterprises. The performance of the public sector relative to the share of national resources available to it is weak, both in terms of output and cost-effectiveness. Although a few public enterprises–notably those involved in extractive industries, financial intermediation, and manufacturing–have generated surpluses, others, especially in the agricultural marketing sector, have become a financial burden, requiring subsidization or loans from the domestic banking system.

Managerial capacity is poor in sub-Saharan Africa due to insufficient training and supportive infrastructure such as data bases and hard and software. Whereas many countries have made advances in education and training, the supply of skilled managers remains short of requirements. Most countries are still dependent on foreign technical capacity for the formulation of investment programs, the preparation of investment projects, and even the design of development plans and policy reviews. This shortage is evidenced by the widespread involvement of the World Bank and bilateral donors in the formulation of sectoral programs, and of foreign companies at the enterprise level.

Reliance on foreign technical capacity has given rise to several problems. First and foremost is the absence of a unified managerial system. The multiplicity of technical groups operating in a given country has frequently led to a situation where national investment programs have become a catch-all for projects originating from different sectors and enterprises. Balancing macro-economic resources, therefore, has been difficult, often resulting in capacity underutilization and high opportunity costs when expensive resources are left idle.

Second, given the differing and changing perspectives of the technical groups, discontinuity in economic management has become the norm over time, sometimes leading to drastic changes in development strategies. Third, costly time lags between formulation of programs and their implementation develop, partially because of lack of follow-up from the technical teams who often consider the program document their final task. Since the participation of local technical cadres in the preparation of programs has been limited, time is wasted over simply digesting the key facets of the programs to be implemented.

Effective economic management has also been hindered by the scarcity and poor quality of data required for planning and policy formulation. Information is not only essential for technical policy analysis and projections, but also for generating confidence in and gaining acceptance of projects. Unsupported by hard data on their likely impact on the economy and interest groups, reforms have a poor chance of gaining acceptance. Statistical bureaus in many countries are short of both qualified personnel and support systems for collecting and processing data. Whereas some ministries with independent sources of finance have tried to develop their own statistical base and some research institutions have become involved in statistics compilation, what often results is a multitude of disorganized and contradictory data.

The overcentralization of the state and the expansion of its activities have diluted its ability to focus on priority areas. However, many administrators believe that decentralization would relegate authority to inadequately trained, incompetent, and dishonest cadres (Jones, 1982, p. 557). While there is some basis for this perception, thinly spreading the more competent managers would not suffice either. Moreover, job accountability is not improved when bureaucratic structures are so encumbered with layers that locating the source of a decision or action is virtually impossible. Since 1972, several countries, including Tanzania, Sudan, and Senegal, have attempted government decentralization. These efforts, however, have increased administrative costs and have proven ineffective in expanding domestic participation in economic planning (Rondinelli, 1981, case of Sudan; N. Blues and Weaver, 1977, case of Tanzania).

Two approaches to correcting the problems presented above are proposed: first, reducing the size of the public sector and decentralizing management responsibilities to lower levels of government and to community groups; and second, strengthening local technical managerial expertise through training and improved data collection and dissemination systems.

REDUCING THE SIZE OF THE PUBLIC SECTOR

Reducing the size of the public sector can be accomplished by its withdrawal from certain commercial and production activities, specifically agricultural marketing, industry, and road transport.

Agricultural Marketing   Public sector withdrawal from agricultural marketing would have high payoffs. However, the lack of adequate infrastructure is a critical constraint. Transportation, storage, and information systems are prerequisites to efficient marketing, yet they have received less attention than the existing marketing institutions. Second, many countries have undergone a number of changes in their marketing arrangements since independence, from control by private interests to cooperatives to parastatals, creating an uncertain atmosphere for producers. As a result, any new changes should be carefully considered.

Not only do parastatals represent a budgetary burden on the state, but they have also become increasingly ineffective, as their share of marketed output, particularly in foodstuffs, has declined over time. Parallel markets that offer higher prices and prompt payment have rendered parastatals non-competitive.[6] Even as the volumes handled by parastatals have declined, their size has remained the same, causing unit overhead costs to shoot up. Hence, substantial losses were incurred. Food marketing parastatals, therefore, have benefited neither the producer nor the urban consumer, as they are unable to deliver the required quotas at the subsidized prices.

Private marketing agents and voluntary cooperatives could fill the gap created by public sector withdrawal from marketing, as both existed in many countries prior to extensive government intervention. The role of private agricultural marketing agents has grown with the development of parallel markets, which in some countries, channel as much as 70 percent of food supplies.[7] Historically, the development of indigenous private agricultural marketers has faced a number of constraints. Under colonial rule, foreign companies, notably Lebanese and Asian, dominated agricultural marketing. Indigenous private traders were largely confined to localized trade in perishables and suffered from lack of access to credit.[8] Only through registered producer cooperatives were Africans able to make any headway in agricultural trade. As a result, at independence, private agricultural trading capacity was underdeveloped.

In the immediate post-independence period, "nationalistic" regimes sought to replace the "alien" or foreign private traders with either government-initiated cooperatives or state/parastatal agencies, further impeding any development of indigenous private trading institutions. However, with increasing food shortages and the apparent inefficiencies of the parastatals, "clandestine" markets in which both operating costs and profits are high have attracted indigenous traders to agricultural marketing both at the local and national levels.

In the early 1970s, official consumer prices were maintained by importing food to meet excess demand, but this is no longer feasible as limited foreign exchange reserves have necessitated reductions in imports. The market share of parastatals in export crops has remained high, however, because of the lack of internal parallel markets for these goods, although there has been some smuggling across borders.

In the area of export trade and bulk handling, therefore, governmental control is likely to continue. As most large processing plants that serve several regions are publicly owned, expertise in procuring export crops from both private marketers and cooperatives will take some time to develop. Due to the critical importance of foreign exchange earnings in public sector allocations, governments will be loathe to relinquish control over these functions.

Short of a complete state withdrawal from agricultural marketing, a possible interim measure calls for the coexistence of marketing parastatals, cooperatives, and private agencies, each specializing in different areas. Streamlined marketing parastatals might concentrate in productive areas where infrastructure is poor, transport costs are too prohibitive for profit-motivated private agencies, and cooperatives are not yet well-formed. Where cooperatives are strong and members have autonomous control, the need for private and public agencies would be negligible. For their part, private marketing agencies might concentrate in easily accessible areas where cooperatives do not exist or are weak, and, at the national level, in interregional trade of foodstuffs. As infrastructure and training are gradually improved, cooperatives and private trading agencies will replace public marketing enterprises on the primary levels. The growth of independent marketing cooperatives should be encouraged for two reasons. First, strong cooperative societies and unions in agricultural marketing provide an organized forum for rural communities and represent a political force to be reckoned with (Lofchie and Cummins, 1982, p. 24), making it difficult for policy reforms to be reversed once economies are beyond the crisis period (Bates, 1983, chapter 5).[9] Second, strong marketing cooperatives prevent the development of private local marketing monopolies. Voluntary cooperatives can be used as a means of expanding the free market in mixed economies, provided they are able to cut loose from governmental control (Andreou, 1977, p. 70).

Appropriate pricing policies and adequate infrastructure are critical to the efficient operation of cooperatives and private marketing agencies. Food prices should be decontrolled and trading channels opened. The state's regulatory role should be confined to preventing monopolies from forming and to guaranteeing minimum prices to stimulate food production in areas that face severe infrastructural bottlenecks. Exchange rates must be adjusted to compensate for domestic inflation and to prevent the erosion of real producer prices for export crops.

Lastly, while improvements in marketing and thus prices for crops will encourage higher output levels, the use of advanced technologies in crop husbandry must be similarly encouraged. A second important function of marketing agents, therefore, is to ensure a smooth and cost-effective supply of production inputs. Given the relationship between the timely supply of inputs and increased productivity, a much more flexible supply system than that of the parastatals is required. If input distribution costs are decreased, profitability and hence productivity will increase.

Industrial Sector   The benefits of public sector withdrawal from the industrial sector are less apparent, given that activities in this domain are generally large-scale and private foreign capital involvement is limited. Considering foreign capital's perceptions of the high political risks associated with investment in industry and the limited availability of private local capital, the gap left by public sector withdrawal would be difficult to fill.[10]

In small- and medium-scale industries, however, there is room for a gradual expansion of local private business, with the public sector concentrating on large-scale industrial activities. Upgrading the performance of public industrial enterprises requires improved project appraisal and a national structure allowing for more operational autonomy and accountability in these enterprises. However, the shortage of skilled personnel remains a problem in both private and public sectors.

Operational autonomy of public industrial enterprises is critical to their commercial viability. While many enterprises are run according to legal charters defining the limits of their commercial activities, the line of accountability is firmly tied to the central authorities in parent ministries, allowing for frequent interference of a non-commercial nature. As a result, management cannot be held directly accountable for overall performance and lack of initiative is a common problem. In addition, channels of communication and overhead costs have been burdened unnecessarily by the proliferation of holding companies, which have expanded rapidly and exhibit monopolistic behavior.

Therefore, public sector industrial enterprises must be streamlined, granted autonomy over their own operations, and held accountable for their performance. Enterprises that cannot perform competitively should not be subsidized or otherwise protected.

Road Transport   African governments are heavily involved in the road transport sector, as public transport companies service most major cities, in some cases as monopolies. They also operate freight and passenger services interregionally, but often in competition with the private sector. Public transport and freight/passenger companies have been operating at losses for many years. Subsidized fares have led to real declines in revenues, generating budgetary deficits. Lacking surpluses, these companies rely heavily on government revenues to replace and expand their fleets. Although the urban transport companies offer subsidized services, their performance has deteriorated. Those public companies involved in cross-country freight and passenger services face the additional problem of servicing regions with poor roads, yet the rates they charge are significantly below the operating costs commensurate with road conditions. Private sector transport services, on the other hand, have fared comparatively better, concentrating in areas with better roads; when they do operate in poor road areas, they are able to charge higher rates.

Liberalization of urban transport services is underway in many countries, such as Tanzania and Zambia, and should be supported. Private companies are working with the public sector, charging higher rates, and the availability of services has improved noticeably. To keep pace with expansion in demand, the size of fleets will have to be increased by both types of operators. Public transport companies should be allowed to charge competitive rates, so that they can develop self-financing capabilities. For freight and passenger services operating in areas with poor road conditions, both public operators and cooperative transport companies will have to continue to play the developmental role until such time as road infrastructure is improved.

DECENTRALIZING ECONOMIC MANAGEMENT

If the responsibility for infrastructural services such as primary health care and education, feeder roads, and primary agricultural support services is shifted to local governments and communities, much of the pressure on centralized management can be alleviated. This is not a new idea–local government existed under British colonial rule and during the early independence period. The dismantling of these local structures and centralization of management was aimed at gaining control over national development under the leadership of newly independent states in order to build national cohesion (Jones, 1982, pp. 553–54).

Whereas this pattern of state control allowed for the pooling and allocation of national resources irrespective of the ability of specific areas to raise their own revenues, it also removed from local communities a sense of accountability for resource use and hence increased the level of dependency on the "omnipotent" government, stifling community initiative. Long lines of communication developed in administration, causing costly delays in decision-making and inflexibility in action. At the top levels of management, attention to priority areas was distracted by the necessity of routine supervision of activities which could have been handled effectively at the subordinate level.

Administrative decentralization and strengthening the role of local governmental structures are essential, given the failure of central governments to develop and maintain primary level services, and in view of the budgetary pressures on central government. Reintroducing the concept of local government can allow for a more appropriate linkage between infrastructural expansion and maintenance on the one hand, and resource mobilization capacity on the other, fostering a spirit of self-help and accountability in local communities. Decentralization also frees the central planning authority to concentrate on priority areas of national development.

STRENGTHENING AND STREAMLINING OF MACRO-ECONOMIC MANAGEMENT CAPABILITY

A key deficiency in economic management in Africa is the insufficiency of competent local planners with experience in policy analysis, project formulation, and balancing of resources. While formal training must continue, the provision of practical experience, through apprenticeships with foreign specialist teams, has a high rate of return in terms of skills imparted and continuity in programs that have been implemented.

In addition to personnel training, efforts should be directed at encouraging policy analyses and research in independent research institutions, including universities. These institutions can provide the structural loci for more serious and focused studies which short-term specialists and ministries may not be able to undertake. African planning agencies' capacities and stature should be enhanced. As most have been involved mainly in the elaboration of medium-term plan documents, they have not been able to play an effective role in scrutinizing and evaluating projects from the ministries. The overriding sway of technical and financial ministries in determining the future of a particular plan must give way to permit planning agencies to contribute advice and program analyses. Development of a strong data base and dissemination system is a critical prerequisite for sound policy analysis and effective planning. Statistical bureaus must be strengthened in manpower, authority, data collection and analysis, and supportive infrastructure.

STATE MARKET INTERVENTION AND PRICE DISTORTIONS

The manipulation of prices to facilitate allocations of resources has been a common practice of many sub-Saharan African governments. Although the extent to which price controls are used varies according to the degree to which the state intervenes in the markets, in general, such practices have generated price distortions that result in inefficient use of resources. Allocations to unproductive sectors have engendered even greater dependence on subsidies and have stifled growth in key productive areas such as agriculture. Significant negative correlations have been demonstrated between price distortions and growth (World Bank, 1983, p. 63).

With the decline in state control over economic spheres and the rise in "unofficial" mechanisms over the last five years, the merits of manipulating prices to influence political interest groups have diminished. Moreover, price controls often have unintended results. Maintaining overvalued currencies, for example, has offset the degree of protection afforded by tariffs; consumer subsidies, though moderating pressures for higher wages and protective of real wage levels for urban workers, have been inflationary. While low interest rates and subsidies for transportation and inputs have been maintained to raise rural incomes, these are more than counterbalanced by low producer prices linked to overvalued exchange rates.

In order to eliminate price distortions, actions will have to be taken with regard to all key prices which create biases against trade and agriculture. Regular adjustment of the exchange rate to reflect changes in inflationary conditions and the availability of foreign exchange; raising real interest rates to encourage savings; reducing trade restrictions and relying more on indirect taxation for revenues; and removing tax structures which distort resource allocation at the production level are required.

Current price distortions are the result of cumulative interventionist actions of the past; therefore, alleviating the distortions will be a long-term process. A gradual and sustained correction will involve lower adjustment costs and produce less political opposition to reform.

EXCHANGE RATES

Average effective exchange rates in sub-Saharan Africa appreciated by 44 percent between 1973 and 1981 (World Bank, 1983, p. 58), with the sharpest increase occurring after the second oil shock in 1979. Governments failed to respond with counter-cyclical adjustments in spending (see Wheeler, 1984, p. 11, fig. 3 for cases of Tanzania, Mali, Ghana, Uganda, Zaire, and Somalia), and the overvalued currencies undercut increases in producer prices, resulting in declining export earnings and ultimately, reductions in exports.

Real producer prices for agricultural exports had begun to fall before 1978, due to export taxes and growing parastatal costs, but in the high inflation period that followed, the situation was severely aggravated by non-adjustment of exchange rates. Some governments resorted to deficit financing, but the results of raising prices paid to producers included accelerating rates of inflation and further declines in real incomes. In effect, maintaining overvalued exchange rates penalized those sectors dependent on exports, such as tourism and manufacturing, and made imports more attractive. Excess domestic demand, generated by below-equilibrium prices for foreign exchange, has had to be curbed through the application of import re-

strictions, fueling corruption, diverting the efficient allocation of resources, and reducing flexibility in resource allocations (Wheeler,
1984, p.12).

Exchange rate adjustments are an important instrument in stimulating trade and agriculture, and in reducing governmental budgetary
pressures. There is widespread skepticism on the short-term benefits
of devaluing exchange rates, given the limits to import reductions
and the slow-responding export sector. However, if exchange rate
adjustments are viewed as part of the long-term structural adjustment process, the systemic bias against trade and agriculture can
ultimately be removed. Protection of agricultural incomes and increases in the profitability of exports represent incentives in revitaliz-
ing the economies and fostering sustained economic growth.
Whereas devaluations tend to be inflationary in impact, in many
countries dependence on government subsidies, overvalued currencies, and recurrent budget deficits have been no less inflationary and
counter-growth.

TRADE RESTRICTIONS

Trade restrictions have also been widely used in sub-Saharan Africa, primarily as a means of protecting nascent industries against
foreign competitors. In a study of 31 developing countries, the World
Bank (1983, p. 63) found that in the subset of nine African countries,
four exhibited high distortions from protecting their domestic manufacturing sectors, with only two countries registering "low" distortions. By contributing to overvalued exchange rates, certain restrictions have also indirectly discouraged exports and agricultural
output.

Most countries invoke the "infant industry" argument in defense
of trade restrictions, as, ideally, these measures would allow for the
development of integrated industrial linkages. But recent experience
shows that in many instances, permanent infancy results from increased protection. Indeed, removing trade barriers alone does not
necessarily open domestic markets to foreign competition. The current limits on import capacity are sufficient to insulate a number of
domestic enterprises from foreign competition.

Import substitution industries, providing higher cost commodities
relative to unrestricted alternative supplies from foreign sources, depend upon transfers from other sectors–in effect, subsidies or foreign

capital inflows. With the decline of both of these areas, these industries are seriously jeopardized. More emphasis must be placed on
raising domestic productivity and on reducing the costs of production. The latter can be accomplished through opening up markets to
foreign competition by lowering tariffs and levying sales taxes for
revenue purposes. In order to increase productivity, improvements
will have to be made in training, management capacity, and infrastructure, including transport, power systems, and water.

Another aspect of trade liberalization involves reductions in import controls that have been imposed as a result of declining foreign
exchange reserves. In the past, the artificially low cost of imports, due
to overvalued exchange rates, produced severe excess demand for
foreign exchange. As a result, rationing schemes were introduced by
governments attempting to balance supply and demand pressures
for foreign exchange (Wheeler, 1984, p. 9). While all countries have a
policy on the allocation of foreign exchange earnings, in general,
allocations have favored imports of capital goods, food, and raw
materials.

In the face of foreign exchange shortages, many economies were
slow in adjusting to the need to restrain import allocations. When
they did, sizeable backlogs in applications for import licenses resulted, leading to crisis-oriented allocations and the proliferation of
corruption. Whereas adjustment of the exchange rate will contribute
toward reducing excess demand, recent experiences in Uganda have
shown that flexible exchange rates do not alone produce desired
development goals under conditions of extreme structural deterioration. The structure of imports favors luxury goods and flight of foreign exchange may result. Infrastructural support services, raw materials, and other basic goods needed for revamping the agricultural
sector do not receive adequate allocations. Therefore, during the recovery period, some aggregate allocations will have to be made to
stimulate growth in these priority areas. Once such allocations have
been made, detailed controls should not be necessary as the adjusted
exchange rate is allowed to affect the markets.

INTEREST RATES

Another problem widely cited is the effect of fairly constant or
marginally rising nominal interest rates in the face of high inflation.
Negative real interest rates have been prevalent in several countries,

including Tanzania, Kenya, Ghana, Zaire, and Nigeria. These distortions have discouraged domestic savings and encouraged subsidization of investment, particularly in industry.

In tandem with overvalued exchange rates and low tariffs on capital goods imports, depressed real interest rates have fostered capital-intensive techniques and excess demand for credit. In those countries where excess demand for investments was met by foreign private capital or foreign aid, over time, the lack of recurrent resources to maintain capacity utilization resulted in declining returns on investment and in falling productivity rates.

In a study of 16 eastern and southern African countries (Gulhati and Datta, 1983), declines in investment rates and productivity were reflected in falling rates of growth. Furthermore, savings rates in these countries fell from the median level of 11.7 percent in 1973 to 7.7 percent in 1978. Although foreign capital inflows rose as a percent of total investment, as national savings dropped, investment growth slowed to 2.4 percent a year on average after 1973, from 6.4 percent prior to 1973. Incremental capital-output ratios (ICOR) increased from a median level of 4.3 for the period up to 1973, to 5.2 in the 1973–79 period. In a subset of countries including Ethiopia, Somalia, Zaire, Madagascar, Uganda, Zimbabwe, and Zambia, the median ICOR rose from 5.7 to 24.3, while Zaire, Uganda, and Zimbabwe registered negative ICORs.

For low income African countries, the rate of return on investment (the reciprocal of ICOR) declined from an average 24.6 percent in the 1960–70 period to an average of 10 percent in the following decade (World Bank, 1983, p. 38). Capacity underutilization, stemming from infrastructural constraints and inadequate supplies of raw material imports, was the key factor behind declines in investment productivity.

While positive real interest rates empirically failed to mobilize domestic savings in sub-Saharan Africa in the decade up to 1973 (income levels and financial intermediation at the margin were found to be more significant factors), when they turned negative in the high inflation period that followed, savings rates declined (Rwegasira, 1983, pp. 89–90). Low interest rates encouraged excessive borrowings, and mounting debt burdens, as governments attempted to bridge domestic financing gaps. Raising real interest rates will suffice to at least reduce the number of projects undertaken, particularly those with low rates of return.

COUNTER-CYCLICAL MANAGEMENT

Proper macro-economic management requires long-term measures that address issues of growth and development, and short-term counter-cyclical or stabilization policies that redress sudden fluctuations or shocks in the domestic market. Such demand management policies have been sorely underused in Africa over the past decade. In the steady growth period of 1960–70, few pressures warranted such measures. Most stabilization efforts were directed at offsetting losses in the mining and agricultural sectors due to climate-related declines in output or depressed world prices. Prior to 1970, many countries ran fiscal surpluses and inflation rates averaged 2.7 percent a year, with the terms of trade growing an average of 1.8 percent a year (World Bank, 1983). After the second oil price hike, world recession and declining terms of trade called for counter-cyclical demand management policies; in their absence, many of the effects of external shocks have been exacerbated.

The current situation is complex, as both structural adjustments and stabilization measures are required, but resistance to such reforms is widespread and implementation is difficult.[11] For example, while increased government spending is needed to break up bottlenecks, stabilization programs call for reducing fiscal deficits. In view of the weakened revenue base and rising debt-servicing obligations, it is no wonder that cutting budget deficits has proven to be the most difficult requirement of stabilization programs (Nelson, 1984, p. 991).

While government spending rose sharply when prices for primary commodities boomed in the mid-1970s, it failed to be adjusted downward in the bust period, adversely affecting the oil-importing countries in sub-Saharan Africa (World Bank, 1983, p. 22). As a result, governments resorted to financing their spending by borrowing, running deficits, or both; inflation rates accelerated as money supply expanded rapidly and production stagnated.[12]

Recurrent budget deficits as a percentage of GDP rose from –3.3 percent in 1972 to –5.9 percent in 1981 on average for all countries in sub-Saharan Africa (World Bank, 1983, p. 88). Subsequently, there have been numerous debt reschedulings in several countries. Over-expansionary fiscal policies can be attributed at least in part to the support of foreign donors who made resources available, often in grant form. In some instances, investments were unproductive as recurrent resources for maintaining capital utilization were unavailable. "White elephants" were the result.

Improved counter-cyclical management calls for restraining spending and building reserves during upswings, and reducing expenditures to levels that reflect available resources during downswings. Through such demand management policies, inflationary pressures and expectations can be moderated.

THE ROLE OF DONORS IN REFORMS

International organizations and bilateral donors have an important role to play in the initiation and implementation of policy reforms in Africa and have recently sought more direct involvement through their training programs, technical assistance, and policy dialogues (Nelson, 1984, p. 990). The current urgency of policy reform and the more favorable environment offer the best opportunity for these organizations to cooperate with specific countries in undertaking the necessary changes. In view of the vast sums these creditors have committed, it is imperative that they become involved in efforts to efficiently use the resources. However, it is absolutely necessary that the key "initiator" role be assumed by the concerned governments if reforms are to be sustained.

Bilateral and multilateral aid agencies have initiated reforms through two main channels: policy dialogues and conditionality. Both instruments have merits and shortcomings in achieving the desired results. Policy dialogues have been deemed to be politically preferable, as they involve less "interference" and recognize the government's ability to undertake independent action. However, in the absence of consensus, dialogues have produced delays. Given the depth of the current crisis, conditionality–"rewarding" those who undertake specified reforms–has increasingly become a means of instigating changes in policy. But conditionality should not be considered a substitute for the will and commitment to change if reforms are to be sustained. Purely imported reforms have limited effectiveness (Callaghy, 1984, p. 76). Moreover, the supervision costs to donors could be extremely high and frustrating if reforms are undertaken in an environment of unwillingness.

While conditionality in aid disbursements can be used to encourage change, the main impetus to reform must come from concerned governments. Working cooperatively rather than admonishing is central to donors' success in speeding up the process of economic change. The current situation calls for more active donor participation in policy formulation, but not as a substitute for local efforts and commitment.

Apart from the traditional areas of support–technical assistance and training–there is an increased need to support institutional reform. There is also a need to coordinate aid disbursements in order to ensure a balance between expanded capacities and recurrent resource availability. Available resources must also reach national priority areas and be efficiently utilized. This will require donor support for the improvement of technical capacity of ministries, and the channeling of their resources into programs that have already been adopted. Providing aid for projects that fall outside the accepted framework encourages irresponsible spending by local independent institutions, undermining the entire planning exercise and the efficient use of resources.

On the other hand, however, donors must agree on proposed programs. This can be achieved through coordinated dialogues with concerned governments on policy frameworks and determination of priority areas. Increased use of joint analysis with the host country can help thrash out key areas of disagreement. However, once an agreement is reached, donors and governments must abide by it, with flexibility limited to mutually agreed upon changes.

The success of policy reform in the long run depends on achieving some immediate results if political support is to continue. The process of getting prices right and removing structural bottlenecks and institutional barriers to growth and development will take a long time to bear results. To arrest further deterioration in the short term, therefore, a substantial injection of resources will be required. Such infusions will generate support for reform. Import capacity must be raised, and agricultural inputs, capital goods for industry, spare parts, and machinery for the rehabilitation and maintenance of infrastructure are needed to speed the process of structural adjustment. The required resources will depart from the traditional project-tied aid, supporting the utilization of current capacity, with new investments limited only to a few areas such as transport and storage (World Bank, 1984, p. 44).

SUPPORTING INSTITUTIONAL REFORMS

Donor support of reforms in agricultural marketing could be channeled toward strengthening voluntary cooperatives in marketing skills, financing, and training. It is critical that aid to these societies come from non-governmental sources in order to prevent the reemergence of government control. In addition to supporting cooperatives, donor assistance could be directed at expanding the ability of private traders to handle bulk volumes to promote economies of scale.

It is critically important that assistance be provided to improve infrastructure, especially transport, storage, and information collection and dissemination. By and large, infrastructural improvements will remain the responsibility of the state, but self-help schemes could be sparked by the provision of technical assistance at community levels. Continued support of industrial promotion institutions will help expand the activities of small-scale industries. Where cost considerations allow, construction of industrial estates for rental could be supported. Increased access to credit and the banking system, as well as support for the procurement of materials and marketing of products, would promote the development of more labor-intensive private or voluntary cooperative small-scale industries.

One important change in the disbursal of assistance is necessary if decentralization is to be achieved. The majority of aid thus far has been channeled through the central governments. However, there is a need to develop outlets through which assistance to non-governmental institutions, such as individual communities and organizations, can be provided. While the administrative cost advantages of dealing with one central institution, the Treasury, for example, are obvious, the independent development of non-governmental sectors can best be achieved if assistance to them is free of government control. In some cases, it might even be possible to offer assistance to cross-national and intercommunity programs, such as "sister city" projects, where urban councils or local government authorities in donor and recipient countries exchange ideas on how to raise revenues or manage expenditures.

Although donor support has to be focused on rehabilitating and increasing the utilization of installed capacity, some project-based support is still necessary in the area of infrastructure. Improvements in rural roads, development of small-scale irrigation schemes, and expansion of agricultural extension services are critical for increased agricultural productivity. Another area for productive project support is reforestation to curb the rapid deterioration of the environment, and especially desertification, which is progressing rapidly in both arid and semi-arid areas of the continent.

Training and technical assistance must continue, but they should be reoriented toward a building of local capacity. As mentioned earlier, apprenticeships are an effective way of imparting practical skills, as well as providing local participants with insights into political-economic constraints.

It is also important that assistance be given to building local research capacity. Collaborative research with institutions in donor countries would complement traditional funding support. Statistical bureaus require support in the training of technical staff and infrastructural facilities for collection, compilation, and dissemination of data. In most cases, continuation of support by various international and bilateral agencies in setting up a national statistical system is required. There is also the need to acquire hard and software for analysis of data and to reduce the time lag between completion of surveys and the publication of results. Many countries still depend on facilities abroad for policy and planning purposes.

In order to provide more continuity and effectiveness in practical training of various technical cadres, specialists working for donor agencies could be given longer assignments. This would help them to acquire a better feel for political-economic conditions, and thus increase their potential effectiveness in advisory roles.

CONCLUSIONS

The current economic deterioration in sub-Saharan Africa has partly been caused by internal economic mismanagement. Wide state intervention in the productive spheres and in markets for resources and products has led to inefficient use of scarce resources not only in the "Pareto efficiency" sense, but also in relation to the development goals adopted by those countries. Serious biases against the development of the export and agricultural sectors have produced stagnant economic growth, arrested social development, increased dependence on food imports, and debt burdens requiring frequent reschedulings. Indeed, the current balance of payments crisis prevailing in African economies, rooted in this structural bias, has been exacerbated by the external shocks of the late 1970s and early 1980s. Protected import substitution industries have not produced the anticipated results, as resource constraints became binding and productivity declined. Instead, the process of industrialization has generated debt burdens and fueled inflation.

Economic deterioration has also undermined state control over economic spheres. Price controls and quantitative restrictions have become increasingly superfluous as parallel markets and corruption are rampant. Rapid expansion of public enterprises is not sustainable as they have become budgetary burdens and a damper on growth. Expansion in public sector employment now faces serious constraints due to reductions in transfer resources from the key productive sectors and foreign aid. Thus the very basis on which patron-client political networks were traditionally served has been undermined.

It is in light of these experiences that policy change is inevitable. The current political-economic situation is not sustainable, but political constraints to change do exist. Nevertheless, the professed distribution of resources and power among various groups has been eroded and a more malleable situation has emerged as unofficial adjustments are being made by different groups in reaction to changing conditions. The changing political calculus is not, however, uniform across the countries. In those countries in which there is little state intervention, fewer changes will have to be made. Structural reforms are less drastic and elites are invariably more accommodative to the recommendations of international financial institutions. For those countries in which state management of markets and participation in productive spheres has been more intensive, departures from the status quo are more dramatic on the surface, but, nevertheless, unofficial activities have largely begun the process of reform.

The main changes required are getting prices right, undertaking institutional reforms, and reducing the size of the public sector to a level commensurate with effective state managerial capacity. Structural adjustments of these economies are long-term undertakings and although stabilization efforts are currently required, they should not form the backbone of reform.

An appreciation of these points will help governments carry out sustained reform programs without necessarily raising high expectations for spectacular short-term results. However, there is a need for some immediate resources and efforts to arrest the trend of deterioration and to reduce hostility and political constraints to reform. This is an interim measure since sustained growth can only be achieved through structural adjustment.

The role of donors in reform efforts includes providing an "interim" injection of resources to raise import capacities, supplying technical and training assistance, and supporting policy and institutional reforms through advice and dialogue with specific governments. The catalytic role in initiating and sustaining reforms is as important as the traditional supportive role as long as it remains clear that the main actor in the process of change is the concerned country. Better coordination among donors will ensure more rational and efficient use of resources and strengthen consistency in planning. Project support by donors in infrastructure, especially in the rehabilitation of the transport system and basic social infrastructure, is of critical importance for revamping the agricultural sector and increasing productivity of investment.

As the UN's review of the "Critical Economic Situation in Africa" (1984:44) suggests, "It will now be necessary to move forward from reflection to concrete action. In this transition, Africa should not stand alone: Its economy is still too fragile to withstand the enormous stresses of moving from crisis to reconstruction and development."

NOTES

1. The World Bank's 1981 report, Accelerated Development in Sub-Saharan Africa, and Toward Sustained Development in sub-Saharan Africa (1984), have placed much emphasis on internal policy reforms to correct structural deficiencies and to reduce negative impacts of external shocks. David Wheeler's study (1984) has attempted to estimate the costs of internal mismanagement for several economies in sub-Saharan Africa and provides strong statistical evidence of significant foregone growth exceeding 2 percent per annum for 16 out of 24 countries studied. There is also a general consensus among bilateral and international aid agencies that improved efficiency and effectiveness in macro-economic management would significantly increase resource productivity.

2. Structural issues have been stressed in the joint report by the African Development Bank and the Economic Commission for Africa (1984), ECA study (1983) and by several specific studies commissioned or undertaken by individual countries, such as the Structural Adjustment Programme (Tanzania Government, 1982), Sessional Papers no. 10, and the more recent no. 4 of 1982 (Kenya Government).

3. In his study of Ivory Coast, Cohen (1974) concludes that access to government is very critical in the accumulation of private property and power.

4. Sandbrook (1982) distinguishes three main typologies prevalent in Africa: neo-colonialist regimes (e.g., Ivory Coast) dominated by foreign capital interests with a relatively weak role for domestic interest groups; "nationalist" regimes with dominant domestic/national interests and a mixture of

private and state capitalism; and "national collectivist" regimes aspiring to transition to socialism.

5. Nelson (1984), citing case studies of Ghana, Kenya, and Zambia among others, stresses the important role political cost/benefit of economic reforms plays in both the "will" to initiate and sustain reform programs.

6. In a report by Club du Sahel/CILSS, "Marketing Price Policy and Storage of Food Grains in the Sahel," for example, it is pointed out that despite government efforts to dominate food marketing through parastatal monopolies in Mali, Senegal, Niger, Chad, and Burkina Faso, these monopolies actually handle only a third or less of food produced and marketed domestically. Similar proportions were obtained in Tanzania (Ellis, 1982).

7. See note 6 above.

8. Barbara Lewis (1980, p. 115) emphasizes this point in her paper when she writes that the origin of barriers to private sector development in agricultural marketing (in West Africa) predates national independence. Colonial policy and practice favored French commercial houses and Lebanese merchants and also set up public institutions which limited the scope of private African merchants. The following independence governments expanded the role of public agencies reducing private traders' market share, at times reducing them to largely clandestine activity. Thus private trading systems remained underdeveloped in terms of specialization, quality control, and market integration. The situation in East Africa was quite similar under colonial rule.

9. Lofchie and Cummins (1982, p. 24) argue that one of the most important problems confronting peasant movements in Africa is to overcome rural-urban conflicts over food policies. The realization of (organized) power would assist in the creation of effective channels of communication with government agencies, and with organizations representing the interests of the urban-based social classes.

Again, Grindle and the Temples (in Grindle, 1980) agree separately that the most promising means of increasing the ability of popular sectors to receive benefits from public policies is through direct organization.

10. The potential of indigenous private industrial entrepreneurship is still largely unknown. Although case studies are available on small-scale private industries, the capacity of the indigenous private sector to undertake large-scale ventures remains unassessed. It is also not clear whether the private sector would escape the political, social, and ethnic calculus which has impinged on efficiency in the public sector.

11. Nelson (1984, p. 989) makes the same point when she writes that exogenous shocks and cumulative ill effects of domestic policies have been concentrated in the decade since 1974 with implications of complex and difficult policies. The fairly brisk growth of the first decade of independence has not provided experience on stabilization management.

12. UNECA, "Survey of Economic Conditions in Africa 1979–80" puts the average annual rate of increase in money supply in the post-1972 period at 25.8 percent per annum compared to the average of 13.6 percent during 1967–72. Given deceleration in real growth, this higher rate of monetary expansion fueled inflation.

REFERENCES

ADB and ECA. 1984. *Economic Report on Africa, 1984.*

Andreou, P. 1977. "An Economic Appraisal of the Role of Cooperative Institutions in Different Economic and Political Systems," in Andreou, P. (ed.), *Cooperative Institutions and Economic Development in Developed and Developing Nations: Selected International Readings in the Economics, Marketing and Management of Cooperative Institutions and Their Role in Economic Development.* Nairobi: East African Literature Bureau.

Bates, R. H. 1981. *Markets and States in Tropical Africa.* Berkeley: University of California.

Bates, R.H. 1983. *Essays on the Political Economy of Rural Africa.* Cambridge: Cambridge University Press.

Beveridge, W.A and M. R. Kelly. 1980. "Fiscal Content of Financial Programs Supported by Stand-by Arrangements in Upper Credit Tranches, 1969–78," *IMF Staff Papers* (June) 7 (2).

Bienen, H. and V. P. Diejomaoh, eds. 1980. *The Political Economy of Income Distribution in Nigeria.* New York: Holmes and Meier Publishers.

Blues, N. and J. H. Weaver. 1977. "A Critical Assessment of the Tanzanian Model of Development." *Agricultural Council Reprints.*

Callaghy, Thomas M. 1984. "Africa's Debt Crisis," *Journal of International Affairs* 38: 61–79.

Cleaves, S. 1980. "Implementation Amidst Scarcity and Apathy: Political Power and Policy Design," in Grindle, M.S., ed., *Politics and Policy Implementation in the Third World.* Princeton: Princeton University Press.

Cohen, M. 1974. *Urban Policy and Political Conflict: A Study of Ivory Coast.* Chicago: University of Chicago Press.

Delancey, M. W. 1980. "Cameroon National Food Policies and Organizations: The Green Revolution and Structural Proliferation." *Journal of African Studies* 7(2).

ECA. 1981. "Survey of Economic Conditions in Africa 1979–80." Freetown.

ECA. 1983. *ECA and Africa's Development 1983–2008: A Preliminary Perspective Study.* Addis Ababa.

Ellis, Frank. 1982. "Agricultural Price Policy in Tanzania," *World Development* 10(4).

Grindle, S., ed. 1980. *Politics and Policy Implementation in the Third World.* Princeton: Princeton University Press.

Gulhati, R. and G. Datta. 1983. "Capital Accumulation in Eastern and Southern Africa: A Decade of Setbacks," *World Bank Staff Working Papers*, no. 562.

Jones, D.B. 1982. "State Structures in New Nations: The Case of Primary Agricultural Marketing in Africa," *Journal of Modern African Studies* 20(4).

Kuria, M. Chege. "The Role of Cooperatives in Agricultural Development of Small Scale Farmers," in Andreou, P., ed. op. cit.

Lewis, Barbara C. 1980. "Political Variables and Food Price Policy in West Africa," paper prepared for the USAID.

Lewis, S., Jr. 1984. "Africa's Development and the World Economy," background paper prepared for the Committee on African Development Strategies.

Lofchie, M. and K. Cummins. 1982. "Food Deficits and Agricultural Policies in Tropical Africa," *Journal of Modern African Studies* 20(1).

McKinlay, R. and A. Cohan. 1975. "A Comparative Analysis of Political and Economic Performance of Military and Civilian Regimes," *Comparative Politics* (October) 8(1).

McKinlay, R. and A. Cohan. July 1976. "The Economic Performance of Military Regimes: A Cross-National Aggregate Data Study," *The British Journal of Politics* (July) 6(3).

Nelson, J. M. 1984. "The Political Economy of Stabilization: Commitment, Capacity, and Public Response," *World Development* 12(10).

Reichmann, T. and R. Stillson. 1977. "How Successful are Programs Supported by Standby Arrangements," *Finance and Development* (March) 14 (1).

Rondinelli, D. A. 1981. "Administrative Decentralization and Economic Development: The Sudan's Experiment with Devolution," *Journal of Modern African Studies* 19(4).

Rwegasira, R. 1983. "Adjustment Policies in Low-Income Africa: An Interpretation of the Kenyan and Tanzanian Experiences, 1974–78," IMF mimeo.

Sandbrook, R. 1982. *The Politics of Basic Needs: Urban Aspects of Assaulting Poverty in Africa*. London: Heinemann.

Stewart, B. A. 1980. "Peanut Marketing in Niger," *Journal of African Studies* 7(2).

Wheeler, D. 1984. "Sources of Stagnation in Sub-Saharan Africa," *World Development* 12(11).

World Bank. 1981. *Accelerated Development in Sub-Saharan Africa: An Agenda For Action*. Washington, D.C.: The World Bank

World Bank. 1983. *World Development Report, 1983*. Oxford: Oxford University Press.

World Bank. 1984. *World Development Report, 1984*. Oxford: Oxford University Press.

World Bank. 1984. *Toward Sustained Development in Sub-Saharan Africa: A Joint Program of Action*. Washington, D.C.: The World Bank.

PART II

THE PEOPLE AND THE LAND

CHAPTER FOUR

Guarding Africa's Renewable Resources

Lloyd Timberlake

By mid-1985, a continent-wide calamity had left some 30 million Africans in 20 nations unable to feed themselves and had forced 10 million people to leave their homes in search of food and water. While often described as "environmental," the crisis was largely the result of poor policy decisions on the part of both African governments and donor and aid agencies.

In nations where over half of the population lives in the rural areas, governments have invested disproportionate amounts of financial support in the cities and their inhabitants. Examples abound. In Ghana and the Gambia, 64 and 82 percent of their populations, respectively, live in the countryside. Yet between 1978 and 1982, domestic agricultural spending in both countries declined by more than 10 percent a year (FAO, 1983).

An FAO study which looked at domestic per capita spending on agriculture found that for 17 African countries, such spending declined by 0.1 percent per year over 1978–82, whereas in all other regions of the developing world, it rose—by 7.3 percent in the Far East, by 3 percent in Latin America, and by 1.9 percent in the Near East (FAO, 1984).

Institutionalized rural poverty has played a major role in the so-called environmental crisis. Rural populations, with little to invest, have been depleting the natural resource base faster than it can be regenerated. The poor impoverish the land and the poor land further impoverishes those who rely upon it. This downward spiral has led to environmental bankruptcy in some regions of Africa.

Describing Africa's "renewable resource" crisis poses a semantical problem. Environmentalists refer to the crisis as "environmental," while agronomists and others refer to it as "agricultural." Both are correct. While few of Africa's farmers are purely in the subsistence sector—completely uninvolved in the marketplace—the vast majority survive on the "environment" or the renewable resource base.

Most of a family's food comes directly from the ground, and perhaps some from livestock. Its energy comes from the ground in the form of fuelwood. [Trees supply well over 90 percent of the total energy used in poorer countries and 80 percent even in oil-rich Nigeria (Timberlake, 1985).] Its water comes directly from the ground or from streams and lakes—all of which rely to some extent on the protection afforded by trees and other greenery.

In Africa, the environmental crisis, renewable resource crisis, and agricultural crisis are one and the same, resulting in a threat to survival. Governments have tended to emphasize the gross national product rather than the "green national product," little of which is ever figured into the official GNP, but which is actually more important to the lives of most citizens. Efforts to put Africa's agriculture on a sustainable basis amount to steps toward preserving the environment. More important, conservation of environmental resources is a first step toward sustainable agriculture.

DESERTIFICATION

Resource degradation in Africa is often equated with "desertification." A number of ecologists and geographers are losing patience with this term because it is scientifically imprecise. A recent World Bank report defines it simply as "a process of sustained decline of the biological productivity of arid and semi-arid land" (Gorse, 1985). Most of Africa's arable land is semi-arid (Avery, 1985).

Since the UN Environment Programme's 1977 Conference on Desertification, most definitions of desertification emphasize the human role in causing it. Indeed, the recent World Bank report took the position that "desertification is a complex, still poorly understood process. . .caused by interactions between drought and human abuse of the environment." British environmentalist Alan Grainger put even more blame on human actions: "Drought triggers a crisis, but does not cause it. Overcultivation and overgrazing weaken the land, allowing no margin when drought arrives. Thus high human pressure will continue during the drought, leading ultimately to even greater and more visible damage to the land and the deaths of large numbers of people" (Grainger, 1982). This view suggests that while the roots of Africa's crisis may not be environmental, environmental degradation deepens any crisis and makes people more vulnerable to the next natural shock.

In 1984, UNEP assessed progress in countering desertification and found virtually none. Desertification of rainfed croplands and dry forest woodlands was accelerating across the Sudano-Sahelian region, while accelerating or continuing in the region's rangelands and irrigated lands. South of the Sahel, desertification was accelerating in rangelands, rainfed croplands, and woodlands, and holding constant at best in irrigated areas. Nowhere was there progress in containing desertification over a wide area (Walls, 1984).

Equally disturbing, the assessment was largely guesswork because so few nations had any idea of the rates at which they were losing productive lands, despite considerable investment in such studies by the UN. UNEP Executive Director Mostafa Tolba complained: "Assessments of the problem have generally not been made nor have national priorities been established" (UNEP, 1984).

Harold Dregne (1983) summed up the political approach to desertification: "Governments do not see desertification as a high priority item. Rangeland deterioration, accelerated soil erosion, and salinization and waterlogging do not command attention until they become crisis items. Lip service is paid to combating desertification but the political will is directed elsewhere. There seems to be little appreciation that a major goal of many developing nations—food self-sufficiency—cannot be attained if soil and plant resources are allowed to deteriorate."

The direct causes of desertification are usually identified as overgrazing, overcultivation, and deforestation. Yet poorly planned and maintained irrigation schemes can also cause desertification as land becomes waterlogged and salinized. While this problem is not extensive in Africa—evident only in Egypt, South Africa, and Sudan, with more than one million irrigated hectares each—it is a big problem in terms of wasted money and opportunities. In 1982, more than one-sixth of all project aid to the Sahel was going for irrigation, yet irrigated land was going out of production due to salinization and water-logging as fast as new land was being irrigated (Grainger, 1982).

SOIL CONSERVATION AND THE REALITIES OF AID

Many solutions to overcultivation focus on intensification of agriculture—getting more produce from a given area of land—in a continent where most systems have traditionally been extensive and where rapid population growth has spilled over to more marginal land. Irrigation offers hope only for the very long term because of problems of high initial investment, recurrent costs, and demographic mismatches—the densest rural populations are often far from areas that can be irrigated.

A World Bank report found that 20,000 new hectares a year could be irrigated effectively in the Sahel and Sudano-Sahelian zones by the mid-1990s, but the number of farming families that would be accommodated by this extension would equal only one-half of the current annual population growth rate in the region (Gorse, 1985).

Getting more without overtaxing the land will depend on individual farmers finding solutions they can afford, such as no-till or low-till cropping, mixed cropping, agro-forestry techniques, water-harvesting, small-scale irrigation, and efficient recycling of crop residues and dung. Many of these technologies are widely tested and understood, though all will need more reserach before being of use in many locations in Africa.

Constraints to on-farm research into these techniques tend to be political rather than scientific. After the 1968–73 Sahel drought, Sahelian and donor governments agreed on food self-sufficiency as a national goal. Yet of the over $11 billion in development aid which went into the region between 1974 and 1982, only 4 percent went to rainfed food crops, and only 1.5 percent went to projects for soil and water conservation and ecological stabilization which would make food self-sufficiency a realistic goal (Giri, 1984).

Governments often appear to be working toward short-term goals which can never be realized because of degraded resource bases. Many African government have relied on exports of agricultural commodities to earn foreign exchange and balance budgets, while the soil is gradually losing its fertility. Egyptian biologist Mohammed Kassas, former president of the International Union for Conservation of Nature and Natural Resources (IUCN), has found that measures to fight desertificaiton are simply incompatible with "rational" financial strategies. In Egypt, the reclamation of one hectare of desertified land costs about $13,000. Yet if deposited in a bank, such a sum of money could earn about $1500 per year in interest. Land "can never give those returns," Kassas noted (Timberlake, 1984).

Donors are no less short-sighted. Though their provision of aid increases purchases by African countries of donor countries' goods, the nature of aid programs per se does little to improve the ability of countries to buy. Britain cut bilateral aid for projects of direct benefit to African agriculture by about one-third in real terms between 1979 and 1984, while maintaining aid to rural road-building and power projects which may benefit agriculture indirectly but benefit British suppliers and contractors directly (All Party Parliamentary Group on Overseas Development, 1985).

In 1985, Canada was tying 80 percent of its bilateral aid to the purchase of Canadian products and was working to increase this figure (Sabatier, 1985). While generous with relief aid, the United States focused more aid where there were "free market" approaches, for military support, or for politically motivated reasons (Shepherd, 1985). Aid for agriculture and rural development from all the Organization for Economic Cooperation and Development nations fell by 20 percent in real terms between 1980 and 1983 (Madeley, 1985).

There are other constraints to investing in the environment. British development analyst Piers Blaikie has compiled a list of essential elements of conservation programs, comparing each item on his list with the realities of the ways in which aid agencies and recipient governments approach such programs. The two columns line up as opposites. Conservation requires efforts over many years, perhaps a decade, but aid-financed or government-run conservation projects require measureable benefits within three to five years. Success in conservation requires diverse, timely, and highly coordinated inputs, but projects usually work through only one ministry. The output of a successful conservation project will be diffuse and difficult to measure, but executing agencies must have quantifiable benefits predicted at the proposal stage. Success requires sustained political will by the central government; projects on the other hand are run through short-term consultancies, usually one to three years (Blaikie, 1985).

One program which has recently been praised in development circles is soil conservation efforts undertaken by the Swedish International Development Authority (SIDA) in Kenya. Having allegedly benefited half the farmers in Kenya, this program has been underway for 10 years, a time frame over which most other Western development agencies will have changed their fashions, philosophies, goals, and even country emphases several times.

WHERE ARE THE ANTHROPOLOGISTS?

Anthropologists have been underutilized in development efforts because their views are often an embarrassment. They are prone to look carefully at the socio-political realities of a project and offer a reasoned explanation of why a project is unlikely to work. In reality, aid project documents typically begin with a page uncritically praising a given recipient government's dedication to rural development and people, and then launch into the technicalities of the project.

Anthropologists and sociologists often feel "that their findings are cast in a negative light—that certain conservation measures will not succeed or will actually do harm—and also that they are frequently overridden or relegated to writing a disparate chapter in a project document or report entitled 'Social constraints to soil and water conservation'" (Blaikie, 1985). Sociologists are often forced into the role of public relations officers, required to persuade the local population to go along with something forced upon them from outside.

Two senior workers at Britain's Overseas Development Administration identified ignorance of what farmers were doing and their motives for doing so as the major causes of disappointing results after a decade of work on integrated rural development projects across Africa (Morris and Gwyer, 1983). The two offer many examples, but in projects in Malawi, Swaziland, and Tanzania, research into local farming methods was not begun until after the projects were initiated.

The science of anthropology is not a cure-all for development mistakes. In fact, natural scientists are justified in complaining that anthropologists spend too much time on marriage customs and kinship links and not enough on current problems, and that they often avoid political realities.

Yet an anthropologist's approach—rooting change in already existing human resources—seems to be the soundest way to bring about change. It has proven very difficult to get farmers to suddenly begin planting trees in large numbers. One of the most successful of such efforts was carried out in Haiti by an anthropologist who, in his own words, "did not know which end of the tree to put into the ground." Former attempts to implement afforestation programs had failed. Paid to plant trees, farmers let their goats eat them so they would be paid to plant more. Told that the government owned all the trees, farmers cut them so the government would have no claim to their land.

Anthropologist Gerald Murray studied Haitian smallholders. He found that farmers owned their own land, even though their plots were small. He found that most were engaged in small-scale market gardening and sold small quantities of beans or corn. He also found a large national market for charcoal. He suggested that trees be encouraged as a cash crop. Put in charge of the program by the Pan American Development Foundation, Murray set up a distribution system, giving trees to peasants who planted at least 500. His workers advised on species and intercropping techniques, but left technical choices to the peasants, only encouraging them to cut and sell for cash after about four years (Timberlake, 1983). Between 1981 and 1984, 20,000 farmers planted 13 million trees, and it was expected that 16 million, double the original goal, would be planted by the project's end (International Task Force, 1985).

One does not need to be an anthropologist to base one's actions on local human resources. One of the most often cited tree-planting successes in Africa, funded by the private voluntary organization CARE, involved the planting of 400 kilometers of double-row windbreaks to protect some 4000 hectares of cropland from wind erosion. These trees not only conserve soil, but provide fuelwood and building poles when pruned. The project was initiated in 1974 by a Nigerien forester and a Peace Corps volunteer; the forester had been the area's forestry extension agent for years. CARE established nurseries, dug wells, purchased fencing, and paid people to guard young trees from livestock for the first three years after planting. The labor was done by farmers, principally traditional young men's groups called "samaria." Initial studies of the project suggest it has increased grain yields by 23 percent.

CARE attributes success (which took some eight years) to several factors: the forester's rapport with the villagers; the backing of local authorities; the project's response to a problem the villagers had identified themselves; and its small scale, expanding only after initial encouraging results (Kramer, 1985). CARE did not list among these factors choice of species or expertise in forestry and soil conservation techniques.

In fact, the much-praised success of many private voluntary organizations (PVOs) in Africa is based on an anthropological approach: cooperation with local people, basing projects on farmers' perceived needs, changing plans according to local priorities. In praising PVOs as the most effective agencies in the campaign against desertification, UNEP said in 1984: "Their high record of success is related to the small-scale and local direction of their projects and the requirements for local community participation, as well as their flexibility in operation and their ability to learn from earlier mistakes. The dominance of field activities gives these actions an impact out of proportion to the money invested" (UNEP, 1984).

According to this description, governmental and multilateral development agencies suffer from overly large scales, direction by outsiders, lack of local participation, inflexibility, and an inability to learn from mistakes. The only way to resuscitate the environment is through individual farmers. Until large aid agencies can include anthropologists, or better still, soil, water, and forestry technocrats who are willing to implement their projects with local people, little aid will get to the grass roots upon which African agriculture is based.

TREES FOR THE FORESTS

Trees outside of those in forests provide most of Africa's fuelwood, and thus most of Africa's energy for cooking and heating. Often described as "bush" or "scrub" of "open forest savannah," these trees tend to be omitted in official accounts because they are not in forests. There was a time when they were classified by foresters in West Africa as "brousse inutile"—useless bush. These trees not only play a role in conserving soil and water, but also provide considerable amounts of food and fodder, and thus are under pressure both from fuelwood cutting and from clearing land for agriculture.

Improved woodburning stoves may make homes safer and healthier, but a study by Earthscan raises serious questions as to whether they are likely to save many trees (Foley et al, 1984). Farming families have little incentive to buy stoves as long as the three-stone fire and its fuel—wood and crop residues—remain free. As local wood supplies dwindle, people use wood more sparingly for fires. Metal stoves tend to be too expensive for agencies to give away, while mud stoves tend to fall apart in six months to a year.

Yet, given the difficulties in getting farmers to conserve fuelwood or plant trees for fuelwood, it becomes increasingly clear how important fuelwood is as a determinant of carrying capacity in dryland areas. A World Bank report (Gorse, 1985) has concluded that in the Sahelian climatic zone—defined here as the northern limit of cultivation south to the 350mm rainfall isohyet—the sustainable human population in terms of crop and livestock production is seven people per square kilometer. The sustainable population in terms of fuelwood production, however, is only one person per square kilometer. In the Sudano-Sahelian belt (350 to 600mm of rainfall per year), crop and livestock production can sustain 15 people per square kilometer, but fuelwood can sustain only 10 people per square kilometer. The report finds that "the natural forest cover is therefore the most vulnerable part of the ecosystem."

Farmers are more easily persuaded to plant trees for agricultural purposes than strictly for fuelwood purposes. The development of various types of agroforestry for specific locations—alley cropping, intercropping, contour rows of trees, and even more effective forest fallow systems—will spur such agriculture-related tree planting. Of course, a side benefit of the conservation is increased supplies of fuelwood and building poles.

The loss of enclosed forests, especially the moist tropical forests of West Africa and the Zaire basin, is a different problem. The major cause of losses here is not fuelwood gathering, but mismanagement of logging, unsustainable rates of logging, and clearing for agricultural land. Only in exceptional cases such as central Tanzania where fuelwood is needed for tobacco curing are forests disappearing to provide energy. Ivory Coast, Africa's biggest timber exporter, saw the area of its closed forest decline by two-thirds between 1956 and 1977, with agriculture destroying 4.5 times more than logging, a ratio which may be similar in other forested parts of Africa (Timberlake, 1985). Ivory Coast's timber exports, which earned foreign exchange worth over $300 million in 1980, are expected to begin to fall before the end of the decade. Nigeria was once a timber exporter, but has now banned exports and may have to start importing to meet domestic needs. Cameroon is logging at a rate which would clear its forests in 90 years, but there are plans to double this rate.

There is hope for the future as governments realize that over-logging their forests is bad business, and that there is more long-term profit to be made from sound, sustainable management. Techniques for such management exist, and there are signs that they are being adopted. Over the past two decades, Zambia has established industrial plantations which it believes can meet its projected industrial timber needs through the end of the century. By 1983, over 45,000 hectares of plantations, mainly pines and eucalyptus, were established, helping "to reduce pressure on the country's diminishing natural forests and developing a highly productive source of round-wood needed in its copper mines and other industries" (International Task Force, 1985).

Another hope is that African governments and foreign agricultural advisers will learn and then stress the value of natural forests in watershed protection and thus to agriculture near these forests. Perhaps the most spectacular example of such natural protection is in Rwanda, Africa's most densely populated country. Efforts by international conservation groups to save the 12,000-hectare Parc des Volcans on the Zaire border centered around convincing Rwandans of the role these forested mountains play in soaking up annual rainfall and releasing it slowly for agricultural use. Clearing would have led to cycles of flood and water scarcity below the mountains, and would have provided enough agricultural land to support only two months' national population increase.

Yet governments have been slow to learn. In early 1985, Kenya's minister of environment and natural resources announced that 17,000 hectares of Kenya's natural forests in 10 districts would be cleared for government tea plantations. Some of this clearing was to be done on the slopes of Mt. Kenya, and foresters were predicting erosion and reduced groundwater on and below those slopes. Kenya already suffers severe fuelwood deficits, and only 3 percent of the nation remains under natural forest (*New Scientist*, 1985).

Unsustainable rates of logging and land clearances raise the suspicion that the exploitation of natural resources by some African states may be due in part to high debts and the desperate need for foreign exchange. If true, a charitable approach to Africa's debt burden may be one of the most effective ways in which donor governments can help Africa safeguard its natural resources. Other ways include education in sound forest management and techniques of watershed protection and rehabilitation.

THE HERDS AND HERDERS

Some 15 to 24 million people in Africa depend on livestock-based incomes. Most of them inhabit the drylands—across the Sahel and through the Horn of Africa to the semi-arid lands of East and southern Africa. The vast majority of these people rely on natural forage rather than on cultivated fodders and pastures, and in the drylands they must move to keep their herds supplied with food.

The nomadic pastoralist system makes a tremendous amount of sense. In areas where natural resources are scarce, the system allows humans to move through those resources, harvesting them and "storing" them in the bodies of their mobile livestock. It may be the only and the most effective way of making a living in land too dry for cropping. Kenyan ecologist David Western has conducted studies in southern Kenya which suggest that nomadic pastoralism is a more efficient way of exploiting dryland savannah than the as-yet unrealized potential of "game ranching." "Contrary to commonly held views, the results do not show natural wildlife ecosystems to be more efficient than pastoralist-dominated systems; quite the opposite in fact. Both appear more efficient than commercial systems" (Western, 1984).

Yet no sector of African agriculture has been as badly treated by development efforts as nomadic pastoralism. African governments find nomads difficult to tax, educate, draft into the armed services, and generally to control. They are suspicious of large numbers of people who traditionally travel armed and who have more respect for ecosystems than for national boundaries. Countries such as Niger have traditionally suspected "nationalistic tendencies" on the part of the Fulani people.

The wet years in the early 1960s, before drought set in, encouraged settled farmers to migrate northward from their usual zones in the south. When drought began in the late 1960s, nomads found their usual refuges in the wetter south blocked by settled agricultural development. Other types of agricultural development took rangelands from herders elsewhere in Africa. For example, the development of the Awash River basin in Ethiopia for cash crops in the late 1960s led to widespread famine among the Afar pastoralists in both 1973–74 and 1984–85.

Because there has been very little offtake from the nomadic herds in terms of increasing GNP or providing domestic protein intake or beef exports, pastoralists have had very low standing with both their governments and aid agencies. Together with other factors, this has led to a widespread policy of "sedentarization"—the encouraged or enforced settlement of nomads.

If nomads settle, but maintain their large herds in dry areas, rapid desertification often results, and when drought occurs, large losses of livestock are incurred because of starvation rather than lack of water. After studying the effects of sedentarization, UNESCO's Integrated Project on Arid Lands in northern Kenya concluded that "it will only be possible to increase human welfare of pastoralists and to stop desertification if the mobility and dispersion of livestock can again be increased considerably, and if overall numbers of livestock can be better controlled through a greatly improved marketing system" (Lusigi and Glaser, 1984).

Fitting pastoralist societies into national development strategies will pose a problem for governments. Solutions will depend on their willingness to decentralize their authority to more traditional social organizations. Work by British rangeland expert Jeremy Swift and USAID's Niger Range and Livestock Project has shown that pastoralist societies can be organized into collectives that are responsible for the bulk purchasing of essential goods that link pastoralist groups to the local government.

Improved beef marketing systems are not likely in the near future. Pastoralists will have little reason to sell large numbers of animals until the consumer items they require are made available to them. With the large distances between nomadic pastoralists and trading centers, governments may have to settle for the more realistic goal of keeping citizens healthy and employed in livelihoods in regions where no other economic strategies work.

International aid agencies and the UN system have made a sudden about-face in their views of pastoralists. The 1968–73 Sahel drought caused agencies to focus on developing herds with the hope of turning the Sahel into a "meat-basket" for the region. The failure of these ambitions is documented by the abandoned abattoirs and fattening pens that litter the region. The confusion of agency goals were summed up by Dr. Michael Horowitz of the State University of New York in 1979: "Livestock projects have been supposed, simultaneously, to increase productivity, reverse the ecological deterioration of the range, shift production from dairy to a beef orientation, improve producer income and quality of life, maintain a regular supply of cheap meat for the internal market, and increase the supply of high-quality meat to the export market" (quoted in Timberlake, 1985).

Subsequently, agencies acted as though the large herds did not exist, or that they were a major cause of desertification. Recently, agencies have shown an understanding of the need to return to basic principles. In 1985, USAID set up a committee of rangeland experts to try to determine what was not known about African rangeland management, and what the research priorities were.

CONSERVATION

While it may seem trivial to consider the problems of Africa's national parks and other protected areas at a time when human lives and livelihoods are threatened, the issue of wildlife conservation raises some principles that apply to resource protection in general. First, conservationists' arguments that wild areas must be preserved because of the "genetic resources" they contain or may eventually be found to contain do not impress Africa or other Third World governments. Governments are being asked to spend money on conserving species which primarily benefit industrial countries.

Indonesia's vice-president, Adam Malik, perhaps best summed up the Third World view when he asked: "How much land for the hungry today? And how much for genetic resources to be preserved for tomorrow? In the past, we have neither received a fair share of the benefits, nor have we received a fair share of assistance—other than inexpensive advice or even more inexpensive criticism—in the efforts to save the common global natural heritage. Unless such responsibilities are equally shared, all our good intentions will only lead to global environmental destruction" (Malik, 1982).

Although much of the encouragement and cash for basic wildlife conservation in Africa will have to continue to be provided by the North, African governments have been willing to invest in conservation when it is connected to tourist revenue. As a result of the influx of tourists, however, the fauna of some of the popular parks are under pressure. In preserving areas for tourism, governments have posted armed guards to keep out the locals, and revenues generated by these areas go into national coffers.

The few experiments so far attempted at directing this revenue to local people—giving them a direct stake in protecting the parks— have borne fruit and suggested ways to proceed. The Zimbabwe government developed an anti-poaching scheme called "Operation Windfall" in Chizaria National Park and the Chirisa Safari Area west of Harare. Basically, the proceeds of elephant culling—sales of meat and ivory—were diverted to two local councils who used it as they saw fit—for schools, clinics, and local transport. Between early 1981 and June 1982, the councils received $960,000. Elephant poaching dropped so dramatically that the parks department found it no longer necessary to post wardens in the areas (Side, 1982).

A complex agreement between the Kenyan government and the Maasai herders who have traditionally depended on the Amboseli National Park for dry season grazing gives the Maasai some tourist revenue from the park, compensates them for cattle lost to wild predators, and has established watering points outside the park for the Maasai livestock. The effort, though it continues to be adjusted and refined, is credited with doubling the rhino population in the park between 1977 and 1983, and increasing the number of elephants, buffalo, and many migratory species.

BUT IS THERE TIME?

Much of the above argument appears to have proceeded on the assumption that the rapid degradation of Africa's natural resource base can be reversed. In many areas, it is admittedly not clear that this is the case.

Can sustainable agriculture really continue given the acceleration and continuation of desertification in all agricultural sectors of the Sudano-Sahelian region, considering that the population of that region has risen from 191 million to about 236 million in the seven years from 1977 to 1984 (Berry, 1984)?

Doubts about the long-term viability of the region are heightened by evidence that human activities actually may be changing the climate for the worse. There are three main ways that this could be happening. Stripping vegetation from the land, through deforestation, cultivation, and overgrazing, increases the reflectivity of the planet's surface, bouncing more solar heat back into the atmosphere and preventing the formation of rainclouds.

Loss of vegetation also means there is less evapotranspiration from plants and less moisture in the soil, so less moisture gets into the sky to return as rain. Finally, the increasing amounts of dust blown aloft from cleared ground may also prevent the formation of rainclouds. Increasing levels of atmospheric carbon dioxide around the planet, released by the burning of carbon fuels, are beginning to have their predicted "greenhouse effect," trapping solar radiation and changing weather patterns to make a drier Sahel (see Hare, 1984).

But the evidence for these changes comes mainly from computer models. Given that substantiating these claims requires conducting experiments, the lack of controls means that Sudano-Sahelian governments are unlikely to have proof of permanent climatic change in time to undertake any massive, planned transmigration projects to try to move their people south to more favorable areas. With rapid population growth rates, poor infrastructure, and inadequate organizational capabilities, it is also unlikely that such a scheme will be at all feasible in the near future, or that it could be guaranteed to do more good than harm. Finally, the people are likely to "vote with their feet" before any such scheme is organized. Though not very well documented, there appears to have been a steady movement southwards in the region for some time.

The question of whether the climate is changing raises other issues of a political and almost psychological nature. Travelling in the Sahel today, one hears many politicians and administrators throw up their hands and say, "What can we do? The climate is changing."

A growing number of geographers feel that concentrating on climatology per se is attention and funding misdirected. Kenneth Hewitt goes so far as to maintain that contemporary natural disaster research, with an emphasis on climatology and geophysics, has "become the single greatest impediment to improvement in both the understanding of natural calamities and the strategies to alleviate them" (Hewitt, 1983).

This is not to write off studies of climate, especially of rainfall and hydrology, as a waste of time. Hare (1984) points out that meteorological and hydrological services have severely deteriorated in recent years in arid zones, in part because adverse climate has reduced governments' ability to support them. But then these have more to do with weather and water availability than with climate, and have a part to play in any attempts to improve rural people's abilities to cope. Expensive computer climate models and satellite surveys have less to offer farmers.

Hare concludes that there are no "big science" answers available to the Sahel such as cloud seeding or other forms of weather modification. Though a climatologist, he sees what hope there is in agricultural and political responses. Control of land use, protecting it from livestock, reducing cultivation, planting trees and shrubs can protect the "micro-climate" at ground level upon which agriculture depends. He also recommends that vulnerable nations equip themselves with drought plans to protect people, land, and resources against future droughts. Whether the climate is changing or not, there will be future droughts.

A U.S. MODEL?

In the mid-1930s, a drought struck the Great Plains in the United States at a time when gross farm income was low and falling, and farmers were "overcultivating" to keep up. There was severe wind damage to desiccated soil and almost one in 10 farmers gave up and sold their farms. The period and the area affected became known as the "Dust Bowl" (Warrick, 1984).

The U.S. government did not respond by rounding up Oklahoma farmers and organizing them into gangs to plant huge tree belts across the state. There were no calls for in-depth studies of the climate of the Great Plains as a response to the crisis. What happened instead was that the government set up a framework, based on the needs and capacities of the farmers, encouraging them to take measures in their own individual interest to resuscitate the natural resource base. Organizations such as the Federal Crop Insurance Corporation, the Soil Conservation Service, and the Agricultural Stabilization and Conservation Service were established. There was frantic activity at the local level to conserve water and protect its sources, to encourage contouring, terracing, leaving fields fallow, using drought-resistant varieties, and to enforce land use regulations.

Similar sorts of activities have been tried in Africa, but in the United States, the emphasis was first on the farmers and their farms. The goal was to keep impoverished farmers in the economic and political systems of the nation for the sake of the nation. A side effect of this emphasis was that farmers were given both the incentives and the means to restore their environmental resource base. Also, the burden of the crisis was shared throughout the nation, in the form of taxes paid by people in cities and far from the drought areas.

It would be impossible for Africa to copy the U.S. response. But the response to the African crisis on the part of both foreign and African experts tends to focus too much on ecosystems, crops, trees, terraces, structures, wells, etc.—too much on things rather than people. One general cause of the African crisis is the tendency of many governments to leave its poor farmers outside of national economic and political systems. Instead of spreading the burden throughout a nation, governments have tended to focus the burden on those least able to bear it—the drought and famine victims themselves.

Donor governments, multilateral agencies, and African governments seem to have passed beyond the era of the "big fix" in Africa: continent-girdling tree belts and regional plans for livestock production and marketing. But they have not yet found the means of getting "development" to the majority whose ability to survive depends on the renewable resource base. Doing so will mean radical changes in the way donors operate, and even more radical changes in the ways in which most African governments operate. For the latter, it will mean finding ways of politically enfranchising their poorest and most powerless, and offering them hope that efforts to protect their environment will bring returns.

Unless these changes occur, once "renewable" resources will be squandered past renewing over large parts of the continent, and Africa's crisis will change from acute to chronic.

REFERENCES

All Party Parliamentary Group on Overseas Development. 1985. *UK Aid to African Agriculture*. London, Overseas Development Institute.

Avery, Dennis. 1985. *Potential for Expanding World Food Production by Region and Country*. Washington, D.C.: Bureau of Intelligence and Research, U.S. State Department.

Berry, Leonard. 1984. "Desertification in the Sudano-Sahelian Region, 1977–1984," in *Desertification Control Bulletin*, No. 10 (May). Nairobi: UNEP.

Blaikie, Piers. 1985. *The Political Economy of Soil Erosion in Developing Countries*. Burnt Mill, England: Longman.

Dregne, Harold. 1983. *Evaluation of the Implementation of the Plan of Action to Combat Desertification*. Nairobi: UNEP.

Eckholm, Erik, et al. 1984. *Fuelwood: The Energy Crisis That Won't Go Away*. London: Earthscan.

FAO. 1983. *Preliminary Report on Public Expenditure on Agriculture in Developing Countries*. Rome: FAO.

FAO. 1984. *How Development Strategies Benefit the Rural Poor*. Rome: FAO.

Foley, Gerald, et al. 1984. *Stoves and Trees*. London: Earthscan.

Giri, Jacques. 1984. "Retrospective de l'economie Sahelienne." Paris: Club du Sahel.

Gorse, Jean, et al. 1985. *Desertification in the Sahelian and Sudanian Zones of West Africa*. Washington, D.C.: The World Bank.

Grainger, Alan. 1982. *Desertification: How People Make Deserts, How People Can Stop and Why They Don't*. London: Earthscan.

Hare, F. Kenneth. 1984. "Recent Climatic Experience in the Arid and Semi-Arid Lands" in *Desertification Control Bulletin*, No. 10 (May), Nairobi: UNEP.

Hewitt, Kenneth. 1983. "The Idea of Calamity in a Technocratic Age," in K. Hewitt, ed., *Interpretations of Calamity*. Boston: Allen & Unwin.

International Task Force. 1985. *Tropical Forests: A Call for Action*. Washington, D.C.: World Resources Institute.

Kramer, John Michael. 1985. "Testimony before U.S. House of Representatives Subcommittee on Natural Resources, Agriculture, Research and Environment" in *Congressional Record* for 23 October, Washington, D.C.

Lusigi, W. J. and G. Glaser. 1984. "Combating Desertification and Rehabilitating Degraded Production Systems in Northern Kenya: The IPAL Project," in Di Castri et al., eds., *Ecology in Practice*, Vol. 1 (Ecosystem Management). Paris and Dublin: UNESCO and Tycooly Press.

Malik, Adam. 1982. Speech delivered to Third World National Parks Conference, Bali, Indonesia.

Madeley, John. 1985. *International Agricultural Development*. Vol. 5, No. 5.

Morris, J. and G. Gwyer. 1983. "UK Experience with Identifying and Implementing Poverty-related Aid Projects" in *Development Policy Review*, 1.

New Scientist. 1985. 21 February.

Sabatier, Renee. 1985. "In Canada, The Business of Aid is Business," *Earthscan Feature*, July 1985. London: Earthscan.

Shepherd, Jack. 1985. "When Foreign Aid Fails," *Atlantic Monthly*, April.

Side, Dominique 1982. "How to Stop Poachers," *Earthscan Feature*, September.

Timberlake, Lloyd. 1983. *The Improbable Treaty: The Cartegena Convention and the Caribbean Environment*. London: Earthscan.

Timberlake, Lloyd. 1984. "Alone in the Wastelands," *Earthscan Feature*, June 1984. London: Earthscan.

Timberlake, Lloyd. 1985. *Africa in Crisis: The Causes, the Cures of Environmental Bankruptcy*. London: Earthscan.

UNEP. 1984. *General Assessment of Progress in the Implementation of the Plan of Action to Combat Desertification*. Report of the Executive Director. Nairobi: UNEP, UNEP/GC.

Walls, James. 1984. "A Summons to Action," in *Desertification Control Bulletin*, No. 10 (May).

Warrick, Richard. 1984. "Drought in the U.S. Great Plains," in K. Hewitt, ed., *Interpretations of Calamity*. Boston: Allen & Unwin.

Western, David. 1984. "The Environment and Ecology of Pastoralists in Arid Savannahs," in *Development and Change* 13:183–211.

CHAPTER FIVE

Population and Health: Africa's Most Basic Resource and Development Problem

Fred T. Sai

With a land area two and a half times larger than the United States, sub-Saharan Africa, a region including 45 countries, is considered among the least developed areas in the world. As measured by basic development indicators, much of the continent has regressed over the last 30 years. After growing at an average of 3.8 percent per year between 1960 and 1970, gross domestic product grew at an annual average rate of only 3.0 percent between 1970 and 1982.[1] And as Africa's population growth rates have increased steadily from an annual average of 2.4 percent in the 1960s to a rate of 3.2 percent today,[2] per capita GDP has dropped markedly: from an annual average of 1.4 percent between 1961 and 1970, to 0.4 percent between 1971 and 1979, to –3.6 percent in the early 1980s.[3] Unfortunately, many of Africa's development problems defy rapid solution, as they have no historical precedent.

While Africa lags far behind the rest of the world in its level and rate of economic development, there is one area in which the continent takes the lead—the rate of growth of its population. Africa's future will be profoundly influenced by the demographics of its population, such as birth and mortality rates, as well as by internal and external migration and health and nutritional issues. These questions will continue to interact with other aspects of underdevelopment to make solutions to the continent's economic problems even more intractable.

Africa's population could well double by the end of the century.[4]

Infant mortality rates now average about 125 deaths per thousand births. The percentage of the population living in urban areas has just about doubled since 1960,[5] and this continued rural-urban migration has outstripped the capacity of governments to provide the bare minimum of social services in the cities. Basic health and nutritional problems remain widespread, despite improvements in medical research and technology elsewhere in the world and in places in Africa itself.

Because the present economic crisis has drastically limited the financial resources available to African governments for the future, it is paramount that African governments and foreign donors alike come to grips with the continent's troublesome population trends. What are the policy options that can effectively address these critical issues? In what manner can African states and foreign donors coordinate their efforts to assure the most economic, yet comprehensive approaches? These questions must be addressed now—for their answers will most certainly determine Africa's capacity for sustainable economic and social development in the future.

Major shifts in both policy and in budgetary allocations are required to address the critical questions of population, health, and nutrition. Such changes will occur, however, only by increasing governmental and public awareness of the dangers of neglect in these areas and by by generating sufficient political will on the part of governments. Additionally, increases in foreign assistance, improvements in health education, and a serious commitment to a regional or subregional approach to these questions are needed. This chapter will examine Africa's demographic features and its health and nutrition problems, and conclude with recommendations for African policy-makers and donors, particularly the United States.

AFRICA'S DEMOGRAPHY

The population of Africa south of the Sahara is estimated at over 450 million, with an average density of 18 persons per square kilometer. Given the land area of the region, the size of the population cannot be considered too great. However, a high population growth rate becomes a problem when it surpasses a nation's aspirations and the capacity of that nation's resource base to meet increasing demands. With an annual average population growth rate of 3.2 percent, the number of people in Africa will continue to exceed the support capacity of their economies unless serious efforts at the governmental level are undertaken to attain and maintain economic growth with a better distribution of national wealth (see Tables 5.1 and 5.2).

A number of demographic considerations indicate a worsening of Africa's population problem in the years ahead. First, the African population is very young, with some 19 percent under five years of age and 45 percent under age 15. This indicates that even if the fertility rate were to be lowered considerably, the population would continue to grow through "demographic inertia."[6] The next generation of parents has already been born. Moreover, Africa's population exhibits the highest dependency ratio in the world. The dependency ratio compares the number of very young and very old to those of labor force age who are capable of supporting them.

The consequences of high population growth rates and the age structure of the population are felt most immediately in increased demand for food, education and health services.[7] While in the rest of the world, the growth of food production has remained slightly ahead of population growth, this has not been the case in sub-Saharan Africa. Whereas food production and population in sub-Saharan Africa both grew at a rate of about 2.4 percent in the 1960s, by the 1970s, the population growth rate of 2.8 percent was far ahead of a food production growth rate of only 1.4 percent. While Africa was basically self-sufficient in food in 1970, today more than one-third of its peoples are fed in some part by imports, thus reducing already scarce foreign exchange reserves.[8]

The young and rapidly expanding population in sub-Saharan Africa means increased demands on already inadequate education and health care systems and implies little likelihood of much improvement in the quality of either. Countries already beset by slow economic growth will be hard-pressed to supply job opportunities to all the new entrants into the labor market. Agriculture offers limited prospects for new employment under current and prospective technologies, as land limits are being reached in a number of countries, creating pressure to leave rural areas. The rapidly growing urban areas have not been able to supply employment to a large share of job seekers. For governments then, the net result of the high dependency ratio is to increase the amount of the national product that goes to consumption, leaving fewer resources for productive investments in other sectors of the economy.

TABLE 5.1
SUB-SAHARAN AFRICA: POPULATION ESTIMATES, MID-1984

Country	Population Estimate mid-1984 (millions)	Persons per sq. km.	Birth rate (per 1000 population)	Death rate	Natural increase (percent annually)	Infant mortality rate[a]	Life expectancy at birth (years)
Sub-Saharan Africa, Total	433.5	18	48	17	3.1	112	49
Western Africa	162.3	26	49	18	3.1	120	47
Benin	3.9	35	51	22	2.9	145	43
Burkina Faso	6.8	25	48	22	2.6	145	43
Gambia	0.6	55	48	28	2.0	189	36
Ghana	13.0	54	47	14	3.3	96	53
Guinea	5.3	22	47	23	2.4	155	41
Guinea-Bissau	0.9	25	41	21	2.0	140	44
Ivory Coast	9.5	30	46	18	2.8	119	48
Liberia	2.1	19	48	17	3.1	109	50
Mali	7.8	6	50	22	2.8	145	43
Mauritania	1.8	2	50	20	3.0	134	45
Niger	5.9	5	51	22	2.9	137	43
Nigeria	92.0	100	50	17	3.3	111	49
Senegal	6.4	33	48	21	2.7	138	44
Sierra Leone	3.5	49	47	29	1.8	196	35
Togo	2.8	49	45	16	2.9	110	49

Eastern Africa	174.3	20	49	17	3.2	108	49
Burundi	4.5	161	47	20	2.7	134	45
Djibouti	0.4	18	47	21	2.6	—	—
Ethiopia	35.4	29	49	21	2.8	140	44
Kenya	19.8	34	55	14	4.1	79	54
Madagascar	9.7	17	44	16	2.8	65	50
Malawi	6.8	58	52	19	3.3	161	46
Mozambique	13.7	17	44	16	2.8	107	50
Rwanda	5.9	227	51	16	3.5	107	50
Somalia	5.4	8	46	21	2.5	140	44
Sudan	20.9	8	45	17	2.8	115	48
Tanzania	21.7	23	50	15	3.5	96	52
Uganda	15.2	64	50	14	3.6	91	53
Zambia	6.4	8	48	15	3.3	98	52
Zimbabwe	8.5	22	47	12	3.5	67	56
Middle Africa	60.7	9	45	17	2.8	117	48
Angola	8.5	7	47	22	2.5	145	43
Cameroon	9.5	20	43	17	2.6	114	49
Centr. Afr. Repub.	2.5	4	45	21	2.4	140	44
Chad	4.9	4	44	21	2.3	140	44
Congo	1.7	5	44	18	2.6	121	47
Equatorial Guinea	0.4	14	42	21	2.1	134	45
Gabon	1.1	4	35	18	1.7	109	50
Zaire	32.1	14	45	15	3.0	104	51

TABLE 5.1 (Continued)

SUB-SAHARAN AFRICA: POPULATION ESTIMATES, MID-1984

Country	Population Estimate mid-1984 (millions)	Persons per sq. km.	Birth rate (per 1000 population)	Death rate	Natural increase (percent annually)	Infant mortality rate[a]	Life expectancy at birth (years)
Southern Africa	36.2	13	40	14	2.6	91	54
Botswana	1.0	2	50	12	3.8	77	55
Lesotho	1.5	50	41	16	2.5	107	50
Namibia	1.5	2	45	17	2.8	112	49
South Africa	31.6	26	38	14	2.4	89	54
Swaziland	0.6	35	47	17	3.0	126	49

[a] Infant mortality rate = deaths under age one per 1000 live births in the same year.

sources: Population estimates: United Nations, Population Division, Estimates and Projections Section, *Demographic Indicators by Countries as Assessed in 1982*, medium variant, New York, December 14, 1983, computer printout; Land area: World Bank, *World Development Report 1984* (New York: Oxford University Press, 1984), Table 1 and p. 276; 1983 per capita GNP: World Bank, *1984 World Bank Atlas* (Washington, D.C.: The World Bank, 1985).

Africa's total fertility rates (the average number of lifetime births per woman) are among the highest in the world. The average is 6.6 births per woman[9] (almost double the average of the world as a whole), though in Kenya the number is as high as 8.1. The continent's mortality rates are also high, with an average crude death rate of 17.3 per thousand;[10] only in a few island states is mortality less than 10 per thousand.

What is worrisome about this trend is that it is largely among the very young that the high death rate prevails. Infant mortality rates are still over 100 per thousand live births and in some rural areas, as high as 250. These figures range from 5 to fifteen times the rate in industrialized countries. A high infant mortality rate contributes to overall high fertility rates by encouraging "replacement births" and also by shortening the period of lactation, during which a woman is less likely to conceive. In Africa, death rates of children aged one to four range from 13 to 50 per thousand, with an average of 23, which is some 20 to 50 times that in the United States, where the rate is 0.8 per thousand and the most common causes of death are accidents or congenital abnormalities.[11] The rate of maternal mortality—death directly related to childbearing—is 300 to 600 per 100,000 live births in Africa, as compared to less than 10 per 100,000 in the industrialized world.

INTERNAL AND EXTERNAL MIGRATION

Africa's cities are growing faster than those in any other region of the world, many at a rate of 7 to 10 percent per year[12] (in Nairobi, the figure is as high as 13 percent). This rapid rate of urbanization poses yet another demographic problem for Africa. Concurrent with this population movement are three negative trends: the development of large shanty towns, or bidonvilles, within and around the major cities which pose serious public health threats; increased unemployment as largely unskilled rural laborers seek work in the cities; and along with the unemployment, an upsurge in crime and drug usage, and a concommitant deterioration of the cities.

Rural-urban migration is not a new phenomenon, but its rate of growth is. Africa is still the least urbanized region in the world. But since 1960, the percentage of urban population has almost doubled from 14 to 25 percent today. With the advent of independence and with efforts to expand social amenities, more work became available in and around the major towns, attracting rural residents to the cities.

TABLE 5.2
POPULATION GROWTH AND PROJECTIONS

	Average annual growth of population (percent)			Population (millions)		
	1960–70	1970–82	1980–2000	1982	1990	2000
Angola	2.1	2.5	2.8	8	10	13
Benin	2.6	2.7	3.3	4	5	7
Botswana	2.6	4.3	3.6	1	1	2
Burkina Faso	2.0	2.0	2.4	7	8	10
Burundi	1.4	2.2	3.0	4	5	7
Cameroon	2.0	3.0	3.5	9	12	17
Central Afr. Rep.	1.6	2.1	2.8	2	3	4
Chad	1.9	2.0	2.5	5	6	7
Congo	2.4	3.0	3.8	2	2	3
Ethiopia	2.4	2.0	3.1	33	42	57
Gabon	0.4	1.4	2.6	1	1	1
Gambia, The	2.2	3.2	2.3	1	1	1
Ghana	2.3	3.0	3.9	12	17	24
Guinea	1.5	2.0	2.4	6	7	9
Guinea-Bissau	..	..	2.3	1	1	1
Ivory Coast	3.7	4.9	3.7	9	12	17
Kenya	3.2	4.0	4.4	18	26	40
Lesotho	2.0	2.4	2.8	1	2	2
Liberia	3.2	3.5	3.5	2	3	4
Madagascar	2.2	2.6	3.2	9	12	16
Malawi	2.8	3.0	3.4	7	8	12
Mali	2.5	2.7	2.8	7	9	12
Mauritania	2.3	2.3	2.6	2	2	3

Mauritius	2.2	1.4	1.6	1	1	1
Mozambique	2.1	4.3	3.4	13	17	24
Niger	3.4	3.3	3.3	6	8	11
Nigeria	2.5	2.6	3.5	91	119	169
Rwanda	2.6	3.4	3.6	6	7	11
Senegal	2.3	2.7	3.1	6	8	10
Sierra Leone	1.7	2.0	2.4	3	4	5
Somalia	2.8	2.8	2.4	5	5	7
Sudan	2.2	3.2	2.9	20	25	34
Swaziland	2.7	3.2	3.9	1	1	1
Tanzania	2.7	3.4	3.5	20	26	36
Togo	3.0	2.6	3.3	3	4	5
Uganda	3.0	2.7	3.4	14	17	25
Zaire	2.0	3.0	3.3	31	40	55
Zambia	2.6	3.1	3.6	6	8	11
Zimbabwe	3.6	3.2	4.4	8	11	16

SOURCE: Derived from World Bank, *World Development Report, 1984*, Oxford: Oxford University Press, 1984.

Since the early 1970s, however, much migration has been the result of economic crisis in the countryside, as two decades of governmental neglect of rural develpment needs has made itself felt. Those with initiative rush to the cities to find work and a better life, but they often find their hopes dashed, at best finding low-paid jobs, but most of the time joining the vast number of unemployed in the towns.

Intra-African migration has also become a problem. Whenever opportunities for employment have presented themselves, such as in Nigeria during the oil boom or during Ivory Coast's agricultural expansion, workers from neighboring countries, usually semi-skilled, but sometimes professional and technical, have migrated in large numbers, creating a politically sensitive problem for the recipient country. Refugees from warfare or drought and famine are also part of intra-African migration. Africans account for about half of the world's estimated 10 million refugees.[13] Despite the hospitality of African governments that spend scarce resources to shelter them, most of the refugees live close to the margin of existence and at times contribute to political instability in their host countries. However, external migration is not confined to within Africa; many Africans—sadly, among the best educated in their countries of birth—leave the continent for better opportunities in Europe and the United States.

HEALTH AND NUTRITION PROBLEMS

Africa's main health problems—related to fertility, nutrition, and communicable diseases—continue to plague its population even when technological advances have been able to control or eradicate these same problems elsewhere in the world.

Fertility-related problems for women—hemorrhage and eclampsia, pre-eclampsia, anemia, and kidney conditions leading to hypertension—result from the prevalence of early pregnancies, closely spaced childbirths, late childbearing, and poor maternity care. Childbearing for African women begins in adolescence—from 15 years old—and may continue until about 50. Women who have more than five children, who continue bearing children into their late 40s, and whose pregnancies are spaced closer than two years are endangering their health and their lives as well as those of their babies. Further, each time a woman become pregnant, she suffers a decrease in her immune reaction, particularly to malaria. Both spontaneous and induced abortions and complications that follow from them are also common and dangerous threats to women's health.

The biological, social, and economic problems associated with adolescent childbearing have not been adequately recognized until recently. Extramarital pregnancies are increasing, causing high school dropout rates and other social problems. In many cases those who have children at a very young age are not provided with any opportunities for resuming their education or for acquiring other skills which would make them economic assets to their communities.

The health needs of infants and young children also require substantially increased investments. Africa's high overall death rates are due in part to the disproportionately high mortality rates of infants and young children. In some regions of Africa, children under five constitute about 20 to 25 percent of the population, but contribute 50 to 80 percent of the annual mortality toll, compared to about 3 percent in Western Europe. Diseases with often fatal results which affect children include diarrhea, pneumonia, malaria (responsible for the deaths of over 1 million children annually), measles, and whooping cough. All of these illnesses are even more hazardous to children's health when they combine with marginal or severe malnutrition. For an estimated cost of only $1.20 per child (not including transportation and administration costs), African children could be innoculated against the six most dangerous childhood diseases: measles, diptheria, whooping cough, tetanus, tuberculosis, and polio as part of a major effort to make low cost health care more widely acceptable.

Adults are subject to vector-borne, food-borne, and environment-related diseases which have largely been eradicated or controlled in other parts of the world. Several diseases commonly afflict a single patient, and the so-called apathy of African workers may simply be attributable to poor health and malnutrition. The mosquito vector carries malaria, filiariasis, and yellow fever which still reach epidemic proportions in areas of Africa. The black fly carries onchocerciasis, or river blindness, making many tracts of fertile land, particularly in West Africa, uninhabitable and unproductive. Trypanosomiasis (sleeping sickness), which attacks both humans and animals, is also a hazard to health and agriculture. Bilharzia, carried by snails, has not yet been controlled, and entire villages can be rendered unproductive by guinea worm.

There are also many endemic food-borne diseases—salmonellosis, shigellosis, and cholera—which are transmitted by the house fly or through poor food handling. Introduced in Africa in 1970, cholera has become endemic because of poor environmental sanitation and water and food control, which have facilitated its easy transmission. Poliomyelitis, infectious hepatitis, and various forms of dysentery are also caused by poor sanitation or poor food handling. Hookworms, ascaris, and other nematodes also afflict all age-groups. Tropical ulcers are also common.

Tuberculosis and leprosy are among the more chronic adult diseases in Africa. Tuberculosis is common in cities and industrial establishments, especially in the mining areas, and poor labor health policies encourage its spread to rural areas. Agriculture, the principal occupation of some 70 percent of the population, also carries with it many health hazards. Apart from accidents resulting from improper use of implements, snake bites and tetanus are frequent afflictions of farmers.

NUTRITIONAL PROBLEMS

Sub-Saharan Africa is the only region in the developing world where nutrition has worsened in recent years (food consumption per capita has actually declined in the last 20 years). In late 1984, the FAO reported that 190 million people in 19 countries were still suffering from one of the worst droughts in Africa's history. But apart from such climate-induced fluctuations, the Sahelian region suffers from almost annual food shortages just before the harvest. These annual shortages lead to weight loss in both children and adults, causing such energy depreciation that adults cannot perform the full amount of work required to prepare for the next sowing season.

Protein calorie malnutrition, resulting in kwashiorkor and marasmus, is one of the most serious nutritional problems in Africa, primarily affecting infants and children. Surveys have indicated that 2 to 10 percent of all children aged 1 to 4 suffer from overt protein calorie malnutrition, and 30 to 50 percent of those under five show a weight deficit which can be considered as clinical malnutrition, often resulting in stunted growth.

Protein calorie malnutrition is associated with very high mortality. Without treatment, kwashiorkor may result in 20 to 50 percent mortality. When malnutrition begins in utero, it is known to affect the psychomotor and mental development of the infant, perhaps irreversibly. Kwashiorkor also mentally retards children, and unless rehabilitative measures are undertaken to encourage mental development, the damage can be permanent.

Various degrees of protein calorie malnutrition have been noticed in adult women as well, particularly pregnant and lactating women. Anemia, resulting from iron and/or folic acid deficiencies, is so common as to occur in 20 to 80 percent of all women and in some men as well. Deficiencies of riboflavin, a member of the vitamin B group, are also common, leading to angular stomatisis, cheilosis, changes of the tongue, gum disease, and consequent tooth loss.

Vitamin A deficiency, affecting the eyes, is the most worrisome, causing xerophthalmia, which if untreated, can result in blindness. Its actual extent is not known and a study of its prevalence is needed. In some parts of the continent, goiter, resulting from inadequate iodine supplies, is a major problem. Goiter can cause foetal deficiency in pregnancy; iodine deficiency in the mother can result in cretin births.

POLICY IMPLICATIONS:
POPULATION AND DEVELOPMENT

The problems of population, health, and nutrition are interrelated in sub-Saharan Africa. In fact, the problems of population and development as a whole are linked. An ongoing debate has continued—particularly since the U.S. policy statement to the International Population Conference in August 1984—over the question of which has a greater impact on reducing fertility: economic development or family planning. Many have argued that family planning programs can have no effective impact until a certain level of development has been reached. In fact, some have gone to the extreme of declaring that economic development is the best contraceptive. Historical evidence shows that development, particularly if well ordered and the fruits reasonably spread, can be followed by fertility decline. On the other hand, evidence exists on the impact of well planned, well implemented family planning programs on fertility.

But examples have shown that even in countries such as Mexico with high levels of development as measured by per capita GNP, there have not been the expected reductions in fertility rates. Edward Green has argued that this is because the majority have not enjoyed the benefits of that development and still regard more children as an asset.[14] Therefore, a more equitable economic development is needed before this can have the desired effect on population growth.

By the same token, a reduction in the population growth rate is needed for more equitable development. Green further notes that rapid population growth further exacerbates the disparities between rich and poor. It leads to increased land values, more fragmentation of property, higher rents, and lower wages. Those who already own land and capital grow richer, while the poor get poorer. High population growth generally inhibits efforts to more equitably distribute resources, because it is difficult to improve the lot of the poor while trying to cope with a heavy rise in the total population. As Maudline and Laphan have demonstrated, good family planning programs together with good development programs have the most impact on fertility when working together. The effect of each by itself can be considerable too.

Arguments about either development or population control are likely to prove futile. Both are required. Without active measures to curb population growth rates the fruits of development will prove inadequate for the peoples' needs. The social burden will fall heavier on the very poor and the disparities between the rich and the poor will be exacerbated.

Baum and Tolbert [15] have stated that the main cost of rapid population growth is borne principally by the poor in the lost opportunities for improving their lives. They advance several reasons for this:

1. Rapid population growth slows development by exacerbating the choice between higher consumption now and larger investment towards future benefits for many.

2. In economies (like those of Africa) dependent on agriculture, population growth threatens the balance between people and scarce natural resources.

3. Rapid population growth makes it difficult to manage the adjustments necessary to promote economic and social change.

It needs to be remembered that whereas economic development brings about many improvements in health the direct application of bio-medical technologies help to provide faster and larger improvements; family planning technologies have to be looked at in the same way.

Africa remains far behind other continents in population and family planning programs, as its leaders have inadequately addressed the linkage between population questions and other development issues. At the time of the Bucharest Population Conference in 1974, only Mauritius, Kenya, and Ghana had evolved policies aimed at decelerating population growth rates and providing education and access to health services. Only Mauritius had instituted programs that were readily accessible to the majority of the population.

However, in 1981, eight countries formed the African Regional Council of the International Planned Parenthood Federation. Through their efforts and those of the UN Fund for Population Activities and other agencies, the relationship between population and other developmental issues began to be recognized at the governmental level. By 1984, eight African countries had formulated population policies, and some 24 others have family planning programs.

The tremendous change in perceptions of the issue of population at the governmental level has been brought about in a relatively short period of time. Still, even in those countries where there is sensitivity to population and family planning issues and where policies have been formulated, programs have had little impact. This is due to several factors.

As previously noted, the fertility rate remains high in Africa. Whereas it has fallen everywhere else in the world, it has remained, at least for the last 25 years, at 6.6 in Africa. There are a number of cultural and socioeconomic factors associated with the still high fertility rate on the continent. The Caldwells have extensively documented many of these factors.[16] For example, they have found that many African women still want more children, regardless of how many they already have (a finding confirmed by The World Fertility Survey). This is attributable in part to the great horror of terminal barrenness among women. Men are marked by an equal fear of impotence and both would seem to stem from the fact that having children is in many cases the supreme mark of manhood or womanhood. A woman's prestige is tied up with her children.

However, attempts to find explanations for Africa's continued high fertility err in imposing uniform explanations—usually of an anthropological nature. Essentially the high fertility relates to the socio-economic levels and conditions. At comparable stages in other people's histories they had high fertility too. It was perhaps never as high because external factors—biomedical technology in particular—were not as favorable as they are now.

While there is a great fear of barrenness, that alone does not explain the desire for large numbers of children. This is probably due first to the fact that the family is the agrarian production unit; and secondly in response to the perceived insecurity of a child's life due to high infant and childhood mortality rates.

There are other issues as well. In some societies where land was communally owned, the only investment that could be made was in children. Marriage in many societies was more a contract between families than individuals, and the bride price was understood to be a payment for reproductive and work capacity.

The Caldwells have found that among many Africans, it is thought that contraceptives are evil; they are feared to cause congenital defects, multiple births, barrenness, sterility, or illness. It is also commonly held that they will cause female promiscuity. In fact, they found that in places such as Nigeria, where contraceptives are used with greater frequency, the primary reasons are to reduce the period of sexual abstinence between births (but still not have births too close together), and to allow for extramarital relations.

Nearly universal distrust of contraceptives is fuelled by religious dogma and, recently, by Western (U.S.) policy. Yet the need for family planning is increasingly obvious as the rising rate of abortion shows.

The Caldwells note that in the past, many governments have derided population programs as examples of imperialist or neo-colonial plots to keep Africa down. But they say that this is not the real problem. Rather, these governments know that population programs run counter to the basic spiritual beliefs and emotions of many African societies.

Julian Conde has suggested historical reasons for the continued high fertility rates.[17] He notes that factors such as the slave trade, wars, natural disasters, and epidemics including plagues and yellow fever, have decimated and in some cases depopulated whole regions of Africa. He feels that "the need to make up for these losses experienced in the past may perhaps unconsciously prompt Africans to reproduce more readily than others."

There are, in addition, more practical reasons for the low success rates of family planning attempts. Many programs and personnel are urban-oriented, which means that the rural areas where the bulk of the population lives are often excluded. Further, the health delivery system in most African countries was inherited from the metropolitan power. Hospitals and health centers serving relatively large populations are the focal points of the system, meaning that health care is available to 20 to 25 percent of the population on a periodic basis. But the remainder of the population is required to travel long distances for treatment or make do with untrained or traditional birth attendants and healers. Further, urban-oriented health systems utilize some of the most advanced technology, creating a budgetary burden which constrains efforts to expand health care to the entire population. In Ghana, for example, hospital services take 80 percent of the health budget, while serving only 20 percent of the population.

IMPROVED PRIMARY HEALTH CARE AND FAMILY PLANNING PROGRAMS

Since the World Health Organization's 1978 Alma-Ata conference, many African countries have affirmed their commitment to extending primary health care to the entire population. However, translating their rhetoric into action has not been easy. The existence of fully staffed and equipped hospitals which take about 75 to 85 percent of the annual health budget makes it difficult to allocate sufficient resources to primary health care. Health services for all will be almost impossible to achieve without a shift of priorities away from prestigious, urban hospital-based care, which caters to the politically important urban population, toward rural services.

A major question, therefore, is to what extent governments can reallocate budgetary resources. If it is not possible to do so, it may still be feasible to increase the overall amount going to primary health care or preventive services. Apart from reordering priorities within health budgets, however, it is important to remember that only 5 to 7 percent of total annual budgets are spent on health. Health care cannot be improved unless the political will to free the necessary funds exists.

Only through national public awareness and pressure will such a policy and budgetary shift come about. And unless governments make a conscious change in policy toward focus on primary health care, no amount of external assistance will make a difference. Each country should have a primary health committee or council at the highest levels to collaborate with and coordinate the activities of the ministries of health, community development, economic development, education, and information.

Another priority is to involve women more directly in the entire development process. Providing women with access to both formal and health care education is critical. Educating women is also the surest way of bringing about declines in rates of fertility. As women are involved in about 80 percent of the continent's food production and handling, little can be achieved to improve health and nutrition for children without their involvement. In this context, special attention must be devoted to fostering breast feeding. Fortunately, in rural areas, breast feeding is the rule rather than the exception, and only a small minority of women—primarily working women—bottle-feed their children. However, there is the need to encourage prolonged breast feeding in all health improvement programs.

In other areas of primary health care and communicable disease control, efforts at oral rehydration for children with diarrhea, expanded immunization programs, and weight surveillance should be implemented both at the national and community levels. Focusing on eradication of a single disease or concentrating on a single sector will not serve to solve Africa's health problems. When a disease is a public health menace and the technology to control it is available at little cost, there is no reason why such a disease should not be attacked. Yet unless the people recognize the other factors—poor sanitation, poor nutrition, lack of education—which contribute to the spread of disease, the simple application of technology to cure it will represent only a short-term solution.

Family planning programs must be emphasized and supported, but this will not happen unless African governments accept that this area must be a priority, that such projects are implementable, and that they can yield results. Both autonomous family planning activities and those that form a part of overall health services are important and should be expanded. Autonomous family planning projects have proved useful in stimulating other aspects of the health care system in many communities. Pharmacies in many big cities find the demand for contraceptives to be substantial; however, because of legal restrictions, many methods of birth control are not available to the women who need them. There are few social marketing programs and few community-based distribution outlets for contraceptives.

Access to contraception needs to be expanded, with the medical system providing backup care, referral, and education on its use. However, a single-minded approach to family planning as the major solution to Africa's development problems, as was advocated in the 1960s and 1970s, should be avoided. This attitude sufficiently alienated many Africans as to make the implementation of family planning activities very difficult.

Food and nutritional problems are more intractable, and perhaps the best that can be hoped for at this stage is identification of the groups at risk. Identification and treatment of the more seriously malnourished can help reduce the level of malnutrition at the community level while education and food production programs take hold. But again the political will must be there if lasting changes are to be effected. Government policies which subsidize food prices, political and military conflict, and traditional agricultural practices also represent barriers to increasing food production. These factors are greatly exacerbated by the alarmingly accelerating rates of deforestation and desertification taking place in sub-Saharan Africa and the lack of attention to rainfed agriculture in research.

REGIONAL SOLUTIONS AND GLOBAL PARTICIPATION

In addition to efforts at the individual government level, African countries must cooperate regionally to address issues of population and health. Unfortunately, neither the Organization of African Unity, the UN Economic Commission for Africa, nor the World Health Organization's regional offices have provided adequate leadership on these issues. For many years, these organizations regarded family planning and population activities as too sensitive to be advocated publicly. Of late, advances have been made in data collection, population censuses, and the training of demographers. But it is troubling that the continent's health authorities have not advocated family planning as part and parcel of efforts to improve the overall health and general living standards of the population. Even maternal and child health care services have not had the requisite support at national or regional levels.

The 1984 World Population Conference in Mexico City, preceded by the Second Africa Population Conference in Tanzania, have shown that there is sufficient interest in issues of health, population, and family planning on the part of African governments. Perhaps the continent's regional organizations can join together and begin to take a much more active role in advocating support for population and health programs by exchanging information, documenting experiences, and identifying programs that have worked and under what circumstances. Exchange programs and workshops at which African experts and health care workers can analyze the issues involved in the implementation of population and health policies of relevance to their people should be supported at the national, regional, and international levels.

A joint food and nutrition commission of the OAU, FAO, and WHO has existed for many years in Accra, Ghana, but at no time in its existence has it been adequately financed. Its primary tasks should be to analyze the food and nutrition situation both regionally and at the country-specific level, to help formulate food and nutrition strategies, and to put the issues before the international community to seek financial assistance. If strengthened, the commission could play a role in sounding alerts on famines as they develop and in identifying appropriate strategies to address them.

The opportunities for research through regional instruments and for regional collaboration are vast but as yet untapped. Efforts at regional economic cooperation are reviving and perhaps through organizations such as the Economic Community of West African States and the Southern African Development Coordination Conference, issues of population and health can begin to be addressed.

For international donors, and, in particular, the United States, there first needs to be a clearer understanding of region-wide and national health and population problems in Africa and institutional capabilities that exist and those that need to be created to deal with them. In these efforts, the important role played by non-governmental organizations and universities should not be forgotten. In addition, U.S. leaders should enter into a policy dialogue with African leaders in order to obtain an accurate assessment of how they perceive the issues of population and health.

The real potential of the communities—human resources that can be mobilized—must be explored. Equally, the limitations of the budgetary and financial allocation processes must be understood. This kind of expertise must be gained by visits to the countries and communities, but probably above all through seminars and workshops of U.S. and African experts. These workshops should aim at identifying solutions to Africa's health problems and examining approaches that have already been tried and failed. The scientific community in the United States can work with African scientists in these endeavors.

Human resource development and institution-building should be another area for emphasis. Many of the continent's institutions which have been founded in the post-independence period have not demonstrated any real relevance to Africa's development problems. Medical schools and institutions, for example, have not devoted adequate attention to developing approaches for expanding health care and services to the rural poor. Perhaps the United States could collaborate with the World Health Organization in improving the involvement of African universities in rural health care. A similar approach should be taken to schools of engineering and agriculture. Scholarship monies in the health field should not be spent only in U.S. institutions, but rather they should be granted for research in Africa on African health problems.

African universities and faculty focusing on agriculture are virtually isolated from the practical agricultural problems the continent is facing. Further, social sciences departments which should be in the forefront of studying the interaction of society and technology and innovation are not seriously addressing these issues. If these universities can be encouraged through outside support to involve themselves in non-traditional areas rather than strictly academic areas, they may be able to play a more significant role in Africa's development needs. Some American foundations and universities could break new ground in making African universities more relevant to development issues.

The United States government has recently expressed doubts about the merits of family planning as a separate program in development efforts and about whether the use of artificial contraceptives should be encouraged. It is unfortunate that the United States, which once stood for freedom of choice in personal decision-making, should be interfering in some of the most personal and critical areas of human life. The American government should realize that its policies toward international family planning organizations are dangerous and community and government leaders should speak out against them.

The American government has removed support from the International Planned Parenthood Federation because it spends less than one-fourth of 1 percent of its funds on abortion and related activities, such as medical meetings in which abortion is a topic of discussion. This will have disastrous consequences on family planning in Africa. The IPPF pays between 60 to 100 percent of the cost of family planning programs in some 25 African countries and without that support, or even less support, these services will collapse and institutions that have taken 15 or more years to develop will disappear. A bipartisan approach to health and population issues is required.

The low level of education for girls and women is one of the more intractable developmental problems Africa faces. Support must be mobilized for an assault on illiteracy and for the provision of reading materials for the literate population. While the overall adult literacy rate has nearly tripled (15.7 percent to 42.9 percent) since 1960,[18] the progress made by women has not been nearly as remarkable (literacy among women averages 20 percent).[19] Likewise, whereas 77.6 percent of all school age children attend secondary school, only 9.5 percent of girls do. Perhaps American women's organizations could commit themselves to literacy programs for African women.

The appropriateness of health technology in meeting Africa's needs should be studied. A center to evaluate health technologies and to adapt them to rural needs should be established. Regional centers to train personnel and to research and adapt appropriate health technology should be considered. In this regard, developed countries share the responsibility for having pressured developing countries to use their scarce resources on costly technology of marginal relevance to the problems they face.

The problems faced by the African continent have no historical precedent. The current rate of population growth is unprecedented. At its most rapid period of growth, the rate in Europe never reached above 1.6 percent per annum. A doubling of Africa's population by the close of the century poses very grave problems in the areas of education, health, and employment.

Technologies which can be applied in Africa are available for health and family planning provided the right choices of both the technology and their methods of delivery are made. Unfortunately, Africa has inherited expensive and irrelevant delivery models which have deluded it into becoming dependent on expensive high technology with limited applications.

The time has come for the United States to send a team of experts to Africa to examine, with African experts within each country, the continent's needs in health and population. During the visit or visits efforts should be made to identify individuals and institutions which could play a role in any effort to reverse the decline in Africa. The needs of such individuals and institutions should be first priority in any strategy, as it is from their success that major lessons will be learned. Special attention should be paid to the identification of women in leadership roles and to plan for their further training and critical development. Such women could be encouraged to travel extensively and be assisted in increasing their role in national affairs. Around them stronger women's groups should be created.

Efforts to get regional consensuses on health and population should be intensified. WHO, ECA and others should be assisted in undertaking an analysis of strategies for Africa in health and population, and set out programs and targets with interested nations. The problems are immense. Solutions will take a long time, and both donors and African governments should gear themselves up for long dedicated searches and applications.

Governments are responsible for the education, health, and welfare of all their citizens. The communications revolution has opened Africa to the rest of the world and has made it possible for African leaders to become aware of the technological advances which may be attractive, but of dubious relevance to their countries' economic development. The U.S. media should play a role in responsibly educating Americans as to the continent's needs and Africans to the opportunities. African governments are prepared for genuine dialogue and cooperation. The United States must evolve approaches with as little political partisanship as possible if long-term collaboration is to be assured.

NOTES

1. "Toward Self-Sustained Development in Sub-Saharan Africa: A Joint Program of Action," Washington, D.C.: The World Bank, September 1984, p. 58.

2. Ibid., p. 82.

3. "The Challenges for Sub-Saharan Africa," speech by Robert S. McNamara, November 1, 1985, p. 36.

4. *World Population Prospects*, New York: United Nations, 1985, p. 146.

5. *World Tables*, Washington, D.C.: The World Bank, 1983, p. 142.

6. "Population and Poverty in Sub-Saharan Africa" by Margaret Wolfson, in *Crisis and Recovery in Sub-Saharan Africa*, Paris: OECD Development Centre, 1985, p. 96.

7. Ibid., p. 97.

8. *World Tables*, p. 486.

9. Ibid., p. 142.

10. Ibid.

11. "Black and White Children in America: Key Facts," Washington, D.C.: Children's Defense Fund, 1985, p. 85.

12. "Compact for African Development Strategies," Council on Foreign Relations/Overseas Development Council, New York and Washington, D.C., December 1985. See Appendix II of this volume.

13. Ibid.

14. "U.S. Population Policies, Development, and the Rural Poor in Africa," Edward Green, *Journal of Modern African Studies*, 20 (I) (1982).

15. Warren C. Baum and Stokes M. Tolbert, *Investing in Development: Lessons of the World Bank Experience*, Oxford: Oxford University Press, 1985, pp. 213–14.

16. John C. Caldwell and Pat Caldwell, "Cultural Forces Tending to Sustain High Fertility in Tropical Africa," 1984 draft of an unpublished paper.

17. Julian Conde, "The Demographic Situation in Africa and its Effect on Economic and Social Development," OECD Development Centre, October 1984.

18. *World Tables*, p. 158.

19. *Women of the World: Sub-Saharan Africa*, Washington, D.C.: Department of Commerce, August 1984.

PART III

AGRICULTURE

CHAPTER SIX

Governmental Strategies for Agricultural Development

Bruce F. Johnston

Africa's recurring food crises have forced governments and donor agencies to search for more effective strategies for agricultural and rural development. Increasing food imports to meet the growing gap between demand and domestic production cannot be sustained over the long term. In order to accelerate the growth of agricultural output, a shift from traditional resource-based agriculture to a science-based agriculture will be required, involving the utilization of more productive technologies and increasing quantities of fertilizers and other manufactured inputs.

The predominantly agrarian structure of the economies of tropical Africa and rapid growth rates of population and labor force have critically important implications for the choice of a strategy for agricultural development. Because of Africa's unique demographic features, countries confront a choice between a "bimodal" (dualistic) pattern, in which resources are concentrated in large and capital-intensive farms, or a broadly based "unimodal" pattern of agricultural development. There is now considerable consensus concerning the advantages of agricultural strategies that foster the progressive modernization of small farm units in economies where 50 to 80 percent of the total population and labor force are still dependent on agriculture (Mellor and Johnston, 1984).

Africa's development problems require attention to the following goals: accelerating the rate of output growth; expanding farm and non-farm employment opportunities; reducing the most serious manifestations of poverty, particularly malnutrition and disease; and slowing rates of population growth. Over the next 30 to 40 years, small farm development strategies involving labor-intensive, capital-saving technologies represent the most economical approach to achieving these goals.

However, the diversity of agroclimatic and socioeconomic conditions, even within relatively small countries, is such that a variety of small-farm strategies will be required. For example, farm equipment innovations based on animal draft power are not feasible in tsetse-infested areas; even in savanna regions the feasibility and profitability of achieving wider, more efficient use of animal-powered implements will vary substantially.[1] Indeed, the diversity of environmental conditions in sub-Saharan Africa poses special problems in fostering technological progress and accelerated growth of agricultural production.

THE CHOICE OF AN
AGRICULTURAL STRATEGY

Agriculture's heavy weight in the economic structure is common to all African countries. Fifty to 80 percent of the population and labor force are still dependent on agriculture for employment and income. Rapid population growth ensures that agriculture's large share in the total labor force will continue and that the absolute size of the farm population and labor force will increase for at least several decades. Although between 1960 and 1984, the percentage of the population in urban areas doubled—from 11 to 22 percent—the farm labor force has continued to increase at an annual rate of approximately 2 percent (Gusten, 1984, p. 12).[2]

Because of those structural and demographic features, the countries of tropical Africa confront an unavoidable choice between an emphasis on agricultural strategies that promote large-scale farms and give rise to a "bimodal" (dualistic) pattern of agricultural development or small-farm development strategies leading to a "unimodal" pattern of development. The rapid growth of the farm population in recent decades has already created conditions of land scarcity in a number of African countries. Of more general significance, however, is the "purchasing power constraint" that characterizes a country where the domestic commercial market for agricultural products is small relative to the large number of farm households. The farm units that comprise a large-scale subsector are able to escape that sectorwide purchasing power constraint because they account for the lion's share of commercial sales. That means, of course, that for the great majority of farm households, the purchasing power constraint is intensified.

The widespread tendency to favor large-scale farm enterprises is often related to the vested interests of those who own or manage the farms, whether as private or state enterprises. This bias toward large farms or estates is, however, based upon a belief in the importance of economies of scale in agriculture. A treatise on the political economy of West African agriculture by Keith Hart provides an example of the view that the establishment of "large, capital-intensive estates" (publicly or privately owned) offers the only effective approach to achieving "a long-run dynamic of economic development through labor specialization, capital investment, and productive innovation" (Hart, 1982, pp. 154, 157).

A pervasive belief in the importance of economies of scale (or of farm size) has been reinforced by the experiences of the United States and other industrialized countries where agricultural productivity has grown on increasingly large farms using ever larger quantities of farm machinery and other purchased inputs. Theoretical analysis and empirical evidence, however, point to the existence of significant diseconomies as well as economies of scale.

Evidence of a decline in output per unit area as the total size of farm units increases—an "inverse relationship" between farm size and output—indicates, however, that in countries where labor is relatively abundant, the diseconomies typically outweigh the economies of farm size. The forces that give rise to this inverse relationship derive from what Binswanger and Rosenzweig (1983) refer to as "behavioral and material determinants of production relations in agriculture."

The principal diseconomies of farm size result from the fact that the costs associated with hiring labor exceed the cost of labor supplied directly by the family members of farm households. Because family members have a claim on the net income of the farm enterprise, their self-interest provides an incentive to seek to maximize the farm's profits by hard work, by acquiring technical knowledge and skills, and by exercising initiative and judgment in carrying out their tasks.

Because agricultural production is subject to the uncertainties of weather and other factors, a variety of "on-the-spot supervisory decisions" must be made (Brewster, 1950). The consequence is that various forces act to raise the cost incurred by employers of farm workers and to reduce the net income realized by wage laborers (Johnston and Tomich, 1984, pp. 43–64).

The technical characteristics of certain crops may give rise to genuine economies of scale. Sugar cane is perhaps the best example. Tea was long considered to be the plantation crop par excellence because of the need for close coordination between plucking the leaves and processing them in fairly large factories. However, the institutional innovation represented by the Kenya Tea Development Authority (KTDA) provided a mechanism for coordinating the collection of tea leaves and their prompt delivery to factories. As a result, small farms have been able to compete successfully with estates in the production of tea (Lamb and Muller, 1982).

It is often asserted—or assumed—that economies of scale are so important in agriculture that a small-farm development strategy is bound to be inefficient and can only be justified by invoking non-economic arguments related to income distribution or nutritional improvement. In fact, there is abundant evidence that small farm development strategies can be a more economical approach to achieving sectorwide expansion of agricultural production than a large-farm strategy when the opportunity cost of farm labor is low because of the lack of off-farm employment opportunities. When structural transformation and economic development reach a point where the relative availability and prices of capital and labor warrant a shift from labor-using, capital-saving technologies to labor-saving, capital-using technologies, then the economies of farm size become significant and small- farm development strategies cease to be appropriate.

In brief, historical experience and logic indicate that there are highly significant economic and social advantages in achieving a transition from resource-based to science-based agriculture by implementing small-farm strategies that lead to unimodal patterns of agriculture development. This does not mean that farms should be uniformly small or that different farms and areas should be expected to advance at the same rate.

Japan's experience is of considerable interest in demonstrating the feasibility and desirability of a unimodal pattern of agricultural development. Some 75 percent of the total labor force was employed in agriculture as late as 1880; and the impressive increases in agricultural productivity that played such an important role in the economic development of Japan were achieved among the small owner-cultivators and tenant farmers who continued to dominate Japanese agriculture until the post-World War II period.

As another example, Taiwan was one of the first developing countries to experience the rapid decline in mortality and "explosive" growth of population and labor force that have become commonplace in the decades since World War II. It was not until the late 1950s that the absolute size of the agricultural labor force in Taiwan began to decline, and during the preceding half-century, the farm workforce had doubled. Although that increase was much less than the fourfold increase projected for Kenya over the same period, it meant that Taiwan's farm units became smaller and smaller until the processes of demographic change finally led to a decline in the absolute and relative size of the farm labor force.

It would be absurd to suggest that Japan and Taiwan provide a "model" that can be emulated by African countries. In fact, a major theme of this chapter is that the physical environment for agriculture in sub-Saharan Africa provides a number of unique characteristics including the predominance of rainfed agriculture and an exceptional diversity of agroclimatic and soil conditions. Nevertheless, the experiences of Japan and Taiwan illustrate the critical ingredients of success—each country created an efficient agricultural research system, a good rural infrastructure, an efficient system for the distribution of farm inputs, and a broad educational system.

Impressive increases in agricultural productivity and output were achieved by gradually expanding the use of purchased inputs such as fertilizers that were capable of being used efficiently by small farmers and which enhanced the productivity of a large labor force rather than displacing farm labor prematurely when alternative employment opportunities were not available. Although the post-World War II land reforms in those countries reinforced their unimodal development, the basic patterns of agriculture were set much earlier when land ownership was highly skewed.

The experience of the Asian countries also points to the fallacy in the simplistic but widely held view that African countries are experiencing food problems because land and resources are devoted to production of export crops instead of food crops. In Taiwan, the expansion of export production enabled the country's small farmers to increase their cash incomes more rapidly than would have been possible if demand had been limited to subsistence requirements plus sales to a relatively small domestic commercial market (Johnston and Kilby, 1975, Chapters 6 and 7). The contribution of those exports to foreign exchange earnings also benefited the farm population, directly by financing imports of fertilizers and other essential farm inputs and indirectly by facilitating the expansion of output and employment opportunities in the nonfarm sectors so as to initially slow the increase in the size of the farm labor force and to eventually permit a reduction in its absolute size.

Under a bimodal pattern of agricultural development, the benefits from export expansion are likely to be restricted to the large-scale subsector. Indeed, it appears that the rapid growth of export production in Malawi between 1964 and 1980 was not only confined to the estate sector, but was in large measure financed at the expense of the country's small-scale farmers (Kydd and Christiansen, 1982).

The fundamental reason why small-farm strategies have significant economic advantages is because of the fit between the resource requirements of such strategies and the resource endowment that characterizes late-developing countries where the bulk of the population still depends on agriculture for employment and income. Since the agricultural sector in African countries is subject to a severe cash income or purchasing power constraint, the extent to which expansion of agricultural output can be based on increased use of purchased inputs is limited. This underscores the importance of the forces that determine the rate and "bias" of technical change (i.e., whether the innovations that become available induce the adoption of labor-using, capital-saving technologies or technologies that are capital-using and labor-saving). Hence, generating and diffusing innovations that are complementary to the existing on-farm resources of labor and land are of decisive importance in minimizing the cost of sector-wide expansion of farm output and also in determining the "pattern" of agricultural development.

In brief, the economic advantages of achieving widespread increases in productivity among a country's small-farm units derive from the fact that they are the most feasible and cost-effective means of attaining the multiple objectives of development—the growth of output, expansion of opportunities for productive employment, narrowing income differentials, reducing malnutrition and excessively high rates of infant and child mortality, and slowing the rate of population growth.

The key to the effectiveness of small-farm development strategies in contributing to the attainment of those multiple objectives lies in its potential for achieving a rate of expansion of employment opportunities, farm and nonfarm, that exceeds the rate of growth of the population of working age. The tightening of the supply/demand of labor that results represents the most reliable means of increasing returns to labor because of its combined effect on reducing underemployment and increasing the "price" of labor, including the implicit price of the unpaid labor of family members working on their own farm units.

The employment-generating potential of small-farm development strategies derives from their reliance on labor-using and capital-saving technologies. Such strategies make it possible to increase farm output by fuller and more efficient utilization of the large and growing farm labor force that characterizes African countries—the key to minimizing the agricultural sector's requirements for the particularly scarce resources of capital and foreign exchange. Past expenditures for tractors and tractor-drawn implements have often contributed to severe shortages of capital and foreign exchange; frequently this has meant that the great majority of farm households have not had satisfactory access to hoes and other basic farm implements.

Further, a successful unimodal pattern of agricultural development helps to encourage more rapid expansion of nonfarm output and employment opportunities. Broadly based agricultural development fosters positive interactions between agricultural and industrial development that stimulate more rapid growth of nonfarm output and employment than can be realized under a bimodal pattern of agricultural development. The pattern of rural demand for farm inputs and consumer goods that is associated with widespread increases in farm productivity and incomes fosters the dispersed growth of small- and medium-scale manufacturing firms that use relatively labor-intensive technologies and rely mainly on indigenous resources of labor and raw materials.

But a bimodal pattern of development tends to be associated with a growth in demand for more sophisticated consumer goods and farm inputs (e.g., automobiles and tractors) instead of bicycles and improved animal-powered agricultural implements. The rate of expansion of firms responding to the pattern of demand associated with bimodal agricultural development is inevitably more constrained by the scarcity of capital and foreign exchange than is the expansion of the smaller firms that are stimulated by widespread increases in income under a successful unimodal pattern of agricultural development. The more rapid growth of off-farm employment opportunities that results is also more important in slowing the rate of growth of the farm work force, thus minimizing the adverse effects of diminishing returns to labor as growth of the rural workforce puts pressure on the arable land available for expanding the cultivated area.

Erroneous perceptions about the importance of economies of scale and failure to recognize the extent to which emphasis on large-farm strategies and the effective implementation of small-farm strategies represent mutually exclusive alternatives have no doubt contributed to the failure of virtually all African countries to achieve successful unimodal patterns of agricultural development. The need for a choice between small-farm and large-farm development strategies has been emphasized because successful implementation of small-farm strategies leading to a unimodal pattern requires a conscious commitment to the sustained and difficult effort required to achieve broad-based agricultural development.

More direct obstacles to the successful implementation of small-farm strategies have been related to macro-economic policies that have adverse effects on the agricultural sector in general but especially on small farmers. Weak supporting services for agricultural research, extension, credit, and programs for the construction and maintenance of roads and other rural infrastructure have also been responsible for generally ineffective implementation of small-farm strategies. Excessive investment of scarce resources of money and labor in promoting a subsector of large-scale farm units is only one of a number of reasons for the weakness of those supporting services.

ACCELERATING AGRICULTURAL DEVELOPMENT: MACROECONOMIC POLICIES AND TECHNOLOGICAL PROGRESS

MACROECONOMIC POLICIES

Many critics of the agricultural strategies pursued by African governments come close to suggesting that "getting prices right" is all that is needed to overcome the food and agricultural problems that have become so serious during the past two decades. Some suggest that the difficulties can be attributed to the failure of independent

African governments to manage their economies efficiently.[3] Reality is more complex. For most African countries, it is not accurate to describe the agricultural sector as "stagnant." Many countries have been expanding total agricultural production at rates that are impressive relative to those that were achieved by the industrialized countries, including Japan. But rates of increase of output of some 2.5 percent have been outpaced by population growth rates of 3 to 4 percent per annum.

There is no doubt that many macro-economic policies have had adverse effects on agriculture in Africa. This has probably been due as much to neglect of agriculture in resource allocations as to price distortions. Deficiencies in research and other support services and inadequate finance for the construction and maintenance of rural roads and transport have been very important factors in unsatisfactory rates of output growth.

Macro-economic policies that have adversely affected agriculture have usually included highly protectionist import-substituting industrialization, although other forces that have often led to high rates of inflation and overvalued exchange rates have also been significant. Budget deficits that fuel inflation are also a result of the failure to enlarge tax revenues in keeping with the expansion of government expenditures.

High tariffs and import quotas to protect a "modern" industrial enclave increase the price of most imports and of locally manufactured products and turn the terms of trade against agriculture by raising the cost of farm inputs and consumer goods. Overvalued exchange rates further worsen the terms of trade, especially for producers of export crops. In addition, governments often fix food prices at artificially low levels for the benefit of urban consumers, thus depressing producer prices and weakening their incentive to expand output.

Government measures to offset these negative effects are almost always concentrated on a subsector of relatively large-scale farmers. For example, financial institutions are often directed to make credit available at artificially low interest rates to farmers and manufacturing firms, leading to an "excess demand" situation as the low interest rates stimulate demand for credit while ceilings on the interest paid on deposits discourage savings. The result is administrative rationing of credit from institutional sources. Invariably, the larger and more influential farmers receive the bulk of the subsidized credit. Subsidized distribution of fertilizer has a similar effect in creating an "excess demand" situation.

Policies that enable large farmers or state farms to acquire tractors at artificially cheap prices have particularly adverse effects. Although tariffs on imports are generally very high, tractors and other capital goods are often allowed to enter duty-free. Given an overvalued exchange rate, the price of this imported equipment is already artificially low. When large farmers have access to subsidized credit, the acquisition of inappropriately capital-intensive, labor-displacing farm equipment is encouraged. In addition, government purchases of imported tractors have often been encouraged by the availability of loans under foreign aid programs which temporarily remove the foreign exchange constraint.

Many of these macroeconomic policies were probably adopted initially without recognition of the consequences. Donor countries have encouraged faulty decisions, such as the purchase of tractors, by offering concessional loans. However, such policies are adopted and maintained because they are beneficial to certain powerful group interests. A regime may attach a great deal of importance to strengthening its hold on power by securing the support of large and influential farmers, the bureaucracy, industrialists, and workers in the modern enclaves created by protectionist policies and other preferential measures (Bates, 1981, 1983).

TECHNOLOGICAL PROGRESS: OBSTACLES AND
OPPORTUNITIES

Strengthening National Research Systems   Deficiencies in both the level and orientation of investment in agricultural research have very likely been the single most important factor behind inadequate rates of technological progress and growth of agricultural production in Africa. Among the factors responsible for those deficiencies are overly optimistic expectations about the availability of profitable technical innovations adapted to Africa's diverse environmental conditions and impatience for quick results. These have encouraged large investments by governments and donors in area- or commodity-based development programs that typically have little impact on productivity and output because the "technical packages" on which they are based did not yield the expected returns.

This over-optimism about the potential for direct technological transfer has been influenced by a common misinterpretation of Asia's experience with the Green Revolution. IRRI and CIMMYT played a critical role in the development of semi-dwarf varieties of rice and wheat that spread so rapidly in the mid-1960s. Their role, however, was to support, not substitute, for national agricultural research programs. The point that bears emphasis is that the Asian countries that have benefited from the Green Revolution have had the indigenous research capability to follow up on the direct "material transfer" of high-yield varieties of rice and wheat with the second and third stages of technological transfer—"design and capacity transfer" (Hayami and Ruttan, 1984). Thus they have been able to utilize imported "prototypes" of genetic material and equipment, a growing body of scientific knowledge, and effective methodologies for experimental work, enabling them to develop crop varieties and agronomic practices adapted to local ecological and socioeconomic conditions.

The indigenous research capability in the countries of South and Southeast Asia is the result of a long-term process of institution-building. This process was strengthened considerably in the 1950s, and the result has been a substantial increase in the supply of well-trained agricultural scientists, social scientists, agricultural administrators, irrigation engineers, and other specialists. Indeed, the agricultural progress achieved since the mid-1960s would not have been possible without this augmented supply of scientists and administrators. The development of a network of agricultural universities in India during the 1950s is the most notable example, but similar progress has been made in many other Asian countries which benefited greatly from foreign aid programs with a high priority on the long-term process of institution-building. AID and other bilateral aid agencies provided major support in sustained technical assistance for the new educational institutions and in foreign training of the nationals who now staff university teaching and research programs. Programs of the Rockefeller and Ford Foundations and the relatively modest but strategic efforts of the Agricultural Development Council also made notable contributions to the strengthening of indigenous capabilities for research and administration of agricultural programs.

While similar programs have been carried out in Africa, they began later and the efforts were more limited and of shorter duration. The tragedy is that African countries, which had the greatest need for sustained programs to support institution-building for agriculture, did not begin to receive significant levels of foreign aid until after aid policies had shifted away from institution-building to new priorities such as "integrated rural development," "basic needs strategies," and preoccupation with "the poorest of the poor." And the "extension bias" that has led to a misallocation of resources in all developing regions appears to have had especially unfortunate consequences in Africa (see Evenson, 1978). Substantial domestic and external resources have been devoted to the creation of sizeable agricultural extension programs which have generally been quite ineffective because they have had so little to extend.

Strong agricultural research programs must be supported by an informed constituency which holds the programs responsible for worthwhile results. During the colonial period, such a constituency existed for export crops, but not for food crops. Kenya and Zimbabwe were the principal exceptions because politically influential European farmers were engaged in production of both.

It is noteworthy that Kenya's impressive progress in promoting smallholder agriculture has been concentrated in "high potential areas" and based mainly on high-value export crops. Prior to 1954, African farmers had not been permitted to grow certain high-value crops, ostensibly because they would compromise the reputation for quality of coffee and other export crops grown on European estates. In fact, Kenyan African farmers' production of high quality coffee and tea and management of high quality "grade" cattle for milk production has been very impressive. The success of that program and continued expansion following independence depended in considerable measure on the fund of knowledge accumulated by Kenya's research stations and in the trial-and-error learning by European farmers over many years. Progress in the "high potential" areas suited to those crops was rapid because the knowledge and experience to provide a basis for technically sound plans for accelerated agricultural development already existed (Heyer et al., 1976).

Widespread adoption of hybrid maize in parts of Kenya also demonstrates the readiness of African farmers to innovate when feasible and profitable innovations are available (Gerhardt, 1975). Mazabuka district in Zambia is another area where success has been achieved in introducing high-yield maize varieties among smallholders. To date, however, the success stories are very much the exception; and the lack of an adequate "research base" appears to be the most common cause of limited technological progress (Anthony, 1979, Chapter 5).

African countries face the difficult challenge of simultaneously increasing the effectiveness of their research programs and securing more sustained support for agricultural research. Limited experience with successful agricultural research programs makes it more difficult to mobilize the needed political and financial support for strengthening research both directly and indirectly through graduate training of future agricultural scientists and other specialists. At the same time, however, there is an important opportunity for donors to make a significant contribution in supplementing domestic financial and trained labor resources. Moreover, cost-effective methods for making agricultural research more relevant to the needs of small farmers who are subject to severe cash constraints are also needed.

"Farming Systems Research"   During the past decade, there has been considerable consensus that Farming Systems Research (FSR) represents an appropriate response to the problem of making research relevant to the needs of small farmers operating under the very heterogeneous conditions that characterize rainfed agriculture. Recent papers by Collinson (1982), Byerlee, Harrington, and Winkelman (1982), and CIMMYT economists (International Maize and Wheat Improvement Center, 1984) represent an important advance, for they emphasize "on-farm research with a farming systems perspective" rather than attempts by formal research programs to develop and diffuse complete farming systems. There are especially serious disadvantages in attempting to promote rigidly defined "technical packages" in heterogeneous environments. Indeed, even identifying appropriate components for farmers to fit into their farming systems requires a focus on specific "recommendation domains" that are reasonably homogeneous in terms of their physical environment, major socioeconomic constraints, and the main features of the prevailing farming systems.

Devising better methods to exploit the complementarity between formal experiment station research and farmers' local knowledge and capacity for "adaptive management" represents an especially important challenge in Africa, given the scarcity of agricultural scientists with the training and capacity for the diagnostic analysis required for FSR. As a recent study by Tomich (1984) has shown, farmers are capable of modifying technologies and adapting them to difficult and extremely heterogeneous conditions. Thus, the task of FSR becomes much more feasible.

The opening speech at a "networking workshop" held in Swaziland in October 1983 is of considerable interest in its emphasis on the need to "investigate and diagnose the constraints under which the majority of small farmers operate." The speaker also noted that it is important for social and technical scientists to work together: "Technical solutions to production problems devised by researchers will only be of any value if farmers can put them into practice given the socioeconomic circumstances in which they operate." He further emphasizes that the blame for farmers' failure to follow recommended practices "does not lie with the farmers, but with the recommendations themselves" (Dlamini, 1983).

A well-documented analysis of government interventions in Uganda by Stephen Carr (1982) emphasizes that the extremely limited impact of research on increasing farm productivity over a period of some 60 years is explained by its concentration on individual crops grown under experiment station conditions rather than by alleged stubbornness of farmers in refusing to adopt new practices. Indeed, more carefully designed trials have demonstrated that under actual farming conditions, the practices followed by farmers were superior to the recommended "improved practices."

In general, the potential yield increases that can be obtained from the introduction of high-yield, fertilizer-responsive crop varieties are considerably less under rainfed conditions than those possible with irrigation and greatly increased application of fertilizers. In Africa, however, it is often feasible for small farmers to increase their output by enlarging the area under cultivation as well as by increasing crop yields. Moreover, it is often necessary to improve soil and water management by better tillage methods in order to realize the yield potential of improved varieties. But it is not possible to expand the acreage cultivated per worker or to adopt improved tillage methods when farming depends entirely on the hoe and human labor.

Animal Draft Power and the Evolution of Farming Systems   Price distortions that make tractors artificially cheap and a tendency to view tractors as a symbol of "modernity" have diverted attention away from efforts to promote the adoption of a wider range of animal-powered farm equipment. Historical experience in Asia and recent developments in Africa suggest that for small farmers with limited cash income, wider and more efficient use of animal-powered equipment is a feasible option to increase area under cultivation and crop yields by soil- and moisture-conserving tillage practices and by improving the precision with which planting and other operations are carried out. Tractor-based technologies may appear to be attractive because of their power and speed, but they represent a large investment not feasible for small farmers.

The presence of tsetse is only one of a number of factors that determine whether animal draft power should be introduced in different farming regions in Africa. The recent work of Hans Binswanger and Prabhu Pingali (1984) is a valuable contribution in understanding the conditions under which a shift from handhoes to animal draft power and other aspects of intensification is encouraged. Population growth, increased off-farm demand for agricultural products, and reduced transportation costs are among the important factors that induce such changes. In a companion paper, Pingali and Binswanger (1984) stress that animal traction becomes important only with the intensification from bush fallow to short fallow systems or annual cropping.

The pattern of evolution of technologies in tropical agriculture is also associated with changing soil preferences that lead to a movement away from lighter soils that are easy to cultivate by hand but risky, toward bottom lands. The soils in bottom lands are hard to prepare by hand, but are more responsive to intensification with animal traction, land improvements, and application of manure and fertilizers.

With increasing population density, it becomes more feasible to undertake labor-intensive investments in irrigation, drainage, and stump removal. Trypanosomiasis and other diseases are minimized as intensification leads to a marked reduction in the density of trees and bush. Binswanger and Pingali (1984, p. 28) further note that tractor cultivation requires more complete and costly destumping than animal traction, which is one of the reasons for their conclusion that "it is almost impossible to bypass the animal traction stage and move directly to tractors."

The role of publicly supported research programs in farm equipment innovations is controversial. Historically, most of the research and development that has led to mechanical innovations has been carried out by manufacturers, often small rural-based workshops that have worked closely with farmers in identifying needs and designing implements that met the local requirements as economically as possible.

An important conclusion from the research by Binswanger and

Pingali is that "traditional" farmers "have responded to changes in population densities and external markets with changes in farming systems, land use patterns and technological change along systematic and predictable patterns" (Pingali and Binswanger, 1984, p. 336). Better understanding of those "systematic and predictable patterns" should increase the effectiveness of FSR researchers in facilitating adaptive learning by farmers as they make the transition to science-based farming systems. It is essential, however, for farmers to be involved from the beginning in what is bound to be a fairly time-consuming learning process. A recent study by William Jaeger (1984) documents the fact that it takes several years for farmers to achieve a rate of utilization of animal-powered equipment that ensures a satisfactory return on their investment.

Irrigation   Given the frequency and seriousness of drought in Africa, interest in irrigation as a means of accelerating the growth of agricultural production has increased. Ian Carruthers (1983, p. 12) has rightly warned against being seduced by the "power of a vision of a transformed, controlled, green, fertile desert." With the exception of Madagascar and Sudan, irrigation is currently of such limited importance that expansion of area under irrigation cannot be expected to contribute very much to the growth of agricultural production in the next two or three decades. It is estimated that on from 1 to 5 percent of the cultivated area in sub-Saharan Africa, some form of water control is utilized, ranging from conventional irrigation schemes to traditional "flood recession farming" (using residual moisture) and swamp drainage. (See Eicher and Baker, 1982, pp. 133–39 for an excellent review of the literature on irrigation in Africa.)

A broad consensus has emerged that most large-scale irrigation investments have proven to be expensive, inefficient, and poorly managed and maintained. After the early 1970s, additions to the irrigated area resulting from construction of new facilities were more than offset by others that had to be abandoned or required rehabilitation. Also, because water control is not complete or is poorly managed, not all developed areas are farmed (World Bank, 1981, p. 76). The expected high yields are not being obtained, technical problems continue, planning has been inadequate, health problems are created, and financing of operations and maintenance is woefully inadequate.

Evidence suggests that small-scale, farmer-initiated irrigation efforts are likely to be more beneficial than large-scale public schemes (Carruthers, 1984). These informal schemes have made greater contributions to food production than the larger ones and use rural labor and local materials. In contrast, conventional irrigation schemes are very costly, requiring an investment of some $5000 to $20,000 per irrigated hectare. Skilled management and further financial resources are needed to operate them effectively. The opportunity cost of capital and managerial staff is very high. Thus there is a very real danger that undue emphasis on irrigation will divert scarce resources from the less glamorous but vastly more extensive rainfed sector.

In the long run, irrigation will undoubtedly become more important. There is reason to believe, however, that natural conditions in Africa are less favorable for reliance on irrigation than in Asia. The great rivers of Asia get much of their water and alluvium from headwaters outside the tropics and carry a richer load of nutrient-bearing silt. The permanent snow cover of the Himalayas also represents an enormous resource for recharging underground aquifers, whereas the high rates of evapotranspiration in sub-Saharan Africa reduce significantly available water surpluses. The main economic potential of the Congo and other rivers in the high-rainfall basin is as a source of hydroelectric power. Studies in Kenya, which is probably more typical, suggest that the potential for expanded irrigation is limited (Eicher and Baker, 1982, p. 134).

Clearly, there is a major need for research to guide future irrigation development in Africa, including studies of the economies of rainfed versus irrigated agriculture as a basis for determining development priorities in individual countries. It seems likely that in much of Africa, it will be desirable to utilize water resources selectively, for example, for supplementary irrigation and for high-value crops, including dry season production of fruits and vegetables. Attention should also be given to improving water supplies for domestic use in order to reduce the enormous amount of time spent by women and children in carrying water long distances.

ORGANIZATIONS AND
RURAL DEVELOPMENT

More efficient organizations and managerial procedures are of great importance in achieving better implementation of agricultural and rural development programs. In Africa, there appears to be a particular need for a more pragmatic, pluralistic approach to such issues. Emphasis on the competing "isms"—socialism versus capitalism or "the magic of the marketplace"—tend to polarize the development debate and divert attention from the more mundane but critical choices. In brief, a "shift in focus to technological and institutional details is long overdue. . .the most serious problems lie not in the grand design, but in what has the superficial appearance of details" (A.K. Sen as quoted in Hunter, 1978, p. 37).

The "institutional details" are critical because economic progress requires "a continually widening network of larger, specialized units of collective action" (Brewster, 1967, p. 69). Those "specialized units of collective action" can include private firms and cooperatives and other types of local organizations as well as government agencies. It is useful to view organizations as a framework for calculation and control through which individuals determine what each should do and seek to ensure that each does what is expected.[4] Those social techniques of calculation and control fall into four categories: "hierarchical techniques" on which governments must rely but which are also employed by large private corporations; "exchange techniques" epitomized by price and market mechanisms but which also include patronage systems; "polyarchical techniques" that provide for some degree of accountability, (e.g., through elective local councils and various systems of voting); and the "bargaining techniques" that are so important in small, local organizations such as cooperatives or irrigation associations.

There is now a growing recognition in African countries that the proliferation of parastatals has been a major source of inefficiency and a serious obstacle to agricultural progress. They are also an important symptom of a common problem in developing countries—an imbalance between the responsibilities taken on by the public sector and the resources available for fulfilling them. The imbalance between the responsibilities assigned to African parastatals and their limited administrative capacity has been particularly serious when they have been given operational responsibilities for the production and marketing of food crops.

A blanket condemnation of parastatals is as counterproductive as excessive reliance on such organizations. For example, the Kenya Tea Development Authority has performed a useful role in carrying out functions to facilitate rapid expansion of tea production by smallholders. S. Olayide and Francis S. Idachaba (1983) make the valid point that a parastatal has somewhat greater flexibility than a government ministry (e.g., in being able to pay more attractive salaries). They also suggest, however, that there is a need for a transition from "parastatals that engage directly in farm input supply and food marketing" to "facilitating institutions" which undertake more limited but crucial functions such as providing market information and coordinating price policies.

John K. Galbraith, who is certainly not an ideologue of the price system, has emphasized that market mechanisms "economize on scarce and honest administrative talent," whereas reliance on detailed planning and administratively determined prices jeopardizes the prospects for rapid and efficient growth. "The consequence— reliance on a large centrally planned and administered public sector—is that the greatest possible claim is placed on the scarcest possible resource. That is, administrative talent, with its complementary requirements in expert knowledge, experience, and discipline" (Galbraith, 1979, p. 111).

Discussions on the privatization of functions such as distribution of inputs or marketing of farm products in Africa often stress the weakness and venality of existing private firms. The important point, however, is that it is inherently more difficult for government agencies than for private firms to efficiently carry out essentially commercial operations. A government or quasi-governmental agency such as a grain marketing board must rely on the "discipline" of bureaucratic regulations to limit graft and corruption. Such regulations reduce flexibility and increase costs, although the patronage role of parastatals is also important in inflating their overhead and operating costs. The more general point is that government operations and controls that confer arbitrary and discretionary power inevitably create "rents" because they give certain officials and other favored individuals control over scarce resources. Literature on "the political economy of rent seeking" emphasizes that when government policies and programs create rents, there will invariably be public officials and private firms that engage in rent-seeking activity regardless of whether this involves illegal practices (Kreuger, 1974).

Needless to say, private traders and other entrepreneurs will frequently charge "exorbitant" prices or pay "unfair" prices (e. g., by using scales that underweigh produce delivered by farmers). Playing a regulatory role to minimize fraudulent practices is clearly a valuable one for governments. Competition, however, provides the most important discipline over private firms, spurring them to efficiency and curbing tendencies to cheat farmers or consumers. In isolated rural areas, however, private firms may be relatively immune from competition. Efficient distribution of farm inputs is likely to be especially difficult in the early stages of commercialization when the volume of transactions is low. A parastatal organization for input distribution may therefore play a useful role until the level of demand is sufficient to attract competing private firms and independent cooperatives.

Negative attitudes toward private firms and the price and market system derive in part from "the autocratic legacy of the colonial system" and "the control orientation of the colonial approach to agriculture" (Young, 1984, p. 16; Leonard, 1984, p. 20). Furthermore, it was expected that an activist, independent state would bring the good things of life to the people; the surge in development expenditures at the very end of the colonial period made that hope and expectation seem credible. Post-colonial African states have tended to equate "development and welfare" with direct government involvement in commercial operations as much as in the provision of "public goods" such as education, agricultural research, and health services. This was often reinforced by the very understandable resentment of the extent to which trade was dominated by Asians, Lebanese, or Europeans.

What are the prospects for a more pragmatic approach to the complex and difficult issues of choosing appropriate organizational structures and social techniques of calculation and control? The recent enthusiasm in development literature for "participation" has been a move in the right direction. There has been an unfortunate tendency, however, to take a narrow view of participation, equating it exclusively with "participatory organizations" in which elected officials and members rely on the social techniques of bargaining and voting in carrying out the tasks of calculation and control.

Local organizations such as marketing cooperatives and irrigation associations can perform valuable functions. But it is important to realize that such organizations impose substantial costs on their members in time and energy and they often fail, in part because benefits to be gained are not sufficient to induce the time and effort required for effective participation. Fortunately, fulfilling the two essential functions of participation—providing feedback based on direct, local knowledge and performing a watchdog function against arbitrary abuses of power—does not necessarily depend on the creation of formal membership organizations.

This broader view of participation has been emphasized by Grace Goodell, an anthropologist with extensive experience in developing countries, who focuses on the importance of "routine fields of interaction." Goodell argues that these fields of interaction, which result from frequent contacts between individuals engaged in economic transactions, are "the real locus of initiative and risk-taking, saving and investment, habits of work or laziness, decisions to link with one another for any common endeavor" (Goodell, 1983, p. 9). She emphasizes that it is within such fields of interaction that predictability—so important for rational allocation of resources—becomes possible.

Goodell also notes that predictability and the rational and innovative behavior which it engenders also depend on "the security of bonding" (i.e., the mutual confidence that derives from repetitive contacts and transactions among those who make up a "field of interaction" which becomes a "system"). That system is made up of individuals, firms, rules of behavior, channels, and specific institutions, which are more likely to be informal than formal. The evolution of savings institutions from informal savings clubs in Africa are an interesting example cited by Leonard (1984, p. 24).

These three prerequisites of sustained and vigorous development—rationality, predictability, and bonding—are jeopardized when participants in local fields of interaction are subject to arbitrary action by outsiders. However, as local "systems" emerge and grow more complex, the participants may gradually become sufficiently numerous and well-organized to act as a pressure group against arbitrary actions by government. In African countries, however, the ubiquitous involvement of government in commercial operations has created an environment hostile to such an evolution. Little progress has been made toward creating the positions that make for predictability, rationality, and bonding. To a large extent, economic development has been dependent on government action instead of being generated by the energy and initiative of individual farmers, traders, and a host of other small- and medium-scale entrepreneurs in positions to identify and act upon opportunities for economic and technical innovations.

Much has been learned since the era when the dictum that the government is best which governs least was advanced. We now know that there are many ways in which governments can play a catalytic and facilitating role in fostering economic and social progress. In particular, direct government action is indispensable in making available important "public goods." Because of the nature of public goods such as police protection and education, it is inefficient and inequitable to rely on markets and the response of private firms to demands for such services: They will simply not be made available at socially optimal levels without interventions by publicly supported organizations. In fact, one of the most powerful reasons for reducing government involvement in what are essentially commercial operations is to permit a concentration of its limited administrative capacity on "only those components which are not likely to be undertaken without planned public intervention" (Lele, 1979, p. 191).

Agricultural research systems and extension programs and investments in roads and other rural infrastructure are examples of public goods important to agricultural development. Public support for health, education, and family planning programs are equally important to the broader goal of rural development. Although public health activities have already brought about a drastic reduction in crude death rates, infant and child mortality rates are still excessively high.

It is beyond the scope of this paper to pursue the important issues of health, nutrition, and family planning. Nevertheless, it needs to be emphasized that expanding agricultural output sufficiently to permit improvements in per capita food consumption will become increasingly difficult and eventually insoluble unless progress is made in bringing birth rates into a more manageable balance with the sharply reduced death rates that now prevail. Otherwise, "equilibrium" may be reestablished through a tragic increase in death rates, as growing population pressure on the land and degradation of land resources lead to increasingly frequent and serious food crises.

POLICY IMPLICATIONS

The issues of agricultural and rural development in Africa are enormously complex. In the future as in the past, attempts to find "new" solutions that will be easy and quick will only result in frustration and waste of scarce resources. The compelling need is for determined and sustained efforts to move toward macro-economic policies that are less damaging to Africa's farmers and to accelerate technological progress among small farmers that will predominate in Africa until well into the 21st century. Because of the structural and demographic characteristics of African economies, there is no realistic alternative to an emphasis on small-farm development that will achieve increases in productivity and output based on labor-using, capital-saving technologies. This is not based on some romantic notion that "small is beautiful." Rather, it represents the most economical and realistic means of furthering the multiple objectives of development with which African countries must be concerned.

In the analysis of the problems of agricultural and rural development in the preceding sections, a number of policy recommendations have been implied. The most important of those policy implications are summarized below:

- Strengthening national research systems and increasing the relevance of research to the needs of small farmers is probably the most fundamental requirement in implementing small farm development strategies and in making the needed transition from resource-based to science-based agriculture.

- Farming systems research is certainly no panacea, but it appears to offer promise as a means of taking advantage of the potential complementarities between formal experiment station research and the local knowledge of farmers for adaptive management in modifying their farming systems. On-farm research in collaboration with farmers thus appears to be the most efficient approach to generating sequences of location-specific innovations that will be feasible and profitable given the constraints that small farmers face, including the lack of cash income that limits their reliance on purchased inputs.

- The difficulties of strengthening national agricultural research systems are compounded by the heterogeneity of the rainfed agriculture that predominates in Africa and by severe shortages of trained personnel. Donors have a particularly significant role to play in helping to expand the supply of agricultural scientists, administrators, and other specialists by providing sustained support for long-term institution-building and well-qualified foreign scientists to offset present shortages. The small size of so many African countries complicates these problems because of limited tax bases and special difficulties in overcoming labor shortages. Thus there appears to be a particular need for foreign aid to strengthen national programs and International Agricultural Research Centers with headquarters or regional programs in Africa. A number of countries contain areas with similar agroclimatic conditions which means that external assistance can play a critical role in facilitating

the diffusion among countries of scientific knowledge and technical innovations.

- Because of the overwhelming importance of rainfed agriculture in
  Africa, priority must be given to increasing its productivity rather
  than making costly investments in expanding irrigation. Small-
  scale, locally controlled irrigation or drainage schemes appear to be
  more cost-effective than large-scale conventional projects. Assistance to large-scale projects should concentrate on rehabilitating
  and improving the management of existing schemes. There is also
  a need for research on surface and ground water resources and on
  the economics of rainfed versus irrigated agriculture in individual
  countries.

- Successful implementation of agricultural programs in Africa will
  require a realistic and pragmatic approach to overcoming weakness in administration. Those weaknesses represent what Jon
  Moris (1983) has aptly termed a "systemic problem." In addition to
  their adverse effects on farmer incentives and on resource allocation for agriculture, macro-economic policies have led to acute
  shortages of foreign exchange and revenue crises that have exacerbated the difficulty of achieving efficient administration of agricultural programs. For example, shortages of fuel and spare parts
  often make it impossible for field staff to make field visits. Those
  same shortages also have adverse effects on road maintenance and
  on the availability of farm inputs and the consumer goods that
  influence farmers' decisions to expand production.

- In addition to the need for improvements in macro-economic management, there is a need to achieve a better balance between governmental responsibilities and resources. The common practice of
  creating parastatals to perform essentially commercial operations
  has aggravated this imbalance. Better understanding of the
  strengths and weaknesses of alternative "social techniques of calculation and control" could lead to more realistic and more pragmatic decisions about activities that demand direct government
  action. In the provision of "public goods" such as agricultural
  research, roads, rural infrastructure, education, and social services
  programs related to health and family planning, direct government action is indispensable. There is a need, however, for a
  greater emphasis on administrative decentralization and on the
  role that local organizations can play in the planning and imple-

mentation of agricultural and rural development programs. It is also important to recognize that participation and accountability can often be ensured by price and market mechanisms: Private firms or independent cooperatives are inherently more efficient than government agencies in carrying out essentially commercial activities such as distribution of farm inputs or the marketing of agricultural products.

• Frank and well-informed policy dialogue between policy-makers and donors is probably the most feasible way to promote needed improvements in national strategies for agricultural and rural development and in donor policies and programs. Fruitful policy dialogue, however, requires strengthening indigenous capacities for policy research and analysis, which underscores the importance of the institution-building task emphasized above. It also requires a greater donor effort to recognize the weaknesses of past policies and operating procedures and to achieve a better understanding and a workable consensus concerning the priority needs for external assistance in the future.

ACKNOWLEDGMENT

I am indebted to Elizabeth Foster and Harriet Johnston for research and editorial assistance.

NOTES

1. The introduction to the valuable survey of research on agricultural development in sub-Saharan Africa by Eicher and Baker (1982) contains a useful summary of the major ecological regions and agricultural systems found in the 41 countries included in their survey. See also Johnston (1958) and Ruthenberg (1980).

2. The implications for the choice of an agricultural strategy of this "arithmetic of population growth and structural transformation" are so significant that it is useful to spell out the relationships. The rate of structural transformation (RST) in a country, defined as the absolute increase in the share of nonfarm labor in the total labor force, depends on the existing share of nonfarm labor in the labor force (Ln/Lt), the rate of increase in the nonfarm labor force (Ln'), and the rate of increase in the total labor force (Lt'). Thus:

$$RST = Ln/Lt \, (Ln' - Lt').$$

It is readily apparent from this equation that the rate of structural transformation will tend to increase gradually as Ln/Lt increases (from just over .1 to .35

in the Kenya projections) and also as Ln' increases or Lt' declines. However, a decline in the rate of growth in the total labor force cannot be expected to occur in less than, say, 30 to 50 years because there will be a time lag of 15 to 20 years before a decline in fertility will be reflected in a reduction in Lt'. An even longer time will be required to reach the turning point when the absolute size of the farm labor force begins to decline.

3. In a fine journalistic report on hunger in Africa, David K. Wills reports: "In Mali alone," says a senior (World Bank) official in Washington, "there's potential to feed all of the Sahel. The problem isn't money. That's available. The problem is management. Projects are simply being abandoned" (*Christian Science Monitor*, Nov. 28, 1984, p.23). Management is indeed a problem. But there is reason to doubt whether it is *the* problem—and also whether the "evidence" underlying the assertion that Mali could "feed all of the Sahel" is any better than the evidence that encouraged the French to make huge investments in the Office du Niger irrigation project that was a disappointment for decades before independence.

4. This section draws heavily on William C. Clark's chapter on "Organization Programs: Institutional Structures and Managerial Procedures" in our joint book (Johnston and Clark, 1982, Chapter 5). The view of alternative social techniques of calculation and control derives from Dahl and Lindblom (1953).

REFERENCES

Anthony, K. R. M., B. F. Johnston, W. O. Jones and V. C. Uchendu. 1979. *Agricultural Change in Tropical Africa*. Ithaca: Cornell University Press.

Bates, R. 1981. *Markets and States in Tropical Africa*. Berkeley: University of California Press.

Bates, R. 1983. *Essays on the Political Economy of Rural Africa*. Cambridge: Cambridge University Press.

Binswanger, H. P., and J. McIntire. 1984. "Behavioral and Material Determinants of Production Relations in Land Abundant Tropical Agriculture." Report No. ARU 17. Research Unit, Agricultural and Rural Development Department, Operational Policy Staff. Washington, D.C.: The World Bank.

Binswanger, H.P., and P.L. Pingali. 1984. "The Evolution of Farming Systems and Agricultural Technology in Sub-Saharan Africa." Report No. ARU 23. Research Unit, Agriculture and Rural Development Department, Operational Policy Staff. Washington, D.C.: The World Bank.

Binswanger, H. P., and M. R. Rosenzweig. 1983. "Behavioral and Material Determinants of Production Relations in Agriculture." Report No. ARU 5, Revised October 5, 1983. Research Unit, Agriculture and Rural Development Department Operational Policy Staff. Washington D.C.: The World Bank.

Brewster, J. M. 1950. "The Machine Process in Agriculture and Industry," *Journal of Farm Economics* 32(1) (February): 69–81.

Brewster, J.M. 1967. "The Traditional Social Structures as Barriers to Change," in H. M. Southworth and B. F. Johnston, eds., *Agricultural Development and Economic Growth*. Itahca: Cornell University Press.

Byerlee, Derek, Larry Harrington and Donald L. Winkelmann. 1982. "Farming Systems Research: Issues in Research Strategy and Technology Design," *American Journal of Agricultural Economics* 64(5) (December): 897–904.

Carr, S. 1982. *The Impact of Government Intervention on Smallholder Development in North and East Uganda*. A. D. U. Occasional Paper No. 5. Wye, England: Agrarian Development Unit, Wye College.

Carruthers, Ian. 1983. "Irrigation Investment: A Problem, Palliative or Panacea for Agricultural Development?," Ian Carruthers, ed., *Aid for the Development of Irrigation*. Paris: OECD.

Carruthers, I. and A. Weir. 1976. "Rural Water Supplies and Irrigation Development," in J. Heyer, J. K. Maitha and W. M. Senga, eds., *Agricultural Development in Kenya*. Nairobi: Oxford University Press.

Collinson, M.F. 1982. *Farming Systems Research in Eastern Africa: The Experience of CIMMYT and Some National Agricultural Research Services, 1978–81*. MSU International Development Paper No. 3. East Lansing: Michigan State University, Department of Agricultural Economics.

Dahl, R. A. and C. E. Lindblom. 1953. *Politics, Economics and Welfare*. New York: Harper & Brothers.

Dlamini, Gilbert. 1983. Opening remarks at "Networkshop on Draught Power and Animal Feeding in Eastern and Southern Africa." Networking Workshops Report No. 2. Mbabane, Swaziland: CIMMYT Eastern and Southern Africa Economics Programme.

Eicher, C. K. and D. C. Baker. 1982. *Research on Agricultural Development in Sub-Saharan Africa: A Critical Survey*. MSU International Development Paper No. 1. East Lansing: Michigan State University, Department of Agricultural Economics.

Evenson, R. E. 1978. "The Organization of Research to Improve Crops and Animals in Low Income Countries," in T. W. Schultz, ed., *Distortions in Agricultural Incentives*. Bloomington and London: Indiana University Press.

Galbraith, J. K. 1979. *The Nature of Mass Poverty*. Cambridge, Mass.: Harvard University Press.

Gerhardt, J. 1975. *The Diffusion of Hybrid Maize in Western Kenya-Abridged by CIMMYT*. Mexico City: Centro Internacional de Mejoramiento de Maize y Trigo.

Goodell, G. 1983. "The Importance of Political Participation for Sustained Capitalist Development." Cambridge, Mass.: Harvard Law School.

Gusten, P. 1984. "Agriculture in Sub-Saharan Africa." Washington, D.C.: The World Bank.

Hart, K. 1982. *The Political Economy of West African Agriculture*. Cambridge: Cambridge University Press.

Hayami, Y. and V. W. Ruttan. 1984. *Agricultural Development: An International Perspective*. 1984 manuscript copy; to be published in 1985 by the Johns Hopkins University Press.

Heyer, J., J. K. Maitha and W. M. Senga, eds. 1976. *Agricultural Development in Kenya: An Economic Assessment*. Nairobi: Oxford University Press.

Hunter, Guy. 1978. "Report on Administration and Institutions." Asian Development Bank. *Rural Asia; Challenge and Opportunity*, Supplementary Papers, Vol. IV, *Administration and Institutions in Agricultural and Rural Development*. Manila: Asian Development Bank.

International Maize and Wheat Improvement Center. 1984. "A Report of a Networkshop on Draught Power and Animal Feeding in Eastern and Southern Africa." Report No. 2. Mbabane, Swaziland: CIMMYT Eastern and Southern Africa Economics Programme.

Jaeger, W. 1984. "Agricultural Mechanization: The Economics of Animal Traction in Burkina Faso." Ph.D. dissertation, Stanford Unviersity.

Johnston, B. F. 1958. *The Staple Food Economies of Western Tropical Africa*. Food Research Institute Studies in Tropical Africa. Stanford: Stanford University.

Johnston, B. F. and W. C. Clark. 1982. *Redesigning Rural Development: A Strategic Perspective*. Baltimore: Johns Hopkins University Press.

Johnston, B. F. and P. Kilby. 1975. *Agriculture and Stuctural Transformation: Economic Strategies in Late-Developing Countries*. New York: Oxford University Press.

Johnston, B. F. and T. P. Tomich. 1984. "The Feasibility of Small-Farm Development Strategies." Paper prepared for the AID/PPC. Washington, D.C.: AID.

Jones, W. O. 1972. *Marketing Staple Food Crops in Tropical Africa*. Ithaca and London: Cornell University Press.

Kozlowski, Z. 1975. "Agriculture in the Economic Growth of the East European Socialist Countries," in L. G. Reynolds, ed., *Agriculture in Development Theory*. New Haven and London: Yale University Press.

Krueger, A. O. 1974. "The Political Economy of the Rent-Seeking Society," *American Economic Review* LXIV(3) (June): 291–303.

Kydd, J. G. and R. E. Christiansen. 1982. "Structural Change and Trends in Equity in the Malawian Economy, 1964–80." University of Malawi, Centre for Social Research, Income Distribution Project, Working Paper No. 2.

Lamb, G. and L. Muller. 1982. *Control, Accountability and Incentives in a Successful Development Institution: The Kenya Tea Development Authority*. Staff Working Papers No. 550. Washington, D.C.: The World Bank.

Lele, U. 1979. *The Design of Rural Development: Lessons from Africa*. Baltimore and London: Johns Hopkins University Press.

Leonard, D. K. 1984. "Developing Africa's Agricultural Institutions: Putting the Farmer in Control." Berkeley: University of Calfornia, Department of Political Science.

Mellor, J. W. and B. F. Johnston. 1984. "The World Food Equation: Interrelations Among Development, Employment, and Food Consumption." *Journal of Economic Literature* 22(2) (June): 531–74.

Moris, J. R. 1983. "What Do We Know About African Agricultural Development? The Role of Extension Performance Reanalyzed." Draft No. 1.

Washington, D.C.: Bureau of Science and Technology, Agency for International Development.

Olayide, S. O. and F. S. Idachaba. 1983. "Input Supply and Food Marketing Systems for Agricultural Growth: A Nigerian Case Study." Paper presented at the International Conference on Accelerating Agricultural Growth in Sub-Saharan Africa. International Food Policy Research Institute, Victoria Falls, Zimbabwe. August 29–September 1.

Pingali, F. L. and H. P. Binswanger. 1984. "Population Density and Agricultural Intensification: A Study of the Evolution of Technologies in Tropical Agriculture." Report No. ARU 22. Washington, D.C.: Research Unit, Agriculture and Rural Development Department, Operational Staff, World Bank, October 17.

Ruthenberg, H. 1980. *Farming Systems in the Tropics*. 3rd ed. London: Oxford University Press.

Shah, M. M. and F. Willekens. 1978. *Rural-Urban Population Projections for Kenya and Implications for Development*. Laxenburg, Austria: International Institute for Applied Systems Analysis.

Tomich, Thomas P. 1984. "Private Land Reclamation in Egypt: Studies of Feasibility and Adaptive Behavior." Ph.D. dissertation. Stanford University.

World Bank. 1980. *World Development Report, 1980*. New York: Oxford University Press.

World Bank. 1981. "Accelerated Development in Sub-Saharan Africa." Washington, D.C.: The World Bank.

World Bank. 1984. *World Development Report, 1984*. New York: Oxford University Press.

World Bank. 1984. "Toward Sustained Development: A Joint Program of Action for Sub-Saharan Africa." Washington, D.C.: The World Bank.

Young, C. 1984. "The African Colonial State and Its Developmental Legacy." Madison: University of Wisconsin, Department of Political Science.

CHAPTER SEVEN

Putting the Farmer in Control: Building Agricultural Institutions

David K. Leonard

Looking to the future of African agriculture, debates about the causes of current food shortages lose relevance.[1] Rather, what is important is that African agriculture is at a turning point in terms of the structure of production itself. This structural shift will be caused by two factors. First, the African land frontier soon will be exhausted. In many areas, no significant opportunities remain for adding crop land without irrigation, and in only a few places, such as southern Sudan and parts of Zaire, does it seem that the frontier will extend well into the future. The existence of fallow land should not deceive us into thinking that land is still available. Under current production conditions, Africa's fragile tropical soils require as long as 15 years to recover their fertility after they have been farmed. Already the beginnings of a shift toward increasing output through improvements in productivity rather than land expansion is evident (Berry, 1983, p. 50), and the era of growth through extensive agriculture will have to be replaced by intensification (Eicher and Baker, 1982, pp. 110,116).

The second factor affecting the structure of agricultural production is the high rate of Africa's population growth, which will increase both the demand for food and the numbers working in agriculture. Under the most optimistic assumptions, agriculture will continue to absorb increased absolute numbers of workers for at least another 30 years.[2] This factor will combine with the shortage of new land to create pressures and opportunities for the intensification of production that have been absent in Africa's traditionally labor-scarce agriculture (Hart 1982, p. 133). Demand pressures on food production will also be accentuated. Since very few African states have the capacity to control food prices, a shift in the domestic terms of trade toward food crops can be expected which will support and finance an intensification of production. These trends are also likely to encourage intensification of export crop production, making land more valuable and labor more abundant.

As a result of population growth and land shortage, commercial food production will become increasingly important. Demand will come not only from the growing urban areas but also from the landless and near-landless whose numbers are increasing and who will no longer be able to survive solely by subsistence efforts. Second, agriculture will make much more intensive use of land and labor. In most places, the land frontier will cease to exist and the rural poor will have to work for others in order to make ends meet. Third, profits will increase sufficiently to make science-based agriculture and the use of purchased inputs much more attractive for food crops.

This shift in the structure of production will not overtake all of Africa at once, as there is great diversity in African agriculture (Berry, 1983, pp. 9–11). Nonetheless, with such a widespread and significant structural shift will come a host of new problems and opportunities to which African governments and donors will need to respond. A great many of the insights developed over the years on the behavior of the continent's farmers are beginning to lose relevance.

THE DYSFUNCTIONS OF THE
CONTROL MODEL

To date, most efforts to promote agricultural production in Africa have relied heavily on instruments of control. Some public agency or private firm arrogates monopsony power over a crop and closely supervises its growers (i.e., a monopoly is exercised over purchase). If credit is to be extended for inputs, it is provided in kind and payments are deducted at the monopsony point of sale. This strategy aims at bringing subsistence producers under state control and extracting resources from agriculture for other sectors of the economy (Hart, 1982, pp. 88–90; Heyer, Roberts, and Williams, 1981, p. 10).

This particular method was based on two assumptions, however, which are now invalid. The first is that African smallholders are too unresponsive to market forces to achieve the commodity quality, productivity, or repayment level desired. The second is that only a monopsonistic, integrating organization can assure the simultaneous presence of all of the necessary requirements of commercial production in underdeveloped African economies.

Historically, there may have been some basis for assuming farmer insensitivity to the market, given the availability of land, and the fact that the economic survival of smallholders was not dependent on the market, and the weak price signals given by the commercially underdeveloped colonial economies. In this sense, farmers were autonomous, and administrators who were desperate to establish a rural presence and to finance the state would have felt driven to establish whatever controls they could (Hyden, 1980).

This assumption of price-insensitive producers was probably always overstated, however, and is doubtful today. As commercialization has progressed, evidence of price responsiveness has become striking (Eicher and Baker, 1982, pp. 28–30).[3]

The other assumption undergirding the traditional control approach was a much stronger one. Commercial, science-based agriculture must be supported by an elaborate infrastructure. It is necessary to assure the simultaneous and timely presence of seeds, fertilizer, credit, extension, roads, transport, and markets. Traditional subsistence agriculture did not stimulate adequate supply of any of these services. Therefore, the only way to achieve a breakthrough to commercial production was for all of the services to be provided by a single organization integrated either vertically around a single crop or horizontally for a particular region. Monopoly and monopsony are not intrinsic to this solution—the purpose is to assure that at least one of each service is present, but not only one. In practice, however, monopoly is the result, in part because the assumption of price insensitivity, which encourages control, comes to be mixed in with it. The temptation to use profits from marketing to cross-subsidize the other services makes it unprofitable for private traders to compete against the subsidized services and makes monopsony necessary for the profitable ones. These integrating organizations therefore are generally constructed around marketing monopsonies for a crop or region. These monopoly powers then make it possible for socially uneconomic agencies to survive.

The integrating organization has a powerful logic and has produced many famous successes, such as Ethiopia's CADU, Malawi's

Lilongwe, and the Kenya Tea Development Authority (Lele, 1975). For a variety of reasons, however, it is now counterproductive for agricultural development in most of Africa. First, this method of promoting agriculture tends to create a fragmented and segregated series of support organizations. The integrating organization provides services for only one crop or region and leaves others totally unserved. Ultimately, these integrating organizations inhibit the development of a well-articulated national economic infrastructure, one in which all the parts can relate to one another and have the fluidity to move into whatever promising openings emerge.

Second, the specialized integrating organization approach is prejudicial to the support of food production. It is extremely difficult to enforce monopsony for commodities that are primarily consumed in mass domestic markets. Thus integrating organizations avoid them or support them only when the farmer also has an export crop (the anchor or security crop concept), which is prejudicial to the poorer farmers who grow only food. Both approaches severely inhibit the emergence of good support services for locally consumed crops because they skim off much of the most profitable business with their specialized focus.

Third, monopolies and monopsonies are dangerous if administrative performance is problematic. When an organization that is the sole provider of an essential service delivers inadequately or late, the entire crop will be threatened, even if all the other services are present. Management standards are not high in most of Africa today. Where recurrent finances are in jeopardy, tendering procedures are tangled, personnel administration is hampered by patronage, staff are underpaid and demoralized, or management by crisis is the rule, single channels for supply of services are a recipe for failure. Where several of them must interact for agriculture to progress, the probability of success is very low (Leonard, 1984). Overlapping, competing organizations—public, private, cooperative, or some mixture—provide the reliability of support which is required in an agricultural infrastructure and are thus the ideal (Landau, 1969).

IMPLICATIONS FOR GOVERNMENTAL ACTIVITY

Most African farmers now need a structure of businesses and other organizations which serves the national economy as a whole, rather than in regional or product-specific fragments. African producers, as consumers, are able to choose and coordinate the support services they require by purchasing them in an open market rather than having the decisions imposed by bureaucrats who are all too often distant and ill-informed (Bottrall and Howell, 1980, p. 150). Achieving this new economic infrastructure will require a concentration on institutional development, involving dismantling current monopolistic controls, facilitating the growth of smaller entrepreneurs, promoting improvements in retrenched public agencies, and financing the construction and maintenance of the necessary physical infrastructure. Such changes will have to be phased in gradually and will require only a modest increase in governmental and donor resources.

Much of the required changes are in the area of public policy and a large part of external assistance will be of the non-project variety. By no means will all activity be of this character, however. A simple dose of privatization and getting prices right will not solve the continent's agricultural problems. The problem in the agricultural sector is more the anti-market and control orientation of the state than its presence. The objective is to move it from a control to a service role which promotes a highly competitive private and cooperative sector.

Since the present policies and structures are deeply rooted in the political sociology of contemporary Africa, such institutional changes will be difficult to achieve and will require considerable amounts of project assistance focused on institutional development. Conditions attached to economic support funds may be useful in bargaining over major policy decisions, but they are too blunt an instrument for the finer, day-to-day operations of government agencies, where much of the reform is needed. Institutional change is never easy and only a small part of the process is the initial decision by government leaders that it would be desirable. A great deal of what appears to have been won at the policy level is lost during implementation.

Institutional development requires a good deal of patient waiting and a long time-horizon. More narrowly focused projects may produce quicker results that can be credited to visible, specific donors, but institution-building is the only way to create a set of structures that will sustain dynamic, national agricultural development. It is institutional structures that distinguish Africa's agriculturally successful nations, not the volume of their project activity.

Donors will not have to wait long to begin institutional reform and development. The first openings already exist. The world recession, the African drought, and the recent changes in the development community's analysis of the continent's problems have combined to produce quite dramatic changes in the receptivity of African governments to institutional reform. Nonetheless, these first openings are only the start of a long, difficult process that will take many years and much patient searching for strategic opportunities.

THE MARKETING OF SUPPLIES AND PRODUCE

Science-based agriculture depends upon on a strong set of market institutions. Fertilizer, improved seed, and other inputs have to be bought and produce has to be sold to pay for these purchases. The establishment of these markets is often very difficult in the early stages of commercialization, for the volume of transactions is so small that profits are low for the trader and prices are unattractive to the farmer. Traders are discouraged from developing these markets and farmers from selling. Thus volume remains low and the trade that exists is frequently monopolistic, making prices still worse. Integrating government corporations have often been created to speed the breaking of this vicious circle. The problem is that these organizations tend to become monopolies and eventually exploit producers with poor prices or bad service, as they have little incentive to perform efficiently.

There are other solutions to the vicious circle problem. The development of roads and the improvement of transportation greatly reduce trading costs, boosting prices and competition. Access to credit and other forms of assistance may also help to bring in new entrepreneurs and lower their operating costs. Governments also may encourage the development of larger wholesale commodity markets in some towns (Jones, 1980, pp. 337–39). Trader exploitation of farmers is best prevented by competition, government broadcasting of price information, and regulation of weights and measures. The available evidence indicates that rural traders, being small and competitive, operate on low margins (Lele, 1981, p. 59). Providing roads and assistance to transporters and traders has the additional advantage of being popular with groups that are politically powerful in most African countries.

Despite the general attractiveness of the small trader option, it has not been judged viable in the past. Government marketing operations are acceptable and cooperative ones can be encouraged as long as they do not result in monopoly. African farmers' most effective power is the ability to withdraw their business. When monopoly deprives them of this exit option, they are quickly exploited. African marketing cooperatives performed quite well in the 1950s when they were struggling for their existence, but have done badly since they began to enjoy official protection, as they have been made instruments of government programs and are not permitted to fail. If the weak cooperatives were allowed to go under, incentives for good management would improve dramatically. The major issue is not a public versus private structure for markets but rather a monopolistic versus a competitive one (Peterson, 1982a).

The opening of new markets is not the only reason for government marketing corporations. They have also been used to tax exports and to even out extreme fluctuations in commodity prices. Revenues must be raised from the rural sector in these predominantly agricultural economies, and export producers tend to be the more affluent farmers. Thus the tax function of public corporations is legitimate, although many African states have so overdone it as to harm the very export crop production on which they depend (World Bank, 1981, Chapter 5).

The dampening of price fluctuations is also a legitimate public function, although it is more often proclaimed as a justification than actually practiced. During the commodity boom of the 1950s, this argument was used to withhold full payments from West African producers, but the funds were diverted and the argument was then forgotten when prices turned down. The restriction of price extremes for food grains requires considerable storage facilities, as stocks must be bought in the good years and sold off in the bad. Very few African countries have the storage capacity to even attempt the exercise. Given the likelihood of recurring drought, the expansion of such facilities is worthy of consideration for those countries that do sometimes produce surpluses.

While there is a case for state intervention in produce marketing, it is not an economic one. Taxes have to be raised and welfare needs are often quite pressing. Whether these justifications are sufficiently persuasive to outweigh their economic costs will depend on the particular circumstances of each country.

Nonetheless, none of the arguments for state participation requires intervention in local markets. The state need only be a buyer of last resort to ease price fluctuations or to provide food security. The taxation of export crops can be done at the point of shipment. Ivory

Coast has the most efficient cocoa marketing structure in West Africa because its government marketing corporation never handles physical delivery of the crop, confining its role to regulating and taxing private trade (Gbetibouo and Delgado, 1984, p. 120). In this way the burden that the government places on agriculture is explicit, intentional, and directly benefits the Treasury, rather than acting as a hidden weight on agriculture through inefficient operations that benefit only the patrons that use them to provide jobs.[4]

The logic of the argument for less direct state involvement in the marketing of inputs and outputs is persuasive, but it will not be easy to achieve where a presence has already been established. Once these government corporations exist, they are hard to dismantle, for the political cost of dismissing employees is high. It is easier to reduce their monopoly powers, although even there resistance is fierce.

For most of Africa, food marketing is the main area where it will be possible to limit the role of the state, because its control has always been marginal, and the main task will be to resist its encroachment on these commodities. Since this is the area where the largest proportionate increase in commercial transactions will occur as the continent's agriculture undergoes its structural shift, this segment of the market is no small matter. Food crops are also the easiest for which to stimulate purely indigenous trading activity and are an important focus of market activity for women, especially in West Africa. It should not be difficult to build strong, private, locally controlled marketing systems for food, as long as governments provide infrastructure and some encouragement.

CREDIT AND SAVINGS

Across the continent, the provision of subsidized credit has been one of the most popular methods of inducing agricultural innovation. Its use has been based on the assumption that capital is scarce in the rural areas and that cheap credit can be used to reduce the costs and risks of new investment. Generally, most of the credit has been provided in kind in the form of inputs, and collections have been made when the farmers sell their produce to monopsonistic marketing organizations. The need to provide security for such formal credit has been one of the primary rationales for the registration of land ownership as well. Such credit schemes have been attractive to African governments because they provide a visible and popular way to "do something" for farmers, and donors have supported them because they provide a vehicle through which large amounts of capital can be moved quickly. Nonetheless, virtually every aspect of this traditional approach to rural credit is flawed.

First, it is unclear that capital really is scarce in rural Africa (Hill, 1970; Donald, 1976, p. 164). Although money often is unavailable for needed agricultural investments, rural dwellers can find capital to pay for school fees and for investments in transport and commerce. Instead, the problems are that investments in agriculture have not been sufficiently profitable and rural savings have been poorly mobilized.

Frequently, subsidized credit has been used to induce changes in small farming that are only weakly profitable or even sometimes detrimental (Heyer, Roberts, and Williams, 1981, p. 7; Donald, 1976, p. 36). Credit then is a substitute for improvements in the profitability of a particular crop by raising its sale price or lowering the cost of its inputs. The available evidence suggests that input subsidies provide much stronger incentives to adopt a new technology than do low interest rates (Adams and Graham, 1981, p. 354). They are also more efficient, as they affect a larger portion of the farm population, whereas subsidized credit is likely to be restricted to the most influential.

Furthermore, it is likely that there are substantial untapped sources of savings in the rural areas (Lele, 1975, p. 97) and that access to them is actually being damaged by subsidized credit programs. Not only does such credit divert attention from the task of building rural savings institutions, but it also decreases the incentive to save and so depresses savings. Thus the leading experts on rural financial markets recommend that savings mobilization should come before emphasis on credit in the early stages of rural development (Adams and Graham, 1981, pp. 351, 356).

Second, it has been presumed that the high interest rates charged by traditional money-lenders are usurious and that low-interest government loans will stimulate development. The available evidence indicates that money-lenders' charges are high because of the costs and risks associated with making loans to small borrowers, not because of exploitative profits. Small farmers are frequently prepared to pay this price for the ease of traditional borrowing, for they often choose it over low-interest government-sponsored credit laden with formal procedures. Indeed, artificially low government interest rates are dysfunctional, depressing the incentive for savings and resulting in most of the loans going to the influential. Thus subsidized interest rates neither stimulate rural development nor help the poor. The general consensus today is that credit should carry market interest rates and that subsidies should go instead into the administrative costs of making savings and credit available to the smallholder (Peterson, 1982a, pp. 90–95).

Third, the form in which agricultural credit has been provided traditionally has been dysfunctional. Arising out of the control orientation of the colonially inspired approach to agriculture, farmers are not trusted to make their own investment decisions and are provided with credit in kind. One disadvantage is that this inhibits the use of loan funds for labor costs and so discourages the very intensification of agriculture that is desired. Another disadvantage is that using the capital for non-agricultural purposes is made difficult. Very often a farmer's most pressing need for capital is not for his crops, but for food, school fees, or attractive commercial opportunities (Chambers, 1983, pp. 117–319). The farmer will go to great lengths to convert the in-kind loan into cash (at a discount to its value) in order to meet other pressing needs. As a consequence, the loan will not benefit the farmer as much as it should, it will not lead to increased production, and it probably will not be repaid (for no new income is produced and the farmer will recognize that he or she will not get another loan without evidence of higher yields).

Several of the leading figures in the field now urge that the use of credit for consumption purposes should be accepted as legitimate and that loans should be untied (Adams and Graham, 1981, p. 355; Lipton, 1980, p. 243). Such a policy actually leads to a significant improvement in loan repayment rates, as farmers are extremely anxious to protect their access to general, untied credit sources (Lele, 1975, p. 94; Leonard, 1984a, p. 183). Thus general rural savings and credit institutions, not ones that are tied narrowly to agriculture, should be promoted. Such a strategy would support broad economic development in the rural areas and would probably support agriculture better than the specifically agricultural credit institutions, as farmers would increasingly use loans for agricultural purposes once they have met their other pressing credit needs. Improved functioning of rural financial markets would also result from the higher use and repayment rates.

The fourth disadvantageous aspect of existing agricultural credit policy is methods of assuring repayment. The most common has been to loan only to farmers who grow cash crops that will have to be sold through a monopsonistic outlet and to collect at the point of sale. There are several problems with this "security crop" method: It imposes a known disability on farmers as a condition for a benefit that is not enjoyed by all; it denies credit to those who produce only food; it makes women's access to credit more difficult, as men generally control export crop revenues while women control the production of food crops; and finally, it doesn't work. Once a credit system begins to break down, farmers have proved remarkably adept at getting around their obligations, even with monopsonies. They change their names, sell to other producers for resale, bribe receiving agents, etc. (Leonard, 1984, p. 183).

The other traditional method of assuring repayment is to require that individually owned and registered land be used as collateral, but this has disadvantages as well. The costs of registering land are much higher than the likely benefits of the credit system that will use it. Creditors, particularly governmental ones, also find it difficult and costly to foreclose on land-secured loans. Further, reliance on land as collateral denies women access to credit. Finally, the system encourages central governments to take control of land use and tenure away from local communities.

The most reliable and viable methods for assuring high loan repayment rates are the borrower's knowledge that he or she will need to use the credit system again, and the sanctions of the borrower's neighbors. The first is most readily assured through a general rural credit system. Virtually all rural dwellers have recurrent needs for consumption credit and will go to considerable lengths to protect their access to it. If formal credit institutions were less rigid about tying their loans and if all creditors (traders, money-lenders, banks, and government agencies) communicated with one another about defaults, farmers would have a powerful incentive to repay their debts and to maintain their credit ratings.

The creation of local sanctions for repayment could be highly complementary with the stimulation of rural savings. Informal savings clubs are extremely widespread in Africa, especially among women (Miracle, Miracle and Cohen, 1980, p. 701). With care, these clubs could be developed into small credit unions and could provide the base for small, cost-effective credit operations through links with more formal banking institutions.

Thus the development of effective rural financial markets need not involve the creation of a new set of credit institutions. What is needed instead is assistance with the extension of the functions of an indigenous social institution and its linkage with commercial banks. This would involve subsidies for administrative costs, but not for interest rates. Although it is important that these clubs initially focus on savings, they can evolve into associations in which rural dwellers are lending their own money to one another, thereby having a considerable stake in assuring repayments (Bottral and Howell, 1980, p. 159). The eventual goal would be a well-articulated, integrated banking system, linking rural and urban sectors. Farmers would continue to save but they would also be able to draw on the larger capital resources of urban residents and entrepreneurs (Donald, 1976, p. 95).

This type of credit system is quite different from the usually unsuccessful marketing cooperative credit schemes. The latter associations are not face-to-face institutions, so that people do not know one another well and cannot apply effective social sanctions. Marketing coops also handle the funds they on-lend in such a way that members rarely feel that losses are coming out of their own pockets (even when they are). As a result, there has been room for considerable exploitation in cooperative credit schemes. All of these unfortunate attributes probably could be avoided in the credit union clubs, with the expectation of quite different results. For example, the savings clubs tend to evolve on lines that are rather homogeneous socio-economically (Muzaale and Leonard, 1985). As long as steps are taken to encourage the availability of clubs to even the poorer members of rural society, the homogeneity of the clubs could help to assure that the more influential do not dominate them and use them to exploit the less advantaged, as they have in the marketing cooperatives (Peterson, 1982b). The experience of the Cameroon Cooperative Credit Union League, the Zimbabwe Rural Savings Clubs, and group credit in Malawi are encouraging examples of what can be achieved (Von Pischke and Rouse, 1983, pp. 27–33).

Although not everyone will be able to save or have access to credit through such a system, in practice only a minority have access to loans now. For those who are left out of the rural financial markets, off-farm employment opportunities are needed. The creation of rural financial markets is important precisely to foster such employment generation. State-sanctioned credit is generally directed too narrowly to meet farmers' strong demands for diversifying their investments and strengthening the rural off-farm economy. All of these steps will take much less capital than has been customary in past donor activity and much more patience and investment of time and local energy in building self-reliance. These institution-building investments have a major, albeit indirect, economic rate of return.

RESEARCH AND EXTENSION

Research and extension are essential to science-based agriculture and are necessary areas for state activity; however, research has not received the priority it deserves in Africa. Investments in this area return benefits only over the long term and are therefore easily neglected by governments that are overwhelmed by pressing needs.

Improvements in the quality and quantity of research are needed and here the farming systems approach has a particularly important contribution to make. Many technical innovations have been stillborn because they were inappropriate to the actual conditions of typical small farmers. Farming systems research can make plant breeders, entymologists, engineers, and others aware of the real constraints that smallholders in various ecosystems are facing and so direct their attention to innovations that will relieve them. The task of "on-farm research with a farming systems perspective" is to assist in the feedback and technical development process by making agricultural scientists aware of what farmers' problems really are (Johnston, 1984). Once research breakthroughs have expanded the range of feasible and profitable options, it can be left to smallholders themselves to decide how best to use them.

Extension has a significant role to play in the development and dissemination of appropriate innovations. Researchers cannot possibly be aware of all the intricacies of farm-level problems and must rely on feedback from the extension agents. Unfortunately, Africa's extension systems are deficient and in need of improvement.

Africa's extension services have been built on quite a different model from the American one, which has well-trained professionals serving a sophisticated and condensed farm population. Instead, African systems have a large number of moderately trained paraprofessionals at its base, serving a mass of smallholders. A system based on paraprofessionals is quite difficult to run, for they need to be organized, motivated, and kept informed to a degree that professionals do not (Leonard, 1977; Leonard and Marshall, 1982, p. 9).

The World Bank's Training and Visit (T&V) system represents the best available solution to these management demands, taking a highly disciplined approach to extension management. A set of formal groups is created, among which the extension agent circulates in a regular, predictable, and readily supervised manner. It is also quite systematic in arranging for the monthly training of extension staff by professional specialists and creating opportunities for problems to be discussed, providing feedback to the research system (Benor and Harrison, 1977; Benor and Baxter, 1984). T&V is not without problems but it has achieved successes in an area in which failure is more common.

At the paraprofessional level, improvements in the quality of training are in order. There are several reasons for wanting to hold back on the numbers of staff at the base of the extension pyramid at this stage. First, expenditures on extension can only be justified when there are profitable innovations to diffuse. A higher quality extension service is justified for it will improve feedback and adaptation, however, and thus improve the quality and appropriateness of research. Second, most of the continent's extension systems have suffered from the under-supervision of junior staff, so it is appropriate to hold back on lower-level numbers in order to restore balance. Third, the usual argument for increases in extension is based on the ratio of farmers to agents, which assumes that farmers must be under the continual supervision of government staff who "know better" if production standards are to be maintained. This degrading image of the farmer is inappropriate. Instead, extension should be conceived of as dealing with a chain of farmer groups which are taught innovations in succession, thus obviating the need for agents to be available to all farmers at all times. Governments are often receptive to donor offers to expand extension services even when they are unpersuaded of their economic value, for they see them as a way to relieve the pressure of unemployed school leavers. When good agricultural research is not available, this is not a cost-effective way of dealing with this pressure, especially when Africa's public payrolls are already overburdened (World Bank, 1981, p. 42).

Government and donor support for agricultural research and extension is therefore needed. The priorities should be expanded research, improvements in the appropriateness of innovations through farming systems work, tightened management of extension services by the application of Training and Visit system reforms, and enhanced quality for agricultural education.

LAND

Traditional land tenure systems in Africa were corporate. Land was held collectively in family, kinship, clan and tribal units, and allocated to individual households for their personal use who lost rights to it if they ceased to occupy it. The collectivity periodically distributed land to new claimants. The view is widely held that this type of tenure pattern inhibits economic development. It is believed that it is inflexible in the face of change as it does not permit sale, and that smallholders are reluctant to adopt innovations that would enhance the value of their land, for fear of losing the benefits in redistribution. Thus it is often argued that centrally imposed individualization and registration of land ownership is necessary for agricultural development (Cohen, 1980, pp. 353–55).

It is now clear that these conceptions greatly underestimate the adaptability of collective land tenure systems. Wherever there has been land pressure, individualization has tended to emerge and with it the de facto selling and renting of land rights (Cohen, 1980, pp. 365–61). Thus these "traditional" systems have not in fact inhibited agricultural development. At the same time, the persistence of collective tenure has permitted communities to regulate their own membership, to react to challenges to their common interests, and to assure some minimal degree of welfare for their poor.

Thus there are few costs and many benefits to land tenure systems under the control of local communities. Communities can guide themselves through the evolution of land law with greater flexibility and sensitivity to local conditions than national authorities can. Communities are willing and able to exercise these responsibilities and would be strengthened in doing so if national governments gave legal authority and other support. The greatest threats to land rights occur when individuals within the community use outside institutions to enforce traditionally unacceptable claims or when outsiders begin to encroach on the community's lands. The latter is a particular problem for pastoralists. Often their ability to dry-season graze on land that is marginal for crops is essential to their use of large amounts of other land with no crop potential. These are instances in which central government support is often needed to protect a community's ability to effectively control and adjudicate over its own land.

The argument made for land ownership systems here is an extension of the case made for seeing African farmers as responsible and ready to take charge of their own economic and social fate, this time through communities' legal control of their own tenure systems. This right is fundamental to a community's ability to define and control its own identity.

IRRIGATION

To date, the experience with irrigation schemes in Africa, particularly large-scale ones, has not been happy. Their effect on income distribution has often been negative (Barnett, 1981, p. 323). They also rarely pay for themselves or have economic rates of return competitive with other investments in agriculture (Stryker, et al., 1981, p. 1). Thus major irrigation schemes are not a near-term priority.

Nonetheless, with African agriculture at a turning point irrigation will soon begin to be more attractive. The land frontier is nearing exhaustion; rural population pressure makes intensification inevitable; and the marketing of food is growing and already accounts for a significant portion of production and consumption.

Most of the major irrigation projects that have been attempted in Africa so far have been built on rigid control models, with the state managing every detail of production. Experience with irrigation on the left bank of the Senegal River is instructive. Two successive attempts at centrally controlled systems, based on Asian models, were dismal failures. Yet when local communities were involved in the construction and management of the operation, productivity was greater and the costs of construction were substantially lower, making the project an economic success (Diallo, 1984). The possibilities for local involvement are greatest on small projects; on large systems local control is feasible only at the turnout level.

The geography of the area in which a system is being constructed largely determines its type, but there is still considerable scope for small-scale irrigation projects in Africa (Stryker, et al., 1981, pp. 30, ii). These units will have economic rates of return in the near-term, whereas large systems will generally become attractive only at the turn of the century. Small-scale irrigation has the added advantage of being amenable to labor-intensive construction methods, which pump money into the rural economy where it can be used to finance agricultural innovations.

OFF-FARM RURAL EMPLOYMENT

The generation of increased off-farm employment is vital to the promotion of rural development. It will be especially important to create jobs for marginal groups. The commercialization of agriculture and the disappearance of the land frontier will lead to a growth in rural inequality. Those with access to land, capital, family labor, and entrepreneurial skill are better placed to take advantage of the new opportunities. Already a significant portion of rural dwellers are dependent on employment by other farmers in order to purchase at least some of their food. The rural poor also are short of capital and find it difficult to borrow, making it hard for them to purchase the inputs that would enable them to make the most out of the land.

Thus for the poor it is especially important that agricultural development be accompanied by increases in rural employment opportunities, for their existence will otherwise be even more marginal than it is now. It is also particularly valuable if these jobs are off-farm and concentrated in the seasons in which agricultural work is slack. Not only does such work have direct welfare benefits, but it also contributes to the productivity of the farms of those who are land-poor or have difficulty raising capital. It gives them a source of funds for investment in crop inputs and provides them with the financial breathing space to work their own farms fully.

RURAL ROADS

Attention to the construction and maintenance of rural roads is one of the more important ways in which the state can stimulate agriculture. It also can assist with rural commerce and off-season employment. Of course, road construction by itself will not produce development; it must be accompanied by an economic infrastructure that can deliver inputs and market surpluses (Devres, 1980, pp. 47,54,20,55).

Labor-intensive methods of road construction obviously have the greatest effect on employment and also have a larger impact on community welfare, as the skills demanded are less sophisticated and are more likely to be available locally. USAID's labor-intensive rural roads project in Kenya has been extremely creative in building small, dirt roads with a minimum of heavy equipment.

Road maintenance is at least as important as construction, as dirt roads deteriorate quickly. Both Kenya and Tanzania have had experience with donor-constructed roads that have had to be completely rebuilt because of lack of maintenance. This task can be performed easily by local residents working under the supervision of a government field engineer.

The biggest problems with road maintenance are financial, not technical. Rural roads have a low political priority for national governments once they have been built. Frequently, donors and governments have expected feeder roads to be maintained by local self-help activity. This has been unsuccessful and was unrealistic in the first place. Poor communities are often willing to contribute funds and labor for the construction of new projects, but they find it almost impossible to raise resources for the recurrent costs of public goods on a volunteer basis (Ralston, et al., 1983, pp. 42-43). These have to be paid out of some form of taxation instead. This could well be a purely local tax, for communities are aware of the benefits of infrastructure such as roads, but the authority for its assessment and enforcement must be available.

LIVESTOCK PRODUCTION

Africa's livestock industry is probably best dealt with in two parts—that which is a part of small, mixed farming operations and that which is pastoral. While many donors and African governments expect nomadic stock-keeping to be swept away with the future tides of development, such an attitude is misguided. Pastoralism makes productive use of an environment that is unsuited for any other form of agriculture given current technology (Horowiz, 1979, p. 32). When crop producers do displace pastoralists, their activities generally are marginal, making them especially vulnerable to variations in rainfall. Furthermore, nomadic stock-keeping persists to this day in the western United States and the eastern U.S.S.R. and should not be seen as "unmodern" (Sanford, 1983, p. 31). The issue then is what can be done to improve its productivity.

The record of recent attempts to improve nomadic livestock production is extremely poor. African pastoralists know more than anyone else about their particular type of herding, and efforts to import scientific approaches from the semi-arid areas of the United States and Australia have been a failure. The reasons are simple. Ranchers in the latter areas are concerned solely with beef production and with maximum returns on investments. African pastoralists are operating a dairy system which is designed to support the largest possible human population on the land, and beef production is only a side-product.

Nonetheless, African pastoralism does have problems and assistance in resolving them could improve its productivity. First, the pressure of human and cattle populations on the range has increased dramatically since the turn of the century and ecological damage from overgrazing is sometimes a problem. More serious is the problem of overgrazing in the sense of higher than economically optimal stocking levels. When many herders share a common range, they have an incentive as individuals to stock beyond the ideal carrying capacity of the range (Jarvis, 1984).

Much of this overgrazing has been created or exacerbated by past government efforts to assist pastoralists by construction of new watering points. Traditionally, although African pastoralists have considered the range a common resource, they have treated watering points as the property of well-defined social groups. Access to water effectively determines whose livestock can use a particular segment of the range. Once public watering points were introduced, this traditional mechanism of control broke down. Opening new range by the drilling of boreholes is desirable, but it should be done as a loan to specific social groups, so that traditional methods of ownership and grazing control are reinforced rather than undermined (Horowitz, 1979, p. 40).

A second problem concerns the frequent weakness of the markets serving pastoralists. Almost all of Africa's nomadic herders are involved to some degree in the long-distance movement and sale of stock. The primary function of their herds is to provide for family subsistence needs, however. For East Africa, it has been estimated that an average family needs 30 to 35 adult cattle for this purpose (Horowitz, 1979, pp. 57–58). It is only as these requirements are exceeded that substantial trade in beef becomes a real possibility. The recognition of these needs will foster a more realistic perspective on the limits to commercial beef production in the semi-arid and arid areas. The problem with markets is most serious in times of drought when the prices offered for livestock are so low as to discourage even distress sales. This exacerbates the grazing pressure on the range and raises the family's general calculation of the stock numbers needed in normal times to assure its survival in the harsh ones. State-subsidized market outlets for drought periods may well be appropriate both from a welfare point of view and to support the commercialization of pastoralism.

The third problem for pastoralists is disease control. They are keenly aware of this problem and frequently administer modern veterinary medicines themselves. Given the economics of most contemporary pastoral production, however, sophisticated veterinary services are only justified for disease prevention at present, not for curative treatment. Prevention and the control of outbreaks cannot be made profitable for private practitioners. Thus the veterinary medicine made available to pastoralists must be provided by the state, even if its costs are recovered through taxes on cattle production. Since disease outbreaks often have international implications in Africa, support for government veterinary services is a particularly appropriate area for donor activity.

Livestock production on small, mixed farms has very different requirements from those of pastoralism. Small stock (sheep, goats, pigs, and poultry) are found on small holdings throughout Africa. Most farms in eastern and southern Africa keep at least one cow as well, primarily as a source of milk. Experience in central Kenya indicates that smallholder dairy production can be quite sophisticated. A science-based livestock industry is feasible and economically attractive in many parts of Africa. The requirements for its support are: research, particularly on improved breeds of small ruminants and on disease control; veterinary services; extension on improved feeding and management practices; and improved milk markets. The time is particularly ripe for the development of private curative veterinary practices (Leonard, 1984b).

DECENTRALIZATION

The agricultural development strategy presented above is a decentralized one—but of a complex variety. Central governments on the continent have over-extended themselves. Instead of trying to do and control everything themselves, they need to decentralize many functions to other entities and concentrate on supporting them to perform well. Only rarely does this involve the classic pattern of devolving authority to elected units of local government. There are many differrent forms of decentralization and agricultural development in Africa requires that almost all of them be used (Leonard and Marshall, 1982, Chap. 1).

For marketing functions, the needed form of decentralization is to make a multiplicity of smaller businesses the primary carrier of services, giving farmers control in their customer role. A similar movement to the private sector is appropriate for agricultural services, such as curative veterinary care and plowing.

Credit involves another form of privatization—the organization of small, face-to-face groups of friends and neighbors to save together, to lend to one another, and to serve as guarantors on each other's loans. This network of alternative local organizations would be linked to the banking system for its larger savings and credit needs. The role of stimulating and supporting the local groups would fall either to government or to international voluntary organizations. Both have demonstrated expertise in handling this linkage function in different parts of Africa and it would depend on the country as to which would do the job better.

The effective operation of an agricultural extension system requires deconcentration of authority to the central government professionals working in the field. Only they are close enough to the farmer to be able to make the adaptations to technical advice that Africa's large ecological diversity requires and only they can provide the feedback to the research system that will make it responsive to these local conditions.

Land use, tenure, and water rights are the areas for which devolution of authority to local governments is most needed. The appropriate place for such jurisdiction is with the entities that traditionally controlled land use, which generally are smaller than the district (anglophone) or department (francophone). Often the authority of these local governments has eroded and would have to be rebuilt by central government support. For irrigation systems, such local government entities would have to be created de novo, since the function usually is not a traditional one and would have to be structured specifically around the system itself.

Rural road construction and maintenance were often handled by district and department governments in the colonial period. Frequently the function was then centralized because local governments were diverting resources from roads to health and education. If special taxes were authorized for roads, local governments would perform this function well.

THE POLITICS OF ALTERING
AGRICULTURAL STRATEGY

African governments should accept the consequences of the inevitable commercialization and intensification of agriculture, should abandon their traditional control-oriented strategy of development,

and should concentrate on fostering private firms that would compete with one another and with state institutions whose services to
small farmers would be coordinated through the operations of the
market. But is it politically feasible for African governments to relinquish their direct involvement in and control over much of the agricultural economy? To answer this question, the character of the African state and the alternative ways in which its needs can be met must
be considered.

The state is a particularly fragile institution in most African countries, threatened with military coups and ethnic secessions. African
elites also are linked to particularly large networks of social obligation. The egalitarianism of pre-colonial African society and the relatively meritocratic character of upward mobility in the late colonial
and independence periods have produced African leaders and managers with large numbers of poor relatives and strong ties to disadvantaged communities. The values of the social exchange systems
that villagers employed to insure themselves against risk are still
strong (Hyden, 1983). Consequently, Africans have major patronage
obligations to poorer peoples and feel strong moral pressures to fulfill
them. For these reasons and for selfish ones that are far more universal, state organizations in Africa are used extensively to pursue the
informal, personal goals of their managers rather than the collective
ones that are formally proclaimed.

The relationship of African states to their rural economies is both
close and exploitative. The continent's governments spend large
amounts of money on programs of direct support to agricultural producers, but all too often they simultaneously do damage that far
outweighs the good by imposing inefficient marketing organizations
and extractive prices on the farm economy. At first this seems surprising, particularly given that the credit and subsidized input programs
into which the money is poured are ineffective and the negative
consequences of poor marketing are dramatic.

Robert Bates has demonstrated the political rationality that under-
lies the frequent economic irrationality of these activities. Positive
acts of support for farmers bring gratitude and can be directed to the
clients of a politician or civil servant, thereby bolstering the legitimacy
of the regime and strengthening the patronage networks of those
who work with it. Although good prices are seen by farmers as positive, they produce no patronage. From the point of view of the government, the economic and political costs of creating marketing
boards that effectively tax agriculture are more than offset by the

political benefits of the jobs and "free goods" which they indirectly finance (Bates, 1981). Even Tanzania, which has resisted the creation of personalized patron-client networks, has felt it necessary to extract a dysfunctionally large surplus from agriculture in order to finance expansions in social services and formal sector jobs.

Escape from the unproductive growth of the state will require something more subtle than laissez-faire economics. The performance of public organizations is poor because few of their participants are committed to their formal, stated goals, and are rather pursuing individual or village interests. To propose the discipline of the free market as a cure for this problem amounts to calling for the imposition of a new method of pursuing the national interest. It is true that the market can achieve this end with a smaller number of consenting actors than a hierarchy. (Marris and Somerset, 1971, have shown that African small businessmen start pulling away from social obligations under the pressures of market discipline.) Ultimately, however, why should the politicians who use their hierarchical positions to pursue narrow interests now undertake the difficult task of turning to the market for the sake of the national interest?

It is essential to the survival of their regimes and the interests of their political leaders that African governments produce visible, distributable benefits. African politicians must have projects and patronage to distribute if they are to survive. The priority therefore is not to dismantle the state but to redirect its activities into areas that combine some economic returns with high political pay-offs. If the latter are high enough, it may be possible to contain pressures for still greater state expenditures, thereby preserving incentives for vigorous growth. It is unlikely that the extraction of resources from agriculture to support urban and elite interests will cease. We can aspire, however, to a structure in which resources are extracted and used relatively efficiently, thereby lessening the net burden on farmers.

One way to raise political returns while lowering economic costs is for benefits to be provided in such a way that they can be given again, rather than constituting a permanent drain on resources. The granting of a job has a relatively low level of political productivity, for once it is bestowed the salary will have to be paid for another 30 years while the recipient's gratitude will not last a tenth that long. In contrast, a labor-intensive rural roads project has a much higher political pay-off. From an economic point of view, roads improve access to producers and rural markets, thereby lowering the costs of trade and improving the chances of competition without imposing government controls that could become exploitative. Simultaneously, roads are very popular with rural constituents and when they deteriorate, their construction can be undertaken again. If those employed are drawn from the local area, the jobs given are a limited act of patronage that can be repeated with new jobs in the future.

Innovative thinking is needed about how vital rural services can be provided in ways that will make them politically productive and self-managing, while not becoming a permanent drain on the Treasury. For example, a subsidy could be paid to set up a veterinarian or paramedic in a private rural practice (perhaps by providing housing, equipping the lab, and maybe giving a cash grant). Even if only one out of two of these practitioners worked out, services in the rural areas would be expanded, government would not be left paying for those who do not work, and both communities and practitioners would be grateful for the initial subsidy. The introduction of private practice makes it more likely that competition will develop, lessening the exploitative potential that goes with public and private monopoly.

In this regard, the high failure rate of loans given to new, small, indigenous businessmen in Africa should be re-evaluated. The political returns on these "grants" is quite high, particularly as this social group is much more influential in politics than workers or small farmers. Small, indigenous businesses are particularly valuable in building a strong, rural, commercial infrastructure and in expanding off-farm employment. The cost to the government of such attempts to expand the economy is certainly less than the permanent drain presented by government corporations. Also, even badly administered loans and grants are less damaging to the economy than the manipulation of protective tariffs and licenses. The development community needs a realistic acceptance of the political and economic benefits of support to African small industry and commerce.

The thrust of the foregoing analysis is to identify those aspects of the agricultural development strategy advocated in this chapter that have potential political returns. The state can then use the pay-offs to buy the room within which the other needed policies can be implemented. Although this will not be easy, it is possible. If it is done, more positive forces of economic growth will be set in motion and resources for still more political favors will be generated, permitting an upward spiral that can be followed as long as these resources are used in ways that are both politically and economically productive. It is unlikely that this strategy will produce economic optimality, but then a government's uncompromising pursuit of that ideal is likely to result in a coup attempt.

SPECIAL CONSIDERATIONS FOR DONORS

African governments have been treated as the primary client for the rural development strategy presented in this chapter. Donors have a significant role to play in African development, but it is a supportive one. The policies that the donors should pursue in Africa are the same ones recommended for the continent's governments. Nonetheless, change cannot be forced on an unwilling society. Donors can try to persuade host countries of the wisdom of their advice; they can and should refuse to support policies and projects they believe are misguided. They can keep a sharp eye out for those moments in which an official in some part of a government seems to be moving in the right direction and to single out those programs for special support. If they try to impose their vision of the future, however, the result will probably be counter-productive, for a program that is unwillingly implemented has almost no chance of success.

Nonetheless, this strategy has specific implications for donors, as it is an institution-building approach to agricultural development. As such, it requires that donors see their interventions in light of their impact on the economy's institutions as a whole and not focus narrowly on specific changes in production that can be credited as "their own successes."

Institutional reform and development also require patience, experimentation, and adaptation. There can be no blueprint for progress in this area. A learning process must be created, requiring that the principal actors come to know one another well, assimilate the unanticipated lessons that their experience produces, and make new and adaptive responses (Korten, 1980). None of this can be done in a short period of time. Perhaps the most destructive of American contributions to international development has been the two-year contract. Agencies of social change within the United States consider such a period too brief for a manager to make a significant contribution. How much longer it must take to do something meaningful in a society one must first learn to understand! If donors are serious about influencing public policies in Africa, they will have to find ways to keep their personnel in the field for at least five years and to make it possible for those who have proven themselves particularly adept in a society to return to work in it again.

Once donor representatives can be kept in place long enough to have true insight into their host societies, they should be given substantially greater discretion than they currently have. An adaptive approach to development requires that those who are doing the learning be given the opportunity to experiment. This suggests that country representatives be given greater influence in the selection of projects and that they have discretionary funds for small opportunities with high marginal productivity. At the moment, one of the great problems of development is that whereas good large projects are hard to develop and justify, there is almost no end to small ways in which monies could be spent to overcome bottlenecks in critical institutions and to exploit fast-breaking opportunities. Money could be well spent quickly if the bureaucratic red tape were cut.

Finally, donors must recognize that strong economic institutions depend for their effectiveness on political stability. Many of the economic policies that donors are recommending for Africa today are politically difficult to implement. Much of the needed policy reform can be achieved only if donors assist governments on the continent to deliver at least some projects with a wide political appeal. Thus although donors may be primarily concerned with narrowly defined economic goals, it is important that they remain involved in the areas of education and health. These "old," "soft," and humanitarian basic needs projects have precisely the political attractiveness needed to sweeten the bitterness of much of the laissez-faire medicine being delivered today.

These kinds of trade-offs will not be easy for donors. The idea that a project in one sector might be undertaken in order to make a policy change in another sector possible implies a considerable amount of cooperation among specialists in the donor agency and a willingness to have progress on one's project dependent on progress outside one's primary area of concern. It also implies that a portion of a donor's portfolio would be tied up in projects that did not appear to reflect the agency's top priorities. Obviously this would be difficult for a donor, but then so are the reforms that are expected of African governments. Is it unreasonable to ask for institutional change on both sides of the Atlantic?

African agriculture is at a turning point and is about to enter an era of intensification and commercialization. This change will make the long-awaited wide-spread shift to science-based agriculture feasible and makes it possible to achieve the increases in food production that are needed to stay ahead of population growth. These structural shifts require a fundamental change in the character of the institutions serving African production. The traditional control approach to the continent's farmers is now inappropriate and dysfunctional. Monopoly and centralization are the most destructive forces at work in Africa's rural areas today. What is required, instead, is a new network of overlapping, competing public and private organizations that will provide reliable services and put the farmer as consumer firmly in control. It is to the politically difficult task of creating this new institutional framework that the efforts of African governments and donors must now be bent.

ACKNOWLEDGMENT

I would like to express my appreciation to Julie Howard for her invaluable comments and research assistance and to the Institute of International Studies of the University of California, Berkeley, for its partial funding of this study.

NOTES

1. It is widely assumed that the present shortages of food are a problem of production, that agricultural growth is no longer keeping pace with increases in population (e.g., World Bank, 1981, p. 45). We don't actually know that this is true, however; the aggregate data for Africa is so weak and the variation shown by the good micro studies is sufficiently great that such continent-wide conclusions are subject to legitimate scepticism. The current shortages in food could be caused by marketing, distribution, or weather problems instead (Berry, 1983, pp. 1–5).

2. Such a result is based on the unrealistic presumption that recent trends in urban population growth reflect increased employment opportunities. Some sources put the present rate of growth of formal non-farm employment below that of population, which would increase labor in the agricultural sector ad infinitum (Johnson and Clark, 1982, pp. 39–44; World Bank, 1981, pp. 176–79; UN, 1981).

3. It is true that much of this evidence concerns specific commodities and is inconclusive about the price responsiveness of aggregate farm production (Berry, 1983, pp. 24–25). The latter depends on the development of a research base and an economic infrastructure that permits farmers to expand their

investments rather that shift them from one crop to another. Precisely such an infrastructure is now or can soon be in place in most of Africa, however, rendering outmoded the traditional assumptions about price behavior.

4. The taxes imposed are believed by many experts still to be too high (J. Peberdy, private communication), but the burden would be even greater under a different structure.

REFERENCES

Adams, Dale and Douglas Graham. 1981. "A Critique of Traditional Agricultural Credit Projects and Policies," *Journal of Development Economics* 8: 347–66.

Barnett, Tony. 1981. "Evaluating the Gezira Scheme: Black Box or Pandora's Box?" In J. Heyer, P. Roberts and G. Williams, *Rural Development in Tropical Africa*. London: Macmillan.

Bates, Robert H. 1981. *Markets and States in Tropical Africa: The Political Basis of Agricultural Policies*. Berkeley: University of California Press.

Benor, Daniel and Michael Baxter. 1984. *Training and Visit Extension*. Washington, D.C.: The World Bank.

Benor, Daniel and James Q. Harrison. 1977. *Agricultural Extension: The Training and Visit System*. Washington, D.C.: The World Bank.

Bergman, Kenneth. 1983. "Climate Change," *International Journal of Environmental Studies* 20: 91–101.

Berry, Leonard and Mustafa Khogali. 1981. "The Physical Resource Background to African Development." Paper presented to The Committee on African Development Strategies.

Berry, Sara S. 1983. "Agrarian Crisis in Africa? A Review and Interpretation." Paper presented to the Joint African Studies Committee. New York: Social Science Research Council and the American Council of Learned Societies.

Bottrall, Anthony and John Howell. 1980. "Small Farmer Credit Delivery and Institutional Choice." In Howell, 1980.

Chambers, Robert. 1983. *Rural Development: Putting the Last First*. London: Longman.

Cohen, John M. 1980. "Land Tenure and Rural Development in Africa." In R. Bates and M. Lofchie, eds., *Agricultural Development in Africa: Issues of Public Policy*. New York: Praeger.

Devres, Inc. 1980. *Socio-Economic and Environmental Impact of Low-Volume Rural Roads—A Review of the Literature*. Program Evaluation Discussion Paper No. 7. Washington, D.C.: United States Agency for International Development.

Diallo, Thiousso. 1984. "Participation Villageoise au Développement Hydro-Agricole de la Vallée et du Delta du Fleuve Sénégal (Rive Gauche)." Unpublished paper. Davis, Cal.: University of California.

Donald, Gordon. 1976. *Credit for Small Farmers in Developing Countries*. Boulder: Westview Press.

Eicher, Carl K. and Doyle C. Baker. 1982. *Research on Agricultural Development in Sub-Saharan Africa: A Critical Survey*. East Lansing: Department of Agricultural Economics, Michigan State University, MSU International Development Paper No. 1.

Gbetibouo, Mathurin and Christopher L. Delgado. 1984. "Lessons and Constraints of Export-Led Growth: Cocoa in Ivory Coast." In I.W. Zartman and C.L. Delgado, eds. *The Political Economy of the Ivory Coast*. New York: Praeger.

Hart, Keith. 1982. *The Political Economy of West African Agriculture*. Cambridge: Cambridge University Press.

Heyer, J., P. Roberts and G. Williams. 1981. *Rural Development in Tropical Africa*. New York: St. Martins.

Hill, Polly. 1970. *Studies in Rural Capitalism in West Africa*. Cambridge: Cambridge University Press.

Horowitz, Michael M. 1979. *The Sociology of Pastoralism and African Livestock Projects*. Program Evaluation Discussion Paper No. 6. Washington, D.C.: United States Agency for International Development.

Howell, John, ed. 1980. *Borrowers and Lenders: Rural Financial Markets and Institutions in Developing Countries*. London: Overseas Development Institute.

Howell, John. 1984. "Conditions for the Design and Management of Agricultural Extension." Agricultural Administration Network Discussion Paper No. 13. London: Overseas Development Institute.

Hyden, Goran. 1980. *Beyond Ujamaa in Tanzania: Underdevelopment and an Uncaptured Peasantry*. Berkeley: University of California Press.

Hyden, Goran. 1983. *No Shortcuts to Progress: African Development Management in Perspective*. Berkeley: University of California Press.

Jarvis, Lovell S. 1984. "Overgrazing and Range Degradation: Is There Need and Scope for Government Control of Livestock Numbers?" Paper presented to the Conference on Livestock Policy Issues. Addis Ababa: International Livestock Center for Africa.

Johnsen, S.J., W. Dansgaard, and H.B. Clausen. 1970. "Climatic Oscillations 1200–2000 AD," *Nature* 227 (August 1): 482–83.

Johnston, Bruce. 1984. "Agricultural Development in Tropical Africa: The Search for Viable Strategies." Paper presented to The Committee on African Development Strategies. Washington, D.C. Overseas Development Council.

Johnston, Bruce and William Clark. 1982. *Redesigning Rural Development: A Strategic Perspective*. Baltimore: Johns Hopkins University Press.

Jones, William O. 1980. "Agricultural Trade Within Tropical Africa: Achievements and Difficulties." In R. Bates and M. Lofchie, eds., *Agricultural Development in Africa: Issues of Public Policy*. New York: Praeger.

Katz, Richard W. 1977. "Assessing the Impact of Climate Change on Food Production," *Climate Change* 1: 85–96.

Kleemeier, Lizz Lyle. 1984. "Integrated Rural Development in Tanzania: The Role of Foreign Assistance, 1972–1982." Ph.D. dissertation submitted to the Department of Political Science, University of California, Berkeley.

Korten, David C. 1980. "Community Organization and Rural Development: A Learning Process Approach," *Public Administration Review* 40(5): 480, 512.

Landau, Martin. 1969. "Redundancy, Rationality and the Problem of Duplication and Overlap," *Public Administration Review* 29(4).

Lele, Uma. 1975. *The Design of Rural Development: Lessons from Africa*. Baltimore: The Johns Hopkins University Press.

Lele, Uma. 1981. "Cooperatives and the Poor: A Comparative Perspective," *World Development* 9: 55–72.

Leonard, David K. 1977. *Reaching the Peasant Farmer: Organization Theory and Practice in Kenya*. Chicago: University of Chicago Press.

Leonard, David K. 1984a. "Disintegrating Agricultural Development," *Food Research Institute Studies* XIX (2).

Leonard, David K. 1984b. "The Supply of Veterinary Services." Paper presented to the Conference on Livestock Policy Issues. Addis Ababa: International Livestock Center for Africa.

Leonard, David K. and Dale Rogers Marshall, eds. 1982. *Institutions of Rural Development for the Poor: Decentralization and Organizational Linkages*. Berkeley: Institute of International Studies, University of California.

Lipton, Michael. 1980. "Rural Credit, Farm Finance and Village Households." In Howell, op. cit.

Marris, Peter and Anthony Somerset. 1971. *The African Businessmen*. London: Routledge and Kegan Paul.

Miracle, Marvin P., Diane S. Miracle, and Laurie Cohen. 1980. "Informal Savings Mobilization in Africa," *Economic Development and Cultural Change* 28(4).

Muzaale, Patrick and David K. Leonard. 1985. "Women's Groups in Agricultural Extension and Nutrition in Africa: Kenya's Case," *Agricultural Administration* 19(1).

Nicholson, Sharon E. 1978. "Climatic Variations in the Sahel and Other African Regions During the Past Five Centuries," *Journal of Arid Environments* 1: 3–24.

Peterson, Stephen B. 1982a. "Government, Cooperatives and the Private Sector in Peasant Agriculture." In Leonard and Marshall, 1982.

Peterson, Stephen B. 1982b. "Alternative Local Organizations Supporting the Agricultural Development of the Poor." In Leonard and Marshall, 1982.

Peterson, Stephen B. 1982c. "The State and the Organizational Infrastructure of the Agrarian Economy: A Comparative Study of Smallholder Agrarian Development in Taiwan and Kenya." Ph.D. dissertation submitted to the Department of Political Science, University of California, Berkeley.

Ralston, Lenore, James Anderson, and Elizabeth Colson. 1983. *Voluntary Efforts in Decentralized Management: Opportunities and Constraints in Rural Development*. Berkeley: Institute of International Studies, University of California.

Sanford, Stephen. 1983. *Management of Pastoral Development in the Third World*. Chichester: John Wiley and Sons.

Stryker, J.D., C.H. Gotsch, J. McIntire, and F.C. Roche. 1981. "Investments in Large Scale Infrastructure: Irrigation and River Management in the Sahel." Washington, D.C.: United States Agency for International Development.

United Nations. 1981. *Statistical Yearbook*. New York: United Nations.

Von Pischke, J.D. and John Rouse. 1983. "Selected Successful Experiences in Agricultural Credit and Rural Finance in Africa," *Savings and Development* 1(7).

World Bank. 1981. *Accelerated Development in Sub-Saharan Africa*. Washington, D.C.: The World Bank.

CHAPTER EIGHT

Agricultural Research: Lessons of the Past, Strategies for the Future

Dunstan S.C. Spencer

Sub-Saharan Africa is the only region in the developing world in which per capita food production has declined during the last two decades, with only Rwanda, Central African Republic, Swaziland, Ivory Coast, Mauritius, and Cameroon showing any positive trends. West Africa has exhibited the slowest growth rate in total food production of all regions, as per capita production of all crops, with the exception of rice, has declined. Slight annual increases in total food production are attributable almost exclusively to increases in area under cultivation, indicating that technological change has had little impact on Africa's food production.

Africa's economic crisis has sharply limited governments' abilities to finance essential capital goods imports and recurrent expenditures, such as fertilizers and irrigation systems, needed to increase agricultural production (OAU, 1980). Poor economic management, inefficient parastatals, and misguided pricing policies have undermined the agricultural sector, particularly export crop production, in which Africa's comparative advantage is the strongest (World Bank, 1981, 1984a, b). Less often considered, however, are environmental constraints and a lack of appropriate technologies, which have also played a significant role in bringing about the decline in the agricultural sector. While better internal policies and a more favorable external economic climate might have delayed the current crisis, they would not have prevented it.

Although agricultural research has come up with some answers to environmental and other agricultural development problems, these solutions have not been transferred to farmers because of bottlenecks such as poor extension systems, inadequate pricing policies, and ineffective and inefficient seed multiplication programs and marketing parastatals. Environmental and other constraints on farmers have not been adequately taken into account in research. New technologies rarely correspond to farmers' changing needs and fail to bring about sustainable growth in aggregate output. This chapter will review strategies for Africa's agricultural development and the performance of earlier agricultural systems, and concludes with a critical evaluation of a modern agricultural research strategy.

AFRICAN AGRICULTURAL DEVELOPMENT
STRATEGIES: THE IMPLICATIONS FOR RESEARCH

Ruttan (1980) has provided a useful outline of agricultural development models, some of which are relevant to agricultural development and research in sub-Saharan Africa.[1] In the "frontier model," agricultural development involves expanding area under cultivation in order to increase overall output. While available statistics show that the small increases in Africa's total agricultural output during the last two decades were brought about by expansion of areas cultivated (Paulino, 1983), the increases were not sufficient to keep up with population growth rates. As a result, the frontier model is of little relevance to sub-Saharan Africa, particularly as new, productive lands open for settlement are lacking.[2]

According to the "conservation model," agricultural output is increased by recycling plant nutrients through organic manures and by labor-intensive methods of drainage, irrigation, and other physical facilities, thus more effectively utilizing land and water resources. There is ample scope for this model in many sub-Saharan countries, as substantial areas are unsuitable for cultivation or other human and animal uses due to desert conditions, rock outcroppings, periodic flooding, or diseases such as bilharzia, trypanosomiasis, and onchocerciasis (Matlon and Spencer, 1984).

Second, there is a high degree of micro-variability in land quality and the better soils are often already under cultivation. Third, soils are unstable, requiring a high ratio of fallow time relative to cultivation. In addition, the rapid growth of the African rural population over the last 30 years has led to intense cultivation of land, resulting in stagnant or declining crop yields and a degradation of the land base. Therefore, soil conservation measures are needed to prevent further deterioration in the land base and to increase agricultural productivity.

As Berry and Khogali (1984) point out, two-thirds of Africa's land area is classified as arid, semi-arid, or dry sub-humid. It is ironic, therefore, that the existing surface and ground water resources have remained largely untapped. Despite recent investments in large-scale irrigation in West Africa, only about 3 percent of the land is currently under irrigation (FAO, 1978). Unfortunately, however, assessments of the large-scale irrigation projects have usually revealed economic losses or non-competitive returns (Sparling, 1981). The evidence strongly suggests that in the absence of long-term and highly subsidized donor commitments which include substantial investments in the training of local workers, it is unlikely that large-scale irrigation schemes will play an important role in improving Africa's ability to meet its food needs in the future.

On the other hand, small-scale, labor-intensive projects managed and operated by family and/or community groups have demonstrated attractive returns on investment (Eicher and Baker, 1982). Agricultural development policy will therefore need to focus on dryland agriculture in the short run, while a mixed strategy which also emphasizes irrigated agriculture is appropriate over the longer term.

The loss of vegetation, (i.e., grasses and trees) is another aspect of the deterioration of the environment, as Berry and Khogali (1984) have also pointed out. Livestock productivity is declining because of the degradation of pastures, while reduction of the forest cover is causing profound changes in soil productivity and probably also in the climate. Therefore, sub-Saharan African countries should pursue a development strategy which includes reforestation and maintenance of livestock herds particularly in semi-arid zones. While it is clear that a rigorous application of the conservation model of agricultural development could reverse the downward trend in Africa's agricultural output, it is not likely to bring about rates of growth needed to match projected increases in aggregate demand.

Due to the limitations of the above models, a number of new ones have emerged since the late 1960s. T.W. Shultz (1964) put forward what Ruttan has called the "high pay-off input model," in which investment to make modern high pay-off inputs available to farmers is the key component in transforming traditional agriculture.[3] Hayami and Ruttan (1972) extended this framework by developing the "induced innovation model," in which indigenous technical change is central to the development process. This model is attractive because it clearly shows that improvements in agricultural productivity "can only be made available by undertaking investment in the agricultural research capacity needed to develop technologies appropriate to the countries' natural and institutional environments and investment in the physical and institutional infrastructure needed to realize the new production potential opened up by technological advances" (Ruttan, 1980).

The institutional capacity to generate technical changes adapted to local resource endowments must be in place and there must be a heavy emphasis on a science-based system of agriculture, since there is only limited scope for a natural resource conservation policy to bring about much increase in agricultural output. While many attempts have been made over the last decade to develop models based on African resource endowments and institutions[4], this chapter will focus on two contemporary issues: whether development strategies in sub-Saharan Africa should emphasize small or large-scale farming and export or food crop production.

LARGE-VERSUS SMALL-SCALE FARMING

Available data shows that small-scale farming has a number of advantages over large-scale farming in Africa. Timmer, Falcon, and Pearson (1983) have stressed the need for broadly based programs for small farm households in most food production strategies. Likewise, Mellor and Johnston (1984) have provided strong theoretical arguments for "unimodel" or focus strategies that emphasize small-scale farming. Dualistic strategies, based on rapid modernization of large-scale, capital-intensive farm units together with capital-intensive industrialization, have not worked in many developing countries because they do not take into account the countries' resource endowments. Agricultural development in sub-Saharan Africa is only likely to succeed by gradually increasing the productivity of small farmers through innovations appropriate to their factor proportions.

EXPORT VERSUS FOOD CROP PRODUCTION

The controversy surrounding export versus food crop production is based on the contention of the World Bank and other international organizations that Africa should specialize in export crops in which it enjoys a comparative advantage, and because its agricultural labor productivity is generally substantially higher in export than in food crop production.[5]

John Mellor succinctly summarized the counter-argument as follows:

> First, given the risk aversion common to farmers, the extent to which they are willing to put their resources in export crop production is determined by their ability to produce adequate home food supplies. Thus, food production and export production may be complementary, not competitive. Increased productivity of the former allows increased production of the latter.
>
> Second, a substantial proportion of African labor resources are already in food production. Failure to substantially raise the productivity of these resources in food production means leaving large numbers of people in poverty and malnutrition for the decades required to facilitate a shift to alternative production and distribution systems. Third, and leaving behind the second point, there is great variability from place to place in the food production resource base in Africa. Although the comparative advantage argument against food production may apply in some areas, it seems unlikely in others. Fourth, no government, given reasonable prospects of success in domestic food production, will import the bulk of its basic food sustenance (Mellor, 1984, p. 4).

In addition to the above points, specialization in export crop production with concomitant increases in food imports would require an accelerated change in food preferences in Africa. Rice, wheat, and maize, which are readily available on the world market, would almost completely replace millet, cassava, and other root crops. There would also need to be a significant increase in transportation facilities, including ports, marketing, and storage infrastructure. While the case for substantially increased investment in food crop production is much stronger than that for specialization in export crops, the latter also need to be increased if foreign exchange is to be earned to finance other essential imports (e.g., petroleum) that cannot be produced domestically. A mixed strategy with major emphasis on food crop production is therefore required.

IMPLICATIONS FOR RESEARCH

The main implications for research of the discussion on agricultural development strategies are:

- Sustained agricultural development will result only if technological and institutional innovations are appropriate to the continent's resource endowments. Therefore, research is needed to provide a thorough understanding of the natural resource, institutional, and socio-economic constraints on sub-Saharan African agriculture.
- There is still scope to increase agricultural productivity by conservation of natural resources, especially land and water resources, particularly in semi-arid zones. To this end, research is needed to develop soil conservation, irrigation, and reforestation technologies.
- Given high population growth rates and the poor quality of most land resources, development strategies and research that focus on small-scale farming should be emphasized.
- While attention should be given to increasing export crop production, particularly where there is clear evidence of comparative advantage, major emphasis should be on food crop production and research.

PAST PERFORMANCE OF AGRICULTURAL
RESEARCH SYSTEMS: THE COLONIAL
PERIOD

Colonial governments did not neglect agricultural research; between 1900 and 1920, at least one agricultural research station was established in virtually every country in sub-Saharan Africa (McKelvey, 1965). These research stations, however, concentrated almost exclusively on export crops such as oil palm, cocoa, coffee, and groundnuts, and yielded rather substantial returns. Hybrid oil palms were developed that contributed significantly to the growth of agricultural exports between 1940 and 1960 (Abaelu, 1971), outyielding local wild palms by 500 to 700 percent in West Africa (Eicher, 1967). Research on cotton began in Uganda around 1904 and spread to northern Nigeria and the French colonies in the 1920s and 1930s. In Burkina Faso, for example, substantial yield increases were obtained by applying the results of cotton research under farm conditions (Delgado, 1981). Similar successes were obtained with cocoa due to research which began in West Africa in the 1920s, and to a lesser extent with groundnuts.

Hybrid maize in Kenya and Zimbabwe was the only food staple to which substantial research efforts were directed during the colonial period. Launched in Zimbabwe in 1932 and Kenya in the mid-1950s, these long-term research programs have yielded substantial returns (Eicher, 1984). Otherwise, there has been a near total lack of research on the major food staples (Collinson, 1983).

While most of the colonial research programs on export crops relied heavily on the successful transfer of materials from other regions of the world—plant-breeding materials for oil palm from Asia, cotton from the United States, and coffee from South America—unfortunately, this successful technology transfer was not repeated in food crop research.

As Judd, Boyce, and Evenson (1984) and Oram and Binglish (1984) have shown, investments in agricultural research as a percentage of total agricultural production were much lower in sub-Saharan Africa than in other developing and developed countries. Thus, although there was considerable investment in export crop research during the colonial era, in absolute terms, it proved insufficient to guarantee the long-term profitability of cash crop production.

In the years following independence, public sector expenditures on research increased significantly. Judd, Boyce, and Evenson (1984) estimate that agricultural research expenditures in East and West Africa in constant 1980 U.S. dollars increased from about $57 million in 1959 to $280 million in 1980, while manpower increased from 1636 scientist man-years to 4100. Over the same time period, public sector expenditure as a percentage of the value of agricultural output rose from about 0.37 percent to about 1.19 percent in West Africa and from 0.19 percent to 0.81 percent in East Africa.

These commendable increases have not produced a commensurate growth in research output. The lack of productive agricultural research in post-colonial sub-Saharan Africa can be approached by a review of the operational difficulties that have been encountered by national research systems and an evaluation of the stock of technologies that have been produced.

OPERATIONAL DIFFICULTIES OF NATIONAL RESEARCH SYSTEMS

In order to function effectively, an agricultural research system needs trained personnel, adequate funds to cover fixed costs (e.g., building of laboratories and purchase of equipment), and operating costs, (e.g., purchases of fuel, fertilizers, and chemicals), and payments of laborers. While there has been a substantial increase in the number of agricultural research workers, statistics do not reflect their levels of qualification or competence. In many national research institutions, many researchers hold only bachelor of science level qualifications and at best can only be expected to perform routine experiments and analysis. As a result, many experiments are repeated year after year, long after they have lost any significance. It often takes a team of outside consultants to suggest new areas of research!

Qualifications levels of researchers in many national programs must be raised. Donor agencies sometimes encourage the tendency to staff national research systems with unqualified people by insisting on training counterparts in externally funded short-term research projects. Those with B.S. level qualifications work with expatriate Ph.D. researchers for one to three years; then they are left on their own to carry on and modify the research programs as necessary. Another constraint is the lack of operational funds and poor financial and research management.

The situation has recently been described as follows:

> The effectiveness of research, extension, and training institutions is impaired by the lack of operating resources needed to function as they should. Yet, all too frequently, governments continue to expand programs, hiring more personnel instead of providing necessary resources to those already on the payroll. Poor performance and effectiveness thus go beyond the simple lack of resources. They arise from poor development administration and financial management.
>
> Poor personnel management and work discipline, lack of performance incentives and professional advancement, inadequate operating funds to do a good job, all discourage highly motivated researchers, trainees, and extension agents. The resulting high staff turnover disrupts research programs and institution-building efforts so necessary for creating effective indigenous national research and extension systems. Until these problems are addressed, zonal research and networking programs will not achieve their full potential.
>
> Untimely budgetary allocations frequently disrupt production campaigns, agricultural experiments, and data collection activities throughout the Sahel. Experiments sometimes must be abandoned or curtailed half-way through the season, or are not properly tended because of a lack of gasoline, vehicles, or other resources, or because of the inability to control implementing staff.
>
> Partly these problems arise from unpredictable budgeting exercises over which research and extension institutions have little control.

Partly they arise from legal structures that severely constrain the institutions' ability to control and allocate resources put at their disposal. Partly they arise from poor internal planning and management of resources in the face of what is obviously a highly unstable and unreliable resource situation. Unless these kinds of institutional constraints are appropriately identified, analyzed, and resolved, we risk spending another 10 years making little progress toward increasing agricultural production. . . .(Lebeau, et al., 1984, pp. 5–6)

EVALUATION OF NEW TECHNOLOGICAL OPTIONS

Matlon and Spencer (1984) have recently examined some of the current stock of technological innovations in terms of their appropriateness to small-scale farming. With regard to land and water management, improved systems in the humid tropics—light clearing, in situ burning, and intensive use of surface mulch in combination with herbicides and minimum or zero tillage—which are being developed by the International Institute of Tropical Agriculture (IITA), have yet to prove effective in on-farm testing. Moreover, chemical weed control methods and small-scale equipment for use in low tillage systems pose more immediate research problems (ter Kuile, 1983).

In the semi-arid zones, tied ridges have dramatically reduced runoff and increased yields in on-station trials in both East and West Africa (Ruthenberg, 1980; ICRISAT, 1981), yet the extensive use of this approach remains doubtful due to its substantial labor costs and yield gaps. Because of increasing demands on crop residues for livestock feed, fuel, and other purposes, the potential extensive use of mulches in sorghum and millet production is limited. On the other hand, tests conducted in Burkina Faso have concluded that the introduction of dirt anti-erosion dikes constructed on the contours of farmers' fields has significantly increased short-term yields (ICRISAT, 1983).

Mechanization schemes using tractors have met with limited success in the humid tropics due to the high capital costs relative to available resources, the scale of farmers' operations, and the lack of know-how in equipment use and maintenance. In addition, the potential yield and labor-saving benefits of animal-powered cultivation practices, repeatedly measured at experimental stations, have rarely been confirmed under farmers' management (Sargeant et al., 1981).

Despite the generally poor chemical composition of most African soil and its rapid depletion under continuous cultivation, the use of chemical fertilizers in sub-Saharan Africa has been minimal. This is due to the high cost of fertilizers, low and extremely variable technical response rates, and the need for complementary applications of large quantities of organic matter to achieve and maintain the potential response to chemical fertilizers over the long run (IFDC, 1976; ICRISAT, 1983; Pichot et al., 1981).

With regard to crop improvement, it is clear that with few exceptions such as hybrid maize in Zimbabwe and Kenya, programs concerned with the genetic improvement of food staples are relatively new and have had little success. Although on-station results have often been promising, when most new varieties are cultivated by farmers, yield gaps of up to 60 percent have consistently occurred (ICRISAT, 1980/83). Unacceptable taste and processing and storage problems are also commonly encountered. As a result, probably less than 2 percent of total sorghum, millet, and upland rice area in West Africa is sown with cultivars developed through modern genetic research.

REASONS FOR FAILURE TO PRODUCE APPROPRIATE NEW TECHNOLOGIES

From the previous review, it is clear that the response of new production technologies to the continent's evolving needs has been inadequate. To a large extent, failures stem from two causes: inadequate understanding of small farmer goals and resource limitations. A glaring example of where research objectives were very different from those of its potential clientele is the case of intercropping. Numerous studies have shown that apart from some small areas in East and southern Africa, intercropping is vastly more important than monocrop systems, occupying over 90 percent of cropped area in most countries. Although there was some work done in the 1930s (Belshaw, 1979), it was only in the 1970s that any serious research on intercropping in sub-Saharan Africa began to be undertaken.[6] Even today, less than 20 percent of all agronomic research in the region addresses the issue, yet what little research has been done shows that intercropping is often much more efficient and less risky than monocropping even from the agronomic point of view.

The second major cause was the colonial period's over-reliance on the diffusion or technology transfer of export crop materials from other countries. With the Green Revolution's success in spreading wheat and rice varieties developed by the International Maize Improvement Center and the International Rice Research Institute to Latin America and Asia, the technology transfer model of agricultural development took firm root in sub-Saharan Africa.

Not only was the model adopted by national research systems, which had few alternatives as shortages of staff and funds prevented them from doing more fundamental research, but regional and international research centers also adopted it as a modus operandi. Thus the West Africa Rice Development Association (WARDA) was founded to conduct rice research, development, and training activities in West Africa on the principle that importing varieties from other parts of the world, testing them for adaptability, and selecting the suitable ones was all that was needed in varietal research (Lewis, 1982). Initially, ICRISAT's Africa program relied very heavily on material transfers from Asia, placing scientific staff in one or two-man teams in national programs (CGIAR, 1978).

The extent to which technical solutions developed elsewhere can be imported into Africa is quite limited because of the continent's higher rate of demographic change and more difficult physical conditions which determine technical potential. Consequently, success has been lacking to date in the direct introduction of exotic high-yielding cultivars, with the exception of irrigated rice where the environment can be modified to suit the crop. ICRISAT has had little success in introducing Indian sorghum and millet varieties to West Africa (Matlon, 1983), and after 10 years of variety trials in which over 2000 imported varieties were tried in the mangrove swamps of West Africa, WARDA found only two varieties that performed as well as the best local varieties (WARDA, 1984). As a result, international and regional centers have learned some lessons from these experiences[7] and some national programs are concentrating on the development of local materials to the extent that their resources permit.

ELEMENTS OF A MODERN AGRICULTURAL RESEARCH STRATEGY FOR SUB-SAHARAN AFRICA

POLICY RESEARCH

As suggested earlier, most recent reviews of Africa's economic situation have highlighted the fact that governmental economic policies have been faulty. Effective agricultural policy-making is a complex activity, encompassing efforts to influence and direct actions of millions of producers, consumers, and marketing agencies in order to meet broad social objectives. This process necessarily requires trade-offs which are not always readily apparent. As a result, there is a critical need to examine the potential costs and benefits of alternative agricultural policies on different segments of the population.

Before this can be accomplished, however, a rather large data set is needed.[8] Data is needed on the consumption patterns of urban and rural households in order to identify the numbers and locations of poor and malnourished elements of society who should be the target of food policy, and to determine aggregate demand parameters in order to trace the effects of various price and income policies. Data is also needed on farming systems in order to better understand the characteristics of production systems in terms of seasonality of supply, distribution of output, the decision-making environment of farms, and the potential sources of technological change.

Similarly, information is needed on markets and marketing institutions—storage, processing, and transportation of agricultural commodities—and on exchange rate functions and price formation. There is a general consensus that agricultural marketing parastatals have largely failed in sub-Saharan Africa. But in order to objectively determine what can replace them, more analysis and information on alternative marketing systems are needed. Lastly, data is needed on the relationship between agricultural systems, the macro-economy, and international markets.[9]

In no African country is there an adequate data base to allow for effective and comprehensive agricultural policy analysis. At the very best, the available data allows only partial analysis of the potential impact of alternative policies. Policy-making therefore continues with an inadequate information base. The situation described by (Stolper, 1969) in *Planning Without Facts* still exists 15 years later in virtually all sub-Saharan African countries.[10] At present, policy-making is based more on "gut feelings"—that private enterprise is intrinsically better than parastatals—than on hard empirical evidence. There is no guarantee that many of the current policy prescriptions which lack empirical evidence will be any more successful than the experiments of the past.

Therefore, given the current confusion, analyses of agricultural and particularly food policies need to receive top research priority.

Initially, emphasis must be placed on collecting primary data, as policy researchers in Africa cannot rely as much on secondary data as in other continents. Therefore, most policy analysis will have to be done by local university researchers and associates and other institutions that have a long-term commitment to the continent. Most Western consulting firms employing short-term consultants do not have the necessary expertise or time to first collect the necessary primary data, then to perform the multifaceted analysis required.

RESEARCH WITH A FARMING SYSTEMS PERSPECTIVE

One of the basic flaws in agricultural research in the region over the last three decades has been the omission of resource and other constraints on small-scale farmers who are the clientele of the research. To overcome this problem, agricultural research must be conducted with a farming systems perspective that views the farm in a holistic manner as it interacts within the larger system (CGIAR, 1978). The major objective of this approach is to increase the productivity of farming systems by generating appropriate new technology. It includes location-specific on-farm research with a short-term objective of developing improved technologies for target groups of farmers, as well as longer-term research at experiment stations to overcome the farming systems' major limitations (Byerlee, Harrington, and Winkelmann, 1983; Gilbert, Norman, and Winch, 1980).

On-station research is an integral part of research with a farming systems perspective.[11] Through such research, new technological components—crop varieties, herbicides, and new cropping methods—are developed, screened, and tested on a pilot scale. Unfortunately, by emphasizing the crucial role of on-farm research, most of the literature erroneously gives the impression that such research can stand on its own and that experiment station research has at best a rather unimportant role to play.[12]

In the last five years, a number of farming systems research teams have been set up all over Africa, supported by finance and technical assistance from external donors. National research programs are also being urged and assisted to launch large farming systems research (i.e., on-farm research efforts).[13] These efforts are likely to bring to the attention of researchers and policy-makers the true problems faced by small farmers. While it will be clear that ready solutions to the problems are not yet available, there is a grave danger that research will not move beyond that point if equal emphasis is not placed on necessary experiment station research. Given their poor reputation, these stations now run the risk of being starved of necessary funding and staffing.

CHARACTERISTICS OF NEW TECHNOLOGIES
NEEDED IN SUB-SAHARAN AFRICA

In order to increase Africa's agricultural productivity, new biological, chemical, and mechanical technologies that would allow intensification of agriculture are needed. In addition, new soil and water conservation techniques must be developed. Biological technology adaptable to local conditions is needed; there are very clear indications that varieties of sugar cane, wheat, and rice suitable to Latin America and Asia have limited adaptability in sub-Saharan Africa.

Given small-scale farmers' limited capital resources and input distribution problems, recommended varieties should be highly responsive to low levels of inputs such as fertilizers. Varieties are needed that perform as well or slightly better than farmers' traditional varieties under traditional levels of management, but yield substantially more under slightly improved management. Too many improved varieties require levels of management beyond farmers' existing capabilities before their full potential is realized.

Several corrective prescriptions can be suggested. In the semi-arid tropics, for example, moderate yield increases with substantially greater stability could be achieved through breeding for improved seedling vigor, drought resistance, and resistance to the most common pests and diseases. The development of varieties with different agronomic characteristics, such as shorter crop cycles or modified plant structures, could also increase farmers' management options, such as intercropping or permitting late planting without yield loss (Stoop et al., 1981).

With regard to new chemical technologies, material inputs such as fertilizers should be derived as much as possible from local sources in order to reduce transportation costs. This calls for substantial research on new plant designs and processes that would allow more economical production of phosphate fertilizers from domestic rock phosphate. Given the labor bottlenecks at weeding time in many countries and the demonstrated yield-reducing effects of weeds in many farming systems, cheap, effective, and easily applied herbicides are urgently needed.

Although sub-Saharan Africa can be defined as land surplus, capital-intensive methods of cultivation cannot substitute for labor in a big way. Mechanical technologies, such as processing machines, cannot economically replace hand labor (Timmer, 1973; Byerlee, Eicher, Leidholm, and Spencer, 1983); animal traction or mechanized land cultivation has had only limited success. Nonetheless, labor productivity is quite low compared to that of Asia (Mellor and Johnston, 1984) and there are often severe labor bottlenecks. Therefore, research on appropriate mechanization technology that is within farmers' reach is needed.

Cooperative ownership and management of agricultural machinery has not worked in sub-Saharan Africa, nor have government tractor hire schemes. It appears then that the only open avenue is research on the improvement of farmers' existing tools and equipment. A hand weeder that allows a farmer to weed twice as fast as existing weeding devices would have a big impact on labor productivity. The International Livestock Center for Africa (ILCA) recently designed an animal yoke that allows the traditional Ethiopian plow to be pulled by one instead of two oxen. This innovation is likely to have more of an impact on agricultural productivity in the Ethiopian highlands than all the mechanization research over the last 30 years, which concentrated on replacing traditional cultivation methods with mechanized methods rather than on improving existing ones.

Therefore, research on improvement of farmers' hand tools and equipment, unglamorous as it might seem, is needed. For example, hand-held equipment—not scaled-down models of equipment used in developed countries—is needed for minimum tillage in the humid zones.[14]

In order to identify appropriate technologies, a research strategy that emphasizes in situ development of new plant materials, local sources of chemical and biological fertilizers, and improved hand tools and animal traction is needed. Combined into simple technological packages which would be adopted in stages by small-scale farmers, these improvements would substantially increase rural incomes.

SOIL, WATER, AND FOREST CONSERVATION
RESEARCH

Efforts to conserve soil, water, and forest resources will allow for some gains in productivity. Again, research is needed on improved conservation practices that could be profitably adopted by small farmers. In semi-arid zones, immediate attention should be given to research aimed at improving the management of existing large-scale irrigation schemes. Soils research is also needed to develop economical ways of maintaining or increasing water infiltration and reducing run-off in semi-arid areas. Also, high priority should be given to research which undertakes to develop economical crop rotations including tree crops, leguminous species, and mixed farming.

Reforestation is included under the general concept of conservation because of the alarming rates at which losses in the forest cover are occurring both in the arid zones where desertification is increasing and in humid zones where climatic changes are taking place. There is little hope of reducing firewood demand either by substitution with other fuels or by police actions or taxation. Efforts must be made to increase fuel wood supplies while maintaining the forest cover.

In the past, reforestation programs have relied too heavily on imported tree species and techniques which have rendered projects hopelessly uneconomic (Taylor and Soumare, 1983). Rather, emphasis should be placed on improving traditional forest species and on the identification of fast-growing trees for humid areas as well as those suited to harsh semi-arid conditions. Research into the incorporation of trees into crop and animal production systems should be given high priority.

LIVESTOCK RESEARCH

An important part of farming systems, particularly in the semi-arid zones where crop production takes place alongside rangelands, livestock production requires research, especially on control of livestock diseases. During the colonial period, livestock research was mainly veterinary. Such early endeavors, together with recent work by the International Laboratory for Research into Animal Diseases (ILRAD) and other international organizations, have yielded economical control measures for most of the important diseases except trypanosomiasis.

The available literature on livestock production and productivity[15] shows that unreliable feed supply is probably the most limiting factor on animal production. But there is limited scope for profitably increasing feed supplies by rangeland pasture improvement (Ruthenberg, 1974; Doppler, 1980). As a result, substantial increases in live-stock productivity will have to await increased crop production. Sup-plementary livestock feeding can then be based on crop residues or on feed specifically grown for livestock. Fortunately, increased de-mand for livestock products is likely to occur only after substantial increases in demand for staple food crops, (i.e., cereals, roots, and tubers) (Mellor and Johnston, 1984).

RESEARCH RESOURCE ALLOCATION

In a world of limited resources, decisions on allocation necessarily imply some trade-offs. Given agriculture's contribution to African economies, the amounts invested in agricultural research are inade-quate and should be increased. But even if resources increase, deci-sions will need to be made as to which of the many areas of research covered in this study should be given priority. Should the emphasis be placed on crop or livestock research, on soil conservation research or genetic improvements, on export or cash crop research, on the Sahel or humid zone?

In identifying priorities, it is often argued that research resources should be allocated where the probability for success is highest. How-ever, breakthroughs in agricultural research are often a result of past research in which a great deal of work has already been done and in which many of the elements of the problem have been identified. Minor investments in new research may yield quick and high returns; the probability of success is highest where there is an existing knowl-edge base.

Second, there is no a priori basis to argue that research in areas in which there is a high probability of success are those that are likely to have significant effects on agricultural productivity or on equity. Therefore, considerations of probability of success in agricultural re-search should be put aside in favor of areas of need when allocations of resources are determined.

Research resources should be allocated between various compet-ing needs within a logical framework. Sub-Saharan Africa can first be divided into sub-regions or zones[16] determined by climatic, eco-nomic, administrative, or other factors, assuming that research con-ducted in one sub-region has little relevance for another. Conse-quently, physical and climatic factors should probably be used as the main criteria in making the divisions.[17] Once established, these demarcations can provide the basis for allocation of resources between the regions and among commodities and research topics.

As a simple rule of thumb, commodity and regional research allocations should be proportional to the share of the commodity or region in the total value of output (Boyce and Evenson, 1975; Ryan, 1978). M. von Oppen and J. Ryan (1981) have proposed a list of 10 criteria, using elements that affect the efficiency of agricultural research and the likely equity implications. They provide a composite numerical index which uses all 10 criteria to derive the required allocation of resources for an international agricultural research center.

Unfortunately, no comprehensive study has been undertaken of research resource allocations between commodities and livestock or between sub-regions in terms of the congruence between the actual and ideal allocation. Neither is it possible to perform such an analysis in the context of this chapter. We must therefore rely on indirect and partial analysis.[18]

From such a preliminary evaluation, the following points emerge:

- Diets in sub-Saharan Africa are dominated by consumption of cereals, roots, and tubers. While cereals account for 60 to 75 percent of the caloric intake in the Sahel, roots and tubers are most important in Central Africa, accounting for 50 to 65 percent of caloric intake. In humid West, East, and southern Africa, cereals account for between 20 and 35 percent. Livestock thus contributes less than 25 percent of total caloric intake. As expansion of livestock output is highly dependent on increased crop production, there is a strong case for placing primary emphasis on crop research in the short to medium term. Investment in livestock research should probably be maintained at present levels. Research in the Sahel should focus heavily on cereals, while roots and tubers should receive most emphasis in Central Africa.

- In terms of volume of production, the most important cereals in sub-Saharan Africa are maize, sorghum, millet, and rice, in order of importance. The most important root and tuber is cassava. While per capita food production has declined significantly in the past two decades, growth rates for cereals as a whole have been lower than for pulses or roots and tubers. Among cereals, the growth rates have been particularly low for millet and maize. As a result, the current allocation of available research funds between commodities is not optimum. In particular, there appears to be an insufficient allocation of available resources to millet and sorghum research.

• While population growth rates are uniformly high in sub-Saharan Africa, it is clear that agricultural research resource allocations to the Sahel should receive highest priority, followed probably by West and Central Africa.

• Consideration of allocations on a sub-regional basis and among areas of research underlines the inappropriateness of generalizations. Rather, decisions must be made in relative terms. Broadly speaking, more emphasis should be placed on soil, water, and forest conservation research than on genetic improvement in the Sahel. Conversely, in the more humid areas of West Africa where these factors are less constraining, the reverse is probably true.

THE RESEARCH SYSTEM AND TIME FRAME FOR AGRICULTURAL RESEARCH IN SUB-SAHARAN AFRICA

There is no substitute for national agricultural research. Countries that have made the most progress in agricultural development are also those that have established efficient and effective agricultural research systems (Mellor and Johnston, 1984; Evenson, 1981). Even if a national research system does not conduct "basic research," a substantial investment in national capacity is needed in order to gain access to and effectively use the advances in knowledge (Schultz, 1979; Ruttan, 1983).

While strengthening national research systems should therefore be given highest priority, these systems in sub-Saharan Africa face many operational problems. Oram and Binglish point out in a forthcoming study that many of the smaller African countries, and in Central America and the Caribbean, would not be able to support a national system capable of handling all their potential agricultural research needs even at a substantially higher rate of expenditure. Therefore, the efforts of national systems must be supplemented in the short to medium term by a system of sub-regional and international research centers.

These centers, in turn, should concentrate on research problems common to several countries. But because of variations in environment and natural resources and other constraints already discussed, individual programs will need to be at the most sub-regional in character. For example, sorghum improvement programs should be designed differently for the Sahel and for southern Africa.

If there is one thing that is clearly evident from reviews of research in sub-Saharan Africa, it is that the successful programs have been those that have not only been well-managed, but have also been long-term in nature (Eicher, 1984). Agricultural research must be cast within 10 to 20 year time frames, rather than the two to five years common in the past.

THE ROLE OF EXTERNAL ASSISTANCE

The primary responsibility for economic development in any country lies with its national government. However, many countries in sub-Saharan Africa would not be able to have sufficiently large national systems even if they increased research expenditures significantly. Prospects for domestic financing of research are even worse with the current dismal budgetary situation of many governments. Unless substantial assistance is forthcoming, agricultural research in Africa will be starved of funds, making it impossible to develop the technology on which future growth and development depend.

Indeed, given that the failures of agricultural development projects over the past decade were partly due to the inadequate stock of technologies ready for adoption by farmers, a major shift in donor resources away from extension or production projects and in favor of agricultural research is justified. This shift, however, should not affect emergency aid needed to combat the present famine and to help cover expected food deficits in the immediate future.

Donors should invest in human capital development as part of assistance to agricultural research. With a comparative advantage in high-level formal education and training at the masters and Ph.D. level, Western donors can help improve the quality of staff in national programs and build a stock of trained researchers. In this regard, it should be stressed that the number of people to be trained ideally would exceed the number of positions that must be immediately filled, as provision must be made for unavoidable losses to organizations and private enterprises.[19]

THE ROLE OF THE PRIVATE SECTOR

As the private sector is profit-oriented, industrial firms will undertake only strictly applied research in which they can expect to derive quick results. The private industrial sectors of most African countries are very small, as are the amounts that can be invested, compared to the magnitude of resources needed for agricultural research. Further, because of the long gestation period of agricultural research and the uncertainties of success, multinational corporations cannot be expected to engage in this activity in a big way.

As stated by Schultz (1979): "The only meaningful approach to modern agricultural research is to conceptualize most of its contributions as public goods. As such they must be paid for on public account, which does not exclude private gifts to be used to produce public goods" (reprinted in Eicher and Staatz, 1984, p. 337).

CONCLUSIONS

The dismal record of agriculture has contributed greatly to the poor economic performance of sub-Saharan African countries in the post-independence period. Domestic and international agricultural research systems must share the responsibility, as they have not produced a large enough stock of technological innovation capable of ensuring sustainable growth in aggregate agricultural output.

Researchers have had an inadequate understanding of small farmer goals and resource limitations, resulting in incompatible recommendations. In addition, an over-reliance on the technology transfer model has discouraged work on improving locally available plant materials and farming systems.

To improve the situation and lay the groundwork for future agricultural growth and development, an increase in investment in agricultural research and a change in the direction of research are required. Major increases in agricultural productivity can only be expected from investment in the agricultural research capacity which is needed to develop technologies appropriate to the region's natural and institutional environment.

Since agricultural development can only be brought about by widespread but gradual increases in productivity by small farmers adopting innovations appropriate to their factor proportions, research must concentrate on developing appropriate technologies such as crop varieties that are adaptable to limited areas and respond well to low doses of inputs such as fertilizers. Material inputs should be derived mainly from local sources and mechanization research should concentrate on improving hand tools and animal traction.

Major emphasis should be placed on soil, water, and forest conservation, and particularly on research to develop economical crop rotations including tree crops, leguminous species, and mixed farming. Top priority should be given to food crop research on sorghum and millet in particular. Although an increase in export crop research may be justified in some countries, present levels of investment in livestock research need not be increased until substantial gains have been made in crop output levels. Because many policy decisions are made with an inadequate knowledge base, policy research which includes substantial primary data gathering should be given high priority.

Major emphasis will also need to be placed on developing and increasing the efficiency of national research systems. But in the short to medium term, regional and international research centers must continue to play an important role in agricultural research in sub-Saharan Africa. Substantial donor assistance will be required in the short to medium term to ensure that these centers and national research systems receive adequate funding. Lastly, investment in research must be cast within a longer time frame than has been common in the past. These allocations must reflect a farming systems perspective and embrace the development of human capital.

NOTES

1. There is a substantial literature on this topic, starting with Lewis (1955) and including Ranis and Fei (1961, 1964), Jorgenson (1961), etc. For a review of the application of these and similar models to African countries, see Eicher and Baker (1982), pp. 30–35.

2. The onchocerciasis areas of the Volta River valley being opened up by control of the blackfly will permit limited application of the frontier model in the next two decades. But this will not make much impact on aggregate agricultural output.

3. These inputs were classified according to three categories: the capacity of public and private sector research institutions to produce new technical knowledge; the capacity of the industrial sector to develop, produce, and market new technical inputs; and the capacity of farmers to acquire new knowledge and use inputs effectively (Ruttan, 1980).

4. See Eicher and Baker (1982), Chapter II, for a review of theoretical perspectives.

5. To ensure success in these areas, considerable policy reforms particularly in marketing and pricing policies are counselled by the IMF and World Bank.

6. Three researchers played an important role in regenerating interest in intercropping research in sub-Saharan Africa. David Norman's farm surveys in northern Nigeria in the 1960s demonstrated the importance of the system

(Norman, 1974), while agronomic research, also in Nigeria, by Bede Okigbo and D.J. Andrews gave professional prominence to intercropping research (Andrews, 1972, 1974; Okigbo and Greenland, 1977).

7. For example, ICRISAT has reorganized its sub-Saharan African research program into one regional center in Niamey, Niger, three sub-regional teams in Zimbabwe, Burkina Faso/Mali, and Malawi, and one bilateral program in Mali (ICRISAT, 1984) and WARDA has established special research projects to do more fundamental research (WARDA, 1984).

8. For a good text on the techniques of food policy analysis, see Timmer, Falcon, and Pearson (1983).

9. The need for food policy analysis to consider these macro as well as micro issues is often neglected by many policy analysts.

10. As an example, the Central Bank of Nigeria's new report on the economy could give no figures on total crop production or on crop losses, etc. (Derrick, 1984).

11. Referred to as "upstream research" by Gilbert, Norman, and Winch (1980).

12. See, for example, the manual by Shaner, Philipp, and Schmehl (1982) which gives an otherwise excellent treatise on the methods and modalities of on-farm research.

13. See, for example, the large U.S.-funded Senegalese program with ISRA and the planned Malian program.

14. Perhaps a good example of the inappropriateness of this scaling-down approach to machinery development is the recent series of equipment developed for zero tillage in the humid tropics. To use the equipment requires land clearing techniques not found on small farms. The equipment can thus only be used by large farmers, yet it is billed as small farm equipment.

15. See Eicher and Baker (1982), Chapter VI, for a review of social science research in this area.

16. For allocation of national research resources, analogous subdivisions of a country could also be made.

17. Sub-Saharan Africa could for example be subdivided into Sahel, East, Central, and southern Africa (USDA, 1981).

18. Every research institution or donor agency should systematically examine its research resource allocation between commodities, programs, and regions, as has been done by ICRISAT (Ryan, 1978, von Oppen and Ryan, 1981, and ICRISAT, 1984).

19. Losses could of course be reduced by setting up attractive incentive schemes for researchers. But donor agencies could do little in this regard except try to convince national governments of the need to attract and keep trained researchers at their jobs.

REFERENCES

Abaelu, John. 1971. "The Nigerian Oil Palm Sector and Social Returns From Hybrid Palms." Agricultural Economics Seminar Paper. Chicago: University of Chicago, Department of Economics, January.

ADB/ECA. 1984. *Economic Report on Africa*. African Development Bank and Economic Commission for Africa.

Andrews, D. J. 1972. "Intercropping with Sorghum in Nigeria." *Experimental Agriculture* 8:139–50.

Andrews, D. J. 1974. "Responses of Sorghum Varieties to Intercropping." *Experimental Agriculture* 10(1): 57-63.

Berry, L. and M. Khogali. 1984. "The Physical Background to African Development." Background Paper, Committee On African Development Strategies, Washington D.C.: Overseas Development Council.

Belshaw, D. G. R. 1979. "Taking Indigenous Technology Seriously: The Case of Intercropping in East Africa." *IDS, Sussex Bulletin* 10:24–27.

Binswanger, H. P., and J. G. Ryan. 1977. "Efficiency and Equity Issues in Ex Ante Allocation of Research Resources," *Indian Journal of Agricultural Economics* 32:3.

Boyce, J. K. and R. E. Evenson. 1975. *National and International Research and Extension Programs*. New York: ADC.

Byerlee, D., C. K. Eicher, C. Leidholm and D. S. C. Spencer. 1983. "Employment-Output Conflicts, Factor-Price Distortions and Choice of Technique: Empirical Results from Sierra Leone." *Economic Development and Cultural Change* 31(2): 315-36.

Byerlee, D., L. Harrington, and D. L. Winkelmann. 1983. "Farming Systems Research: Issues in Research Strategy and Technology Design." *American Journal of Agricultural Economics* 64(5): 897–904.

CGIAR. 1978. Farming Systems Research at the International Agricultural Research Centers. Rome: TAC Secretariat.

CGIAR. 1978. Report of the TAC Quinquennial Review Mission to the International Crops Research Institute for the Semi-Arid Tropics (ICRISAT). Rome: TAC Secretariat.

Collinson, M. 1983. "Technological Potentials for Food Production in Eastern and Central Africa." Paper presented at the Conference on Accelerating Agricultural Growth in Sub-Saharan Africa, Victoria Falls, Zimbabwe, August.

Delgado, C. 1981. "Price Policy, Returns to Labor and Accelerated Food Grain Production in the West African Savannah," in *Food Policy Issues and Concerns in Sub-Saharan Africa*. Washington, D.C.: IFPRI, pp. 103–18.

Derrick. 1984. "Decline of Agriculture Shows No Sign of Slowing," *African Business* 76:17.

Doppler, W. 1980. *The Economics of Pasture Improvement and Beef Production in Semi-Humid West Africa*. Eschborn: German Agency for Technical Cooperation.

ECA. 1983. *ECA and African Development, 1983–2008*. Addis Ababa: Economic Commission for Africa.

Eicher, C. K. 1967. "The Dynamics of Long-Term Agricultural Development in Nigeria." *Journal of Farm Economics* 49:1158–70.

Eicher, C. K. 1984. "International Technology Transfer and the African Farmer: Theory and Practice." Working Paper, University of Zimbabwe, Dept. of Land Management, March.

Eicher, C. K. and Doyle C. Baker. 1982. *Research on Agricultural Development in*

Sub-Saharan Africa. East Lansing: Michigan State University International Development Paper, No. 1.

Eicher, C. K. and J. M. Staatz, eds. 1984. *Agricultural Development in the Third World*. Baltimore: Johns Hopkins University Press.

Evenson, R. E. 1981. "Benefits and Obstacles to Appropriate Agricultural Technology." *The Annals of the American Academy of Political and Social Sciences* 458 (November): 54–67.

FAO. 1974. "Provisional Food Balance Sheets, 1972–74." Rome: Food and Agricultural Organization.

FAO. 1978. *Regional Food Plan for Africa: Report of the Tenth FAO Regional Conference for Africa, 18–29 September, 1978, Tanzania*. Rome: Food and Agricultural Organization.

Gilbert, E. H., D. E. Norman and F. E. Winch. 1980. *Farming Systems Research: A Critical Appraisal*. East Lansing: Michigan State University, Dept. of Agricultural Econ., MSU Rural Development Paper No. 6.

Hayami, Y. and V. W. Ruttan. 1971. *Agricultural Development: An International Perspective*. Baltimore: Johns Hopkins University Press.

ICRISAT. 1980–83. *Rapport Annuel*. Ouagadougou, Burkina Faso: Programme Cooperatif. International Crops Research Institute for the Semi-Arid Tropics. ICRISAT/Burkina Faso, 1980, 1981, 1982, 1983.

ICRISAT. 1984. *A Long Term Plan for Developing International Cooperation*. International Crops Research Institute for the Semi-Arid Tropics, October.

IFDC. 1976. *Etude sur les engrais en Afrique de l'ouest*. International Fertilizer Development Center. *Muscle Shoals, USA*: Volume 1.

Jaeger, W. 1984. "Agricultural Mechanization: The Economics of Animal Traction in Burkina Faso." Ph.D thesis, Stanford University.

Jorgenson, D. W. 1961. "The Development of a Dual Economy." *Economic Journal* 71: 309–34.

Judd, M. A. L., J. K. Boyce and R. E. Evenson. 1984. "Investing in Agricultural Supply." *Economic Development and Cultural Change* (in press).

Lebeau, F. J., R. F. Chandler, C. E. Fergusson and T. Zalla. 1984. "Assessment of Agricultural Research Resources in the Sahel." USAID, May.

Lewis, W. Arthur. 1955. *The Theory of Economic Growth*. London: Allen and Unwin.

Lewis, J. K. D. 1982. *West Africa Rice Research and Production: One Crop, Fifteen Nations, and Multiple Ecologies*. Project Impact Evaluation, Washington, D.C.: USAID.

Matlon, P.J. 1983. "The Technical Potential for Increased Food Production in the West African Semi-Arid Tropics." Paper presented at the Conference on Accelerating Agricultural Growth in Sub-Saharan Africa, Victoria Falls, Zimbabwe.

Matlon, P. J. and D. S. C. Spencer. 1984. "Increased Food Production in Sub-Saharan Africa: Environmental Problems and Inadequate Technological Solutions." *American Journal of Agricultural Economics* (in press).

Mellor, J. 1984. "The Changing World Food Situation—A CGIAR Perspective." Paper presented at the International Centers Week, November 5–9, IFPRI, Washington, D.C.

Mellor, J. and B. F. Johnston. 1984. "The World Food Equation: Interrelation

Among Development, Employment, and Food Consumption." *Journal of Economic Literature* 22: 532–74.

McKelvey, J. J., Jr. 1965. "Agricultural Research" in R. A. Lystad, ed., *The African World: A Survey of Social Research*. New York: Praeger, 317–51.

Norman, D. W. 1974. "Rationalizing Mixed Cropping Under Indigenous Conditions: Example of Northern Nigeria." *Journal of Development Studies* 11: 3–21.

Oram, P. and V. Binglish. 1984. "Investment in Agricultural Research in Developing Countries: Progress, Problems, and the Determination of Priorities." IFPRI (forthcoming).

OAU. 1980. *The Lagos Plan of Action for the Implementation of the Monrovia Strategy for the Economic Development of Africa*. Lagos: OAU.

Okigbo, B. N. and D. J. Greenland. 1977. "Intercropping Systems in Tropical Africa" in R. I. Papendick, P. A. Sanchez and G. B. Tyiplett, eds., *Multiple Cropping*, Madison, Wisconsin: American Society of Agronomy, 63–101.

Paulino, L. 1983. "The Evolving Food Situation in Sub-Saharan Africa." Paper presented at the Conference on Accelerating Agricultural Growth in Sub-Saharan Africa, Victoria Falls, Zimbabwe.

Pichot, J., M. P. Sedogo, J. F. Poulain and J. Arrivets. 1981. "Evolution de la Fertilité d'un Sol Ferrugineux Tropical sous l'Influence des Fumures Minérales et Organiques." *Agronomie Tropicale* 36 (2): 122–33.

Ranis, G. and J. C. H. Fei. 1961. "A Theory of Economic Development." *American Economic Review* 51(4): 533–46.

Ranis, G. and J. C. H. Fei. 1964. *Development of the Labor Surplus Economy: Theory and Policy*. Homewood, Ill.: Richard D. Irwin.

Ruthenberg, H. 1974. "Artificial Pastures and Their Utilization in the Southern Guinea Savanna and the Derived Savanna of West Africa. Tour d'Horizon of an Agricultural Economist." (Two Parts). *Zeitschrift für Ausländische Landwirtschaft* 13(3): 216–31.

Ruthenberg, H. 1980. *Farming Systems in the Tropics*. 3rd ed. Oxford: Oxford University Press.

Ruttan, V.W. 1980. "Models of Agricultural Development" in Eicher and Staatz, eds., *Agricultural Development in the Third World*. Baltimore: Johns Hopkins University Press, 38–45.

Ruttan, V. W. 1983. "The Global Agricultural Support System." *Science*: 222.

Ruttan, V.W. and Y. Hayami. 1972. "Strategies for Agricultural Development," Food Research Institute, 9(2): 129-48.

Ryan, J. G. 1978. "Agriculture and Research in the Semi-Arid Tropics." Economics Program, ICRISAT, Hyderabad, India.

Sargent, M. J. Lichte, P. Matlon and R. Bloom. 1981. "An Assessment of Animal Traction in Francophone West Africa." East Lansing: Michigan State University, Department of Agricultural Economics, African Rural Economy Working Paper No. 34.

Schultz, T.W. 1964. *Transforming Traditional Agriculture*. New Haven: Yale University Press.

Schultz, T.W. 1979. "The Economics of Agricultural Research," In C. K.

Eicher and J. M. Staatz, eds., *Agricultural Development in the Third World*. Baltimore: Johns Hopkins University Press, 1984, 335–47.

Shaner, W. W., P. F. Philipp and W. R. Schmehl. 1982. *Farming Systems Research and Development*. Boulder: Westview Press.

Sparling, E. W. 1981. "A Survey and Analysis of Ex-Post Cost-Benefit Studies of Sahelian Irrigation Projects." Department of Economics, Colorado State University (mimeo).

Stolper, W.F. 1969. *Planning Without Facts: Lessons in Resource Allocation From Nigeria's Development*. Cambridge, Mass.: Harvard University Press.

Stoop, W. A., C. Pattanayak, P. J. Matlon, and W. R. Root. 1981. "A Strategy to Raise the Productivity of Subsistence Farming Systems in the West African Semi-Arid Tropics." *Sorghum in the Eighties*, 519–26, ICRISAT, Hyderabad, India.

Taylor, G., and M. Soumare. 1983. "Strategies for Forestry Development in the Semi-Arid Tropics: Lessons from the Sahel." Paper presented at the International Symposium on Strategies and Designs for Afforestation, Reforestation and Tree Planting, Waageningen, September 19–23.

ter Kuile, C.H.H. 1983. "Technological Potentials for Food Production in Humid and Sub-Humid Tropics of Africa." Paper presented at the Conference on Accelerating Agricultural Growth in Sub-Saharan Africa, Victoria Falls, Zimbabwe.

Timmer, C.P. 1973. "Choice of Technique in Rice Milling in Java." *Bulletin of Indonesian Economic Studies* 9(2): 57–76.

USDA. 1981. *Food Problems and Prospects in Sub-Saharan Africa: The Decade of the 1980's*. ERS, Foreign Agriculture Research Report No. 166. Washington, D.C.: United States Department of Agriculture .

Von Oppen, M. and J. Ryan. 1981. "Determining Regional Research Resource Allocation at ICRISAT." Economic Program. Hyderabad, India: ICRISAT

WARDA. 1984. Programme Achievement, Contribution to and Impact on Rice Development in West Africa. West Africa Rice Development Association, WARDA/84/STC-14/17. Monrovia, Liberia.

World Bank. 1981. *Accelerated Development in Sub-Saharan Africa*. Washington, D.C.: The World Bank.

World Bank. 1984a. *World Development Report, 1984*. Washington, D.C.: The World Bank.

World Bank. 1984b. *Toward Sustained Development in Sub-Saharan Africa: A Joint Program of Action*. Washington, D.C.: The World Bank.

CHAPTER NINE

Strategic Issues in Combating Hunger and Poverty in Africa

Carl K. Eicher

"Since most Africans are farmers, raising the productivity
of farmers is a sine qua non of raising the African standard
of living."—W. *Arthur Lewis*, 1955

Hunger and poverty in sub-Saharan Africa are two fundamental
problems that are morally unacceptable to Africans and to world
opinion. Hunger is especially intolerable in a world "awash with
grain," where North America, the EEC, and Japan are competing for
Third World markets and where enough food is produced each year
to provide every person with 3000 calories.

Sub-Saharan Africa[1] is a vast continent that defies easy generalizations. But amid its diversity and complexity, two important facts
stand out: Many African states have slowly lost the capacity to feed
their people, and Africa is the poorest continent in the world economy. In 1985, Africa's famine captured world attention and resulted
in a tripling of the 1983 level of food aid to 7 million tons of grain. But
both the Sahelian famine of the early 1970s and the Ethiopian famine
of 1985 are dramatic manifestations of longer-terms problems that
have been building up for two decades—increasing rates of population growth, lagging food production, malnutrition, and pervasive
poverty (Eicher, 1982).

African states are now receiving generous advice from many quar-
ters on what needs to be done to solve hunger and poverty, but much
of it is based on confusion over the causes of Africa's agrarian crisis.
There is little understanding of the technical and institutional requirements for agricultural change and a tendency to underestimate the

gestation period required to develop human capital, managerial skills, and bio-chemical technology—the prime movers of agricultural change.

This chapter is devoted to a discussion of the strategic issues in combating hunger and poverty in sub-Saharan Africa over the medium term (3 to 5 years) and long term (5 to 15 years); the nature of the problem and the required long-term response; the hunger and poverty battle; the role of agriculture in the macro-economic strategy of African states; the prime movers of agricultural development; food security policy dilemmas; and the role of foreign assistance in African agriculture under conditions of limited absorptive capacity.

THE NATURE OF THE PROBLEM AND THE REQUIRED LONG-TERM RESPONSE

Because the food outlook is bleak for many African countries, additional resources are being mobilized by private groups, charities, and donor agencies. However, before additional funds are pumped into African agriculture, it is important to examine the nature of the problem—the causes of hunger and poverty—and the required long-term response.

Africa-wide generalizations about rates of growth of population, food production, and per capita income tend to cloud many of the remarkable achievements of individual countries. Although Africa's economic performance has been poor, there are bright spots. For example, "Many countries, both middle-income (e.g., Ivory Coast, Cameroon, and Botswana) as well as some of the poorest (Rwanda and Malawi) have performed well for some time, achieving real average annual growth rates from about 5 percent to over 12 percent between 1970 and 1982" (Jaycox, 1985). Life expectancy has increased by 20 percent from around 39 years in 1960 to 47 in 1983.

What are the prospects for Africa's future economic performance? As a general rule, economic projections, even for individual African countries, should be made cautiously. In 1960, Africa was basically self-sufficient in staple foods, and some countries, such as Senegal and Nigeria, were significant exporters of groundnuts to Europe. In the 1960s, Africa's population growth rate was modest—1.5 to 2.0 percent—and new land was more or less automatically brought under cultivation by subsistence farmers without foreign aid-financed food production projects. However, Africa's rapid population growth since independence has raised some important issues. Food production has grown at half the population growth rate since the 1970s. Thus, one of the two core problems examined in this chapter is the food production-population battle.

THE FOOD PRODUCTION—POPULATION BATTLE

The starting point for understanding the food production-population battle is the rate of population growth—not the population density or the total size of a nation's population. In Africa, current rates of population growth of between 2.5 to 4.4 percent are extremely high by historical standards and imply a population doubling over a period of 15 to 25 years. A comparison between Africa and Japan is instructive. Japan is a textbook case of how a country with a poor natural resource base skillfully mobilized smallholder agriculture to finance its structural transformation from a feudal power in 1878 to an industrial nation by 1912. The agricultural sector made a strategic contribution to national development through a land tax that financed 63 percent of the national budget until 1902. Moreover, thanks to improved rice varieties and steady domestic terms of trade, the agricultural sector grew 2.3 percent per year, outstripping the population growth rate of around 1.0 percent over the 1878–1912 period.

In Africa, agricultural output grew by 1.7 percent between 1970 and 1985—a respectable rate in comparison with Japan's 2.3 percent over the 1878–1912 period (Ohkawa and Rosovsky, 1964). But Africa's population is currently growing at roughly triple the rate in Japan over the 1878–1912 period. Hence, there is a significant difference in one of the "initial conditions"—the population growth rate—in the early stage of Japan's modern economic growth and contemporary Africa. Kenya's annual population growth rate of 4.4 percent will require a doubling of food production in 16 years—a rate unprecedented in the early history of Japan and other industrial countries.

One of the simplest measures of population growth is the total fertility rate—a rough proxy for the average number of lifetime births per woman. Currently, the total fertility rate in Africa is 6.9 compared with 1.8 in the United States. But unlike in China, where there is concerted campaign to implement the "one family, one child policy,"[2] there is little debate in Africa today—even among academics—overpopulation and family planning, let alone political support for measures to reduce the average number of children per family from seven to five.

Today, demographers generally agree that family planning programs have been ineffective in Africa in the last 25 years, and that "no nation displays any significant sign of fertility decline" (Caldwell and Caldwell, 1984). Africa's population explosion will result in a doubling of population in 15 to 20 years in most countries, thus increasing pressure on land and natural resources, such as fuel wood, grazing areas, and national parks.[3]

It is time to shelve the misleading cliche that Africa is a land-abundant continent. Because of unequal population distribution in relation to agricultural potential and political barriers to international migration to land-abundant countries, calculating Africa's total food production potential is irrelevant to the ability of a sub-region such as the Sahel or a country such as Kenya to feed its population. The long-term trend is toward increasing population pressure on land and natural resources and growing food dependence on industrial countries (FAO/UNFPA/IIASA, 1982). Three policy implications emerge from this analysis. First, assuming that there will be no significant reduction in fertility over the next 10 to 15 years, the food needs of many African states will have to be partially met through food imports for the next 10 to 20 years, just as India drew on food aid for 15 years from 1956–71. Second, to double food production over the coming 15 to 20 years, many African governments will have to place substantially higher priority on the agricultural sector for several decades—not for one year as President Moi did when he declared 1984 the "Year of Implementation" in Kenya. Third, Africans cannot ignore population growth as they turn to industrial countries for food aid. Food aid and population control measures should be viewed as two sides of the same coin in policy and foreign assistance negotiations.

A PERSPECTIVE FROM INDIA ON THE TIME FRAME

India responded to Ethiopia's 1985 famine by donating 100,000 tons of food grain, but, surprisingly, this generous gift was not picked up by the media—perhaps because there is a perception in Europe and North America that India is still a food aid client of the West. India's achievement of a reliable food surplus in 1980 after two decades of pro-agricultural policies is of broad significance to African governments and donors as they start to pump additional aid into African agriculture.

Thirty years ago, India suffered poor harvests in two successive years, and the food emergency was met by a vast inflow of food aid, primarily from the United States, that extended for 15 years. India's food crisis of the mid-1950s shattered the heavy industry development strategy that was being pursued on the recommendation of the Indian mathematician, Professor P.C. Mahalanobis, head of the Indian Statistical Institute. Mahalanobis' heavy industry model reflected his pessimistic view of the ability of India's peasantry to mobilize agriculture as a leading sector of development, and his admiration for Russia's emergence as a world industrial power in one generation.

The seeds for the "long view" of agricultural reform were planted by a team of American agricultural scientists under the sponsorship of the Ford Foundation. The team's influential study, *Report of India's Food Crisis and Steps to Meet It* (India, 1959), made the case for long-term investments in human capital, research, irrigation, and infrastructure as the foundation for modernizing Indian agriculture; they argued that industrial development would founder without a reliable food surplus. India's policy response to its food crisis of the mid-1950s and bad harvests of 1965–67 led to a deemphasis on heavy industry and increased public investment in the agricultural sector over two decades. The United States and several other key donors linked expanded food aid to basic agricultural reforms.[4]

India became self-sufficient in food production in the early 1980s. But two decades after its concerted drive to modernize agriculture and achieve self-sufficiency in food grain, India has eliminated neither hunger nor poverty. A quarter to a third of the rural population lacks either access to land or income to buy enough calories. India is taking vigorous steps to deal with hunger through rural works programs, fair-price shops serving the urban labor classes, and carefully targeted food subsidies.

What can African states and donors learn from India's experience? There is no single answer, except what can be gleaned from a mosaic of interrelated factors: four decades of political stability without a coup; the skillful use of massive food aid shipments for 15 years until Green Revolution wheat and rice varieties gained widespread adoption; sound and consistent macro-policies for agriculture; investment in agricultural research, rural roads, and irrigation; and the introduction of a new institution—state agricultural universities—modeled on the U.S. system of land grant universities.[5] Although foreign aid to India amounted to a substantial $14 billion over the 1951–70 period, per capita aid was only $1.50 per year (Mellor, 1979, p. 89)[6]—an extremely modest amount compared to Africa today, where aid flows to some West African states are $50 to $75 per capita a year.[7] The main lesson for African states and donors, however, is not the role of aid in India's development, but the concentration on macro-economic policies favoring agriculture, technology generation, human capital, and strengthening agricultural institutions—over 25 years. One of the most painful lessons that has been learned about agricultural development in Africa is that it takes time to develop stable political structures, a competent civil service of high integrity, an indigenous scientific capacity, locally financed agriculture research, biologically stable and economically profitable technology for rainfed farming, and the development of local Masters and Ph.D. training programs to reduce dependence on expatriate assistance. The accumulated evidence of the 25 years since colonial rule suggests that the required response to hunger and poverty in Africa should be conceptualized in a time span of several decades, a period that makes a mockery of donors who are peddling projects—particularly institution-building projects—with three to five-year time spans.

THE HUNGER AND POVERTY BATTLE

Hunger is the lack of adequate nutrition on a temporary or chronic basis. Because there is no accepted agreement on the quantitative cutoff point between adequate nutrition and malnutrition, there is no consensus among specialists and international agencies on the number of hungry and malnourished in Africa. A conservative estimate is that about one-fourth of the African people or about 100 million were hungry and malnourished in 1985.[8] A decade ago, it was commonly assumed that protein shortages were the dominant cause of malnutrition, but recent research has shown that the key to good nutrition for most people is getting enough calories from several different sources.

A great deal has been learned over the past decades about the complex linkages between hunger and poverty. Hunger and malnutrition are caused primarily by one or more of the following: low productivity of family labor on subsistence farms; unstable output levels due to drought; lack of access to land; and lack of income to purchase adequate food on a timely basis. Expanded food production alone, however, will not eliminate hunger and malnutrition, as although the United States and India are self-sufficient in food, neither country has solved its hunger and malnutrition problems. There is increasing recognition that hunger is a function of multiple causes and that the hunger-poverty battle is a complex political struggle over how a society deals with poverty—the root cause of hunger in industrial and Third World countries.

Pervasive in Africa, poverty is a major cause of hunger because it prevents people from purchasing a calorie-adequate diet. The majority of the poor in Africa are subsistence farmers who are producing food at low levels of labor productivity. One of the most effective ways of raising real incomes of subsistence farmers in the short run is to increase the productivity of their main enterprise, staple food production. This can increase the per capita availability of home-produced foods, raise cash incomes through the sale of staple food, or enable family food needs to be produced with less land and labor, thus freeing these resources for other income-earning activities such as cotton production or off-farm employment (see Chapter 11). Historically, however, the only proven long-term solution to rural poverty is economic development, a process that absorbs some farm labor in rural small-scale industry and induces the migration of rural people to the industrial and service sectors.[9]

A few African states and donors are discarding the appealing but potentially misleading concept of food self-sufficiency, replacing it with "food security" as a strategic goal of national development. Food security is defined as the ability of a country to ensure that its population has access to a timely, reliable, and nutritionally adequate supply of food on a long-term basis (Eicher and Staatz, 1984).

THE ROLE OF AGRICULTURE IN THE MACRO-ECONOMIC STRATEGY OF AFRICAN STATES

The neglect of agriculture in most African states since independence raises two basic questions. First, has agriculture been neglected because policy-makers are ignorant about the strategic role of a reliable agricultural surplus as a foundation of industrial development? Second, has agriculture been neglected because policy-makers and researchers are confused about how to solve the dilemma of investing in agriculture to expand its future productivity, while having to tax it to develop other sectors of the economy?

With the growing consensus on the importance of agriculture to African development, one can conclude that agriculture has not been neglected in African policy circles because of ignorance. The second question, on the other hand, has to be answered partially in the affirmative because most policy-makers, civil servants, and donors are confused over how to find the proper balance between investing in and taxing the agricultural sector. This problem has plagued Western development economists for 30 years.[10]

The following illustrates why it is difficult to get African leaders to accept the view that the agricultural sector can be a motor of change in the overall economy:

- In the absence of the petroleum, minerals, or other non-agricultural sources of government revenue and foreign exchange, how does a government accelerate national development from an agrarian base when international trade in agricultural commodities cannot be counted on as a long-term engine of growth?[11]

- How does a government generate consistent political support among urban and military leaders for long-term investment in agriculture when a succession of coups and counter-coups "force" political leaders to emphasize crash programs "to get agriculture moving"?

- How does a government use agricultural pricing policies to achieve multiple objectives? For example, how does a government resolve the dilemma of raising producer prices to stimulate food production in the long run, when higher prices will make it more difficult for net food buyers (e.g., landless and urban poor) to meet their minimum nutrition needs in the short run?[12]

- How does a government promote structural change (e.g., Tanzania's Ujamaa resettlement program and Zimbabwe's land transfer program) without a large loss of production in the short run?

- What are the relative roles of technology policy, price policy, and institutional reform in bringing about increased farm production?

The following country illustrations highlight some successful and unsuccessful attempts at finding a meaningful role for agriculture in macro-economic strategies over the past 25 years. During the first two decades of independence, many African scholars and planners looked to Israel,[13] Yugoslavia,[14] China,[15] and other countries for successful development models that could be imported to assist in the "catching up" process. These imported models invariably failed. The failure of many ranches, state farms, settlement schemes, and government tractor hire schemes over the past two decades was partially a function of the inexperience and incompetence of political leaders and their foreign advisers. As President Nyerere of Tanzania recently reported: "There are certain things I would not do if I were to start again. One of them is the abolition of local government and the other is the disbanding of cooperatives. We were impatient and ignorant" (Nyerere, 1984, p. 828).

An important lesson that has been learned is that whether capitalist or socialist, the ideology of development cannot in and of itself generate agricultural development, as in both systems there have been many failures. Agricultural development is too complex to be a function of any single factor such as climate, ideology, or appropriate technology. Nevertheless, in terms of agricultural production goals, capitalism has proven to be a more reliable strategy than socialism at this stage of Africa's economic history. After 25 years of independence, there are no models of agrarian socialism in Africa that have produced a reliable agricultural surplus. At this early stage, most low-income African states lack the skilled managers and the vast information network required to manage state farms, plantations, or ranches with a high degree of efficiency. Tanzania's experience with agrarian socialism is instructive.

Despite Tanzania's well-publicized pro-agriculture strategy following the 1967 Arusha Declaration, the government compelled farmers to abandon their individual farms and to live in villages while quietly turning the price and income terms of trade against them. In fact, in 1980, farmers received 36 percent less for their food and export crops in real terms (after correcting for inflation) than in 1970 (Ellis, 1982, p. 272). After two decades of promises to get agriculture moving, President Nyerere retired in October 1985 leaving behind the legacy of a stagnant agricultural economy. Tanzania's inability to feed itself is the fundamental reason why African states no longer emulate Tanzania as a model of development.

On the other hand, Malawi, Cameroon, and Zimbabwe are the agricultural success stories of the 1980s. With consistent governmental support for agriculture over several decades, smallholders in Malawi have responded and produced a maize surplus in 8 of the past 10 years. Also minister of agriculture, President Banda systematically makes two "crop inspection" trips throughout the country each year at planting and at harvest time. Even during the 1984 drought year, Malawi produced a large maize crop and sold 50,000 tons to neighboring countries.

Cameroon is another under-reported agricultural success story. President Ahidjo and his successor President Biya have repeatedly emphasized that "the soil is the first and most dependable employer," earning more than 80 percent of the country's foreign exchange. Agricultural achievements in Malawi, Zimbabwe, and Cameroon have given political leaders and policy-makers a feeling of self-confidence. There is a growing sense within Africa that policy-makers should draw on their own experiences to solve their problems—a spirit of collective self-reliance at the heart of the Lagos Plan of Action. It is time to refocus the study of African agriculture, drawing lessons from African successes[16] and failures, as well as from India, Hungary, Brazil, Australia, China, and other countries.

A common denominator in Africa's post-independence history is political instability, which adds to the difficulty of developing and implementing a long-term agricultural development strategy. For example, Nigeria's six coups over the past 19 years have each been followed by a knee-jerk food production campaign under the banner of the Green Revolution and Accelerated Food Production.

PRIME MOVERS OF AGRICULTURAL DEVELOPMENT

Agricultural production must be doubled in many African states in order to catch up with the population growth rate. However, no amount of political will, policy reform, or change in relative prices of single commodities will achieve this unless policy-makers and donors concentrate on the prime movers of agricultural change over the medium to long-term:

- New technology that is produced by public and private investments in agricultural research.
- Human capital and managerial skills that are produced by investments in schools, training centers, and on-the-job experience.
- Accretionary growth of biological capital investments (e.g. improving livestock herds, planting, spraying, pruning and main-

taining cocoa and coffee trees) and physical capital investments in infrastructure such as small dams, irrigation, and roads.

- Improvements in the performance of institutions such as land tenure, marketing, credit and national agricultural research, and extension services.
- Favorable economic policy environment.

The first four of the prime movers require long gestation periods of from five to 25 years. For example, experience has shown that it takes 10 years of research on the average to produce a new plant variety, and another five to eight years in which to gain widespread farmer acceptance. It takes 10 to 15 years of graduate study and on-the-job training for an agricultural research scientist to be productive. Donors, however, are avoiding the long gestation investments required to develop indigenous scientific, managerial, and technical capacity. The World Bank has financed showcase components of human capital projects such as buildings for the faculties of agriculture at the University of Zambia, University of Nairobi, Rural Development Institute in Senegal, and the Kolo School of Agriculture in Niger. The EEC recently provided a $12 million loan for a new building for the Faculty of Veterinary Medicine, University of Zimbabwe, while Japan is financing a $6 million Veterinary Medicine Building at the University of Zambia. Buildings, vehicles, and equipment also weigh heavily in foreign aid loans and grants for agricultural research projects. For example, the World Bank is allocating roughly two-thirds of its $19 million loan to Senegal over the 1982–88 period to develop and rehabilitate six research stations, including laboratories and office space, and 106 houses on the stations; and to purchase 11 trucks, 20 tractors, 27 tillers, 205 vehicles, and 105 motor bikes. But delivering vehicles and constructing buildings can be completed in two to three years. Who will train the research staff after the present multi-donor-financed project is completed in 1988? Who will help the young Senegalese researchers gain experience and maturity in developing new varieties of millet, sorghum, maize, and cowpeas over the next 10 to 15 years?

The preference of donors and African states to finance buildings and equipment illustrates their poverty of thinking in the critical area of institutional development. It reflects a lack of understanding of the accretionary process of human capital formation and institution-building. The second characteristic of the prime movers is their com-

plementary nature. Payoffs to investment in applied agricultural research will be low unless there is an effective extension service to
diffuse the new technology. Likewise, payoffs to investing in agricultural extension services in Africa have generally been low because
many research services have had little to offer to extension agents. Let
us turn to the first prime mover—agricultural research to generate
new technology.

TECHNOLOGY GENERATION

Africa has an under-reported colonial history of crop improvements such as cotton in Sudan, Mali, and Senegal; oil palm in Zaire
and Nigeria, and hybrid maize in Zimbabwe and Kenya (Eicher and
Staatz, 1985). But with the exception of a few crops such as maize,
research in food crops was modest relative to export crops during the
colonial period. This neglect is easily explained because with low
rates of population growth and densities, African farmers could meet
increased family food needs by bringing more land under cultivation.

With a few notable exceptions such as maize in eastern and southern Africa and cassava in West Africa, farmer-tested food crop technology is almost non-existent in Africa. New production technology
for food crops, export crops, and livestock can be an important means
of generating income for farmers, allowing them to purchase an improved diet for their families. In short, hunger can be combatted by
expanding export crops, livestock, the sale of food, and rural off-farm
employment.

USAID has announced an innovative long-term plan to strengthen
national agricultural research services and faculties of agriculture in
Africa (AID, 1985b). Ideally, the World Bank and other donors will
cooperate with AID and work closely with African states in strengthening national research services and regional research networks and
improving the linkages between these institutions and the international research centers. As a first step, donors should design agricultural research and faculty of agriculture projects with a ten-year life of
project and fold many existing farming systems projects into broad-
based efforts to strengthen national research services.

HUMAN CAPITAL AND MANAGERIAL SKILLS

By any yardstick—literacy rates, percentage of school-age population in secondary school and universities, or percentage of expatri-

ates in scientific, managerial, and academic staff positions—Africa is at the bottom of the human resource scale in the Third World. What has been the response of donors? The World Bank approved two education projects for Africa totalling $24 million in 1984, representing 3.6 percent of its worldwide education portfolio of $694 million (World Bank, 1984). Currently, USAID has around 650 bilateral projects in 38 countries (AID, 1985c). Three of the 650 projects are supporting undergraduate and higher degree programs in agriculture in Cameroon, Uganda, and Zimbabwe, and 250 African students are being supported in long-term training (B.S., M.S., and Ph.D.) in various agricultural disciplines (AID, 1985b)—modest responses by two major donors to Africa's crushing human resource problems.

Kenneth Shapiro (1985) recently reported that the stock of human capital in scientific fields per million people in Africa in 1980 was about one-fourth the relative scientific strength of Asia in 1970. The quality and relevance of agricultural training in Africa's universities are coming under increasing scrutiny. Tanzania's bold decision to establish a new agricultural university—the Sokoine University of Agriculture—in 1984 was an outgrowth of President Nyerere's 1981 visit to the Punjab Agricultural University, one of India's 20 state agricultural universities established in the 1960s and modeled after the U.S. Land Grant System. The faculty of agriculture at the University of Dar es Salaam has formed the nucleus of the new university at Morogoro. But Tanzania is ill-prepared to finance a second university at a time when its treasury is almost empty.

Nobel Laureate T.W. Schultz recently reflected on the United States' leadership role in financing human capital in India and its record in Africa to date: "The role that U.S. foreign aid and that of American leadership. . .played in establishing the agricultural universities in India stands as a major achievement of permanent value. It was not a short-term undertaking. It entailed building a new institution (the state agricultural university) for the long-term. But regrettably, U.S. aid has failed to undertake any corresponding enterprises since then; to wit our dismal record throughout most of tropical Africa" (Schultz, 1983, p. 464).

At present, there appears to be little agreement among the departments of education and agriculture within UNDP, USAID, SIDA, FAO, FAC, the African Development Bank, and the World Bank on how foreign assistance can most effectively assist in strengthening Africa's indigenous capacity in food and agriculture. In the 1970s and early 1980s, major donors and U.S. foundations have retreated from investment in human capital. Having allocated 10.6 percent of its Africa budget to education in the 1960s, the World Bank reduced this to 4.1 percent in 1980–84 (Lele, in press).

RURAL CAPITAL FORMATION

In industrial countries, agricultural development was fueled by the mobilization of family labor for clearing land, picking stones, and building fences—an accretionary type of capital formation whereby land and livestock productivity improved over generations. Security of tenure plays a strategic role in converting family labor into capital formation because, with security, farm improvements can be passed on to the next generation. In Africa, there is a tendency for donors to concentrate on financing new agricultural projects while overlooking how to help African farmers and rural communities mobilize savings to finance their own investments.

RURAL INSTITUTIONS

The fourth prime mover is strengthening the performance of rural institutions from land tenure systems to farmer irrigation associations. Not only is there a paucity of literature on how to strengthen rural institutions such as national agricultural research, credit, and extension services, but this topic falls outside the realm of economics—whether neoclassical, political economy, dependency, or marxist. Research, pilot projects, seminars, and workshops are urgently needed to strengthen basic agricultural institutions over the next 10 to 15 years (Bonnen, 1982).

ECONOMIC POLICY ENVIRONMENT

A favorable economic policy environment, the fifth prime mover, is crucially important to facilitate the implementation of the four prime movers already mentioned. Policy dialogue and pricing policies have replaced basic human needs as code words in development circles in the 1980s. For example, Ernest Stern, vice-president of the World Bank, recently challenged the view that drought is the cause of African stagnation, asserting that "it was not nature, but policies which reduced Ghana's cocoa exports from 380,000 tons in 1973 to

160,000 tons 10 years later" (Stern, 1985, p. 5).[17] Aid administrators have commonly focused on policy reform as the fundamental issue in restarting African economies. Several donors have reported that pricing reforms have boosted the production of commodities such as maize in Zambia, sorghum in Somalia, and cocoa in Ghana by 30 to 50 percent. But the crucial point is not what happens to a single commodity but to aggregate farm production. There is solid evidence that favorable pricing policies are a necessary but not sufficient condition for boosting total agricultural production in the long run.[18]

Unfortunately, single commodity responses to higher prices oversimplify and mask the complex set of parallel actions that must be taken to boost the production of a broad range of commodities. For example, smallholders dramatically cut back on cotton production in Uganda in 1983–85 because they had waited for up to one year for the government cotton board to pay them for their crop. Instead, they used their land and labor to produce sunflower for cooking oil and maize for home consumption and export to neighboring countries. Therefore, it is time to shift the debate to the difficult art of gaining national political commitment and consistent donor support for the five prime movers as a policy package.

This analysis has highlighted the strategic importance of long-term investments in the prime movers of agricultural development in order to strengthen the productive capacity of the agricultural sector in the medium to long term. Food aid can be used to buy time until investment in these prime movers pays off. Donors need to come to grips with long gestation investments by making an explicit, up-front commitment to financing human capital and institutional development projects for 10 to 15 years; and by designing, implementing, and evaluating these institutional investments as a "core policy package" under the aegis of a consultative group of donors. But in the final analysis, donors will probably swing their weight behind the prime movers before African states do because the ruling elite in many African countries do not view agriculture as a motor of change. Hence, they are reluctant to shift gears from short-term projects with short-term political results to the prime movers as a coordinated national effort.

FOOD SECURITY POLICY DILEMMAS

As the food production and population race and the hunger and poverty battles are complex and inter-related, they must be analyzed within the political economy framework of specific countries. Neither slogans such as "Food First" nor computer scenarios can identify the complex trade-offs and consequences on production, consumption, nutrition, foreign exchange earnings, and government revenue of pursuing specific food security policies. Country-level research on the interaction between technology, institutions, and macro-economic policies is urgently needed to help resolve some of these policy dilemmas. The first step is to distinguish between food self-sufficiency and food security.

DEFINITIONS OF FOOD SELF-SUFFICIENCY AND FOOD SECURITY

The concept of food self-sufficiency implies the ability of a country to meet all its staple food needs with domestic production and storage under all weather conditions. Food self-sufficiency has a built-in supply (production) bias—increasing the production of food and the reliability of forecasts by installing early warning systems, and increasing grain storage as a hedge against drought and the uncertainty of buying food in international markets.

Food security is defined as the ability of individuals and households to meet their staple food needs on a year-round basis from home production, the domestic market, or imported food. Food security analysis deals with supply issues as well as with a wide range of factors that affect demand for food. A major premise of food security policy is that poverty or the lack of effective demand (purchasing power) is a major cause of hunger and malnutrition. Hence, food security researchers spend considerable time addressing demand factors such as policies and projects for generating income and employment, and income distribution policies that help the poor secure adequate calories. Demand factors are important because even if a country is self-sufficient in food, people can die if there are landless or poor who cannot translate their food needs into access to resources to produce or to buy enough calories to survive.

It is time to discard food self-sufficiency as a policy objective and to replace it with food security. Food self-sufficiency fails to address what combination of home production, domestic storage, food imports, and distribution programs is needed to meet the food needs of all members of society. As a policy goal, food security means that food policies of African governments and donors should not be limited to food production per se, but should encompass a broad range of policies to help rural and urban people increase their incomes and access to a reliable supply of food at all times. But gaining political and technical support for food security as a policy goal will take time.

The influential Berg Report on Africa (World Bank, 1981) helped shift the debate from equity issues to economic growth. Many economists now contend that expanded growth and international trade are key to increasing food security because the benefits from faster growth will "trickle down" to all members of society, thus enabling them to purchase their foods needs. But others believe that it will take too long for an increased rate of economic growth to trickle down to help the poor in the Sahel and northeast Brazil or the landless and unemployed in India. For example, Amartya Sen of Oxford University argues that India's food self-sufficiency is a hollow achievement relative to Sri Lanka and China where political priority has been given to the food needs of the poor. As a result, "the average Sri Lankan or Chinese can expect to live about a decade and a half longer than the average Indian" (Sen, 1984, p. 82).[19]

Many African nations have adopted explicit food security strategies and have prepared food security plans. The strategies of Senegal, a food-deficit state, and Zimbabwe, a food exporter, will be examined briefly to illustrate some of the complex food security policy dilemmas.[20]

SENEGAL AND ZIMBABWE

In recent years, Senegal has imported about half its annual cereal consumption. If present production and population trends continue, it may import about two-thirds of its food grain needs by the year 2000 (Abt Associates, 1985, p.iii). Senegal currently imports about 1000 tons of rice a day, mostly broken rice from Thailand at a relatively low price. Broken rather than long grain rice is the preferred staple of many Senegalese because it is cheap and it absorbs cooking oil during the preparation of the national dish, rice and fish. The Senegalese government is faced with several tough questions: How can food production be increased on rainfed and irrigated land? What role should international trade play in achieving an assured food supply—especially for urban consumers? What are the interactions between short-run and long-run policies to achieve food security? How can urban consumers be encouraged to consume more locally produced millet and sorghum and less imported wheat and rice? How will the food import bill be paid?

Since the 19th century, Senegal has followed a policy of agricultural specialization, exporting groundnuts and importing broken rice to supply both the urban and rural areas. Historically, the state has played a direct role in agricultural trade, legally monopolizing the groundnut trade, rice imports, and, until 1980, grain marketing. Over the past 15 years, drought has reduced domestic food grain and groundnut production. In the early 1980s, the combined effects of drought, a depressed world market for groundnuts, and the worldwide recession forced the government to review its agricultural strategy. To address the worsening food situation, the government announced a "New Agricultural Policy" in 1984 that called for: increased food grain self-sufficiency, primarily through irrigated rice production in the Senegal River Valley in northern Senegal, and millet and sorghum production in the Groundnut Basin; a greatly expanded role for private trade and farmers' cooperatives in input and output marketing; and a reduction in the activities of state-managed regional development authorities and parastatals. The new policy aims at production of 75 percent of the nation's food grain consumption by 2000 (Senegal, 1984, p. 6c).

In implementing the New Agricultural Policy, the government has had to face competing objectives—paying higher prices to farmers to encourage them to produce more and cushioning urban consumers from higher food prices—and the difficulty of developing private trade after years of state marketing. In launching the new policy, the price of imported rice was raised over 20 percent to reduce the budget deficit and to stimulate production of locally produced millet, sorghum, and rice. Yet, when the consumer price of millet and sorghum also rose, some government officials called for strict price controls on these cereals to help protect urban consumers.

The use of pricing policies to increase local food production is producing mixed results. For example, the cost of irrigated rice production on the large government-managed farms in the Senegal River Valley is extremely high by world standards (Ndiame, 1985). Government investment in these perimeters has reduced funds available for the development of rainfed crops such as maize in higher rainfall areas. Because traditional millet and sorghum varieties respond only modestly to fertilizer, an increase in the domestic supply of these food grains in response to higher relative prices is likely only at a high marginal cost. In addition, lacking clearly defined rules, private traders have been hindered from playing the role envisaged of them in the New Agricultural Policy (Sow and Newman, 1985). Senegal's agricultural research system is weak and has generated almost no improved food crop technology for farmers. This experience demonstrates the fallacies of depending almost totally on pricing policy to increase food production both in the short and long term. Senegal is a high cost food producer partially because its technology package is empty and partially because of ineffective government support services. A nationwide survey in 1984 revealed that the government fertilizer agency delivered fertilizer to farmers after 90 percent of them had completed millet planting and 38 percent had finished planting peanuts (Crawford, et al., 1985).

Senegal's failure to get its agriculture moving during the 20 years of Senghor's regime and the five years under President Diouf has imposed a severe hardship on the welfare of the population and has been a severe brake on the entire economy. Senegal is one of the few African countries where per capita incomes were about the same in 1985 as at independence in 1960. Ongoing food security studies suggest that Senegal should abandon its long-run goal of 100 percent food grain self-sufficiency. Since Dakar is a major seaport, it may be more efficient to try to assure food security by importing relatively low-cost broken rice while increasing millet, sorghum, and maize production for rural people. Alternatives to rice production in the irrigated perimeters of the north (e.g., vegetables and tomatoes for canning factories) should be considered as Senegal seeks more cost-effective ways of assuring its food security.

At independence in 1980, Zimbabwe inherited a dual agrarian structure of roughly 5000 large commercial farms and 700,000 smallholders. The fundamental problems in agriculture were the low productivity of smallholders, widespread poverty and malnutrition among commercial farm workers, a large landless population, and a rural infrastructure that had been battered by the guerrilla war (Blackie, 1981). In 1981, the government identified the "achievement and maintenance of food self-sufficiency and regional food security as an important national objective" (Zimbabwe, 1981). One of the fundamental policy dilemmas the Mugabe government has skillfully addressed is the redistribution of land and income to the urban and rural poor while maintaining the productive capacity of its commercial agricultural sector—a major earner of foreign exchange.

Despite poverty and malnutrition among smallholder families and workers on commercial farms, Zimbabwe has maintained its dual production structure in the short run. In 1985, commercial farms produced about 50 percent of cotton and the marketed surplus of maize, and 99 percent of the tobacco crop. The government has tried to improve the food security of the rural poor by raising the minimum wage of farm workers and by purchasing commercial farms on a "willing buyer-willing seller" basis, in order to transfer land to the landless. At the same time, aggressive steps are being taken to help smallholders expand rainfed crop production, especially cotton and maize, and to promote smallholder irrigation.

The government has followed pricing policies which favor agriculture, even though this may have increased the food insecurity of the urban poor in the short run. In 1983/84, the government eliminated Z$100 million in consumer subsidies on wheat bread, meat, dairy products, and refined maize flour—the staple food of civil servants. In an attempt to lessen the impact of these changes on the urban poor, subsidies were retained on their staple, coarse maize meal, and the minimum wage was increased. Following a three-year drought, the government raised maize producer prices 28.5 percent in June 1984,[21] four months before planting time for the 1984/85 crop. With favorable weather, farmers responded with a record maize crop, a large percentage of which came from smallholders. Zimbabwe is now developing inter-African trade agreements to sell its maize surplus.

Although Zimbabwe's experience is frequently cited as an example of the successful use of pricing policies to stimulate maize and cotton production, not all the increase in production should be attributed to higher prices and good weather. Zimbabwe's farmers are able to respond to favorable prices because they have access to well-functioning input and output markets, a seed coop supplied by a network of 200 commercial seed growers, an extension system that has given increasing attention to smallholders in recent years, and one of the strongest agricultural research services in Africa.

In 1949, Zimbabwe became the first country after the United States to develop hybrid maize varieties after 17 years of research (Eicher, 1984). Subsequent research led to the development of a long-season hybrid for commercial farmers—SR52—that can be called the green revolution of southern Africa. Although several hybrid varieties were developed specifically for smallholder growing conditions and made available to them in the mid-1970s, it was only with improvements in the marketing, credit, and extension systems, expansion of private fertilizer distribution facilities, and an end to the disruption caused by war that smallholders rapidly adopted the new varieties. The government of Zimbabwe is skillfully using pricing and technology policy as a package because it has a backlog of proven maize and cotton varieties for both smallholders and commercial farmers and it realizes that pricing and technology policies are complementary. In 1985, smallholders produced 50 percent of the maize and cotton marketed, up from 10 percent at independence in 1980.

Zimbabwe is one of Africa's agricultural success stories of the 1980s. The government has concentrated on the prime movers of agricultural development, walked a tight rope on efficiency and equity issues, devalued its currency to promote industrial and agricultural exports, and harnessed its agricultural sector as an engine of economic change. In spite of its success in increasing total food production and becoming a maize exporter, Zimbabwe's long-term food security also depends on its ability to deal with periodic drought, its rapid rate of population growth, and land hunger in a dual agrarian society.

FOREIGN ASSISTANCE UNDER CONDITIONS OF LIMITED ABSORPTIVE CAPACITY

Calls for more aid to Africa are gaining momentum. Music benefits raised $54 million for Africa in three months in mid-1985. The World Bank's Special Facility for sub-Saharan Africa—to compensate for the shortfall in the resources of the International Development Association (IDA), the Bank's concessionary affiliate—began operation on July 1, 1985. While hunger and famine are powerful magnets for resource transfers, it is important to keep in mind that:

- Although Africa has 16 percent of the population of Asia, Africa received more official development assistance (ODA) ($8 billion) in 1982/83 than Asia received.

- Although Tanzania consumed $2.7 billion of ODA over the 1973–82 period, its economy is stagnant, and Nyerere, like Nkrumah, will be viewed as a failure in domestic economic management.[22]

- Senegal has received a high aid allocation—about twice the level of ODA per capita of other African countries and four to five times higher per capita than Asian countries. However, after 25 years, Senegal's per capita income is about the same as it was at independence. In 1981 and 1982, official aid transfers amounted about one-fifth of Senegal's GDP.

- "The technological basis for increased production on the majority of Sahelian farms does not exist" (AID, 1985a, p. 9).

- In many countries, more aid cannot be absorbed in irrigation, rainfed farming, and livestock projects "with integrity" because of absorptive capacity problems, lack of improved technology, etc.

- African states are flooded with project aid which co-opts scarce human capital, such as African scientists and managers (Morss, 1984). Kenya had 1000 projects in all sectors in 1985; 40 of the 1000 were agricultural research projects or research components in agricultural and rural development projects.

- Technical assistance (expatriate advisers) is being increasingly questioned by Africans because of its cost ($80,000 to $150,000 per person per year), mediocre quality, and frequent turnover.

From this brief overview, foreign aid is faced with a number of serious challenges. The starting point is to examine how efficiently foreign assistance has been absorbed by African states.

ABSORPTIVE CAPACITY

In the 1950s, the phrase "absorptive capacity" emerged "as a rough measure of a society's ability to employ efficiently additional capital resources" (Rostow, 1985, p. 47). Constraints on absorptive capacity were repeatedly flagged during the 1960s because most countries had small pools of skilled personnel to staff their research stations, hospitals, and schools.[23] One of the most perplexing problems that African planners and foreign advisers have grappled with over the past 25 years is how to realize the desire of African political leaders to "catch up" with the industrial world given the modest capacity of most states to absorb available ODA[24] and foreign private investment. Problems of absorbing and using aid efficiently became especially acute when aid was doubled in real terms in just six years from 1975 to 1981.

Following the 40 percent compound rate of growth of foreign aid inflows to the Sahel over the 1971–78 period (Berg, 1983, p. 45), questions were raised about aid absorption. For example, the inspector-general of USAID questioned the Sahel's ability to absorb development assistance at the 1981 level (AID, 1981). Three years later, another team visited the Sahel and reported: "In project after project, one also found that AID project designers overstated the capabilities of the host governments to implement the projects. Despite nine years' experience, this continued to occur. Consequently, the host governments, unable to implement, were overwhelmed and the projects were ineffective" (AID, 1984, p. 20).

The reasons for the chronic absorptive capacity problems in Africa are directly linked to the colonial policies of under-investment in human capital and the failure of foreign assistance to strengthen indigenous training and research institutions while flooding Africa with project aid requiring local managerial capacity to implement, monitor, and meet the audit requirements of donors. Although donors have trained tens of thousands of Africans overseas since independence, this type of training is not a substitute for building local institutions to develop indigenous scientific and managerial capacity. Accordingly, from evidence across Africa, the absorptive capacity problem has been underestimated and skirted by both African states and donors for several decades. This problem should be addressed squarely before additional aid is pumped into African agriculture in the next few years, especially given the hundreds of organizations that are trying to help Africa under the banner of famine prevention.

OBJECTIVES OF FOREIGN ASSISTANCE AND
STANDARDS OF PERFORMANCE

The volume of foreign assistance transferred to Africa overshadows the quality of aid in comparative assessments of donor performance. Why is this the case? Many donors incorrectly assume that the primary objective of aid is to transfer resources from rich to poor countries and that the largesse of a particular industrial country can be ranked by the percentage of its GNP allocated to aid for the Third World. However, the correct criterion is to assure that the absorptive capacity is expanded and matched by the availability of capital for development programs which are in appropriate sectoral balance (Rostow, 1985, p. 330). This leads us directly to issues of absorptive capacity and recurrent cost and the standards of performance used by donors.

The absorptive capacity problem is being studiously avoided by most African states, by donors who typically equate the volume of resource transfers with "helping" Africa,[25] and by some donors who tolerate lower standards of performance in Africa. Edward V.K. Jaycox, vice president of the eastern and southern Africa department of the World Bank, recently reported that perhaps the most important reason for the high failure rate of projects in Africa is the fact that "African countries have not been held to the standards of performance common elsewhere in the world, including other low income countries" (Jaycox, 1985).

RECURRENT COSTS

Recurrent costs are an integral part of the absorptive capacity problem. A few years ago, many donors started to pay the recurrent costs of agriculture and health projects in Africa because of the devastating drought in the Sahel from 1968–73, the oil price shocks, and the general shift in donor priorities to helping the poorest of the poor. Donors' soft position on recurrent costs has been a major mistake because: it artificially elevates the number of projects beyond the ability of African states to manage them and it makes it difficult, if not impossible, to achieve effective donor coordination;[26] it takes the pressure off African states to mobilize rural resources to pay for water supplies, agricultural extension, agents and health services; and it promotes a delusional system of shadow government agencies, offices, titles, and local perquisites that can never be financed by domestic resources after foreign aid is phased out.[27]

A recent study in the Gambia showed that if all donor-financed agricultural projects were continued after their scheduled termination date (normally in three to five years), the operating budget of the ministry of agriculture would have to be increased by 70 percent (Tyner and Billings, 1984). Since the Gambia—like many other countries—is being pressed by the IMF, World Bank, and some bilateral donors to trim budgets and reduce the role of the state, a large percentage of the agricultural projects are likely to be picked up by other donors[28] or will fade away after donor assistance is phased out. The issue raised in the pioneering study by Tyner and Billings is fundamental: Is there a life after donor-financed projects? Addressing the recurrent cost problems at both sectoral and national levels is a major challenge for African states and donors. Most African states are treating the recurrent cost problem casually because they realize that donors have a penchant for starting new projects. As a result, it is relatively easy to repackage projects and get new donors to pick up where others have left off.

TECHNICAL ASSISTANCE: COST, QUALITY, AND TURNOVER

There is no exact figure on the number of expatriate advisers, teachers, scientists, and planners in public agencies in Africa, but the figure is in the tens of thousands. Technical assistance is coming under increasing attack in Africa because its costs are too high, its quality uneven, and its rapid turnover detrimental to institution-building. African states are increasingly using some of their international loans and grants to purchase three person-years of technical assistance from Third World countries for the cost of one person-year from industrial countries.

U.S. FOREIGN ASSISTANCE AND AFRICAN AGRIGULTURE

Since the United States is a large bilateral donor in Africa, it is important to examine what it is doing to combat hunger and poverty. In 1985, USAID channeled about $1 billion to 35 African countries through bilateral assistance and numerous regional programs. This figure does not include the emergency food assistance the United States provided to Africa in calendar year 1985. AID has dramatically reduced the number of its projects from about 900 to 1000 in 1984 to 650 in mid-1985 (AID, 1985c).

The number of African countries assisted by USAID has varied widely over the past 20 years. In 1966, USAID had technical assistance programs in 35 African countries. In the mid-1960s, under pressure from Senator Fulbright to reduce the number of "potential Vietnams," President Lyndon Johnson requested the American ambassador to Ethiopia, Edward M. Korry, to review the U.S. aid program in Africa. The "Korry Report" of 1966 recommended that the United States concentrate its aid program in Africa on a few "development emphasis countries" and lend its support to the World Bank for coordination of external aid.

In 1967/68, AID adopted a new policy that reduced its regular bilateral assistance programs to 10 countries (AID, 1967), following the guidelines of the Korry report. A number of regional programs—some hastily designed—were introduced as a way to channel U.S. assistance to small countries such as Benin, Botswana, and Swaziland. But the number of AID bilateral programs increased rapidly in the mid-1970s, partially in response to the Sahel drought[29] and the emergence of southern Africa as a policy priority. The USAID regional program for Botswana, Lesotho, and Swaziland was replaced by bilateral programs. But 20 years after the Korry Report, the number of AID bilateral programs is back to the 1967 level—35—and the same question remains: Can AID's technical staff and contractors (U.S. universities and consulting firms) in food and agriculture do a credible job in managing agricultural programs and projects in 35 countries?

Some hard choices now confront USAID, Congress, and the Executive branch. But, unfortunately, Congress is not getting sound counsel. The recent Office of Technology Assessment report on Africa is the product of a hurried effort by a team that assembled many facts but glossed over the tough technical, institutional, and political issues in getting African agriculture moving (OTA, 1984). USAID is scattering its limited technical staff across too many projects and too many countries to make a "significant difference" in combating food and poverty in Africa. Moreover, most U.S. ambassadors and their counterparts in other diplomatic missions in Africa are pressing for foreign aid projects that will produce what one U.S. ambassador recently described as "high visibility and quick returns." Currently, USAID is being forced to reduce the number of permanent staff in Africa as part of the budget reduction exercise of the federal government.[30] Unless basic issues of time frame, absorptive capacity, and strengthening the technical capacity of USAID programs are squarely addressed , U.S. foreign assistance in Africa will not achieve its full potential.

AID is now in the process of consolidating its Sahel program (AID, 1985a), reducing the number of projects in Africa, and implementing an innovative plan to strengthen national agricultural research services and faculties of agriculture over the next 20 years (AID, 1985c). Nevertheless, USAID will find it difficult to deliver on its present food and agriculture programs in 35 countries unless its agricultural staff (career and contractors) is increased in quality. AID currently does not have a full-time irrigation specialist in the bureau for Africa in Washington or in its regional offices in Abidjan and Nairobi.

CONCLUSIONS

While famine has faded from much of Asia since the mid-1970s, famine and chronic hunger have become more prominent in Africa, leading not only to massive short-term relief efforts, but also to crash programs to increase food production. In dealing with hunger and poverty in Africa, it is important to recognize that many of the hungry, particularly the chronically hungry, are malnourished not because the aggregate supply of food is inadequate, but because the poor lack the purchasing power to buy a calorie-adequate diet. Improving the food security of the poor requires measures to increase their purchasing power. Food security should replace food self-sufficiency as a policy goal for African states and become the focal point of donor assistance to food and agriculture in Africa.

Further, it is time to stop thinking of Africa as a land-abundant continent. Because of vastly different rainfall levels and patterns and availability of locally adopted technology, there are better prospects for food production outstripping population growth in the temperate climates in southern Africa than in the semi-arid zone of Sahelian West Africa. The message is clear—it is time to focus on sub-regions and examine the problems unique to each region rather than discussing Africa in homogenous terms.

In the long run, given appropriate policies and investments in the prime movers of African agriculture—human capital, agricultural research, bio-physical capital, and strengthened rural institutions—most countries have the physical capacity to feed themselves. But in the short to medium term, population growth is generating food needs in many countries that cannot be met except through food grain imports. Just as India did, African states should learn how to increase the efficiency of food aid. Donors should link long-term food aid to tough policy reforms, including a fundamental reordering of development priorities in favor of agriculture. But this will require a degree of donor coordination that has not been achieved in Africa over the past 25 years.

The issue of aid and African agriculture has raised some fundamental problems that require further analysis, debate, and change. Donors—large and small, bilateral and multilateral—do not have a coherent plan to assist Africa in combating hunger and poverty in the 1980s and 1990s. In many sectors—rainfed farming, irrigation, and livestock—additional aid cannot be absorbed given Africa's limited capacity, lack of profitable technical packages, the project mode of delivering aid, and lip service to donor coordination.

Donor attention should shift from short-term pricing policy reforms to a number of complex and parallel investments in the prime movers of agricultural development. Each must be examined as part of a core investment package covering a period of 10 to 20 years.

It is time to jettison donors' preoccupations with increasing the quantity of resource transfers to Africa. Immediate priority must be given to increasing the efficiency of existing foreign assistance-financed programs and projects. As part of this process, the following problems should be addressed: absorptive capacity, indigenous scientific and managerial capacity, recurrent costs, standards of performance, donor coordination, and marshalling donor support for the prime movers of agricultural development. The large volume of aid enables African political leaders to avoid some hard decisions on food and agriculture. Finally, while the U.S. Congress has encouraged USAID to operate bilateral programs in 35 African countries, unless USAID concentrates on the prime movers of agricultural change over the next 10 to 15 years, the United States will not make a significant difference in helping African countries tap their large agricultural potential.

ACKNOWLEDGMENT

The research supporting this chapter was financed by the U.S. Agency for International Development, Bureau for Science and Technology and Bureau for Africa, under a "Food Security in Africa" cooperative agreement with the Department of Agricultural Economics, Michigan State University.

NOTES

1. Hereafter referred to as Africa.

2. Reports from rural areas of China indicate that there is strong resistance to this policy and a failure of some local authorities to enforce it.

3. In Zimbabwe, the National Park Service is examining how farmers surrounding national parks can harvest some of the game on the edge of the parks while retaining the basic integrity of the parks. Large game have to be culled in Zimbabwe's parks and boreholes supply water at critical times of the year in order to maintain the animal herds for tourists.

4. For two accounts of the constructive role played by donors in bringing about agricultural policy reforms in India in the 1960s, see Rostow (1985, pp. 176–78) and Paarlberg (1985, pp. 143–70).

5. See Mellor (1979); Sen (1981); and Lele (1984).

6. To put this figure of $1.50 per capita aid in perspective, it is worth about $4.00 to $5.00 in 1985 prices.

7. In 1981, the eight countries in the Sahelian region of West Africa, with a total population of 34 million, received $1.96 billion in Official Development Assistance (ODA) or $56 per capita (AID, 1985a).

8. Based on unpublished data from FAO, Rome, June 1985.

9. In China, there is nearly complete prohibition of rural to urban migration. Permitting migration would imply that industrialization and urbanization would eliminate rural poverty instead of the official self-reliance strategy which challenges farmers to escape from poverty by increasing farm productivity and encourages villages to improve social services to hold people in rural areas (Perkins and Yusuf, 1984, p. 200).

10. For a synthesis of agricultural development ideas in historical perspective, see Staatz and Eicher (1984). See Delgado and Mellor (1984) for an analysis of required structural changes in African agriculture.

11. See World Bank (1983) and Duncan (1984).

12. See Timmer, Falcon, and Pearson (1983) for a seminal analysis of the food price dilemma.

13. Chief Akin Deko, then minister of agriculture, Western Nigeria, led a delegation to Israel in 1959 to study Kibbutz and Moshav settlements. Based on their favorable impressions, Nigeria imported the Moshav model and spent about $50 million before the schemes collapsed in the late 1960s.

14. A team of planners in Yugoslavia prepared Ethiopia's first development plan and sent the plan to Addis Ababa via the diplomatic pouch.

15. A steady stream of African heads of state, including President Mobutu of Zaire, visited China to find the key to agricultural development. When President Mobutu returned to Zaire, he declared agriculture to be the "priority of priorities" for 1974. In Kinshasa in 1974, civil servants spent Saturdays tending their gardens and farm plots following directives from the Presidency.

16. See Lamb and Muller's (1982) account of the highly successful Kenya Tea Development Authority, a parastatal that assists 18,000 smallholders in tea production, processing, and marketing.

17. Stern's comments are echoed by a plea for policy reform by the Nordic countries (Nordic Delegation, 1984). For an influential study of the political rationale for seemingly irrational agricultural policies, see Bates (1981).

18. The late Raj Krishna (1982) of Delhi University contends that if price policy alone is used as the sole instrument to raise agricultural output in the long run, the inflationary effects would be untenable on both economic and political grounds. Krishna is of the opinion that "a balanced policy should stress a technology policy more than price policy, while the price environment is kept as favorable as possible" (p. 256).

19. The 1983 life expectancy is as follows: India, 55; China, 67; Sri Lanka, 69 (World Bank, 1985a).

20. This section draws on Eicher and Staatz (1984).

21. Since inflation was running about 20 percent per annum, the real price increase received by farmers was positive.

22. But the donors are an integral part of Tanzania's stagnation. T.W. Schultz contends that "the relationships among the official foreign aid donors of the high income countries are all too cozy. . . .For example, a compe-

tent analysis of the actual harm that has been done by the aid of the World Bank, the IMF, and other multilateral UN agencies to the economy of Tanzania, would be exceedingly instructive" (Schultz, 1983, pp. 460–61).

23. For example, in 1964, there were only three African scientists in all of the agricultural research stations in East Africa (Kenya, Tanzania, and Uganda), (Johnston, 1964, p. iii).

24. ODA refers to concessional transfers for development purposes with a grant element of at least 25 percent.

25. The concept of "moving money" has been used as a proxy for "helping the Sahel." The Club du Sahel, OECD, Paris, reports that "with respect to the volume of donor assistance to the Sahel, it is possible to make a specific assessment of the Club's contribution. Donor flows have clearly increased since the creation of the Club du Sahel in 1975. In 1976 , ODA commitments for Sahel countries were $817 million. Soon after the Club's inception, donor commitments began to grow, rising from $817 million in 1975. . .to $1.9 billion in 1981" (De Lattre and Fell, 1984, p. 80).

26. For example, in the Eastern region of Burkina Faso in March 1981, there were 10 different donor projects providing credit funds to the government extension agency: USAID, 4; UN, 3; France, 2; and the Swiss, 1. Moreover, the quantum jump in donor assistance for integrated rural development projects increased the number of extension agents in the region from 24 in 1978 to 149 in 1981. In Kenya, there are roughly 20 different kinds of water pumps in rural areas that have been supplied by donors. Getting spare parts is a nightmare.

27. For example, the World Bank has established a "shadow" statistical organization in Nigeria to collect data for Bank-financed agricultural projects.

28. Since Italy is a relative newcomer in the donor community in Africa, it is common knowledge that it has taken over many marginal projects that other donors have "shed" from their portfolios.

29. For example, in Burkina Faso, the United States opened a small bilateral aid mission after independence but terminated it in the mid-1960s. In 1973, the United States provided $12 million of emergency food relief and launched 16 short-term recovery and relief projects totalling $3.2 million. In September 1974, USAID opened a small Country Development Office and began to implement larger-scale, longer-term development projects. In May 1978, with the increased scale of development programming, the Country Development Office was turned into a full USAID bilateral mission. But in 1985, USAID is cutting back its program in Burkina to a skeleton operation because of policy differences with the Burkina government.

30. USAID is planning to reduce its worldwide direct-hire (career) staff in 1986 and again in 1987.

REFERENCES

Abt Associates. 1985. *Senegal Agricultural Policy Analysis*. Report to USAID/ Senegal. Cambridge, Massachusetts.

AID. 1967. *U.S. Foreign AID in Africa*. Washington, D.C.: Agency for International Development.

AID. 1981. *Improvements Must be Made in the Sahel Regional Program*. Washington, D.C.: The Inspector General, March 10.

AID. 1984. *Inadequate Design and Monitoring Impede Results in Sahel Food Production Projects*. Washington, D.C.: The Inspector General, January 31.

AID. 1985a. *Sahel Development Program: Annual Report to the Congress*. Washington, D.C., March.

AID. 1985b. *Plan for Supporting Agricultural Research and Faculties of Agriculture in Africa*. Washington, D.C., May.

AID. 1985c. *Agriculture and Rural Development: Functional Review FY 1978-86*. Washington, D.C.: Africa Bureau, Office of Technical Resources, Agriculture and Rural Development Division, July.

Bates, Robert. 1981. *Markets and States in Tropical Africa: The Political Basis of Agricultural Policies*. Berkeley: University of California Press.

Berg, Elliot. 1983. *Absorptive Capacity in the Sahel Countries*. Paris: OECD, Club du Sahel, April.

Bingen, R. James. 1985. *Food Production and Rural Development in the Sahel: Lessons From Mali's Operation Riz-Segou*. Boulder: Westview Press.

Blackie, Malcolm. 1981. "A Time To Listen: A Perspective on Agricultural Policy in Zimbabwe." Harare: University of Zimbabwe, Department of Land Management, Working Paper 5/81.

Bonnen, James. 1982. "Technology, Human Capital and Institutions: Three Factors in Search of an Agricultural Research Strategy." East Lansing: Michigan State University, Department of Agricultural Economics, Ag. Econ. Staff Paper No. 82-117.

Busch. L. and W. Lacy, eds. 1984. *Food Security in the United States*. Boulder: Westview Press.

Caldwell, John C. and Pat Caldwell. 1984. "Cultural Forces Tending to Sustain High Fertility in Tropical Africa." Australian National University (draft).

Carter, Gwendolen and Patrick O'Meara, eds. 1985. *African Independence: The First Twenty-Five Years*. Bloomington: Indiana University Press.

Chigaru, P. R. N. 1984. "Future Directions of the Department of Research and Specialist Services, Ministry of Agriculture, Zimbabwe." Harare: Ministry of Agriculture, Department of Research and Specialist Services, November.

Crawford, Eric, Curtis Jolly, Valerie Kelly, Philippe Lambrecht, Makhona Mbaye and Matar Gaye. 1985. "A Field Study of Fertilizer Distribution and Use in Senegal, 1984: Final Report." Dakar: Institut Sénégalais de Recherche Agricole.

DeLattre, Ann and Arthur M. Fell. 1984. *The Club du Sahel: An Experiment in International Cooperation*. Paris: OECD.

Delgado, Christopher and John W. Mellor. 1984. "A Structural View of Policy Issues in African Agricultural Devlopment," *American Journal of Agricultural Economics* 66(5):665-70.

Duncan, Ronald, ed. 1984. "The Outlook for Primary Commodities, 1984 to 1995." Staff Working Paper No. 11. Washington, D.C.: The World Bank.

Eicher, Carl K. 1982. "Facing up to Africa's Food Crisis." *Foreign Affairs*, Fall.

Eicher, Carl K. 1984. "International Technology Transfer and the African Farmer: Theory and Practice." Harare: University of Zimbabwe, Department of Land Management, Working Paper 3/84.

Eicher, Carl K. 1985. "Agricultural Research for African Development: Problems and Priorities for 1985–2000," paper presented at a World Bank Conference at Bellagio, Italy, February 25–March 1.

Eicher, Carl K. and Doyle C. Baker. 1982. *Research on Agricultural Development in Sub-Saharan Africa: A Critical Survey*. MSU International Development Paper No. 1. East Lansing: Michigan State University, Department of Agricultural Economics.

Eicher, Carl K. and John M. Staatz, eds. 1984. *Agricultural Development in the Third World*. Baltimore: The Johns Hopkins University Press.

Eicher, Carl K. and John M. Staatz. 1985. "Food Security Policy in Sub-Saharan Africa," paper presented at the XIXth Conference of the International Association of Agricultural Economists, Malaga, Spain, August 25–September 5.

Ellis, Frank. 1982. "Agricultural Price Policy in Tanzania," *World Development* 10(4).

Evenson, Robert E. 1984. "Benefits and Obstacles in Developing Appropriate Agricultural Technology." in Eicher and Staatz (1984), pp. 348–61.

FAO/UNFPA/IIASA. 1982. *Potential Population Supporting Capacities of Lands in the Developing World*. Report of Project INT/75/P13, Land Resources for Populations of the Future, FAO, Rome.

FAO. 1984. *SADCC Agriculture: Toward 200*. Rome.

Higgins, Benjamin. 1959. *Economic Development: Principles, Problems and Policies*. New York: Norton.

India, Ministry of Food and Agriculture. 1959. *Report on India's Food Crisis and Steps to Meet it*. New Delhi.

Jaycox, Edward V. K. 1985. "Africa: Development Challenges and the World Bank's Response." Lecture, Woodrow Wilson International Center for Scholars, Smithsonian Institution, Washington, D.C., August 6.

Johnston, Bruce. 1964. "The Choice of Measures for Increasing Agricultural Productivity: A Survey of Possibilities in East Africa," *Tropical Agriculture* 41(2):91–113.

Kerr, Richard. 1985. "Fifteen Years of African Drought," *Science* 227 (March 22).

Krishna, Raj. 1982. "Some Aspects of Agricultural Growth, Price Policy and Equity in Developing Countries," *Food Research Institute Studies* 38(3):219-60.

Lamb, Geoffrey and Linda Muller. 1982. *Control, Accountability and Incentives in a Successful Development Institution: The Kenya Tea Development Authority*. Washington, D.C.: World Bank, Staff Working Papers, No. 550.

Lele, Uma. 1984. "Rural Africa, Modernization, Equity and Long-Term Development," in Eicher and Staatz, pp. 436–52.

Lele, Uma. In Press. "Growth of Foreign Assistance and Its Impact on Agriculture," in Mellor, Delgado and Blackie.

Lewis, W. Arthur. 1955. "The Economic Development of Africa," in *Africa in the Modern World*. Calvin W. Stillman, ed. Chicago: University of Chicago Press, pp. 97–112.

Lewis, John P. 1985. "Aid, Structural Adjustment and Senegalese Agriculture." Princeton: Princeton University, Woodrow Wilson School (draft).

Mellor, John W. 1979. "The Indian Economy: Objectives, Peformance and Prospects." *India: A Rising Middle Power*, ed. John W. Mellor. Boulder: Westview Press, pp. 85–110.

Mellor, John W., Christopher Delgado and Malcolm J. Blackie. In Press *Accelerating Food Production Growth in Sub-Saharan Africa*. Baltimore: The Johns Hopkins University Press.

Morss, Elliott. 1984. "Institutional Destruction Resulting from Donor and Project Proliferation in Sub-Saharan African Countries," *World Development* 12(4): 465–70.

Ndegwa, Philip. 1985. *Africa's Development Crisis and the Related International Issues*. Nairobi: Heinemann.

Ndiame, Fadel. 1985. "A Comparative Analysis of Alternative Irrigation Schemes and the Objective of Food Security: The Case of the Fleuve Region in Senegal," unpublished M.S. thesis, Department of Agricultural Economics, Michigan State University.

Nordic Delegation. 1984. "Policies in Agriculture and Rural Development: A Nordic View," Nordic position paper, SADCC conference, Lusaka, 1–3 February.

Nyerere, Julius. 1984. "Interview," *Third World Quarterly* 6(4):815–38.

Office of Technology Assessment, U.S. Congress. 1984. *African Tomorrow: Issues in Technology, Agriculture and U.S. Foreign Aid; A Technical Memorandum*. Washington, D.C.

Ohkawa, Kazushi and Henry Rosovsky. 1964. "The Role of Agriculture in Modern Japanese Development," in *Agriculture in Economic Development*, eds. Carl K. Eicher and Lawrence Witt. New York: McGraw-Hill, pp. 45–68.

Paarlberg, Robert L. 1985. *Food Trade and Foreign Policy: India, the Soviet Union, and the United States*. Ithaca: Cornell University Press.

Perkins, Dwight and Shahid Ysuf. 1984. *Rural Development in China*. Baltimore: The Johns Hopkins University Press.

Reutlinger, Shlomo. 1984. "Project Food Aid and Equitable Growth: Income-Transfer Efficiency First," *World Development* 12(9):901–11.

Reutlinger, Shlomo and Marcelo Selowsky. 1976. *Malnutrition and Poverty: Magnitude and Policy Options* (World Bank Staff Working Paper No. 21). Baltimore: The Johns Hopkins University Press.

Rostow, W. W. 1985. *Eisenhower, Kennedy and Foreign Aid*. Austin: University of Texas Press.

Schuh, G. Edward. 1985. "Strategic Issues in International Agriculture." Washington, D.C.: World Bank, Agriculture and Rural Development Department, draft.

Schultz, T. W. 1983. "A Critique of the Economics of U.S. Foreign AID," in *Issues in Third World Development*, eds. K. C. Nobe and R. K. Sampath. Boulder: Westview Press.

Sen, Amartya K. 1981. *Poverty and Famines: An Essay on Entitlement and Deprivation*. Oxford: Clarendon Press.

Sen, Amartya K. 1984. "Food Battles: Conflicts in the Access to Food," *Food and Nutrition* 10(1):81–90.

Sénégal, République du. 1984. *Nouvelle Politique Agricole*. Dakar: Ministère du Développement Rural, Mars–Avril.

Shapiro, Kenneth. 1985. "Strengthening Agricultural Research and Educational Institutions in Africa." Hearings, the Subcommittee on Foreign Operations, the Senate Committee on Appropriations, U.S. Senate, Washington, D.C., March 26.

Sklar, Richard. 1985. "The Colonial Imprint on African Political Thought," in Carter and O'Meara, pp. 1–30.

Sokoine University of Agriculture. 1985. *The Mission of Sokoine University of Agriculture*. Morogoro: Tanzania, April.

Sow, P. Allansane and Mark D. Newman. 1985. "La Réglementation et l'Organisation des Marchés Céréaliers au Sénégal: Situation des Campagnes de Commercialisation 1983:84 et 1984:85." Dakar: ISRA/BAME Document de Travail 85-2.

Staatz, John and Carl K. Eicher. 1984. "Agricultural Development in Historical Perspective." in Eicher and Staatz, pp. 3–30.

Stern, Ernest. 1985. "Speech at the Overseas Development Council," Washington, D.C., February 20.

Timmer, C. Peter, Walter P. Falcon and Scott R. Pearson. 1983. *Food Policy Analysis*. Baltimore: The Johns Hopkins University Press.

Tyner, Wallace and Martin Billings. 1984. "Recurrent Costs of Agricultural Sector Projects in the Gambia." Abidjan: USAID, November.

Valdes, Alberto, ed. 1981. *Food Security for Developing Countries*. Boulder: Westview Press.

World Bank. 1981. *Accelerated Development in Sub-Saharan Africa: An Agenda for Action*. Washington, D.C.

World Bank. 1983. *The Outlook for Primary Commodities*. Washington, D.C.: Staff Commodity Working Papers, No. 9.

World Bank. 1984. *Annual Report, 1984*. Washington, D.C.

World Bank. 1985a. *Ensuring Food Security in the Developing World: Issues and Options*. Washington: Agriculture and Rural Development Department, November 15.

World Bank. 1985b. *World Development Report 1985*. Washington, D.C.

Zimbabwe, Government of. 1981. *Growth With Equity*. Harare.

PART IV

INDUSTRY

CHAPTER TEN

Can Africa Industrialize?

A.M. Hawkins

"Industrialization is the main hope of most poor countries trying to increase their levels of income." Expressed 30 years ago by Hollis B. Chenery, this view continues to hold sway among economists, planners, and policy-makers for whom industrialization and economic development are synonymous. The development of a dynamic manufacturing sector has typically marked a country's transition from low to intermediate income levels. However, since the 1950s, only a handful of countries—the so-called newly industrializing countries (NICs) of East Asia and Latin America—have achieved such a change in status. In sub-Saharan Africa, only Zimbabwe, where manufacturing output contributes one-quarter of the gross domestic product (GDP), comes close to having attained such a transformation.

Africa lags far behind the rest of the developing world in industrial development. Although the share of manufacturing in sub-Saharan Africa's GDP has risen since 1960, it remained under 10 percent by 1980—well below the average share of other developing regions. To some extent, the rising share of manufacturing actually reflects sluggish agricultural performances rather than vigorous industrial expansion, as taxation and subsidies have artificially shifted price factors in favor of manufacturing. On the other hand, however, existing data almost certainly understates the extent of industrialization in Africa, as official statistics do not include most small-scale manufacturing industries which account for an estimated 20 percent of Africa's total manufacturing output.

While Africa's share of the world's manufacturing value added (MVA) rose by 32 percent, from 0.41 percent in 1963 to 0.54 percent in 1981, and its share of MVA in all developing economies rose slightly from 9.5 percent in 1963 to 10.4 percent in 1983, a closer look at the geographic distribution behind these figures reveals an uneven pattern. In 1981, five sub-Saharan African countries—Nigeria, Zimbabwe, Ivory Coast, Ghana, and Kenya—accounted for more than 60 percent of MVA; 21 countries accounted for 7 percent of the region's MVA; and the remaining 17 countries, 31.5 percent.

While MVA in all developing countries, excluding the least developed, grew an average 8 percent a year in the 1963–73 period, falling to 5.1 percent in the next decade period (1973–82), in sub-Saharan Africa, MVA in constant terms (1975 base year) rose 8.5 percent a year through the 1960s, slowing to just over 5 percent per annum in the 1970s. Furthermore, out of a total set of 40 African countries, per capita MVA between 1973 and 1981 declined in more than half.

The 1975 conference of the United Nations Industrial Development Organization (UNIDO) established the Lima Target by which developing countries' share of global industrial production was to reach 25 percent by the year 2000. In 1983, however, the UNIDO Secretariat estimated that developing countries were unlikely to exceed a 13.5 percent share by the turn of the century, with Africa's share amounting to no more than 1.2 percent. While per capita MVA in Africa in 1980 was comparable to the rates of South and East Asia, UNIDO projects that by the end of this century, Africa's MVA will be less than half that of Asia (UNIDO, 1984a).

Industrialization has barely begun in many sub-Saharan African countries, particularly as low incomes and populations in small countries and high costs associated with transportation and other distribution sectors in larger economies effectively limit market size, discouraging industrial investment as economies of scale cannot be achieved. Moreover, in contrast to Chenery's view, there is a host of evidence to support the argument that manufacturing is unlikely to become a self-propelling and leading economic sector in countries that lack certain "threshold" levels of per capita income.

SOURCES OF INDUSTRIAL GROWTH

The three traditional sources of industrial growth are: production for export, including the processing of primary products; production for domestic markets; and production to replace imports, or import substitution. Africa's share of world exports, falling from 2.7 percent in 1970 to 1.9 percent in 1983, is both small and restricted to a limited range of primary commodities (UNCTAD, 1984). Rather than diversifying its export base, the continent has become increasingly dependent on exports of primary products for its foreign exchange earnings. Whereas in 1970, 68 percent of Africa's exports were resource-based, by 1978, this figure had risen to 72 percent. For developing countries as a whole, the comparable figures were 53.3 percent and 53.1 percent (UNIDO, 1983a).

Africa's share of world exports of manufactured goods, estimated at 0.36 percent in 1980, has been falling despite rising levels of output, while its share of total world industrial output increased from 0.83 percent in 1970 to 0.97 percent in 1980. These UNIDO calculations suggest that the main impetus to increased manufacturing output has been growing domestic demand, including import substitution industries, rather than exports. As manufacturing valued added per capita was growing faster than GDP per capita until the mid-1970s, import substitution was the more significant source of demand expansion.

Reinforcing the observation that import substitution industries provided the main stimulus to industrial growth, data for 5 countries confirms that, with the exception of Nigeria, import-substituting industries contributed to at least one-third of industrial growth rates in the 1970s. If the five countries are at all representative, then Africa appears to have been more reliant than average on import substitution as a source of demand growth.

STRATEGIC OPTIONS

To date, the three main strategies to industrialization have been the import substitution option; the export orientation option, including the further processing of primary products; and the agricultural demand-led option. Although these options are not necessarily mutually exclusive, there is evidence that import substitution as a strategy for industrialization has jeopardized and delayed the development of export industries and could also have adverse effects on the agricultural demand-led approach.

African manufacturing is dominated by firms producing simple consumer goods import substitutes—notably foodstuffs, beverages, and tobacco, accounting for 31 percent of MVA, followed by clothing and textiles, contributing 21 percent (Table A.2 in Appendix I). The ʿconcentration on products that are income inelastic in demand partially explains the slowdown in industrial growth during the 1970s. Once the initial "easy" phase of import substitution was completed, countries experienced difficulties in either expanding their import-substituting bases or entering the world export markets. Unfortunately, industries with low income elasticities of demand—food, beverages, clothing and textiles, wood and furniture products, and paper products—are the sub-sectors in which less developed countries (LDCs) clearly have a comparative advantage as they are labor-intensive and low-skilled industries.

Contributions to total manufacturing growth in world markets were dominated by skills-intensive industries between 1960 and 1980. The expansion of the chemicals and machinery industries accounted for 63 percent of world manufacturing growth in the 1966–73 period and 70 percent between 1974 and 1980, while industries such as foodstuffs and clothing accounted for only 7 and 12 percent, respectively. Heavy industry and high-tech industries are expanding more rapidly than light industries, with adverse implications for the LDCs in terms of increasing their share of world manufacturing value added and employment, given the capital-intensive nature of the faster growing industrial sub-sectors.

IMPORT SUBSTITUTION VERSUS EXPORT
ORIENTATION

The debate on import substitution versus export orientation has dominated contemporary discussions on African development strategies. But the impressive growth performance of the handful of newly industrializing countries in the 1960s and early 1970s has spawned the new conventional wisdom that export-led growth is likely to be the more efficient path for sub-Saharan Africa.

The shortcomings of the import substitution strategy in Africa have been documented, and the experience of Kenya, regarded in the 1960s and 1970s as one of the continent's few economic success stories, underlines the validity of this assessment. Between 1964 and 1978, Kenya's real industrial output grew at an average 9.5 percent a year, outstripping annual real GDP growth rates of 5.9 percent. Similarly, wage employment in manufacturing doubled between 1966–1978 to 130,000.

Advances in industrial growth stemmed from heavy protectionist policies, such as foreign exchange quotas, licensing, and tariffs, resulting in local manufacture of simple import substitutes, particularly those goods consumed by middle and upper-income groups. The primary beneficiaries were not Kenyan firms, but foreign multinationals who were assisted by direct loans and equity capital contributions from the government, access to foreign exchange at an overvalued exchange rate, and bureaucratic encouragement.

As a result, manufactured goods imports as a percent of total domestic supplies fell from 44.3 percent in 1972 to 31.5 percent in 1978, while exports of manufactured goods as a percent of gross output were more than halved. Further, value added dropped as a percent of gross output from 28 percent in 1972 to 18.2 percent in 1978. Essentially, the "easy" phase of the import substitution strategy had wound down by the end of 1970s, confronting the government with the necessity of either breaking into export markets or developing an expanded import substitution base, including intermediate goods and capital equipment.

The pattern of industrial growth was strongly biased against export expansion because high protection levels made import replacement substantially more profitable than exporting, especially given the requirement that exporters use high cost and often sub-standard local inputs. Low (1979) notes that the export food processing sector had to pay high prices for local packaging materials, a sugar price twice as high as world prices because of unrebated excise taxes, and in some instances higher prices for raw materials.

Alluding to the Kenyan experience, the World Bank found the import control system "complex, cumbersome, and inconsistent," with a "wide latitude for abuse." Furthermore, the effects of import restrictions on local prices were found to be "uniformly upward" (Low, 1979, p.410). The agricultural sector suffered from negative protection "to the extent that almost all the locally manufactured items the farmers buy are protected"; the Kenyan motor vehicle assembly plants undoubtedly raised the cost of transportation in the country (p.415).

More significant perhaps, protectionist policies in Kenya have favored large-scale and often foreign firms. As a result, the industrialization process has been skewed toward capital-intensive techniques and the production of goods more appropriate to higher income markets.

Import-substituting strategies that include protectionist policies have encouraged a pattern of industrial growth that precludes export expansion. Evidence from a number of countries, including Nigeria and Zimbabwe, illustrates that import substitution tends to shift the pattern of imports away from final consumption items to raw materials and intermediate and capital goods, rather than reducing dependence on imports altogether. As a result, the degree to which a country can compress its imports is reduced, giving rise to the mounting adjustment problems since 1974, and the necessity of depressing consumption, income, output, and employment.

The manufacturing industry in Africa has also been a formidable net user of foreign exchange. This sector has contributed to a nearly fivefold increase in import elasticity of GDP in the last two decades. The African Development Bank (1985) notes that the manufacturing industry in a majority of sub-Saharan countries is "overly dependent on imports and sometimes structurally inefficient."

Import substitution policies also require detailed and efficient administration. As Galbraith has argued (1979), while market mechanisms "economize on scarce and honest administrative talent," interventionist strategies, such as operating a complex system of import licensing, place "the greatest possible claim on the scarcest possible resource."

BEYOND IMPORT SUBSTITUTION

Three key prerequisites for African economic growth for the remainder of the century will be increased savings ratios, higher returns on investment, and substantially enhanced net foreign exchange inflows. Industrialization programs will have to focus on savings of foreign exchange, the creation of new jobs, and the achievement of increased per capita incomes along with a more equitable pattern of income distribution. In light of the region's poor economic performance since 1973, it is argued that emphasis should be placed not on income redistribution now, but on policies designed to raise average incomes and above all policies that generate employment, as these will indirectly improve income distribution. Given the record of import substitution not only in Africa but in LDCs as a whole, it is clear that a new approach must be taken.

Export-led industrialization has been widely acclaimed to provide a more sustainable basis for efficient economic growth in sub-Saharan Africa. The rapid growth rates of the newly industrializing countries (NICs) during the 1960s and 1970s, and their apparent ability to weather two oil price rises have been "somehow closely related to factors associated with the rapid growth of exports" (Krueger, 1984). Economic growth rates in the NICs accelerated appreciably after export-oriented policies were undertaken and were clearly not the consequence of one-shot injections of resource allocations. Switching to an export orientation not only accelerates industrial expansion, as Krueger argues, but it can lead to major new primary exports, as has been the case in Brazil, reducing dependence on capital inflows and foreign borrowing—the so-called "indebted industrialization" that has contributed to the current debt crisis (OECD, 1984).

Theoretically, export-led growth improves the efficiency of allocations and increases the supply of foreign exchange, paving the way for more liberal and sustainable import regimes. Moreover, it has been shown to be more labor-intensive than production for domestic consumption, with the unskilled labor component estimated to range between 50 to 100 percent higher than in import-substituting industries.

Although export growth stimulates overall output levels and incomes, thereby generating additional employment, a number of resource-based industries, particularly those in basic processing and exports of minerals, are not labor-intensive. These activities often require significant capital outlays to sustain relatively few jobs. Rather, an indirect stimulus occurs as the subsequent increase in foreign exchange allows for looser import controls and therefore higher output levels and job creation elsewhere in the economy.

When export-led industries draw on unskilled and semi-skilled labor, they have a direct impact on primary as well as secondary employment. It is precisely because they have a comparative advantage in labor-intensive manufactures that developing countries show positive employment trends in their export-led industries. In addition, an emphasis on export-led growth has encouraged transfers of technology. Korean industry, for example, enjoyed "virtually free access" to technological and managerial information through foreign buyers who were the most important source of information on product development and who contributed to improved production and managerial techniques (World Bank, 1983a).

THE VIABILITY OF EXPORT-LED GROWTH

Even if the rationale underlying export-led growth is acceptable, its applicability to sub-Saharan Africa is less certain. Hypothetically, if all LDCs exhibited similar export intensities to those of Singapore, Hong Kong, Korea, and Taiwan, this would translate into a 700 percent increase in manufactured exports from developing countries, increasing their share of industrial countries' import markets from 16.7 percent in 1976 to more than 60 percent. In effect, as Cline concludes, the Asian export-led growth pattern cannot be replicated "without provoking a protectionist response ruling out its implementation" (1982, p. 89).

Further, the rapid export growth of the NICs in the 1960s and 1970s coincided with a period of sustained, rapid expansion in world trade—a phenomenon unlikely to be repeated in the next 10 to 15 years. The slowdown in world trade since the late 1970s and the rise in protectionism in developed economies suggest that export-led growth will be more difficult to achieve in coming years, particularly as protectionism is most evident in labor-intensive manufactures—precisely the area in which LDCs have comparative advantage (Baldwin, 1970).

Compounding the problem of entry into markets are advances in technology. In several industries such as electronics, transnational firms have been able to relocate production to final markets rather than maintain presences in developing countries (Kaplinsky, 1984, pp. 79–84). A recent UNIDO study acknowledges these barriers to export-led strategies, urging industrialized countries to grant favorable quotas to the LDCs to enable them to secure a market foothold. Given high levels of unemployment in many industrial economies, however, this suggestion is likely to meet with strong opposition. No less contentious is UNIDO's companion recommendation that the NICs relinquish their efforts in labor-intensive manufactured exports and venture into more technologically advanced export areas.

More fundamental questions arise as to the ability of low-income African economies to replicate the Asian model, given small domestic markets and therefore high unit costs, inadequate access to technology, and limited entrepreneurial capacities.

RESOURCE-BASED INDUSTRIALIZATION

The popularity of a variant of the export-led model—resource-based industrialization—has dwindled in recent years given the sluggish performance of primary product prices on world markets. Natural resource exploitation, particularly of minerals and petroleum, has often created export enclave economies characterized by a high-wage, capital-intensive sector with limited employment as an island of prosperity in a sea of underemployment, unemployment, and rural poverty. Dependence on a single resource has also encouraged governments to neglect their agricultural sectors and to maintain overvalued exchange rates, which militate against industrial growth and deter much-needed export diversification.

There are, however, some instances where resource-based industrialization has been successful—Ivory Coast, Malawi, and Zimbabwe are examples. In each case, industrialization has been partially encouraged by protectionist strategies and agriculture has played a critical role either as the primary foreign exchange earner or as creator of a market for the outputs of domestic industry while simultaneously earning foreign exchange from raw material or semi-processed exports.

The drawbacks of resource-based industrialization, however, are vulnerability to exogenous shocks, such as international prices for exports and adverse weather conditions. However, this strategy is more attractive than import substitution or dependence on export of manufactures because it exploits comparative advantage; it can be highly labor-intensive; and it does generate net foreign exchange revenues.

AGRICULTURE-LED GROWTH AS AN ALTERNATIVE

If both import substitution and the export orientation are ruled out, is there a third way? Adelman (1984) has advanced the agricultural demand-led approach to industrialization as a means of "buying time" to enable the industrial countries to overcome protectionist pressures and open the door to renewed growth in manufactured exports by NICs.

To be adopted by those LDCs that have few or no prospects for developing or expanding non-traditional exports, that are net food importers, or that have an already established industrial base, this strategy is based on the underlying assumption that a domestic mass market will develop as a result of increased agricultural productivity. Small-scale and medium-sized farmers, many of whose inputs can be supplied by domestic industry, will produce goods that can be processed by manufacturers and rising incomes will generate further demand for local goods. Again, the pitfalls of this approach, similar to those of import substitution, concern the ability of domestic industry to provide inputs at competitive prices and to thrive either domestically or in foreign markets without government subsidies.

But recent experience in Zimbabwe lends some support to this strategy. Government supply-side policies aimed at increasing productivity particularly among small-scale farmers included improved access to farm credits; investment in boreholes, marketing depots, roads, bridges, and irrigation schemes; incentive pricing; and expanded extension services. As a result, there was a substantial increase in smallholder cotton and maize output in the 1984/85 season; the cotton is ginned locally and about 30 percent is absorbed by domestic clothing and textile manufacturers, with the balance exported as lint. Similarly, maize is milled domestically and the surplus is exported. As the Standard Chartered Bank of Zimbabwe reports, increases in production of consumer goods in 1984 reflected rises in the spending power of peasant farmers.

THE POLICY DEBATE

As the foregoing review of various options indicates, the debate on appropriate strategies of industrialization is far from closed. Although in theory, it might be possible to proceed simultaneously on all three strategies, practical obstacles to such a comprehensive approach are formidable. For example, export promotion in practice implies some degree of discrimination against industries producing for the domestic market; protecting manufacturing activities breeds high cost export sectors; and strong domestic markets encouraged by the agriculture-based strategy conflict with the development of export markets since it is more profitable to engage in manufacturing for the home market.

Since the 1960s, economic policy in Africa has largely focused on macro-economic planning without due consideration to micro-economic issues. Successful economies, like sound businesses, are essentially those that have a diverse portfolio of investments. Rather than basing decisions on artificially high rates of return that are a function of import barriers, insulated monopolies, subsidized interest rates, or other investment incentives, they should reflect the perceived net economic worth of projects. Accordingly, a broadly neutral economic environment is desirable, in which policy-makers can encourage savings and investment in various sectors of the economy.

Such a purely neutral approach to economic planning, however, is unlikely to be adopted in Africa, given a strong commitment to state intervention reflecting a belief that political independence is meaningless without economic self-determination and self-sufficiency. Realistically, the smaller the market, the greater the likelihood of state participation in any major venture. In those cases where the limits of import substitution have been reached, some degree of public sector intervention must come into play if incentives to exports and agricultural output are to be implemented.

Given the varying levels of industrialization in Africa, gross generalizations on policy initiatives are dangerous. But in effect, small, least developed economies have few options other than to retain the infant industry protection they already enjoy, while endeavoring to eliminate discrimination against small-scale, labor-intensive, or export-oriented industries. In these countries, import substitution is a dead-end strategy since the smaller the domestic market, the faster the saturation point will be reached and the greater the danger of establishing high-cost inefficient industries. The Malawian model, with its emphasis on self-sufficiency in foodstuffs and agricultural exports as a springboard for resource-based industrialization, is commendable from the viewpoint of small, resource-poor nations.

In larger, relatively more prosperous countries such as Nigeria, there is a dire need to shift focus from import substitution to agricultural rehabilitation, which in the long run will enhance the competitiveness, viability, and growth prospects of existing industries. This will involve temporarily downgrading the role of manufacturing in the economy, along with the implementation of policies designed to restructure incentives toward an outward-looking bias.

Experience over the last decade suggests that African policy-makers are reluctant to undertake such a corrective strategy until it is forced upon them by crisis conditions. But the longer the policy transition is delayed, the more difficult it will be to achieve.

The typical policy package involves devaluation of the currency to bring domestic prices more in line with those on world markets; gradual removal of quantitative restrictions on imports and other non-tariff barriers and their replacement with tariffs; a general reduction in the average tariff level; and a move toward tariff uniformity that no longer favors the importation of intermediate and capital goods. Such a policy package is more likely to be implemented successfully, however, if linked to balance of payments support from donors.

EXPORT INCENTIVES

As tariffs will have to be maintained during the transitional period, it will be necessary to provide counterbalancing export incentives. The typical export incentive program embraces preferential credit lines and access to foreign exchange for imports of industrial inputs, tax concessions to industries promoting exports, outright subsidies and exemptions from import duties for exporters, and provision of subsidized export supplier credits to exporters of machinery and capital equipment. These programs, however, should be seen as ancillary rather than mainstream efforts to increase foreign exchange earnings. Specific incentives to boost exports have been found to be less effective than the creation of an economic climate that encourages efficiency and competitiveness. In a study of 27 LDCs, Love (1984) concludes that successful export programs depended significantly on supply side variables in all but four countries, rather than on export incentives per se.

Further, domestic monetary and fiscal policies should be reformed to eliminate biases against labor-intensive industries and against small-scale enterprises. In the past, policies such as tax concessions on new investment, minimum wage legislation, restrictions on the "hire and fire" policies of private companies, and the encouragement of investment by means of negative real interest rates have distorted factor prices in such a way as to lead industrialists to adopt capital-intensive techniques.

TECHNOLOGY

Two distinct problems arise with regard to transfers of technology to Africa. First, there is a need to ensure that appropriate technologies are adopted in industry, and, second, that more rapid technological progress be made in order to avoid the danger of African industry being left behind and forced to compete, using outmoded technologies, in the mature, slow-growth sub-sectors.

The trade regime adopted by a country has a significant bearing on productivity, growth, and technological advance. Import substitution programs tend to dissuade technological advance when they allow highly concentrated or monopolistic industries to form. Operating at low capacity, these industries generate a cost-permissive atmosphere of "x-inefficiency," in which goods are produced at high costs because industrialists are free of open market competition. International competition, on the other hand, induces a "challenge response" mechanism whereby efforts to minimize costs lead domestic industry to adopt more efficient new technologies (Nishimizu and Robinson, 1984).

Foreign exchange constraints similarly deter technological transfers, as modern capital equipment and intermediate inputs become more costly. Policies that promote export-led expansion through easier access to foreign exchange can lead to higher productivity through increased availability of imported technology, economies of scale, and competitive incentives.

At the same time, appropriate technologies have been found to be both available and viable in LDCs. The Pickett study of choice of technologies in 12 industries concluded that a significant range of efficient technologies existed in virtually all the industries under review, and in some instances were labor-intensive. In those instances where labor-intensive techniques were used but were less than optimal, the opportunity costs were found to be invariably small. For 430 of the 486 technologies studied, the net present value, at a 10 percent discount rate, of the most labor-intensive technology was within a mere two percent range of the most profitable technique, implying that the rate of return from a sub-optimal technology is only slightly below the profit-maximization technique.

These and other research findings suggest that choices of technology in LDCs are often sub-optimal, reflecting lack of familiarity with available techniques; a tendency to imitate developed economies in their choice of technologies; the inclination of transnational corporations to employ the same techniques they use at home; a distorting structure of incentives—negative real interest rates, subsidized loans, and tax incentives—and the over-pricing of labor. Although well-intentioned, many industrial relations policies, including minimum wage levels, raise the implied cost of labor by restricting the private sector's freedom to manage its employment policy.

The solutions to these problems must include measures to eliminate biases against labor-intensive techniques and to encourage entrepreneurial decision-making in choosing appropriate technologies.

State intervention in this field is desirable, given its access to the requisite data.

THE ROLE OF FOREIGN INVESTMENT

Transnational corporations remain the most effective means of transferring technology across international borders. With the slowdown in foreign direct investment since the 1970s and Africa's deepening liquidity crisis, there has been a renewed interest in foreign private investment on the part of African governments. As a result, two negative trends have become apparent. First, countries have begun to compete against one another for new investments, with the result that concessions granted have reduced the value of the project in terms of tax revenues, net foreign exchange earnings, etc. Second, fierce competition for new investment has led to the implementation of inappropriate projects.

The main advantage of direct foreign investment is not the inflow of funds, which in net terms has been substantial in only a relatively small number of LDCs and very few in Africa, but its associated benefits in transfer of skills and technology and access to world markets.

Over the last decade, joint ventures in which foreign equity does not exceed 50 percent have been on the increase. Indeed, a number of contractual arrangements now involve some investment by the foreign firm, but no equity participation at all. Turnkey operations, subcontracting, licensing arrangements, management, service and production-sharing contracts are examples.

These new forms of investment offer potential advantages to host governments concerned about limiting the foreign presence in their economies and their dependence on foreign capital, management, and technologies. They offer the host country increased control over investment decisions, job creation, technology choice, and exports, without the disadvantages of foreign ownership and control.

The issue of dependency is central to an industrialization strategy for sub-Saharan Africa. Five forms of dependence can be identified: market dependence, technological dependence, managerial dependence, dependence on foreign capital, and economic inflexibility (Roemer, 1981). Industrialization strategies in Africa in the past have reflected efforts to reduce such dependencies; import substitution was seen as an obvious way to reduce dependence on foreign trade while indigenization decrees were adopted to increase the authority of local management.

However, the record of the last 25 years shows that not only has a new kind of foreign trade dependence arisen in the form of import dependence, but reliance on foreign capital—indebted industrialization—has also increased. Technological and labor dependence remains acute, as does economic inflexibility as evidenced in the severe difficulties in adjustment to external shocks.

Trade, aid, and investment underline international interdependence in economic relationships. Economic interdependence for developing countries is primarily vertical—volumes of north-south trade, aid, and investment are much more substantial than south-south flows. Given the weaknesses of export-led growth, it is imperative that sub-Saharan Africa develop south-south trading links with other developing economies. But for the remainder of this century, opportunities created by access to industrial country markets, capital, technology, and expertise must be exploited. The challenge for African governments is to design a framework within which foreign investment will take place on a substantial scale, but without setting off fierce competition between host countries.

EMPLOYMENT

Industry's contribution to job creation in most LDCs has been disappointing; its share of the total labor force has averaged 14 percent in low income countries and an estimated 12 percent in sub-Saharan Africa (Squire, 1979). In contrast, in the United Kingdom in the mid-19th century, 40 percent of total employment was provided by the manufacturing sector. With some notable exceptions in East Asia, the insignificant role of industry in employment generation in developing economies reflects an emphasis on capital-intensive techniques (World Bank, 1982).

Between 1960 and 1980, industrial employment in sub-Saharan Africa grew by 4.5 percent per year, exceeding the estimated 2 percent annual growth rate of the labor force. However, even if the growth rate in industrial employment were to double, manufacturing's share would amount to only half of the growing labor force. As a result, manufacturing alone is unlikely to solve Africa's growing unemployment crisis.

Nevertheless, small-scale enterprise is considerably more labor-intensive than medium and large-scale businesses. Accordingly, policies should promote the small-scale sector wherever possible. Second, the labor intensity of exports of manufactures has been found to be greater than that of producing for the domestic market or for import substitution. Export-oriented policies stimulate industrial employment, as higher profits in the export sector lead to increased investment, employment, and output levels throughout the economy. Third, increased industrial employment yields external economies in the form of higher productivity per worker than in agriculture or services, along with improvements in the quality of labor that arise from skills acquired on the job.

It is clear that the region faces a deepening unemployment crisis resulting from rapid population growth and low levels of investment. It is essential therefore that policy should be directed at raising capital-labor ratios in existing enterprises and ensuring that, where possible, new investment should be labor-intensive. Getting prices right for capital and labor is an obvious step in the right direction.

WAGES

Labor in sub-Saharan Africa is generally considered to be overpriced. Historically, high wage levels were the consequence of colonization which imported wage structures from the metropole. Structurally, rapid productivity growth in enclave export sectors, such as copper in Zambia and Zaire and oil in Nigeria, gave rise to a distorted wage structure, as average wages throughout the economy were linked to those in the export sector. A third reason has been income redistribution goals of African governments, who often use statutory minimum wage policies toward this end.

High wage levels—partially a result of overvalued exchange rates—and lower productivity have deterred employment growth and undermined Africa's relative comparative advantage in labor-intensive activities (Table 10.1). If Africa is to replicate the experiences of certain Asian and Latin American countries that have attracted foreign investment in assembly plants, for example, a more comparative cost advantage in wages is essential. But it would be wrong to place undue emphasis on the role of low wage levels in attracting industrial investment. UNIDO describes average wage levels as at best ambiguous determinants of industry location or in the prediction of changes in world industry. Recent advances in the microelec-

TABLE 10.1
AVERAGE WAGES IN MANUFACTURING: SELECTED COUNTRIES

Country	Average Wage per Month US $ (1980)
Pakistan	60
Tanzania	71
Ghana	130
Nigeria	170
Kenya	174
Singapore	215
Zambia	229
Korea	242
Zimbabwe	325
United States	1,250

SOURCE: International Labor Organization. *Yearbook*, Geneva, 1984.

tronics industry and in robotics have enabled firms in the developed economies to overcome unfavorable wage differentials through a combination of increased productivity and quality improvements.

Nevertheless, appropriate labor pricing remains important. Continued distortions which extend beyond explicit wage costs to industrial relations policies will adversely affect choices of technologies and encourage capital-intensive methods at the expense of creating jobs.

CAPITAL UTILIZATION

In sub-Saharan Africa, capital utilization rates tend to be very low in comparison with other LDC regions, with industry largely dependent on imports of raw materials, intermediate goods, and spare parts, and on small, low income domestic markets. To a large extent, underutilization of capital stems from industrial capacity growth rates that outstrip both the supply of imported inputs and domestic demand. Encouraged by high profits in protected and uncompetitive domestic markets, the rapid expansion in industrial output ceased in the late 1970s when imports became too costly or simply unavailable. As a result, industries became unprofitable, operating at high unit costs but at low levels of capital utilization. The situation was exacerbated on the demand side by falling per capita incomes in a number of countries.

The importance of capital utilization cannot be stressed enough. Low rates not only mean low returns on capital, thereby discouraging new investment, but also wasted resources. Raising capital utilization rates is both a quick and an inexpensive way of increasing output, productivity, and employment without new net investment, freeing savings for investment elsewhere in the economy. In addition, such a policy works well in tandem with export-led growth. Given the relatively high costs of inputs and limited domestic markets, companies operating with substantial excess capacity—for example, the manufacturing industry in Nigeria was operating at only 50 percent capacity in 1984—can increase their output for export purposes with no additional investment.

Winston (1984) has shown that high capital utilization rates are determined in part by wages, interest rates, and technology. Negative real interest rates and high wages encourage large-scale, capital-intensive investments that will tend to have low utilization rates. Positive real interest rates and market-determined wages on the other hand will force companies to utilize their capital more efficiently, resulting in higher employment and output per unit of capital.

In the near-term, donors will continue to have an important role to play through commodity import programs, which have, for example, contributed significantly to maintaining output and employment in Zimbabwean industry since 1983. Donor countries should consider program aid which enhances utilization of existing capacity as part of a general policy reform package, in preference to project aid designed to create new capacity.

In the medium-term, efforts must be made to expand export markets and to develop stronger domestic markets, tapping local sources for input supplies. This will require adjusting overvalued exchange rates and imposing tariffs on imports of raw materials and intermediate goods.

STATE-OWNED ENTERPRISES

In the post-independence period, Africa's public sector has grown rapidly, extending into the mining, manufacturing, and services sectors. The record has not been a happy one, as Killick (1983) notes: "A large industrial public sector will contribute little to dynamic industrial growth, will tend to become a drain on public finances, will require a net inflow of resources to cover its capital requirements, and will discourage the growth of private industry."

In a sample of 70 developed and developing countries, Africa's public sector contributed an average 33 percent of investments in the 1970s, against 16.5 percent in the other countries (Short, 1984). Even these statistics, however, understate the role of government in a typical African economy. Governments exercise far-reaching controls over their economies by way of regulations governing the private sector, such as import restrictions, monetary and fiscal policies, labor and wage legislation, and indigenization decrees.

Although less than in the utilities and mining sectors, the share of public ownership in the industrial sector has exceeded 25 percent in many sub-Saharan African countries (Table 10.2). State-owned enterprises are found to use both more capital and labor than private companies for the same or even lower outputs. In Tanzania, for example, the more capital-intensive public sector has had slightly lower output per worker and lower productivity of capital, while in Ghana, labor productivity in public enterprises was only 55 percent that of the private sector in 1969/70 (Killick, 1983).

Nevertheless, the privatization of industrial ownership must be approached cautiously, as inefficiencies are not a result of public ownership per se, but rather a function of the degree to which the state interferes in daily decision-making, the degree of decentralization of decision-making, the flexibility of management structures, and the policy environment in which public enterprise operates.

There is a danger that privatization strategies will merely shift ownership and control from one inefficient management to another, given scarce managerial and entrepreneurial skills. As long as the policy environment is hostile to business efficiency, as long as managerial and entrepreneurial skills are scarce, and as long as there is overt political interference including a requirement to satisfy non-commercial goals, enterprises will remain inefficient regardless of ownership.

Above all, state-owned enterprises cannot be assessed on purely economic criteria, but rather must be judged against the social and political goals they are required to attain. It has been argued that a more practical policy goal in Africa would be to make the public enterprise sector more efficient and development-oriented rather than reducing its size.

State-owned enterprises were established because of a perceived

TABLE 10.2
PUBLIC AND PRIVATE SHARES IN MANUFACTURING VALUE ADDED: PERCENTAGE FOR SELECTED COUNTRIES

Country	Early/Middle 1960s	1969	1972–73	1979–80
Ghana				
State-Owned	13.3	16.0	17.2	27.1
Joint Ventures	7.9	19.7	18.0	25.6
Private	78.9	64.5	64.8	47.3 [a]
Zambia				
Public/Parastatal	n.a.	n.a.	53.2	56.4
Private	n.a.	n.a.	46.8	43.6
Tanzania				
Parastatal	5.0	22.5	33.2	31.0
Private	95.0	77.5	66.8	69.0
Kenya				
Public	15.5	13.2	18.0	n.a.
Private	84.5	86.8	82.0	n.a.

[a] consisted of 25.7% private Ghanaian, 12.7% private foreign and 12.7% private mixed (domestic and foreign).
SOURCE: W. F. Steel and J. W. Evans: *Industrialisation in Sub-Saharan Africa*. Technical Paper No. 25 (Washington, D.C., The World Bank, 1984.)

need to gain control of strategic sectors and to become involved where private enterprise was either unwilling or unable to launch a new venture, and where entrepreneurial know-how was absent. State participation was often required by foreign investors as a means of gauging creditworthiness and ensuring security for foreign sector interests.

In the mid-1970s, the budgetary burden of public enterprise deficits in Africa averaged 3.3 percent of GDP, reaching 10 percent in Zambia (1978/80) and 4 percent in Tanzania (1974/77) (Short, 1984). These public sector deficits have contributed to balance of payments problems because they are partially financed from foreign borrowings, thereby increasing the debt-servicing burden, and because of the sector's high propensity to import. Financing their deficits from domestic bank credit has clearly been an important factor contributing to high rates of money supply growth and therefore high inflation rates.

Given the disappointing performance of the state sector, most African governments have been reluctant to launch new parastatals and a number of countries—Ghana, Nigeria, and Zambia—have adopted a privatization approach. In May 1985, Tanzanian President Julius Nyerere was quoted as saying that sisal plantations will be returned to private ownership, as production had fallen from 220,000 tonnes in 1970 to 47,000 tonnes in 1984.

Whether the solution lies in this approach or in better management of public sector enterprises remains to be seen. In any event, privatization will not be a viable option unless public enterprises are seen by the private sector as potentially profitable. It is doubtful whether private sector funding exists in most countries to take over state-owned enterprise. A more promising approach would be to restructure economic policy along market-oriented lines and to revise the guidelines within which public enterprises will operate in the future.

FINANCE AND CAPITAL MARKETS

Efficient capital markets, in which interest rates and yields on financial assets are determined by competitive supply and demand forces, are central to industrial development. Pegging interest rates below rates of inflation in order to control the cost of credit and encourage investment has often been counterproductive, in effect deterring savings and generating excess demand for credit. This in turn requires direct control over bank lending policies which tend to favor large rather than small enterprises and which frequently allocate funds to inefficient low-return investments while encouraging capital-intensive projects.

Efficient capital markets on the other hand increase both savings and investment, channeling them to productive uses throughout the economy on the basis of the highest rates of return, and ultimately generating employment and overall economic growth.

Unfortunately, governments in many developing countries have placed their emphasis on attracting foreign investment via investment codes and incentives to multinational corporations rather than on developing efficient capital markets which would to some extent reduce dependence on foreign capital.

Reviewing the development programs of 16 sub-Saharan countries, the African Development Bank concludes that dependence on foreign capital is as high as 80 to 100 percent for some of the least developed states, averaging 56 percent for the entire sample. Only Guinea, Sudan, Uganda, Botswana, and the Gambia had investment plans where the bulk of financing was to be met from domestic sources. Furthermore, the bank found that domestic savings ratios have stagnated, except in oil-exporting countries, and investment rates have declined. Net investment as a percent of GDP is reckoned to have been below the 15 percent gross investment ratio of GDP estimated for 1984 because of the serious deterioration of capital stock in many parts of the region.

In the low income countries, the domestic savings ratio fell from 10.9 percent in the 1960s to 8.8 percent in the 1970s, and is expected to drop to an average of 8.6 percent over the next decade (ADB, 1985). Although partially explained by stagnating real income levels, this trend also reflects policies and institutional structures that are not conducive to savings and investment. Structural deficiencies in the banking systems also explain the failure to mobilize even low levels of savings and to channel these funds into productive investment. In terms of investment, low rates of return on capital in manufacturing and problems within the investing institutions themselves, such as development banks, are among the more glaring shortcomings.

Suffering from lack of resources, development banks have been hard hit by the international debt crisis and the subsequent reluctance on the part of international lenders to invest in Africa. Further, bottlenecks in some countries have arisen at the project proposal stage. When submitted to development banks and other investing institutions, proposals have been found to be so poorly prepared that their chances of acceptance are considerably reduced (UNIDO, 1984b).

Although provision of long-term finance for capital investment is not within the domain of commercial banks, they could assist the development process by providing working capital which can be the critical factor in the success or failure of the small-scale enterprise sector. The deterioration of the fiscal balance in the region poses another on-going problem. Large fiscal deficits mean that a substantial proportion of available savings is being absorbed by the public sector—partly to finance the deficits of state-owned enterprises—which reduces the availability of capital for investment in manufacturing and indirectly imposes a severe balance of payments strain since a fiscal deficit is frequently mirrored by an external payments deficit.

ENTREPRENEURSHIP

African governments have justified nationalization of industry on the basis of a lack of indigenous entrepreneurship, and an ADB/OAU/ECA report supports this claim, stating that entrepreneurial ability is probably "the most important scarce skill in sub-Saharan Africa." Although this may be true, the environment in which policies are made—high rates of domestic inflation, overvalued exchange rates, and lack of access to technology—have made it more attractive for entrepreneurs to engage in the trade and services sectors such as transport, than in manufacturing. It is therefore arguable that Africa's problem is not a shortage of entrepreneurs, but of industrial entrepreneurs.

Governmental ambivalence toward private enterprise has also contributed to the lack of private participation. Whereas in some francophone countries, leaders have openly stated a preference for foreign investors over local entrepreneurs because they come equipped with finance, foreign exchange, technology, expertise, and market access, other governments have actively discouraged private enterprise. However, government regulations and restrictions have both discouraged indigenous enterprise and favored the larger firms which are invariably foreign-controlled.

Efforts to indigenize foreign-owned businesses have tended to create a small new elite or have further enriched the existing military or bureaucratic elite. The Kenyan government's drive to reduce the Asian presence in the economy in the early 1970s was unsuccessful because, as a Kenyan minister subsequently conceded, "We didn't have enough financial backup, nor did we have the management skills to operate the shops we pushed the Asians out of." Ten years later, Asian entrepreneurs were estimated to account for one-quarter of Kenya's GDP, 55 percent of manufacturing output, and three-quarters of retail activities (Baker, 1983).

While there is no easy solution to this problem, there is room for improved business education and extension programs for manufacturing industries. However, as long as the public sector and international companies continue to offer greater security and financial remuneration, they will attract the best entrepreneurial talent. As most indigenization efforts have failed, African governments should exploit the entrepreneurial talents of the "permanent" expatriate community—the Asians in East Africa, the Lebanese in West Africa, and the whites in southern Africa. The most promising policy would be to focus on education, training, and extension along with access to credit and technology that are designed to help the successful small-scale manufacturers make the difficult transition to medium-scale activities.

FUTURE POLICY

That the onus for reversing the current trend in African economies rests squarely with the governments and people of the continent is widely recognized. The assistance that the donor community can realistically be expected to provide is limited, given the disappointing results of the substantial aid flows over the last two decades. Numerous studies, including those undertaken by African institutions, emphasize the need for improved policies, management, and institutions within the continent itself. This will require, first and foremost, a restructuring of the domestic policy environment.

POLICY REFORM

Stated time and again by multilateral agencies such as the World Bank and International Monetary Fund, policy reform must include a system of incentives that is as uniform as possible across different sectors. Such a neutral policy environment allows industrialists to make decisions on the basis of perceived long-term returns rather than on the basis of a protected domestic market or tax holiday. While laissez-faire policies cannot be embraced totally or import-substituting policies completely relinquished, it will be necessary to move gradually toward a uniform incentive package, counterbalancing the existing biases by special incentives to export industries as well as agriculture. Future industrial investments will be determined by the country's resource endowment and its comparative advantage.

Even if a restructuring of incentives, including the adoption of a realistic exchange rate policy, fails to stimulate export-led expansion, investments in import-substituting activities or those aimed at satisfying domestic demand will be more soundly based and more efficient than under a system of high levels of effective protection.

Effective supply-side strategies that eliminate existing obstacles to investment and growth are also needed. These include the creation of essential infrastructure, access to credit, supply of complementary inputs—raw materials, intermediate items, skilled personnel, technology, marketing expertise, and entrepreneurial capacity—and legislative, monetary, and fiscal policies that combine to create a positive environment for investment. Moreover, political stability is required to create a conducive investment climate. Above all, African governments can stimulate industrial growth by accentuating incentives and curbing regulatory and restrictive programs.

TRADE RATHER THAN AID

The donor community's most valuable contribution to industrialization in sub-Saharan Africa would be to remove protectionist and particularly non-tariff barriers to trade. According to a GATT estimate, about 35 percent of world trade is subject to non-tariff barriers of some kind, while the Leutwiler Committee's report (Leutwiler, 1985) calls for fairer and clearer rules in agricultural trade in order to allow efficient agricultural producers to compete.

In effect, policies such as the EEC's Common Agricultural Policy discourage exports in LDCs and fuel skepticism over the viability of an export-led growth strategy. If donors wish to see economic policy reform in Africa, they should reverse the present trend toward protectionism and provide balance of payments and technical support to help countries through the difficult period of adjustment toward an outward-looking industrial strategy. It is pointless for bilateral and multilateral donors to insist on conditionality for financial support during a period of structural adjustment, if export market opportunities are restricted by protectionism.

Second, given excess capacity in sub-Saharan industry, donors should focus their efforts on provision of commodity import assistance and balance of payments support rather than on aid for new industrial capacity. Third, Western donors are particularly well-placed to assist developing countries in the screening of new projects, in building African capacity in negotiating skills with transnational corporations, in providing technological guidance and advice, and in offering business school training to entrepreneurs and managers.

Donors also have a responsibility to improve communications between African governments and business on the one hand, and their own multinational corporations on the other. Donors can help promote investment opportunities, draw attention to market openings, and use moral suasion against implementation of inappropriate projects and techniques on the part of LDCs. It is in the interests of the countries in the region to terminate competition for new investment.

Firms in the Western countries are the foremost source of technology and donor governments should take steps to speed up the rate of technology diffusion, while ensuring that transfer costs are minimized. Lastly, Western businesses could provide direct assistance in entrepreneurship development by offering on-the-job training to African managers or by seconding staff to operate extension services in the region. Such technical assistance will yield greater rewards than expertise at the macro-economic or planning level.

CONCLUSIONS

In the mid-1980s, it is apparent that many of the ambitious targets outlined in the Lagos Plan of Action are unlikely to be achieved. Given the weak performance of agriculture, it is unfortunate that the Lagos summit designated the 1980s as the "Industrial Decade for Africa," as industrial expansion will continue to be hampered by a weak agrarian base. The Lagos Plan of Action's emphasis on self-reliance and self-sustained growth is ironic because agricultural failure has made sub-Saharan Africa more rather than less dependent on developed market economies for aid, capital, skills, and even food.

For at least the remainder of this decade, the manufacturing sector will be secondary to agriculture in most of the continent. Therefore, priorities should be redirected toward agriculture as the continent's leading sector. Further industrialization should be dependent either on domestic market growth resulting from rising farm output and incomes, from export expansion, or preferably from a combination of the two. Manufacturing value added is likely to grow as a result of increased production for domestic demand, renewed emphasis on resource-based industry, and, it is hoped, increased exports, primarily to other developing countries, but also to the developed market economies.

Although self-reliance and self-sufficiency in agriculture and resource-based industrialization are worthy objectives, no country or trading bloc can claim to be self-sufficient in a world of increased economic interdependence. Further, the danger is that the quest for self-reliance and self-sufficiency will spark another round of inward-focused industrialization based on comparative disadvantage rather than advantage, with adverse effects on efficiency, growth, exports, employment, and income distribution.

The strength of an outward-oriented economic strategy lies in its reliance on market signals to achieve an efficient or at least more efficient allocation of economic resources. In the long run, an agriculture-led growth strategy, accompanied by national economic policies which provide incentives and limited restrictions, is more likely to enhance economic stability and flexibility in sub-Saharan Africa, reducing the degree to which countries are dependent on foreign aid and capital.

REFERENCES

Adedeji, A. 1982. "Development and Economic Growth in Africa to the Year 2000," in Timothy Shaw, ed., *Alternative Futures for Africa*. Boulder: Westview Press.

Adelman, Irma. 1984. "Beyond Export-Led Growth," *World Development* 12(9) (September).

African Development Bank. 1985. *Annual Report 1984*. Addis Ababa.

Baker, Pauline. 1983. "Obstacles to Private Sector Activities in Africa." Report for the U.S. Dept. of State (mimeo).

Baldwin, R.E. 1970. *Non-Tariff Distortions in International Trade*. Washington, D.C.: Brookings Institution.

Cline, W. R. 1982. "Can the East Asian Model of Development be Generalised?," *World Development* 10(2).

Financial Times. 1985. "Why Steps are Needed to Safeguard Free Trade." *Financial Times,* March 28, 1985.

Fransman, M. 1984. "Explaining the Success of the Asian NICs: Incentives and Technology," *IDS (Sussex) Bulletin* 15(2).

Galbraith, J. K. 1979. *The Nature of Mass Poverty.* Cambridge, Mass.: Harvard University Press.

Kaplinksky, Raphael. 1984. "The International Context for Industrialisation in the Coming Decade," *Journal of Development Studies* 21(1) (October).

Killick, Tony. 1978. *Development Economics in Action: A Study of Economic Policies in Ghana.* New York: St. Martin's Press.

Killick, Tony. 1983. "The Role of the Public Sector in African Developing Countries," *Industry and Development* 7. New York: UNIDO.

Krueger, Anne. 1983. *Trade and Employment in Developing Countries.* Chicago: University of Chicago Press.

Krueger, Anne. 1984. "Comparative Advantage and Development Policy Twenty Years Later," in *Economic Structure and Performance, Essays in Honor of Hollis B. Chenery.* Orlando: Academic Press.

Leutwiler, Fritz. 1985. *Trade Policies for a Better Future.* Geneva: GATT.

Livingstone, Ian. 1984. "Resource-based Industrial Development: Past Experience and Future Prospects in Malawi," *Industry and Development* 10. New York: UNIDO.

Love, J. 1984. "External Market Conditions, Competition, Diversification and LDC Exports." *Journal of Development Economics* 16(3).

Low, F. 1979. "Export Potential in the Kenyan Fruit and Vegetable Processing Sector." Nairobi (mimeo).

Nishimizu, M. and S. Robinson. 1984. "Trade Policies and Productivity Change in Semi-Industrialised Economies," *Journal of Development Economics* 16(1-2) (September-October).

OECD. 1984. *New Forms of International Investment in Developing Countries.* Paris.

Organisation of African Unity, African Development Bank, Economic Commission for Africa. (undated). *Accelerated Development in Sub-Saharan Africa: An Assessment by the OAU, ADB AND ECA Secretariats.*

Pickett, J. 1979. "A Consistent Approach to the Choice of Technology," *World Industry Since 1960.* New York: UNIDO.

Roemer, Michael. 1981. "Dependence and Industrialisation Strategies," *World Development* 9(5).

Schaatz, S. P. 1977. *South of the Sahara; Development in African Economies.* Philadelphia: Temple University Press.

Shirley, M. M. 1983. "Managing State-Owned Enterprises." Staff Working Paper No. 577. Washington, D.C.: The World Bank.

Short, R. P. 1984. "The Role of Public Enterprises: An International Statistical Comparison," in *Public Enterprise in Mixed Economies.* Washington, D.C.: IMF.

Squire, Lyn. 1979. "Labour Force, Employment and Labour Markets in the Course of Economic Development." Staff Working Paper No. 336. Washington, D.C.: The World Bank.

Standard Chartered Bank. 1984. *Zimbabwe Economic Bulletin* (November). Harare, Zimbabwe.

Steel, W. F. and J. W. Evans. 1984. "Industrialisation in Sub-Saharan Africa." Technical Paper No. 25. Washington, D.C.: The World Bank.

UNCTAD. 1984. *Handbook of International Trade and Development Statistics*.

UNIDO. 1979. *World Industry Since 1960*. New York.

UNIDO. 1981. *World Industry in 1980*. New York.

UNIDO. 1983a. *Industry in a Changing World*. New York.

UNIDO. 1983b. "A Strategy of Industrial Development for the Small Resource-poor, Least-developed Economies," *Industry and Development* (8).

UNIDO. 1984a. *A Statistical Review of the World Industrial Situation in 1983*. New York.

UNIDO. 1984b. *The Role of National Development Financial Institutions in Organisation of the Islamic Conference Countries in Promoting Industrial Development*. (mimeo).

Winston, G. 1984. "The Utilisation of Capital in Developing Countries." UNIDO working paper (mimeo).

World Bank. 1982. *Trade and Development Policies for Industrial Development*. Washington, D.C.

World Bank. 1983a. *World Development Report 1983*. Washington, D.C.

World Bank. 1983b. *Kenya: Growth and Structural Change. Vol. 2*. Washington, D.C.

World Bank. 1984a. *Towards Self-Sustained Development in Sub-Saharan Africa*. Washington, D.C.

World Bank. 1984b. *World Development Report 1984*. Washington, D.C.

Zimbabwe Banking Corporation. 1985. *Economic Newsletter*. Harare.

CHAPTER ELEVEN

Small-Scale Industry

Carl Liedholm and Donald C. Mead

The role of small-scale industries in African development has recently emerged as an important concern among policy-makers, international donors, and researchers. The Lagos Plan of Action, for example, argues that as part of their industrial strategies, countries should aim at creating "a network of small and medium-scale industries as well as actively promoting and encouraging the informal sector." Even today, however, relatively little is known about these activities in Africa.[1] Consequently, policy-makers and planners charged with formulating programs to assist small-scale industry are frequently forced to make decisions "unencumbered by evidence."

This chapter aims to help fill the knowledge gap by setting forth what is known about small-scale industries in sub-Saharan Africa and the implications of these findings for policies and programs. Our coverage of industry includes manufacturing (ISIC codes 31–39), as well as the repair of manufactured goods (ISIC code 951), a treatment consistent with most manufacturing censuses and studies.[2] "Small-scale" is defined as those establishments with less than 50 workers. Although somewhat arbitrary, such a limitation excludes most foreign-owned firms and those with more modern and sophisticated management skills, more capital-intensive production techniques, and greater access to capital, technical assistance, and government incentive schemes.

DESCRIPTIVE PROFILE

OVERALL MAGNITUDE AND IMPORTANCE

The available evidence indicates that small-scale firms are a significant if not dominant component of the industrial sectors of most African countries. Not only are the overwhelming majority of industrial establishments small, but they account for the vast bulk of industrial employment. Small-scale firms in countries with the required data generally account for two thirds or more of total industrial employment; indeed, for one country, Sierra Leone, with quite complete and accurate data, the figure is 95 percent. Moreover, most of the employment is concentrated at the smallest end of the size spectrum, with relatively less employment found in firms in the 10 to 49 worker size range. Small-scale firms also generate an important portion of the value-added of Africa's industrial sectors, although their share of value-added is not as great as their employment contribution.

COMPOSITION

An examination of available data indicates that clothing production—primarily tailoring—predominates in most countries, ranging from 25 percent of all establishments in rural Burkina Faso to 52 percent in Nigeria. Wood production—primarily furniture-making—follows, with metal-working (usually blacksmithing), food production (primarily baking), and vehicle, shoe, electrical, and bicycle repairs also found with some frequency. In the rural areas of several countries, such as Burkina Faso and Botswana, beer brewing is a dominant activity, usually undertaken by women. In general, small-scale firms are involved in the production of "light" consumer goods—clothing, furniture, simple tools, food, and drink.

LOCATION

A surprising yet significant finding is that, in most countries, the vast majority of small industries are located in rural areas.[3] Moreover, employment in small rural manufacturing industries often exceeds that generated by all urban manufacturing firms. In Sierra Leone, for example, 86 percent of total industrial sector employment and 95 percent of industrial establishments were located in rural areas

(Chuta and Liedholm, 1985). Similar findings have been reported elsewhere in Africa and in other parts of the world (see Liedholm and Mead, 1985). These figures may actually understate the true magnitude of rural industry because country censuses often fail to register the smallest of the rural industries.[4]

SIZE

The overwhelming majority of these firms are very small, with most employing fewer than five persons. Studies in Nigeria (Aluko, 1972), Sierra Leone (Chuta and Liedholm, 1985), and Ghana (Ghana, 1965) have found that 95 percent or more of the small-scale firms employ fewer than five individuals. Many are simply one-person enterprises. In rural Burkina Faso (Chuta and Wilcox, 1982), for example, 52 percent of the small-scale firms were one-person activities, while in Sierra Leone (Liedholm and Chuta, 1976), the figure was 42 percent. Such findings indicate that most small-scale industrial firms in sub-Saharan Africa are tiny. In view of their large numbers and generally low incomes (see Chuta and Liedholm, 1985), they constitute a potentially important target group for policy-makers concerned with the poor.

OWNERSHIP

The available evidence indicates that the overwhelming majority of small firms are organized as sole proprietorships. In Nigeria (Aluko, et al., 1972), Sierra Leone (Chuta and Liedholm, 1985), and Burkina Faso (Chuta and Wilcox, 1982), for example, over 97 percent of the small firms are set up in this fashion. Female sole proprietors dominate certain small industries in a number of countries, such as beer brewing in Burkina Faso (Chuta and Wilcox, 1982), Botswana (Haggblade, 1984), and Ghana (Steel, 1981), gara dyeing in Sierra Leone (Chuta and Liedholm, 1985), and clothing production in Ghana. There are a few limited liability companies, partnerships, and cooperatives, but almost no small enterprises in the public sector. Indeed, the vast majority of the private industrial establishments in sub-Saharan Africa are small scale.

LABOR AND CAPITAL

A review of the available data, which is summarized in Table 11.1, indicates that hired labor is generally a minor component of the labor force in small enterprises. An interesting finding is that apprentices play a dominant role in parts of West Africa (Nigeria, Ghana, and Sierra Leone), but are quite minor elements of the labor force in East

TABLE 11.1

LABOR FORCE CHARACTERISTICS OF SMALL-SCALE MANUFACTURING FIRMS
(PERCENTAGES)

Country (Area Covered)	Proprietors and Family Workers	Hired Workers	Apprentices
Sierra Leone entire country [1976]	41	17	42
Nigeria			
Western Region [1970]	39	11	50
Mid-West Region [1971]	30	7	63
Lagos [1971]	33	10	57
Ghana			
Kumasi [1975]	29	6	65
Accra [1972]	39	9	52
Burkina Faso			
Eastern ORD [1980]	94	2	4
Tanzania			
Dar and 20 townships [1967]	52	41	7
Kenya			
Rural industries (RIDC clients) [1977]	20	69	11

SOURCES: Sierra Leone: Liedholm and Chuta, 1976; Nigeria: Aluko, et al., 1972; Kumasi: Aryee, 1977; Accra: Steel, 1979; Burkina Faso: Chuta and Wilcox, 1982; Tanzania: Schadler, 1968; Kenya: Child, 1977.

Africa, where the tradition of an organized, indigenous apprentice-ship system is lacking. Proprietors and family workers play a key role in small-scale industries. Most entrepreneurs have little formal edu-cation, have learned their technical skills as apprentices in other small-scale enterprises, and lack extensive training in marketing, fi-nancing, or management (see Chuta and Liedholm, 1985).

The overwhelming source of capital, either for establishing or ex-panding firms, is personal savings, relatives, or retained earnings (Table 11.2). In these countries, less than 4 percent of the funds come from formal sources such as the commercial banking system or the government.

GROWTH

Although systematic information on industrial growth is limited, available evidence indicates that small-scale industrial activity in Af-rica has been increasing. Small-industry employment, for example, grew at a 6 percent annual rate during the 1960s in Ghana (Steel, 1981), and at the same rate over the 1974–80 period in Sierra Leone (Chuta and Liedholm, 1982). Whether small-scale industry has been increasing at a faster rate than large-scale is not clear. In Sierra Leone, small-scale employment grew at a faster rate than large-scale, but in Ghana, the opposite pattern occurred.[5] Nevertheless, since small-scale industries account for such a large portion of industrial employ-ment, even if small producers were to grow at slower rates than the large, the absolute increases in small-scale employment could still be substantial. In Ghana during the 1960s, for example, small-scale in-dustries absorbed five times as many workers as the large-scale firms, although the latter grew at a faster rate.

What kinds of small-scale enterprises are growing the most rap-idly? By firm size, limited evidence from Sierra Leone and from other developing countries outside of Africa indicates that one-person firms are increasing the least rapidly (indeed, in Sierra Leone they were declining), while those in the 10 to 49 size group are growing the fastest.[6] The number of and employment in small firms appear to be growing the most rapidly in the urban areas. In Sierra Leone, for example, small-industry employment grew at a 6 percent annual rate from 1974 to 1980 in urban areas, but at less than half that rate in rural areas.

By enterprise types, food-related activities (such as baking and

TABLE 11.2

SOURCES OF FINANCE FOR INITIAL INVESTMENTS BY SMALL ENTERPRISES IN SOME AFRICAN COUNTRIES

(Percentage of Initial Investment by Source)

| | Nigeria | | | | | | | |
Source	Western State	Mid-West State	Kwara State	Lagos State	Tanzania	Sierra Leone	Uganda
Own savings	98	88	96	98	78	60	78
Relatives	2	10	[a]	2	15	20	—
Banks	[a]	[a]	2	[a]	1	1	1
Government	—	1	2	[a]	1	—	—
Money lenders	[a]	1	—	—	—	1	—
Other	—	1	—	—	6	18	21

[a]less than 1 percent

SOURCES: Nigeria: Aluko, et al., 1972; Tanzania: Schadler, 1968; Sierra Leone: Liedholm and Chuta, 1976; Uganda: Bosa, 1969.

milling), tailoring and dressmaking, furniture-making, and metal-working have generally grown rapidly, even after large-scale domestic factory production in these sub-sectors has begun. Moreover, several newer activities, such as bicycle, auto, and electrical repair, have grown especially rapidly. On the other hand, activities such as spinning and weaving, shoe and leather goods production, and pottery generally appear to have been declining in importance. These differential growth patterns are important in designing policies and programs directed toward small-scale enterprises.

DETERMINANTS OF THE ROLE OF SMALL-SCALE INDUSTRY

DEMAND PROSPECTS

What is the major source of demand for the products of small-scale industry in sub-Saharan Africa? The overwhelming bulk of products made in small firms are simple consumer goods that cater primarily to the needs of relatively low income urban and rural households. Consequently, a key issue is whether the demand for these products increases as local incomes increase. Most entrepreneurial surveys in Africa indicate that lack of demand is an important constraint facing most small firms. Although some have argued that these types of products are inferior (i.e., demand for them would decline as incomes increase), the few empirical studies indicate that there is a strong, positive relationship between local income and demand for small-scale industry products.

In Sierra Leone, for example, King and Byerlee (1978), on the basis of their pioneering survey and analysis of rural expenditures, reported that an income increase of 10 percent would increase the demand for the products of small-scale firms by almost 9 percent. Consequently, the growth of demand for small-scale industry products would appear to be closely linked to corresponding increases in household incomes, particularly among the rural and low-income segments of the population.

Are there important sources of demand for small-industry products that stem from their backward and forward production linkages with other segments of the economy? In general, these sources of demand appear to be less developed in sub-Saharan Africa than in other parts of the developing world. The strongest of these production linkages in sub-Saharan Africa, however, are found in the agricultural sector, where the processing of several crops, such as rice and oil palm in West Africa (see Spencer, et al., 1976, and Miller, 1965), and the production of implements for traditional agriculture (see Chuta and Liedholm, 1985) are frequently undertaken by small-scale firms. Production linkages with large-scale industry appear particularly weak in sub-Saharan Africa; very few sub-contracting relationships between large and small industrial firms appear to have been developed as yet.

Further, foreign demand for small-industry products is relatively small, limited to a few specialty products such as gara-dyed cloth from Sierra Leone (Chuta and Liedholm, 1985) and baskets from Botswana (Haggblade, 1984).

SUPPLY FACTORS

Small-scale industries are generally more labor intensive than their larger-scale counterparts. Since in sub-Saharan Africa, capital and foreign exchange are relatively scarce, and labor, particularly unskilled, is relatively abundant, those firms that generate more employment per unit of capital would appear to represent activities or techniques most appropriate to the country's factor endowments. Both aggregate and industry-specific data consistently show that small firms in sub-Saharan Africa generate more employment per unit of scarce capital than their larger-scale counterparts (see Chuta and Liedholm, 1979, and Page and Steel, 1984).

A key related issue is whether these same labor-intensive small-scale firms use the scarce factor of capital more effectively than their larger-scale counterparts. Aggregate data are limited and do not show consistent results. A few industry-specific studies have been completed in which firms in the same industry are grouped together. The findings from these studies indicate that small-scale firms in these industries generate more output per unit of scarce capital than their larger-scale counterparts.

Do these same small enterprises also generate a higher rate of "economic profit" than their larger-scale counterparts? The economic rate of return to capital, a measure that reflects profit when all inputs including family labor and capital are valued at their opportunity cost, may be a better measure of economic efficiency or total factor productivity than the output-capital ratio, which assumes that labor and other factor inputs have a "shadow price" of zero. Although economic profitability data are limited, the available results are consistent with the previous capital productivity findings: small-scale firms generated higher "economic" rates of return to capital than their larger-scale industrial counterparts. While not conclusive, these findings do indicate that in several lines of activity, small-scale industries are economically efficient.

POLICY AND PROJECT ISSUES

The preceding discussion makes clear that small enterprises are widespread and diverse in sub-Saharan African economies and that they are apparently quite efficient in their use of resources. In view of their potential contribution to future growth in income and employment, they should be the target of policy and project-focused attention from African governments and donors. A focus on small producers also corresponds with the U.S. Agency for International Development's current interest in private enterprise, one of the "four pillars" of emphasis in current aid programs.

However, questions arise concerning the design and implementation of policies and projects to support the growth of small producers. In this section, we make a distinction between policies which are designed to affect broad classes of producers on the one hand, and projects which are based on a patron-client relationship to provide assistance to particular designated firms, on the other. For each of these, it is helpful to separate policies and projects that operate on the "supply side" (i.e., which focus on the availability of inputs and production conditions), as distinct from those whose major focus is on demand considerations.

POLICIES

Industrialization was a major development goal in virtually all sub-Saharan African countries in the immediate post-independence period. In large measure, this meant an emphasis on large-scale firms, generally using the most modern technology with a high level of capital intensity and an import substitution focus (see Ewing, 1968). This approach subsequently came under attack on two related counts: it often involved considerable economic inefficiency in resource use; and it led to only minimum absorption of labor in the manufacturing sector (see Frank, 1968, and Morawetz, 1974). The result was a widespread disillusionment with large-scale industrialization as a central focus for development policy.

This disillusionment also led to a renewed interest in exploring the possibilities of industrialization through small enterprises. While most governments in sub-Saharan Africa have stated that they favor and support the growth of small producers (see, for example, OAU, 1982), there are only few policies that might be considered as directly supportive of the growth of small firms. In fact, the most pervasive impact of current government policies on small producers arises from their unintended side-effects. In large measure, the central impact of these policies on small producers is negative, operating in ways which discriminate against them rather than encouraging their development. First, a considerable amount of assistance is provided to large producers through policies that are restricted in their design and specification. A typical example is the Development Ordinance enacted in Sierra Leone in 1960, which gave income tax holidays and import duty exemptions to firms planning to invest $50,000 or more in plant and equipment, but no comparable assistance to smaller firms. (Chuta and Liedholm, 1985).

Second, even for policies which in principle apply equally to all types of enterprises, implementation is often undertaken in such a way as to have strongly differential impacts on producers of different types and sizes. In Rwanda, for example, small enterprises generally do not import their inputs directly, but buy them from local importers, who are subject to higher tariff rates. In a similar way, in other countries, small firms find it difficult if not impossible to act as suppliers to the government, since the procurement packages are too large and there are no provisions for partitioning of contracts. In this situation, the most important first step in instituting a policy regime supportive of small enterprise growth is to eliminate the existing policy biases against the small producer.

SUPPLY SIDE POLICY ISSUES

There are a number of different policy areas that concern the availability and costs of inputs and related questions pertaining to the production process. The first of these relates to credit. Interest rate ceilings are an important area where policies have a major impact on small enterprises. Studies suggest that it generally costs more per dollar lent to process loans to small compared to large borrowers; risks of default may also be higher than for more established firms. In such a situation, interest rate ceilings may make it unprofitable for financial institutions to lend to small producers at all. The result is that small enterprises are often forced to turn for their credit needs to informal sources that generally charge much higher interest rates.

In Sierra Leone, for example, the maximum official interest rate in 1974 was 12 percent, but the informal market rate was over 160 percent (Byerlee et al., 1983). Official interest rate ceilings in Africa generally run from 10 to 20 percent, while informal rates frequently are 100 percent or more (see Chuta and Liedholm, 1979). Therefore, efforts to protect small borrowers from bearing the full costs of their credit needs means that they are forced to rely on even higher cost alternative credit channels.

The policy implications here are straightforward. It is important to work toward the elimination of interest rate ceilings as a move toward ensuring that interest rates more closely approximate the opportunity costs of capital for small borrowers.

Second, small producers often find themselves at a disadvantage in access to foreign exchange. Obtaining an import license often requires skills and contacts with government bureaucracies which small firms do not have. Beyond this, tariff rates are generally set in a decision-making context based on a response to pressures; small firms often find that they do not have the requisite influence. In the case of tariffs on textile machinery in Sierra Leone, for example, large garment producers were covered by the country's industrial incentive package and were able to import their machines duty-free; small tailors, by contrast, found that the sewing machine, their basic capital input, was classified as a luxury consumer good and taxed accordingly with no duty relief. Similarly, dyes used in large-scale textile firms were admitted duty-free, while the dyes used in the making of gara cloth were subject to the full import tariff (Chuta and Liedholm, 1985). Such differential treatment of large and small firms with respect to foreign exchange access and tariffs should be eliminated.

As a third supply-side policy issue, governments in many countries exercise extensive control over the distribution of industrial inputs. This may reflect a suspicion of unscrupulous merchants and their excessive mark-ups or it may be a part of a policy aimed at the control and regulation of supplies of imported inputs. There is often a bias in favor of the larger producers in the implementation of such controls.

Unless the government makes a conscious effort to ensure that these inputs are equally available to smaller firms, the larger producers will generally end up benefiting from the controlled markets. These problems arise most clearly in relation to imported inputs handled by public sector distribution systems; they also appear for local products distributed through public sector channels. In both cases, the most common picture involves unequal access to inputs between the large and small users. The most effective way of removing this bias is to work toward a system based on reduced governmental control and intervention in the distribution system.

A fourth area of concern relates to governmental rules and regulations. There has been considerable interest in exploring the position of a category of small producers referred to as the "informal sector" in Africa. While we have not found this categorization to be particularly helpful, it has one important characteristic related to government regulations (Page, 1979). In many ways, small producers fall outside government assistance programs, but also outside taxation, regulation, and control mechanisms. In some cases, the laws explicitly state that they do not apply to small producers (small firms are not required to obtain certain kinds of licenses, to obey certain labor regulations, or to pay certain types of taxes). In many other cases, however, the laws are written as if they apply to all producers regardless of size. This is often the case even when all agree that enforcing the laws for very small producers is quite unrealistic.

Stating the law in broad terms but then interpreting it more restrictively has not only bred contempt of the law, but has also exposed small producers to threats that unless they "pay off" the appropriate officials, the law in question will be put into effect against them with the risk that they can be put out of business. Frequently, the implementation of such laws for small producers is highly arbitrary and erratic, making it virtually impossible to engage in sensible business planning. Industrial regulations should be screened carefully to ensure that there is a workable and equitable way of implementing them for small producers or that these small producers are explicitly exempted from coverage.

DEMAND SIDE POLICY ISSUES

Numerous studies have made clear that perhaps the single most important constraint facing small producers, particularly in the rural areas, is the problem of finding markets for their output. Many of these producers sell only in local or regional markets. Conversely, a significant share of the low-cost consumer goods sold in such rural markets are produced by small enterprises located in the same region. This means that policies supportive of increasing income in rural areas will have significant multiplier effects through expanding demand for the output of small manufacturers. Probably the most important set of policies for the encouragement of small manufacturers particularly in rural areas concerns the expansion and equitable distribution of agricultural incomes. Policies slanted against agricultural development lead not only to a stagnant agricultural sector, but also to stagnant demand for products of rural small manufacturers.

PROJECTS

Until recently, most of the attention of African governments and donor agencies on small enterprise development has been focused not on the overall policies that affect small businesses generally, but on targeted projects or programs that involve some form of patron-client relationship with individual establishments. In the 1950s and early 1960s, most of these projects in Africa focused on the provision of an integrated package of inputs to a relatively limited number of "modern" small businesses, following the "Indian model" developed and applied earlier in Asia and Latin America by the Stanford Research Institute and the Ford Foundation (see Staley and Morse, 1965).

After a hiatus of about a decade, interest in small industry in sub-Saharan Africa reemerged under the guise of appropriate technology and the informal sector. Currently, most of this interest surrounds firms at the lower end of the size spectrum, typically with a rural orientation and involving subsidized assistance for a small minority of producers. Perhaps reflecting the normal lag between theory and practice, however, many projects are still designed on the earlier model, with relatively high cost assistance being provided to a relatively small number of firms.

SUPPLY SIDE PROJECTS: CREDIT AND TECHNICAL ASSISTANCE

In recent years, credit projects have been the most common method of providing direct assistance to individual small enterprises in sub-Saharan Africa. These programs have been designed to overcome small firms' lack of access to formal credit sources (Table 11.2)—the greatest "perceived" constraint as viewed by the producers themselves. A number of countries in sub-Saharan Africa, such as Cameroon, Zambia, and Kenya, have designed special credit programs aimed specifically at the small producers (Kilby and D'Zmura, 1985). Very often, though, they have been directed toward the top end of the small enterprise sector, leaving the smaller producers with limited access to institutional credit. These programs are often based on a tranche of funds from outside donors lent to a certain category of borrowers at subsidized interest rates. These below-cost interest rates also raise the potential danger of spreading to small producers the same perverse excessive capital intensity which has often characterized the larger firms. They also make it unlikely that local funding agencies will step in to continue this credit flow when external assistance is no longer available.

Only a few of these credit projects in sub-Saharan Africa have been evaluated. It is frequently argued, however, that the administrative costs and risks of lending are much higher for small than for large firms (see World Bank, 1978). Concern is also expressed regarding the extent of small industry's demand for credit and the effectiveness of the delivery channels. Two recent reviews of several small industry credit schemes such as the Partners for Productivity Rural Enterprise Development Project in Burkina Faso indicate that several have been successful, generating benefit-cost ratios consistently above one, and frequently with administrative costs and arrears rates below 10 percent of the loan value (Kilby and D'Zmura, 1985, and Liedholm, 1985).

Most of the successful projects have some common characteristics that should be considered when designing new schemes. First, they have primarily provided working capital rather than the fixed capital that is the focus of most lending schemes,[7] consistent with the findings of most recent small industry studies that point to the lack of working capital as a primary financial constraint facing most small-scale firms.

Second, the delivery mechanisms of these successful credit projects differ markedly from the standard credit schemes. Loans are screened on the basis of character rather than on project feasibility and/or collateral. Moreover, the institutions are locally based with decentralized decision-making; the initial loans are small for short periods; and loan volume per loan officer is high. Finally, interest rates are high enough to cover operating expenses including the cost of funds. In several countries, formal credit institutions, including commercial banks, have been able to modify their loan procedures to meet these characteristics.

Two steps may be taken to encourage formal sector financial institutions to lend to small firms. One would be to pay a share of the administrative costs for commercial banks or other financial institutions, and provide loan guarantees. This could be done on a temporary basis, with the share of costs covered from outside and/or the magnitude of the guarantee declining over time. Second, consideration might be given to providing technical assistance to financial institutions to enable them to develop lower-cost screening mechanisms for lending to very small producers (Liedholm, 1985).

Technical and managerial assistance schemes have also been a popular method of providing direct project support to small firms in sub-Saharan Africa. As early as 1962, industrial development centers designed to provide technical and managerial assistance to small businesses were established in Zaria and Owerri, Nigeria, with USAID assistance. Similar centers were subsequently established in many other African countries, including Ghana, Botswana, Tanzania, and Kenya (Livingston, 1977). Although there have been a few evaluations of individual centralized assistance centers (see, for example, Hawbacker and Turner, 1972), there has not yet been a systematic analysis of their experiences or of the effectiveness of technical assistance schemes for sub-Saharan Africa. It is frequently argued, however, that business' demand for such services is very small.[8] Another often-heard criticism is that such programs have ended up concentrating a large volume of resources on a relatively limited clientele and that their delivery costs per client are therefore unduly high (see Kilby, 1982).

A review of a number of projects in sub-Saharan Africa makes it possible to isolate several common characteristics that seem to accompany successful technical assistance activities. First, these projects tend to be industry- and task-specific, such as the highly regarded training program in Botswana that imparted joinery skills to carpenters to enable them to produce coffins for the local markets (Haggblade, 1982). Second, these projects addressed situations where only a single "missing ingredient" needed to be supplied to the firm rather than an array of ingredients.[9]

The Botswana mud oven training course, which was designed to teach women to make mud ovens and bake bread for sale, provides a graphic example. The women in the scheme who previously had baked other products for sale were able to increase their incomes substantially, while those women without any prior commercial baking experience failed because there were too many "missing ingredients" (Haggblade, 1982). Projects assisting existing firms are therefore more likely to be successful than those that attempt to establish new firms.

Third, before successful projects were launched, prior surveys of industries had been undertaken to uncover the demand for the activity and the number and type of "missing ingredients." Such surveys are important because evidence is accumulating that the constraints facing small-scale industries in sub-Saharan Africa vary significantly from country to country and from industry to industry (see Chuta and Liedholm, 1979).

Finally, successful projects tend to be built upon proven existing institutions. Although these may often be formal institutions, existing informal institutions should not be overlooked. The apprenticeship system is an example of an informal institution that can provide a low-cost alternative for the delivery of technical and management assistance to small firms in sub-Saharan Africa. One of the striking features of the labor market in West Africa, illustrated in Table 11.1, concerns the central role of the apprenticeship system in the training of workers in small enterprises. The contrast with East Africa (as well as with most other countries of the world) is quite marked. Thus in East Africa, government training programs play a particularly important role in supplying skilled personnel to the small enterprise sector.

Care is needed to ensure that training programs are designed with the needs of smaller producers in mind. Beyond this, the expansion of apprenticeship systems in East and West Africa should be explored. A comparison of apprenticeship systems and government vocational training programs demonstrates that the former can be far more effective—and particularly more cost-effective (Mabawonku, 1979). Policies aimed at encouraging the expansion of apprenticeship systems might include rewarding their graduates in public and private sector hiring practices; regularizing the terms of service; and recognizing the implications of their activities (i.e., those who provide the training cannot always capture its benefits, since trained workers are free to move to a different employer). Other types of training programs might also be instituted through the apprentice-ship system, particularly to help develop managerial skills among small producers.

In a number of African countries, a key aspect of small enterprise development policy has centered around industrial estates, provid-ing construction of sheds with basic utilities which are then rented or sold to small enterprises. Two arguments have been advanced to justify the construction of such facilities. First, currently available space with the required utilities is inadequate; in some cases, this is explained in terms of problems of establishment of clear land titles. Second, grouping firms together in such an estate makes it possible to provide common trading programs and facilities, such as machine shops, (i.e., various types of industrial extension services.)

While these arguments sound convincing, in practice most indus-trial estates have proven to be an expensive means of subsidizing the work-space costs of a limited number of existing enterprises (see, for example, Kilby, 1982). They have also been ineffective in facilitating the development of new firms. For the firms they do help, their assistance is high cost, involving a wide range of assistance, much of which will not be needed by the client firms. In general, industrial estates have not proven to be effective channels for providing assist-ance to small enterprises in sub-Saharan Africa.

DEMAND-SIDE PROJECTS: MARKETING ASSISTANCE

One common characteristic of small producers in Africa and else-where is that they are often more skilled in production than in prod-uct design and marketing. As a result, they often produce standard-ized products for sale in local markets that may be growing only slowly. In such situations, an appropriate focus would be to assist small producers to establish more effective links to outside markets. This could be done through sub-contracting arrangements, either with larger manufacturers or with merchants.

Sub-contracting arrangements among producers are said to be rel-atively rare in Africa, although arrangements based on contracts be-tween small producers and merchants or traders can be found in some African countries, often for the marketing of craft products. An excellent example is Botswanacraft, which in the 1970s provided the single missing marketing link that was needed to support the com-mercial production of basketmaking in the rural areas (see Haggblade, 1982). Where they are effectively carried out, such contract production and sub-contracting systems can play an important role in establishing linkages between isolated producers and more dynamic markets. Consideration should be given to exploring ways of expanding the nascent role of sub-contracting in sub-Saharan Africa (Mead, 1985).

IMPLICATIONS FOR AFRICAN GOVERNMENTS AND DONOR AGENCIES

Small enterprises are of considerable importance as sources of employment and income in sub-Saharan Africa today. This importance is likely to increase over time, as population growth puts strains on available cultivable land, and as the number of people seeking work outside agriculture exceeds the absorptive capacity of large-scale industrial and service enterprises. This discussion has suggested a number of measures to facilitate the expansion of small enterprises and to channel this expansion in productive directions.

Three major conclusions can be drawn concerning small enterprise policies, the ways these policies currently impinge on small producers, and the need for more effective policy support in the future. The first is that the impact of current policies on this group of enterprises has generally been negative, resulting in discrimination against small producers and in favor of their larger-scale and better-connected competitors. This discrimination arises both from the ways in which laws are written and the ways they are implemented. African governments and donor agencies need to better understand the ways in which existing policies operate in practice, with the aim of eliminating this discrimination and establishing more equal competitive conditions for large and small enterprises.

The second major conclusion is that the key constraint hindering the growth of small enterprises, particularly in rural areas, is related to a deficiency of demand. The government's overall development policies can play a key role in overcoming this deficiency. In particular, agricultural policies aimed at a rapid growth of rural incomes are important not only in their own right, but also because they contribute in a major way to the growth potential of non-agricultural, rural small enterprises.

Efforts to establish pricing systems that provide incentives to farmers to increase their output, to encourage the development of effective marketing systems for selling their products, and to institute agrarian reform leading to an equitable sharing of the benefits of increasing agricultural output can all contribute in important ways to the potential for growth among small non-agricultural producers.

The third major point, closely related to the previous two, involves a recognition that, in thinking about the effects of policies on small producers, African governments and donor agencies must adopt a comprehensive view, looking far beyond the traditional sphere of industrial policy to agricultural pricing and income policies and the general foreign exchange regime of the country.

Projects or client-specific programs in sub-Saharan Africa have primarily focused on eliminating or reducing supply constraints. African governments and donor agencies have a useful continuing role in this area. The majority of projects directed at the support of small enterprises have been in the area of credit, partly reflecting the fact that many small enterprise projects are best designed as small projects, requiring only limited amounts of funding. However, donors are often under pressure to "move money," and one of the few ways of doing so in significant volume is through concentration on credit activities.

A review of successful credit projects suggests the following guidelines to facilitate the growth of small enterprises in sub-Saharan Africa as elsewhere in the world: concentrating on working capital rather than fixed capital; screening of loans based on the character of the applicant rather than the characteristic of the project; decentralizing decision-making to local institutions and local individuals; and granting loans in small amounts, for short periods, to encourage and facilitate high repayment rates.

Among the key findings concerning small enterprise projects in areas other than credit, the following may be singled out as being of primary importance in the design and implementation of future projects. First, useful projects will generally be carefully targeted to a limited range of enterprises, probably in one or a few closely related industries. Second, projects are more likely to succeed if they can be targeted to deal with one or a limited range of missing components, rather introducing a complex range of changes all at once. Third, it is generally advisable to start from existing institutions, rather than attempting to begin from scratch with a new locus and staff. Fourth, projects aimed at establishing more effective links between dispersed producers and more dynamic and often more distant markets can provide useful contributions. Fifth, there is a need for careful field research to determine the needs of small producers in particular situations so that projects are effectively targeted.

POLICY REFORM AND IMPLEMENTATION ISSUES

The process of policy reform is a complex one, involving pressure groups and compromises which are difficult for an outsider to understand, much less lead. Experience suggests some rules about the most effective way of working toward policy change. First, policy change is generally a long-term process. Almost any change will mean that some groups benefit while others lose. Efforts to move things too rapidly can cause great social turmoil, during which all possibilities of improvement may be frozen.

Second, the most effective route to policy reform often involves participation by actual and potential policy-makers in analyses of the ways in which policy currently works and how alternative policy configurations might operate. Well-focused policy-oriented studies can provide important insights into the ways policies are currently working, thereby supplying a firmer base of understanding for those who wish to effect changes. With judicious governmental policies and carefully formulated direct assistance measures, the already sizeable contribution of small-scale industries to sub-Saharan African development can be further enhanced.

NOTES

1. For a review of existing studies, see Liedholm (1973), Page (1979), and Page and Steel (1984).

2. Mining, construction, trading, and transport are not included in this review.

3. The UN definition of rural localities with fewer than 20,000 inhabitants is used in this chapter. The conclusions do not change markedly if other definitions are used.

4. Rural manufacturing employment had been underestimated in Sierra Leone by almost one-half (Liedholm and Chuta, 1976).

5. In Tanzania, it appeared that small industry's share of industrial output fell from 1966 to 1974 (Wynne-Roberts, 1980).

6. In Sierra Leone, over the period 1974–80, one-person firms were declining at a 4 percent annual rate; firms in the 2 to 9 workers category increased at a 3.5 percent annual rate; while those firms with from 10 to 49 workers increased at a 12.7 percent annual rate (Chuta and Liedholm, 1982).

7. The emphasis on fixed capital stems from aid donors' interest in lending schemes with high foreign exchange components, an orientation of academic economists toward fixed assets, and a paucity of requisite statistics.

8. See, for example, Page and Steel(1984) and Liedholm and Chuta(1976) and the Economic Commission for Africa (1982), which states that "it must be kept in mind that most small-scale enterprises are unaware of the need for these services."

9. Peter Kilby (1982) developed this notion when reviewing ILO/UNDP small-enterprise projects worldwide.

REFERENCES

Aluko, S. A., O. A. Oguntoye and Y. A. O. Afonja. 1972. *Small Scale Industries: Western State Nigeria*. Ile-Ife: Industrial Research Unit, University of Ife.

Aryee, George. 1976. "The Inter-Relationships Between the Formal Sector and the Informal Manufacturing Sector in Kumasi, Ghana." Geneva: ILO.

Bosa, George R. 1969. *The Financing of Small Scale Enterprises in Uganda*. Nairobi: Oxford University Press.

Byerlee, D., Carl Eicher, Carl Liedholm, and D. Spencer. 1983. "Employment-Output Conflicts, Factor Price Distortions, and Choice of Techniques: Empirical Evidence from Sierra Leone." *Economic Development and Cultural Change* 31(2): 315–36.

Child, Frank C. 1977. *Small Scale Rural Industry in Kenya*. Los Angeles: UCLA, African Studies Center, Occasional Paper No. 17.

Chuta, E. and Carl Liedholm. 1979. "Rural Non-Farm Employment: A Review of the State of the Art." East Lansing: Michigan State University, MSU Rural Development Paper No. 4.

Chuta, E. and Carl Liedholm. 1982. "Employment Growth and Change in Sierra Leone Small-Scale Industry, 1974–80." *International Labour Review*. 121(1) (January–February): 101–13.

Chuta, E. and Carl Liedholm. 1985. *Employment and Growth in Small-Scale Industry: Empirical Evidence from Sierra Leone*. London: Macmillan Co.

Chuta, E. and D. Wilcox. 1982. "Employment in Rural Industries in Eastern Upper Volta." *International Labour Review*. 121(1) (July–August): 455–68.

Economic Commission for Africa. 1982. *Programme for the Industrial Development Decade for Africa*. New York: ECA/OAU/UNIDO.

Ethiopia, Government of. 1980. *Statistical Abstract, 1980*. Addis Ababa: Central Statistics Office.

Ewing, A. F. 1968. *Industry in Africa*. London: Oxford University Press.

Frank, Charles. 1968. "Urban Unemployment and Economic Growth in Africa." *Oxford Economic Papers*. 20(2) (July): 250–74.

Ghana, Government of. 1965. *Area Sampling Survey of Small Manufacturing Establishments-1963*. Accra, Ghana: Central Bureau of Statistics.

Haggblade, Steve. 1982. *Rural Industrial Officers' Handbook*. Volume II, District Planning Services, Ministry of Commerce and Industry, Gaborone, Botswana.

Haggblade, Steve. 1984. "The Shabeen Queen." Ph.D. dissertation, Department of Economics, Michigan State University.

Hawbacker, George and H. Turner. 1972. "Developing Small Industries: A Case Study of AID Assistance in Nigeria, 1962–1971." Washington, D.C.: AID.

Kilby, Peter. 1982. "Small Scale Industry in Kenya." East Lansing: Michigan State University, MSU Rural Development Paper #20.

Kilby, Peter and John D'Zmura. 1985. "Searching for Benefits," AID Evaluation Special Study No. 28, Washington, D.C.: USAID.

King, Robert and D. Byerlee. 1978. "Factor Intensities and Locational Linkages of Rural Consumption Patterns in Sierra Leone." *American Journal of Agricultural Economics* 60, (2): 197–201.

Liedholm, Carl. 1973. "Research on Employment in the Rural Nonfarm Sector in Africa." East Lansing: Michigan State University, African Rural Employment Paper No. 5.

Liedholm, Carl. 1985. "Small Scale Credit Schemes: Administrative Costs and the Role of Inventory Norms." East Lansing: Michigan State University, MSU International Development Working Paper (forthcoming).

Liedholm, Carl and Enyinna Chuta. 1976. "The Economics of Rural and Urban Small Scale Industries in Sierra Leone." East Lansing: Michigan State University, African Rural Economy Paper No. 14.

Liedholm, Carl and Donald C. Mead. 1985. "Small Scale Enterprises in Developing Countries: A Review of the State of the Art" (draft).

Livingston, Ian. 1977. "An Evaluation of Kenya's Rural Industrial Development Programme." *Journal of Modern African Studies* 15: 494–504.

Mabawonku, Adewale. 1979. "An Economic Evaluation of Apprenticeship Training in Western Nigerian Small Scale Industries." East Lansing: Michigan State University, African Rural Economy Paper No. 17.

Mead, Donald C. 1985. "Subcontracting Systems and Assistance Programs: Opportunities for Intervention." East Lansing: Michigan State University, MSU International Development Paper (forthcoming).

Miller, W. L. 1965. "An Economic Analysis of Oil Palm Fruit Processing in Eastern Nigeria." Ph.D. dissertation, Michigan State University.

Morawetz, D. 1974. "Employment Implications of Industrialization in Developing Countries: A Survey." *Economic Journal* (84): 491–592.

Norcliffe, G. B. and Freeman. 1980. "Non-farm Activities in Market Centers of Central Province, Kenya." *Canadian Journal of African Studies* 14(3): 503–17.

Organization of African Unity. 1980. *Lagos Plan of Action for the Economic Development of Africa, 1980 to 2000*. Addis Ababa: OAU.

Page, John. 1979. "Small Enterprise in African Development: A Survey." Staff Working Paper No. 363. Washington, D.C.: The World Bank.

Page, J. and W. Steel. 1984. *Small Enterprise Development: Economic Issues from*

African Experience. Technical Paper No. 26. Washington, D.C.: The World Bank.

Spencer, Dunstan, I. May Parker, and Frank Rose. 1976. "Employment Efficiency and Income in the Rice Processing Industry in Sierra Leone." East Lansing, Michigan: Michigan State University, African Rural Employment Paper No. 15.

Staley, Eugene and Richard Morse. 1965. *Modern Small Industry for Developing Countries*. New York: McGraw-Hill.

Steel, William F. 1977. *Small-Scale Employment and Production in Developing Countries: Evidence from Ghana*. New York: Praeger Publishers.

Steel, William F. 1979. "The Urban Artisanal Sector in Ghana and the Cameroon: Comparison of Structure and Policy Problems." *Journal of Modern African Studies* 17(2): 271–84.

Steel, William F. 1981. "Female and Small-Scale Employment Under Modernization in Ghana." *Economic Development and Cultural Change* 30(1) (October): 153–67.

World Bank. 1978. "Employment and Development in Small Enterprises." Washington, D.C.: The World Bank.

Wynne-Roberts, C. R. 1980. "Small Scale Industry Development in Sub-Saharan Africa." Washington, D.C.: The World Bank (mimeo).

CHAPTER TWELVE

Private Investment and African Economic Policy

Niles E. Helmboldt, Tina West, and Benjamin H. Hardy

The achievement of self-sustained economic development in Africa depends on the policy decisions of its governments. The policies of the United States or any other outside party, although they can be a help or hindrance to development, are secondary. Without an appropriate, consistent set of economic policies that favor the growth of local, private production to meet local and external demand, African governments will find only temporary escape from the conditions that constitute the African economic crisis. Harnessing the energies of the private sector to help Africa achieve its development objectives seems to be the appropriate strategy.

The choice of a particular development strategy, particularly one as heavily laden with ideological connotations as the free market, is a political decision. This chapter does not presume to direct national leaders on how to decide these issues. However, given recent efforts of a number of governments to revitalize their economies—including giving a larger role to the free market—we can point to various practical steps that can increase the benefits and perhaps diminish the ills of this approach.

The focus of this chapter is on actions African governments can take to achieve their goal of self-sustained growth. Current policies that constrict the growth of the domestic private sector seem an easier obstacle to address than those presented by the structure of international trade. This is not to deny that factors beyond the control of African governments—weather, the slow growth of world trade, and weak commodity prices—have played a large role in causing their economic problems. While African officials have been calling for the industrialized countries to create a more favorable trading environment, current trends of protectionism and political conservatism in the United States and elsewhere make such action unlikely in the near future.

Our analytical schema addresses near-term prospects—two to four years—for investment in Africa, mobilized both domestically and from abroad. We make three basic points. First, little new capital, especially foreign private capital, will be available for Africa during this period, for reasons largely related to African government policies. Therefore, reforms in these policies may help make Africa more attractive to capital investors, particularly over the medium to longer term.

Second, even in the absence of new capital, Africa can begin to recover and to generate new economic development because development does not depend on capital alone. The apparent disarray of African economies often blinds us to existing resources both in the modern and the traditional sectors. Investments already made in manufacturing and commercial agriculture need only foreign exchange for rehabilitation, or, in many cases, removal of the controls and disincentives that currently limit productivity. Small farmers, small entrepreneurs in the informal sector, and small manufacturers already possess the capacity to increase production and the demand for goods exists.

While it is reasonable to assume that the private sector is the most significant source of investment capital, incentive structures in many African countries have not encouraged the private sector to take investment risks. Again, short-term policy reforms can produce salutary results quickly. Governments can stimulate production by reallocating resources to improve the productivity of their own capital investment and by removing some of the existing disincentives to private sector investment. They can also increase the private sector's access to foreign exchange.

The third point is addressed to the U.S. government and the international donor community, which can lend support to African governments in these efforts by their advice on policy and by standing ready to help in practical ways. If promotion of the private sector is not to become another development fad, donors must assist in African governments' efforts to resolve the political problems which can result from economic policy reform and with the pervasive problems of foreign exchange shortages. Structural adjustment will be achieved not only by advocating theories, but by devising creative solutions to practical problems.

THE SHORT-TERM INVESTMENT OUTLOOK

PRIVATE CAPITAL INFLOWS AND FOREIGN PRIVATE INVESTMENT

Unless Treasury Secretary James Baker's initiative is fully implemented, which now seems unlikely, external capital is unlikely to increase from any private source over the next several years, given changed institutional outlooks on the part of banks and multinationals and the investment climate to which African government policies have contributed.

The most authoritative projection of near-term external capital flows to sub-Saharan Africa is contained in the World Bank's *Toward Sustained Development in Sub-Saharan Africa*. Net capital inflows are forecasted to drop from an annual average of $10.8 billion during 1980–82 to $5 billion for 1985–87. Gross capital flows from official and private sources (excluding the IMF) remain roughly the same, at $8.9 billion and $4.2 billion, respectively, but debt amortization payments increase from $2.3 billion to $8 billion—$5 billion of which is owed to private sources.[1]

Although the gross figures imply that repayment of private loans is a major problem, most African countries rely far more on official grants and loans. Based on the data in the 1985 edition of *World Debt Tables*, at end-1983 official lending to 36 sub-Saharan countries made up more than 75 percent of total public or publicly guaranteed debt, including undisbursed debt.[2]

Private and official debt are roughly equal in only two countries, Benin and Congo, with only four countries more heavily indebted to private lenders: Gabon (67 percent), Ivory Coast (59 percent), Nigeria (80 percent), and Zimbabwe (64 percent). Private borrowings by these four countries amount to $20.6 billion, or 71 percent of the total of $29.2 billion in private external lending to sub-Saharan Africa. Similarly, debt service payments of these four countries constitute the bulk of repayments to private lenders—74 percent of the total due between 1985 and 1987. For the remaining countries, new inflows depend largely on their relationships with official lenders.

Our observation that new investment from the industrialized

countries is unlikely to increase substantially in the next few years is confirmed by available data on private sector investment. Although measuring the value of total foreign private sector investment is an inherently difficult process,[3] the OECD Development Assistance Committee (DAC) has compiled a time series that is reasonably consistent.[4] Direct investment by DAC members in sub-Saharan Africa (excluding South Africa) grew from approximately $4.9 billion in 1967 to $7.1 billion in current dollars in 1972—an average annual growth rate of 7.7 percent in nominal terms. By the end of 1981, investment totaled about $11.6 billion, and the annual rate of increase had slowed to 5.6 percent.

However, the average annual growth rate of investments in all developing countries between 1970 and 1981 was 10.7 percent, suggesting that DAC-member investment is increasing more slowly in sub-Saharan Africa than in other developing areas.[5] If these growth rates were adjusted for inflation, they would probably show very little increase in the value of DAC-member investment in Africa.

Investment in Africa from newly industrialized countries, particularly Brazil and India, is increasing more rapidly than that of DAC members. Brazilian companies have invested widely in Nigeria (telecommunications and ethanol) and in the Lusophone countries, while Indian companies have invested in paper and machine tool manufacturing in Kenya. Africa ranked second as a recipient of Indian foreign investment in 1980, according to data quoted in Wells (1983).[6]

The bulk of new investment from industrialized countries is coming from companies that already have long-term commitments in Africa—the 1983 Heinz purchase in Zimbabwe being one of several exceptions. Such companies are more likely to seek funding for new investments than those with no previous experience in Africa. African governments, leery of dishonest investors, can take some comfort in dealing with firms that have established track records. During good times, committed companies are likely to reinvest a significant portion of their profits. Goldsbrough (1985) reports that in a group of developing countries, reinvested earnings averaged 39 percent of recorded investment during 1973–1982, noting that over 50 percent of direct investment from the United States and the United Kingdom was in the form of reinvested earnings.[7]

Although these companies form a hardy band of long-term investors, many others have become disillusioned with their investments in Africa. The Japanese withdrawal from SODIMIZA—a joint copper mining venture with Zaire—and the closing of the American Motors assembly operation in Kenya are recent examples.

A potential source of investment, though not of foreign exchange, is blocked currency held by external private investors and trade creditors. Halting the legal repatriation of funds is a disincentive to new investors. However, a number of governments have already blocked repatriation of large sums, including dividends and short-term trade debt. This money, which the central bank usually declares to be temporarily nonconvertible, may remain blocked for many years. If governments can persuade foreign investors and debt holders to continue holding these blocked funds in local currency, however, the money can become a source of new investment.

While most foreign creditors and investors have no interest in using their blocked funds to invest in a country, others may consider the cost of waiting to be higher than the risks of investing. Several governments are designing incentives to encourage these companies, such as allowing access to the foreign exchange earned by new exports. Although if these investors undertake new projects, they will probably bring in only the minimum amount of additional foreign exchange needed for the project, the investments are otherwise similar to direct foreign investment projects.

By declaring that these foreign investments will be treated as new direct foreign investments, governments may enable investors to obtain insurance or other guarantees from their home country. In African countries where there is a bilateral investment agreement, American investors can obtain OPIC coverage on the same terms as new investment. The foreign government approval letter need only state that the investment from blocked funds will be treated as new investment.

DECLINING FOREIGN INVESTMENT: CAUSES AND REMEDIES

There are a number of reasons why prospects for foreign capital inflows are poor today. African governments can address the internal problems more effectively than the external ones. New policies might well improve the investment climate and its attractiveness to foreign investors in particular. In the text below, we outline prescriptions for policy reform; they are, however, intended for governments that have already decided to increase the scope of the private sector in their economies.

EXTERNAL FACTORS

Bank Lending   Increased lending from private commercial banks is unlikely. After peaking at $8.6 billion in 1981, new commitments from private creditors dropped to $5 billion in 1983, according to the *World Debt Tables*.[8] Probably they declined further in 1984 and 1985.

Commercial banks are reluctant to lend to Africa for reasons not necessarily related to African economies. Major American banks with international portfolios are currently reviewing their exposures, particularly those in energy, agriculture, and other weak spots in the domestic economy, as well as in Latin America. Under these circumstances, they are not aggressively seeking new lending opportunities in developing countries. Lending within the United States is more profitable than it has been for some time thanks to a larger than usual spread between the prime rate and the cost of funds. A recent estimate shows that U.S. bank lending abroad dropped by $13 billion during 1984.[9] Reinforcing bankers' reluctance to add significantly to their Third World lending is the fear that it would send up a red flag to Wall Street financial analysts, adversely affecting bank stock prices. Given the poor profit performance of some of the largest banks over the past three years, analysts are now especially watchful.

Regional banks in the United States that participated in syndicated loans in the boom years are more unhappy about reschedulings than are the money-center banks that have long-term commitments to African markets. The regional banks would like to get their money out and stay out. By contrast, a few money-center banks are willing to maintain their exposures and will increase their lending again when African opportunities become relatively attractive. Among their clients are multinational companies, many of which are also in Africa for the long haul. By staying in Africa, these few money-center banks have remained close to opportunities for collateral business, such as deposits from customers and fees for letters of credit and funds transfers. However, both European and American banks are looking for guarantees from their export credit agencies or at least for the comfort of World Bank and IMF programs which impose financial discipline on creditor governments.

Private Investment   In a parallel change in institutional perceptions, multinational investors from industrialized countries are increasingly unwilling to set up operations in the low and middle-income developing countries if more prosperous and stable countries are available. Even if it is more expensive to locate and operate a plant in Australia, for example, rather than Jamaica, Thailand, or Kenya, many investors are taking the safer route.

For their part, Africans no longer have high expectations of foreign investment. Each side has been hurt by abuses of trust. International contractors have delivered shoddy products, including entire turn-key projects; corrupt or capricious African officials have milked contractors or thwarted programs. It will take time to undo this damage; investors who have been burned once will not clamor to return at the first sign of reform.

INTERNAL FACTORS

Investment Climate   Perceptions of high risk act as a barrier to new foreign investment and are based on the entire economic picture, especially the investment climate. For private investors, the sine qua non of their involvement is profitability as measured by return on capital. They perceive Africa not only as a place where business costs are high, but also as a relatively unpredictable environment.

Ultimately, the investment climate reflects investors' perceptions of the government's ability to maintain stable policies that allow viable, prudent investments to operate profitably. Such confidence is more a function of the government's reliability over time than its ideology; some socialist governments have excellent reputations for dealing fairly and effectively with foreign investors.

That the investment climate in African countries is a specific deterrent to foreign investment is clear from surveys of potential foreign investors in DAC-member countries. Baker (1983) estimated that as of 1982, American investment in sub-Saharan Africa totaled less than $6 billion—about 3 percent of total U.S. foreign investment.[10] Baker's survey of U.S. investors reveals that their attitudes toward African risk are shaped not only by structural and environmental factors, but also by more immediate, day-to-day operational problems.

She reports that investors who had decided not to invest in Africa gave six major reasons: markets were too small, the response of the host governments was too slow or requirements were too complicated, the ideology of the host country government seemed hostile to private investment, there were prospects for political instability, credit-worthiness (as indicated through mounting debt, a shortage of foreign exchange, sudden import bans) was lacking, and government intervention in the economy was excessive. It is significant that very few firms indicated that they were concerned with nationalization or expropriation. Instead, companies seem to realize that indigenization is likely to be undertaken by countries seeking greater control of their economy and that insurance can be obtained against nationalization. Hence, in evaluating political risk, "the trend is away from studying macro-political stability to studying a country's regulatory process and its likely choices."[11]

Baker also found that the complaints most frequently voiced by firms already in or planning to operate in Africa had to do with the inefficiency, capriciousness, and/or corruption of bureaucratic processes and government decision-making.[12] A crucial step toward improving the investment climate lies in streamlining government procedures where they touch upon routine relationships with business.

For example, some central banks have worsened their relations with private lenders and damaged their credit standings through slow, inefficient procedures, clerical mistakes, and what appears to lenders to be a reluctance to cooperate. A poor reputation with creditors decreases the ability to obtain loans on the lowest terms. In some countries therefore, central bank efforts to improve debt administration would yield large benefits at relatively modest cost.

Domestic investors also find arbitrary regulations a major obstacle. One successful African entrepreneur told us recently that half his time is spent dealing with government bureaucrats rather than on managing his operations. Uncertainty about changes in regulations limits the amount of investment he is willing to undertake.

Legal Climate   Investor confidence in the rule of law is perhaps the most important single determinant in any investment decision. Legal protection is one area in which the government's performance must match that of other countries if the nation wishes to compete successfully in attracting investors. It is in the government's interest to provide and adhere firmly to a legal code that provides fair and equitable treatment to all businesses. In particular, multinational firms invest widely throughout the industrial world where legal protections are routinely available; such firms expect developing countries to replicate that legal environment as closely as possible.

Unquestionably, the government has the right to demand that foreign and domestic businesses conform to its laws. However, investors compensate for uncertainty by increasing the threshold rate of return required to elicit a positive investment decision. In uncertain environments, they require high short-term profits that may not be in the country's long-term interest. The investor is as concerned with consistency of application as with the content of laws. A foreign investor can live with a wide range of "rules of the game," but prefers to locate a project in a country where arbitrary changes in economic or legal policies do not occur. They want to be assured that the government will treat them fairly, and they want a number of explicit legal guarantees. Among these are equitable and prompt compensation in case of nationalization; the same protection for patents, trademarks, and designs that industrial nations offer; equality before the law for domestic and foreign-owned firms; and clearly agreed upon processes for resolving disputes with the government.

The Investment Code   The legal system and governmental policies concerning private sector investment meet in the investment code. The investment code should clearly specify the laws with which the investor must comply—indigenization schedules, local equity provisions, local value added requirements, labor laws—so that the investor can include the cost of compliance in the calculation of expected profitability. As far as possible, the code should contain or identify clearly all the information the investor needs for these calculations, and should make clear what the government expects from the investor.

Both governments in search of foreign exchange inflows and investors looking for more certain profits may take actions that are not justified by their economic return. While highly desirable from the investor's point of view and cheap to grant on the government's part, protection from competition distorts the economy. Tariff exemptions encourage investment in capital-intensive, import-dependent enterprises. Attempts to compete with the financial incentives—such as tax holidays and free land—of other developing countries may raise costs to the government without attracting any more investment than market opportunities warrant already.

Baker and other scholars have found that foreign investors weigh the overall investment climate far more heavily than financial incentives in their decisions.[13] Surveys of investors over the past 30 years have consistently found that legal guarantees are more important than special financial incentives.[14] Guarantees of the investor's right to repatriate investment capital and dividends, interest on approved loans, and expatriate salaries are also major primary concerns.

Foreign vs. Domestic Investment African governments may be tempted to view these issues as relevant to only a small group of foreign actors whose role in the domestic economy is limited and who must be restrained in any case. What troubles us more than the slow-down in foreign investment is the slow growth of investment in manufacturing by African investors. While foreign investment has the drawback of using substantial amounts of foreign exchange, there are others as well, such as the use of inappropriately capital-intensive technology, or the difficulties of linking imported enterprises with the local economy. While foreign capital should not be discouraged, in many cases its contribution to development is not as substantial or permanent as the growth of the informal sector and increased domestic investment in light manufacturing would be. However, the same disincentives to investment that frustrate foreigners also discourage Africans.

REINVIGORATING AFRICAN PRODUCTION

We disagree with the African finance minister who recently said, "A developing country always finds itself in a vicious circle. There is no development without investment, no investment without equipment, and no equipment without getting indebted."[15] The implicit assumption is that development is imported and that it stops when the ability to borrow or attract equity investment is curtailed. This statement overlooks the potential for increased productivity that African economies already possess. African countries can begin moving now toward the Lagos Plan of Action goal of building self-reliance independent of massive foreign capital.

THE NEED FOR FOREIGN EXCHANGE

The most serious constraint today on the growth of the private sector is the lack of foreign exchange—needed less for new investment than to preserve the capacity to import essential goods for maintaining production. Without policy changes, the private sector appears unlikely to generate sufficient foreign exchange because of weak international demand for most of Africa's major exports, heavy debt service burdens, large food and fuel import bills, and a myriad of smaller bills for imported goods and services needed to keep the economy from deteriorating further.

The public sector continues to absorb the major share of foreign exchange. Over the years, governments, mainly through foreign borrowing and aid, have undertaken massive capital investment programs, many of which are perpetual foreign exchange drains, as they often rely heavily on imports for production and maintenance. These projects seldom produce exportable goods and services, thus generating no foreign exchange themselves. Some private investment projects share these characteristics, and although others provide net foreign exchange inflows, all make some demands on foreign exchange for dividends and loan repayments.

Both African governments and foreign investors have borrowed heavily abroad to finance projects. Only when projects generate foreign exchange through new exports or save it through import substitution is there a net foreign exchange gain. Certainly, inflows of direct foreign investment and foreign loans initially ease the balance of payments deficit, but their long-term benefits depend on the project's net foreign exchange effects, which take some time to be felt. Only if the project's foreign exchange earnings or savings exceed repatriated flows will it contribute toward a favorable balance of payments. On the other hand, where foreign borrowing fails to generate increased foreign exchange earnings, foreign exchange shortages are exacerbated.

If foreign exchange is insufficient, existing capital is underutilized. Factories that depend on imported raw materials or spare parts often operate at 10 to 20 percent of capacity or shut down altogether. Lack of imported agricultural inputs reduces yields and increases the difficulties of harvesting and processing crops. The continuing shortage of foreign exchange must cause a shake-out of those organizations most dependent on imports, although some public sector organizations performing vital economic and social functions will correctly be protected from market forces. For the private sector, governments can make access to foreign exchange the incentive to find local substitutes and to export. As has been demonstrated in Zambia, such an incentive increases both production and investment.

Improving access to foreign exchange can be the most powerful incentive currently available to governments to encourage investment. Zambia's provision of foreign exchange incentives over the last 18 months demonstrates the value of such an approach. Extremely limited since the end of the copper boom in 1975, the private sector's access to foreign exchange was expanded in July 1983, with the central bank's announcement that exporters of agricultural goods would be allowed to retain 50 percent of their foreign exchange earnings and use them for goods imported under valid import licenses. The government later extended the incentive to all exporters, except those of minerals. The private sector's response was a marked increase in activity; farmers found markets for fruit and vegetables in Europe and beef in other African countries. Manufacturers found new markets for textiles, uniforms, bicycles, and pottery in neighboring countries. Foreign-owned companies with large blocked local currency holdings began to search for profitable export-oriented investments in manufacturing and agricultural processing.

DEVELOPMENT WITHOUT FOREIGN CAPITAL

During the 1960s, many development economists assumed that scarcity of capital was the critical constraint to growth in developing countries.[16] However, countries that increased capital stocks without achieving much growth have demonstrated that the role of capital is more complex. In his classic article, "The Place of Capital in Economic Progress," Cairncross avers that "the biggest single influence on capital formation is market opportunity."[17] He suggests that rapid growth of investment and income can arise from the same set of favorable circumstances and that indeed growth in income can precede growth in investment.

The point is relevant to Africa today. Government economic policies that encourage production in the private sector can initiate growth. Productive units in the private sector include small farms, small enterprises in the informal sector, and larger, privately owned manufacturing, service, commercial agriculture, and agricultural processing firms. Under-used productive capacity in all segments of the private sector, combined with existing demand and fueled by increased agricultural incomes, could produce a fairly rapid increase in incomes and output. It should in turn encourage successful producers to expand in response to opportunities. African countries have succeeded in adding to both their physical and human capital stocks during the past 25 years; what is needed now is to make fuller use of them.

In Africa's present circumstances, the dearth of foreign investment capital need not preclude economic development. Economic development is measured not only by rising national income but also by increased capacity for self-sustained growth. Development is a process of augmenting the ability to add value, and it results from new combinations of existing natural resources, labor, capital, and ingenuity to produce needed goods and services. It is not a checklist of investment projects or heavy industries, and it cannot be bought.[18] While shortages of investment funds increase difficulties, they need not bring development to a stop.

If African governments encourage the productive sectors in their economies, working with rather than against them, development will take place. Private producers need consistent economic policies. These include realistic exchange rates that favor local production and exports over imports; positive real interest rates that ration scarce capital and encourage domestic savings; some immediate access to foreign exchange so that the lack of a $50 spare part does not shut down production for a month; and government regulations that promote open and competitive markets and minimize bureaucratic delay and arbitrary enforcements.

MOBILIZING DOMESTIC CAPITAL

Fostering existing productive capabilities in agriculture, the informal sector, and manufacturing involves a somewhat different set of governmental responsibilities. African governments have tried to shoulder the major responsibility not only for directing their economies toward long-range goals, but also for acting as the main engine of economic development. The Chinese have found that governments cannot afford to do it all, that centralized decision-making becomes inefficient, and that therefore it makes sense to harness private energies to help in the effort. Governments should encourage the growth of competitive markets in goods and services by reducing the number of state-owned monopolies, but they should retain (and in some cases strengthen) their role as arbiter of last resort on issues of economic power and justice.

Governments can see the effects of their economic policies in the behavior of their citizens. If it is more profitable to import than to produce locally, few citizens will invest in production. If trading produces a more secure and reliable income than manufacturing, most people will become traders. If it is more profitable to invest in real estate or abroad than in factories, farms, or services at home, money will flow into buildings and foreign bank accounts. Where officials' speeches contradict their policies, the people will respond to the realities, not to the rhetoric. National economic priorities must be reinforced with real incentives that reward desirable economic behavior and make undesirable behavior unprofitable.

CREATING OPTIONS FOR DOMESTIC INVESTORS

Investment Funds   African governments limit opportunities for domestic private sector investment by constricting the supply of funds. Sources of investment capital for the modern private sector are limited to bank lending, foreign investors, and self-financing. The mobilization of investment funds through domestic capital markets is not possible today, as the only formal capital markets are in Kenya, Nigeria, Ivory Coast, and Zimbabwe, and these are stagnant, if not contracting.

Without functioning capital markets, investors who might be willing to take an equity position in another firm have no assurance that they can sell that position when they so desire. The inability to "cash out" at will reduces the number of potential investors and forestalls the development of venture capital activities. Governments should encourage the creation of capital markets and provide the oversight necessary to prevent their abuse.

Government interference in financial markets also reduces the supply of funds and investor options. When governments raise money by issuing bonds with negative real interest rates, the purchasers tend to be only those who are legally obliged to hold a portion of their assets in government bonds, primarily insurance companies and pension funds. The bonds thus represent a subsidy by the holders to the government—not an attractive investment alternative—while holding government bonds also reduces funds available to the private sector. Finance ministry officials should price bonds so as to provide real rates of return, thus encouraging the development of a free market in government securities.

Similarly, government ceilings that hold bank interest rates lower than the inflation rate eliminate bank savings accounts as an economically rational alternative, preventing banks from playing their traditional intermediary role between savers and investors. Artificially low interest rates create a demand for loans that cannot be met. Banks or government agencies then control the allocation of loans, usually with the result that large borrowers find it easier to raise funds than small ones, and foreign firms are preferred over indigenous ones. Again, bank interest rate levels should move freely or at least be set with the objective of creating a modest real rate of return to encourage savers.

African businesses rightly complain that they have less access to bank loans than the government and foreign firms. In our experience, banks have turned to the smaller businesses only when more secure opportunities have dried up, preferring the lower risk of lending to government agencies and foreign multinationals. However, a higher level of savings would force banks to put their funds to work. One result would be an interbank market in which banks with lending opportunities borrow from banks with surplus funds. Another would be a wider range of acceptable borrowers. Improving smaller business access to loans can be accomplished by increasing savings levels, which encourages banks to make riskier and more profitable loans, and by encouraging small cooperative lending schemes.

Investment Choices   Domestic entrepreneurs in search of profits have only three choices—to go into business for themselves, to invest in real estate, or to invest abroad, which often entails using illegal means to get their money out of the country. Despite vigorous efforts, governments have not succeeded in preventing transfers of funds abroad. As in many other economic contexts, the regulated are better at finding loopholes than the regulators are at designing controls.[19] This problem stems in part from overvalued exchange rates. Not only do they drive domestic capital out of the country, but they also allow foreign goods to compete unfairly, undermining local production and precluding otherwise profitable enterprise, especially in manufacturing. Governments can allow exchange rates to reach realistic levels and then maintain them there.

Without reforms, few citizens will invest in manufacturing because it takes a relatively long time to produce a return, it demands a substantial initial investment, and its operations are highly vulnerable to disruption. As a Nigerian journalist has written, "The logic of investing in productive industry is considered warped in the face of the ability of a trader with much less capital to turn over so much money as to make the return on investment for the industrial entrepreneur seem pitiful."[20]

Lastly, in many parts of Africa, there is no commonly shared set of business practices which would provide a basis for mutual trust. For example, young, foreign-educated MBAs have little in common with wealthy traditional landowners, although as business partners, they could accomplish much. An important task for African governments and business communities is to develop a business code that reinforces the legal code of ethical behavior. Clearly, the responsibility for forging such a consensus lies with Africans, not outsiders, but it is necessary if the private sector is to thrive.

THE DOMESTIC PRIVATE SECTOR AS AN ENGINE
OF GROWTH

The largest and possibly the only short-term sources of increased production and investment are the three productive segments of the existing domestic private sector. Smallholder agriculture accounts for the bulk of the population's employment, the informal sector for the major share of employment in manufacturing, and the larger enterprises for a substantial portion of GDP. In the aggregate, each sector's economic decisions are crucial to the overall health of the economy.

CALLING EXISTING CAPACITY BACK INTO
PRODUCTION

Like the modern manufacturing sector, the agricultural and informal sectors are producing at less than capacity. In agriculture, unused capacity can be defined in terms of the ability to increase overall production at a given market price using existing farming methods. Unused capacity in the informal sector is even more difficult to quantify, but the availability of appropriately skilled labor and its ability to respond quickly to increased demand are rough measures.

Increasing production by putting existing productive capacity to work does not require large amounts of investment capital, but rather working capital and market opportunities, coupled with the producer's efforts. Some working capital can be supplied in domestic currency through credit institutions. Foreign exchange auctions allow manufacturing firms to purchase (albeit at a premium) those items vital to profitable production and those using mainly local inputs needing only modest amounts of foreign exchange have an advantage over firms that have to import most of what they use. This system can stimulate firms to find local substitutes or to do more local processing.

Structural adjustment is called for when the existing capital stock does not match opportunities and new investment capital is required to expand existing capacity, or to create new capacity. Here, governments should favor private activity that yields early, high output-to-capital ratios. Africa's private agriculture and light manufacturing accomplish this better than the public sector which is concentrated in utilities, public works, and heavy industry. When the economy is stagnant, stimulating the private sector and postponing all but the most urgent capital-intensive public investments may be the best way to get the economy moving again. This is not to suggest that the government should neglect social welfare programs in favor of the private sector, but rather that heavy industry, public building, and major dams and irrigation projects must wait.

A recent study by two IMF economists supports a strategy of encouraging the private sector in developing countries. Blejer and Khan (1984) analyzed the behavior of public and private investment between 1971 and 1979 for a varied group of 24 developing countries.[21] Their preliminary findings suggest that developing countries which allowed the private sector a relatively large investment role achieved higher levels of overall savings and higher average rates of growth. They found clear evidence that the level of private investment varies with the flow of credit to the private sector, and that short-term government investment tends to crowd out private investment, while long-term government investment in infrastructure encourages it.

Such government investment can achieve multiple objectives. Rural infrastructure development projects making use of local labor during slack seasons can increase rural incomes and achieve improved output-to-capital ratios. The highly successful Kenyan Rural Access Road Program, for example, has built roads with high engineering standards at low cost for 15 years. Forty-two local construction units supervise road building in their areas, providing training, hand tools, and guidance to seasonally available workers. The program's diverse group of foreign donors minimizes demands on the government's administrative resources by setting standardized procedures and meeting annually to review progress.

SMALLHOLDER AGRICULTURE

The potential for increasing small farm productivity is limited at present to what can be achieved with existing technology. Farmers could certainly benefit from better availability of inputs—credit, seed, pesticides, and fertilizers—but there are no economical, high-tech, quick fixes because technological breakthroughs for rapid increases in the production of African food crops (other than maize) have yet to be made. At the same time, there is no doubt that African smallholders respond swiftly to price incentives.

In Zambia, the small farmers of Central Province clearly understand that payment now is worth more than payment later. Normally, maize is a slightly more profitable cash crop than cotton, which is much more labor-intensive. Cotton production, however, is expanding rapidly. Farmers choose cotton partly because of its resistance to drought, but more because the cotton parastatal takes only three weeks to pay, while the maize parastatal takes three months. Here, where farmers are powerless to make their own selling arrangements, the incentive is the relative efficiency of one parastatal over another. This arbitrary situation does not reflect a conscious policy decision by the government, and it may not correspond to the needs of the economy.

Our recommended strategy to increase investment is to increase market opportunities. Many governments have already committed themselves to increasing producer prices for agriculture and to foreign exchange rate devaluation. A healthy agricultural sector is the foundation upon which to rebuild, as it relieves foreign exchange shortages to the extent that domestic foodstuffs replace imports and agricultural exports increase. It provides purchasing power to the largest segment of the population and when they buy locally manufactured goods, they create opportunities for farsighted, energetic local businesspeople.

That agricultural policy affects the growth rate of the entire economy is evident in a recent FAO comparison of nine African countries between 1970 and 1981. The four countries whose domestic terms of trade were relatively most favorable to agriculture (Malawi, Kenya, Ivory Coast, and Cameroon) had rates of agricultural and GDP growth at 4.2 percent and 6.0 percent, respectively—higher than the five remaining countries (Ghana, Tanzania, Ethiopia, Senegal, and Nigeria), whose growth rates averaged 1.3 percent and 2.7 percent, respectively.[22]

Since 1981, many governments have changed their pricing policies. While some have seen positive results, drought has obscured the effects in other cases. Even if harvests improve, farmers and governments will face bottlenecks in harvesting, transport, and storage. The United States should be prepared to provide funds temporarily, as a logical extension of drought relief, for the purchase of spares, tires, and fuel for transport, bags for harvesting, and temporary storage, including tarpaulins and sheds. African governments and local private firms should carry out these activities in the future.

African governments have an important role to play as guarantors against the exploitation of smallholders and as providers of infrastructure. It is not enough for governments to increase prices for food and export crops in order to stimulate smallholder production. They must also take steps to ensure competitive markets that provide the farmers with an adequate flow of inputs, services, and consumer goods, allowing the private sector to provide the credit, seed, fertilizers, pesticides, and other goods. The new system must leave the bulk of the profits from agricultural sales in the producers' hands, in order to encourage expansion. Otherwise, from the small farmer's point of view, it makes no difference whether his profits go to the marketing board or to the local trucker or retail store. If retail prices rise because farmers with higher incomes seek more non-agricultural goods, middlemen's efforts to re-stock will ensure that wholesale prices also rise, increasing manufacturers' incentives to produce more goods. There must be competition among traders if higher agricultural prices are to stimulate long-lasting increases in farm output.

In a free market, farmers need information about prices if they are to hold their own against traders and transporters. The government can provide this through radio broadcasts,[23] in which regular bulletins announce prices prevailing in various regions. This device will work only if there are competing buyers and sellers of goods and services.

Farmers' needs for additional sources of funds must be met. At present, commercial banks find rural lending unprofitable because small loan administration is prohibitively expensive. Therefore rural lending schemes are good sources for this money. Farmers and small businessmen, particularly in West Africa, have developed their own credit schemes.[24] Government or PVO-funded lending is yet another alternative to commercial banking. In their analysis of five small enterprise lending projects, Kilby and D'Zmura (1984) report that these are among the most successful of all foreign aid projects, generating exceptional rates of economic return if loan administration is kept simple, local, and inexpensive. They find that the simplest systems are the most effective; technical assistance often adds more cost than benefit.[25]

THE INFORMAL SECTOR

Outside of the so-called modern sector—commercial agriculture and manufacturing based on imported technology—there is a broad range of small-scale, non-farm economic activities, including trading, crafts, simple manufactures, and services, which comprise the informal sector. Those activities in which investment would raise overall output are those which produce goods and services, and not those performed by middlemen. Sharing many of the problems of the small farmer, entrepreneurs in the informal sector would benefit similarly from the policy changes already discussed. In this sector, which employs so many workers and facilitates the spread of skills, the growth in the number of enterprises and their income levels can serve as an important measure of economic development.[26]

Page and Steel (1984), using another way to differentiate traders from producers of goods and services, define an informal sector micro-enterprise as one characterized by some barriers to entry, but too small to have access to bank finance or public agency programs.[27] These barriers may be limited capital or skill requirements. Such an enterprise avoids management and organizational issues because it is small enough to be run by one person. Its size precludes participation in industrial estates or other government assistance aimed at larger enterprises. Therefore, the best way to help the small entrepreneur, like the small farmer, is to change the general economic environment.[28]

As they stand today, government policies tend to discriminate against informal producers. A government that rations imports rather than devalues favors large firms over small ones, as do artificially low interest rates; in both cases, the small firm is crowded out. Burdensome regulations and taxes encourage the informal enterprise to operate in the gray market, outside the official nets (both the tax net and the safety net of social services). The informal entrepreneur operates on the fringes of legality, harassed or victimized by the police. A simple tax system, minimal regulation, and an end to harassment would allow the informal sector to grow in response to increases in rural demand and to contribute to government revenues.[29]

Bank lending to the informal sector faces the same obstacle as lending to small farmers: administrative costs per loan are too high to allow profits. However, loans that provide working capital to buy the inputs needed for production can contribute importantly to growth. The same lending schemes recommended for small farmers can serve the urban informal sector. African governments should encourage the formation of informal sector lending projects.

The U.S. government could also expand funding to lending schemes administered by PVOs or local groups, some of which have developed good banking mechanisms.[30] However, training in simple banking techniques should accompany funding to PVOs. In at least one of the cases studied by Kilby and D'Zmura, untrained expatriate administrators wasted resources and time reinventing workable systems.[31] Assuring repayment is not necessarily a problem, but strict sanctions against delinquents remain essential.[32]

THE MEDIUM- AND LARGE-SCALE MANUFACTURING SECTOR

The existing modern manufacturing, service, and agribusiness sectors have been among the focal points of development efforts in most countries. Ownership is shared to varying degrees between the public and private sectors and within the private sector, between foreign, immigrant, and African investors. The performance of many firms has fallen short of both government and investor expectations. Well-run, profitable parastatals are rare. Firms granted protection from competition have failed to produce goods at competitive prices. Development of local intermediate inputs has been slow. In countries where policy reformers choose to expand the private sector, market forces ultimately must sort out the viable enterprises from those which can only operate with subsidies or protection.

Private Sector Response to Incentives   The Zambian foreign exchange retention incentive mentioned earlier has dramatically improved the investment climate because it addressed a number of problems simultaneously. It has encouraged increased use of local inputs and has created new demand that mobilizes local funds for investment. It has also encouraged producers to learn to compete effectively in international markets.

With a radical change in the attitudes of the local business community in Zambia, an interest group may be created which, having benefited from economic change, will support further reform. The central bank has provided a valued incentive, and has ensured that exporters face a minimum of red tape and have unimpeded access to their foreign exchange entitlements. This incentive alone will not solve all of a country's problems, but it is a simple, pragmatic step to encourage growth, an opportunity made possible by the economy's own distortions. It is not a complete solution, but it is an encouraging move toward diversifying exports and increasing productivity.

In a number of African countries, the private sector has demonstrated its ability to respond to opportunities created by changes in government policies. As the response of medium and large-scale entrepreneurs has been less well-documented than that of the smallholder agricultural and informal sectors, we present below a few examples from our experience.

In 1978, the government of Zaire ended Air Zaire's monopoly on domestic air passenger and freight service. As a result, there are now several new, profitable airlines offering scheduled service between Kinshasa, Lubumbashi, Goma, and Kisangani. These successful companies are either solely owned by private Zairean businesses or are joint ventures with foreign partners. Private air transport in Nigeria has been similarly successful, with recent foreign joint venture partners providing equity contributions. By contrast, despite rising tourist demand for air safaris, Kenya's sales tax and customs duties, which nearly double the cost of aircraft, have stifled the growth of private air transport and postponed the replacement of aging aircraft.

The Nigerian government has acted to increase returns on large-scale agriculture and has forced manufacturers to try to develop local raw material inputs. A startling new phenomenon—the Lagos lawyer or accountant turned farmer—has recently appeared; these would-be entrepreneurs are attracted by promising profit potential created by the military government's policy changes. Manufacturers now receive import licenses only for production of essential goods with high local content.

In sum, Africa's private manufacturing sector is dynamic enough to respond to opportunities if the government is willing to change its economic policies. The costs will include a painful shake-out among the medium- and large-scale enterprises, hardships for urban workers, and some loss of direct control over economic resources by the government. The benefits of increased growth accrue to both the private sector and the government. The government will begin to show its people that earlier social welfare promises can be made good, and the success of the private sector will gradually relieve the pressure on government to employ more people than it needs. As private sector activity increases, its skills and its ability to meet new demands increase as well. This rocky road can lead to self-sustained growth.

IMPLICATIONS FOR U.S. POLICY

The most appropriate short-term investment strategy for Africa today requires policy reform in four broad areas:

- The removal of barriers and uncertainties to doing business in the domestic economy.
- Encouragement of the growth of competitive markets in goods and services, reducing the number of state-owned monopolies, but retaining or even strengthening the government's role as arbiter of last resort on issues of economic power and justice.
- Encouragement of economic activity that yields early, high output-to-capital ratios.
- Maintenance of a flow of real credit to private investors and directing government investment as much as possible to infrastructure.

Even in the expected absence of large private capital inflows from overseas, these reforms will soon yield economic benefits because they call into production existing capital resources—idle plant and skilled labor.

The United States can play a useful role in bringing about these reforms. At a time when past economic policies are being questioned, some African governments are ready to experiment with new approaches. However, the reforms must show benefits quickly—within one or two years—and they must not threaten the existing political order.

The United States should provide concrete financial assistance during the period of transition. The most important first result of increasing production from re-employed resources will not be wealth, but the restoration of hope; a substantial surplus for economic development will come later. Two recommendations made earlier for harvest support and assistance in creating small lending schemes can have the speedy results that are urgently needed.

Foreign aid will have to continue indefinitely. As domestic production increases, moreover, the need for basic infrastructure and social services will increase. African government will have to coordinate multilateral and bilateral aid in support of these essential activities.

During 1985, the United States provided more than $1 billion in emergency drought and famine relief, over and above the $1.166 billion in non-military aid. Even if the emergency conditions abate, the administration should request that Congress continue this assistance. The economic justification for continuing assistance is that growth in Africa will contribute to greater world trade, providing new markets for American goods. From an ideological standpoint, a program of policy-based assistance that encourages economic development through free market mechanisms is likely to appeal to the administration, the Congress, and the electorate. On humanitarian grounds, those who have supported famine relief should also support assistance that will help to prevent a recurrence of famine.

We advocate deemphasizing new American private investment in Africa until there are genuine opportunities on the appropriate scale. Rather, the role of the United States should be that of adviser and supporter of the free market system, the success of which will call forth increasing investment from all sources. AID economic support funds must continue as a means of persuading African leaders to adopt economic reforms and rewarding those who do so. The African Development Foundation can assist Africans at the village and community levels in development projects that will contribute to productivity and Congress should ensure that the Foundation is adequately funded. As Treasury Secretary James Baker explicitly recognized at Seoul in October 1985, the United States should support the funding of World Bank and other multilateral programs that promote policy reforms intended to increase the scope of private economic activity.

In addition to providing policy-based aid, the U.S. government can help simply by maintaining existing institutions that foster American investment, lending, and trade in Africa. The Export-Import

Bank, the Overseas Private Investment Corporation, USAID's Bureau for Private Enterprise, and similar entities can facilitate private American activity that supports expansion of the private sector in Africa. As part of its general campaign against protectionism, the administration should resist pressures to erect trade barriers to new African manufactures and semi-processed goods.

The easiest element of the American role is advocacy. Since the Reagan administration has a strong ideological commitment to the free market, it should not be difficult to find spokesmen who can argue tactfully and persuasively and who can give cogent advice about the economic effects of specific steps. Advocacy and advice should be provided in the person of a temporary special ambassador—a highly visible public official who can concentrate the energies of the United States on practical action. This person should be an experienced Africanist and a strong advocate of productive free enterprise. He or she should concentrate on devising appropriate ways for American foreign assistance programs to reinforce positive steps toward building the private sector.

NOTES

1. World Bank, *Toward Sustained Development in Sub-Saharan Africa* (Washington, D.C.: The World Bank, 1984), p. 47.

2. World Bank, *World Debt Tables: External Debt of Developing Countries*, 1984–85 Edition (Washington, D.C.: The World Bank, 1985), pp. 26–119.

3. For a good discussion of the difficulties, see Reginald Herbold Green, "Foreign Direct Investment and African Political Economy," in Adebayo Adedeji, ed., *Indigenization of African Economies* (New York: Africana, 1981).

4. The 1967 and 1972 figures are quoted in Helge Hveem, "The Extent and Type of Direct Foreign Investment in Africa," in Carl Widstrand, ed., *Multinational Firms in Africa* (Uppsala: Scandinavian Institute of African Studies, 1975), p. 83. The 1981 figure is from OECD, *Investing in Developing Countries* (Paris: OECD, 1982), p. 25. It assumes that investment in sub-Saharan Africa continued to represent 75% of total investment in Africa, as was true for the 1967 and 1972 DAC estimates.

5. OECD, op. cit., p. 22.

6. Louis T. Wells, Jr., *Third World Multinationals: The Rise of Foreign Investment from Developing Countries* (Cambridge, Mass.: MIT Press, 1983), p. 169.

7. David Goldsbrough, *Foreign Private Investment in Developing Countries*, Occasional Paper No. 33 (Washington, D.C.: IMF, 1985), p. 6.

8. World Bank, *World Debt Tables*, op. cit., p. 26.

9. *The Economist* 294(7382) (February 23, 1985): 84.

10. Pauline H. Baker, *Obstacles to Private Sector Activities in Africa*, unpublished, prepared for U.S. Department of State, January 1983, p. 6.

11. Ibid., p. 50.

12. Ibid.

13. Among those who make this point are Richard D. Robinson, *National Control of Foreign Business: A Survey of Fifteen Countries* (New York: Praeger, 1976); Isaiah Frank, *Foreign Enterprise in Developing Countries* (Baltimore: Johns Hopkins, 1980); and several studies quoted in Alice Galenson, *Investment Incentives for Industry: Some Guidelines for Developing Countries* (Washington, D.C.: The World Bank, 1984). This last is an excellent discussion of African investment incentives and their economic effects.

14. The above group; also Jurgen Voss, "The Protection and Promotion of Foreign Direct Investment in Developing Countries: Interests, Interdependencies, Intricacies," *International and Comparative Law Quarterly* Volume 31 (October 1982), pp. 686–708.

15. Michael Griffin, "Madagascar's Finance Minister Reflects on the Economy," *African Business* (April 1984): 29.

16. UN, ECAFE, *Programming Techniques for Economic Development* (Bangkok: 1960), quoted in Gerald M. Meier, ed., *Leading Issues in Economic Development*, 4th ed. (New York: Oxford University Press, 1984), p. 219.

17. A.K. Cairncross, "The Place of Capital in Economic Progress" (1955), quoted in Meier, op. cit., pp. 225–229.

18. Jane Jacobs, *Cities and the Wealth of Nations* (New York: Random House, 1984), p. 119. She is not alone in describing development as a process, but her description of the organic growth of new skills from older work is particularly clear.

19. Jonathan David Aronson in *Money and Power: Banks in the World Monetary System* (Beverly Hills: Sage, 1977) gives the example of the U.S. banks' ability to circumvent U.S. regulation in order to enter the Euromarket.

20. Pat Utomi, "Nigerian Bankers Prefer Trade to Industry," *African Business* (May 1984): 61.

21. Mario I. Blejer and Mohsin S. Khan, "Private Investment in Developing Countries," *Finance and Development* (June 1984): 26–29. (None of the countries in the sample is African; the sample is clearly not random and the results are not necessarily representative of developing countries as a group.)

22. Food and Agriculture Organization of the United Nations, "Agricultural Price Policies in Africa," paper for the Thirtieth FAO Regional Conference for Africa held in Harare, Zimbabwe, July 16–25, 1984, p. 19.

23. David K. Leonard also makes this point in Chapter 7.

24. Marvin P. Miracle, Diane S. Miracle, and Laurie Cohen, "Informal Savings Mobilization in Africa," *Economic Development and Cultural Change* (August 1980) 28:4.

25. Peter Kilby and David D'Zmura, "Searching for Benefits," unpublished, May 1984, pp. 2–4.

26. We thank Peter Kilby and John Harris for this measure of growth.

27. John M. Page, Jr., and William F. Steel, *Small Enterprise Development:*

Economic Issues from African Experience (Washington, D.C.: The World Bank, 1984), p. 11.

28. Ibid., pp. 37–39.
29. Ibid.
30. Miracle, Miracle, and Cohen, op. cit.
31. Kilby and D'Zmura, op. cit., p. 21.
32. Ibid., pp. 125–27.

PART V

HUMAN RESOURCES

CHAPTER THIRTEEN

African Education: Problems in a High-Growth Sector

David Court and Kabiru Kinyanjui

In a continent characterized by tumult and change, the persistent and seemingly insatiable public demand for formal education has been one fascinating constant. The abiding faith of African governments and individuals in education as a means of advancing economic and social well-being has been found to be well-placed, since, in the absence of other modernizing institutions, schools have been found to have more profound beneficial implications than earlier recognized.[1]

From this perspective, low levels of investment in human resources must account in part for the apparent stagnation and decline of African economies. While the need for more education is thus accepted, urgent questions remain. What kind of education should be provided? What policies should govern its provision? What means are available for its finance?[2] These concerns are significant in the calculations of individuals, governments, and international agencies which place education at the center of the debate about fostering development in Africa.

THE HISTORICAL CONTEXT OF EDUCATION IN AFRICA

The educational systems inherited by the newly independent African nations in the early 1960s were designed to serve colonial and minority interests. Overall provision of education was grossly inadequate given the needs of modern nationhood, with enrollment of the relevant age groups little more than one-third in primary schools, less than 3 percent in secondary schools, and a minute fraction in the few institutions of higher education that then existed on the continent.[3]

In countries with colonial settlements, education systems were characterized by racially segregated structures and by corresponding imbalances in patterns of expenditure. Educational opportunities were unevenly spread within countries and dependent on proximity to areas of colonial settlement, missionary presence, and levels of economic development. Curricula were infused with European content, practice, and ethos and were administered and largely taught by expatriates at the secondary levels. There was little technical or agricultural education and girls were hardly represented at all at secondary and higher levels.

Given that these systems were ill-designed for the economic and social needs of newly independent African countries, achievements in the field of education since 1960 have been truly dramatic. From a small base, enrollment in primary education is virtually universal in many countries, accompanied by more extensive secondary enrollments (Table A.3 in Appendix). This expansion reflects the removal of racial structures and the incorporation of groups that previously had no access to formal education and was made possible by the allocation of sizeable public funds and community efforts.

Accompanying the quantitative expansion were important qualitative improvements, including the adaptation of inherited structures and content to reflect national circumstances and culture, first at the primary level and more recently in secondary schools. In many countries, a variety of educational and training institutions has been created to meet the growing need for skills and services. Adult education has become an important component and in several countries, such as Tanzania and Ethiopia, massive and repeated national campaigns have succeeded in reducing illiteracy.

Increased attention has been given to agricultural education through, for example, the expansion of farmer training centers. The greater emphasis on technical training is evident in the establishment of polytechnics and a range of technical and professional courses under private and government auspices. Most African countries have established at least one national university, but several have developed multi-layered systems of higher education.

The localization of staff has proceeded apace. Educational administration and the teaching force at the primary and secondary levels

are now almost entirely in national hands, while the number of expatriates in tertiary education has been steadily reduced. At the same
time, attention has been given to improving the qualifications of educators. Research to further understanding of the functioning of educational systems in Africa has expanded. Most countries have become more adept at monitoring increasingly complex systems of
education. In particular, systems have been sustained by the dedication of innumerable teachers who are improving the lot of the next
generation, often through improvisation in the face of diminishing
resources.

Great strides in improving the external efficiency of education systems are evident in the extent to which staffing targets have been met
and in the less tangible but no less important benefits that accrue to a
nation that increases its literate population. These socio-economic
outcomes of education are difficult to quantify, but there is increasing
recognition of the wider impact of education on development, beyond staffing provision. It is clear that one of the most important
effects of expanded education has been to foster achievement which
in turn has helped to hold the nation-state together throughout most
of the continent.[4]

DIMENSIONS OF THE CURRENT SITUATION

Despite the impressive achievements that have been made in education systems in many African countries, the present situation provides little grounds for complacency. Symptoms of decline are evident throughout the continent. The central problem is that the
expansion of enrollments has exceeded the capacity of African economies to sustain their educational systems. After a period of advance,
the efficiency of educational provision and the quality of instruction
are deteriorating in most African countries. Several broad dimensions of the problem can be identified.

First, the overall provision of education in Africa remains inadequate in terms of both economic requirements and issues of equity
(Table A.3). There is a growing consensus that the low level of human
resource development in Africa relative to other inputs accounts for
poor economic conditions in most of the continent. Empirical evidence substantiates this claim. Throughout Africa, institutions and
projects are languishing or inoperable for lack of trained personnel to
run them.

Moreover, research on the economic benefits that result from extended education in the form of greater agricultural productivity, labor efficiency, and so forth supports this observation.[5] Education also produces major non-economic benefits in improved community health, nutrition, fertility control, and general responsiveness to technological innovation.[6]

Second, due to rising numbers of students, a sizeable part of the primary and much of the secondary school sectors have degenerated into little more than facades of learning institutions.[7] Many such schools have large classes—often of 100 students—and no desks, chairs, chalk, blackboards or other teaching aids. Textbooks are unavailable or inappropriate and untrained teachers are common. Grade repetition and drop-out rates are high. Although evidence is scanty, it is almost certain that average academic performances have declined because of deteriorating facilities, declining resources, and admissions of disadvantaged groups.

More serious than the presence of untrained teachers is the decline in teacher morale. While in the past, teachers enjoyed great status in the community and the profession was a sought-after one, today teachers are a beleaguered and dispirited force. Those that cannot leave the profession seek ways of supplementing their incomes, adversely affecting the quality of their instruction.

Associated with the decline in the quality of the state system is the erosion of public confidence. Those with resources opt out of the system at all levels from nursery school to university, with an increasing number of children being sent to Europe or America for secondary and higher education.

Third, access to educational opportunities in most countries is still not evenly distributed across the sexes and across regional and social groups, and sharp differences in performances on national examinations have been observed. Educational policy in the early years of independence tended to ignore these types of disparities, thereby reinforcing them. Correcting the imbalance was not viewed as a priority because of the absolute shortage of those with educational qualifications and the need to fill positions in the expanding economy which led to an emphasis on secondary and higher education for those who were already in the system.[8]

Regional inequalities in the provision of education assume a particularly critical importance in Africa because they tend to be synonymous with ethnic differences. Especially at the secondary and higher levels, several countries have been forced to adopt regional quota systems as a way of responding to the threat to national integration posed by differing educational access. However, even in those countries that have made major efforts to restructure their societies along egalitarian lines, data suggests that regional inequalities have persisted and indeed increased.[9]

Data concerning access to education of different social groups is less conclusive. Initially, systems were relatively "open" in terms of affording opportunities to children from rural or poor areas. However, with the increasing differentiation of African societies resulting from the spread of monetary economies, a corresponding differentiation of schools has resulted and socio-economic factors are becoming more important in determining access to better education and subsequent mobility.

From a developmental standpoint, the most important aspect of present inequalities in education concerns the restricted opportunities for girls, particularly at the higher levels. At the primary level, the number of female enrollments has risen substantially—from 24 percent of the age group in 1960 to approximately 60 percent in 1985—with an increase at the secondary level from 3 to 15 percent. However, there are notable differences in these ratios in the various countries. The need remains to increase enrollments in those countries where it is low in the first cycle.

However, the more fundamental problem of gender inequality has to do with the limited access of girls to quality secondary schools, universities, science and certain professions, and training opportunities and scholarships of all types. Research shows that the education of women outweighs all other factors, including income, in its beneficial impact on a range of development-related areas such as childcare, nutrition, and health.[10] Thus, continuing restrictions on educational opportunities for women are not only a matter of inequity, but a serious impediment on national development.

The dramatic expansion in formal education was a response to a shortage of middle-level personnel, but ironically its most visible consequence has been the "school-leaver problem." Graduates of primary and secondary schools have faced increasing difficulty in finding employment in the modern wage economy, as the number of students in the system has surpassed the capacity of African economies to provide the kind of employment school-leavers had been led to expect.[11]

The pressure was felt first by primary school students whose certif-
icates no longer guaranteed employment. Following a period in the
mid-1960s when a period of shortage of those with secondary school
education merged with an equilibrium in supply and demand, unemployment among some secondary school-leavers was noticeable for
the first time in the mid-1970s.

As the jobs for which school-leavers felt prepared were in the
towns, urban migration became an integral part of the problem.
Worsening employment prospects have intensified rather than reduced the demand for education and triggered the now-familiar phenomenon of qualification escalation. This is a rational response to an
educational structure in which students must complete one level before being allowed to enter the next and to a social structure where
there are few alternative channels for mobility. Since only a minority
of students can pass from one stage to the next and the rewards to
gaining entry are high, the result is a system characterized by competition and exclusion. With the majority at each level of the hierarchy
unable to proceed with further education, schooling is inevitably
geared to the interests of the minority.

At the lower end of the scale, only about half of African youth
complete the basic seven-year cycle of primary education, of which
approximately 23 percent continue on to any kind of formal secondary level education. Consequently, most of Africa's youth are left at
an early age to fend for themselves in small-scale farming and rural
enterprises. The challenge for the school systems is to find ways of
preparing them for productive lives in the rural sector.

For those at the upper end of the hierarchy, the expansion has not
produced self-sufficiency in high-level personnel in most African
countries. A shortage of highly trained people, especially in the scientific and technical fields, continues to plague most countries and, as a
result, many remain dependent upon outside professionals.

A final consequence of the growing number of students is the
strain on management capability. Keeping the system afloat, much
less making qualitative reforms of curricula or structures, has become
the all-consuming preoccupation of ministries of education. Compounding management problems are incomplete, unreliable, or unavailable data bases that are essential for effective management and
reform. Nor is there the necessary research expertise for making good
use of existing data.

From an educator's viewpoint, the critical problem facing Africa at present is the poor quality of education available for society in general and the shortage of those highly trained individuals who can be the designers, implementors, and catalysts of development policy. Quality improvements and cost-saving innovations—central to any educational strategy for Africa—require sustained attention to improved planning, analysis, and management capacity.

NATIONAL POLICY RESPONSES

Three distinct responses to the problems just described are discernable in the educational policies of African nations over the last 25 years: adaptation of the inherited structure, creation of a parallel system, and rejection and transformation of the old system.

In the first group are those countries which have kept the structure of the system inherited at independence largely intact and have concentrated on adapting it to meet new circumstances and on nationalizing its content and personnel. Characteristic of these systems are a retention of a metropolitan language, a stress upon examinations, international standards, higher education, and overseas training, and a relative lack of emphasis on adult literacy and the incorporation of previously neglected groups. These systems are highly academic and elitist and do not cater to the employment and skills needs of large segments of the population.

The perception in many countries that the formal system of education was not providing the relevant skills and values needed for employment and economic development led to the growth of parallel structures of non-formal education. A variety of out-of-school learning activities exists in most countries in sub-Saharan Africa. Sponsored by a host of non-governmental agencies, they include literacy classes, vocational skills, agricultural extension, paramedical training, and a number of other skill-imparting programs.

In many cases, these training programs provide a valuable means of improving the lives and employment opportunities of participants and have been especially successful in developing community leadership and social mobilization. They also provide an ideal alternative to conventional schools for organized learning. Yet surprisingly little is known about the efficiency and cost-effectiveness of individual programs. Where assessments have been made, the record is mixed. The varied learning activities carried on outside the formal school system have proven to provide neither alternative education nor a short-cut to rapid education. As a result, the parallel structures have remained a second-best choice in the eyes of the population.[12]

The third type of response, based on a fundamental questioning of the appropriateness of inherited structures to African circumstances, is an attempt to replace them with a different and more relevant system. In some cases, the radical critique and the formulation of alternatives emerged during the struggle for liberation from the colonial power. Necessitated by conditions of the struggle, such changes were part of a larger rejection of the type of society that was seen as embodying the oppression of Africans, as was the case in Mozambique, Guinea-Bissau, and Zimbabwe.[13] In Tanzania and Ethiopia, on the other hand, reformulation and experimentation were the result of the state's ideological premises and policy positions.[14]

In both cases, however, the reform of education was part of a wider effort to transform the economic and political structures of the society. Education was expected to develop a new consciousness and new skills that would contribute to this transformation. Emphasis was therefore placed on mass education—both adult and primary— rather than on secondary and higher levels, and extensive use was made of literacy campaigns. Educational content stressed political understanding, practical experience, and a pedagogical approach to productivity in agriculture, health, and nutrition. Prominent among the structural emphases were the importance of integrating schools into the surrounding community, collective decision-making, the utility of manual labor, and the necessity of educating women.

A critical assessment is long overdue of the experiences of countries that have attempted fundamental educational change in face of economic or political circumstance. In several instances, these countries have anticipated educational emphases that other countries have come to recognize as important, such as the significance of women's education, productive work, and local culture. Second, the experiences of those countries that have recently emerged from a liberation struggle are relevant to the future experiences of Namibia and South Africa that have yet to attain majority rule. Third, it is clear that whatever their political orientation, governments are grappling with issues of general concern to the continent. Because their experiences are instructive, they should not be ostracized by Western donors on political grounds.

THE CONTEXT OF THE POLICY RESPONSE

Before turning to some of the specific critical issues in education, it is necessary to identify the particular features of the socio-political environment that most condition the formulation of educational policy. Africa has the highest fertility rates and the fastest rate of population growth of all regions in the world. The population is expected to double its present size shortly after the turn of the century. This increase will exacerbate the pressures already described by raising the demand for education and intensifying the pressure on limited resources.

By the year 2000, children in the 5–14 age group will account for one in seven of the population in the industrial world, but one in four in Africa. This suggests that "not only is there a bigger school expansion job to be done in Africa, but that there are proportionately fewer people in the working population to carry the burden of that schooling."[15]

The pressures created by population growth are intensified by economic crises. The recent economic recovery seems to be bypassing African countries and a rapid improvement in economic conditions cannot be expected. As a result, public spending on education relative to numbers of students or in absolute terms is unlikely to increase. Many African countries are already spending as much as 20 percent of their national budgets on education. The pressure on educational budgets comes not only from the per capita decline in available resources, but also from escalating costs. Further, the current expansion of education systems is occurring at the post-primary level, requiring more expensive teachers, plant, and equipment than at lower levels.

Another less obvious but harmful constraint on quality improvements stems from the political context. Twenty-five years after independence, there are few governments in Africa that are not still striving to create a sense of nationhood and to break down the parochial ties that threaten national unity.

The paramount preoccupation is establishing a unified economic and social system and synthesizing traditional and modern administrative institutions. Lacking a unified economic and political base, governments are required to invest large amounts of productive capital in institutions that hold society together.[16] Among the most important of these institutions, schools are the focal point for divergent political interests. As education at the upper levels is regarded as a means of attaining future status, schools are an important arena for political competition.

Uneven distribution of educational facilities in African countries is therefore a considerable source of political vulnerability and finding ways of reducing these disparities is a continuing preoccupation. Another pervasive feature of the socio-cultural context in which educational policy is made is the loosely termed phenomenon of "tribalism," which has more aptly been characterized as the "economy of affection."[17] This system of reciprocal relationships based on kinship, residence, and religion tends to override other loyalties, constituting a powerful social force which penetrates all spheres of life. Its impact on education has been positive, providing the driving force to act collectively, raise resources, and build and run schools in homogeneous communities.

The impact of the economy of affection in the national context is less positive, however. The strength of established familial loyalties tends to weaken the legitimacy of national institutions assigned to develop educational policy. For example, individuals and groups in which the economy of affection is strong have tended to direct public resources to private and community purposes.[18] Institutions become subject to patterns of conflict between interest groups and positions within them become part of localized power struggles that have little to do with the qualities required for a particular job. Frequently, actors in key policy positions are moved in or out with little regard for the health of the institution.

In its broader manifestation, the economy of affection leads to styles of decision-making, attitudes toward authority, assumptions about community, and notions of merit that heavily constrain management and can render ineffective otherwise productive inputs of skills and training. In this climate, Western notions of management are not easily introduced, explaining the ineffectiveness of so many aid projects that are predicated upon management styles and assumptions about the behavior of bureaucracies that simply do not apply in the African context.[19]

The varied participation of donors in the development of African education has created a relationship with recipient ministries that heavily conditions the formulation of policy. Aid has undoubtedly made massive contributions to the development of African education, but some of its effects have been less noteworthy. Problems have arisen from the volume of aid and the multiplicity of donors, each with its own style, timetable, project orientation, information requirements, and demands for accountability.

By definition, the aid relationship is an unequal one. The volume of external funds creates a dependency relationship in which the "real" preferences of countries rarely emerge. The willingness of some African countries to adopt external models and experimental projects that were preordained to be irrelevant or inadequate in terms of any conceivable national purpose is explained largely by ministries' weak bargaining position in the aid negotiation process.

Moreover, the different styles and information requirements of various donors pose an immense burden on recipient ministries.[20] Servicing these diverse needs frequently absorbs most of the time of scarce ministry talent. Common to many donors is the desire to make a quick and distinctive impact. This dissuades support for the simple, routine, and the proven, and encourages buildings and bounded projects rather than long-term measures involving recurrent costs. Africa has been host to innumerable projects, experiments, and models which in some cases reflect the wholesale transplant of established foreign models—Swedish folk development colleges, Cuban agricultural schools, British libraries, Canadian technical colleges—and, in others, reflect the powerful and often passing fashions of donor conviction. Consequently, in many African countries, the national system of education is a patch-work quilt of semi-autonomous projects of diverse national hue.

While donor agencies proclaim their commitment to project replication, in practice they often pay insufficient attention to the relevance of a project to the wider system. Indeed, in response to management problems, donors have emphasized the autonomy of their projects. While additional aid is undoubtedly part of the solution to some of the educational problems of Africa, past aid has been part of the problem. Rationalizing aid coordination, practice, and style can improve the situation, as can efforts to increase the capacity of African nations to participate more "equally" in the negotiations that determine aid patterns and practice.

CRITICAL ISSUES IN EDUCATIONAL POLICY

While greater investment in Africa's human resources is needed, governments lack sufficient funds to finance the development or even maintenance of their school systems. This is because education is highly subsidized and the proportion of the total budget allocated to education is already high, with unit costs of further expansion likely to be greater than before. In permitting further expansion of education to proceed unquestioned in response to popular demand, there is a danger that the steady deterioration of facilities, the demoralization of teachers, and the ritualization and impoverishment of the learning process already evident in several countries and many schools will continue. New ways of organizing resources and channeling demand are therefore essential.

Modifying demand for education so that it accords more with social needs and with what is financially feasible is a major challenge. Demand for education has evidently not been weakened by those who have been unable to get the high-paying jobs they had hoped for. Demand is sustained by the high rewards that are rigidly tied to educational attainment and by the propensity of employers to consistently upgrade the qualifications required for any given job level. As long as one type of formal schooling monopolizes access to positions of prestige, influence, and wealth, demand for that type of education is unlikely to be altered by exhortation, curriculum change, or the mere provision of other types.

Eventually, unemployment among the educated may reach a level where people will begin to doubt the wisdom of their investment in education. But until that point is reached, the only way to modify demand is to alter the incentive structure in order to bring private calculations of the costs and benefits of education more in line with social benefits.[21] One means to this end is to transfer more of the cost of education from the state to the individual and to reduce the pay differentials that are currently tied to higher level qualifications.

Adjusting public sector salary structures as a means of modifying educational demand is fraught with political implications, as it involves a self-denying ordinance on the part of civil servants. A more practical approach is to seek new sources and patterns of finance.

In most African countries, the national educational system is heavily subsidized by the state at all levels. Based on studies of the rates of return, primary education has relatively greater social benefits than secondary and higher levels.[22] Therefore, in terms of both equity and cost considerations, reducing subsidies to secondary and higher level education and channeling the saved resources to primary education is desirable. It is not yet clear how shortfalls at the upper levels can be met, but imposing tuition fees and charges for accommodation and food, providing student loan programs, developing private schools, and involving the private sector in the provision of bursaries are suggested.[23] Another method that has been successful in several countries is the development of productive activities in schools—particularly farm production—as a means of supplementing diets and offsetting food costs.[24]

An additional means of expanding resources available for education is to use existing facilities more efficiently. Establishing economies of scale—increasing class size, raising student-teacher ratios, expanding the school day, using new technologies such as the radio, teaching fewer subjects, taking advantage of alternative types of schools such as Koranic schools, and modifying the school calendar to accord with seasonal changes—provide a few options.[25]

Cost reduction must be accomplished with an eye to the effect on quality. Research findings show that factors inside the school—curriculum, facilities, qualifications of teachers—are more important determinants of student achievement than in the industrialized world where social factors have more influence.[26] Therefore, given the poverty conditions of most African classrooms, simple improvements have an inordinate effect on quality.[27] Measures that are especially beneficial include raising the morale and knowledge of teachers and providing textbooks and examinations.[28]

The link between schooling and jobs in the wage economy has forced educational planners to reexamine the purpose of education to see how it can anticipate the conditions of rural life that most students will encounter. As the ratio of students to job opportunities has risen, a new rationale for schooling other than preparation for a paid job must be developed. Anticipating self-employment has become one of the most popular re-interpretations of the purpose of schooling in Africa.[29] The expectation is not that schools can create self-employment any more than they can create paid jobs, but that they can improve the quality and variety of the skills that students bring to their rural communities. Three concepts have emerged among African educational planners: terminal education, vocationalization, and productive school work.

Recognizing that most African youth will be exposed to no more than the basic cycle of primary education, some planners believe that primary education should be complete and terminal in itself. It should stress the skills needed by the terminating majority rather than the requirements of those continuing on to secondary levels.

The major problem with this approach is in determining which skills are most relevant to self-employment in agriculture and petty trading and which school subjects can provide them. Defined in such terms as the provision of "survival skills" and "basic competencies," the essential cognitive prerequisites for agricultural productivity and productive self-employment are not yet known.[30] Two equally questionable experiments in African countries have been expanding the number of subjects studied in the hope that broad coverage will include items of relevance, and increasing the vocational and practical content of the curriculum.[31] To date, however, there is little evidence to suggest that these responses will provide useful skills to students.

Achieving terminal education is not simply a question of finding the right curriculum and combination of subjects. More fundamentally, it requires de-linking primary and secondary schools in the minds of students and the general populace. As long as secondary education is perceived to be the route out of rural poverty and into the security of an urban wage-paying job, it will be difficult to replace the lure of secondary education with the notion of terminal primary education.

In the search for relevant schooling, a number of African countries are integrating productive work activities into the more academic aspects of the school syllabus.[32] The rationale is partially economic—to recover some costs through the sale of produce or the production of food—but it also involves helping to ease the move from school to work by beginning the transition at school. However, the socialization goals of school production have proved less easy to accomplish due to the difficulty of reconciling the pedagogical and economic aspects of productive work.[33]

Perhaps the most common response of ministries of education to the widening gap between students and jobs is the increasing emphasis on the vocational aspect of education.[34] Structures parallel to the academic system—technical, agricultural, and industrial schools which provide intermediate level skills for the wage economy—are one example. A second approach has been to set up a compulsory vocational training component in the curriculum to encourage acquiring employment skills. In a third approach, vocational education occurs in non-formal, post-primary training programs.

A central aspect of colonial policy, vocational training has also received substantial resource commitments from post-independence governments and has been a central plank of much donor assistance.

Ironically, the current drive toward vocational and technical training coincides with emerging research results which reveal that they are more expensive than general education and do not seem to achieve the economic and labor market goals that are sometimes claimed.[35] Although there may be strong political grounds for emphasizing vocational education at all levels, the economic and financial constraints argue against such an approach.

When attempting to increase the relevance of education, a distinction must be made between two types of knowledge and skills as the content of basic education. On the one hand are those skills which need to be acquired by all and can be prescribed centrally—literacy, numeracy, and a common level of political knowledge. In a different category are more specific skills which relate to the dominant economic activities in a local setting. The latter at the very least should be identified and implemented by the local community. In practice, however, it is difficult to distinguish between the different types and consequently to decide how much time should be allocated to each.

Finding an appropriate balance between local and national learning needs is complex and can be illustrated by the running debates over teaching foreign languages in primary schools and the proportion of school time which ought to be devoted to practical and farm work. In most African countries, an international language—English, French, or Portuguese—is taught to all students, although for most it is a second or third language with little immediate relevance to rural life. It is argued that this requirement burdens young pupils and introduces the risk that the international language and the culture it embodies will foster an external perspective inimical to the development of locally relevant skills and frames of reference. Others maintain that to abolish it would deprive the majority of students of access to an inestimable store of knowledge and medium of communication which may be relevant in the long-term to the goals of improved rural development.

If the language question poses the danger that access to the outside world may detract attention from local realities and priorities, emphasizing practical work and farm production raises the opposite concern. Excessive attention to meeting school production targets or assisting with community work may detract from the minimum amount of classroom time needed for long-term self-education and hence contributions to rural development. The general dilemma, then, is that of finding a balance in curriculum content and allocations which ensures that long-term intellectual development is not sacrificed on behalf of a spurious short-term practicality.

At the heart of the need for a balanced approach to local and national learning requirements is the issue of administrative responsibility for education.[36] It is one thing to acknowledge that community participation in educational decision-making requires decentralization of administration and quite another to effectively divide responsibilities between the capital and the regions.

In most countries, the administration of education is highly centralized because of earlier efforts to train high-level personnel and relate it to national economic plans, a belief in the need for a uniform curriculum both to ensure minimum national standards and encourage desired socialization, and a view of educational resources as political assets. The dilemma resides in the fact that effective educational reform demands localization as an objective and centralization as a mechanism.

Examinations are an effective instrument that can be utilized by ministries of education to control, direct, and monitor quality, while encouraging the development of locally relevant self-employment skills and knowledge. In most African countries, national examinations are held at each level, in effect weeding out the majority of students. With opportunities decreasing sharply at each successive stage and a small number of wage-earning jobs, the selection process based on a national examination system is inevitable in a pluralistic context where it is essential to have a procedure appearing "objective."[37]

In resource-poor countries, it is important that those selected for further education and training are those best equipped to make good use of it. Consequently, the selection function of education tends to dominate the broader goals of schooling. Subjects taught heavily reflect the contents of the examination rather than the nominal syllabus or the broad ideals of society. Nevertheless, the power of examinations over teaching staff and pupils can be used to influence what is taught in a positive direction.

By careful analysis, it is possible to ascertain which concepts and skills are being mastered by most pupils and which present difficulty. Teachers who are especially effective in passing on difficult skills can be identified. Because the examination is standardized and national, it can be used for important diagnostic and monitoring purposes both over time and between areas. This capacity for analysis and diagnosis is complemented by a feedback system in which schools and teachers are informed of which areas require further work.

It is therefore possible to use an examination not only for identifying an elite through selection, but also for developing skills and competence among the school-going population. It is also possible to focus attention on curriculum content relevant to terminal primary education irrespective of individual motivations for secondary education. Examinations provide a means of defining, encouraging, and evaluating quality.

While needing to respond to the circumstances and development goals unique to African countries, the educational systems must also maintain and encourage internationally acceptable standards. This issue is significant at every stage of the education system, but it is encountered perhaps most acutely at the university level in the debate over appropriate structures and practices for the national versus universal role of universities.[38]

The debate about the internationalism of African education has been clouded by perspectives on both extremes. One argument posits that whether international standards are a product or a cause of the technological dominance of the industrial world, their mastery is a prerequisite for understanding and dealing with that world. The opposite view holds that to aspire to foreign standards is to perpetuate Africa's cultural and technological dependency and to ignore the needs of the majority of people.

In reality, this is not an "either-or" situation. Some educational practices and goals—particularly those involving a technology of research and teaching in languages, science, and engineering, for example—seem to be universally applicable and useful. Others, such as Western concepts of medical qualifications, may be inappropriate to African circumstances and needs. The question should be what to borrow in the light of associated costs.

At this historical juncture, isolationism in education cannot be Africa's creed. The challenge is how to develop a cadre of scientists, professionals, researchers, and managers who reflect the best skills that international training has to offer, but who are also committed to the development of their own societies.

The role of universities has been a central issue in the debate about the contribution of education to national development.[39] In the 1970s, national leaders and international agencies had high expectations and stressed the singular responsibility of the university to serve society in direct, immediate, and practical ways that would improve the well-being of the national population.[40]

Despite efforts at reform, universities in general remain in financial and political trouble. Criticisms have increased that universities are not justifying their high costs by either a corresponding contribution to the improved well-being of their people or to the transformation of their societies. Their adherence to the metropolitan model was seen to inhibit their ability to respond to the needs of their own societies, leaving them as detached islands in a sea of poverty.

As cost-benefit analyses showed relatively greater returns from other forms of education, the tide of assistance turned against universities and toward primary, secondary, and technical education.[41] At the same time, the expansion of lower levels of education has brought about irresistible pressure for more places at the university which in turn produces overcrowding and the inevitable dilution of quality.

Government pressure on universities to emphasize vocational and professional courses runs up against university concerns over autonomy and scholarship. In the face of increasing student dissension, insistence on higher levels of political conformity and on government involvement in university decision-making has fostered even greater staff demoralization. This is further exacerbated by financial pressures which keep salaries at declining values and in many cases deprive universities of the very tools of their existence such as books, journals, and paper.

It is clear that the expectations that universities would transform their societies were inflated and misplaced. In the 1970s, the newly established universities were preoccupied with institution-building and were in no position to address complex developmental tasks. Nor are universities the most appropriate institutions for providing vocational training or leadership in developmental projects. Critics have tended to lose sight of the contributions universities have actually made, judging them by their failure to realize a set of preconceptions that may have had limited applicability in the first place.

The main achievement of African universities has been to establish their legitimacy as valued institutions by improving the relevance of teaching and research to the national environment and by training their own staff. From being based largely on imported texts and theories, curricula have now developed a degree of autonomy and research is now an integral part of the university purpose. Now that questions of staffing and institutional identity have been resolved, universities are able to assume a role in development based on commitment, conviction, and consensus rather than as an artificial response to governmental or external expectations. The challenge of the 1980s is for universities to convince their governments and national populace that beyond meeting staffing targets, they have a responsibility to train the minds that can advance development.

The challenge for donors is to support this purpose. Universities in Africa are languishing for want of resources and new sources need to be found. For all their problems, universities remain the principal means of regenerating scientific and professional expertise and represent one of the few havens of reflection and critical thought in Africa. Donor agencies helped to bring them into being and for those from societies where universities are part of the national fabric to conclude that similar institutions in Africa are irrelevant luxuries on the basis of their brief history is to condemn the continent to perpetual intellectual dependency.

RESEARCH ON EDUCATION

Implicit in much of what has been said is the need for additional and improved research on education. The development of Africa's universities is the most significant institutional advance from the perspective of research over the last ten years. Despite the need for constant refurbishment, universities in the major countries of the region have developed to the point where they represent a significant resource and source of expertise.

Concomitantly, national research units in governments and parastatals have emerged, including research and evaluation units in ministries of education, central statistical bureaus, and national councils of science and technology. The emergence of these research institutions has been followed by the formation of national educational research associations in various countries.

An important outgrowth of the national institutions is the spread of regional networks for research on education where the region's leading educational researchers meet periodically to review research findings and methodologies. By identifying and assessing research that is not generally accessible in international publications, they help to correct the imbalance between north and south in research on African education. Another important institutional development has been the increasing interest of a variety of non-governmental organizations—notably religious and women's organizations—in establishing an improved research base for their work in education and rural development.

Despite the vigor and depth of the research infrastructure, some significant problems remain.[42] Poor research, particularly from the education departments of colleges and universities, is common. The very few able researchers are scattered among different institutions, affecting the depth of overall research capability. Further, educational research has been beset by isolationism and territoriality. Researchers have shown little inclination to move beyond issues of classroom pedagogy; therefore, links with corresponding institutions in community health, agriculture, and population are virtually nonexistent. There is thus an overriding need to strengthen local institutional capacity for research and analysis in education and for better research focusing on the relationship between education and different aspects of economic and social development.

Considering the amount of public and external funds allocated to education, the proportion dedicated to research and to research training is minuscule. External support for doctoral work overseas has declined, adversely affecting the regeneration of the educational research community. However, the U.S. Agency for International Development's (USAID) interest in education and training appears to be growing. Described in the USAID policy paper, "Basic Education and Technical Training," a strategy is set forth which calls for the "institutionalization and long-range improvement of the indigenous information base and the strengthening of LDC capability for analysis, resource allocation, and policy determination."[43]

USAID has recently announced a ten-year commitment to improve the efficiency of education and training systems in five countries—Niger, Somalia, Liberia, Botswana, and Cameroon. This project will support research, planning, and analysis of education, build host country capacity to undertake these activities, and focus initially on the formal primary system. A network for both information exchange and cooperation with other agencies is expected to emerge from this undertaking.[44]

The International Working Group on Education (formerly the Bellagio Group) has also been notable in developing and utilizing research on education in Africa. Held annually to bring together the representatives of the main donor agencies supporting work on education, meetings of this group have provided an opportunity for exchanges of information and for concentrated attention on important themes such as literacy, the financing of education, and basic education. During the past three years, "new" donors—particularly the Scandinavians, Dutch, and Germans—have joined the group, as have more African educationists.

The relationship between education on the one hand and agricultural productivity and other developmental indicators such as health, nutrition, and fertility on the other is one of the most important areas in which research is needed. While it is acknowledged that education has some bearing on economic and social development, the mechanisms that account for its impact remain unclear.[45] The next step is to clarify how the process of schooling affects an individual's later ability to adapt to the technological requirements of agriculture, health, and other development domains.

A second area requiring urgent research are the impediments to and development consequences of women's education. Similarly, investigations of those factors that influence student achievement and of policy options that can improve it are needed. Research is also needed on the financing and administration of educational systems. Expanding enrollments have placed a heavy financial burden on central government, causing it to devolve some of the costs upon local communities. Therefore, both new forms of educational finance and major reorganizations of administrative structures and loci of control will be required.

STRATEGIES FOR ACTION: THE ROLE OF NATIONAL GOVERNMENTS

African governments remain the prime movers in their nations' economic development, and particularly in educational development, because their decisions not only shape the direction, utilization, and management of available resources, but also determine the parameters for action by local communities, non-governmental agencies, and donors. Given the state's central role in the operation of educational systems, several strategies can be identified.

• One of the most urgent priorities of national governments is to improve the management and administration of the ministries of education. This task involves the exploitation of available technologies such as more efficient information systems and better use of research. More attention must be paid to the human resource side of management, which is currently characterized by a disregard for professional knowledge, unplanned and ill-formed interventions, expenditures without justifiable benefits, arbitrary staff transfers, and a consequent instability in the system as a whole. Improving utilization of human resources for increased professionalism in ministries requires a decision-making system that encourages participation and a reward system that encourages commitment on the part of a professional staff.

- The quality of management at the school level has a significant bearing on student and teacher motivation and hence on academic performance. Recruitment, salary, and promotion policies that encourage the most capable administrators and teachers, and in-service training that permits their constant refurbishment can go a long way in improving the quality of education. Along with such policies, measures to strengthen the sense of teacher accountability to parents, the community, and ministry officials are needed. Where morale is high and commitment strong, inspection and supervision are likely to lead to increased efficiency and accountability.

- In the last two and a half decades, ministries have been preoccupied with problems of quantitative expansion. With the current rate of population growth on the continent, the demand for education will intensify to the point where concern for quality is likely to be a secondary issue. However, if the current trend toward disillusionment with the state system and the emergence of a dual structures is not to become irreversible, ministries must take deliberate measures to ensure the quality of educational output and to strengthen the conditions that promote and increase high standards at strategic points within the public system.

- Growing demands for education pressure governments to allocate resources to education at the expense of other productive sectors of the economy. The expansion of education needs to be placed in the context of increased food production and employment creation. This is not simply a matter of balancing the allocation of resources between different sectors, but of fostering those types of education that have a demonstrated impact upon productive behavior in different development domains. Given the absence of such knowledge at present, it is advisable to pursue general education at the primary level rather than programs that target industrial, agricultural, or vocational goals.

- With the dominant role of national governments in education, there has been a lack of organized, alternative views that would invigorate debates on educational policies. Such debates are important for the development of sound strategies and require the encouragement and involvement of relevant interest groups, including teachers' unions, parent and student associations, and women's groups. Essentially, a democratization of the education system is called for, which would stimulate initiatives and experiments by non-governmental and community organizations.

- African governments today have a more qualified pool of professional talent that can be harnessed for improving education. However, policies in hiring, promoting, training, and utilizing this scarce resource often lead professionals to seek opportunities outside their country. Discriminating measures to identify and encourage high-level professionals need to receive more attention.

- The quality of governance is central to the likelihood of improved educational performance. The challenge is to encourage governments to take a hard look at the systems they have been operating for the last 20 years and to explore ways of making them more quality-oriented and rewarding to teachers and pupils. Financial stringency often deters change, but much can be achieved without incurring additional costs. In fact, the most effective changes are those concerned with improving existing practices rather than a radical transformation of existing structures. However, changes in social attitudes and behavior will be necessary before any reforms can be implemented successfully, and this challenge is primarily a political one.

STRATEGIES FOR INTERNATIONAL ASSISTANCE

The future of education in Africa ultimately depends on reducing the rate of population increase and reviving economic growth.[46] However, improving education both in qualitative and quantitative terms can further both these goals. While national governments are ultimately responsible for the contribution of education to national development, international assistance can facilitate and accelerate the process.

Donor agencies considering innovative strategies must take into account what has been tried in the past. Africa has a sorry history of educational innovations that were highly touted at the time of their inauguration, but are now commemorated in broken radios, missing batteries, dust-covered science kits, immovable tractors, unworkable lathes, and forgotten syllabi. The recent World Bank review, "Basic Education and Agricultural Extension," is an important reminder of the need to take account of historical experience.[47]

If we have learned anything about the development process in the last 20 years, it is that technological change is rarely a complete solution. Education is critical in improving the non-technical aspects of technological change, although education itself seems to be infertile terrain for technological interventions. Anderson's dictum of 10 years ago that "the educational process is unlikely to experience a major technological breakthrough" has been confirmed by donor experience since then.[48] For reasons spelled out recently by C.E. Beeby, improvements in education are more likely to occur as a result of incremental increases in understanding rather than from a sudden technological discovery.[49] New technologies such as micro-computers and cassette recorders can contribute to improvements in teacher training and the management of education systems, but it is unlikely that they can be of widespread use as classroom tools in systems that have trouble ensuring supplies of chalk, exercise books, texts, and chairs.

Swings in emphases in education have occurred over the years. Lifelong learning, non-formal education, community education centers, and education and production have come and gone with bewildering rapidity, illustrating a tendency to treat the part as a whole.[50] When a chosen route fails to achieve what was expected, attention shifts to another element that is not yet discredited. Within donor agencies, the broad problem of the African country becomes defined in terms of the narrow administrative category in which the agency works. The agency then becomes captive in its approach to a problem. Avoiding this requires a broad-gauged strategy of what one is trying to achieve and an underlying institutional philosophy demonstrating long-term commitment, permitting flexibility within a framework, and offering a coherent image to prospective beneficiaries of assistance.

Education systems do not exist in a vacuum, but are rather embedded in a web of values, interests, and institutional relationships. As agencies think about new forms of research and training, they need to take account of what exists in prevailing institutions, cultural styles, and incentive systems. For much of the 1970s, non-formal educational activities were viewed from outside the continent as a relatively cheap and more rapid means of "delivering" education, and substantial aid resources were devoted to this goal. Yet research and experience have not vindicated this approach—whereas these activities may be a useful supplement to formal education, they cannot replace it. The primary school remains the principal means of providing literacy and numeracy. Thus, donors could have a greater impact if reforms are directed toward the existing primary school system rather than alternative institutions or technology.

Another example of the benefits of building upon existing incentive structures is provided by the history of examinations in Africa. Looked at from the perspective of Dore's "diploma disease," examinations would not appear to be a very appropriate vehicle for donors in trying to improve the content and relevance of basic education.[51] Yet, examinations are and will remain a central part of the incentive structure in Africa. Donor attention to strengthening national examination councils in Africa could have a significant impact upon the quality of education in Africa. Reform has the most chance of succeeding if it is based on what exists and on what is important in the prevailing educational context.

National institutions for research and training fare better than regional ones. With one or two notable exceptions, the experience of donors has been that while economies of scale may frequently point toward regional centers of excellence, these have been extraordinarily difficult to sustain given problems of coordination and national sensitivity. However, the greater strength of national over regional institutions should not obscure the importance of seeking ways to foster regional interchange. Focused research in education is particularly necessary, as is the creation of networks that can provide a means for sharing regional experience.

There is a need to go beyond the ritualistic commitment to replication toward building a concern for system-impact into initial project designs. This will require some serious thinking about the long-term consequences of a given aid activity including the recurrent cost implications. More broadly, it may require new ways of organizing projects so that lessons are gained from the project experience.

In the past, some donors have tended to focus more on the end product of assistance—a well-prepared plan, a convincing evaluation, a well-constructed building, or an elegant curriculum—than on the process from which these products emerged. Lately, however, the importance of the empirical and analytical bases for policies has been acknowledged. Above all, research and training that can improve understanding of educational problems require the development of strong national and regional research institutions.

Local institutional capability is a prerequisite for effective educational reform and a priority in any assistance strategy. Local institutions are sensitive to the context of a problem and the likely consequences of proposed reforms. More important, however, it is imperative that the sense of dependence that currently inhibits self-motivated reform in Africa be reduced. A degree of achieved self-awareness and self-confidence is a necessity for effective educational reform.

A degree of local capacity in research policy and management is needed that can strengthen the recipient's ability to set priorities and argue counter-priorities and lead to policies that the people will accept. The strategy paper of the Africa bureau at USAID is notable for its recognition that universities offer one of the best sources for developing this skill.[52]

Another area in which aid can make a major contribution is in improving the data-gathering and processing capabilities of education ministries. In most African countries, there is an urgent need for the establishment of a system for the regular collection and publication of basic statistics. Part of this task is the development of management tools such as resource allocation criteria, indicators of performance, and principles of cost-effectiveness which lead to better administration of the system as a whole.[53]

Donors have emphasized quantitative expansion in education in keeping with the priorities of African governments. Now, however, more attention must be paid to what happens inside schools and how this relates to other dimensions of human welfare. It is clear that many of the central issues in education are questions of values and motivation rather than numbers. Hence, there is a need for new forms of research that focus on content, quality, and motivation— what is being learned and why—rather than on the numbers passing through.[54]

Closely related to new styles of research is the need for new forms of training. Donor agencies have supported training in the past, but it is clear that neither the right number nor the right type have been produced. There are some respected external training programs—the

IIEP in Paris, the EDI in Washington, and a number of university-based programs—which have provided adequate training in research methods. But some have been preoccupied with education system efficiency itself or with narrowly defined economic and political outcomes. To date, training of analysts and managers has not been concerned with the relationship between education and other aspects of human welfare, nor has it focused on identifying an appropriate balance between local and external training.[55] The problem is less a shortage of money than of good ideas and institutions with an appropriately trans-sectoral outlook.

In stressing the need for more and improved training, we need to guard against the notion that training alone can bring about institutional reform. It is common for returned participants in donor training programs not only to fail to bring about institutional reform, but to be constrained in their individual contribution because of the absence of a supportive infrastructure. However, it is now recognized that relatively modest resources made available to returnees and their institutions can help offset some of the constraints.

It has been fashionable outside the continent to deride African universities as irrelevant or expensive. But within the continent, they are valued and influential and will continue to be the principal source of local expertise for research and analysis. Given their importance, it is clearly unwise for donor agencies to view them as undesirable luxuries. Because they have an enormous potential influence over the rest of the education system, it is necessary to seek ways in which they can be assisted in providing the leadership and resources in research and training that they are uniquely placed to offer.

Resistance among African policy-makers to outside prescriptions on the treatment of women has been common. Consequently, donors must exhibit particular sensitivity in this area. The imperative of expanding educational opportunities for women comes as much from the goals of development as from concerns about equity. Supporting government plans for expanding educational opportunities for women is one of the single most important strategies for African development.

Williams has equated the "learning-resource famine" with more familiar food famine in the gravity of its impact upon Africa's future.[56] Aid agencies are in a good position to help resolve this type of famine because they can supply the foreign exchange needed to purchase equipment, books, paper, transportation, fuel and so forth which are crucial to the educational enterprise in Africa. Learning resources within schools, colleges, and universities must be strengthened to increase the possibilities for independent study.

There is an urgent need for greater coherence in the overall aid process; however, tension is inevitable between the priorities and styles of individual donor agencies and the goals of coordination. One area where greater coordination may be possible is in reducing the burden of information demands placed upon recipients by greater standardization in their requests. Another means is by structuring increased African participation in the inter-agency dialogues about aid that occur in a variety of gatherings such as the International Working Group on Education.

CONCLUSIONS

The essence of the problem facing education systems in Africa is that the expansion of enrollments is exceeding the capacity of African economies to maintain educational quality. The gap in learning achievements between African students and those of industrial countries is widening to unbridgeable proportions, threatening a condition of permanent dependency. Educational deficiencies have long-term implications for the health, fertility, as well as agricultural productivity of the African populace and therein lies much of its significance. The empirical relationship between educational attainment and the increase in human well-being and potential is now clear, but much remains to be discovered about the mechanisms which can strengthen it. Associated with the practical problems of inadequate mass education and research inadequacies is the shortage of trained analysts and researchers who can provide the problem-solving capability for African nations.

To restate the gravity of the problems facing education in Africa is neither to imply past failure nor to countenance despair for the future. The accomplishments of the past 20 years—increased literacy and enrollments, sacrifices made, and commitment demonstrated—give hope for addressing the challenges of the future. The new problem is how to accommodate the increasing numbers and how to relate education to improvements in the quality of life through better health and more productive self-employment.

Attention has been drawn to a series of issues that merit consideration by those who will frame responses to current problems. Above all, the primary school remains the best hope for providing the kinds of skills needed to equip people for meaningful lives. National and international resources should therefore be concentrated on methods of improving the quality of primary education. This can be done by the provision of books, the improvement of management, the involvement of communities, and the stimulation of teacher morale. Measures that stress the incorporation and education of girls are especially important.

It is doubtful that many of the new information technologies offer hopes of a breakthrough in improving cognitive attainment. However, they do hold the potential of complementing and enriching educational experience and merit continued systematic experimentation. The needs and opportunities for education to affect the well-being of the population are clear. Further improvement in the human resources of the continent is an urgent requirement. The challenge facing African governments and the international community is finding the finance and applying it strategically and imaginatively.

NOTES

1. This is the conclusion emerging from a series of research reviews and studies conducted by the World Bank. Many of the most significant pieces of work are reviewed in Steven Heyneman, "Research on Education in the Developing Countries," *International Journal of Educational Development* 4(4)(1964): 293–304.

2. G. Psacharopolous, "Education Research Priorities in Africa." Washington, D.C.: The World Bank, 1984.

3. D. Court and D.P. Ghai, *Education, Society and Development: New Perspectives from Kenya*. Nairobi: Oxford University Press, 1974.

4. P. Williams, "Education Priorities in Sub-Saharan Africa," paper prepared for Conference on Education Priorities in Sub-Saharan Africa, Windsor, 3–7 December 1984.

5. D. Jamison and L. Lau, *Farmer Education and Farm Efficiency*, Baltimore: Johns Hopkins University Press, 1982.

6. C. Colclough, "Primary Schooling and Economic Development: A Review of the Evidence," Staff Working Paper No. 399, Washington, D.C.: The World Bank, 1980.

7. K. King and D. Court, "The Interaction of Quantity and Quality in Primary Education," paper prepared for conference on Primary School Effectiveness, Arusha, Tanzania, 1982.

8. K. Kinyanjui, "The Distribution of Educational Resources and Opportunities in Kenya," Discussion Paper No. 208, Nairobi: Institute for Development Studies, 1974.

9. D. Court and K. Kinyanjui, *Development Policy and Education Opportunity: The Experience of Kenya and Tanzania*. Paris International Institute for Education Planning, 1978. D. Court, "The Education System as a Response to Inequality in Kenya and Tanzania," *The Journal of Modern African Studies* 14 (4)(1976).

10. J. Grant, *The State of the World's Children 1985*. New York: UNICEF, 1984.

11. K. King, "Education and Youth Unemployment: Some Propositions," paper presented at the Ninth Conference of Commonwealth Education Ministers, Nicosia, Cyprus, 23–26 July 1984.

12. D. Court, "Dilemmas of Development: The Village Polytechnic Movement as a Shadow System of Education in Kenya," *Comparative Education Review* 17(2) (1974).

13. C. Diaz, "Education and Production in Guinea-Bissau," *Development Dialogue* II (1978): 51–57. F. Ganliao, "The Struggle Continues: Mozambique's Revolutionary Experience in Education," ibid: 25–36. N. Shamuyarira, "Education and Social Transformation in Zimbabwe," ibid: 58–72.

14. J.K. Nyerere, "Education for Self-Reliance," Dar es Salaam, Government Printer, 1966.

15. P. Williams, op. cit., p.4.

16. G. Hyden, *No Shortcuts to Progress*. London: Heinemann, 1983.

17. G. Hyden, op. cit.

18. G. Hyden, op. cit.

19. J.R. Moris, "The Transferability of Western Management Concepts and Programs, An East African Perspective," in L.D. Stifel, et al., *Education and Training for Public Sector Management in Developing Countries*. New York: The Rockefeller Foundation, 1978, 73–83.

20. K. King, "Problems and Prospects of Aid to Education in Sub-Saharan Africa," paper presented at Conference on Education Priorities in Sub-Saharan Africa, Windsor, 3–7 December 1984.

21. E.O. Edwards and M.P. Todaro, "Educational Demand and Supply in the Context of Growing Unemployment in Less Developed Countries," *World Development* 1 (3 & 4)(1973).

22. G. Psacharopolous, "Returns to Education: An Updated International Comparison," *Comparative Education* 17: 321–41.

23. J.C. Eicher, "Educational Costing and Financing in Developing Countries: Focus on Sub-Saharan Africa," Staff Working Paper No. 655. Washington, D.C.: The World Bank, 1984.

24. D. Court and K. King, "Education and Production Needs in the Rural Community: Issues in the Search for a National System," Paris International Institute for Educational Planning, 1979.

25. J.C. Eicher, op. cit. A. Fowler, "Seasonal Aspects of Education in East and Southern Africa," Nairobi mimeo, 1982.

26. S.P. Heyneman, "Influences on Academic Achievement: A Comparison of Results from Uganda and More Industrialized Societies," *Sociology of Education* 49(3)(July 1976): 200–11.

27. S.P. Heyneman, "Research on Education in the Developing Countries," *International Journal of Educational Development* 4(4)(1984): 293–304.

28. S.P. Heyneman, "Improving the Quality of Education in Developing Countries," *Finance and Development* 20(1983): 18-21.

29. K. King, op. cit.

30. S.P. Heyneman, op. cit.

31. D. Court and K. King, op. cit.

32. K. King, *The Planning of Technical and Vocational Education and Training*, Paris International Institute for Educational Planning, 1984.

33. D. Court and K. King, op. cit.

34. K. Lillis and D. Hogan, "Dilemmas of Diversification: Problems Associated with Vocational Education in Developing Countries," *Comparative Education* 19 (1)(1983).

35. G. Psacharopolous and W. Loxley, "Diversified Secondary Education and Development," Report on the Diversified Secondary Curriculum Study, Washington, D.C.: World Bank, 1984.

36. D. Court and K. King, op. cit.

37. D. Court and K. Kinyanjui, op. cit.

38. The issue of the "academic gold standard" is reviewed at length in E. Ashby, *Universities British, Indian, African: A study in the Ecology of Higher Education*, Cambridge, Mass.: Harvard University Press, 1966. See also E. Shils, "The Implantation of Universities: Reflections on a Theme of Ashby," *Universities Quarterly*, XXII (2)(1968): 142–66, and T. Eisemon, *The Science Profession in the Third World*. New York: Praeger, 1984.

39. D. Court, "The Development Ideal in Higher Education: The Experience of Kenya and Tanzania," *Higher Education* 9(1980): 657–80.

40. J.K. Nyerere, "The University's Role in the Development of New Countries," opening speech, World University Assembly, Dar es Salaam, June 27, 1966. Aklilu Habte, "Higher Education in Ethiopia in the 1970s and Beyond: A Survey of Some Issues and Responses," in C. Ward, ed., *Education and Development Reconsidered*, New York: Praeger, 1974, pp. 214–40.

41. J.C. Eicher, "Education Costing and Financing in Developing Countries," Staff Working Paper No. 655, Washington, D.C.: The World Bank, 1984.

42. See S. Shaeffer and J. Nkinyangi, eds., *Educational Research Environments in Developing Countries*, Ottawa: IDRC, 1984.

43. USAID, "African Bureau Strategy Paper: Education and Human Development." Washington, D.C., 1984.

44. R.M. Morgan and V.J. Cieutat, "Improving the Efficiency of Educational Systems: Project Introduction and Summary." Florida State University, 1984.

45. D. Court, "Education and Socio-Economic Development: The Missing Link," mimeo, 1985.

46. P. Williams, op. cit.

47. H. Perraton, et al., "Basic Education and Agricultural Extension: Costs, Effects, and Alternatives," Staff Working Paper No. 564. Washington, D.C.: The World Bank, 1983.

48. C.A. Anderson, "Fostering Educational Research in the Third World," in F.C. Ward, op. cit.

49. C.E. Beeby, "The Quality of Education in Historical Perspective,"

paper presented at seminar on the Quality of Education, The World Bank, Washington, D.C., mimeo, 1983.

50. B. Robinson, "The Sector Approach to Education and Training." Nairobi: USAID, RESDO/ESA, 1984.

51. R. Dore, *The Diploma Disease: Education, Qualifications and Development*. Berkeley: The University of California Press, 1976.

52. USAID, op. cit.

53. P. Williams, op. cit.

54. F. Method, "National Research and Development Capabilities in Education," in F.C. Ward, op. cit.

55. J.L. Moock, "Overseas Training and National Development Objectives in Sub-Saharan Africa," *Comparative Education Review* 28 (2)(1984).

56. P. Williams, op. cit.

CHAPTER FOURTEEN

Women's Role in Development

Jane I. Guyer

Ten years ago, policy-making for African women's activities and concerns was necessarily "planning without facts." The fund of information on the status of women was thin and scattered, and in only a few countries were there organizations at the national and local levels with the expertise and political influence to articulate women's interests. As a result of a wide variety of efforts undertaken during the UN Decade for Women, this is no longer the case. There has been a great improvement in African women's access to education, and in the number, independence, and sophistication of women's organizations. For policy and aid purposes, there has been a major improvement in the documentation of women's economic and familial roles, and in understanding the obstacles in the path of policy implementation for women from the international to the local level.

This increased knowledge, experience, and organizational expertise suggests that development policies must build on women's potential and improve the conditions under which they work, or suffer losses and foregone opportunities which Africa cannot afford at this juncture. The fact that women's work is a crucial resource in African rural economies, particularly in food production, has been known for decades. What has been almost completely lacking, however, has been a long-term, sustained attempt to develop and implement an agricultural and social policy with this fact in mind.

It would be naive to suggest that the same set of policies could be pursued throughout such a diverse continent. Indeed, one of the central arguments of this chapter is the need to work with the differing national and regional realities in a flexible manner. There are, however, certain general guiding principles: first, we need to accept the fact that women's African agricultural production will continue to depend heavily on women for the foreseeable future; second, promote women's interests in the context of broader development objectives; third, shift the emphasis in policy-relevant work on women and by women, toward measures which go beyond the rubric of "the development project."

A strategy for the future must be based on the following principles:

- *Facts*: Women's enterprise is critical in Africa's agricultural economy, particularly in food production for domestic use and the home market, and in local and regional trade. Their successes have been achieved with negligible foreign or national aid, and with little political representation. Women's legal and practical disabilities are increasingly at odds with the urgent needs of economic and population policy.

- *Aims*: Optimal conditions for promoting welfare, employment, and technical innovation depend on the promotion of diversified regional economies in which opportunities for occupational specialization, income generation, and property-holding are available to women. Women's optimal participation in production and in family and national life depends on the protection and promotion of their legal rights and the recognition of their organizations.

- *Implementation measures*: There are three organizationally independent ways in which women's interests should be represented at national and international levels: a) policy research devoted to analyzing the effect of past and prospective social policy on women's activities, b) women's bureaus devoted to legal and political representation, and c) technical expertise on women's concerns represented in specific projects and policies within the specialist services or ministries.

The three parts of this chapter illustrate and expand on each of these arguments.

THE RECORD ON WOMEN IN ECONOMY AND SOCIETY

AGRICULTURE AND RELATED ACTIVITIES

The majority of the African population continues to work in primary production, and, in almost all rural areas, women outnumber men.

Official figures compiled from official sources suggest that a little under half of the rural labor force in Africa is female (FAO, 1982; Dixon, 1982).Impressive as this may sound by world standards where the comparable proportion is about one-third, there are reasons to believe that this figure underestimates women's importance. For example, in Malawi, women constitute two-thirds of the full-time farmers (FAO, 1982), and their seasonal labor input is often more consistent and exacting than that of their male counterparts. In a Liberian study, men worked on the farm more than 80 percent of the available days only one month out of the year, whereas women worked beyond 90 percent capacity in five months (Carter, 1982, p. 103). And they often work longer hours in the fields; in a Burkina Faso study, women spent 80 percent more time than men in production, supply, and distribution (McSweeney, 1979, p. 381, see Appendix 1). This picture of hard work on an exacting daily and seasonal rhythm characterizes much of the African woman's productive labor.

Women's work is concentrated in certain tasks and crops. In a breakdown of 13 duties, from clearing new fields to provision of cooked food, women were found to provide half or more of the labor for 10 of those tasks (FAO, 1982, p. 4). Women provided 70 percent or more of the labor in hoeing and weeding, farm to village transport, storage, processing, and the provision of water and fuel. Men provided 70 percent or more of the work in cutting the forest, staking out fields, turning the soil, and hunting.

While men's tasks are declining in importance due to decreasing heavy forest cover and declining game resources, the tasks associated with female labor are becoming increasingly important. The re-cultivation of short-fallow land requires increased weeding; the increasing distance of fields from villages demands transport; and the growth of regional food marketing places a premium on processing and storage of the raw crops from the field. Therefore, even without male outmigration or male specialization in export crops, there is increasing pressure on the agricultural tasks associated with women. In areas where men migrate out to work, women are required to take over male tasks as well.

Women tend to specialize in food crops for home consumption or regional markets, whereas men concentrate in export crop production. This division is the most marked in the forest areas of West and Central Africa. In commercial tree crops, particularly cocoa and coffee, men provide 80 percent of the labor, while they do as little as 9 percent of the work in root crop cultivation for food. Figures from other countries, however, suggest a considerably higher women's contribution to export crop production; they provide 35 percent of the labor on tobacco in Swaziland, 47 and 37 percent in two different cases of cotton production in Malawi, and 70 percent in coffee production in Rwanda (FAO, 1982, p. 4). According to Rodriguez, "most cashew workers in Mozambique are women" (1983, p. 130).

Conversely there are some areas in which men produce food crops for the local market. In parts of Nigeria and Ethiopia men are the principal farmers. Men provide 36 percent of labor in hybrid maize production, and 45 percent in upland rice and 60 percent in swamp rice in Sierra Leone (FAO, 1982, p. 4).

In recent years, one important innovation has been truck farming of European vegetables, highly perishable fruits, flowers, and other fragile crops in the peri-urban areas. Women have figured prominently in this type of cultivation, for example, producing onions in Ghana and vegetables in Abidjan. Intensive farming requires relatively small areas of land and little clearing labor, and is therefore quite manageable by women when they have restricted access to resources.

Despite rising food imports, urban food supply in large parts of Africa is still ensured in the regional productive and trading economy. Throughout the continent, small-scale processing and trade is dominated by women, while men predominate in transport. Major cities such as Ibadan, Brazzaville, and Kinshasa have been fed through women's trade. In the 1950s and 1960s, economists P.T. Bauer (1954) and W.O. Jones (1972) found the food trade to be highly competitive and efficient within the restrictions imposed by poor infrastructure and access to capital.

Outside the coastal regions of West Africa where women have dominated trade for centuries, women's self-employment in processing and trade has been a fairly recent development. Since the rapid growth of urban areas after 1945 and particularly after independence in the 1960s, women have responded to the opportunities presented by expanding markets, in part as a result of income incentives, but also due to the exigencies of low incomes and insecure access earnings. According to Dixon, 43 percent of the workers in the self-employed sector in Africa are women (Dixon, 1982). Most urban centers are now heavily dependent on the services provided by these women.

THE FORMAL SECTOR

Information on women's formal sector employment has been gathered only very recently. As late as 1977, Lucas noted that the data were so poor and inconsistently collected that "generalizations about African women are scarcely possible" (p. 36). Studies now confirm what was intuitively clear—women's representation in formal sector employment is much lower than men's at all levels. At the top, there are a few highly educated women in law, politics, medicine, and other professions. Many of these women come from prominent families, however, and hardly represent the possibility of upward mobility for the brilliant girl from an ordinary background.

At a lower professional level, recent figures for Liberia, for example, show that 16.7 percent of the working male population were formal sector employees, as compared with 1.1 percent of working women (Carter, 1982, pp. 1–9). In Tanzania, women were 5 percent of the employed labor force in 1951, and 9 percent in 1974, a negligible increase when one considers the substantial shift in investment from large-scale agriculture to industry over the same period (Bryceson and Mbilinyi, 1978).

Some of the limitations on women's employment were set during the colonial period and, in some countries, the "traditional" Western female occupations are dominated by men. Nursing and midwifery are generally male occupations in francophone countries as a result of the military medical tradition of the colonial period. Domestic service is predominantly male in Zambia, again due to the colonial tradition (Hansen, 1984). There are more male school-teachers in Africa than in Europe.

When women do find steady employment, it therefore tends to be in unskilled jobs, for example in certain categories of plantation labor, such as tea-picking in the CDC plantations in Cameroon, ancillary work in rubber and oil palm estates in Liberia, and nursery work, weeding, mulching, and gathering in Kenya.

The overall pattern of women's employment reflect the following set of factors. First, women's educational levels have lagged far behind men's until very recently, so that women now in their productive years tend to have poorer formal sector skills, including mastery of the official language. Second, occupational structures were established fairly long ago, and under conditions of high unemployment, thus it is difficult for women to break into the old "preserves." Finally, in some places, there are the familiar cultural constraints on women in technical fields and managerial positions.

WOMEN'S EARNINGS

In the formal sector women earn lower wages than men. Steel and Campbell suggest that in Ghana, men's wages are as much as 90 percent higher than women's, largely due to women's over-representation in low status work (1982, p. 239). In agricultural labor, the differential is somewhat narrower; women on a Cameroon rubber plantation, for example, earn about three-fourths the salary of men (Koenig, 1977, p. 94). The differential, in earnings between men and women appears to be considerably higher, however, in the small-scale, self-employed or family labor sector than in formal sector agricultural wage labor.

Efforts to estimate returns to labor by sex in self-employment are fraught with methodological problems, but the critical factor in determining differentials appears to be access to resources. Certain crops, especially cocoa and coffee, provide much higher returns than others, and farming of these crops is almost universally male. The Liberian study showed that cocoa and coffee bring three or more times the returns per labor day as rice, and up to twice as much as cassava. Both men and women produce rice; cassava is cultivated predominantly by women (Carter, 1982, p. 113). In other words, the differential in returns is not a simple direct function of the gender of the farmer or trader. The returns to men's labor, however, are in a higher range even though there is considerable overlap. There can be as much as a 4:1 differential between men's returns from cocoa and women's from food crops, as was the case in southern Nigeria during the 1952 cocoa boom (Galletti et al 1956).

Women tend to control less capital than men, and this may account for their lower returns to labor in some cases. In the plow economies of southern Africa, where women have access to oxen only through men. In Botswana, Lucas reported that women's farms tend to produce similar yields per unit area as men's farms, but at a much higher labor cost (1979). Without timely use of the plow, deficiencies have to be compensated for by increased hand labor. The same pattern of increased labor to make up for disabilities to other inputs is evident in Kenya, where women farmers have suffered from limited access to official agricultural services, extension, credit, and improved seed (Staudt, 1982).

In the processing and trade sectors, women's enterprises tend to be somewhat smaller than men's, and their access to markets tends to be more geographically limited (Dulansey and Austin, 1985, p. 99). Given these restrictions, most of which are a function of lower status, it is not surprising that women's earnings are lower than men's.

PRODUCTIVITY, INNOVATION AND
RESOURCE ACCESS

There is evidence that given the same resource endowments, women can be as productive and innovative in their work as men (Moock, 1976). Fortmann shows that women farmers are responsive to new techniques as men who grow the same crop (Fortmann, 1982). Muntemba relates how a Zambian production scheme for women "mushroomed" when it was provided with extension services (1982, p. 94). Women themselves have introduced various innovations independent of government, particularly in marketing organization. In Ghana and Nigeria, where women's enterprise has a long history and where women have developed their own credit organizations, many women have gained prominence as entrepreneurs.

There is nothing "natural" about the marginalization of women into low- status, poor return occupations. It is a question of resource control, itself a legal and policy issue which, in the past has been rendered unapproachable by the association of local practices with the idea of "custom."Closer examination shows that "customary" provisions can be quite recent inventions, often shaped by central policy. The effective exclusion of women from the planning machinery and the restriction of women's extension education to home economics in Malawi cannot conceivably be thought of as "African tradition" (Hirschmann, 1985). In some cases, the limitations on women's access to formal sector resources are even contrary to local "customary" practice. The various provisions that restrict women's access to capital, extension, and higher level decision-making must be seen as, in principle, changeable through the political process.

Beyond its effects on production, a further benefit from encouraging improved income and resource control for women is its influence on their patterns of consumption and savings. Women's interest in saving and in technical and productive investment may be greater than men's at the same income level. They appear to devote less money to social and ceremonial expenditures, due to their marginal position in local power structures. Women's credit associations have spring up when female incomes rise, offering credit and investment opportunities in those situations where women can translate improved incomes into increased resource control.

WOMEN, FAMILY WELFARE, AND POPULATION

African family structures present a different configuration of elements than those of Europe and Asia, with their own economic and demographic implications. Within the "extended family," there is a separation of functions. A child is socialized and fed within the very small unit centered around the mother, while at the same time being a full member of a larger group which provides a house site and ensures political, legal, and social support in relation to outsiders. Women's claims, like men's, are defined by this context, although generally through marriage rather than descent. Many of the characteristics of marriage derive from polygyny, even though the present rates of polygyny are much lower than in the past. A man assumes only certain defined responsibilities toward each wife and her children, and the wives themselves have both the right and duty to fulfill the others. Women therefore expect to support their own children within the mother-child unit which Ekejiuba has described as the "hearth-hold," to distinguish it from the household (1984).

When they search for ways of earning an individual income, women see themselves as pursuing their children's and broader familial interests. All sources suggest that the simplest answer to the classic question, "What do women want?" would include independent control of income. It is imbued in women that provision of their children's material needs rests largely with them. Their husbands are generally expected to pay for religious, political, and occupational education.

The combination of the two principles—nested familial structures and the relative economic autonomy of the hearth-hold—makes it imperative for women to earn an income. Studies have shown that women tend to choose a reliable source of personal income over uncertain access to a possibly larger sum in their husbands' or fathers' pockets. Dey quotes Gambian women rice farmers as preferring work on their own plots to their husbands', even for a wage (1981, p. 120). Jones shows that women in northern Cameroon shift their work from their husbands' to their own crops unless adequately rewarded (1972). Dupire describes women in Ivory Coast refusing to provide free porterage of their husbands' crops to market (1960, p. 14) and Obbo has written about women's "struggle for economic independence" in the urban setting of Kampala (1980).

This pursuit of individual income is a corollary of the division of labor, income, and responsibility between husband and wife. Under present conditions of insecurity, including probelms of resource access, high divorce rates, late marriage, or destitution at widowhood, there is an even greater incentive than in the past to insure such an income.

Besides providing for themselves, women's work and incomes are disproportionately devoted to children's nutrition and basic welfare. In the forest region of southern Cameroon, women provide most of the staples from their fields and devote up to three-fourths of their cash income to food supplements and household needs such as soap, matches, and kerosene (Guyer, 1984). In four ecologically different rural areas in Ivory Coast, Berio shows that "women supply between 48 and 63 percent of the most important food groups" (1983, p. 65).

In welfare terms, any deliberate or inadvertent measure which inhibits women's access to income and resources is likely to have swift effects, certainly on nutrition.

It would also affect fertility. In theory, women's employment is expected to provide anti-natalist incentives if work is in the formal sector and pro-natalist if it is in the informal and peasant sector. Neither correlation seems to hold true in Africa (Cain, 1984). Three West African studies find practically no reduction in desired or actual family size among women who work (Lewis, 1982; Fapohunda, 1982; Kollehlon, 1984). Rather, it is argued that fertility is likely to remain high wherever women have no alternative support in widowhood and old age (Cain, 1984). In this case, improving women's security of access to resources may be one plank of population policy. It certainly

appears that demands for family planning are coming far more from
women than from men.

WOMEN IN LAW AND POLITICAL LIFE

African nations have quite varied constitutional provisions and
policies with respect to women's status, ranging from the militant
promotion of women's equality in Mozambique (Urdang, 1984), to
the exemption of family law and the position of women from the anti-
discrimination clause of the new Zimbabwean constitution (May,
1982). Even where there is official support for women's organizations, as Feldman describes in Kenya, "economic and political
crises. . .have tended to displace attention" (1984, p. 67). Foreign
donors have shied away from the interventionist implications of taking a strong, explicit stand on a topic as imbued with passion and in
some cases religious fervor as the position of women.

The record here is discouraging. First, in many African countries, it
is unrealistic to call for increased participation of groups of citizens,
whether male or female, because of political restrictions. Second, in
some countries, there has been an effort to redefine "tradition" with
respect to the position of women in quite misleading ways. Under
Mobutu's ideology of "authenticity," the women's groups which
sprang up after 1960 were banned, then selectively affiliated with the
party. In the legal system, "the combination of the Belgian legal code
and 'traditional' laws has resulted in a hodge-podge of some of the
worst aspects of both" (Wilson, 1982, p. 164).

Finally, even with militant ideologies of one sort or another, all
African countries recognize local "custom" with respect to family
law. Rarely does the civil code cover all possible contingencies of
marriage and inheritance. This means that even when a woman is
married under the civil code and earns an income in the formal sector,
her property rights may be subject to customary practice. The main
points which need emphasizing here are that "custom" has often
been reworked to serve particular interests and no longer bears a
strict relationship to precolonial practice. The following are brief illustrations chosen to throw some light on women's legal problems.

In Kenya, land law has been changed in order to promote individual tenure. In the Luo region, men own the land, but women acquire
permanent use rights by virtue of marriage. Individual tenure creates
a whole series of unresolved problems in relation to women's rights,

largely because inheritance is still judged in terms of "custom." The security of a woman's rights in case of inheritance, sale, or lease of the land on which she works, the right of an inheritor to dispossess his father's widow in favor of his own wife, and the rights of unmarried women to farm land are all ambiguous and disputable (Pala, 1980). While women provide the main agricultural labor force, their rights to the land are insecure.

In Zimbabwe, inheritance is governed by custom, which in this case means that if the children are minors, the entire estate goes to the brother or lineage next-of-kin. A widow who has worked to develop her husband's business, built and furnished his home, and educated the children can be left totally bereft (May, 1983).

In both these cases, as in many others, the version of customary law which has been sanctified over the years constitutes a barrier between the female producers and the incentives to production. Very few women serve as assessors on the tribunals through which "custom" is interpreted. Short of radical legal change, provisions to represent women's interests in these courts might provide means for local reforms and innovations.

Women's political organizations at the national level are quite varied in their power, representativeness and formal affiliation within the larger political arena. While one cannot be unrealistic about the possibilities they offer, they may be the only context in which women can rise to political prominence and in which women's issues can gain a national audience.

One encouraging prospect in women's rights is that education levels for females have greatly increased, especially at the primary level. The change is most striking for Tanzania, where the percentage of women aged 15 to 49 who have enrolled in primary school rose from 18 to 93 percent between 1960 and 1981 (Poats, 1984). The Sahelian countries remain at a lower level, but the increase is still significant (see Table A.3 in Appendix I).

The gains at higher levels and in adult education are less impressive. There are still very few women with technical expertise. Rural courses for women have tended to concentrate on home economics skills, instead of building on new levels of literacy to advance technical knowledge and accounting. At a Zambian farm institute studied by Muntemba, courses were given to 704 men and only 288 women, and most of the women's curriculum revolved around sewing and knitting (1982, p. 93). In a comparable case in Malawi, over half of the course hours for "farmers' wives" were devoted to home skills (Hirschmann, 1985).

The possibility of improvement on all social fronts has been strengthened by the expansion of women's organizations. Increased literacy and increased collective representation for women are the two conditions under which national debates about economic, welfare, and legal policy toward women can develop.

OBSTACLES TO WOMEN-IN-DEVELOPMENT
POLICIES

The scope of the problems concerning women-in-development programs in donor countries can be indicated by Staudt's stark figures on the Women In Development Office (WID) of the U.S. Agency for International Development (U.S. AID), where "a million dollar budget (was) allocated to WID in a multi-billion dollar agency" (1985, p. 139). U.S. AID records show that projects in Africa which were women-specific or had women's components accounted for only 4.3 percent of regional bureau funding, and only four out of 45 agricultural projects mentioned women as beneficiaries (Staudt, 1985, pp. 97, 100). The 1982 report of the administrator of the United Nations Development Programme showed that between 1974 and 1980, only 4 percent of projects approved were considered to "involve women's participation," and in over half of these, the female participation was "minor" (1982, p. 4). On the list of recipients of projects involving women by continent, only the Arab states and Europe rated lower than Africa (1982, p. 7).

Given the importance of women's labor in African economies, why is it so consistently bypassed? One way in which African social change has been understood and its future projected is through a theory of social evolution. In this model, women's involvement in farming is considered "backward," to be replaced by peasant "household" production. By implication, women's farming and their independent enterprises are expected to disappear "naturally" and therefore neither is worth careful consideration or the investment of scarce resources. The way forward is thought to be promotion of large-scale enterprise in which Western scientific farming can be practiced without the intricate incumbrances of family law, women's time budgets, etc.

It is not the emphasis on plantation agriculture per se which is wrong with this theory, but rather the elimination from consideration of those currently farming the land and who will continue to do so barring massive urban migration, for the foreseeable future. In fact, the fragmentary evidence suggests that women's importance in rural economies continues to increase. It is not a question of whether women's farming will still exist in the year 2000 and beyond, but whether it will be carried out under optimal conditions. These would ideally include the use, by scientific research, of women farmers' expertise in managing a tricky environment.

Another view holds that as long as agriculture is associated with female labor, it will remain low in status, receive poor returns, and be relatively distant from the formal sector. This situation is perceived as alterable only by favoring the increased participation of men.

Both these views are outdated, based on simplistic assumptions that African development in the late 20th century will or can necessarily repeat the same "stages" as other parts of the world at other moments in history. Women's improved organization and modern education offers the possibility of lifting some of the restrictions on women's enterprise. The realization in development circles that indigenous farming techniques have great adaptive strengths, offers the possibility of productive engagement for the first time.

A third negative view might link the "crisis" state of African agriculture to female farming. In fact, there is no correspondence between areas in particular distress at the moment and the gender-specificity of food cultivation. As the current worst case, Ethiopia has plow cultivation systems run by men, which is otherwise quite unusual in sub-Saharan Africa. Depending on the traditional short-handled hoe, women's farming in southern Cameroon feeds its own rural population at close to adequate levels, and also urban centers from Gabon to eastern Nigeria. World Bank estimates of changes in productivity by crop over the past 20 years indicate that cassava, a crop grown almost entirely by women, has been the only staple to keep up with population growth (IBRD 1981, pp. 168–9).

These hidden erroneous assumptions prevent constructive consideration of possibilities for strengthening women's enterprise as a component in diversifying rural economies. Whereas women's farming, processing, and trade cannot be the entire answer to Africa's agricultural needs, neither are they the major source of the problem.

SUMMARY

The collected knowledge about women in Africa is not only a list of facts or an account book of successes or failures, but a collection of information in support of a set of complementary ideas. Development policies which fail to address women's current economic activities are running against the tide with respect to women's participation, and are potentially setting up serious ripple effects in children's welfare, fertility, and the poor use of development resources. Women's interests are optimally furthered when allied with general measures to to promote rural employment and strengthen regional diversity. Policies which support and promote women's activities have to be part of such a broad development strategy.

Policies promoting women must also be varied and flexible enough to address different constraints at the national level. No single policy can possibly apply everywhere; alternative routes and strategies must be available to circumvent particular setbacks and limitations in order to avoid abandonment of the goals themselves.

The work by and about African women has generated a far better-documented policy debate than was possible 10 or 15 years ago. This is a very short period of time in relation to the enormous breadth of the issues, and can only pay off in the longer term over an extended period of continued work and active experimentation.

STRATEGIES AND PRIORITIES

Framing a coherent approach to the role of women in African economies demands developing a set of goals, from the most general to the most particular. At the most general level, research on women's activities and incomes supports a development policy in which current indigenous practices and small-scale intensive enterprises are seen as a potential strength. To a considerable degree, the interests of women can be met within a "small-scale farmer" policy; by contrast, they are less likely to be served by large-scale, specialist commercial plantation agriculture or a strong export crop focus. The economic and welfare returns tend to be higher for more women when productive economies are diversified, where local and regional trade can develop, and where the avenues to diffusion of technologies are open.

A specific focus on women, however, considerably sharpens the parameters of such a policy. The following discussion outlines both the convergences between a general approach to diversification and an approach with women's concerns as the central focus, and the modifications which the latter imposes. It is critical that women-in-development advocates engage in the debate in this manner as both allies and critics, because the ultimate goal must be the promotion of greater general welfare and economic vitality.

INTERNATIONAL AND NATIONAL TRADE POLICY

African products have held a weakened position on world markets for some time. Rising food imports have caused particular concern since around 1975, when the combined effects of drought, escalating petroleum prices, and civil disturbances undermined the regional and urban-rural food trade. Since women figure prominently in the domestic food supply sector, they are deeply affected by the way in which this situation is managed. Research and political representation should be undertaken on this crucial issue by those concerned with women's economic interests.

Two main dangers are in evidence. First, at the international level, there is a possibility of state-subsidized competition for new grain markets by the farmers of the developed world. This has been advocated recently by Orville Freeman (1985). The argument that the de-control of African grain prices would lead to improved incentives for African farmers no longer holds if cheap imports are unrestricted. Trade is just as much a "woman's concern" as population policy or civil rights, since decisions on this matter will affect women's access to income.

Material and technical inputs for the productive processes are the more urgent imports. Small-scale industry and agriculture can be blocked by the lack of one particular ingredient required from abroad—chemicals for soap production, sheet metal for tool-making, spare parts for machinery, improved seed and planting materials, vaccine for livestock, solar pumps for irrigation, etc. If trade with Africa is to be promoted—as Secretary of State Shultz has suggested (1984)—it should be in types of goods which stimulate local enterprise and raise the productivity of both men and women, not in consumer goods which replace their products on the market.

Studies of income generation projects for women are unanimous in their findings that the high cost of imported inputs and the low cost of imported competing products militates very strongly against success (Buvinic, 1984, p. 2). Such projects cannot realistically be pursued without a supportive trade policy. Many of the so-called failures of women's projects may be due to the policy environment rather than the structure or purpose of the project itself.

At the national level, regarding staple grain markets, women will benefit most if the small-scale sector can strengthen its niche in the distribution system. At present, the small-scale parallel market is discouraged in a variety of institutionalized ways—through high vehicle taxation, discriminatory market access, market taxes, prohibition of inter-regional transport of certain crops, and police controls. In Guinea and Ghana, there has been outright hostility between the government and women traders. If these measures and attitudes are left unaddressed when markets are decontrolled, large-scale business will be greatly favored over the smaller scale operations which Bauer showed to be more competitive and efficient in their use of resources and in their ability to bring market incentives to relatively scattered rural producers. It is very important that the potential effects of decontrol on employment and incomes, as well as consumption, be examined under varying national conditions.

PROMOTION OF TECHNICAL CHANGE

Among those who advocate agricultural policies that favor the small-scale farmer, there seems to be quite profound disagreement over whether "technical solutions" for improving African agriculture already exist "on the shelf." Attention to the role of women in rural economies helps to focus the question. There are some known and successful technologies, particularly in the predominantly female spheres of processing, storage, small animal husbandry, and truck farming, whose diffusion is too slow. Although based on sophisticated scientific and technical research, they tend not to be of the "package" variety, but rather specific innovations. For example, animal vaccination removes a general constraint on husbandry; the introduction of intensive truck crops in peri-urban areas makes use of potentials for land and labor reallocation; and mills for processing cassava remove a particular labor and management bottleneck.

Information about new crops and methods has diffused across the continent throughout its history, and continues to do so. Staudt, for example, reports that "the diffusion of information was found to occur among women's networks" in Kenya (1982, p. 221). But much more work needs to be done to speed the adaptation of known technologies to local situations.

Experimentation and adjustment of appropriate technologies offer enormous potential in the medium-term, not solely by means of expanding adoption of such methods, but through the participation of the producers in making their own social and technical modifications. A graphic example of an effort to improve potato storage is given by Rhoades (1984). From one side of the globe to the other, farmers have incorporated the principle that storage in diffused light results in shorter sprouts and less weight loss than storage in darkness, although the techniques used to achieve this vary from place to place. Olga Linares provides the example of Diola rice farmers' rapid adoption of a rice variety with a sharp spike which inhibits pre-harvest losses to birds and releases the female and child labor otherwise devoted to bird-scaring.

The possibilities seem quite wide, but it remains largely a question of planning, orchestrating, and financing such a program of participatory information dissemination. Since women would be a major category of participants, the research on women suggests some of the constraints and possibilities.

Public Identification of Technologies   Studies by and about women identify problems of safety regarding the use of some technologies, particularly chemical poisons such as insecticides and herbicides, which must be spread under much more controlled conditions. Having such substances and their containers around in the environment of African villages, where the level of vigilance over children is low when all adults are working, poses serious public health problems. Technologies for diffusion should be low-risk in physical and financial terms in order to promote maximum experimentation with minimum damage.

With regard to other possibilities for lifting technical constraints, an analysis of work patterns suggests bottlenecks around particular tasks (Cloud, 1985). Women find it difficult to recruit extra labor (Johnny et al., 1981), and often rely on their children's help in solving the need to be in two places at once (Pala, 1979). Large-scale capital and technology does not lift these constraints and in fact often creates new ones. For example, when larger areas can be plowed by tractor, the weeding and harvesting are often left to women to manage with the old hand techniques (Boserup, 1970; Anderson, 1985). In the short to medium term, the "labor shortage" is task-specific and often associated with the availability of women's labor.

Technologies that remove particular constraints can promote expansion. For example, ILO studies of cassava-processing in southern Ghana show that even during economic crisis, diesel-powered graters are used and processing capacity now outstrips production (ILO, 1984, pp. 8, 272). In Central Africa, by hand-processing cassava, not only are women working extremely hard (Adam, 1980), but surplus production is often left in the ground unharvested. There is no point in lifting the production constraint if the processing constraint is not removed.

Many problems identified in artisanal processing are amenable to technical solutions already known. Some improved techniques are already employed, but again, in limited areas: solar driers for fish preservation, diesel mills for cassava-grating, energy-efficient stoves for cooking, and drying platforms for cassava flour (ILO, 1984).

Certain crops and cropping systems are particularly amenable to technical change through participatory dissemination. Truck farming for urban markets has spread quite widely, often with minimal needs for on-going intervention. Experimental systems, such as alley cropping developed at the International Institute for Tropical Agriculture in Ibadan, could be attempted throughout the humid zone. Leguminous trees are planted in widely spaced rows, and perform the dual function of maintaining soil fertility and providing mulch and fodder for animals. The system is well-suited to areas where the population density is too high to permit long fallow cycles. Such low-risk techniques could be attempted in a wide variety of social and ecological environments.

The choice of known technologies worth promoting must also include certain services which will only be available through the government, such as livestock vaccination. From women's perspective, particular attention should be given to small ruminants such as goats and sheep, since women more often own this kind of animal for both investment and food.

While the situation varies across Africa and the rest of the tropical world, it is hard to believe that a vast technical wisdom does not already exist with actual prototypes which could be tried out. The inventory of potential technologies needs to be matched with the actual bottlenecks in production and processing to serve as a basis for dissemination and comparison of results. It is not a question of doubting the importance of crop/fertilizer packages, but rather of placing them within the total labor and technology context. Far more can be done beyond developing new strains of crops, and many other innovations can directly address the constraints on women's work.

Formation of National and International Networks   Some form of organizational structure is required for semi-controlled dissemination of technology and for the collection and evaluation of results in different areas. No innovations can be diffused without channels of information, yet women have not been well represented in those channels in the past. Women's formal and informal organizations which exist almost everywhere in Africa may provide the conduit. Working with women's organizations ensures that where techniques apply to women's tasks and crops, women will be involved in the field trials. The experimental activity itself strengthens these organizations' interest and expertise in technical issues.

Outlets   Inexpensive inputs should be sold, with subsidies only for the cost of maintaining a broad enough inventory to allow for experiment. Studies in many regions show that as poor as people are, some resources do exist in the rural areas and savings and credit clubs are growing. Commercial sale of items such as seed, grinders, containers, and storage materials obviates the very difficult problems presented by formal sector credit—the small size of loans, the need for collateral, and the difficulty of enforcing repayment. For larger items, however, new forms of credit will have to be made available.

Credit   Lack of access to credit has been identified by a variety of sources as a major obstacle to the adoption of new techniques by women (ILO, 1984, p. 371; Loutfi, 1980, p.42, Fortmann, 1982, p. 193). Where credit is an essential component of a project or program, a means of extending it to women must be developed. Many of the barriers women face in this regard are due to their disabilities with respect to the sole source of collateral recognized by banks—title to property.

The provision of formal sector credit poses a problem both to customers and to the banks and parastatals which try to enforce repayment. More goods could be sold outright if retail outlets for productive inputs could be made a profitable endeavor, leaving the small-scale credit to local rotating credit associations. Whereas credit has been used for other purposes, such as tying farmers to monopsony purchasers of the product, parastatal control is likely to be limited in the future. Distribution of inputs through commercial outlets may provide women with better access than cooperatives because female membership in formal cooperative groups is limited.

Commercial access has often benefited women; in fact, the picture of women as "traditional" is far from accurate. Rural life is more commercialized in some respects than the stereotypical views suggest: The West African food processors studied by the ILO purchased 34 to 35 percent of their firewood (1984, p. 224), and a sample of Ghanaian female cocoa farmers hired 44.3 percent of the labor required on their farms, 10 percent more than their husbands (Okali, 1983, p. 85). Alternatives to "traditional" resource access tend to favor women, who often turn to the market with great alacrity.

Education/Extension   Women's access to extension services is poor in Africa. In general, women are less mobile than men, less able to set aside large blocks of time for training, and unable to spend long periods of time on the farm with a male extension worker. In addition to ensuring that women farmers are included in any extension network, some investment should be made in developing new means of transmitting technical information to them. Radio broadcasts in local languages are one possibility, but written material should not be ruled out altogether as female literacy rates rise. Training of women extension agents with levels of technical expertise comparable to men should be a priority in higher education.

RESEARCH

Processing and Storage   Reliable processing and storage are critically important in order to make full use of current production, especially since improved transport and infrastructure are unlikely to be affordable under present circumstances. If a policy focusing on small-scale farmers succeeds, it will eventually generate more marketable surpluses which in turn will place heavier demands on those who are primarily responsible for processing and storage, namely women.

In the short to medium term, improvements in processing techniques are of greater strategic importance than improvements in production itself. This is especially true for cassava, one of Central and West Africa's major staples. Cassava is highly perishable unless reduced to flour, which takes at least twice as much labor time as cultivation. Cassava could become price-responsive if processing techniques, market prices, and market access were more favorable.

An ILO study of cassava processing provided a number of useful observations. It found that women were not necessarily unreceptive to innovations which involved moving their activities out of the home; rather, they made an explicit trade-off between technical benefits and social losses (1984, p. 370). The group work which resulted from sharing expensive capital obtained higher levels of labor productivity.

At the moment, tons of fruit rot in all but the most efficiently commercialized or most densely populated rural areas. Fruit processing could generate employment for rural women. The enormous fruit surplus produced in the humid zone and the low level of fruit trade to the savanna is in part a problem of consumer tastes, as preserves and jams are not part of the diet, but dried fruit could be one alternative.

In other words, there are still unworked opportunities and women are not necessarily intransigently conservative. Present technologies may be programmed into a particular rhythm of daily life, but this does not mean that women are unwilling to change.

Agriculture   Research on women's work suggests several priority concerns in agriculture itself. First, a positive approach to multiple cropping and mixed farming is far more likely to benefit women farmers than crop-specific research for large-scale production. Intercropping has technical advantage in Africa and also fits in with the family dietary requirements which form the basis, though not the limit, of most women's farming.

Second, where women share tasks and fields with men, it is often the (misnamed) "secondary crops" which are controlled by the women. The importance of "secondary crops" cannot be overestimated. A study in Sierra Leone found on average 21 intercrop species per farm plot. "Crops in addition to the main crop (rice) accounted for 54 percent of the market value and 73 percent of the food energy value of the total output of such farms" (Richards, 1983, p. 27). Research to develop varieties for multiple-cropped fields, rather than for maximum production under controlled, monocropped conditions, has been promoted recently and should be further encouraged.

Despite men's association with monocropping and export crops, the barriers to women's development of monocropped fields have

more to do with local and national discrimination against access to
large stretches of land, capital equipment, and permanent trees than
with the technical potential of the current division of labor by sex.
Women's peri-urban market gardening can be very successful without running up against such barriers. Adaptation of truck vegetables
to new environments, the diffusion of other tropical vegetables from
tropical Asia, and development of indigenous vegetables are useful
areas for research.

No major staple is more associated with women's cultivation and
primary processing than cassava. Cassava has many assets as a crop:
It is the staple whose productivity in Africa compares most favorably
with yield levels elsewhere in the world; it is more nutritious than
often asserted, especially if the leaves are eaten as a green vegetable;
and it has always been marketed through the "private sector" at "free
market" prices. Technical improvements in cassava cultivation
would benefit women more than improvements in any other single
crop. Research on cassava and other root crops has been carried out at
the International Institute for Tropical Agriculture in Ibadan and
should continue to be funded at a level comparable to the major cereal
crops.

WOMEN IN LAW AND SOCIETY

As earlier stated, the record here is among the most discouraging.
Women's access to and control of resources is consistently more limited than men's in projects, in legal statements, and in customary
practice. Donors can exert influence in these areas by funding female
students for higher and technical education; by developing equitable
resource access in projects; by funding women's projects, networks,
organizations, and publications; and by providing technical advice
on civil rights and legal issues.

The major funding agencies do not have a good track record in any
of these areas. Dey describes women who have been cut off from
access to land as a result of development projects (1981); Conti shows
how women assumed to be free of family labor (1979); and Rogers'
book (1979) is a litany of the ways in which women have been side-
lined, sometimes out of the sheer myopia of Western thinking. Policy
can be at serious variance with the views of local men. Lapido, for
example, quotes Yoruba farmers as being pleased "that something
progressive might also reach their wives" (1981, p. 131).

While impressive gains were made in primary education during the 1970s, during the same period, the number of women trained by U.S. AID halved and over half of the remaining number were trained in population and health (Staudt, 1985, pp. 95-96). At the same time, there is a shortage of trained people to do technical work (ILO, 1984, p. 287) and of female teachers to work with female farmers and artisans on experimental trials of new technologies.

Critical legal work on women's status has been needed for a long time. Anomalies in current legal frameworks are sometimes glaring. Family law is the basic framework of any "peasant" or small-farmer strategy; continuing disputes about inheritance, the legitimacy of marriage, the seniority of children, the rights of widows and so on are debilitating and counter-productive (Okali, 1983). There are no simple answers here, but the lack of attention given to legal issues in recent years and the potential of drifting into de facto attenuation of women's rights is serious. Women's organizations within African countries need the resources to research and monitor their own situations and to implement policy reforms—as limited as ensuring female assessors on all customary tribunals or as radical as guaranteeing women's rights to land. This is not only an issue of civil rights, but a prerequisite for improving women's ability to respond to incentives.

IMPLEMENTATION STRUCTURES

In the past decade, the concern with women has been institutionalized in multi-purpose offices with the particular mandate to research and represent women within larger organizations. The Women In Development Office of U.S. AID and the UN Voluntary Fund for Women are two examples within the donor community. Some African countries have ministries or bureaus for women's affairs, while others have only a small understaffed office or committee. Most political parties have women's branches.

Over the years, the limitations of this approach have emerged. Staudt's book on the AID office shows that in terms of the numbers of projects concerned with women, the output has been disappointing. The WID endeavor has been poorly funded in terms of the resources of the agency. The UN fund is voluntary—not a regularly budgeted item—dependent on the annual commitments of individual countries. National organizations run into the same sort of problem— enough resources to function, but not effectively. They depend to a much greater degree than comparable organizations on voluntary labor (Buvinic, 1984, p. 22) and get stuck in small-scale, pilot-stage activities.

The lack of financial commitment is only one aspect of the problem. Some of the obstacles are clearly attitudinal: simple lack of interest on the part of the professional staff, a certain inertia in the organization of the field offices, and diffidence about "intervening" in family issues. Others include poor institutional links to technical sectors such as agriculture and lack of a firmly grounded disciplinary basis on which to evaluate results. Briefly put, "women's affairs" are susceptible to being relegated to an inconspicuous corner of the bureaucracy, with few connecting links of reporting or authority.

Regardless of existing institutional and personal resistance to a concern with women, it is clear from reports of those working within such structures that they are very awkward and perhaps unworkable. Women's issues span health, education, nutrition, and agriculture and yet the women's office has no authority with regard to projects funded in those areas. This may be one powerful reason why a great deal of recent successful work on women has focused on small-scale technology, an area not really captured by any other department and one which is slightly anomalous, neither industry nor agriculture.

Women's offices seem to have intrinsically incompatible aspects to their mandates. Research in technical areas, from tax policy to crop rotations, requires integration into the rest of the technical community. Political action, on the other hand, such as advocacy of a women's perspective within the organization as a whole, lobbying for more funding for women's projects, or the maintenance of links to other women's groups, demands cross-disciplinary organization and a somewhat more confrontational collective stance. Working on project administration involves yet another kind of structure defined by authority and cooperation. Individuals may be able to do all of these at once, but an organization runs up against the limits to flexibility in level of expertise, loyalty, collective morale, and so on. This is all the more problematic when the issue itself is as controversial as that of "women," and adversaries are looking for ways to avoid dealing with it.

Staudt suggests abandoning this overburdened, underfinanced, and understaffed type of organization in favor of a "loosely knit but diverse front" (1985, p. 139) of people located mainly within the technical sectors. Buvinic argues that the form of a "women's organization" should be retained, but used solely for research and evaluation (1984, p.22). Staudt adds that consultation with such an office ought to be a compulsory part of all project formulation and evaluation. In summary, a division of labor among those concerned with women's status should be actively sought.

At the very least, three functions are needed: broad policy research, representation, and technically specific expertise. Separation of these functions has the merit of improving organizational functioning and flexibility in the face of shifting politics and funding, and also achieves a critical transition from project-based to policy-based work. The broad question of women and development must be liberated from the tyranny of the "project."

Throughout this discussion, it has been implicit that those concerned with women's role in development can and should urgently address policy at the national and international levels as well as being involved with the formulation and implementation of development projects. Women gain and lose from trade and pricing policies, wage and benefit policies, changes in family law, and the narrow focus of agricultural research at the international centers. Local and international scholars and experts need to carry out the necessary research to suggest alternative courses of action. Ideally, there should be forums for local constituencies to comment on the implications.

Policy research shows that women's status can be addressed irrespective of the vexing problems of accessibility, obstacles to project organization, and the inertia of bureaucratic structures. The perception that "projects" have not worked very well for women is no valid reason for continuing to bypass the female side of economic and domestic life.

Projects themselves are likely to remain a major feature of aid—they are discreet, fundable, amenable to sub-contracting, and focus on measurable results. As pointed out in the introduction, there has been a significant improvement in the knowledge of why projects for women succeed or fail (see, for example, Overholt et al., 1985). The work of the next decade is to address the findings—that women tend to be second-class citizens with respect to access to resources for development, that they can, on the contrary, be highly effective as aid recipients, and that women's networks and organizations can function as sources and disseminators of information, promoters of credit associations, and potential lobbies for agricultural interests.

ACKNOWLEDGMENTS

The following people's suggestions and comments on earlier drafts are gratefully acknowledged, without committing them to any of the views expressed: Sara Berry, Christine Jones, Margaret Jean Hay, and Pauline Peters.

REFERENCES

Adam, Michel. 1980. "Manioc, Rente Foncière et Situation des Femmes dans les environs de Brazzaville (République Populaire du Congo)." *Cahiers d'Etudes Africaines* 20(1-2): 5–48.
Anderson, Mary B. 1985. "Technology Transfer: Implications for Women." In C. Overholt, et al., *Gender Roles in Development Projects*. West Hartford, Conn.: Kumarian Press, pp. 57–78.
Bauer, P.T. 1954. *West African Trade*. Cambridge: Cambridge University Press.
Berio, Ann-Jacqueline. 1983. "The Analysis of Time Allocation and Activity Patterns in Nutrition and Rural Development Planning." *Food and Nutrition Bulletin* 6(1): 53–58.
Boserup, Ester. 1970. "The Changing Role of Tanzanian Women in Production: From Peasants to Proletarians." Unpublished paper, University of Tanzania.
Bryceson, Deborah F. and Marjorie Mbilinyi. 1978. "The Changing Role of Tanzanian Women in Production: From Peasants to Proletarians." Unpublished paper, University of Tanzania.
Buvinic, Mayra. 1984. "Projects for Women in the Third World: Explaining their Misbehavior." Washington, D.C.: International Center for Research on Women.
Cain, Mead. 1984. "On Women's Status, Family Structure and Fertility in Developing Countries." Washington, D.C.: The World Bank.
Carter, Jeannette E., assisted by Joyce Mends-Cole. 1982. *Liberian Women, Their Role in Food Production and Their Educational and Legal Status*. University of Liberia: Profile of Women in Development Project.
Cloud, Kathleen. 1985. "Women's Productivity in Agricultural Systems: Considerations for Project Design." In C. Overholt, et al., op. cit., pp. 17–56.
Conti, Anna. 1979. "Capitalist Organisation of Production through Non-Capitalist Relations; Women's Role in a Pilot Resettlement in Upper Volta." *Review of African Political Economy* 15/16: 13–52.
Dey, Jennie. 1981. "Gambian Women: Unequal Partners in Rice Development Projects?" In Nici Nelson, *African Women in the Development Process*. London: Frank Cass, pp. 109–122.
Dey, Jennie. 1983. "Rice Farming Systems. Case Studies of Current Developments and Future Alternatives in Upland Rice and Inland Swamp Rice."

Expert Consultation on Women in Food Production. Rome: Food and Agriculture Organization of the United Nations.

Dixon, Ruth. 1982. "Women in Agriculture: Counting the Labor Force in Developing Countries." *Population and Development Review* 8(3): 539–66.

Dulansey, Marianne and James E. Austin. 1985. "Small Scale Enterprises and Women." In C. Overholt et al., op. cit., pp. 79–131.

Dupire, Marguerite. 1960. "Planteurs autochtones et étrangers en Basse-Côte-d'Ivoire orientale." In *Etudes Eburnéennes* VIII: 7–237.

Ekejiuba, Felicia. 1984. "Contemporary Households and Major Socio-Economic Transitions in Eastern Nigeria." Paper presented at the workshop on "Conceptualizing the Household: Issues of Theory, Method and Application." Cambridge, MA.

Fapohunda, Eleanor. 1982. "The Child-care Dilemma of Working Mothers in African Cities: The Case of Lagos, Nigeria." In Edna G. Bay, ed., *Women and Work in Africa*. Boulder, Colorado: Westview Press, pp. 277–88.

Feldman, Rayah. 1984. "Women's Groups and Women's Subordination: An Analysis of Politics Toward Women's Groups in Kenya." *Review of African Political Economy* 27/28: 67–85.

Food and Agriculture Organization of the United Nations. 1982. "Follow-Up to WCARRD: The Role of Women in Agricultural Production." Rome.

Fortmann, Louise. 1982. "Women Work in a Communal Setting: The Tanzanian Policy of Ujamaa." In Edna G. Bay, ed. op. cit., pp. 191–205.

Freeman, Orville. 1985. "Opening Markets for Food Abroad." *New York Times*, May 15th.

Galletti, R., K.D.S. Baldwin and I.O. Dina. 1956. *Nigerian Cocoa Farmers; An Economic Survey of Yoruba Cocoa Farming Families*. London: Oxford University Press.

Guyer, Jane I. 1984. *Family and Farm in Southern Cameroon*. Boston University, African Research Series #15.

Hansen, Karen Tranberg. 1984. "Negotiating Sex and Gender in Urban Zambia." *Journal of Southern African Studies* 10(2): 219–38.

Hirschmann, David. 1985. "Bureaucracy and Rural Women: Illustrations from Malawi." *Rural Africana* 21:51–63.

International Bank for Reconstruction and Development. 1981. *Accelerated Development in Sub-Saharan Africa* Washington, D.C.

International Labor Office. 1984. *Technological Change, Basic Needs and the Condition of Rural Women*. Geneva.

Johnny, M. M. P., J. A. Karimu and P. Richards. 1981. "Upland and Swamp Rice Farming Systems in Sierra Leone: The Social Context of Technical Change." *Africa* 51: 596–620.

Jones, Christine Winton. 1983. "The Mobilization of Women's Labor for Cash Crop Production: A Game Theoretic Approach." Unpublished Ph.D. dissertation, Harvard University.

Jones, W.O. 1972. *Marketing Staple Food Crops in Tropical Africa*. Ithaca: Cornell University Press.

Koenig, Dolores B. 1977. "Sex, Work and Social Class in Cameroon." Unpublished Ph.D. thesis, Northwestern University.

Kollehlon, Konia T. 1984. "Women's Work-role and Fertility in Liberia." *Africa* 54(4): 31–45.

Lapido, Patricia. 1981. "Developing Women's Cooperatives: An Experiment in Rural Nigeria." in Nici Nelson, ed., op. cit., pp. 123–36.

Lewis, Barbara. 1982. "Fertility and Employment: An Assessment of Role Incompatibility among African Urban Women." In Edna G. Bay, ed., op. cit., pp. 249–76.

Loutfi, Martha. 1980. *Rural Women, Unequal Partners in Development*. Geneva: International Labor Office.

Lucas, David. 1977. "Demographic Aspects of Women's Employment in Africa." *Manpower and Employment Research* 10(1):31–38.

Lucas, Robert. 1979. "The Distribution and Efficiency of Crop Production in the Tribal Areas of Botswana." African Studies Center Working Paper No. 20, Boston University.

McSweeney, Brenda Gael. 1979. "Collection and Analysis of Data on Rural Women's Time Use." *Studies in Family Planning* 10(11/12): 378–82.

May, Joan. 1982. *Zimbabwean Women in Colonial and Customary Law*. Gweru: Mambo Press.

Moock, Peter. 1976. "The Efficiency of Women as Farm Managers." *American Journal of Agricultural Economics* 58: 831–35.

Muntemba, Maud Shimwaayi. 1982. "Women and Agricultural Change in the Railway Region of Zambia: Dispossession and Counter-Strategies." In Edna G. Bay, ed., op. cit., pp. 83–104.

Obbo, Christine. 1980. *African Women: Their Struggle for Economic Independence*. London: Zed Press.

Okali, Christine. 1983. *Cocoa and Kinship in Ghana. The Matrilineal Akan of Ghana*. London: Kegan Paul International.

Overholt, Catherine, Mary B. Anderson, Kathleen Cloud and James E. Austin. 1985. *Gender Roles in Development Projects: A Case Book*. West Hartford, Conn.: Kumerian Press.

Pala, Achola Okeyo. 1979. "Women in the Household Economy: Managing Multiple Roles." *Studies in Family Planning* 10: 337–43.

Pala, Achola Okeyo. 1980. "Daughters of the Lakes and Rivers." In Mona Etienne and Eleanor Leacock, eds., *Women and Colonialization: Anthropological Perspectives*. New York: Praeger, pp. 186–213.

Poats, Rutherford. 1984. *Development Cooperation*. Paris: Organisation for Economic Cooperation and Development, Chapter 12.

Rhoades, Robert E. 1984. "Tecnicista versus Campesinista: Praxis and Theory for Farmer Involvement in Agricultural Research." In P. Matlon, R. Cantrell, D. King and M. Benoit-Cattin, eds., *Coming Full Circle: Farmers' Participation in the Development of Technology*. Ottawa: International Development Research Centre, pp. 139–50.

Richards, Paul. 1983. "Ecological Change and the Politics of African Land Use." *African Studies Review* 26(2): 1–72.

Rodriquez, Anabella. 1983. "Mozambican Women after the Revolution." In Miranda Davies, ed., *Third World—Second Sex: Women's Struggles and National Liberation. Third World Women Speak Out*. London: Zed Press, 127–34.

Rogers, Barbara. 1979. *The Domestication of Women, Discrimination in Developing Societies*. New York: St. Martin's Press.

Shultz, G. 1984. The U.S. and Africa in the 1980s. Current Policy No. 549. February 15. Washington, D.C.: U.S. Department of State.

Staudt, Kathleen. 1982. "Women Farmers and Inequities in Agricultural Services." In Edna G. Bay., ed., op. cit., pp. 207–24.

Staudt Kathleen. 1985. *Women, Foreign Asistance and Advocacy Administration*. New York: Praeger.

Steel, William F. and Claudia Campbell. 1982. "Women's Employment and Development: A Conceptual Framework Applied to Ghana." In Edna G. Bay, ed., op. cit., pp. 225–48.

United Nations Development Program. 1982. "Integration of Women in Development." Report of the Administrator. New York.

Urdang, Stephanie. 1984. "The Last Transition? Women and Development in Mozambique." *Review of African Political Economy* 27/28:8-32.

Wilson, Francille Rusan. 1982. "Reinventing the Past and Circumscribing the Future: Authenticite and the Negative Image of Women's Work in Zaire." In Edna G. Bay, ed., op. cit., pp. 153–70.

CHAPTER FIFTEEN

Manpower, Technology, and Employment in Africa: Internal and External Policy Agendas

Kenneth King

The local and external agendas on the role of manpower in African development look very different. The external agenda is concerned with "getting the numbers right," the dangers of over-expansion and under-utilization of labor, and the training of very specific subgroups to address the problems of agricultural productivity, population control, and other development issues. The local manpower agenda, conditioned by the traditions of scarcity of skilled labor and exclusion from training that prevailed in the colonial era, is fundamentally suspicious of labor over-supply.

A comprehensive approach to manpower development is lacking both locally and among external donors. On the external side, this is partially due to donors' preoccupation with projects and their preference for building on their comparative advantage in particular sectors. Thus, one donor is concerned solely with increasing formal apprenticeship in industry and another with agricultural extension, the engineering faculty, or the training of rural artisans. The provision of manpower is invariably a justification for regional projects, but in practice, this amounts to little more than an assertion that national development is impeded by shortages of specialized manpower.

No less difficult to grasp, the local manpower agenda has little to do with whether the state does or does not have a ministry of manpower development or whether there is a tradition of carrying out manpower surveys. As is the case with the donor agencies, the implicit manpower assumptions of the state have to be deduced from a wide variety of sources, many of them far removed from the official manpower planning apparatus. The actual manpower policies of the state consist of many uncoordinated initiatives such as guaranteeing graduates employment, measures which favor science over arts in tertiary education, concern about the ratios of men to women in modern sector jobs, and others. These policies in turn determine the expansion of polytechnics, secondary schools, and universities.

Overlaying these forces, the official apparatus of manpower planning seeks to control the politics of the domestic manpower agenda. Manpower planning units have won few rounds in this contest over the last 20 years, but it is nevertheless useful to regard these official units as a negotiating forum between the external and internal agendas for manpower development. In many countries, the existence of an official apparatus represents the hope that if only the different categories of manpower could be ascertained, they could be scientifically managed.

ASPECTS OF THE LOCAL MANPOWER AGENDA

In the 1980s, local agendas continue to be preoccupied with expanding education at all levels. Since there are virtually no signposts from manpower planning ministries or elsewhere as to the appropriate size of secondary, polytechnic, or university education, the lure of universal primary education has given way to that of universal secondary, and eventually to open higher education.

Underlying increasingly open educational systems is the assumption that opening opportunities to compete for the few good jobs available is more equitable than shaping educational policy to the pyramid of well-paid jobs. Therefore there is little correspondence in size between the education and training system (the supply) and the wage and salary sector (the demand). The increasing determination of a number of African countries to build colleges of technology, polytechnics, and technological or agricultural universities in the face of strong negative pressure from external agencies illuminates the tensions between local and foreign agendas.

Countries are determined to provide access to scientific and technological careers, particularly during one of Africa's worst recessions. Consultants carrying out feasibility studies on the need for more polytechnic or university graduates are in a peculiarly difficult position. Investigating something that is already feasible in local eyes, they represent agencies that are skeptical of the country's ability to fund or absorb further graduates.

Nowhere is the conflict between manpower agendas more fierce than over the issue of pre-vocational skills for all. With their increasingly cross-national research base, donors believe that offering pre-vocational skills in general schools cannot succeed in developing countries. But what to external donors is yet another example of the vocational training fallacy is to local decision-makers a relevant and logical extension of educational opportunity.[1]

A corollary of the dispute over basic skills is the differing attitudes of donor agencies and national governments toward training in the informal sector of the economy. The ILO and other bodies were fascinated by the open access system of training and skills in the shanty towns, roadsides, and villages—local, low-cost skilled manpower development. By contrast, governments could barely be constrained from sweeping the informal sector out of sight, destroying shanty workshops, and in some cases trying to prevent young apprentices from developing their skills.[2]

While dramatic evidence of local manpower agendas is found in access to different levels of education, other elements in the informal manpower agenda concern the relationship between skills and scientific knowledge. Of particular importance are relations between artisans, technicians, scientists, and engineers in the industrial sector, and between the various grades of agricultural staff in the rural sector.

One example of the relationship between skills and knowledge is the application of the 1:5:30 ratio as suggested proportions of engineers, technicians, and artisans. While this ratio is widely argued over and has been used to support the expansion of technician and scientific careers, for all the decades of manpower planning, there has been no rule of thumb to give direction to university expansion. Ministers are guided by rather simple but compelling manpower agendas and not least by the evidence of massive social demand for higher education of the sort evident in Southeast Asia.

In many African countries, there are entire shadow university populations overseas that often exceed the number of home-based students. This is central to manpower planning, for very few of the shadow university students are on government scholarships. Unlike the home situation where there is some attempt to "get the numbers right" for arts, computer science, agriculture, and so on, in the shadow university system, tens of thousands of students are deciding their own course of study.

In the United States in 1983-84, at least half of the 330,000 foreign students chose just three disciplines: engineering, management, and computer science.[3] For the carefully controlled schools of engineering and computer science in a national university of an African country, the implications of these figures do not need much explanation. Therefore, African ministers are as much guided in their plans for local university expansion by the evidence of a 1:1 ratio between their home-based and overseas students as by donor arguments about the impossible costs of further higher education.

In Tanzania for almost 20 years, a very different educational model has been in operation—neither a pyramid nor a square, but a low, flat rectangle with a tiny, thin spire. President Nyerere has preached that secondary education is a privilege not a right, and that a poor country cannot afford to have more than 1 or 2 percent of its primary school leavers attend secondary school. In proportion to the number of children in primary school, Tanzania consequently has the smallest secondary school population in the world. This controversial model was widely praised by the donor community. Now, however, it must be admitted that this particular manpower approach is in ruins; there are shortages of educated people at all levels.[4]

Both Kenya and Tanzania's systems of further education were planned by a colonial power determined that higher education in Africa should not be influenced by the Indian model with its ever-expanding associated colleges.[5] Now, with more than 5000 East African students studying in Indian colleges and universities, African decision-makers are clearly impressed by India's claim to have the third largest contingent of scientific and technical manpower in the world, and have considerable admiration for the investment in science that they associate with India, Singapore, Hong Kong, and South Korea.

African policy on higher education for development is now at a peculiarly difficult crossroads. Lacking signposts, policy-makers have to fall back on very basic intuitions, of which the most compelling is the conviction that they have dramatically under-invested in science and technology since independence.

By contrast, many African countries have been content with Africanizing the public service, approaching the localization of the industrial and extractive sectors with extreme caution. As a result, in the mid-1980s, many of the scientific careers where Africa offers opportunities are still dominated by white science. Rangeland management, ecology, archaeology, palaeontology, renewable energy, mining, and specialized agricultural research are only a few of the fields where technological capability is predominantly in expatriate hands. It is not surprising, therefore, that at their recent Harare conference, African ministers of education targeted science and technology education as the next great advance.

The real manpower agenda is increasingly determined to extend provision of science and technology at all levels, as well as agricultural skills and sciences. Some argue that saturation with skills and science is the only way around the dilemmas of scarcity, but whether through mobility or misallocation, small cadres of trained people have not utilized their skills in jobs for which they were trained.

A fundamental issue is identifying the local meaning categories of skill and technical knowledge. The time-honored European distinctions between skilled and semi-skilled labor, between artisans, technicians, and scientists do not apply in Africa at all. Unlike the European and Asian skilled workers whose attitude to their craft has been hardened by caste, community, or union traditions over many generations, the majority of African artisans, technicians, and scientists are still first generation.

As a consequence, there is little disposition to think of these occupations as lifelong or family concerns. Polytechnic students are not necessarily settling down to 25 years as contented technicians, any more than technical or vocational school students are planning to stay in skilled work throughout their lives. Assumptions about the connection between training facilities and subsequent careers seldom take into account local perspectives. In reality, it is entirely possible that some polytechnics are full of shadow university students, and that some technical schools are full of students identical to those found in the ordinary high schools.[6]

The lack of connection between the training facility and the category of work aspired to makes a good deal of difference to calculations of skilled manpower supply. Therefore, understanding how skill and knowledge hierarchies are viewed locally is important for any analysis of the need for middle-level manpower. A similar case could be made for the distinctions between certificate, diploma, and graduate qualifications in agriculture.

Another important element in gaining a sense of the local manpower agenda is the difference between the small number of modern sector paid jobs and work in subsistence agriculture or in the urban and rural informal sectors. In many African economies, only 10 percent of the labor force is employed in the paid wage and salary sector, with more than half of this number in the public service.

Workers in the modern sector are few and relatively privileged. In one sense, people inside this favored sector have more in common with each other than with the large majority who work outside, both in terms of different traditions of training and education and the jobs themselves. Thus a carpenter in the modern sector, employed by a multinational or the ministry of works, has more in common with a clerk or other middle-range civil servant than with a carpenter who is working on his own in the informal sector of the economy.[7]

The most dramatic examples of belonging to the fortunate few come from those very systems like Tanzania's where secondary school children are virtually guaranteed jobs because of the exclusion from government secondary school of 98 percent of primary school leavers. In this situation, whether students pursue agriculture or home economics in secondary school is of minimal importance when compared to those not in school at all. Loyalty to these "disciplines" is consequently very weak and it is therefore not surprising to find little correlation between education and subsequent employment. The rather high mobility among those who are inside the modern sector can foil attempts to relate training to job classifications.

A second very crucial aspect of the distinction between jobs and work is that the bulk of those practicing a particular trade—automobile mechanic, builder, carpenter—fall outside the modern sector and are not captured by statistics. This would not be significant if the modern sector was a self-contained system separate from the 90 percent working outside. The reality, however, is quite the opposite. The vast number of shadow artisans and workers in the informal sector are incorporated into the modern sector at many points. For example, it is common for formal sector construction companies to use low-paid, non-unionized labor from the informal sector in regular building contracts, having an obvious impact on the "demand" for formally trained artisans. This raises problems for approaches to manpower that treat the modern sector as independent from the larger system.[8]

A crucial element in the local manpower perspective is related to the moving educational frontier between "real" jobs and ordinary work. In a situation where only 10 percent of the workforce have real jobs, the universalization of primary or secondary education and the moves toward open higher education can have unforeseen consequences. In the inevitable democratization of primary education after independence, the marketability of the primary school certificate was devalued almost overnight. Consequently, following a short-lived political concern about the "educated unemployed" primary school leaver, new generations of secondary school graduates became the focus of political concern, giving way in turn to the higher secondary and college graduates. By the mid-1980s in many developing countries, primary school leavers could no longer be described as educated unemployed.

Primary school leavers were no longer seriously considered for modern sector jobs. Widespread concern about the political threat of several million "jobless" school leavers proved unfounded; the expected demoralization of youth did not materialize. As these school leavers lacked any incentive to register as unemployed, it became difficult to quantify them. They vanished back into the informal and unregistered occupations of their parents.[9]

The consequence of this moving educational frontier is that in many countries, primary and secondary school leavers are politically irrelevant, apart from some regular exhortations to use their school skills for self-employment. Only graduates are sufficiently politically important to warrant job-creation schemes. This does not necessarily mean that governments regard the eight or 12 years of education as wasted, but concern with how such education is being used is not very high on the manpower agenda. Where government ability to create jobs is restricted to the public service and parastatals, the most popular political alternative is to create educational opportunities to compete for these jobs.

ASPECTS OF THE EXTERNAL MANPOWER AGENDA

Although more is known about the external than the internal manpower agenda, the external map for particular countries is not clear. It can be deduced from the mass of official and voluntary projects and technology and investment decisions of foreign companies operating in the country.[10]

External agencies have strong views about their own comparative advantage in manpower training in Africa, tending to support a particular sector in a style peculiar to them. Some agencies are exclusively concerned with rural artisans, others with a particular type of agricultural extension or maternal and child health. While all provide training components in-country, overseas, and in third countries, except where donors share a sphere of influence, there is virtually no knowledge of what other donors are doing, or any attempt to coordinate.

THE TEMPTATIONS OF SCALE

Donors' interest in promoting manpower initiatives in Africa is due to the relative smallness of most of the countries. With single universities and polytechnics and easy access to most of the senior decision-makers, individual countries appear open to influence compared to South and Southeast Asia. External agencies seem to believe that the manpower situation can be corrected with the right delivery system. What cannot be grasped in a few weeks, however, even in a very small country with a handful of training institutions, is the local significance of skill and knowledge—a sense of how parents, pupils, and politicians are using particular institutions.

THE DESIRE FOR RATIONALIZATION

By the mid-1980s, even a country whose first trade school dates only from the 1920s is likely to have a whole range of government, private, parastatal, and NGO bodies involved in skills training at different levels. The donor community tends to think that this apparent duplication must be rationalized and coordinated. Given the highly political nature of many of these educational decisions, such demands for rationalization strike very close to local political nerves.

In the colonial period, independent educational initiatives were frequently halted. With independence, however, a number of African achievements in education and training have been treated with great skepticism by donors on pedagogical or fiscal grounds. External skepticism to measures in Kenya, for example, can be documented in the outright condemnations of the Harambee secondary school movement, free primary education to Standard Four, the development of some 15 Harambee institutes of science and technology, free primary education to Standard Seven, and many other educational initiatives.

By reason of its enormous commitment to the expansion of education, Kenya has encountered this clash between internal and external manpower agendas more than other nations. Yet even countries with quite different priorities, such as Tanzania, are frequently given recommendations for rationalization. The paradox of these recommendations is not only that there is virtually no rationalization of donor priorities, but that donor priorities often shift dramatically within the space of two or three years. Donors end up competing for projects they had earlier declared foolhardy, or deciding that local priorities they once admired are simply no longer tenable.

DIFFERENT MANPOWER RESEARCH AGENDAS

While there is no common external approach to manpower research, some of donor interests in this area are derived from fundamentally different concerns than local ones. The types of manpower research projects considered as important are often those that contrast the cost and effectiveness of two parallel "delivery systems" in technical, vocational, or agricultural education. The working assumption is that research may point to where rationalization is needed.

The temptation for external research to rationalize is particularly acute when four or five different institutions are involved with broadly similar types of training. But the "scientific" rationalization of what appear to be illogical LDC systems often fails to take account of the history and specificity of the institutions under review.[11]

Efforts to associate particular amounts of education with particular development outcomes are also common among external donors. Donors are preoccupied with identifying what increments to agricultural or industrial manpower can be derived from particular sequences of education. Possibly the single best known example is the assertion that four years of education is basic to worker productivity.[12] Some studies have been very influential within the donor community in making the case for increased support to basic education.

Donors' concepts of human resource development and deployment are a world apart from the local agenda on education and manpower. The commitment to universal primary or secondary education originates from quite different sets of assumptions in many

African countries. There are too few studies which look at the impact of three years of higher education on the nature of graduates' work, perhaps because research has been preoccupied with legitimizing the priority of primary education, rather than with analyzing what a country may hope to reap from its new generations of graduates.

Thus, one of the challenges to African researchers is to develop a local research agenda for education, manpower, and employment. On the external research agenda it is already clear that some priority research will be concentrated over the next decade upon clarifying how schooling affects an individual's later ability to adapt to the technological requirements of agriculture.[13] Based on their own insights into manpower policies, African researchers have the opportunity and obligation to lay out and implement a different set of solutions than those currently proposed.[14] In the absence of local initiative, the grounds on which manpower discussions take place in developing countries will be claimed by the Western research community.

MANPOWER POLICIES, UTILIZATION, AND THE TECHNOLOGICAL ENVIRONMENT

Having sketched some features of the foreign and local manpower maps, it may be useful to look more closely at current manpower planning in some African countries and what new approaches are being developed. Regarding the protracted and unproductive debate about particular techniques for manpower planning, Hollister has summarized the present rather unimpressive state of the art admirably:

> In looking back over these (20) years, I am struck by how little progress seems to have been made: the literature on manpower planning seems little different to what was written two decades ago, and, more important, the practice of manpower planning seems hardly to have changed at all.
>
> It is my impression that the plans made by manpower planners have rarely had any effect on the policy decisions actually made. The methods used, however, have had the effect of discouraging the development of information which could have been used to improve the policy-making process.[15]

Given the amount of information actually collected by different agencies, it seems quite likely that under-utilization of existing information is as serious as the absence of information. However, a priority of any new approach to manpower must be a concern with utilization of existing personnel rather than quantitative projections of those who are not yet hired. Officials in manpower ministries often assume that if a manpower survey were available, the shortages and surpluses would be evident and it would then be simple to argue for more technicians (and in turn for more polytechnics), or more artisans (and more training schemes).

Nothing could be further from the truth. There is virtually nothing that can be deduced from knowing how many engineers, technicians, and artisans there are in a particular country. Instead, therefore, we shall explore a number of ways for looking at the complex issue of utilization, which itself is inseparable from the technological environment.

THE FARM, FIRM, AND FACTORY

A prerequisite for understanding how manpower is actually used in Africa is to examine a few case studies in the main sectors of the economy. For the purposes of illustration, three sectors—farm, firm/office, and factory—could be looked at in each of four modes: public, multinational, local, and informal.

Manpower surveys often concentrate on what is measurable, large-scale, and modern sector, routinely excluding the bulk of employment. It is critical that smaller local and informal sector enterprises are included in these case studies, because their pattern of labor use directly affects the pattern in the wage and salary sector. It is also critical to include the public sector (i.e., a ministry) because no less than half of the modern sector works for the government. The purpose of these case studies is to uncover different patterns of utilization of labor in different sectors, and to note how these are affected by education, training, and technology policies, as well as by elements in the two manpower agendas.

GOVERNMENT OFFICE OR MINISTRY

Understanding the labor process and the culture of the civil service is central to any broader goals of manpower analysis, since in several countries the state sector absorbs all the graduates of certain training institutions, and 75 percent of many crucial occupational groups, such as engineers. Among the more salient features of work organization are:

- The rise of oral decision-making and a measure of retreat from reliance on literacy. For field ministries like education and agriculture, the retreat from literacy has forced headmasters into headquarters and brought ministry officials to the province and district. It also dramatically reduces workloads for secretaries and typists. In addition, though French and English remain immensely popular in schools, they are not an easy or effective medium for many of the secretarial staff.

- Constant delegation of decision-making to higher levels has reduced the written output in lower professional cadres and the number of decisions made because of over-centralization.

- The absence of effective induction systems for new entrants can mean the destruction of the morale of both school and university graduates within a matter of weeks.

- The technological environment is not elaborate, but irregular supplies of paper, ribbons, servicing, and even electricity combine with unwieldy and ineffective filing and registry systems to make evaluations of office efficiency rather complex.

- Finally, the public sector alone offers scope for limited job creation within patronage systems; hence there is a greater expectation of over-staffing and under-utilization in ministries than in most other areas.

The colonial civil service tradition bequeathed to the continent has clearly undergone a major transition since Africa's independence, yet almost no thought has been given to the personnel implications of these changes. The civil service is more educated but less trained and skilled in some ways than it has ever been. Twelve years of basic education may now be the norm for civil service secretaries in many countries, but this does not necessarily translate into increased efficiency if education is underutilized on the job. The state of the civil service is part of a much wider set of political issues. No simple manpower formula for altering ratios of secretaries and professionals or exposing everyone to some system of management will do more than scratch the surface of the problem.[16]

The local and external manpower agendas converge at the level of the African civil service, which is likely to be a common point of conflict between the two. Donors perceive that their own manpower priorities in particular projects or programs have to be made system-proof by special executive committees or by expatriate teams. While one agency would reintroduce expatriate manpower, another believes that the introduction of new information technology might make manpower planning possible. While new technology may simplify the management task, it will have little or no success if one of the explicit manpower policies of the head of state is that all graduates must find work, if need be, in the civil service.

In this case study, it is clear that the techniques of manpower planning are not relevant, nor are improved national manpower surveys which identify crucial shortages and surpluses. Nothing is more important to the deployment and employment of technical manpower in a country than understanding the under-utilization of the still rather good general education of those who enter the nation's largest "firm."

SMALL-SCALE LOCAL ENGINEERING WORKSHOP

While local engineering firms differ dramatically from one country to the next with the salient features of manpower utilization altering accordingly, the following points might emerge from case studies of small-scale skilled engineering firms. First, this sector is still dominated by expatriates or non-African management. Second, in some cases it has the potential to make tools, dies, spare parts, and components of great variety, but it is plagued by low levels of capacity utilization.

Third, some of this under-utilization of capacity is directly linked to the technology policy of the state. The range of imported goods is so great that there is little incentive or comparative advantage to increasing local manufacturing. Thus, the investigation of under-utilization of manpower is sometimes inseparable from the under-utilization of capacity in the firm itself, which in turn is influenced by national policy.

Firms tend to use "shadow" technicians and artisans who are trained on the job by skilled European or Asian machinists, rather than hiring formally trained technical school and polytechnic graduates and/or utilizing the formal apprenticeship system. This strategy reduces the salary bill and the danger of poaching by providing limited skills to the African artisans. If such firms really wanted to enter the field of components manufacture, they would find that the new technologies and associated quality controls dictated by the industrialized countries require an investment in machine tools and a labor process that actually undervalues their existing improvisational skills.

The manpower analysis implications of these critically important small engineering workshops are complex. The concentration of skills in expatriate hands renders the pursuit of the ratio of engineer to technician to artisan meaningless. Informally trained technicians and artisans will not even show up in manpower surveys that assume that these categories can only be produced in formal training institutions. Hence, understanding the constraints of the small engineering sector is a precondition to interpreting any data that a wider survey of engineering manpower might produce.

The absence of trained African technicians and artisans in small-scale engineering workshops cannot be construed as a "demand" for such people, to be met by polytechnics or other formal training schools. On the surface, Africans who acquire a modicum of skills in expatriate engineering workshops would improve on their expertise by leaving and starting their own workshops. But for that to happen at the level of a skilled machinist, for example, access to capital and equipment is necessary, reinforced by a technology policy that makes local manufacture of spare parts and components worthwhile.

As an essential means for deciphering data collected on a wider scale, case study work on the labor process and work organization in one or two representative engineering firms should be conducted. In a 1982 manpower survey in Kenya, some 75,000 individual workers were interviewed and information about their work experience and training was collected. The titles used by the workers to describe their own positions were then "translated" into the numerical codes of the Kenya National Occupational Classification System.

Most of the classic problems of relating job titles in particular firms to larger occupational classifications can be presented in a small table relating to one category of engineering worker (Table 15.1).[17] It is virtually impossible to sort out the skilled from the semi-skilled workers because many semi-skilled machine operators are lumped in the same category as skilled machinists, turners, or fitters. A machine operator can be working on a machine which routinely punches out identical pieces of metal throughout the shift, or he can be on a machine where a great deal of skill is required.

Where coders translating worker titles into national codes do not know the engineering industry or do not have strong English skills, miscoding can take place. One indication is when the category "other worker" is preferred to a specific description. Another is when the very crucial distinction is missed between "tool maker" and "hand tool operator." Such surveys tend to aggregate findings so that all the specific job groups within different sectors are lost in a single category of production, maintenance, and factory workers. Even if education and training are cross-tabulated with this large work group, there is no way of knowing the different levels of education and training in each of the sub-groups. From a policy viewpoint, it would be important to know whether only in the multinational and parastatal sectors workers had completed secondary education and institutional training, or whether the level of certification was rising throughout the productive sectors.

TABLE 15.1
METAL WORKING MACHINE OPERATORS AND MACHINERY FITTERS

Code	Job Group	Number
7110	Leading hand	16
7121	Metal working machine setter/operator	116
7122	Lathe setter/operator/turner	119
7123	Milling machine setter/operator	22
7124	Planing machine setter/operator	12
7125	Boring machine setter/operator	5
7126	Tool sharpener, saw doctor	31
7129	Other machine tool setter/operator	339
7131	Machinery assembler (production)	5
7132	Machinery fitter/maintenance	153
7140	Hand tool operator	37
7150	Precision instrument maker/repair	10
7190	Other metalworking machine oper./ftr.	1698
Total in this sub-group		2556

THE MULTINATIONAL INDUSTRIAL SECTOR

Because the multinational sector is by far the most studied, we will focus on the way it is regarded by governments as the ideal representative of attitudes toward training and manpower utilization. The multinational sector is generally highly responsive to formal training, accepting regular apprentices, seconding them to the local training schools and later to polytechnics, and accommodating levy-grant schemes. It supports institutionalized training both at home and abroad and has the personnel and managerial capacity to organize in-house induction and training systems.

Large multinationals are naturally at the forefront of the local training lobby; they are represented on tripartite training committees and provide a very visible ideal that is hard to follow. Even governments find it difficult to emulate them, for although ministries are very responsive to demands for institutional training, they do not have the capacity to utilize productively the levels of training in which they invest so willingly.

Government technical ministries, parastatals, and multinationals account for almost all the apprenticeship places, scholarships, and sponsorships to national polytechnics, and main users of the levy-grant system where it operates. Therefore, almost all high quality, high cost training efforts are situated at the tip of the iceberg, reinforcing and legitimizing higher pay and benefits.

The danger of multinationals' "responsiveness" to those forecasting demand for formally trained technical labor is that it is easy to assume that other sectors should follow suit. Unlike the situation in Denmark, Scotland, or Germany, where rural workshops have regular apprentices, the imported apprenticeship system has no roots at all in the small urban or rural firms. Attempts to this end distract attention from existing and developing local systems of skill acquisition. The close liaison between the formal technical training system and this restricted group of parastatal, government, and multinational enterprises more importantly deflects attention from measures that would allow low-cost access to formal training and upgrading to firms that cannot afford sponsorship or day release.

THE SMALL AND MEDIUM-SIZED FARM

Numerous manpower studies address the size of various groups of graduates leaving the agricultural training system and the need for improved agricultural extension systems. However, there is little knowledge of the skill levels of those who run their own farms or are employed as small-scale farm managers, nor is there much sense of the availability of jack-of-all-trades workers who can weld farm equipment and do basic carpentry, building, and plumbing.

These skills are of crucial concern to many farmers, and it is quite possible that the specialized skills offered by the regular training institutions do not fit the bill at all. Formal agricultural skills are basically monopolized by the government, multinational estates, and agro-related industries, scarcely penetrating to the level of the local farm manager. Case studies of manpower utilization in the small and medium farm sector could provide some insights into the relationship between the formal training system and the utilization of agricultural skills in the rest of the farm sector. They might also be of value in considering the relationship between new systems of agricultural extension and the skill and knowledge needs of those running small mixed farms.

MANPOWER AND THE INFORMAL SECTOR

Most manpower surveys in Africa have assumed that for skills to be taken note of, they must be located in regular enterprises with a given minimum of employees. In many surveys of high- and middle-level manpower, skilled artisans were captured if they worked in modern sector firms and excluded if they worked elsewhere. In recent years, the manpower potential of the informal sector has come to the attention of national governments and has led to calls for productive self-employment. However, there is no clear pattern of how young people learn to become self-employed or how skills are acquired and extended in different fields. Fortunately, there is now a growing number of case studies from both francophone and anglophone Africa which could be taken advantage of by planners who wish to understand the dynamics of labor use and which could eventually begin to alter the local political rhetoric about education for self-employment.[18] Some of the lessons for manpower planners from this literature include the following:

- There is no such thing as a mass program of training for self-employment.
- It is exceedingly hard for governments (always so closely associ-

ated with the formal employment sector) to promote self-employment.

- NGOs, accustomed for decades to working on small budgets close to the grassroots, stand a better chance of developing small-scale programs in support of self-employment.

- In many cases the political rhetoric in favor of training for self-employment is a good deal stronger than government commitment to its development.[19]

It is exceedingly important that manpower analyses extend beyond matters of training and low-cost access to formal institutions to incorporate the technological dimension that is so vital to understanding capacity utilization in the small-scale industrial sector. In some ways, the rate of technological change has been more marked in the informal sector than in Africa's formal industrial estates. More work needs to be undertaken on the role of technology in labor processes. The external manpower agenda relating to the informal sector also needs to address the impact of basic primary education on informal productivity. If some causal connection can be found, this would certainly be valuable in maintaining external support to primary education.[20]

MANPOWER POLICIES IN EDUCATION,
TRAINING, AND PRODUCTION:
IMPLICATIONS FOR PLANNING

Having outlined some of the connections between technological change and particular patterns of labor utilization in different sectors, it may now be useful to underline some of the consequences of adopting these approaches. The challenge to planners working with manpower or human resource policies is that they must operate with a knowledge of the three crucial areas—education, training, and production.[21]

Traditional discussions about manpower have described the task of the planner as achieving a fit among these three spheres, yet they must also acknowledge that there are limitations on matching these three activities because of the powerful inherent differences in their modes of operation. For example, similar skills exist in each of the spheres, such as metal work, computing, or secretarial skills. For the planner, this situation has frequently been described as "substitutability"—that the welder trained on the job can replace the welder trained in a vocational training center, or someone who has picked up welding in the machine shop of a secondary school.

Obviously, this situation immensely complicates the task of anyone trying to work out the sources and quantities of expertise in different areas. The crucial point is that few skills are easily transferable. Agriculture, carpentry, or office practice learned in school cannot be compared with or substituted for similar disciplines offered in training institutions or acquired directly on the job. This is not to apply value judgments on school-based skills versus on the job skills, but rather to suggest that the context and "feel" of skills acquired in the areas of education, training, and production are significantly different.

In addition, therefore, to a concern about how labor is utilized, there needs to be an awareness of the environment in which the skill was first produced. Instead of totalling up mechanics or other trades coming out of secondary schools, trade schools, and industrial or parastatal training units, it is important to discern the different combinations of exposure to skills and specialized knowledge that young people can gain as they move through the spheres of education, training, and production.

In some situations, it may appear that a young person has been exposed three times (in school, training center, and in the firm) to what may sound like a similar skill, but the different contexts and purposes of the institutions concerned can mean that there is no redundancy. Identifying the various combinations and tracks that are favored by students, governments, and employers is probably more vital than head counting school graduates and seeing if they utilize their skills. The emphasis needs to be less on the title of the course or the skill and more on the specific contributions of the school or industry.

In some of the older studies based on assumptions of substitutability, the focus was on whether someone educated in technical studies or agriculture was in an occupation related to that discipline. Our present schema would be much more concerned with assessing the quality and specificity of the school's contribution before even deciding whether it could be legitimately traced from the world of education to the world of production.

This new approach to manpower not only appreciates what are likely to be the very different contributions of school carpentry courses, training center modules, and carpentry acquired in a furniture firm, but also the impact and the often unanticipated effects of government intervention in these three spheres of education, production, and training. There are also powerful political interventions within the three spheres to rearrange these patterns. Industry may be pressured to undertake a great deal more training, and schools may be required to undertake production or orient their students through more specific training for the world of jobs or self-employment.

Concern about unemployment usually is more evident in the sphere of education than in training or production because the state has more direct control over that sphere. Lacking the power to intervene very effectively in industry, it often seeks to affect employment or industry indirectly by directly affecting schools. There are therefore a series of interventions in many African states to reorder relationships among education, training, and production.[22] These are the cutting edge of the local manpower agenda. In relation to these initiatives, the primary task of the manpower analyst should be less to calculate how many thousands of fresh vocational graduates there might be than to study the way that innovations are incorporated and adapted by the larger system.

The process of incorporation eventually determines whether or not a political initiative for vocationalization of education gets turned into a routine school subject. This implies that the planner must be well aware of the local traditions of education, training, and production, if new attempts to rearrange the pattern of relations are to be set within this historical context. The nearer the planner gets to the local traditions of training, education, or production, however, the clearer it becomes that there is no such thing as a single training tradition or training lobby. The training sphere is itself an accretion of particular interest groups, institutions, and organizations whose origins often reflect a particular historical issue or negotiation.

African traditions of training, education, and production are also complicated by the legacies of colonial and post-colonial external manpower agendas. While the original rationale for their adoption has passed and they have been indigenized, they may still represent a particular training lobby of non-governmental organizations, specific donors, or local companies.[23]

From the perspective of the 1980s, while it may appear that there is no such thing as a national training system, but a bewildering array of semi-autonomous training initiatives, it would be premature to stress rationalization and reduction. One of the chief characteristics of the training systems in Africa is their smallness in numbers and coverage. National youth services, industrial vocational training centers, and polytechnics may well have only a few thousand students altogether.

The challenge to the planner is to uncover the logic of this scattered system—what determines its size, what are the advantages of fragmented bodies responsible for training, and what are its organizing principles. Planners must also understand the important relationship between manpower trained in the workshop and the informal sector on the one hand, and manpower produced in modern sector firms and their related training system on the other.

It must be acknowledged that the circle of production contains an enormously greater variation in a developing country than in a developed one. A majority of producers are located in subsistence self-employment or in petty production (which includes services, agriculture, and industry), while only an extremely influential minority are in the modern sector. After more than a decade of study on the informal sector, a great deal is known about the types of work, people, technologies, incomes, and training patterns in the informal sector.

As a result, the informal sector has finally become a policy item on the local manpower agenda; previously it was only part of an external agenda. This development merely underlines the gap between the formal and the informal sectors, as well as the difficulty of communicating to governments the complexity of the informal sector and its patterns of labor and technology utilization.

Tapping the informal sector as a means of solving unemployment is a compelling approach. There is an acute shortage of jobs, and the informal sector is mostly composed of the self-employed and seems able to expand. Therefore, if there is more education and training for self-employment in the school system, there will be less educated unemployment. The "logic" of this argument has led to attempts to reorient the education system with the insertion of a training function and sometimes even a production element.

MANPOWER POLICIES: THE METHODOLOGICAL CHALLENGE AND AN AGENDA FOR ACTION

Currently, the possibilities of producing a series of techniques that will facilitate manpower policy planning appear limited, while the constraints of research information in effecting change are also recognized. Following are some of the key areas for further analysis and action.

The relation of the local manpower agenda to a labor utilization perspective is most important. As we have defined it, the local manpower agenda is a composite of the interrelationship between local traditions in education, training, and production. These traditions are obviously dynamic, but typically involve generalizations about whether training is sponsored or open, whether local communities expect to build schools or have governments provide them, how parents and young people view the distinction between paid jobs and self-employed work, and so on.

The local agenda also includes political interventions in the spheres of education, training, and production, and the logic behind them. In many African states, these interventions are driven by concern over unemployment, tending to be system-wide initiatives based on snapshot insights into labor relations, as illustrated above.

The political agenda often includes such items as more primary school skills for self-employment; more science and technology courses in higher secondary and university; and more training facilities for middle-level technicians. It is important to stress that this type of political manpower agenda is not derived from the national plan (which is often written with an eye to the external manpower agenda), but from the priority interventions of government in these spheres.

Finally, by far the weakest component of the local agenda is the research wisdom of planners and analysts in ministries and in university research centers about human resource development strategies. This is not just a question of doing better research, but of closing the gap between the research culture on the one hand and the policy culture on the other. Although it is clearly possible at certain points to inform policy-makers, it must generally be acknowledged that the priorities of the world of policy are different from those of research. Hence, even if more analysis gets done within the framework we have been proposing, the process of translating it into policy will not be rapid or easy.

KEY ELEMENTS IN AN INTEGRATED LABOR
UTILIZATION PERSPECTIVE

Manpower utilization can be defined as the intersection point of education, training, and technology policies, as well as of part of the local and external manpower agendas. The explicit policies in each of these areas are relatively useless in analyzing labor use. Just as the local manpower agenda has never been stated explicitly but must be deduced and mapped out, so too the implicit policies of education, training, and technology must be laid bare if the nature of labor use in any particular sector is to be understood.

This requires looking at sector-specific utilizations of education, training, and technology. All sectors are likely to have some common job categories such as mechanics, clerks, and accountants, but it is unnecessary to total these up. Rather, what must be understood are the series of local negotiations about education, training, and technology that define differently these similar-sounding jobs in each sector, and how the local manpower agenda of the government has an impact on that firm-level negotiation.

In many countries, even a brief examination of these intersection points would reveal some very salient features of the local labor utilization systems. For example, there are local hierarchies of skill and knowledge, and local titles to define them in the different sectors; the ministry's hierarchy of labor classification is intimately connected to certification in the national polytechnic system, to which there is sponsored access; the small firm is resisting inclusion in the new training levy system; in the large farm, there has been no connection with any off-farm training except at the level of management. From this approach, a series of sector utilization studies can emerge, identifying the technical form of the large farm, the engineering shop, the technical wing of a ministry, or the urban informal repair sector, and so on.

SECTOR UTILIZATION STUDIES AND THE TWO MANPOWER AGENDAS

Some essential differences between the local and external manpower agendas have been outlined; both are powerfully affected by political considerations, and in many ways are pulling in different directions. Therefore, it may be worth examining to what extent the proposed utilization emphasis can more creatively alter or build upon the two manpower agendas. The first advantage of the utilization approach is that it gives a sector snapshot of a particular set of interrelations. This could be extremely timely in small farm sectors affected by drought, or in giving an accurate reading of the mix of employment, education, and training policies as they affect the public sector employers.

Without some careful analysis of how farming and public service traditions are being affected by the local manpower agenda, it is easy for external actors to jump to conclusions about the need for more agricultural extension or for drastic steps against over-manning in the civil service. The second way that the approach could be incorporated by the two manpower agendas is where the two meet—for example, where there is a powerful local bid to expand higher technical education and the donor community is approached.

At present, this is typically a situation where the external agenda requires justification of the project through some manpower forecasting. Instead, there would be merit in looking at the utilization and non-utilization of certain groups of graduates from the existing polytechnics operating in the firms surrounding the proposed technical college. For example, clarifying why no small manufacturing workshop ever employs a polytechnic leaver or ever sponsors an employee to attend such a college is potentially more important than a general guesstimate about the need for ever more middle-level technician manpower.[24]

THE INTERDISCIPLINARY UTILIZATION ISSUE

The other methodological shift associated with this approach is that although manpower policy analysis is clearly a mix of education, training, technology, and employment policies, these disciplines are seldom integrated. In traditional employment missions, there may appear to be an interdisciplinary team, but educators look only at the schools, the training experts at the training system, and the economists at factories. In the approach we have proposed, the term "labor utilization" includes the utilization of school skills and knowledge from training centers, but it also involves understanding employer attitudes toward education and training, and how they relate to learning and available technology in the world of production.

Given the crucial separation between the spheres of education, training, and production, an interdisciplinary team would be able to guard against inappropriate evaluations, such as the use of school knowledge in firms as though it was designed to be vocational, and similarly with the training curriculum. Instead of researching what proportion of school math, science, or university engineering is actually used in industry or agriculture, an examination is needed of what relearning and adaptation has to take place in different sectors, what are the discontinuities between the culture of the school and that of the firm, and between school science and the presence or absence of an atmosphere of technological innovation.

ACTION AND ANALYSIS FOR THE EXTERNAL MANPOWER AGENDA

In the last few years, the manpower and human resource development theme has occupied an increasingly important place in donor planning—Britain's ODA has a new policy on its manpower assistance to Africa; Canada's CIDA has put human resources planning at the forefront; and the World Bank has devised a human resources agenda for action. However, as of yet, none of these external agendas for specific African countries have been analyzed. Individual projects are known, but their underlying assumptions have not been examined.

Advice to decentralize, reform the public sector, train management, privatize, and improve planning is abundant, but the different implicit agendas behind donors' fascination with manpower at this point are less clear. Some are of the view that African public sectors do not function effectively because of overmanning, nepotism, abandoned standards, or politicization. From these kinds of assumptions, policies aimed at increasing expatriate manpower and management training are derived.

But there are other assumptions based on the view that it may take at least 20 years for the corner to be turned on African management capacity in public administration and on research capacity in science, agriculture, and other fields—views which could result in a commitment to more training at every level. While some recommend training as near to the production site as possible, it is difficult to know whether this implies a disillusionment with the quality of higher education or merely a more rapid way of getting a project started.

Precisely because of the magnitude and complexity of the external manpower agenda, both governments and donors would benefit if there is a careful mapping of its contours. Currently, the project focus and special interests of each donor prevent a clear view of the overall picture. It would therefore be extremely timely if a map of where human resource development aid is going and why could be developed for two or three African states.

Such a review would reveal uneven emphases reflecting different aid traditions and particular preferences for relations between education, training, and production, as well as unpredictable political interventions in the scale and priorities of assistance in manpower development. If African manpower agendas appear irrational and overly political at times, the same can be said of the often unexplained shifts in aid policies.

It may also be useful to highlight a small number of activities that relate directly to the issue of manpower utilization. For example, several donor agencies might wish to support small-scale labor utilization studies for sectors in which they intend to invest. The precise method employed would depend on the sector and task, since, as Hollister has argued, "There is no uniform method applicable across the entire public sector, and the procedure should be to shape the analysis to the character of the manpower problems in each sub-sector. The character of the problems and the appropriate methods for analyzing them will vary substantially from one sub-sector to another."[25]

Although context-specific, undertakings by external agencies in the manpower field should address such salient themes as open and closed training, the science and technology content of key training courses, on-the-job training in key industrial and agricultural sectors, and the role of job recruitment and certification systems, such as trade testing or the public service commission. These issues affect a large number of jobs, and understanding them could provide useful insights into the local manpower utilization systems. Another high priority would be a review of the functions and leverage of the various manpower planning units in ministries such as agriculture, education, health, and finance—obvious foci of interest for any attempt to reshape the manpower analysis system.

REVIEW AND DISSEMINATION OF RESEARCH TO POLICY

Any review or revision of an approach to manpower must take the local and donor decision-making environments into account. Admittedly, the process of changing traditional attitudes to manpower assessment cannot happen overnight. The research community must take the first step, and there is now evidence of a shift in approaches by the very variety of perspectives on the manpower assessment task. There has also been an enlargement of the concept of manpower policy to include the role of science and technology, education, training, and employment policies.[26]

The new approaches will then have to be applied, for although the older manpower paradigms are in many ways discredited, the alternative methods have not yet been tried. The new methods could be implemented either at the sub-sector level, or could involve labor utilization studies in crucial sectors; analyses of key themes cutting across the local manpower agenda; mapping the external manpower agendas in selected countries; and reviewing current manpower planning units across ministries.

Since donors are more open to research findings than hard-pressed national governments and ministries, it is likely that some of the new approaches will first be adopted by the donor community. The World Bank's manpower research may eventually become part of discussions with lenders and other agencies. But progress in changing approaches to manpower training will be even slower when members of the national research community in developing countries seek to influence their policy-makers. Dissemination of relevant research to the policy-making community is not yet highly developed; hence, the time horizon for change will be very long.

In the meantime, the methodological challenge is to develop new tools and more appropriate concepts to describe African manpower issues. This will necessitate an understanding and incorporation of traditions of labor use in Africa, a clarification of the implicit relationship between education, training, production, and technology, and more coherent options for revisions of both the internal and external manpower agendas.

NOTES

1. K. King, "The Planning of Technical and Vocational Education and Training," IIEP, occasional paper, 1985, p. 35; P. Foster, "Some Policy Implications of the Tanzanian and Colombian Studies," Washington, D.C.: The World Bank, September 1984 mimeo.

2. K. King, The African Artisan (London: Heineman, 1977).

3. K. King, "Open and Closed Universities: North-South Contrast," Society of Hong Kong Scholars Conference: Current Development in Higher Education, January 1985, Hong Kong.

4. K. King, "The End of Education for Self-Reliance?" occasional paper, 1984, Centre of African Studies, Edinburgh University. Also, "Education

Research in Tanzania, Summary Comments," report of a seminar, August 1984, Dar es Salaam University, Department of Education.

5. Eric Ashby, *Universities, British, Indian, African. An Ecology of Higher Education* (London: Weidenfeld and Nicolson, 1966).

6. K. King, "Technology, Education, and Employment for Development (TEED). The Research Context and the Methodological Challenge," seminar paper, IDRC, Nairobi, January 1985.

7. K. King, "Education for Self-Employment" in IIEP (UNESCO), *Education, Work and Employment*, II (Paris: UNESCO, 1980).

8. K. King, *The African Artisan*, op. cit.

9. Ninth Conference of Commonwealth Education Ministers, "Education and Youth Unemployment: Some Propositions," working paper by K. King, Nicosia, 23–26 July 1984.

10. For a more detailed analysis of the ecology of aid, see K. King, "Problems and Prospects of Aid to Education in Sub-Saharan Africa," lead paper, Conference on Education Priorities in Sub-Saharan Africa, Windsor, England, 3–7 December 1984.

11. Jon Moris, *Managing Induced Rural Development* (Bloomington: University of Indiana Press, 1981) passim.

12. D. Jamison and L. Lau, *Farmer Education and Farm Efficiency* (Baltimore: Johns Hopkins University Press, 1982); D. Jamison and P. Mook, "Farmer Education and Farm Efficiency in Nepal: The Role of Schooling, Extension Services and Cognitive Skills," *World Development* 12, 1: 67–86.

13. S. Heyneman, "Research on Education in the Developing Countries," *International Journal of Educational Development* 4 (4) (1984): pp.301–302, quoted in K. King, "Technology, Education, and Employment for Development" op. cit., p. 5.

14. See K. King, "Technology, Education, and Employment for Development. The Research Context and the Methodological Challenge," op.cit.

15. Robin Hollister, "A Perspective on the Role of Manpower Analysis and Planning in Developing Countries," in "Manpower Issues in Educational Investment," Staff Working Paper No. 624 (Washington, D.C.: The World Bank, 1983), p. 59.

16. Jan Loubser, *Human Resource Development in Kenya: An Overview* (CIDA), Hull, November 1983, pp. 119ff. Also, Republic of Kenya, Working Party on Government Expenditures: Report and Recommendations, Nairobi, July 1982.

17. K. King, "Preliminary Reactions to the Interpretation of Manpower Data in Kenya: Toward a Qualitative Approach," 31.8.84, Nairobi, mimeo.

18. N. Ngethe et al, "Technology Policy and Planning in the Informal Sector" in Workshop on Technology Policy and Planning in the Informal Sector: the Case of Food, Agriculture and Energy in East Africa Sub-region, Economic Commission for Africa, December 1984. J. Odurkene, "Indigenous Apprenticeship and On the Job Training Practices in Uganda," paper to Workshop on Technology, Education, and Employment for Development, IDRC, Nairobi, January 1985. See also Workshop on the Informal Sector in Francophone Africa, University Institute for Development Studies, Geneva, March 1985.

19. K. King, "Planning of Technical and Vocational Education," op. cit., pp. 77–78. Also, Wim Hoppers, "Skill Training and Self-employment" (The Hague: CESO, 1983) mimeo.

20. Ongoing work by P. Moock on the informal sector in Peru, Washington, D.C.: The World Bank, Education Department.

21. For an elaboration, see K. King, "Education with Production: Approaches to a State of the Art" in Workshop on Education and Production in Theory and Practice (The Hague: CESO, 1985), reprinted in *Education with Production* (Gaborone) Autumn 1985.

22. For a valuable analysis of patterns of intervention in Latin America and the Caribbean, see Noel McGinn et al., "Recent Experiences in the Coordination of Education, Employment and Technology in Latin America and the Caribbean," draft mimeo, Harvard University Graduate School of Education, April 1, 1985.

23. See K. King, "Educational Transfer in Kenya and Tanzania," *Compare* 13 (1), (1983), pp.81–87.

24. For a similar perspective, see Robin Hollister, op.cit. pp. 72–74.

25. Ibid., p. 73.

26. See, for example, the series of workshops on Technology, Education, and Development organized by IDRC in East Africa, January 1983, August 1983, and January 1985.

PART VI

AFRICA AND THE WORLD ECONOMY

CHAPTER SIXTEEN

Africa's Debt: Structural Adjustment with Stability

Chandra S. Hardy

The crisis atmosphere that followed Mexico's moratorium on principal payments in 1982 has abated somewhat over the past three years with economic recovery in the industrialized world, stretched out repayment schedules for the major debtors, and the willingness of borrowers to undertake very tough adjustment policies. However, for most developing countries and especially those in sub-Saharan Africa, financing their external debt continues to pose very serious difficulties.

Estimated at around $100 billion, Africa's total external debt is not large, amounting to less than that of Brazil alone, but it is extremely burdensome. Comparable to those of the largest borrowers, debt service payments in Africa account for 50 to 60 percent of export earnings. In low-income Africa, total external debt amounts to more than half the value of output and six times the value of exports.

Despite these telling figures, Africa's debt has received less international attention than that of the major Latin American debtors, for example. Accounting for only 10 percent of total developing country debt and for less than 5 percent of debt owed to commercial banks, Africa's external debt is not perceived to pose any systemic risk. Significantly, however, the majority of those countries that have been accumulating arrears and rescheduling debt have been African. And despite repeated reschedulings, Africa's debt burden has increased rather than eased, suggesting that the problem is one of deep-rooted poverty and insolvency, not temporary illiquidity.

Few attempts have been made to devise a comprehensive solution to Africa's debt problems. This chapter reviews the nature and dimensions of the debt, recent economic conditions and future prospects, the inadequacy of rescheduling operations, and the role of the International Monetary Fund. It concludes with a recommended policy agenda.

GROWTH OF EXTERNAL DEBT

Between 1973 and 1983, Africa's debt increased six-fold, growing at an average annual rate of 22 percent, substantially in excess of the rate of growth in output or exports (Table A.5 in Appendix I). For low-income Africa, long-term indebtedness grew at a relatively more modest, but still alarming rate, increasing more than four-fold, from $5 billion to $22 billion.

Over 90 percent of Africa's debt is owed directly to or is guaranteed by official sources in the creditor countries (official debt). By the end of 1983, medium- and long-term debt in sub-Saharan Africa amounted to $58 billion.[1] Another $5 billion was owed to the International Monetary Fund (IMF), with short-term debt and arrears reaching $18 billion. By year-end 1983, therefore, total external debt amounted to $81 billion. Other estimates range from $107 billion to $150 billion, reflecting the inclusion of additional countries.

Over the same period, the structure and composition of Africa's external debt changed markedly. As a share of total outstandings, official and concessional loans declined, while private and commercial bank loans rose. For sub-Saharan Africa as a whole, concessional loans fell from 43 percent to 36 percent of total outstandings between 1973 and 1983, with loans carrying variable interest rates increasing from 9 percent to 22 percent of the total.

Whereas long-term debt owed to private creditors accounted for 40 percent of total outstandings in 1973, by 1983 it amounted to 46 percent. Behind this increase, the debt owed by the public sector to the financial markets rose nine-fold over the decade to $19 billion in 1983; its share of total outstandings climbing from 21 percent in 1973 to 33 percent in 1983. Of the long-term debt owed to official creditors, the portion owed to multilateral agencies rose from 27 percent in 1973 to 41 percent ten years later. More important, the share of "preferred creditors" (multilateral lenders and the IMF) in total long-term external liabilities grew from 18 percent in 1973 to 28 percent in 1983. In low-income Africa, this shift was more dramatic, rising from 18 percent to 37 percent.

The changes in the structure of external obligations are reflected in the hardening of the average terms. Maturities and grace periods on new commitments became shorter while interest rates rose over the decade. As a result, the grant element or degree of concessionality fell from 32 percent in 1973 to 16 percent in 1982.

Debt service payments grew rapidly from $1.2 billion in 1973 to nearly $6 billion in 1983. In effect, debt service payments increased at a slower pace than absolute debt levels because of an accumulation of payments arrears and reschedulings. In 1983, payments of interest and amortization amounted to only 40 to 50 percent of the total debt-servicing costs falling due that year. Further, with hardening terms, the composition of the debt service altered. Interest payments rose from 25 percent of the total debt service paid in 1973, to 39 percent in 1978, and to 43 percent in 1982. Interest payments continue to account for one-third of projected debt-servicing costs.

The increase in indebtedness over the past decade, however, has not been matched by an increase in Africa's capacity to pay. A look at the principal indicators of debt—the external debt/export ratio, the external debt/GDP ratio, and the ratio of interest and principal payments to total exports of good and services (debt service ratio)—reveals that in comparison to other regions, Africa and low-income Africa in particular is the most heavily indebted.

Over the past decade, all of these debt ratios deteriorated sharply in Africa. The debt service ratio jumped sharply from 9.2 percent in 1975 to 17.3 percent in 1981. In low-income Africa, this ratio rose from 9.2 percent to 22 percent over the same period. Moreover, these figures understate the true extent of the burden. Omitting short-term debt obligations and arrears and payments to the IMF, the data includes only the debt service that was paid on public medium- and long-term debt. When the former are taken into account, the debt service ratio exceeds 50 percent for sub-Saharan Africa overall and surpasses 100 percent for many individual countries. Even with an incomplete data base, the toll of debt-servicing costs on low-income African economies is apparent in the ratio of interest payments to GNP, amounting to 2.1 percent as compared to 0.3 percent for low-income Asia.

Another indicator of Africa's perilous financial situation is the drastic fall in the level of foreign exchange reserves. In 1982, Africa's gross foreign exchange reserves amounted to less than one month of substantially reduced imports, below their 1973 levels. In net terms, reserve levels were negative by several billion dollars. The lack of foreign exchange reserves heightens the continent's vulnerability to exogenous shocks. For example, even a slight delay in the receipt of export earnings can hold up food and oil imports since banks are unwilling to provide unconfirmed letters of credit, and can cause delays in payments to official creditors who in turn can suspend disbursements on existing loans.

The current situation is desperate and is not likely to improve without major and concerted action on the part of Africa's official creditors. Much of the recent increase in debt has been due to the capitalization of arrears—either unpaid interest payments are added to the stock of debt and thus "capitalized," or new loans are extended to cover unpaid interest and principal payments falling due—and declining net capital inflows. Between 1979 and 1983, outstanding debt grew by $20 billion, but net inflows rose by only $1 billion, and net transfers declined in nominal terms, implying an even greater fall in real terms (Table A.5 in Appendix I). The recent drop in net inflows reflects a rise in amortization payments and a decline in new commitments. In 1973, the ratio of scheduled principal payments to disbursements was 31 percent; by 1983 it had risen to 58 percent.

More ominously, between 1980 and 1983, new commitments to all developing countries fell by 21 percent, while those to low-income Africa plunged 45 percent, with commitments from private sources dropping from $1.5 billion in 1979 to just $137 million in 1983. The 31 percent decline in new commitments from official sources poses a more serious problem as these represent the principal source of funds for low-income Africa. The impact of falling levels of commitments is likely to be expressed in depressed net inflows, and debt service payments are expected to remain high. In 1983, net transfers from private sources to low-income Africa were negative by $300 million. Unless these trends in capital flows are reversed, net transfers from official sources will also be negative in a few years.

ECONOMIC SITUATION AND PROSPECTS

Declining output levels, rising inflation, and widening current account deficits are symptoms of the overall deterioration in economic activity in Africa over the past decade. Since 1974, per capita GDP has dropped nearly 1 percent per annum; inflation has jumped from an annual rate of 10 percent to over 20 percent in 1984; and the combined current account deficit has increased from $4 billion to $14 billion in 1984. These deficits were not financed by a net inflow of medium- and long-term debt, but rather by what are called monetary transactions—a build-up of short-term debt, a drawdown on reserves, purchases from the IMF, and the accumulation of payments arrears.

Africa's deteriorating economic situation is largely due to a series of shocks, each more devastating than its predecessor. Over the past decade, in addition to wars and two prolonged periods of drought, Africa has experienced a five-fold increase in the price of grain, a seven-fold increase in the price of oil, recession and inflation in the industrial countries, high and volatile interest and exchange rates, and a collapse in commodity prices.

Of these, the most adverse in scope and duration have been trends in the international economy. The sharp decline in output and accelerated rates of inflation in the industrial countries after the first oil shock resulted in reduced demand for Africa's exports and a weakening of commodity prices. As a result of low world demand for exports, declining terms of trade, and inelastic demand for imports of food, fertilizers, oil, and producer goods, African economies experienced widening current account deficits.

Domestic policies have also played a part in Africa's economic decline given weak institutional structures, overblown bureaucracies, and governments committed to overambitious spending programs that could no longer be funded by trade revenue. Unable and in some cases unwilling to cut expenditures to meet declining revenues, governments resorted to deficit financing, fueling the inflation created by acute shortages, particularly of imported goods.

The severity of the external environment can be gauged from the fact that income losses due to the deterioration in Africa's terms of trade were as much as 10 percent of GDP in 1974–75 and again in 1979–82. Some countries registered losses as high as 25 percent of GDP during the latter period. By contrast, the income loss to the industrial countries due to adverse terms of trade was 2 percent of GDP after each oil shock.

DOMESTIC POLICY ADJUSTMENT

Adverse terms of trade reduce the purchasing power of export earnings. As a result, incomes fall, costs rise, and larger current account deficits are incurred. In order to finance these deficits, reserves are drawn down and borrowings increase. In an effort to reduce the need for external financing, domestic policy adjustments are undertaken to reduce imports, increase exports, dampen consumption, and raise investment levels. In poor countries, however, the social costs of cutting public spending can be high and changing the structure of production is a lengthy process, requiring additional resources.

Adjustment in low-income Africa has largely entailed cuts in consumption and investment, causing higher rates of unemployment and falling real incomes and output.

Reductions in spending have often been accompanied by accelerated rates of inflation as the domestic prices of imports rise as a result of scarcity or devaluation. As a result, governments have been unable to cut spending at the same rates as declining revenues, leading to wider fiscal deficits financed by monetary expansion.

By the time a country requests assistance from the IMF, the financial situation is often desperate. The need for stabilization is thus not in question, but rather at issue are the scope and speed of adjustment and the required policy mix. Some key questions must then be asked: Do all domestic policy failures have to be corrected simultaneously? Must the time period required for assessing the success of stabilization periods be three years rather than five or 10 years? Can stabilization programs be designed that provide some minimum protection of basic human needs?

As most governments are unable to mobilize the political consensus needed to implement stabilization programs that require further cuts in living standards, an alternative policy package would include a higher level of net capital inflows needed to carry out structural change. In this way, the conditionality required by the IMF would be retained, but with greater flexibility in the prescribed period for achieving the targets and in the monitoring of performance criteria (Williamson, 1983). At present, the IMF does not have the resources needed to finance longer-term adjustment programs. Therefore, unless these funds come from other creditors, sooner or later drastic adjustments, perhaps including debt repudiation, will have to take place.

FOREIGN BORROWING AND ADJUSTMENT

The growth in external indebtedness in Africa may suggest that increased reliance on foreign resources was a means of avoiding adjustment. However, this is not the case. Many African countries adjusted by cutting imports and output growth, borrowing to maintain investment levels and to cushion the fall in consumption. In fact, borrowings proved insufficient to check a widespread erosion of the physical and human capital stock.

After the first oil shock, the international donor and financial communities responded promptly and generously to Africa's financing needs. The IMF established an oil facility and a trust fund to make concessional loans to low-income countries. However, increased borrowing from official sources was not sufficient to offset a decline in the purchasing power of exports, and thus to prevent a decline in imports and output growth.

In 1976–77, recovery in the industrial countries, a frost in Brazil that damaged its coffee crop, and good weather in many parts of Africa led to an increase in export volumes and prices and a modest decline in current account deficits (Table A.8 in Appendix I). But the recovery was unsustainable, and even before the second oil price increase in 1979, the terms of trade had started to deteriorate sharply.

Adjustment to the second oil shock was borne almost entirely by a reduction in imports and output. As the industrial economies fell into the worst recession since the 1930s, demand for Africa's exports collapsed and commodity prices plummeted to their lowest levels in 25 years in 1980. Although more severe than the first, the second oil shock met with a cooler official donor response. A number of countries scrambled for funds by resorting to government-insured or guaranteed funds from export credit agencies and banks. Facilitated by industrial countries' efforts to expand their exports, these suppliers' credits in effect financed the current account deficits after 1979, along with a further reduction in reserves and an accumulation of arrears.

Existing arrangements for meeting the financing needs of developing countries fail to recognize countries' unequal capacity to adjust to payments imbalances. The biggest debtors had enjoyed rapid growth rates before running into debt-servicing difficulties. Their economies are diversified; their domestic savings rates are high; and they have demonstrated the political and economic ability to run trade surpluses in the midst of a prolonged recession at home and abroad. Their weight in international financial markets has drawn attention to their problems; thus they and their creditors have cooperated to find imaginative and flexible solutions to their debt-servicing problems.

Although on the order of the major Latin American borrowers, Africa's debt burden has received less attention because it is not considered a threat to the international financial system (Table A.6 in Appendix I). However, Africa's debt problems warrant attention because its economies are more vulnerable to liquidity crises:

- Their share of trade to GDP and the ratio of debt to exports are much higher than for low-income Asia, and therefore they are more exposed to international fluctuations.
- African economies are predominantly agricultural and therefore more subject to climatic variations.
- Primary commodities account for nearly 80 percent of Africa's exports and primary commodity producers suffer sharper terms of trade swings than exporters of manufactured goods.
- Poorer economies are also less able to withstand shocks. Given rigid production structures, African economies cannot quickly move out of one kind of export to another when international prices deteriorate, nor can they reduce imports in favor of domestic substitutes. Unlike the major borrowers, African economies are less able to smooth adjustment to shocks by borrowing, as they lack access to balance of payments financing from banks; their quotas in the IMF are small; their net reserve levels are negative; and their administrative and institutional capacity for crisis management is weak.

FUTURE PROSPECTS

Even if there is a sustained recovery in OECD growth, most African economies are unlikely to see any improvement in living standards over the coming decade. Even given a modest improvement in the terms of trade, net annual inflows of 7 percent of GDP, and substantial increases in official development assistance (ODA) and commercial flows, low-income Africa is projected to show no increase in per capita GDP for the rest of this decade, according to the 1985 World Development Report.

In the absence of any remedial measures by the international community, the prognosis for Africa could be even worse. First, the international environment remains hostile. A set of unfavorable price trends, including high real interest rates, an overvalued dollar, and adverse terms of trade, greatly increases its real debt burden.[2] Real interest rates are at unprecedented levels in the United States, and when the nominal rates applicable to Africa are adjusted for the movement in real export prices, real rates of interest of 20 percent have been estimated.

The high value of the dollar in relation to the other major trading currencies adversely affects Africa's trade with Europe—its principal market—and its debt-servicing costs, as the loans are denominated in dollars.

World Bank projections indicate that even with faster growth in the industrial countries, commodity prices may only reach 1980 levels in 1995. Some commodities will show no recovery in real terms over the coming decade. However, a more disturbing development is the failure of commodity prices to revive with the U.S. recovery. In February 1985, the World Bank's commodity price index stood at 87.3 (1977/79 = 100), 13.5 percentage points below the level of a year ago and 1.4 percentage points below the level in October 1982, the bottom of the 1981–82 recession. In short, the combination of high borrowing costs and the collapse of commodity prices in spite of the U.S. recovery is not improving the manageability of Africa's debt burden.

Second, the trend in capital flows is not consistent with a recovery in African output. Since 1980, net lending to developing countries has been declining. In 1983, the net inflow was $1 billion and probably negative in 1984. The drastic decline in the level of commitments suggests that net lending will remain depressed.

Third, projected debt service on public and publicly guaranteed debt is estimated at $10 to 11 billion per annum through 1987, twice the level of the annual debt service paid in 1980–83, while repayments to the IMF are estimated at $1.2 billion per annum. There has been no progress in reducing trade arrears, estimated at $18 billion, and gross revenues are less than one month's imports.

DEBT RESCHEDULINGS

With balance of payments deficits amounting to 9 percent of GDP in 1984 and limited scope to correct these imbalances, Africa clearly requires higher levels of net capital inflows and longer periods for adjustment. To date, however, the policy response to Africa's debt-servicing problems has been short term and piecemeal, consisting largely of annual debt reschedulings which fail to address the need for additional aid.

Since 1975, 15 African countries have rescheduled debt in multilateral negotiations with official creditors or commercial banks on 47 occasions. An even larger number of countries are accumulating arrears on payments since not all with debt problems have requested or been able to satisfy the conditions needed to obtain debt rescheduling. According to the IMF, Gambia, Ghana, Guinea, Mali, Sierra Leone, Tanzania, Zaire, Zambia, Benin, Chad, Guinea-Bissau, Mauritania, and Nigeria are all in arrears on payments, while a few have also had debt reschedulings.

Reschedulings of debt to official creditors normally are discussed under the auspices of the Paris Club, an ad hoc group of Western creditor governments which has met under the chairmanship of the French Treasury since Argentina's 1956 request to replace bilateral negotiations with a multilateral meeting of its creditors. Over the years, the Paris Club has evolved a set of unwritten governing procedures and practices which have also been adopted by the Bank of England (London Club) and the OECD.

These procedures include agreement among creditors to meet only after payments arrears have arisen and the debtor country has agreed to an IMF stabilization program; only the principal creditors and the debtor are invited to the meeting; relief is limited to officially insured export credits and government loans; debt relief is limited to about 80 percent of the principal payments due over a three-year period; and debts are rescheduled for three to 10 years at market interest rates.

Since 1979, the pace of debt reschedulings has accelerated. In the period 1979–82, over half of the multilateral debt renegotiations (20 out of 38) were for African countries and 16 out of 17 which took place at the Paris Club over this period were African. In addition, 11 countries have had to reschedule their commercial bank debt under separate agreements, including Ivory Coast and Nigeria, which had enjoyed high credit ratings in the mid-1970s.

The Paris Club mechanism has not been effective in easing Africa's debt difficulties, as the relief provided has been too little and too costly. Designed to keep debtors on a short leash, Paris Club procedures apply strict limits on the definition of debts eligible for relief. Excluded are debts owed to Eastern Europe, the multilateral development banks and the IMF, debts previously rescheduled, interest payments, and arrears on short-term debt. As a result, more than half of most countries' debts are ineligible. In addition, since the amount of relief provided suffices only to ease liquidity problems for a year or two, repeated reschedulings have been common. Most countries have experienced three or more debt reschedulings over five years.

The effect of repeated reschedulings has been to increase the debt burden. While debt relief has been provided by stretching out maturities at market rates of interest, interest charges on debts incurred at original average interest rates of 6 percent have increased to an average 10 percent. As a result, interest payments have risen from $429 million in 1973 to an estimated $3.3 billion in 1984, with interest charges accounting for one-third of the debt service due over the next three years. The capitalization of overdue principal (and, in a few cases, interest charges) and short-term debts have added $21 billion to debt outstanding since 1979. Over the same period, net inflows increased by only $1 billion per annum.

Further, Paris Club reschedulings have failed to mobilize additional public and private funds for Africa. The existing arrangements for debt rescheduling thus point to an asymmetry in the treatment of large and small debtors. At the urging of the IMF, rescheduling packages and IMF assistance to the major debtors were contingent on "new" lending from existing creditors and a re-opening of short-term lines of credit. This approach has not been evident in the case of Africa's major creditors. While an IMF stabilization program is required before the Paris Club will reschedule debt, new aid and credits are not part of the Paris Club procedures.

The level of net inflows to Africa is largely decided by official sources, usually coordinated at aid group meetings. As a result, after 21 reschedulings since 1979, the level of net inflows of ODA declined from $12 billion to $6 billion in 1983, and net inflows from private sources have turned negative.

Paris Club reschedulings have also failed to normalize short-term trade financing arrangements. Official export credit agencies which provide guarantees on private sources of credit to developing countries go "off cover" for countries accumulating arrears or requesting debt reschedulings. While until about 1979, once a country had agreed to an IMF program and had rescheduled part of its long-term debt, its creditworthiness for some portion of insured credits was restored, this is no longer the case. Particularly in Africa, acceptance of an IMF program and restructuring debt at market rates only provide temporary relief and do not guarantee new trade lines of credit.

THE IMF IN AFRICA

Over the past decade, the IMF has helped African countries finance growing balance of payments deficits. In 1975, purchases from the IMF's oil facility furnished 53 percent of the total gross flows from the IMF to Africa, cushioning the impact of the first oil shock. In addition, the IMF used part of the profits from the sale of gold holdings to set up the Trust Fund and an interest-subsidy account to provide low-cost loans to its poorest members. After 1979, when commercial bank lending to Africa virtually dried up, the IMF became Africa's only source of balance of payments (non-project) financing.

Between 1979 and 1983, the average volume of IMF lending to Africa increased more than three-fold. By 1983, net purchases from the IMF were equivalent to 34 percent of net flows of public and publicly guaranteed debt. However, the nature of the support offered by the Fund was quite different after the first and second oil shocks. In 1975 and 1976, low conditionality funds accounted for 80 percent of Africa's purchases, but after 1977, higher conditionality lending steadily increased, amounting to 75 percent of IMF lending to Africa.

Another major change has been the reduction in Extended Fund Facility (EFF) arrangements or medium-term adjustment programs in favor of standby arrangements 12 to 18 months in duration. Despite the IMF Board's 1981 claim that "the adjustment process in many countries is under growing external pressure and longer periods of assistance under the EFF will continue to be increasingly important," the EFF has been used less and less. At the end of 1981, five African countries held EFF drawings, four of which were signed that year. That same year, however, three were cancelled. In 1982, two more African countries signed extended EFF agreements, but these were also cancelled a year later. Thus, of seven African countries which signed EFF agreements between May 1979 and April 1982, only Ivory Coast and Gabon retained the facility. At present, Malawi is the only African country to have an EFF agreement. Standby arrangements have been the far greater source of funds. In 1979, some 29 African countries had standby agreements; today only 13 are in effect.

In addition to its higher conditionality lending, the IMF has increasingly exercised a leadership role in the international financial community vis-à-vis Africa. A consensus has emerged among bilateral and multilateral donors and official export credit agencies that all financial arrangements now hinge upon recipients' adoption of an IMF adjustment program. Similarly, requests for debt rescheduling at the Paris Club are not approved unless the borrower has concluded an agreement with the Fund, and require continual satisfaction of IMF performance criteria. This enlarged IMF function has aroused a great deal of controversy; therefore it may be useful to briefly review the applicability of IMF operations to Africa's debt problems.

IMF OPERATIONS

The IMF's resources are held in a revolving fund that is augmented through periodic quota increases, the most recent of which was in 1981. Members of the IMF enjoy drawing rights—use of Fund resources—that are determined in relation to the size of their quotas. As of December 1984, the value of all quotas in the Fund was SDR 89 million ($91.5 million). The industrial countries accounted for 62.8 percent of all quotas; the non-oil developing countries accounted for 26.3 percent, and the oil-exporting countries for 10.9 percent. The IMF can also supplement its resources by borrowing from governments; the General Agreement to Borrow is one such means by which industrial countries agree to make additional funds available for special situations.[3]

Whereas the World Bank was established to help countries achieve longer-term economic growth, the Fund's task was to prevent member countries experiencing cyclical balance of payments problems from adopting the deflationary policies and competitive devaluations prevalent in the 1930s. To qualify for Fund assistance, a member was required to agree to correct its payments imbalance. Until the early 1970s, the principal borrowers from the IMF were the industrial countries.

As stated in a recent staff paper, the Fund's basic objectives are to promote economic growth, to reduce inflation, and to improve the current account position in the medium term. Consequently, IMF programs involve setting specific quantitative targets for output, inflation, and current account deficits; selecting the mix of instruments to achieve these objectives; and determining the intensity with which each instrument is used. While no two Fund programs are identical, the principal policy instruments generally involve exchange rate adjustment, credit controls, fiscal measures to reduce expenditure and increase taxes, and the removal of arrears.

Critics of the IMF contend that its prescriptions and funding are unsuitable for Africa. IMF programs stress demand management (expenditure cuts) to correct external payments imbalances. While measures to stimulate domestic production are included, they have lower priority when they conflict with the need to cut imports. However, after a decade of declining import and output growth rates, further belt-tightening measures are no longer viable solutions for Africa.

Second, critics argue that current Fund programs require countries to show improvements in their external payments position in three to five years, and, under standby arrangements, within one year. But the required structural reforms take time to implement and require additional investment. Third, IMF funds are costly—interest is slightly below market rates and repayment periods average five years.

Fourth, reaching agreement with the IMF does not ease the liquidity constraint. Very often net inflows from the IMF to Africa are zero or even negative during the course of a stabilization program. Moreover, the IMF does not play a catalytic role in mobilizing additional aid for Africa. In fact, since 1979 net ODA flows to Africa have declined by 50 percent and private flows have turned negative.

Lastly, the IMF's record of effectiveness as measured against its own agreed targets or results after the program has ended is not encouraging. After a decade of increasing IMF involvement, Africa has fallen deeper into crisis.

The IMF does not discriminate against Africa per se. Its policy prescriptions are the same for all its members, whatever their stage of development and causes of their external payments imbalance. Rather, criticism of the IMF rests on its generalized solution to a problem which cannot be generalized—the indebtedness of developing countries. Whatever the merits of the IMF's approach to the correction of payments imbalances, performance criteria should be tailored to the needs of specific countries. Africa needs longer-term structural balance of payments financing on concessional terms.

Conditionality itself is not the issue; urgent measures are needed to restore order to Africa's financial transactions. Rather, the controversy centers on how and over what time period these required policy measures can be put into effect. Whereas IMF programs are deemed successful if external account imbalances are reduced, unless structural reforms and some stimulus to production result, such balance of payments "improvements" are apt to be transitory. Structural transformation in Africa requires measures to raise the productivity of smallholder agriculture and increase export volumes. These reforms cannot be accomplished in the short run, nor can they be realized without higher levels of investment and agricultural imports.

Resources available from the IMF can only provide a fraction of Africa's needs for balance of payments financing. Africa accounts for only 3.3 percent of IMF quotas, and since the 1981 quota increase, access to the use of Fund resources has been reduced twice, from 150 percent to 95 percent of quotas under "normal" circumstances (115 percent in exceptional circumstances) and from 600 percent to 408 percent cumulatively. In net terms, sub-Saharan Africa has significantly lower access limits in 1985 than before the general quota increase. Access to the Compensatory Financing Facility has been reduced from 100 percent to 83 percent of quotas, and the practice that up to 50 percent of quotas was available on low conditionality terms has been withdrawn.[4]

Africa's total use of IMF resources cannot exceed $12 billion, or about 20 percent of its imports in 1980. As of January 1985, Africa's use of Fund resources totalled $5.1 billion, with much of the increase in lending taking place after 1979. Net IMF credit made available to Africa between 1979 and 1983 equalled $3.7 billion, sufficient to offset only about one-quarter of the cumulative shortfall in the purchasing power of exports resulting from the 20 percent deterioration in the terms of trade over this period.

Further, the use of Fund resources is too costly for Africa. Because of the rapid increase in its lending since 1979, the IMF has become one of Africa's main creditors, with repayments estimated at over $1 billion in 1984. The IMF was also owed 50 to 75 percent of the debt service paid in 1984.

Between 1985 and 1987, repayments to the IMF are projected at $1.2 billion per annum, in addition to the $10 to 11 billion per annum due on public and publicly guaranteed debt. If the average volume of purchases remains at the 1984 level of $1 billion, net transfers from the Fund will be negative by $200 million per annum over the next few years. The IMF will then become part of Africa's debt problem rather than part of its solution. Already, a few countries—Chad, Sudan, and Tanzania—are falling into arrears on their IMF loans and this trend is likely to continue unless action is taken to increase net official flows to Africa.

Expanded use of Fund resources did not prevent an overall decline in total resources available to Africa, and, given the short maturity and high cost of IMF loans, it is not surprising that the IMF's involvement in Africa has so far met with little success. An IMF staff review (Zulu and Nsouli, 1985) of programs in operation in Africa in 1980 and 1981 showed that the targets for output growth and reduction of fiscal and balance of payments deficits were met in 20 to 30 percent of the cases; the targets for reducing inflation and net credit expansion were met in 50 percent of the cases. The slippages in implementation were attributed to unforeseen developments, lack of political will, administrative weakness, over-optimistic targets, and delays or shortfalls in net inflows of development assistance.

CONCLUSIONS

While external debt is not the most serious problem confronting Africa, failure to resolve its debt-servicing difficulties limits the continent's ability to confront the more urgent problems of growing poverty and economic decline. Not only has the absolute level of external debt increased over the past decade, but the burden of financing increasingly nonconcessional and shorter-term loans has mounted. By 1982, the grant element on new borrowing had fallen to 16 percent from 32 percent in 1973, and debt service payments due had risen from $1 billion to $10 billion over the same period.

Africa's debt-servicing difficulties are evident in the rapid increase in arrears on payments and in the number of debt renegotiations. Between 1956 and 1974, there were 30 renegotiations for 11 countries, of which Ghana was the only African country, accounting for four renegotiations between 1966 and 1974. Since 1975, however, 15 African countries have rescheduled their external debt on 47 occasions, and payments arrears have approached an estimated $18 billion, about one-third of outstanding public medium- and long-term debt.

African countries could do very little about rising international interest rates, the appreciation of the U.S. dollar, the decline in aid flows, and adverse terms of trade movements. As a result, attention was focused on the decline in export volumes which was largely attributable to domestic policy failures—inefficient pricing and marketing arrangements, particularly those affecting agriculture. However, insufficient attention has been given to two additional constraints: Africa's high import dependence and its low level of agricultural productivity.

In relative terms, African economies exhibit higher import elasticities of demand than most other developing countries. Ratios of imports to GDP range from 19 percent to 30 percent, with both industry and agriculture highly dependent on imports of intermediate goods. The decline in export volumes should therefore be examined in the context of the 50 percent decline in intermediate goods imports over the past decade.

Second, while existing government structures and agricultural policies share part of the responsibility for the overall decline of this sector, it would be simplistic to view pricing and marketing measures as sufficient to reverse negative trends. The crisis in African agriculture preceded its financial and economic crisis and it is not easily overcome. Thus, while African countries exhibit short-term liquidity problems common to other countries with debt-servicing difficulties, these arise from structural weakness and require different solutions.

PATTERNS OF ADJUSTMENT

In contrast to the adjustments African countries were able to make to the first oil shock mostly by virtue of positive external factors, no comparable adjustment has taken place following the 1979 oil shock. Commodity prices continue to be depressed, weather conditions unreliable, and aid flows declining. The failure to provide Africa with the resources needed to offset the loss in income due to adverse terms of trade movements has led to widespread erosion of physical and human capital stock in every sector which, unless reversed, will adversely affect future growth rates.

The response to Africa's debt crisis has entailed a series of annual Paris Club reschedulings contingent upon agreement on a standby program with the IMF. The method and terms of these renegotiations, however, do not take into account Africa's requirement for long-term net resource inflows to halt the economic decline and stimulate a recovery in production. In addition, in many countries that have been unwilling or unable to reach agreement with the IMF, the crisis has deepened. Debt service payments are consuming an increasing share of Africa's declining export earnings and net capital inflows, despite the fact that almost the only debts currently being serviced are those to the World Bank and the IMF.

At present, the international environment remains unfavorable to Africa and prospects will not improve without a concerted effort by major creditor countries. According to World Bank projections, even with modest improvements in world commodity prices, a declining U.S. dollar, and renewed aid inflows, per capita income in 1990 may be no higher than in 1970, and the debt burden will remain high. Over the next several years, scheduled debt service payments are projected at nearly $10 billion per annum, with 70 percent of the debt owed to the IMF falling due over the next three to four years. Africa's export potential is insufficient to finance long-term development on conventional terms or even to service much of its existing ODA debt.

SUGGESTED POLICY AGENDA

There is an overwhelming need to approach Africa's debt problem with a more comprehensive consideration of both the financial and non-financial aspects of the problem. African debtors could be divided into many categories—oil exporters, low- and middle-income countries—to which different sets of policy could be applied. But such an approach is unnecessary because what is striking about Africa's plight is its universality. The same post-independence pattern of high growth, stagnation, and crisis has emerged in most countries because of the considerable homogeneity of African economies— small populations; tropical environments; dependence on commodity exports and on foreign trade; agrarian bases; and high infant mortality, low literacy, and low life expectancy.

Second, Africa's economic problems cannot be separated into the problems of food, population, ecology, refugees, debt, as all are aspects of the deep-seated obstacles to growth. Unless progress is made on all fronts, the achievements are likely to be few and ephemeral.

Third, Africa's payments problems cannot be divided into short-term balance of payments and liquidity issues and longer-term growth and development issues, and hence parcelled out among the relevant international institutions. Africa's balance of payments problems pre-date the oil price increases and other shocks of the 1970s. The continent's debt problem has been internationally recognized as one of long-term poverty and therefore must be addressed in that context. Against such a comprehensive and longer-term setting, special actions must be taken to reduce Africa's mounting debt burden, including some of the following.

Debt Cancellation   The most effective solution to Africa's debt problem would be to cancel its obligations. High debt service payments are in part due to the amortization of old debt. If all bilateral creditors adhered to UN resolution 165 of March 1968 to cancel or retroactively adjust the terms of past ODA debt, some needed relief would have been provided. Only a few countries—Canada, Sweden, Switzerland, and Holland—have fully complied with the agreement. While the United States has legislation in place that allows for conversion of debt into local currency, this has not been implemented.

A precedent for a more comprehensive debt write-off exists in the 1970 renegotiation of Indonesia's debt. On that occasion, all of Indonesia's obligations to Western creditors were rescheduled for 30 years at no interest. Repayments of interest on originally contracted debt were to begin during the latter half of the repayment period and the country was given the option of deferring principal payments due in the first 8 years to the last 8 years of the agreement for a modest charge. The agreement also provided for a review of these arrangements in 10 years, at which time the country's economic situation and debt-servicing ability would be reassessed.

For those lenders unwilling or unable to cancel debts, there are the options of allowing debts to be paid in local currency or refinancing existing debt on softer terms. Specific action, however, is needed by the IMF, World Bank, and regional development banks which account for almost half of the projected debt service. They are not allowed to reschedule debts and are permitted by other creditors to be excluded from debt rescheduling operations; hence their preferred creditor status. However, debt relief measures that apply to only 30 to 50 percent of the debt service due do not ease the liquidity constraint.

With 1984 trends indicating that the IMF is reducing its net exposure in Africa, not only will net transfers from the Fund be negative, but other sources of balance of payments financing will be needed if IMF debts are to be paid on time. If, on the other hand, IMF lending to Africa were to increase, it should be on concessional terms. A specially funded trust fund could be established that would both extend concessional loans and refinance IMF debts over the long-term, on the order of a similar IMF program after the first oil shock.

Multi-year Rescheduling   Repeated debt reschedulings will not adequately address Africa's debt problem. They have merely added to the debt burden, constrained access to trade financing, and failed to bring about an increase in import levels. In May 1984, the London Summit endorsed multi-year reschedulings, which have been acted upon for the major debtors and which allow for part of the debt owed to private sources to be rescheduled for 12 to 14 years at existing rates but with reduced spreads and fees. Applied to Africa together with an option to adjust payments in line with terms of trade movements, such an approach would ease immediate debt burdens. In recognition of the structural reforms needed, concessional debt relief could be considered a legitimate form of development assistance. To counter the argument that those countries that have borrowed the most would benefit most, measures could be instituted to ensure that such countries receive less additional aid. The total resource package would be determined by current needs and performance criteria, with debt relief only one component of the overall policy package.

It may also be more effective to alter the forum for debt rescheduling for the poorest countries from the Paris Club to aid group meetings. Since 15 of the 21 countries which rescheduled debts between 1970 and January 1983 were low-income countries, aid group meetings could have provided better multilateral forum for consideration of debt problems in relation to the minimum level of inflows needed to restore normal trade arrangements and import capacity.

Increased Aid   Higher levels of imports and investment are needed to restore Africa's productive capacity. The need for increased aid to Africa must be examined in the context of the significant decline in net inflows from official and private sources. Official flows declined by 25 percent in 1981 to below the 1979 level in nominal terms. Net transfers declined by 30 percent. Total commitments to low-income Africa fell by 42 percent in 1981. If these trends are not reversed, net flows and net transfers from officials sources may soon be negative. Net transfers from private sources have been negative since 1979, despite the accumulation of commercial arrears which can account for up to a year's export earnings, as in the case of Zambia and Tanzania.

For the future, Africa will not be regarded as creditworthy for commercial bank lending and will have to rely largely on official concessional aid. Given the small size of the markets, equity investment in non-extractive industries is not likely to be profitable unless governments provide high rates of protection. And increased reliance on suppliers' credits since the mid-1970s has contributed to the rapid increase in the debt burden and the proliferation of uneconomic projects. An additional $6 billion in annual ODA flows to the poorest countries could be achieved if bilateral donors complied with the multilaterally agreed target to raise their share of ODA from the current level of 0.08 percent to 0.15 percent of GNP. This could be achieved by a reduction in the share of ODA to middle-income developing countries.

Improved Aid Quality   It would be misleading to conclude from Africa's desperate economic situation that much of the aid it has received over the past decade has been wasted. There have been some success stories in some countries, in some sectors, and at different times. However, three years of drought at the end of a decade of shocks has created an unbearable burden and many distortions. Domestic policy failures and lack of effectiveness in some of the past aid to Africa, documented in many recent reports, further underscore the need for improvements in the quality of aid.

The need for domestic policy reforms must be continually stressed, but donors also need to take a number of measures that would improve aid effectiveness: bringing aid flows more in line with the current financing priorities of the recipients; raising investment and recurrent expenditures on agriculture; rehabilitating existing projects; and restructuring the debt more in line with its debt-servicing capacity. Other measures could include a decline in the number of projects, a reduction in tied aid, and increased financing of local currency and recurrent expenditures.

It is estimated that about one-half of bilateral ODA is tied to purchases in the donor country. Aid-tying can add up to 20 percent to the cost of projects in addition to creating projects that are not suitable to local conditions and also result in the lack of standardization of machinery and spare parts. Finally, many projects are started that place heavy demands on local currency and recurrent expenditures and intermediate goods imports. Donors' doubling of the share of existing ODA which goes to the poorest countries and implementation of measures to improve the quality of aid would produce enormous benefits at no additional budgetary costs.

Improved Debt Management   The debt crisis has exposed the need in all developing countries for better systems to collect and process debt information, and for closer coordination of the pattern of borrowing and investment. But African governments also need to consider that the risks of borrowing are greater for smaller, poorer, and heavily indebted regions, and special efforts need to be taken to control the growth and composition of future indebtedness. Good debt management is a part of good economic management and while better systems for controlling debt do not prevent crises from occurring, they do minimize the real economic burden of financial disruptions.

The following guidelines would contribute to improved debt management: utilizing available computer facilities to improve the recording and processing of data on all foreign exchange receipts and payments; establishing systems to coordinate the flow of the above information with decisions taken by the country's financial managers, especially at the Central Bank and the Ministry of Finance; giving final borrowing authority to a financial management team; foregoing borrowing for investment if the returns or requirements are questionable; limiting borrowing which is not long term and concessional; and recognizing that borrowing on market terms is especially hazardous for primary commodity producers.

SDR Allocation   In addition to increased resource transfers, Africa also needs a stable source of reserve creation and access to short-term trade financing. Its lack of liquidity is evident in the low level of gross reserves and the build-up in trade arrears. During the 1970s, the global need for liquidity was largely met through the dramatic increase in the price of gold and the expansion of commercial bank lending. These developments did not help the poorest countries, as their only source of balance of payments financing is the IMF. However, IMF quotas are very low. A special issue of SDRs is needed pending increased quotas and enlarged access to Fund resources. An agreement could also be reached by which the industrial and oil-exporting countries would forego their allocation of SDRs in favor of the poorest countries. Trade arrears could be taken up by the IMF and refinanced along with the debt owed to the IMF. Alternatively, the special SDR issue could be used to consolidate these arrears and replenish reserve levels. Africa's liquidity could also be enhanced by increased access to an enlarged Compensatory Financing Facility.

Existing arrangements for meeting the financing needs of developing countries are not adequate. At present, these arrangements are not working well for either creditor or debtor countries—a pre-condition for international monetary reform. However, even within the present unstable and risky framework, special attention needs to be given to the financing needs of the poorest countries which bear a disproportionate share of the burden of adjustment to global payments imbalances. They have experienced the biggest cuts in living standards and the decline in official flows is accelerating their economic decline.

NOTES

1. The data on Africa's debt is not complete. The data from the World Bank's Debtor Reporting System are the most comprehensive source, but they exclude IMF drawings, short-term loans, trade arrears to non-financial

enterprises, and private non-guaranteed borrowing. For many countries, these obligations are quite large.

2. The real debt burden is measured by the number of export units—tons of coffee, cotton, etc.—needed to meet a dollar of debt service.

3. Including use of the General Agreement to Borrow, whereby the industrial countries make additional funds available for special situations.

4. Access to the Compensatory Financing Facility has been reduced from 100 percent to 83 percent of quotas and the practice that up to 50 percent of quota was available on low conditionality terms has been withdrawn.

REFERENCES

Adedeji, A. 1984. "Foreign Debt and Prospects for Growth in the Developing Countries of Africa in the 1980s." Addis Ababa: United Nations.

Balassa, B. 1982. "Adjustment Policies and Development Strategies in sub-Saharan Africa, 1973-78." Discussion Paper No. 41. Washington, D.C.: The World Bank.

Balassa B. 1982. "Policy Responses to External Shocks in sub-Saharan African Countries." Discussion Paper No. 42. Washington, D.C.: World Bank.

Duncan, R. 1983. "Quarterly Review of Commodity Markets." Washington, D.C.: The World Bank.

Griffith-Jones, S. and R. H. Green. 1984. "African External Debt and Development: A Review and Analysis." Mimeo. Sussex, England: Institute of Development Studies.

Hardy, C. S. 1982. "Rescheduling Developing Country Debt, 1956-1981: Lessons and Recommendations." Monograph No. 15. Washington, D.C.: Overseas Development Council.

Helleiner, G. K. 1984(a). "Outward Orientation, Import Stability and African Economic Growth, and Empirical Investigation." Department of Economics, University of Toronto. Mimeo.

Helleiner, G. K. 1984(b). "Aid and Liquidity: The Neglect of the Poorest in the Emerging International Monetary System." Department of Economics, University of Toronto. Mimeo.

Hope, N. 1984. "Notes on the Debt and Debt Prospects for sub-Saharan Africa." World Bank. Mimeo.

Loxley, J. 1984. "The IMF and the Poorest Countries." Ottawa: North-South Institute.

Williamson, J., ed. 1983. IMF Conditionality. Cambridge: Institute for International Economics/MIT Press.

World Bank. 1981. Accelerated Development in Sub-Saharan Africa: An Agenda for Action. Washington, D.C.: The World Bank.

World Bank. 1983. World Development Report 1983. New York: Oxford.

World Bank. 1984. Toward Sustained Development in sub-Saharan Africa: A Joint Program of Action. Washington, D.C.: The World Bank.

World Bank. 1985. World Development Report 1985. New York: Oxford.

World Bank. World Debt Tables, 1984-85. Washington, D.C.: The World Bank.

Zulu, J. B. and S. M. Nsouli. 1985. "Adjustment Programs in Africa." Occasional Paper No. 34. Washington, D.C.: International Monetary Fund.

CHAPTER SEVENTEEN

Africa's Trade and the World Economy

Stephen R. Lewis, Jr.

Africa's relationship to the world economy over the past four centuries has failed to instill confidence in the workings of international trade. The first two centuries were dominated by the human plunder of the slave trade. Then, the 19th-century scramble for Africa by European commercial and political interests began, in some regions, an exceptionally exploitive system. The cash crop economy and African labor's involvement in production for the international market were expanded in the 20th century. But development was limited to primary production: Africa was to provide hewers of wood and drawers of water for the industrial world, and trade and international commerce often was controlled by foreign minorities. In the post-independence period, shocks from the international economy have reverberated more strongly in Africa than in other regions of the world.

Despite this rather dismal record of contact with the world economy, the small size of most African countries means foreign trade must play an important part in their development strategies, even for those countries whose long-term objective is to reduce their vulnerability to the international economy.

THE RECORD OF GROWTH AND TRADE IN AFRICA

FOREIGN TRADE

In the 1960s and through the commodity boom of the early 1970s, Africa's export performance was quite satisfactory, but after the first oil shock, it slipped badly both absolutely and in comparison to other developing regions (Table A.9 in Appendix I). Low-income African countries have suffered a consistent deterioration in their external terms of trade since the mid-1960s (Table A.10). Overall, Africa's terms of trade have held fairly constant since the mid-1960s, reflecting a rise in the continent's oil exports.[1]

While Africa appears to have fared slightly better than "non-oil developing countries" as a group, it has coped less well with declining terms of trade than the low-income countries of Asia. The purchasing power of exports (the volume of exports adjusted for changes in the terms of trade) rose substantially in low-income Asia, but fell modestly in low-income Africa. While all non-oil developing countries experienced a 137 percent expansion in the purchasing power of their exports between 1967 and 1983, this indicator rose by only 36 percent in Africa.[2]

One possible reason for Africa's greater difficulties is the steeper decline in the terms of trade for low-income African countries in comparison with low-income Asia in the two recession periods of 1973–76 and 1979–82. Viewed over longer time periods, however, movements in the terms of trade in these two groups were much closer. Since external shocks hit poor countries harder, the sharper downward fluctuations contributed to the relatively poorer African showing. Consequently, short-term stabilization efforts may be more important for Africa than elsewhere.

A fairly consistent pattern of declining export shares of Africa's important commodities is shown in Table A.11. In four of the eight important metals and minerals (copper, zinc, tin, and lead), Africa's share of developing country exports declined between 1960 to 1978, and in two more (iron ore and bauxite), the share declined during the 1970s. For 10 important food commodities, African shares declined in six (cocoa, groundnut oil, palm oil, bananas, and maize) over the entire period, with its share of coffee falling during the 1970s. Further contractions in Africa's share of world exports occurred in timber, cotton, tobacco, rubber, and sisal over the longer period, with its contribution of hides and skins decreasing in the 1970s.

Had the decline in these export shares been associated with a concomitant rise in output of other commodities, there would have been little cause for concern. However, overall stagnant export performance (shown in Table A.9) and poor GDP growth rates indicate that other types of production were not increasing.

Import volumes have not suffered to the same extent as export volumes in Africa largely because of a rising share of capital inflows. However, both the variability of imports and the inadequate import growth rate (1 percent per year since 1976) have constrained growth in most African countries. The financing of imports, both on a long-term and on a counter-cyclical basis, is a matter of greatest importance to income growth and to trade policy reform.

CAPITAL FLOWS, DEBT, AND RESERVES

Capital inflows have become more important in Africa than in the low- and lower-middle income countries of the rest of the developing world. While Africa has suffered from foreign exchange constraints in recent years, its external debt build-up, most of which is long term and non-commercial, has been very substantial. Given slow growth in both GDP and exports, the rapid accumulation of debt even on concessionary terms will eventually prove to be a serious burden. Africa's debt service ratio has tripled over the past decade, with debt service payments in excess of a quarter of export earnings for a number of countries.

Insufficient liquidity to cope with external shocks such as changes in terms of trade or weather has imposed a certain inflexibility on governments, not only inhibiting economic growth,[3] but also forcing the adoption of import and foreign exchange control systems.[4] Thus, not only have African countries suffered from long-term shortages of foreign exchange, but they have also been confronted with critical day-to-day problems that inhibit sound decision-making.

CAPITAL FORMATION

Rates of capital formation and productivity of capital give particular cause for concern. Africa has a lower ratio of investment to GDP than other regions, although the ratio did rise modestly in the 1970s. Both the share of savings in GDP and the share of investment financed by domestic savings are low and deteriorating as compared with other regions. The rising deficits of domestic saving mirror the growing balance of payments deficits which must be financed by foreign capital.

Perhaps of greater importance, investment has failed to generate significantly higher levels of output and incomes. Marginally rising investment ratios and declining output rates in the 1970s strongly suggest that the productivity of new investment was negative. Rates of return on investment in low-income Africa fell dramatically as compared with other regions. Such low productivity of new capital inflows is a major cause for concern, especially when investment is financed by extended debt. If there is to be a brighter future for Africa, increasing the productivity of resources will have to form a major part of the solution. Africa cannot continue to require twice as much investment as other regions in the world to generate the same increase in incomes.

EXTERNAL FACTORS AND DOMESTIC POLICIES

DEBATE OVER THE PAST RECORD

Apportioning blame for Africa's poor economic performance has spawned a rather vigorous debate over whether the principal causes are beyond the control of African governments (i.e., the poor state of the world economy, associated declines in commodity prices, and drought) or due to adverse government policies on key issues such as exchange rates, imports, and pricing structures.

In reality, however, Africa's poor performance can be blamed almost equally on both factors. Its economic performance could have been substantially better over the past decade if either the exogenous environment had been more benign or if African governments had adopted more appropriate policies.[5] In fact, some studies suggest that, on average, African governments could have offset most of the adverse effects of the external environment of the 1970s by optimal policy choices.[6] Further, a good many of the external factors could have been mitigated by different policies on the part of industrial countries and international institutions. Since both external and domestic policies could be improved, there is some basis for optimism when considering the future prospects of the region.

ENVIRONMENTAL FACTORS

There is no doubt that African countries have been at a disadvantage due to poverty, characterized by low levels of literacy, less diversified economic structures, low savings rates, etc. These features of underdevelopment make it more difficult to respond to adverse exogenous trends such as drought, declining export prices, or increased energy prices. Further, Africa's relatively newer machinery of government has limited its ability to respond to the adversities of the 1970s. Many African countries have also had to confront the instability of domestic or international violence in the relatively short period since independence.[7]

The international economy has also had a substantially negative effect on Africa in the past two decades, particularly since the first oil price shocks. In the 1970s, greater fluctuations in primary commodity prices and a downturn in real prices (both associated largely with the performance of the OECD economies) made Africa's external economic environment exceptionally difficult. According to one estimate, only two variables—the growth rates in the OECD's imports and Africa's barter terms of trade—account for over 80 percent of the variations in Africa's growth rates over the two decades 1960–1980. From such evidence, many observers have concluded that environmental or external factors are the principal cause of Africa's poor performance.[8]

DOMESTIC POLICIES

The issue of domestic policies pursued by individual African countries is a complex one, often generating heated debates. The key policies include exchange rates, tariff structures, import and other direct control systems, government wage policies, pricing policies (especially for agricultural commodities and parastatal or government-owned corporations), and a variety of macro-economic policies, including adjustments to fluctuations in external conditions. To a large extent, the debate divides between those who advocate market-oriented and outward-looking policies, and those who suggest that reliance on market forces and greater involvement in international trade will inhibit equitable growth and increase Africa's political and economic vulnerability and dependence.

A balanced reading of the evidence suggests that domestic policies do play a major role. Studies by independent scholars and analyses by the IMF and the World Bank substantiate the view that certain measurable policies lead to improved economic performance. Specific policy measures that are conducive to improvements in overall economic performance include exchange rate adjustments to avoid excessive overvaluation,[9] altering import levels in response to changes in export earnings,[10] and adoption of more appropriate policies during adverse movements of foreign exchange reserves.[11]

On the other hand, overvalued currencies that discriminate against exports and import controls that starve key productive sectors of needed inputs appear to be major determinants in Africa's declining share of many commodity exports. Further, failure to maintain more balanced macro-economic management over the trade cycle has led to variations in import rates which have also detracted from economic performance.[12]

A quicker payoff from improved trade and macroeconomic policies is more likely to come in countries that have already reached a somewhat higher level of income and diversification, however, a point emphasized by Helleiner and by the IMF's 1983 studies.[13] Since African countries are predominantly lower income, the short-term benefit from adopting the "prescribed" policies could be less significant than elsewhere.

BALANCING ENVIRONMENTAL AND POLICY
VARIABLES

David Wheeler (1984) presents some intriguing results that have a bearing on the current debate. "Environmental" variables—terms of trade, civil disturbances, presence of minerals, and lack of initial diversification—generally have a greater impact on performance than "policy" variables, such as exchange rate adjustment and adapting to changed circumstances. His calculations show what the performance of 24 African countries might have been had either the environmental factors or policy choices been "optimal."[14]

For the average country, the environmental cost on economic growth was about 3.3 percent per year, while the cost of non-optimal policy choices was about 2.4 percent per year. While environmental factors clearly dominate, a typical country could have eliminated over two-thirds of the costs imposed by external conditions by changing its domestic policies. Sixteen countries could have added at least 2 percent per year to their growth rates by changing policies, and in 11 countries, optimal policy choices would have more than offset the costs of adverse environmental factors. One factor classified by Wheeler as "environmental"—the presence of mining activities—

seems to me to be more policy related. The poor performance of mining economies is not purely a function of external factors, although the character of mining economics does present problems for policy makers.[15]

In sum, evidence suggests that despite the low-income nature of many African economies and the adverse external climate of the past two decades, it was within the power of African governments to significantly affect economic performance by appropriate policies on international trade—exchange rates, tariff and tax structures, import control mechanisms, and macro-economic policies bearing on balance of payments management.

OPPORTUNITIES AND CONSTRAINTS OF TRADE

DEVELOPMENT OBJECTIVES

Given low levels of per capita output in most African countries, raising output levels so that the average person will benefit directly must be the first major objective of policy reform. Maximizing GDP growth alone is not enough—growth must be broadly based and accessible to the currently disadvantaged—which in most African countries means the rural majority.

The scarcity of key factors, including arable land, capital, water, skilled labor, and foreign exchange (and the likelihood that these will remain key constraints in the coming decade) means that a second priority must be to increase the productivity of these factors. More output per unit is essential if there is to be a significant and sustained improvement in the level of well-being of the majority of Africans.

Third, with substantial excess capacity in many productive sectors—underutilized industrial and infrastructure projects and high unemployment and underemployment of labor—policies should aim at expanding output rather than reducing demand as a means of addressing balance of payments problems. While stabilization programs are important, they must exhibit a bias toward growth.

These three propositions are at the core of any search for improved policies and performance, regardless of judgments about likely levels of external assistance. Indeed, without higher productivity, there is little sense in borrowing larger volumes of external resources.

CONSTRAINTS AND OPPORTUNITIES

The constraints posed by international trade relate primarily to the traditional export commodities: these cannot provide for rapid growth of per capita income in Africa on a sustained basis. Fluctuations in international demand for African primary commodities will continue, and no demand projections suggest that a sustained and dramatic upward trend is likely. While some countries may yet be able to increase output and real incomes from growth of traditional commodities (including petroleum), traditional exports cannot be assigned a leading role in Africa's economic recovery.

Another source of constraints on international trade is inaccessible markets. Even if production meets competitive quantitative, qualitative, and pricing criteria, protection in the export markets of the developed or the developing world, credit terms, and lack of knowledge of overseas markets all present obstacles to growth through international trade. These constraints on trade tend to be stressed by opponents of "outward-looking, market-oriented" policies as a preferred regime.[16]

Nevertheless, it is virtually impossible for Africa to contemplate significant progress in economic development and genuine economic independence without exploiting more fully the opportunities offered by the international economy that complement domestic economic structures. These include access to cheap sources of products needed for development and profitable added markets for goods that can be produced at home. The key issue is not whether to trade, but rather what, how, and when to trade. What are the conditions under which the domestic economy should be linked to or integrated with the international economy? And when and how should portions be de-linked or partially or totally isolated from international trade?

Both the constraints and the opportunities inherent in the international economy express themselves largely in terms of price structures. While declining commodity prices or rising energy bills may represent a constraint on domestic policy, they also represent opportunities for converting domestic production of some commodities into domestic consumption of others at an attractive rate of exchange. A key issue is how to be certain that both the constraints on and the opportunities for national gains through trade are made apparent to domestic producers.

POLICY ALTERNATIVES AND EMPHASES

With nearly four-fifths of Africa's population dependent on agriculture for its livelihood, increased agricultural production is essential for any meaningful improvement in living standards. Given high rates of population growth, the size of farm populations will grow for the next 30 to 40 years even if there is an extraordinary growth in Africa's non-agricultural economy.[17] Growth in agricultural output and productivity as the sine qua non of development is substantiated by the experience of virtually every middle or upper-income country. Agriculture has provided the savings, foreign exchange, markets for new domestic manufactures, labor force for the towns, and food for the labor force over the history of virtually every developed country.

In addition, changing the industrial structure—in particular the manufacturing sector—is intimately related to overall economic development. Achieving structural change involves balancing incentives to, and investment in, agriculture and manufacturing. This question cannot be put in terms of import-substituting versus exporting industries: Excessive dependence on internal markets is a dead-end especially for small countries; and in virtually all successful cases, industries were established initially for a domestic market and later broke into exports. Therefore, the key issues are first balancing the incentives given to production for the home versus the export market both for agricultural and for manufactured goods, and then how to provide incentives for productivity growth that can lead to competitiveness in export industries.[18]

Finally, issues of trade orientation and agricultural growth have been linked in a somewhat pointless discussion over cash versus food crop production. Such a question cannot be answered in the abstract, as the right balance in agricultural production depends on the economics of producing specific commodities in a specific country and the markets for those commodities at home and abroad. It makes no more sense to encourage production of export cash crops that face declining prices abroad than it does to encourage production of food crops where the productivity of labor, land, capital, and water is relatively low. As markets and technology change, so do optimum cropping patterns. The objective should be the growth of farmers' real incomes and of the economy as a whole.

PRICING AND INCENTIVES

All developing countries must choose pricing incentives for producers, consumers, and traders. Since individuals and enterprises make most crucial decisions on the basis of prices, sound national economic management requires prices that promote sustained development. Pricing policies can adversely affect income distribution, production of both food and export crops, and employment opportunities in both agriculture and industry, but can also play a positive role. Evidence from Africa shows that peasant farmers are rational economic calculators, adjusting their behavior to react to changes in prices and known technologies, and to the uncertainties and constraints faced in their economic lives.[19]

In the industrial sector, response to price is less precisely established, but sectors with increased profitability and greater certainty of markets and profits have shown increased investment and output, while those that are discriminated against in terms of profits, prices, and certainty are less likely to expand. Even parastatal bodies (unless finance is no constraint) must pay attention to the prices of inputs and outputs, and must cover operating costs—thus they will enter production lines when they can be sure to influence the prices paid or received, and will not produce products or provide services where they are at substantial risk.[20]

DOMESTIC PRICING AND INTERNATIONAL TRADE

Domestic price structures should be based on an implicit cost-benefit calculation made from a national economic standpoint. Most resources have a variety of potential economic uses and international prices generally represent a set of opportunities for buying and selling which the country must accept as given.[21] Consequently, the national calculus should aim at producing those goods with the highest payoff in terms of the real value of domestic output, usually measurable in terms of net import savings or net export earnings.

The national calculus must also take into account international market conditions for major products, the necessity of learning by doing in newly developing sectors, and the value of diversifying away from traditional sectors. All these points are critical for African countries, as there are limits to the payoff from expanding traditional export products. Diversification both within agriculture and into other sectors is important to permit expansion of economic activities without facing market limitations and to reduce risks associated with concentration in a few products and markets.

As new activities often require higher start-up costs, a successful diversification program must aim at productivity growth rates and cost reductions that outpace those of traditional activities. Thus, uninhibited free trade, with a domestic price structure identical to world prices, is not the best policy, particularly for the lowest income countries.[22]

Nevertheless, domestic prices that deviate too drastically from international prices have been inimical to African development objectives. This is due in part to a failure to recognize one of the constraints of international trade: whatever domestic prices are set, the international price structure is what it is. Ostensibly protected against foreign competition, one local industry is simply favored over other local industries. Protection is a subsidy; consumers could have purchased the protected product more cheaply abroad, but were forced to trade with the domestic producer. As a result, income is transferred from the domestic consumer to the local producer.[23]

More important, the protected sector always appears to be saving more foreign exchange than is actually the case. Differences between apparent savings—after purchases of local inputs and income payments for wages and profits—and the amount actually saved must be made up by a subsidy payment exacted from the consuming sector.[24] In extreme cases, the contributions of protected industries can be negative, as the foreign exchange needed for inputs is greater than the foreign exchange value of the output. As a result, real national income falls and the balance of payments worsens although physical production increases.[25]

How long can such subsidies continue? As protected sectors grow, their needs for subsidies also mount unless their rate of productivity growth is very rapid. If the protected sectors grow more rapidly than those providing the subsidies (as has been the case in virtually all of Africa), then growing sources of transfers, such as agriculture, mining, and tourism, must be found. But with stagnant output in agriculture and mining, protected sectors have no source of subsidy to support their expansion.[26]

Capital inflows have also permitted protected domestic industry to make factor payments that exceed foreign exchange savings. Much of the non-agricultural growth in Africa in recent years has effectively been subsidized by rising capital inflows. This approach, too, is a dead-end unless there are rapid productivity increases in the protected sectors, both to remove the need for continued subsidy and to earn or save enough foreign exchange to repay the foreign loans.

Pricing structures adopted by many African countries have tended to favor protection for manufacturing industries that produce only certain goods, notably luxury and semi-luxury consumer goods, for the domestic market. Consequently, industries which manufacture exports, many essential import substitutes, and agricultural products all have been heavily penalized. In agriculture, pricing discrimination is evident not only for traditional exports,[27] but for new agricultural exports and food crops. The issue, then, is not merely sectoral discrimination, but also a systematic bias toward production of selected manufactured goods for the domestic market.

It has been argued that the scope for growth outside import-substituting industries has been negligible in most African countries which inherited monocultural economies, and, therefore, that there are no alternatives to subsidies for import-substituting industries. While there is some truth to this argument (production in a new industry is most likely to first serve the demands of the home market), in the absence of exceptionally rapid productivity growth, the present structure of incentives is both impossible to reconcile with development objectives and completely self-limiting. When industries producing manufactures for the home market are paid 10, 20, or 50 times as much as producers of agricultural goods in order to save foreign exchange, no reasonable productivity growth differential will eliminate the need for perpetual subsidies.[28]

African countries must encourage the expansion of non-traditional exports and the manufacturing sector. Modest amounts of protection for new products in the domestic market and modest assistance for new exports are justifiable as incentives when changing economic structures.[29] This point must be understood and accepted by Africa's trading partners, international institutions, and donors. But it is the extent of discrimination against all exports and against agriculture that has caused interventions in the pricing system to become pernicious rather than productive.

What products could be exported and to which markets? It is impossible to answer this question with any precision. The nature of diversified growth is that a variety of sectors and industries are engaged in producing for both the home and external markets. With

balanced incentives, a wide mix of activities emerges, capable of satisfying both domestic and foreign demand.[30]

OTHER DOMESTIC POLICIES

In addition to pricing structures of internationally traded goods,
domestic price distortions and overall fiscal and monetary policy can
help or hinder growth and diversification of international trade. Domestic wage and parastatal pricing policies have adversely affected
economic performance. With real wages in the modern sector much
higher than in agriculture, for example, newer sectors have faced
difficulties in becoming internationally competitive. When prices for
the output of parastatals are kept low, shortages, under-investment,
inefficient use of resources, and deficit operations result, adding to
the burden on public financing.

Aggregate monetary and fiscal policies have also played a role.
Currency overvaluation often can be attributed to excess money creation, as monetary authorities respond to the requirements of financing fiscal deficits. As public expenditures have risen faster than tax
revenues, the public sector has borrowed from the banking system.
As a result, excess demand has put pressure on domestic wages and
prices. In the absence of exchange rate adjustments, domestic prices
have risen above the domestic currency equivalent of similar goods
traded internationally. The resulting balance of payments problems
have accelerated the adoption of import control systems and tariff
structures which discriminate against new exports and duty-free imports such as food.

OPTIONS FOR IMPROVED PERFORMANCE

As indicated earlier, Africa's economic performance could be considerably improved by actions undertaken by the countries themselves and by international institutions and donors. A number of
suggestions are presented here.

THE ENVIRONMENT OF THE NEXT DECADE

The pattern of economic history suggests that world economic
performance in the next decade is likely to be considerably better than
in the preceding one. While a commodity boom is not likely in the

next decade, commodity markets are expected to be healthier based on modest assumptions of growth in industrial countries and lower real interest rates. Further, I think that the current forecast of recovery in the OECD countries is too pessimistic. Given the close relationship between Africa's trade and growth prospects and OECD growth, the next decade should show improved African economic performance, even if policy changes are not undertaken by African governments or the international community.[31] Indeed, renewed growth of the OECD economies should help reduce current protectionist trends and provide opportunities for new African exports.

Having stated that African trade opportunities are expected to expand, it would be wrong to conclude that Africa will automatically reach an acceptable growth rate by virtue of the world recovery. African exports are primarily those commodities subject to the constraints of trade, and the need for diversification will remain. In most African countries, the opportunities for successful, low-cost import-substituting industrialization will not be sufficient to trigger output of non-traditional exports from agriculture and manufacturing on the required scale. Import substituting agriculture and non-traditional exports from agriculture and manufacturing are both essential and possible.[32]

Another lesson from the past is that volatility in primary commodity markets will continue. African governments must adopt policies and employ resources to buffer their economies from cyclical fluctuations more effectively than in the past.[33]

ACTION BY AFRICAN GOVERNMENTS

African government must review their price and tax structures to:

- eliminate major pricing anomalies, particularly of foreign exchange and basic foods, and excessive protection for import-replacement industries that result from import controls,
- provide modest discrimination in favor of exports and import replacement activities in manufacturing and agriculture,
- reduce the extent of discrimination against traditional exports,
- substitute sales and excise taxes for tariffs to ensure that consumption restraints and revenue needs do not result in unwarranted protection.

Countries need to improve their macro-economic management by adopting counter-cyclical balance of payments and budgetary policies in both upswings and downswings.

Administrative reforms are needed to encourage a more productive role for foreign trade, especially:

- minimizing administrative barriers to exporters,
- increasing encouragement of exports through provision of adequate credit, information on markets and procedures abroad, etc.,
- easing producers' access to imported components, spare parts, and capital goods.

The reform of price structures is a necessary, though not sufficient condition for improving Africa's economic performance. The pricing of foreign exchange is an extremely powerful policy tool and the incentive system is an effective means both of increasing agricultural output and shifting its composition toward productive use of resources. Excessive protection has also contributed to Africa's economic problems. The proposed agenda would first involve removing the most extreme distortions in each country. However, modest penalties are required on the production of most traditional export commodities and on other goods in which countries have established cost advantages.[34]

Restructuring prices should provide some advantage for the newer sectors of the economy. Modest levels of protection on all import-replacement activities and modest encouragement to all non-traditional exports are called for. To this end, relatively uniform tariff levels on different types of products and modest subsidies to new exports are recommended.[35]

There is always a concern that in restructuring prices, excessive demand for consumer goods, particularly luxuries, will be created. Countries should utilize sales and excise taxes, rather than tariffs and import controls, to regulate consumption. While reduced tariff and quota protection will mean lower prices to producers, higher sales and excise taxes will keep prices facing higher-income consumers at penalty levels.

Proposal pricing reforms are not new, but would provide greater incentives to agricultural production, increase the lowest income groups' share of GDP, and raise output from the agricultural sector, hence improving incomes, output, and the balance of payments. They would also restructure the output of manufacturing sectors toward lower cost industries. The success of countries such as Malawi and Ivory Coast in diversifying their economies and exports over the past decade highlights the positive use of incentives.

Improved macro-economic management is also a high priority, particularly in smoothing the peaks and troughs of international commodity markets. Most of the financing burden of this exercise should be underwritten by the international community, although individual countries must exercise monetary and fiscal restraint when commodity prices are relatively high, in order to conserve resources when they are low. The argument that developing countries can ill afford to keep resources "idle" in foreign exchange reserves is based on the assumption that the productivity of other uses of resources is greater than the use of resources to avert extreme restrictions when commodity prices decline. However, the evidence suggests that the damage done by severe restrictions is greater than the output foregone by building up modest international reserves.[36] Further, if countries had greater resources at the beginning of periods of stringency, the need to resort to extreme trade-restricting measures would be less likely.

Exchange rate adjustments are an essential element of reform, but adjustments made without budgetary and monetary discipline will simply feed inflation. And, such modifications must be part of long-term planning, not crisis management. In addition to better pricing of foreign exchange, tariff reforms, and modest subsidies to new exports, export activities require other types of support. In many African countries, despite the extreme scarcity of foreign exchange, it is almost as difficult to get permission to export as to import. Documentation requirements and other clearance procedures must be minimized, and export activities should receive preference in credit allocations as countries appraise private and parastatal projects.

Finally, a persistent problem in most of Africa is the import control and allocation system. Scarce imported goods often do not reach the sectors that could use them most productively. Exporters and producers of highly valued import substitutes, including food, are often starved of access to imported inputs and capital goods. To complement pricing structure reforms, greater flexibility in the allocation of imports is also needed.[37]

The suggested changes face a host of obstacles. Altering the pricing structure will change the distribution of rewards. In countries in which the urban and often mining workers have benefited from the policies of turning the domestic price structure against agriculture, reforms which raise agricultural prices will meet objections from employed workers. Licensing systems have created their own circle of wealth and privilege that will not easily be given up. Nor is it easy to pursue budgetary and balance of payments management policies which involve more restraint in cyclical booms in order to avoid the stop-and-start effects that have had a negative effect on overall economic performance. Governments will need considerable support in making these reforms, and the assistance of the international donor community is essential.

Countries with already diversified economies may see the quickest benefits from improved policies. But the need to realign the incentive structures in the poorest and least diversified economies is equally important, as the loss of real output from inefficient projects is more critical in the low-income countries.[38] Stabilization policies to avoid stop-and-start growth will improve the efficiency with which investment is used and increase growth rates for the poorest countries which have no access to commercial capital for counter-cyclical financing.

ACTIONS BY THE INTERNATIONAL COMMUNITY

The following actions by the major donor countries and multilateral institutions are recommended.

Donor assistance should be shifted toward greater non-project financing by:

- Debt relief, particularly from bilateral donors,
- Increased non-project aid in support of reform programs undertaken by recipient countries,
- Increased resources for compensatory financing, either through the IMF or another source, operating on a more automatic basis for both drawdowns and repayments,
- Provision of new financing vehicles for non-traditional exports to African markets and elsewhere.

Industrial countries should continue to reduce tariff and non-tariff barriers on African exports and should not retaliate when African countries use modest subsidies on non-traditional exports.

The mix of external assistance should be shifted toward a higher share of non-project aid, as the perceived bias of donor agencies toward project assistance may have contributed to both the low productivity of new investment and the crisis management of the foreign trade sector in Africa. When countries are short of foreign exchange, they are likely to accept any donor-financed project. In providing the host country's contribution, domestic resources are then diverted from other uses irrespective of relative productivity. When completed, the project requires scarce resources for its operation, runs at less than its optimal level, and yields lower returns on investment.

Shifting the aid mix would make possible higher productivity of both existing and new projects and more rational macro-economic planning on the part of African governments. In addition, non-project aid could be budgeted to support the domestic policy reforms that must be undertaken if external assistance is to have improved productivity rates.

The shift to greater non-project assistance might take different forms, depending on the planning and implementation capacity and economic structure of the country. In a country with high debt burden and considerable planning and implementation capacity, a substantial debt rescheduling could provide enough resources and sufficient breathing space for needed reforms and recovery while other aspects of the aid and investment program remain unchanged. In other countries, greater use of structural adjustment loans and comparable aid from the bilateral donors might accomplish a similar goal, with somewhat more focus on sector policies and projects. And in a low-income country with fewer management capabilities, greater automatic compensatory financing to facilitate better macro-economic management over the trade cycle could greatly enhance aggregate performance.

Relieving the official external debt burden of low-income Africa in particular would free up much needed resources. A major advantage of debt forgiveness or of significant rescheduling is that the released resources are not tied to projects. While the multilateral institutions, particularly the IMF and the World Bank, do not reschedule or forgive obligations falling due, the bilateral donors could make a substantial contribution. Several billion dollars a year could be provided in this manner, augmenting Africa's "untied" aid substantially and possibly increasing net capital flows by 50 percent.[39]

Increased concessionary financing to facilitate reform of pricing and incentives is an essential component of the process of moving toward higher rates of output growth and productivity. The World Bank's structural adjustment loan program is a step in the right direction, but its resources are limited. Additional funds from bilateral donors would strengthen the impact on the overall development program and if such assistance were available on a continuing basis rather than only at time of crisis, the process of matching policy reforms with aid would be less politically charged than at present.

The IMF's short time horizon and the fact that it is usually called in when the situation is already desperate places too great a burden on the difficult process of policy reform. In such circumstances, discussions can be acrimonious and misunderstandings are common. If more development and stabilization assistance were put in a context of long-term policy reforms, less emphasis would be placed on meeting a particular condition by a specified date. Further, the entire process could be tailored to the particular needs of individual countries, rather than being bound by the IMF's relatively rigid rules.[40]

A third category of resources would be used for meeting cyclical fluctuations in commodity prices. Declining import capacity has directly retarded African development, and the policies adopted in times of crisis have made matters worse in the longer run. No less problematic have been cyclical management policies when commodity prices are on the upswing. Countries have been quick to spend increases in foreign exchange earnings, postponing the repayment of short-term stabilization funds that are borrowed on a fixed repayment schedule.

While holding higher average levels of reserves would be a good solution, this seems to be nearly impossible in most countries. As an alternative, the size of IMF compensatory financing arrangements could be increased and the terms modified. More financing would become available automatically when a country's major exports declined by specified amounts or when cereal or energy imports increased due to external factors.

Further, repayment would be scheduled over a relatively long period independent of the behavior of the major exports, but would be automatically converted to a shorter schedule if export earnings improved by a specified amount. The automatic allowance for larger drawings would remove some of the pressure on governments and central banks when export earnings are depressed or import payments surge. At the same time, with the automatic repayment schedule, there would be some assurance that countries would not become over-committed in times of temporary abundance.

The fourth set of measures involve aid flows aimed more directly at increasing Africa's non-traditional exports. Two elements are important in this effort. First, financing non-traditional exports from African countries, both to other African countries and to the rest of the world, would involve providing credit to central banks so that the exporter could extend normal trade credits. The central bank would provide credit to the exporter through normal banking channels which would be repaid by the exporter and by the central bank when foreign exchange was received from the importing country. The credit line could then be drawn down again for more non-traditional exports.

From a national point of view, there would be substantial interest in making sure such exports increased to assure that the credit lines to the central bank were fully tapped. The country would have the incentive to establish procedures that would be readily accessible to exporters and would improve on the competitiveness of African suppliers. It would also ensure that domestic credit favored export diversification and expansion.

Second, assistance to increase trade should include the extension of credit for regional payment clearing arrangements. The clearing arrangements of the Preferential Trade Area for East and Southern Africa provide for the central banks of the member countries themselves to extend credit and take the risk of receiving hard currency at the end of the settlement period. If financing were available for the settlement of such intra-African trade debts, countries would have a much more powerful incentive to utilize the exports of their neighbors. The small size of intra-African trade suggests a low cost to such financing; yet the small size of individual national markets suggests the potential from regional integration would be fairly large.[41]

Finally, the continued extension of preference for all exports from African countries to the United States and other OECD countries is an essential ingredient of any program to increase Africa's benefits from international trade. The size of African exports, under the most optimistic assumptions about export performance over the next decade, is so small that relaxation in the OECD countries could be accomplished without measurable hardship in those countries, while the benefits to Africa in terms of increased export earnings and output could be very substantial.[42]

ACTIONS BY GROUPS OF AFRICAN COUNTRIES

Cooperation among African countries in removing barriers to in-tra-regional trade is another imperative. Regional groupings repre-sent the best vehicle if they work toward limited goals, such as reduc-ing licensing requirements and improving payments clearing arrangements before dealing with tariff reductions, and not attempt-ing to agree on "rationalization of industrial location." If the donor community provides funding to cover the foreign exchange risks of trade liberalization of trade among African countries, African govern-ments would be more willing to engage in such practices. Since closer economic cooperation among African countries is an important prin-ciple throughout the continent and a key element in the Lagos Plan of Action, donors and African governments should work together to achieve a greater measure of cooperation in trade expansion.

CONCLUSIONS

Africa's record of economic growth has been dismal for the past decade or more. GDP growth has lagged, GDP per capita has fallen, export growth has been slow, the productivity of investment has declined, and dependence on capital inflows has risen, leading to sharply rising ratios of debt to both GDP and exports. Agriculture, in particular, has grown slowly, resulting in declining yields per hectare and output per capita.

The likely payoff of better domestic policies is quite high, and if combined with adjustments on the part of the industrialized coun-tries, more rapid growth in Africa than is now forecast is possible. The package of policies for sustained growth involves actions by both the African countries and the donor community. African countries need to adopt reforms of exchange rates, import controls, and agri-cultural pricing systems to remove the extremes of subsidies and penalties inherent in their current arrangements. They must also adopt better counter-cyclical macro-economic management. An in-crease in non-project aid, such as the World Bank's structural adjust-ment loans, would be highly desirable to support such policy re-forms.

Trade policies can play a key role in determining African economic performance. Genuine progress toward greater economic independence will only come through adoption of policies which lead to a more effective and efficient use of Africa's resources—land, capital, people, foreign exchange, water. Not only must policies maximize the opportunities inherent in international trade, but they must also limit the effects on domestic economies of adverse movements in foreign markets. The international donor community can assist in the process of reform both by directly financing reform efforts and by reducing trade barriers to African exports.

NOTES

1. Measurements of the terms of trade are more complex and difficult to interpret than many other economic magnitudes, whether for a particular country or a group of countries. While the basic notion is simple (the import purchasing power of a given volume of exports), measuring prices of non-standardized goods is difficult, and any significant change in the composition of either imports or exports raises questions about the weightings to be used. Since success in economic development implies that the composition of both imports and exports will change dramatically, the weightings will necessarily change rapidly, and fixed weight indices may give misleading results.

2. The data used in these comparisons are taken primarily from World Bank sources. IMF data are also used. Although the groupings of countries are slightly different between the two sources, the overall results as judged from the two institutions' data are not affected by the differences in coverage and definitions. Detailed information on definitions and on the classifications of the countries can be found in the various issues of the World Bank's *World Development Report*, or the IMF's *World Economic Outlook*.

3. Evidence on this point is provided by Helleiner (1984).

4. The sequence of foreign exchange crises leading to trade policy regimes of a highly restrictive and distorting nature is spelled out well by Bhagwati (1978) and Krueger (1977) and confirmed by case studies undertaken for their joint efforts, as well as in earlier comparative studies of Little, Scitovsky and Scott (1970) and Balassa and Associates (1971). Kenya's resort to controls in successive foreign reserve crises in the 1970s is a clear case of a control system that arose largely in response to short-term emergencies, and where the certainty of direct controls in restricting imports was a decisive factor in their adoption over other measures that were considered. However high the costs, industries that promised to "save imports" could successfully recommend that competing imports be banned.

5. This judgment refers to the two decades ending around 1980. The most recent two to three years have not yet been included in any rigorous statistical analysis.

6. Alternatively stated, in some of the cases of lowest economic performance, the effect of an adverse external environment was made considerably worse due to the choice of policies by the countries involved.

7. Wheeler (1984) shows that lack of economic diversity and domestic political instability were major factors affecting the performance of African countries in the 1960s and 1970s, while Helleiner (1984) illustrates how import instability deteriorates economic performance in less diversified, low income countries.

8. Wheeler (1984) distinguishes between several measures of the quantity of OECD imports, using both simultaneous and lagged variables, and a single measure of the net barter terms of trade. The analysis is carried out for Africa as a whole, and there are numerous data problems in producing plausible variables for a diverse continent and its similarly diverse markets. However, the underlying relationships seem extremely strong, and the significance of each coefficient and the accuracy with which both the trend and the turning points of African growth are predicted are impressive.

9. The *World Development Report 1982* and *1983* both contain analyses pointing to the power of exchange rates in encouraging or discouraging economic performance; Balassa's (1983) work on Africa and on other countries' responses to external shocks gives the same result. Wheeler's analysis of African countries points to the power of the exchange rate, as does the IMF's analysis in its *World Economic Outlook* in 1983.

10. Wheeler's studies as well as those of Balassa show that the ability or willingness to adjust to changed external circumstances is important in Africa. Note, however, Helleiner's cautionary note that the lowest income countries may be unable to adjust import levels without substantial penalty to economic activity. This important issue is discussed below.

11. Harberger and Edwards (1982) compared countries, including African countries, which had to deal with falling international reserves. They concluded that "crises countries" which adopted policies to deal with falling reserves too late in the cycle demonstrated worse economic performance than countries which managed reserves with better anticipation of the consequences, and took actions earlier to stabilize their external positions.

12. Helleiner's studies are a major source of evidence here, though he would stress the need for externally financed liquidity to allow countries to ride out the cycles.

13. The 1983 *World Economic Outlook* contained an analysis of the effects of exchange rate changes on the trade balance in various groups of developing countries. In general, significant improvements were found in the countries that depreciated their currencies, relative to those that appreciated, during periods of adjustment to crisis. The least significant relationship was for the low-income country groups.

14. "Optimal" values were determined from the economic performance *within the 24 African countries themselves*. Thus, the results are based solely on conditions and performance in seventeen low-income and seven lower-middle-income countries of Africa. While Wheeler's results are extremely interesting and suggestive, they cannot be called definitive. For example, the civil

disturbance variable is a dummy variable used when there are coups or civil wars. The precise definition of any such variable is obviously a difficult empirical problem. The measurement of some of the other variables, too, such as those showing the ability to adjust to changed economic circumstances, could also be questioned. The effort is a most imaginative one, however, and is the best available.

15. I have described and analyzed elsewhere (Lewis, 1984) an "automatic adjustment mechanism" in mining economies. Based on the nature of mineral enterprises and the political economy of mining developments, the mechanism will tend to give mineral-rich countries a poorer record of performance than those without minerals. However, this mechanism can be circumvented to capture the potential gains from mineral developments (e.g., through preventing the effects of mineral export earnings from dominating the exchange rate, and ensuring that wage settlements in mining and government reflect conditions in the rest of the economy), rather than having them serve as a negative influence. I find it difficult to regard the presence of economically exploitable, non-renewable resources as necessarily retarding economic performance.

16. Such opponents often have other items on their agendas—for example, the conviction that such policies will retard the movement toward more economic independence and self-reliance, that market related solutions are inherently likely to generate unequal distributions of income, or that such policies are likely to lead to larger or more pernicious roles for transnational companies.

17. This general theme is elaborated in the recent survey of the world food equation by Mellor and Johnston (1984).

18. Achieving a better balance between export production incentives and import substitutes will not necessarily lead to a rising ratio of exports to GDP. As productivity rises, and real GDP per capita increases, domestic markets will grow. In some countries, prospects for substantial import replacement may exceed the prospects for major export growth, so that growth with more diversified output would result in a falling share of exports and imports to GDP. On the other hand, to the extent that there are substantial domestic spin-offs from a rapidly growing export sector, "export led" growth need not result in an increased ratio of exports to GDP either. Countries that have pursued a better balance of incentives have generally achieved more diversified economies, regardless of whether they have become more open or closed as measured by ratios of trade to growth.

19. Eicher and Baker (1982) point to over twenty studies (covering cotton, coffee, cocoa, palm oil and kernels, tobacco, rubber and groundnuts) which together provide "irrefutable evidence that smallholders are economic men," and incorporate price factors into production decisions (p. 90). They also conclude more generally (p. 30) that "there is unambiguous evidence that African farmers, traders and migrants will respond to economic incentives."

20. The growth of the manufacturing industry in Kenya in the 1970s was very closely related to the incentives provided by the tariff and import licens-

ing system. Indeed, the quickest and most accurate way of finding out what Kenya produces is to examine either the tariff schedule to identify the highest tariff rates or the import licensing schedules to see which goods are subject to the tightest restrictions.

21. When a country faces less than perfect elastic demand for its exports, then it is marginal revenues, not prices, which are given, and the country will affect its price by the quantities it attempts to sell. There are also circumstances, sometimes a matter of contract, where a country is limited in the quantity of the commodity it can sell at a given price. For relatively small producers, or for producers just entering a market, these constraints are less likely to apply.

22. In the strictest formal economic terms, if there were perfect capital markets and a variety of other condidtions, private decisions on profit maximization would lead to optimal investment patterns even for new industries with higher costs. Such conditions are not present in developing countries, particularly in Africa. Consequently, there is a strong case for government intervention in the pricing system.

23. After Ghana opted for heavily protected industrialization in the 1960s, for example, producers of all non-cocoa exports were being paid about one new cedi to earn a dollar, while they had to pay at least one and a half new cedis to purchase a dollar's worth of clothing produced by local industry.

24. This is a simple restatement of the principle of the effective rate of protection to an industry. For elaboration, and one of the first applications in Africa, see Steel's work (1972) on import substitution in Ghana.

25. Steel (1977) and Leith (1974) report cases in Ghana, Phelps and Wasow give examples in Kenya, and the World Bank gives an anonymous African example of such perverse results from excessive protection.

26. This factor is explicitly recognized by the Kenya government and is outlined carefully in the 1984 budget speech explaining the reform in tariff and indirect tax structure. Note that *if* productivity had grown rapidly, the new sectors could export and the problems of stagnation and balance of payments deterioration would be avoided.

27. *Some* discrimination against traditional exports is justified in many cases on both demand inelasticity and diversification grounds.

28. Ratios of this magnitude appear in a number of countries. The most well-documented cases are those reported by Leith, Steel, and Phelps and Wasow. Such relative rewards could not be defended in terms of differences in demand elasticities, either.

29. Note that discriminating modestly in favor of new import substitutes and new exports necessarily means modest discrimination against traditional exports in which a country has established cost advantages.

30. Botswana, which was dominated by mineral developments for fifteen years, has had growth rates of real manufacturing output and employment in excess of 10 percent per year throughout that period. The new industries sold partly in domestic and partly in export markets (primarily but not exclusively

regional). Botswana has the least restrictive import control system in Africa, and has provided little in the way of specific protection to new industrial activities until very recently, when a system providing equal incentive payments to import replacement and exporting industries was adopted.

31. The 1984 IMF *World Economic Outlook* and the World Bank's 1984 *World Development Report* both forecast recoveries in the OECD countries that are, in my view, a bit pessimistic. I think both fail to take account of the fact that many of the structural problems of the 1970s, including adjustment to a much higher level of energy prices and coping with some institutionalized aspects of inflation in the high-income countries, seem to be behind us. Since developments in the OECD countries are crucial to the forecasts for the developing countries, my view of the forecasts for the developing world is more optimistic as well. John Kendrick's recent article (1984) focusing on productivity growth in the United States articulates a number of reasons why the current forecasts of the OECD growth rates may be too pessimistic.

32. Eicher and Baker (1982) point out that the large volume of illegal and unrecorded trade among African countries is indicative of substantial potential trade if the penalties on international exchange were removed.

33. Neither the IMF nor the World Bank 1984 forecast addresses what, from Africa's viewpoint, may be a key issue: *Whatever* the trend in the next five to ten years, there is bound to be a cycle around it. Managing the cycles well is at least as important as the trend. The 1984 *World Development Report* (p. 31) also points to the serious consequences in Africa of poor management during the upswings of commodity markets in the 1970s.

34. "Modesty" may be in the eye of the beholder, but, in both penalties for traditional exports and protection for new industries, one should be skeptical of proposals for departing from international prices by more than twenty-five percent. I have no "scientific" basis for this, but the results of the comparative studies by Balassa and Associates (1971), Little, Scitovsky and Scott (1970), and Bhagwati (1978) and Krueger (1977) are suggestive of such limits.

35. It is important for the high-income countries to accept that some modest form of what appear to be subsidies will be required in most developing countries for their new exports. New activities have initially higher costs, and the tax, tariff, and exhange rate systems in Africa generally penalize domestic producers relative to world market prices. If the developed countries are serious about their desire to have Africa become more self-reliant, less dependent on aid, more attuned to using prices to guide their economies, and better able to buy exports from the industrial countries, then they will have to accept that African countries must give special encouragement to new exports aimed at all markets, and not retaliate with tariffs or quotas.

36. Helleiner's analysis stressing the importance of stability in import coefficients, and the adverse consequences of import instability adds strength to this point. Further, given the recent record in Africa on the productivity of investment, accumulation of reserves in order to avoid sharp reductions in imports would probably have resulted in more growth than the

use of those resources to undertake unproductive investments. If capital inflows had been aimed less at creating more projects and had been devoted instead to stabilizing import levels during low commodity prices, African economic performance would have been better over the past decade.

37. Zimbabwe's recent experience with a World Bank credit that provides for significantly easier access of exporters to necessary imports is a good example of one step toward administrative reforms that would support the objectives of using trade to promote growth. Zambia's experiment with allowing exporters to retain a portion of their foreign exchange to meet requirements for imports of raw materials and spare parts also appears to be quite successful.

38. The use of "efficient" here simply refers to the amount of real goods and services produced, as valued by the costs facing the country. Under exceptionally distorted pricing structures projects are chosen that simply deliver much less value for money from a national viewpoint, even if they are privately profitable (or, if undertaken by a parastatal, completely cost-covering). And, projects which would provide more real goods per unit of capital, foreign exchange, or highly skilled labor, are not taken up because they are not cost-covering (or privately profitable) at the existing set of prices.

39. In the early 1980s the gross capital flows to Africa were around $12 or $13 billion, of which $8 or $9 billion was from bilateral and multilateral grants and loans. Amortization was about $2 to $3 billion on total debt, but only around $0.5 to $1 billion on debt to bilateral and multilateral aid agencies. The amortization figure is rising rapidly, however, and in the next two or three years will rise to between $6 and $9 billion on total debt, and around $3 billion on aid to official agencies. It is this latter figure that could be significantly affected, and if it were to be done through forgiveness, the interest burden could be reduced as well. These numbers are based on IMF and World Bank sources.

40. Helleiner, one of the most persuasive of the critics of the IMF activities in Africa, has aimed much of his criticism at the Fund's failure to consider individual characteristics of the countries it is called to help. Having greater flexibility to craft the solutions to the problems would increase the likelihood that reforms would be entered into with greater conviction on the part of African governments.

41. There could be more elaborate forms of this payments clearing arrangement, which owes its concept to the European Payments Union and the mechanism for distributing assistance under the Marshall Plan. I have in mind something a good deal less elaborate, and, given the relatively small size of existing intra-regional trade, a good deal less expensive.

42. The World Bank reported that in the 1976–78 period the traditional primary commodities listed in Table A.3 (Appendix I) accounted for about 83% of Africa's total exports, leaving about US$4.5 billion in other exports. The total is not a great deal larger today, given the disastrous export performance noted earlier. This compares with a figure for 1982 imports into the industrial market economies of $US 1,200 billion.

REFERENCES

Balassa, Bela, and Associates. 1971. *The Structure of Protection in Developing Countries*. Baltimore: Johns Hopkins University Press.

Balassa, Bela, and Associates. 1983. "Policy Responses to External Shocks in Sub-Saharan African Countries," *Journal of Policy Modelling* 5(1)(March).

Bhagwati, Jagdish N. 1978. *Foreign Trade Regimes and Economic Development (XI): Anatomy and Consequences of Exchange Control Regimes*. Cambridge, Mass.: Ballinger.

Eicher, Carl K. and Doyle C. Baker. 1982. "Research on Agricultural Development in Sub-Saharan Africa: A Critical Survey," East Lansing: Michigan State University, International Development Paper, No. 1.

Gordon, David F. and Joan C. Parker. 1984. "The World Bank and Its Critics: The Case of Sub-Saharan Africa," Ann Arbor: University of Michigan, Center for Research on Economic Development Discussion Paper No. 108.

Harberger, Arnold C. and Sebastian Edwards. 1982. "Lessons of Experience Under Fixed Exchange Rates," in Mark Gersovitz, Carlos F. Diaz-Alejandro, Gustav Ranis and Mark R. Rosenzweig, eds., *The Theory and Experience of Economic Development: Essays in Honor of Sir W. Arthur Lewis*. London: George Allen.

Helleiner, G. K. 1983. "The IMF and Africa in the 1980s," *Princeton Essays in International Finance* 152(July).

Helleiner, G. K. 1984. "Outward Orientation, Import Instability and African Economic Growth: An Empirical Investigation," in Sanjaya Lall and Frances Stewart, eds., *Paul Streeten Festschrift*, forthcoming.

IMF. 1980. *World Economic Outlook*. Washington, D.C.

IMF. 1984. *World Economic Outlook*. Occasional Paper No. 27. Washington, D.C.

Kendrick, John W. 1984. "Productivity Gains Will Continue," *Wall Street Journal*, August 29.

Krueger, Anne O. 1977. *Foreign Trade Regimes and Economic Development (IX): Liberalization Attempts and Consequences*. Cambridge, Mass.: Ballinger.

Leith, J. Clark. 1974. *Foreign Trade Regimes and Economic Development (II): Ghana*. New York and London: Columbia University Press.

Lewis, Stephen R., Jr. 1984. "Development Problems of the Mineral Rich Countries," in M. Syrquin, L. Taylor and L.E. Westphal, eds., *Economic Structure and Performance: Essays in Honor of Hollis B. Chenery*. San Diego: Academic Press.

Lewis, W. A. 1980. "The Slowing Down of the Engine of Growth," *The American Economic Review* (4)(September).

Little, Ian, Tibor Scitovsky, and Maurice Scott. 1970. *Industry and Trade in Some Developing Countries*. Paris: Oxford University Press.

Mellor, John W. and Bruce F. Johnston. 1984. "The World Food Equation," *Journal of Economic Literature* XXII(2)(June).

Phelps, M. G., and D. Wasow. n.d. "Measuring Protection and Its Effects in Kenya." Working Paper No. 37. Nairobi: Institute for Development Studies.

Steel, W. F. 1972. "Import Substitution and Excess Capacity in Ghana," *Oxford Economic Papers* 24(2)(July): 212–40.

Steel, W. F. 1977. *Small-Scale Employment and Production in Developing Countries: Evidence from Ghana*. New York and London: Praeger.

Wheeler, David. 1984. "Sources of Stagnation in Sub-Saharan Africa," *World Development* 12(1)(January): 1–23.

World Bank. 1982. *World Development Report*. New York: Oxford University Press.

World Bank. 1983. *World Development Report*. New York: Oxford University Press.

World Bank. 1984. *World Development Report*. New York: Oxford University Press.

CHAPTER EIGHTEEN

Foreign Aid in Africa: Here's the Answer—Is It Relevant to the Question?

Robert J. Berg

By almost any measure, sub-Saharan Africa is extraordinarily dependent upon the goods, services, and funds supplied by foreign aid. Except for the radical right and left, almost all analysts concerned with Africa's deep developmental crisis believe that future aid flows will be of continuing and perhaps growing importance. Africa's development partners have played an important role in the continent's economic development and must take both some of the credit and some of the blame for its current predicament. Africa is where it is today in part because of aid, and its future will be strongly shaped by what donors do and how they do it.

In this chapter, the effectiveness of aid to Africa will be described and recommendations will be made for increasing the benefits aid can bring to African development. While other chapters in this volume make recommendations on what development options present the most promise for Africa, this study is restricted to the mechanism through which many of these options are likely to be financed.

DESCRIPTION OF FOREIGN AID TO AFRICA

For decades, the developing countries have been the recipients of major flows of resources from the developed world, averaging over $100 billion per year in the last four years.[1] Nearly two-thirds has been nonconcessional and has recently included major roll-overs of past private debt. The remaining one-third is development assistance, of which about $35 billion a year is official aid and $2 billion a year from non-governmental organizations.

Africa is dependent upon the aid flows provided from official and private donors. Total financial flows to Africa are estimated to have averaged $13 billion in recent years, just over half of which has been concessional. While Africa's 369 million people constitute approximately 12 percent of the people in the developing countries,[2] Africa receives 22 percent of official development assistance (ODA).[3]

Twenty-five of the 45 countries in sub-Saharan Africa depend upon aid for over two-thirds of their total externally provided financial receipts. Of these, 15, including many of the smallest countries, are dependent by more than 90 percent on aid. According to the UN Economic Commission for Africa (ECA), aid to this area equalled almost 40 percent of its total imports and over half its total investment in 1981.[4]

In 1982, official aid averaged 5.85 percent of Africa's GNP[5] (excluding Nigeria, the average was 7.52 percent), although there were wide variations, running from .05 percent for Nigeria to 51.4 percent for Cape Verde. In 1982, ODA made up 19 percent of total gross domestic investment in all of sub-Saharan Africa. Excluding the oil-exporting countries, however, ODA was 44 percent of gross domestic investment.[6]

Africa's precarious international debt situation heightens the importance of foreign aid. No other part of the world has as serious a debt burden relative to GDP. While the total debt is relatively small compared to that of Latin America, Africa has beaten a path to the Paris Club to reschedule its debts with far greater frequency than any other area of the world.[7] Half of Africa's debt arises from past foreign aid, as compared to only 15 percent for Latin America.

While Africa's external finance situation is extremely serious now, barring unexpected changes in Africa's terms of trade, it is very likely that this situation will deteriorate. Without a major push, aid levels are likely to remain constant, while repayments from past loaned aid will rise. Hence, net aid levels are likely to decline over the rest of the decade. Similarly, substantial repayments to the IMF and commercial creditors are due in the short and medium term. New investment in Africa has tailed off in recent years and few expect much in the way of a recovery over the next several years.

Finally, it should be noted that Africa is far more dependent than any other part of the world on foreign sources for the goods and services most often required for development. Other parts of the world, reaping the benefits of their past development, can tap local sources of industrial and service production to a far greater extent. The need for a larger proportion of foreign exchange to carry out development initiatives and the absence of a strong and reliable export base has made Africa highly dependent upon foreign aid to finance its development efforts.

Aid is traditionally categorized by type: technical assistance, capital assistance (both project and non-project aid), and food aid. Capital assistance accounts for two-thirds of concessional aid to Africa, some $4.6 billion a year. This transfer of foreign goods to Africa is largely packaged in project aid. For many years, African officials have called for this aid to be switched to a non-project, budgetary support basis. To an increasing extent, this is occurring, but not to ease administration as much as to increase donor leverage in economic policy discussions.

Technical assistance is still of great significance in Africa; indeed, the area may receive up to 75 percent of all technical assistance provided by donors.[8] While the financial sum involved is large—about 25 percent of all aid to Africa[9]—what is of greater significance is the sheer number (perhaps 20,000) of resident foreign technicians in Africa, particularly in the francophone countries. While the days when major African development issues were decided solely by foreign-supplied technicians are largely over, the influence of foreign consultants is still great, particularly when new initiatives are designed or launched. And the costs are very large indeed—two to three times the cost in their home countries and 10 to 25 times the cost of sometimes comparable local experts.

Food aid to Africa normally amounts to about $650 million a year, but in the 1984–86 emergency, it is running at over $2 billion a year.[10] Emergency food programs have played a crucial role in meeting African food needs in the 1973–74 and current droughts, providing about half of total net cereals imports. Non-emergency food aid, used for school lunch and food-for-work programs, for example, has also been a continuing part of donor programs.

Because of this book's special interest in U.S. policy, it is worth paying particular attention to the size and composition of U.S. aid to Africa. Such assistance comes through bilateral aid channels and through major U.S. contributions to multilateral programs that benefit Africa. Bilateral U.S. aid to Africa has grown fairly rapidly in the last several years and now is over $1 billion excluding sizeable emergency aid (another $1 billion in 1985–86). The main components of this aid are noted in Table A.12 in Appendix I, showing changes since 1980. Military aid has been included in this calculation to indicate that along with Economic Support Fund assistance, the United States now gives about 46 percent of its non-emergency assistance to Africa for open political and military purposes.

TRENDS AND ISSUES IN AID TO AFRICA

Public and private international donors operate through or with the consent of national governments in developing countries. This is more than a diplomatic nicety to African governments: It is a sign that Africans want to be and in most cases are in charge of their development.

Donors have respected and helped to underwrite Africa's development goals, in part because donors have often participated in the planning process, but also because it is clearly in the donor's short-term political interest to support the development aspirations of local political leaders. With perhaps a stronger commitment to reinforcing national plans, multilateral donors have also strengthened and subsidized national planning efforts of African officials. Some continue to do so, but others, most notably the World Bank, have been seeking to modify national planning strategies. By and large, however, local development planning has been backed by donor finance. When planning has been good, this has been beneficial; when it has been incompetent or corrupt, the donor has been an accomplice.

DONOR TRENDS

The development aims of African governments have evolved from a post-independence preoccupation with basic infrastructure and institution-building to a more recent concern with the rural sector and its accompanying infrastructure and service needs.

Donors have not been passive observers of changes in development trends in Africa, however. They have their own agendas and interests which often change. Some of these changes have come about through normal learning and adjustment to new problems, but other shifts have resulted from changes in the donor's political environment, new personnel, the need to present a new face on programs to sell them to legislatures, or simple-minded impatience with existing programs.

Incomplete data from the Development Assistance Committee of OECD indicates some of the major changes that have occurred. Table 18.1 shows a major increase in support to agriculture over the past few years, sizeable increases in health and education, and a decline in general economic support, the latter having been reversed more recently. For the United States, the shifts from infrastructure and institution-building in the 1960s to basic human needs in 1973 and back to institution-building and policy reform in 1981 were far more abrupt than was warranted.

While in the past, these shifts in donor preferences have sometimes been at odds with African planners, in the last year a new pattern of convergence has occurred. The major donors and African planners agree at least rhetorically on the major priorities for Africa's development: emergency assistance now emphasizing food aid and debt reform; rehabilitation emphasizing balance of payments aid; and long-term development based on population planning, agricultural development (especially food self-sufficiency), and related supporting development of human resources and non-agricultural sectors. The agreed-on agenda contains a huge dose of policy and structural reform. All of this presents a tremendous opportunity to undertake reinforcing actions and to greatly increase the effectiveness of domestic and foreign development assistance.

In so doing, there are also very great opportunities to capitalize on the lessons of previous development experiences. The evidence of past experience is more readily available now than in any previous period, because in recent years donors have heavily invested in evaluation of their aid programs. A main question is whether policymakers will consult this evidence as they consider and undertake policy changes, or operate in the absence of an informed reading of the past and future.

Donors influence the outcome of activities they support not only by choosing sectors and strategies, but by how they act individually and as a group. Over the last few decades the following has occurred in donor aid to Africa.

More Donors and Projects   There are many donors active in Africa now and there are likely to be more in the future. If it is hard to match

TABLE 18.1
SECTORAL ALLOCATION OF OFFICIAL DEVELOPMENT ASSISTANCE (ODA) TO AFRICA, 1978–82
(in current $ millions)

Sectors	1978	1979	1980	1981	1982	1978–82 Sectoral Total
Energy	137	221	534	267	287	1,446
Food & Agriculture	866	1,078	1,359	1,655	1,880	6,838
Health	158	281	266	414	543	1,662
Education	165	186	187	340	299	1,177
Social Infrastructure & Welfare	133	91	162	177	205	768
Transportation, Storage & Communication	833	827	981	811	990	4,442
Industry, Construction & Mining	126	89	215	138	276	844
Trade & Tourism	24	66	42	20	72	224
Gen'l Economic Support	1,650	1,054	1,509	1,229	1,157	6,599
Other & Unallocated	195	75	144	118	225	757
Total	4,287	3,968	5,399	5,169	5,934	24,757

SOURCE: Data from an unpublished study by OECD, Paris. Because of gaps in information relating to sectoral allocations, yearly aid totals from this table do *not* equal total ODA assistance to Africa.

program needs and donors now, it will be harder in the future, as donor-financed projects and entities continue to clutter the physical and public administration landscape.

More Field Staff   More donors are recognizing that international assistance cannot be administered solely from the home country with only infrequent trips to the field to consult with African governments. Placing more and better people in the field has enabled some donors to delegate more decision-making to their field staffs which often helps speed implementation.

Greater Flexibility in the Rules   Too much aid is tied to home-country procurement and legislated or administrative rules which seem reasonable in the abstract but are difficult to carry out in practice. In spite of almost interminable negotiations, the Development Assistance Committee of the OECD has failed to achieve landmark reforms. Some individual donors have increased their flexibility to permit more local buying and more ease in adjusting projects mid-stream. But there are disturbing counter-trends toward more tied aid, engendering more corruption and less value.

Some Softening of the Terms   Donors were slow to react to Africa's need for soft credit, but made generally appropriate changes in the 1970s. Some donors have even forgiven past ODA loans to the poorest countries, but the United States has refused to do so.

Increased Coordination of Aid   Efforts to coordinate African aid have been in direct response to the trauma of its crises. As a consequence of the 1973–74 drought, the Club du Sahel was created to coordinate donor work in the Sahelian states. A back-to-back grouping of Sahelian governments—the Permanent Interstate Committee for Drought Control in the Sahel—was also created to facilitate working with the donors. Both institutions have been useful and have worked together admirably. In the late 1970s, seven countries which account for some 65 percent of bilateral aid to Africa (Belgium, Canada, France, Italy, United Kingdom, United States, and West Germany) formed the Cooperation for Development in Africa to jointly analyze sectoral strategy questions and to coordinate their donor programs. In addition, since 1984, UN agencies have drawn closer together under the stimulus of the UN Secretary-General, and the World Bank has also been more active in coordinating donor assistance. More donors and

African governments now recognize that a better coordinated donor effort is required and the barriers to coordination are beginning to fall.

All of the above characteristics and trends greatly affect how well the donors are able to contribute to African development. At present, however, two major factors overshadow all others in their impact on African development today: the drought and how it has affected African needs and the consequent new demands on donors; and, second, a great shortage of recurrent finance and an absence of development finance generated from domestic sources. Host country counterpart staff and funds have always been in short supply. Now, where such staff are available, their salaries, fuel, and support rations have been cut so drastically that their effectiveness is greatly impaired. Donor agencies are faced with aiding institutions which do not have the financial capacity to undertake anything new. To a major extent, the donors inadvertently exacerbated the recurrent finance problem by shifting in the 1970s to types of development activities requiring large amounts of recurrent support. While in theory, major donors now are willing to finance more recurrent costs, in practice a major shift in financing formulas has not occurred.

U.S. AID IN PERSPECTIVE

Among the donor programs that have changed the most is that of the United States. While there has been some consistency of approach beneath changes in rhetoric (hence long-time programs in Liberia and Zaire and support to many institutions in Africa, and a consistency, at least on paper, in functionally concentrating on agriculture, health, education, and population), there has been a great amount of real shifting. The following are notable:

- A tilt toward Africa: more budget; an attempt to upgrade field leadership and staff in key Washington posts; more leadership internationally on some African development issues; and creation of the African Development Foundation to work with grassroots organizations.

- A more politicized program: Politically justified economic aid is not only 34 percent[11] of U.S. economic aid to Africa, but it is so mixed in with "Development Assistance" (non-political aid funds) in many country programs that the motives for the entire U.S. aid program have become confused. To an increasingly large extent, the quid pro quo for U.S. aid is political loyalty rather than economic performance. The United States' reluctance to respond quickly to emergency food needs in Ethiopia and Mozambique in 1983 is held up by the American religious and NGO communities as evidence of the heavy political basis of U.S. aid.[12]

- A major shift in content: From the concentration on basic human needs that was evident in the 1970s and remains at the core of USAID's legislative mandate, interest has now shifted to programs emphasizing the private sector and market forces, changes in developing country pricing policies, human resource development, and science and technology. While it has been argued that the shift was more in interpretation than in basic philosophy, the shift in rhetoric was major and a large number of USAID programs in Africa have been changed as a result.[13]

AID ISSUES RAISED BY THE WORLD BANK

In contrast to the U.S. program, which as of early 1986 had produced no clear, long-run game plan for aiding Africa, the World Bank developed a fairly clear program in 1981 on how it wished to assist African development. In its celebrated *Accelerated Development in Sub-Saharan Africa: An Agenda for Action*,[14] the Bank focused on a number of strategy issues. Uppermost were policy reform to provide more incentives for farmers and the private sector; emphasis over the medium term on agriculture for export; more efficiency in agricultural and human resources; reduced emphasis on industrialization; more efficiency and expansion of energy resources; and greatly increased aid levels in order to facilitate recommended policy reforms.

Public reaction to questions of policy reform recommended in the "Berg Report" has been so strong that its recommendations on aid have almost entirely escaped critical attention. The report implies that aid is perhaps the major vehicle for rich countries to help Africa. While the report did not analyze the effectiveness of past aid to Africa, it did offer several important suggestions on how aid can be made more useful in the future, some of which have been acted upon by the World Bank, others which have not. The suggestions include:

- Increasing assistance in formulating and supporting policy reforms through such mechanisms as technical assistance and nonproject aid (acted upon).

• Continuing major reliance on project assistance (acted upon).

• More flexibility in project design and administration, including evolutionary design models such as pilot projects.

• Increasing local cost and recurrent cost financing over relatively longer periods of time.

• More harmonization of donor procedures and more donor coordination in general, although the report (p. 130) cautions that "some African governments are unenthusiastic. They fear 'ganging up,' as well as a loss of 'maneuverability'."

• Continuing substantial technical assistance to increase the local management of aid-funded projects.

These suggestions will be revisited after consideration has been given to a question that has been absent from many discussions on aid to Africa: How effective has aid been? In brief, is it an answer to the kinds of questions facing Africa?

HAS INTERNATIONAL ASSISTANCE BEEN EFFECTIVE IN AFRICA?

We can now answer the question better than ever before. Until recently, opinion on the effectiveness of aid was based on anecdotal evidence often collected by writers representing the political extremes. Evidence has also been provided from econometric studies such as the famous Bariloche model. In 1976, the Fundacion Bariloche concluded that aid was only modestly helpful in improving socio-economic well-being, a finding that many intellectuals in developing countries interpreted to mean that aid was a luxury most countries could live without.

The Bariloche researchers asked the right question: Are countries better or worse off with aid? Unfortunately, this question cannot be answered for Africa in general since so few states have been without aid. Further, it would be meaningless to relate economic performance only to inflows of aid. The next best level of analysis would be to ask whether aided projects perform better or worse than unaided projects. This is possible in some African settings where larger portfolios of unassisted development projects exist, but little evaluative work has been done on them.

While whether or not aided projects and programs work may not be the most perfect question, for the first time donors are in a position to answer it. For over a decade, the World Bank has been collecting evaluative information on its portfolio. USAID has been conducting an important series of impact evaluations since 1977,[15] as have Canada, West Germany, Netherlands, United Kingdom, and the EEC. Some of the major NGOs also have evaluative information on their portfolios. In addition, the Western bilateral donors have begun to compare their evaluation results through the Evaluation Experts Working Group of the OECD's Development Assistance Committee.[16]

A number of the donors have recently begun to aggregate their findings in very useful ways. The available information permits a large number of observations about the effectiveness of aid in general and to Africa specifically.[17]

ECONOMIC AND SOCIAL RESULTS

The general economic setting of the past two decades is well-known: Although overall GNP growth rates are not very different from other regions of the world, Africa's tremendous increase in population has meant very slow growth and even declining per capita GNP. While we do not have the techniques to judge aid's effect on GNP growth, aid has been an important mainstay of development budgets and has been responsible for a great amount of new investment. As noted above, in 1982, for example, ODA represented 19 percent of overall gross domestic investment in Africa. Excluding the oil exporters, ODA was 44 percent of gross domestic investment.

Non-Project Aid   Donors have tried to influence the macro-picture through their overall aid programs, particularly through non-project aid, most of which has provided general budgetary support intended to foster specific reforms. This is a difficult type of intervention to evaluate since the donor's funds blend into general foreign exchange holdings and government budgets so the additional development uses cannot be traced. Even so, it is surprising that so little is known about the effectiveness of non-project aid, given the current emphasis on facilitating policy reforms through this mechanism.

Bilateral donors have not kept a very good evaluation record on their non-project assistance, as the Development Assistance Committee's evaluation group discovered. An exception is the USAID study of program aid to Zimbabwe in 1981, which found very efficient and effective use of post-independence funds provided by the United States to help meet a backlog of import needs.[18]

The World Bank's record of assessing its non-project lending is a good deal better, but much of it concentrates on South Asia.[19] The Bank's analysis claims that countries receiving major non-project Bank aid performed substantially better than non-recipients (e.g., a GDP growth rate of 4.5 percent in 1981–83 versus 2 percent for all other oil-importing developing countries, and a greater reduction in current account deficits than other countries).

Two recent studies shed additional light on non-project assistance. Innovative work by Joan Nelson[20] highlights the importance of taking national political and administrative features into account when crafting strategies of structural reform. Donors have not been sensitive enough to these factors.

In a review of the World Bank's structural adjustment program, former Bank official Stanley Please maintains that the Bank enjoys a comparative advantage over other donors in helping develop and negotiate policy reforms in such regions as sub-Saharan Africa.[21] He argues that Bank project lending often calls for the same kind of analysis given to non-project assistance, but that projects are an awkward way of achieving policy reforms and may indeed undercut simultaneously given non-project assistance. Please believes that the World Bank ought to concentrate far more on non-project assistance to achieve policy reforms. Other donors, he feels, are able to carry the bulk of project assistance needs.

The evidence from project lending bears this out to the extent that project outcomes are influenced by the sectoral and policy setting. Donors have frequently found that projects could not be effectively carried out while the sectoral setting was unfavorable or needed adjustment.

While there is a clear need for non-project aid in a large number of African settings due to urgent requirements for inputs and to help foster basic policy reforms, it is important to realize that the evidence of final impact of such lending is almost non-existent. It is simply an informed article of faith that the poor will be better off if non-project assistance is given rather than project aid. Such articles of faith are not permitted in project lending.

The question is whether the sole quid pro quo for aid ought to be policy adjustment or whether aid ought to accomplish more or other things. The case for more reliance on non-project assistance is considerably enhanced if there is proof that a government is able to administer programs well, delivers goods and services to those who need them, and even has the capacity to expand its administrative reach by undertaking new activities. This is a case which has long been made in India, but can be made only rarely in Africa. Indeed, it is project aid which can best build the administrative capabilities needed to be able to use non-project aid.

It is equally clear, however, that the project system upon which most donors will rely in Africa is not without its distortions of the macro-economic scene. Unlike non-project assistance, project assistance negotiated through the national government (the aid mode official donors and NGOs use) has drawbacks, as was pointed out in an EEC study of the results of four of its Africa programs. Project aid was bound to "fragment the development process, create development enclaves isolated from the economic, social, and administrative context, make it more difficult to carry out development experiments, particularly in rural areas, and make implementation of the national plans more hazardous."[22]

Thus, both non-project and project assistance have defects and advantages. Historically, there has been a pendulum swing between the two kinds of aid. We are now in a period where the swing is toward non-project aid. What kind of aid best suits Africa must be answered through country-specific analysis, but there are some relevant observations:

- Non-project aid may well be necessary for the short run due to the need for import finance and policy reform which should be instituted soon. In a well-ordered world, such assistance would be abundantly available under longer-term financing from the IMF. The argument by Please that the Bank has the ability to best argue through policy reform may be correct, but that ability ought to be more apparent in the IMF.

- The need for technical aid can in no way be met by non-project aid.

- The requirement for longer-term capital assistance can be supplied through non-project aid, but this takes very well-established administrative staffs. In Africa, there will still need to be a significant amount of project aid to help form and administer new and particularly larger development investments.

The bulk of aid to Africa now ought to be non-project, but ought to return soon to project assistance. There is no question that the relationship between the two kinds of aid must be more complementary. Good non-project aid ought to enable projects (however financed) to function well, and good larger projects ought to be crafted to reinforce the policy changes more centrally sought by non-project aid. Better coordination between donors and better collaboration with African states will improve the art of using these aid mechanisms.

Project Aid   For many years, it was thought unnecessary to compile evidence on the effectiveness of projects aided by donors. After all, ports, highways, universities, elementary schools, airports, health clinics, industrial plants are all in clear evidence, built, being used, and often accompanied by signs attributing the financing to specific donors. But some of the buildings are empty. And some of the trained staff are no longer around. And some projects didn't turn out the way they were intended and may unintentionally harm the well-being of people.

Most major donors conduct case study evaluations after the donor involvement in the project has ended. Critics have questioned the objectivity of evaluations prepared by the donors themselves, but in reality, the reports are often very hard-hitting and include discussions of "failures" which biased organizations would never circulate.

ECONOMIC RESULTS

The results of a large number of evaluations indicate that aid has generally been put to productive purposes, but that aid to Africa has yielded a lower economic return than in most other areas.

The World Bank has assessed a large number of projects in its Post-Project Audit Reports. These project evaluations pay particular attention to estimating the economic rate of return[23] of projects a year or so after the Bank has finished disbursing funds for the activity. IDA credits are particularly relevant to Africa.[24]

On the basis of discussions with other donors, it is fair to conclude that projects in Africa do not perform as well as projects in more robust economies. Aided projects generally do succeed in Africa—although not by as large a margin as in other parts of the world—but this relative success is not well appreciated.

The World Bank's reports are large enough in number to permit a useful analysis of economic results by sector of activity. The ex post economic rates of return for Bank projects started and completed in the 1961–81 period are shown in Table 18.2.[25]

There is not a sufficient volume of evaluation data from other donors to meaningfully aggregate African results by sector. But it is worth noting what is available. Canada has compiled the results of 62 project evaluations, 33 of which are from Africa. The summary results are shown in Table 18.3.[26]

The study of USAID data, using a 1-10 rating system (1 worst, 10 best), showed the sectoral results in Table 18.4.[27] From this data, one begins to gain a small idea of donor diversity and differences in sectoral performance. Perhaps surprisingly, agriculture in West Africa and transport in general come out well. Education projects are the best sector in AID's analysis, but are a source of problems to Canada (and are not assessed by the Bank in this analysis). The 92 IDA/IBRD West Africa projects score far higher than Latin America in three of four sectors, but East Africa projects score low in a number of sectors. USAID and World Bank data indicate that neither institution has had much success with potable water projects, perhaps because tracing their economic benefits is a complex business.

Other studies and an examination of individual reports illuminate the sectoral results more clearly.

Irrigation   A large number of the Bank's agricultural projects are in irrigation. Bank and USAID experiences are about the same: These projects are expensive, difficult to carry out, frequently have management problems, and yield less satisfactory results than other sectors.

Rural Development   World Bank results in Africa up to the late 1970s were mixed, averaging a 15 percent return, but have since deteriorated significantly, particularly in East Africa where fully half of Bank agricultural projects evaluated in 1974–85 were judged to be failures.[28] Integrated rural development projects have faced very tough problems everywhere, but they have not been replaced by a more logical theory of rural development.

Livestock   Almost all donors report major problems with livestock projects, particularly those aimed at improving the economic lot of nomadic herders in Africa, an area of work where social knowledge is particularly important and often lacking among donors. African livestock projects could be improved, however, by treating them as experiments—drawing them up and staffing them carefully and monitoring them closely.

TABLE 18.2
IDA/IBRD LOANS AND CREDITS: ECONOMIC RATES OF RETURN, 1961–81
(Average by Project Estimated at Audit)

Sector	East Africa	West Africa	Europe/ Middle E./ No. Africa	Latin America/ Carib.	East Asia/ Pacific	South Asia	Total	No. of Credits
Trans.	14.5	20.1	18.6	22.6	21.9	22.2	20.0	185
Agric.	9.7	15.4	18.0	12.7	21.7	27.7	16.8	221
Power	14.0	12.7	15.8	11.7	13.2	30.0	13.5	62
Indust.	3.0	—	16.3	13.6	25.0	14.3	14.6	21
Telecom.	14.0	—	26.0	18.0	19.1	19.9	19.9	28
Water	9.1	9.9	10.0	6.7	5.0	—	8.4	21
Total	11.7	17.4	17.6	15.8	20.1	23.7	17.3	538
No. of Credits	78	92	85	138	92	53	538	

SOURCE: World Bank data prepared by Clarence Gulick, Task Force on Concessional Flows, work in progress.

Agricultural Research and Extension   USAID's study of agricultural research programs showed relatively good results, as did a far more comprehensive Bank report of 128 projects in 10 countries, four of them in Africa.[29] Both studies indicate the need to carefully identify research priorities and to better link them with national agricultural planning and implementation. The USAID report stressed the value of a multi-disciplinary approach in planning such interventions (farming systems research).

Education   USAID studies corroborate World Bank and other findings that educational activities are often quite productive and satisfactory donor projects in Africa. The 1980 *World Development Report* concluded that investments in education were one of the highest pay-off options in the field of development.

TABLE 18.3

CANADIAN AID (CIDA) PROJECT EVALUATIONS: IMPACT ON TARGET GROUPS

Sector	Projects	Percentage of Total (234) Findings		
		Positive	Mixed	Negative
Agric. & Rural Development	15	64	4	32
Water Supply	3	74	10	16
Forestry	3	89	—	11
Education	16	52	9	39
Health	3	62	13	25
Cooperatives	1	25	25	50
Energy	2	67	—	33
Transportation	4	62	3	35
Mining	2	33	33	33
Environment	2	88	—	12
Others	11	53	23	25
Total	62[a]	62	9	29

[a]33 Africa; 18 Latin America; 11 Asia

Health and Population   Health and population interventions could benefit from greater systematic assessment. A frequent stumbling block for village health programs has been the inability to cover recurrent costs. Charging user fees for health and other social services may be one way out of the dilemma. Potable water is one of the very few areas in which comparative evaluative work has been done on all donors in one field. In a survey in Tanzania,[30] it was found that the Netherlands ran especially good programs, the Australians ran very costly and inappropriate programs, and nine other donors fell in between. The survey highlighted the great costs to a poor country of carrying multiple supply and maintenance systems instituted by donors using separate approaches and procurement channels. An out-

TABLE 18.4
OVERALL RATING OF U.S. AID PROJECTS BY REGION
AND SECTOR

Region/Sector	Rating[a]
Africa	6.45
Near East/North Africa	6.21
Asia	7.50
Latin America/Caribbean	7.88
Total	7.28
Agr. Research	7.37
Irrigation	6.55
Rural Elec.	7.82
Rural Roads	7.14
Education	7.99
Potable Water	6.60
Other	7.21
Total	7.28

[a]Scale: 1 (worst) to 10 (best)

come of this survey was the adoption of a national policy in Tanzania favoring low technology (hand-dug village wells) which can be maintained with locally available materials and skills.

Infrastructure   The record is mixed to good. Donors are generally skilled in planning the technical aspects of infrastructural projects. Donor-supplied contractors and/or supervisory services have assured the completion of many "concrete" projects throughout Africa. Numerous studies have emphasized the need to better maintain such projects, but the record of deterioration of Africa's infrastructure is more complex than what is apparent at first glance. It is easy to see if roads are used. But infrastructure projects have also brought a set of social and economic issues such as shifts in land holdings as greedy urbanites benefit from their knowledge of planned new roads by buying up rural land and displacing the planned beneficiaries (Liberia, 1981); or falling standards of living as useless trinkets from the urban economy reach rural residents while new ways of earning money to pay for these luxuries do not (Ethiopia, 1972). Infrastructure is often necessary, but inadequate by itself to improve standards of living. The political role infrastructure projects can play in linking parts of new nations together has not been well analyzed in donor evaluations, but ways of increasing the social and economic value of such projects are identified in these studies.

Food Aid   Assessments of food aid point to the particular importance of child feeding, emergency, and food-for-work programs in areas where food stocks are low to nonexistent or where the poor lack the purchasing power to obtain food. There has been difficulty, however, in effectively targeting the benefits from long-term projects aimed at improving the nutritional well-being of selected groups. Many improvements are needed in this area.[31] Chronic food shortages in Africa in recent years have made food aid a permanent feature of assistance to the continent.[32] Food aid has negative side effects on recipients, however, causing a shift in urban consumer tastes from indigenous to imported foods and, in turn, a foreign exchange drain in the future. Negative effects of bulk food aid are noted but are considered avoidable and not pervasive.[33]

This rapid survey has not covered evaluations published by the United Nations, which tend to be consistent with the findings of the bilateral and other multilateral donors. A word should be added about the evaluation evidence from non-governmental organizations (NGOs), particularly in view of the large number of American NGOs in Africa and the significant amount of funding handled by them. At best, NGOs display commendable economy of action, flexibility of implementation, and effective results with small, community-oriented projects. But these organizations can also be careless, easily over-extended, not well-coordinated with other activities, and economically inefficient. As with official donors, organizations have different strengths and the same organization can perform well in one area and very poorly in another.

While the previous section highlighted a part of the growing literature on the economic impact of assistance to developing countries, the equally important social results of foreign aid must also be considered.

Africa's economic woes are well-known, but its social situation is less well appreciated. A useful yardstick is the Physical Quality of Life Index (PQLI), an aggregate of infant mortality, life expectancy at age one, and literacy. It is clear that Africa has the greatest difficulty in meeting basic social needs of life, literacy, and health. The area with the highest PQLI is North America with 96, whereas Africa's PQLI is 43. A measure of closing the gap in the index, the Disparity Reduction Rate (the rate at which the disparity between a country's level of performance in the social indicators and the best performance expected anywhere in the year 2000 is being eliminated) shows a fair amount of progress over the period 1960–82: 1.6 percent per year for low-income Africa (versus 0.9 percent for low income Asia) and 1.4 percent per year for middle-income Africa (low in comparison with Asia and Latin America).

Despite this progress and the fact that many donor programs aimed at improving the quality of life have been implemented throughout Africa, a major deterioration in social gains has taken place recently given the severity of Africa's crises. Gains over the rest of this century in the Sahelian belt in particular will be very difficult.

Among the major donors, social concerns became more prominent in the early 1970s. Notable were the World Bank's policy changes announced by Robert McNamara in Nairobi in 1973 and the New Directions legislation for USAID in 1973, along with AID's subsequent requirement that each of its project feasibility studies include a social soundness analysis to assure that benefits go to intended recipients. During this time, major donors also became more concerned with bettering the condition of women, and very recently with setting goals for improvements in child well-being.

Donors have had difficulty in translating their concerns about equity into well-crafted programs, perhaps not realizing quickly enough that even in low-income countries, there is ample opportunity to divert intended benefits from the poor. Recent World Bank evidence indicates that where the poor have been especially targeted as beneficiaries of rural development projects, the overall economic results have been competitive with non-targeted projects, although the former required greater amounts of staff time for design and monitoring. As noted, education projects have had particularly important equity effects, particularly those which bring education to new areas and open up opportunities for girls and women.

But all is not positive in this area of concern. In fact, the EEC found that all of their agriculture projects produced gains in producers' incomes, but that most of these went to the male landholders. "Projects rarely aim at improving the welfare of the young or of women, and still more rarely achieve it."[34] And it can almost be categorically stated that donors find that the very poorest groups in countries are difficult to reach.

This is not to say that the means of enhancing the social effectiveness of projects are unknown. Greater participation by the poor in the design and implementation of projects has been shown to increase the effectiveness of aided projects[35], but the added costs entailed have discouraged donors from more widespread replication of these experiments.

Donors and African states have better technical than social knowledge. Since the on-board strength of social scientists in donor and recipient governmental organizations is low to non-existent, a turnaround in the mediocre social results of aided activities is not apt to come soon.

POLITICAL IMPACT

For the few donors, particularly the United States, which invest significant aid funds largely to yield political benefits, little evidence exists as to whether intended political payoffs actually materialize.

On the basis of scanty evidence, the following is put forth:

- Measureable political goals are seldom formulated and never articulated as part of a donor's development plans.
- Development initiatives funded with political monies are seldom specifically designed to achieve articulated political ends.
- Political aims are often shorter term, while development aid is a long-term proposition (projects take six to 10 years to show real impact, non-project aid two years); hence there is a risk of mismatching the demand and the supply.
- The greater the political urgency, the less rigorous the design of the development intervention, and the greater the chance that it will not succeed in its development objectives.

The net result is that development assistance aimed at political ends runs a high risk of failing to achieve both specific political desires and development goals.

EFFECTS ON INSTITUTIONS AND MANAGEMENT

There can hardly be any objection to Africans managing their own economies in more effective ways. Donors have had this high on their agendas both in recognition of the importance of managerial capacity in the development process and for the simple selfish reason that life is easier for the donor when a country has the ability to implement development projects.

The challenges in this field have been great. Evaluations of donor projects in Africa are replete with complaints about administrative problems. The few countries where donors find life easier in Africa seem to be ones that have given up some of their autonomy to troops of foreign advisers (e.g., Malawi, Botswana, Ivory Coast) who are often quite skillful in organizing information for donors.

It is almost impossible to gauge accurately whether institutional and managerial performance has improved in Africa, but a case can be made that it has. Independence brought new institutional needs and an exodus of important talent—two challenges which the new governments were poorly prepared to meet. Donors responded by providing tens of thousands of technicians and great volumes of technical assistance and institution-building projects. The impression is that the volume of such assistance has somewhat declined recently (although it is still notably high in francophone Africa). This assistance seems also to have changed in character as Africans have gained more experience in institutional management. The days when any and all technical advice was accepted are long over. African officials may need advice, but the needs are far more sharply and professionally defined and technical recommendations are more critically screened now than in the past. One very important factor is that the current crises have led to a new tone of realism about the policy environment in Africa. More African officials are discussing and acting on the kinds of administrative and policy reforms long advocated by many development observers and participants.

Donors have always been involved with institutional reform and growth in Africa, but in recent years, even greater attention has been given to this need, particularly by the World Bank and USAID. To what extent this new emphasis has incorporated lessons from past programs is not known.

The scoreboard from past programs has not been encouraging. Two major reviews of institution-building projects in Africa have been produced in recent years. USAID reviewed a sample of 183 of its Africa projects (active from 1974 to 1982) which had institution-building components.[36] While in about 50 percent of the projects, the positive findings outweighed the negative, fully 42 percent of the projects had negative results outweighing positive results (versus an average of 33 percent world-wide).

Results from a more thorough World Bank survey of 118 institutional development projects in Africa are even less positive.[37] Most of the projects had serious implementation problems; over half were considered to have had little or no impact; and only one in 10 was considered to have been very effective.

In a study of 62 projects, including 33 African projects, Canada's CIDA found that while 60 percent had improved managerial capabilities, fully two-thirds had not enabled the institution being helped to become significantly more self-reliant.[38] Indeed, evaluators of EEC aid stressed that it had to focus far more on creating the "capacity for self-development."[39] In view of this poor record, it is perhaps commendable that donors have maintained their technical assistance and institution-building programs, as the need has not evaporated. But there is little evidence that donors have changed the way they provide technical assistance. Repeated criticisms that experts float in and out, thereby precluding the possibility of sustained dialogues, that provision of expertise is very costly, and that foreign technicians are culturally insensitive, have not been acted upon. Nor has there been much creativity in providing management options for situations where a policy dialogue is useful but doesn't require full-time technical assistance.

Donors must also recognize that the donor mode of operation has negative institutional development effects. Donors have frequently end-run African institutions by creating special enclaves for their projects. What makes good sense in each individual project case creates cumulative chaos and undermines good public administration.[40] Thus donors are both part of the problem and given Africa's shortage of skills and resources, a necessary part of the solution to institutional and managerial reform.

Most basically, the need to help improve Africa's institutions and management demands a better calculus by donors as to whether foreign help or training of Africans will be most effective. There is little disagreement that training of Africans will be most effective and a far cheaper and more enduring solution to solving institutional problems in Africa. Why this solution is not turned to more often calls for a complex explanation involving such factors as real and perceived needs for quick fixes, the unavailability of candidates for training, and in some cases a subtle need to have troops of foreign technicians in order to justify high standards of living for African managers. Of course, there are urgent short- and medium-term institutional and management needs where foreign help will be very useful, but these must not preclude donors and Africans from placing greater emphasis on more enduring solutions. These solutions will undoubtedly involve heavy reliance on project aid, but also require better management of such aid by both sides.

REPLICATION AND SPREAD EFFECTS

Most often donor staff commence a program, policy, or project initiative with the idea that it will lead to a widespread ripple effect in the national application of a policy, replication by the government or private sector, or diffusion of the benefits. Unfortunately, evidence of project replication and spread in Africa is very scanty.

A vigorous private sector and a well-funded government are important catalysts in expediting the spread of social and economic innovations, but both institutions are weak in Africa. This explains in part the paucity of evidence on replication/spread in Africa today, but the complexity of gathering the evidence itself must also be recognized. Difficulties include the long time periods involved and problems associated with sorting out the many influences acting on project diffusion.

There is some hopeful evidence that even in Africa's difficult setting, diffusion of innovations can take place. Numerous simple technological innovations in agriculture, health, and education have spread well on a local or regional scale in Africa. Further, the literature on diffusion and spread indicates that projects and programs can be better designed to encourage ripple effects. Both experiences with small-scale diffusion in Africa and this literature have important implications in helping to design future assistance programs in Africa.

IMPLICATIONS: CAN PROJECTS IN AFRICA
COMPETE?

In this rapid review of aid effectiveness in Africa, it has been clear that aided activities in Africa perform less well than elsewhere. Economic rates of return are lower, failure rates are higher, management problems are greater, and the social context is less well understood and hence not handled well. The averages mask the losers which haunt aid officials—the white elephants, the "showpiece investments. . .made possible largely by generous financial support from the donor community,"[41] and the earnestly invested careers which have left little behind.

Contrast this with aid to South and East Asia—great results to impress parliaments, an easy lifestyle in the field, careers which are bound to look good. Why should donors bother with Africa? The wonder is that most still do and are increasing their concern and programs. But some are not, particularly those emphasizing the private sector and those normally drawn to larger infrastructural investments, areas where prospects in Africa are often regarded as poor.

If the shift by some donors away from Africa was the result of a rational thought process, this might be better understood. But where this has occurred, it is more because African projects do not compete as well as other options and hence a major strategic question is being decided in the absence of real policy discussion.

For those donors wishing to continue major activities in Africa, there is a tendency to mask the real problems by adding an extra dose of fiction to decisions that lead to commitments of new development investments, but also to quite unrealistic expectations and plans.

For both donors switching out of Africa with little hard thought and for those staying but with unrealistic expectations, the relevant question may well be: Should donors adjust their standards in order to respond to Africa's development needs with more candor? The embodiment of these standards is the economic rate of return. Is too much reliance being placed on this calculation in deciding whether and how to assist Africa?

These concerns are perhaps best illustrated by the case of the Manantale dam in the Senegal river basin, a major scheme to assist Senegal, Mauritania, and Mali by regulating the flow of the Senegal River and creating major opportunities to foster irrigated agriculture. After lengthy and expensive feasibility and environmental studies, AID and the World Bank decided that the project could not be supported. Although the need—regulating the supply of water in one of the most difficult and drought-prone areas in Africa—was great, the fatal fact was that the economic rate of return forecast for the $1 billion investment was zero. Yet Germany and several Middle East donors put up the money because they saw no other more feasible option for the area.[42]

The Manantale dam is a dramatic example of what donors face in Africa. The economic rates of return on past donor investments have been satisfactory, but future development investments look poor given clouded economic prospects in a number of countries. Donors are now faced with the choice between sticking with relatively stringent standards and shifting away from Africa, or staying in Africa but sitting out on tasks which someday must be undertaken, such as development of Africa's relatively few large-scale water resources. If donors are to effectively respond to Africa's long-term development crises, a fresh approach to project selection criteria is imperative. Donors must recognize that standard measures of feasibility such as rates of return are not accurate indicators of a project's importance to the development of a resource-starved area. The need for simultaneous development to raise the general level of economic performance means that if any given project is weighted by itself, it may not seem worthwhile. It may take a nexus of what now seem like marginal investments in order to create a renewed momentum to development in Africa.

RECOMMENDATIONS

How can Africa take advantage of more donor programs while avoiding the burden of a more chaotic development pattern? And what can donors do to be of better assistance to Africa? In this section, recommendations are addressed to donors and to African governments.

LEVELS OF AID

In both the short and longer term, aid will play a key role in Africa's development. External finance is critical to Africa's survival and growth, but most sources apart from aid are drying up. Trade prospects are uncertain, private investment has decreased, new net capital resources are unlikely, and domestic resources are shrinking and unlikely to recover soon. Short-term needs include food requirements not available on the continent, spare parts to restore existing production, and help to restore basic services.

At the same time, larger longer-term development investments are needed to lay a better base for agricultural production and many other fundamental building blocks of development. Again, no other resources, particularly from the foreign sectors, are in sight to provide major new funds for these purposes.

In the short run, Africans are faced with finding new aid resources and seeking debt forgiveness for past aid. It also may be possible for some donors to institute legislative changes permitting repayments of past aid loans to be cycled back to Africa.[43]

In the longer run, however, new donor funds might well come from switching of traditional aid allocations from other regions to Africa. The switching should come about naturally as currently aided countries in Latin America and other better off areas evolve into stronger trading and financial partners.

Some respected analysts of African development argue that Africa receives too much aid and is having difficulty absorbing the flow of resources it now receives. There are abundant problems which reinforce this viewpoint: Aid is poorly coordinated; African states are hard put to find counterpart funds and staff; and new long-term programs cannot easily take root in the midst of all the crises Africa is facing.

Attacking the constraints affecting the absorption of aid is needed and holds more hope for Africa's development. This view has shaped a number of the following recommendations. Simply put, it is very hard to see how Africa would be better off with less aid. The best solution would be more aid and much better quality in the handling of that aid by donors and African governments.

African states themselves can help to expand resources from donors. Better management of resources will attract more aid. In addition, African governments need to become more cognizant of donor interests and more proficient at marketing their own programs. Nevertheless, increasing aid levels obviously will be difficult. It will take concerted leadership by Africans, international organizations, and politicians in the donor community.

IMPLEMENTING FOR SURVIVAL AND FOR QUALITY

The prolonged development crisis in Africa dramatically highlights the most basic reason for aid to Africa—survival. This must be the first priority for donors and African states. There are three critical ingredients: balance of payments support to finance imports of critical goods necessary to keep economies afloat; assistance to maintain and restore the public infrastructure; and food aid.

Africa's current economic crisis requires an adjustment of the content and financial formulas of donor aid programs. The main requirement in Africa now is to keep the economies running instead of starting new projects. Spare parts and maintenance of infrastructure, industry, and services will be far more important in the next few years than financing new efforts.[44] Finance for foreign exchange and local currency recurrent costs is critically needed in many countries.

Because food aid is a special kind of assistance, a few added recommendations are in order. To plan effective short-term strategies, Africans require more assurance that food aid will be supplied by the donors in adequate volume and with sufficient logistical support to meet emergency needs. The food surplus countries have a special obligation, and the United States is in far better shape than other major supplier countries such as Canada, Australia, and Argentina. Non-governmental organizations have repeatedly pointed to the need not only for increased food supplies, but for financial support to provide in-country logistical support for food deliveries. Another improvement takes more political courage. Donors could help to reinforce local African markets by supplying food aid from local supplies when there is a surplus.

The crucial strategy decision for African governments and donors is how to carry out the survival tasks and still lay a basis for longer-term growth. Just as it would be wrong to continue putting the great bulk of resources in long-term development investments, it would be wrong to finance only short-term needs.

This chapter reviewed data showing that many kinds of aided activities perform satisfactorily. But it has argued that donor investment standards might have to be adjusted in order to permit some kinds of basic, needed initiatives to be carried out in Africa. Development in Africa must proceed on the assumption that the name of the game remains to implement for quality—reinforcing what works and weeding out or altering what doesn't.

The underlying recommendation is that African governments be assisted in gaining the capacity to fully manage their own development. It is worth reflecting on this goal in the context of improving the quality of development programs. Governments which implement for quality need the ability to judge how development is going in their country. An unbiased flow of information must be generated inside the government and must reach top political levels quickly. Some governments have impressive capabilities in these matters which ought to be studied. For example, the government of Sri Lanka's Ministry of Plan Implementation has been extremely resourceful in identifying bottlenecks holding up development projects across the country. Because the head of state holds the ministry's portfolio, there is an appropriate audience for key recommendations to enhance the quality of development.

African governments and donors can take a number of actions to improve public administration by helping create local monitoring and evaluation units (as is being done in a very few African countries now) to assess development performance and search for economical ways to reach desirable goals.

COORDINATION

Foreign aid will not be seen as an unqualified asset as long as there are mismatches between demand and supply and as long as the costs of dealing with donors continue to be so large. There is considerable agreement that foreign assistance requires better coordination to improve the quality of aid to Africa. The question is how best to do this. The problems seem to be field-centered and the solutions tried now generally are not.[45]

The largest donors will resist being coordinated and will need to be involved in sectoral strategy consultations with African states. This is appropriate since these donors can help underwrite entire sectoral strategies. African states and the World Bank have a special role in actively promoting this kind of consultation in the field. For the larger number of project-oriented, medium- and smaller-sized donors, field-centered options are needed which expedite coordination and are under the lead of African ministries, yet save time for officials on all sides. These ideas are suggested:

- Special coordination units could be formed on a sector-by-sector basis within each country. While there has already been some use of sector coordination committees, the concept could be expanded to make an entity the sole bargaining unit between all donors and a ministry. The unit would identify demands for donor involvement, help "recruit" donors, assign donors by geographic area, and negotiate master agreements with the ministry. The coordinating unit would then arrange a series of agreements with donors and would be the conduit to raise implementation issues/complaints/suggestions with the ministry for the set of donors involved. The unit might also be the holder of counterpart funds. This kind of unit could permit donors to staff projects for field duty instead of having to assign staff for capital city negotiations. The costs and staffing of such units would have to be carefully considered in order to be acceptable to all sides.
- Rather than sector-by-sector units, smaller countries might find it convenient to create one unit intended to be the intermediary for all but the largest donors. Such an entity might have sole responsibility for negotiating with donors which finance any project or program. An example is the Institute for Solidarity in Cape Verde which has been highly successful in attracting funds to the island republic.
- The soundest way, in theory, to consolidate initiatives by Africans and donors would be for almost all initiatives to be carried out under line ministry auspices. An alternative would be for the donors to pool funds for specific endeavors to be carried out under the leadership of one of them.

It will take political courage from all sides to effect better systems of coordination. Donors will need to suppress some of the ego value of aid and African states will have to suppress their fears of being locked into an unequal partnership.

CHOICES OF DONORS BASED ON MERIT

African states ought to be in a position to match development financing needs to the abilities of donors in a specific area. African officials should have access to the significant amount of information available regarding which donors do what best. More candid exchanges of information can lead to useful mutual pressure to improve performance and to allocate resources where donors can make the most valuable contributions.

Bilateral donors also have a range of choices along the continuum of channeling their aid through bilateral mechanisms or multilateral institutions. Many of the bilaterals ought to be more supportive of the multilateral agencies. A number of the bilaterals are not very competent donors and ought to recognize that their aid will continue to be of inferior quality unless they make major improvements soon. Even the largest bilaterals must concede certain advantages to the World Bank, with its unique abilities and power, and to the International Fund for Agricultural Development, UNICEF, and the UN Fund for Population Activities, all of which are effective and germane to Africa. Bilaterals have been negligent in helping these institutions secure the funds to assist Africa now and into the future.

While the World Bank has its faults, the bilaterals can more quickly effect instititutional changes there, given their powerful roles as Bank executive directors, than they can change their own aid institutions. A thorough review of evaluation information ought to help bilaterals better decide where comparative advantages lie.

LEARNING MODEL APPROACH FOR DESIGN AND IMPLEMENTATION

For some time, leading authorities have espoused the virtues of the learning model approach for development. This approach emphasizes model and pilot projects as well as evolving designs of projects during implementation. Evaluation evidence reinforces both the need for this kind of approach and the value of making well thought-out changes during the life of projects and programs.

A key implication of the learning model approach is the need for more flexibility by governments and donors to permit mid-stream project changes; in fact, such course corrections should be encouraged. Encouraging easy ways to make justified mid-stream changes is important and generally can be accommodated in bureaucracies. However, it is particularly difficult to alter a project at the very end of an agreement when the project reverts to a country's sole technical and financial care. During implementation, donors must focus more on whether a recipient country will be prepared to take over assisted endeavors when the donor funds expire and/or when foreign technicians leave. If it will take some additional input of funds or staff to assure a smooth transition to African management, the donor must be prepared to decide well in advance of termination dates so that all involved can plan accordingly.

In the private sector, financing changes during implementation is less of a problem. Corporations have contingency funds. Given the high frequency of cost and time overruns in Africa, it is a pity that donors have so far been unable to devise a similar mechanism of prudent management. In the absence of a quick-disbursing contingency fund, there is a premium on timing evaluation and monitoring teams at useful points and well enough in advance of key dates in order to be able to act prior to the dreaded cutoff date.

LEARNING MODEL IN POLICY AND PROGRAM DESIGN

Reference was earlier made to the large number of evaluation findings which are now being brought together more systematically by the major donors. Typically, these reports identify a large number of weaknesses in project designs which are translated into special sector reports and guidelines as to how to improve projects. While this may be necessary, it is far from a sufficient response.

Donors should take the evaluation evidence far more seriously. The most inexcusable donor action is to keep repeating mistakes. Some donors have instituted regular reviews of the findings of their own evaluations. It would be even more useful for donor executives to regularly review evaluation evidence generated from the wider donor community.

Meeting with African officials to review the validity and implications of major evaluation findings is also important. This would allow for a more "hands-on" approach to professionalizing staff and would emphasize that both sides must learn the lessons of experience.

In both African and donor establishments, development policy ought to evolve based on actual experience. Donors have an obligation to factor in African officials' participation when policy decisions are being considered. One looks to the day when donor coordination meetings will be run by African governments and will center on hard evidence from their own development experience along with analysis of its implications on development policy and donor assistance.

STAFFING FOR DEVELOPMENT

Staff composition in the donor organizations and within African governments must be looked at carefully. As there is a repeated finding that projects operate without accurate social and institutional knowledge, then it seems logical for African governments and donors to put more emphasis on hiring social scientists, institutional change experts, sector policy analysts, and implementation planning experts.

TERMS AND CONDITIONS OF ASSISTANCE

As donors contemplate future assistance to Africa, they will need to consider the terms of their assistance more carefully. Reviews of the effectiveness of past aid programs to Africa have already provided keys to needed improvements.

- Investment for the long haul is needed, particularly if spread effects, replication, and other diffusion are anticipated. A large proportion of assistance to Africa involves technical, managerial, and institutional development goals that require longer-term approaches. There must be recognition that in many kinds of programs, particularly agricultural development, a great deal of experimentation is needed. Carefully paced pilot, research, and model programs require time to be carried out and the assurance that, if they succeed, there will be a responsive follow-up.
- Any responsible review of Africa's financial situation will lead to the conclusion that only soft financial terms are appropriate. The only question is whether more donors can shift funds to a grant basis. Many already have.
- Both World Bank and USAID policy now recognize the need for more recurrent cost financing for developing countries.[46] The issue

is particularly germane since many analysts recommend that donors back existing activities rather than start new ones in Africa, in
recognition of the imperative of keeping the existing economies
going, of building from whatever strength exists, and of reinforcing existing institutions in preference to creating new ones. The
financial implication for donors is that such projects call for far
greater emphasis on recurrent and local cost financing. This type of
financing is never popular with donor treasuries and central
banks. Therefore, the decision to undertake more financing of existing activities is at root a political one.

• The "Berg Report" correctly recommends that donors harmonize
  their aid procedures.[47] Who could disagree, but who could be optimistic after the OECD Development Assistance Committee has
  tried unsuccessfully to do so for at least 20 years? From time to
  time, one or another of the major donors has unbashfully volun-
  teered its own procedures as the standard to which others should
  conform, but there have been few if any takers. A solution, of
  course, is for donors to pay far greater attention to host country
  procedures and to harmonize around them to the greatest extent
  possible. In some cases, this is done, but in most cases donors
  seem completely unaware that the aid recipient has its own system
  of design or monitoring projects.

If a country lacks an adequate system for development management, then it is imperative that donors work to help recipient governments achieve this capacity. In the interim, donors can involve national officials far more in the routine tasks of project management,
(e.g., by including local officials in the reviews and evaluations of
donor-financed projects and by sending them copies of key donor
reports on that country's projects).[48]

LESSONS FROM THE EEC: LINKING AID AND TRADE

Through the Lome Agreements, the EEC states have entered into
comprehensive aid and trade relationships with a large group of African, Caribbean, and Pacific Basin states. The agreements offer some
examples of innovations in donor behavior well worth considering:

• The agreements are the products of negotiations that emphasized
  equal bargaining power on all sides. The renewable agreements

run for five years each. There is a strong feeling that the EEC has entered into predictable and responsible "contracts" for development with the African-Caribbean-Pacific states involved.

• The Lome Agreements link aid and trade, as does the U.S. Caribbean Basin Initiative. To a limited extent, the agreements also cover investment promotion. While U.S.-African trade ties are not strong, the reinforcing potential of coordinated trade-aid-investment policies can serve as a constructive dynamic in Africa's development and can effectively further longer-term U.S. interests. Aid has an important long-term development role which, if done well, can greatly increase the long-range potential for trade and investment. The long-term benefits of aided development should not be sacrificed to short-term considerations which leave little developmental residual. Aid should not be turned into front money for short-term trade and investment deals. The Lome Agreements, in financing trade promotion and a large number of other aid-trade linked ideas, point the way to a number of initiatives which are of longer-term value and which might be considered by other donors.

THE CONCEPT OF SHARED RISK

Africa is in a terrible plight. Given the bleak economic outlook and the lack of financial alternatives, aid flows are of fundamental importance to the survival of peoples and to prospects for their betterment. While the quantity of aid must be increased to brighten Africa's prognosis, so must its quality. Efforts to improve the quality of aided and unaided development have tremendous importance. The likelihood of huge increases in aid levels is not strong: More must be achieved with existing resources. In any case, a better quality performance will enhance the prospects for aid.

None of the recommendations in this chapter will be easy to bring about, but some seem simpler and will encounter less resistance than others.

The underlying theme of this chapter is that two kinds of risks are going to have to be taken in greater measure. First, African leaders and donors must take steps aimed at a more rational use of aid resources and at placing Africans more at the center of their own development. There must be a greater willingness to enter into coordination, to implement for quality, and to make decisions based more on actual performance.

The second kind of risk is to keep trying to do the difficult. No clear-eyed reading of the evaluation evidence would leave one sanguine about continuing current practices in fields such as livestock and institutional development. But does that mean that the donors should abandon such fields? To agree to this would imply ceasing to care about problems such as the fate of 30 million pastoralists in Africa.

It would be easy to improve the record by dropping the risky projects. The more responsible task is to recognize openly that in a number of areas, there are fairly high risks and that prudent management is imperative. Riskier programs and strategies raise questions about existing donor standards and they certainly entail higher overhead costs in design, supervision, and field management time. These projects and programs predictably will need to be changed and they often will be frustrating. They will probably be on the books longer than most projects and will have to withstand pressure for termination. But if the projects in risky areas are sensitively managed, they may prove far more valuable than standard approaches ploddingly carried out or bright fads that come and go with few lasting results.

It will take unusual political courage to bear the burdens of these kinds of risks. But if donors and African governments can work together more in a sense of partnership and with as much professionalism as possible, the burden of risk can be shared and peer support can be found to help see African leaders and their peoples through very difficult times.

ACKNOWLEDGMENT

I acknowledge with great thanks abundant help from Julie Howard and Marguerite Turner in preparing this chapter.

NOTES

1. In this chapter, "foreign aid" will refer to official flows from bilateral and multilateral sources and grants from private agencies (private aid). "Official flows" are composed of: (1) Official development assistance (ODA), that is, grants or loans; undertaken by the official sector; with promotion of economic development and welfare as main objectives; at concessional financial

terms (if a loan, at least 25 percent grant element); (2) Technical cooperation: grants or loans to nationals of developing countries receiving training abroad and to cover costs of developed country personnel serving abroad; and (3) Other official (non-concessional) flows.

2. Mid-1982 estimates from: United Nations, *Demographic Yearbook 1982*, New York, 1984. Department of International Economic and Social Affairs, Statistical Office. International Bank for Reconstruction and Development, *World Development Report 1984*, New York: Oxford University Press, 1984.

3. According to OECD's Development Cooperation 1984, in 1983, total ODA receipts for less-developed countries were $33.6 billion. For sub-Saharan Africa alone, ODA totalled $8 billion.

4. United Nations Economic Commission for Africa, *Survey of Economic and Social Conditions in Africa, 1982–1983*, Document E/ECA/CM.10/4, 9 March 1984.

5. Weighted by population.

6. World Bank, *Toward Sustained Development: A Joint Program of Action for Sub-Saharan Africa*, Washington, D.C., August 1984. Calculated from Table A.Z.

7. In the period 1975 through March 1984 there were 45 Paris Club debt reschedulings. Thirteen sub-Saharan African Countries accounted for 32 of these reschedulings. (Briefing paper prepared by L.M. Goreux of the IMF, April 30, 1984.)

8. Uma Lele, "Rural Africa: Modernization, Equity, and Long-term Development," *Science* 211 (4482) (February 6, 1982).

9. World Bank, *Accelerated Development in Sub-Saharan Africa*, op.cit., p. 165.

10. The average cost of providing U.S. food aid to Africa has been estimated at $300/ton (including transportation). Personal communication, USAID.

11. See page 9, "U.S. Official Bilateral Assistance to Africa," op.cit.

12. For example, see "Bread for the World Report on the U.S. Responses to the African Famine," released May 3, 1984.

13. There is some confusion in this. For example, recent Africa Bureau leaders in USAID have publicly called for a deemphasis in population programs in Africa while approving budget increases for such programs.

14. World Bank, 1981. The report was written by an African Strategy Review Group coordinated by Elliott Berg. It is often referred to as "The Berg Report."

15. I initiated this series in 1977 and managed it until 1982.

16. I chaired the predecessor of this group fropm 1980 to 1982.

17. Unfortunately, most of this information is not publicly available at this time. One can only encourage donors to release these analyses for public discussion. In any case, I am grateful to have been given access to much of the existing information.

18. Gary Wasserman et al., *U.S. Aid to Zimbabwe: An Evaluation*, AID Program Evaluation Report No. 9, August 1983.

19. "Structural Adjustment Lending-Progress Report," draft, April 1984.

20. "The Politics of Stabilization," in *Adjustment Crisis in the Third World*, Richard E. Feinberg and Valeriana Kallab, eds., Overseas Development Council, Transaction Books, 1984.

21. *The Hobbled Giant: Essays on the World Bank*. Boulder: Westview Press, 1984.

22. Commission of the European Communities, staff paper, "Initial Report of the Results of Overall Evaluation of Community Aid," SEC (81) 189, Brussels, February 1981.

23. The rate of return is the remuneration to investment stated as a proportion or percentage. The financial rate of return is the internal rate of return based on market prices; the economic rate of return is the internal rate of return based on economic values.

24. The International Development Association (IDA) is the World Bank's soft-loan window, providing most of its concessional finance for the poorest developing areas, including Africa.

25. World Bank, calculations prepared by Clarence Gulick, Task Force on Concessional Flows, 1984.

26. CIDA, "Bilan des Evaluations Bilaterales, 1981–83."

27. R. Cohen, op.cit.

28. See World Bank, "Rural Development Projects: A Retrospective View of Bank Experience in Sub-Saharan Africa" (Report 2242), 1978 and World Bank, "Tenth Annual Review of Project Performance Audit Report 1984," published 1985.

29. Josette Murphy, *Strengthening the Agricultural Research Capacity of the Less Developed Countries: Lessons From AID Experience*, U.S. Agency for International Development Program Evaluation Report No. 10, September 1983. World Bank, "Agricultural Research and Extension: An Evaluation of the World Bank's Experience," forthcoming.

30. Daniel Dworkin, *Rural Water Projects in Tanzania: Technical, Social, and Administrative Issues*, AID Evaluation Special Study No. 3, November 1980.

31. David E. Sahn and Robert M. Pestronk, *A Review of Issues in Nutrition Program Evaluation*, USAID Program Evaluation Discussion Paper No. 10, July 1981.

32. World Food Programme, *World Food Programme in Africa*, Rome, June 1984.

33. Edward J. Clay and Hans Singer, *Food Aid and Development: The Impact and Effectiveness of Bilateral PL480 Title I-Type Assistance*, USAID Program Evaluation Discussion Paper No. 15, December 1982.

34. Commission of European Communities, op.cit.

35. Kurt Finsterburch and Warren Van Wicklin III, "The Contribution of Beneficiary Participation to Development Project Effectiveness," a review of 52 USAID evaluations, draft, July 1985.

36. Barnett and Engel, *Effective Institution Building*, AID Program Evaluation Discussion Paper No. 11, March 1982.

37. World Bank, "Institutional Development in Africa" (report no. 5085), May 1984.

38. CIDA, op.cit.

39. Commission on the European Communities, op.cit., p. vii.

40. Robert J. Berg, "The Long-run Future of Donor Planning, Monitoring, and Evaluation," *Development* XXII, (2–3), 1980.

41. Uma Lele, op.cit.

42. Whether recessional agriculture depending on annual floods, dry land, or small irrigation systems would be more feasible is hard to tell particularly due to a poorer understanding of such systems among Western and Western-trained African technicians.

43. Debt forgiveness is an issue for the United States. It is legally permissable for the United States to forgive official debts to least developed countries, but this option has never been exercised perhaps out of fear that a precedent would be set for the huge debt owed by India and a few other major recipients of past USAID loans. But surely the crisis in Africa is of an order not faced by these other past recipients. Debt forgiveness for Africa and reinstituting the ability to use reflows to fund new aid programs would be very useful steps for the United States to take.

44. Reginald Herbold Green and Mark Faber, "Sub-Saharan Africa's Economic Malaise: Some Questions and Answers," *Journal of Development Planning*, forthcoming.

45. "Review of Coordination among Multilateral Agencies in Support of World Food Conference Objectives: Report by the Executive Director," World Food Council/1984/3, January 27, 1984.

46. The Bank and AID encourage recipients to finance recurrent costs out of user charges wherever possible. The point that user charges are often too low (see Jacob Meerman, "Minimizing the Burden of Recurrent Costs," *Finance and Development*, December 1983, pp. 41–43) is well taken, but in these years of crises it may be a poor time to rigorously institute that policy. See also "Recurrent Costs," AID Policy Paper, May 1982.

47. *Accelerated Development in Sub-Saharan Africa*, op. cit., p. 130.

48. A non-African example: Until the late 1970s, there was no donor contact with the highly professional evaluation staff of India's National Planning Commission, a staff which was established in 1952 and controls a professional network of 900 trained evaluators. The Indians were not asked to carry out, participate in, or read an evaluation prepared to meet a donor need. There are numerous parallels in Africa, but no African government has such a well-established evaluation system. Given other perceived priorities, it is unlikely that good monitoring and evaluation systems will be established in Africa in the absence of donor encouragement.

Tabular Appendix

TABLE A.1
LAND USE IN AFRICA
(As Percentage of Total Land Area)

	1967–71	1974	1977	1980
Arable and permanent crops	5.58	5.75	5.92	5.97
Permanent pasture	25.91	25.91	25.87	25.86
Forest and woodland	23.99	23.59	23.27	22.95
Other land	42.31	42.55	42.75	43.02

SOURCE: *FAO Production Yearbook 1981*, v. 35, p. 65.

TABLE A.2
DISTRIBUTION OF MVA IN AFRICA—1975
(Percentage)

Food, Beverages and Tobacco	31
Textiles, Clothing and Leather	21
Wood and Furniture	4
Paper, Printing, Publishing	5
Chemicals, Petroleum, Coal, Rubber and Plastics	16
Non-Metallic Minerals	5
Basic Metals	4
Fabricated Metal Products	13
Other	1

SOURCE: UNIDO (1983).

TABLE A.3
COMPARISON OF ENROLLMENTS AT DIFFERENT EDUCATION LEVELS FOR SUB-SAHARAN AFRICAN COUNTRIES, 1960–81

| | Number enrolled in primary school as percentage of age group | | | | | | Number enrolled in secondary school as % of age group | | Number enrolled in higher education as % of population aged 20–24 | |
| | Total | | Male | | Female | | | | | |
	1960	1981	1960	1981	1960	1981	1960	1981	1960	1981
Angola	21	—	28	—	13	—	2	—	(.)	(.)
Benin	27	65	38	88	15	42	2	18	—	1
Botswana	42	102	35	94	48	110	1	23	—	—
Burkina Faso	8	20	12	26	5	15	1	3	(.)	1
Burundi	18	32	27	40	9	25	1	3	(.)	1
Cameroon	65	107	87	117	43	97	2	19	—	2
Cent. Afr. Rep.	32	68	53	89	12	49	1	13	—	1
Chad	17	35	29	51	4	19	—	3	—	(.)
Congo	78	156	103	163	53	148	4	69	1	6
Ethiopia	7	46	11	60	3	33	—	12	(.)	1
Gabon	100	202	124	207	76	198	5	34	—	—
Gambia, The	12	52	17	67	8	37	3	14	—	—
Ghana	38	69	52	77	25	60	5	36	(.)	1
Guinea	30	33	44	44	16	22	2	16	—	5
Guinea-Bissau	25	101	35	141	15	61	3	20	—	—
Ivory Coast	46	76	68	92	24	60	2	17	(.)	3
Kenya	47	109	64	114	30	101	2	19	(.)	1
Lesotho	83	104	63	84	102	123	3	17	(.)	2
Liberia	31	66	45	82	18	50	2	20	(.)	2

Madagascar	52	*100*	58	—	45	—	4	*14*	(.)	3
Malawi	—	*62*	—	*73*	—	*51*	1	*4*	—	(.)
Mali	10	*27*	14	*35*	6	*20*	1	*4*	—	1
Mauritania	8	*33*	13	*43*	3	*23*	—	*10*	—	—
Mauritius	98	*107*	103	*107*	93	*106*	24	*51*	—	—
Mozambique	48	*90*	60	*102*	36	*78*	2	*6*	—	(.)
Niger	5	*23*	7	*29*	3	*17*	—	*6*	—	(.)
Nigeria	36	*98*	46	*94*	27	*70*	4	*16*	(.)	3
Rwanda	49	*72*	68	*75*	30	*69*	2	*2*	—	—
Senegal	27	*48*	36	*58*	17	*38*	3	*12*	1	*3*
Sierra Leone	23	*39*	30	*45*	15	*30*	2	*12*	—	*1*
Somalia	9	*30*	13	*38*	5	*21*	1	*11*	(.)	*1*
Sudan	25	*52*	35	*61*	14	*43*	3	*18*	(.)	2
Swaziland	58	*110*	58	*111*	58	*109*	5	*40*	—	—
Tanzania	25	*102*	33	*107*	18	*98*	2	*3*	—	—
Togo	44	*111*	63	*135*	24	*87*	2	*31*	—	(.)
Uganda	49	*54*	65	*62*	32	*46*	3	*5*	(.)	2
Zaire	60	*90*	88	*104*	32	*75*	3	*23*	(.)	1
Zambia	42	*96*	51	*102*	34	*90*	2	*16*	—	1
Zimbabwe	96	*126*	107	*130*	86	*121*	6	*15*	(.)	2

NOTE: Figures in italics are for years other than those specified.
SOURCE: *Towards Sustained Development in Sub-Saharan Africa* (Washington, D.C.: The World Bank, 1984).

TABLE A.4
SUB-SAHARAN AFRICA: SHARE OF MANUFACTURING IN GDP 1981
(Percentage)

Zaire	2.5	Uganda	4.2
Angola	2.6	Namibia	4.4
Gambia	2.6	Lesotho	4.7
Guinea	3.1	Sao Tome & Principe	4.7
Reunion	3.5	Sierra Leone	4.8
Equatorial Guinea	5.1	Seychelles	6.6
Liberia	5.2	Sudan	7.1
Niger	5.3	Gabon	7.7
Benin	5.4	Chad	7.8
Cape Verde	5.4	Mali	7.8
Comoros	5.4	Mozambique	8.8
Botswana	5.6	Somalia	8.8
Nigeria	6.1	Tanzania	9.0
Togo	6.4	Cameroon	9.8
Madagascar	10.1	Cent. Afr. Repub.	13.5
Burundi	10.9	Burkina Faso	13.8
Ivory Coast	11.0	Ghana	13.9
Rwanda	12.7	Senegal	14.7
Kenya	13.3		
Malawi	15.2	Swaziland	24.3
Mauritius	15.5	Zimbabwe	26.5
Zambia	15.8		

SOURCE: UNIDO data base.

TABLE A.5
AFRICA: GROWTH OF INDEBTEDNESS
(U.S. $ billion)

	1973	1979	1983
Debt outstanding[a]	9.9	36.7	57.8
Disbursements	2.2	8.8	10.6
Net inflows	1.3	6.2	7.4
Principal repayments	0.9	1.6	3.1
Interest	0.3	1.3	2.6
Debt service	1.2	2.8	5.7
Net transfers	1.0	5.0	4.8
Exports	13.3	40.5	28.0
Debt-service ratio	8.8	7.0	20.3

[a] Public and publicly guaranteed medium- and long-term debt only.

SOURCE: *World Debt Tables*, The World Bank.

TABLE A.6
1983 DEBT INDICATORS
(percent)

Principal Ratios	Major Borrowers	Sub-Saharan Africa	Low-income Africa
Debt/export	167	197	598
Debt/GNP	29	32	37
Debt service/exports	22	20	31
Interest/GNP	2.3	1.5	0.9
Gross reserves (months)	3.2	1.5	3.3

SOURCE: *World Debt Tables, 1984*, The World Bank.

TABLE A.7
STRUCTURE OF THE LONG-TERM EXTERNAL DEBT OF SUB-SAHARAN AFRICAN COUNTRIES, 1973–1983
(U.S. $ billion)

	1973	1978	1979	1980	1981	1982	1983[a]
Total debt outstanding and disbursed	9.9	29.2	36.7	43.3	47.5	51.4	57.9
A. Public and publicly guaranteed	9.3	27.4	34.4	40.4	44.5	48.1	53.8
Official creditors	5.9	15.7	19.8	24.1	26.3	29.2	31.1
Multilateral, of which	1.6	5.6	6.7	8.4	9.8	11.4	12.6
Concessional	0.6	3.1	3.8	5.0	5.8	6.8	n.a.
Bilateral, of which	4.3	10.3	13.1	15.7	16.5	17.8	18.5
Concessional	3.7	8.0	8.9	10.2	10.9	11.6	n.a.
Private Creditors	3.4	11.7	14.6	16.5	18.2	18.9	22.7
Suppliers	1.3	3.5	3.7	3.5	3.5	3.4	3.8
Financial Markets	2.1	8.2	10.9	13.0	14.7	15.5	18.9

B. Private Nonguaranteed	0.6	1.8	2.3	2.7	3.0	3.3	4.1
Memorandum							
Concessional Loans %	43.4	38.1	34.6	35.1	35.2	35.8	n.a.
Variable Int. Rate Loans %	8.8	15.6	17.8	19.2	21.0	22.0	n.a.
Debt to preferred creditors	1.8	6.7	8.4	10.4	13.2	15.4	17.4
Multilateral[b]	1.6	5.4	6.7	8.4	9.8	11.4	12.6
Use of IMF Credits	0.2	1.3	1.7	2.0	3.4	4.0	4.8

[a] Estimates.
[b] Multilateral includes the IMF Trust Fund.
SOURCE: The World Bank.

TABLE A.8

AFRICA: SELECTED ECONOMIC INDICATORS, 1973–82[a]

	1973	1974	1975	1976	1977	1978	1979	1980	1981	1982
					(in percent)					
Economic growth	2.39	6.27	2.75	5.85	2.82	1.84	1.52	2.69	1.84	1.90
Inflation	9.86	17.07	15.84	16.63	24.30	18.95	22.32	23.29	25.84	16.25
Terms of trade	8.30	7.63	-12.19	7.16	17.64	-7.25	-0.35	-7.09	-6.21	-4.74
Ratio of external debt to GDP	24.90	25.87	27.50	32.82	35.10	36.90	38.96	42.36	23.41	50.63
Debt service ratio	—	8.00	9.50	9.50	11.40	15.00	15.50	17.20	20.50	27.40
					(in billions of U.S. dollars)					
Current account	-4.50	-4.00	-7.20	-6.50	-6.60	-9.40	-9.90	-12.90	-14.00	-13.20
Net official transfers	1.10	1.50	1.70	2.00	2.30	2.50	3.10	3.20	3.60	3.20
Net capital inflows	3.80	2.60	4.90	4.40	4.90	6.30	6.40	7.10	6.80	6.80
Overall balance of payments	0.50	0.30	-0.60	-0.10	0.70	-0.40	-0.20	-2.40	-3.60	-3.20
Total outstanding debt	11.60	14.75	18.40	23.40	30.22	37.20	45.54	57.23	61.84	67.70

[a] This follows the IMF's International Financial Statistics classification of the African countries. These include all the African member countries, with the exception of Algeria, Egypt, Nigeria, and Libya, which are classified under different headings. In this table, South Africa is also included.
SOURCES: IMF, Current Studies Division; *World Economic Outlook*, Occasional Paper No. 9.

TABLE A.9
EXPORT VOLUME GROWTH RATES

	1960–70	1970–79
All low-income countries	5.4	–1.0
All low-income excluding		
China and India	5.7	–1.1[a]
Low income Africa	5.3	–1.9
Semi-arid	5.9	4.4
Other	5.0	–2.7
All middle income countries	5.4	4.3
Oil exporters	4.4	2.6[a]
African oil exporters	6.6	–0.1
Oil importers	6.7	4.1[a]
African oil importers	7.1	–0.5
Sub-Saharan Africa	5.9	–0.8

[a] 1970–80

SOURCES: *World Development Report*, 1984, p. 234; *Accelerated Development in Sub-Saharan Africa*, 1981, p. 149; *World Development Report*, 1982, p. 124.

TABLE A.10
TERMS OF TRADE AND PURCHASING POWER OF EXPORTS
(Average Rates of Change)

	Terms of Trade		Purchasing Power of Exports	
	1961–70	1970–79	1961–70	1970–79
Sub-Saharan Africa	2.9	2.5	7.6	1.0
Oil exporters	1.2	14.7	7.7	12.6
Oil importers	3.4	–1.5	7.6	–2.7

SOURCE: World Bank, *Accelerated Development in Sub-Saharan Africa*, 1981, p. 18.

TABLE A.11
SUB-SAHARAN AFRICA'S SHARE OF DEVELOPING COUNTRY EXPORTS
OF SELECTED COMMODITIES
(Percentage)

	1960	1970–72	1976–78
Fuels			
Petroleum	0.3	7.6	8.6
Minerals and Metals			
Copper[a]	47.3	52.1	38.8
Iron ore[b]	10.8	30.3	19.7
Bauxite	5.7	4.7	31.7
Phosphate rock	0.6	13.3	14.3
Manganese ore[b]	22.2	53.1	36.9
Zinc[a]	27.7	25.9	18.7
Tin[a]	11.7	9.7	3.6
Lead[a]	12.9	19.4	6.6
Food and beverages			
Coffee[b]	19.3	29.3	29.1
Cocoa[a]	72.8	80.1	72.3
Sugar	4.6	5.6	11.0
Tea	7.1	15.7	19.4
Groundnuts[a]	87.1	74.8	63.5
Groundnut oil[a]	77.3	72.2	56.8
Beef	4.5	4.0	8.6
Palmoil[a]	65.7	22.6	6.7
Bananas[a]	11.3	7.2	4.9
Maize[a]	4.8	4.4	2.5
Nonfood			
Timber[a]	44.7	22.8	18.5
Cotton[a]	23.2	28.8	22.4
Tobacco[a]	40.6	25.4	19.4
Rubber[a]	7.4	7.9	4.9
Hides and Skins[b]	21.2	33.7	23.7
Sisal[a]	68.5	58.3	52.8

[a]Africa's share declined 1960 to 1976–78.
[b]Africa's share declined 1970–72 to 1976–78.
SOURCE: World Bank, *Accelerated Development in Sub-Saharan Africa*, 1981, p. 21.

TABLE A.12
U.S. OFFICIAL BILATERAL ASSISTANCE TO AFRICA
(Commitments, in $ millions)

	1980	1984	1985
Economic Assistance			
Development Assistance	282	349	356
Economic Support Fund			
(Economic aid given for			
political purposes)	133	338	425
P.L. 480	268	295	334
Emergency Food Aid	—	—	1,000 *est.*
Total Economic Assistance	683	982	2,115
Military Assistance	77	157	170
Total Assistance	760	1,139	2,285

NOTE: Military aid has been included in this calculation to indicate that along with Economic Support Fund assistance the U.S. now gives about 46% of its non-emergency assistance to Africa for open political and military purposes.

SOURCE: (Economic Assistance) USAID Policy Bureau Analysis, May 13, 1984; (Military Assistance) 1980: USAID, U.S. Overseas Loans and Grants, Washington, D.C., 1983; 1984 and 1985: Personal Communication, Bureau of Political Military Affairs, Department of State.

TABLE A.13
OFFICIAL DEVELOPMENT ASSISTANCE PER CAPITA BY REGIONS
(current dollars)

	1961	1971	1981	1982	1983
Africa	$4.21	$5.10	$20.27	$19.68	$19.10
Latin America					
(exclusive of W. Indies)	3.78	2.30	6.57	6.69	6.44
Asia					
(including China)	1.08	1.77	3.34	2.95	2.64
Asia					
(excluding China)	1.96	3.19	5.90	5.14	4.38

SOURCE: Overseas Development Council calculations based on OECD, *Development Assistance and Development Corporation*, 1964–1983; and United Nations, *Demographic Yearbook*, 1982.

Compact for African Development

Report of the Committee on African Development Strategies

CO-CHAIRMEN

*Lawrence S. Eagleburger
  Kissinger Associates, Inc.

*Donald F. McHenry
  Georgetown University

COMMITTEE MEMBERS AND
ENDORSERS OF THE REPORT

Morton Bahr
  *Communications Workers of
  America*

*Douglas J. Bennet, Jr.
  *National Public Radio, Former
  Administrator, USAID*

---

*Member, Committee on African
Development Strategies.
Affiliations are for identification
only. Committee members and
endorsers are acting in their
individual capacities.

*Elliot Berg
  Elliot Berg & Associates

*Louis Berger
  Louis Berger, Inc.

Marjorie Craig Benton
  Save the Children Federation

*Tom Bradley
  Mayor of Los Angeles

Andrew F. Brimmer
  Brimmer & Co., Inc.

*Robert S. Browne
  Economic Consultant

Prescott Bush
  Prescott Bush & Company

*Goler T. Butcher
  Howard University

William H. Bywater
  *International Union of Electronic,
  Electrical, Technical, Salaried and
  Machine Workers*

*Frank C. Carlucci
  Sears World Trade, Inc.

Joseph R. Daly
Doyle Dane Bernbach, Inc.

*John C. Danforth
U.S. Senate

*Ralph P. Davidson
TIME, Incorporated

Peter J. Davies
InterAction

John Diebold
Diebold Group, Inc.

*Julian C. Dixon
U.S. House of Representatives

Thomas R. Donahue
AFL-CIO

*Donald B. Easum
African-American Institute

*Thomas L. Farmer
*Prather, Seeger, Doolittle, and
Farmer*

*Richard E. Feinberg
Overseas Development Council

*Louis B. Fleming
Los Angeles Times

*J. Wayne Fredericks
Ford Motor Company

*Paul Fribourg
Continental Grain Company

*David A. Hamburg
Carnegie Corporation of New York

*Niles Helmboldt
Equator Holdings Limited

*Jesse Hill, Jr.
Atlanta Life Insurance Co.

*Benjamin L. Hooks
*National Association for the
Advancement of Colored People*

*Robert D. Hormats
Goldman, Sachs & Co.

Vernon E. Jordan, Jr.
*Akin, Gump, Strauss, Hauer &
Feld*

*Elizabeth T. Kennan
Mount Holyoke College

*Paul H. Kreisberg
Council on Foreign Relations

*Carol Lancaster
Georgetown University

*Mickey Leland
U.S. House of Representatives

*John P. Lewis
Princeton University

George N. Lindsay
Debevoise & Plimpton

*Bruce Llewellyn
Philadelphia Coca Cola Bottling Co.

*C. Payne Lucas
Africare

*Alex Massad
Mobil Oil Corporation

*Paul F. McCleary
United Methodist Church

Robert S. McNamara

*William Grawn Milliken
*Former Governor, State of
Michigan*

Erwin Millimet
Stroock & Stroock & Lavan

*Richard Moose
*Shearson-Lehman, International,
Inc.*

Victor H. Palmieri
The Palmieri Company

Peter G. Peterson
The Blackstone Group

*Charles W. Robinson
Energy Transition Corporation

*Randall Robinson
TransAfrica

David Rockefeller
Rockefeller Brothers Fund

Fred Rosen
Fred Rosen Associates

SUMMARY

The drought, famine, and debt emergencies in Sub-Saharan Africa have demonstrated the depths of the continent's fundamental development crisis. Perhaps because of the crisis, African leaders and their donor friends in the Western world and the multilateral organizations have arrived at a new consensus about what needs to be done for Africa's development. This Committee strongly believes that this consensus creates an historic opportunity. Africa, the United States, and other nations of the world should now make a strong, long-term commitment to help Africa help itself.

Humanitarian and political interests require that the United States take a leading role in creating a Compact for African Development. The cost of such a compact, especially in a period of budget stringency, is significant: some $3 billion a year in long-term assistance from the American public and private sectors. But the costs later would be higher still if African economies were to slide into full-scale economic collapse.

The Compact requires a mutual undertaking: A U.S. commitment to long-term support in exchange for an African commitment to implement reforms and improve economic performance. Only such reforms can guarantee greater external support; yet greater resources must be made available before reforms can lead to growth.

A comprehensive approach for Africa's development must address remaining emergency needs, rehabilitation of economies, and longer-term development problems. The program set forth in this report addresses these needs. Specifically, the Committee on African Development Strategies recommends actions to:

MEET THE IMMEDIATE FOOD NEEDS OF HUNGRY
PEOPLE WHILE FOSTERING DEVELOPMENT

1. Using food from the United States and other donors, African states should initiate food-for-work and other food programs to foster agricultural development and increase productivity.

2. The United States and other donors providing assistance should negotiate longer-term food aid arrangements in Africa, covering up to five years at a time and guaranteeing support—in the event of shortfalls during that period—to those governments that are working vigorously to reform policy and increase investment for higher agricultural productivity.

STOP THE DETERIORATION IN AFRICA'S
ECONOMIES

3. In exchange for the reaffirmation by African states of responsibility for their debt, the United States government should re-program, or stretch out over an extended period of time, its share of most African debt.

4. The United States should pledge $250 million to the World Bank's Special Facility for Sub-Saharan Africa.

INITIATE STRATEGIES AND ACTIONS FOR THE
LONGER TERM

5. The United States should lead a drive for increased investment in environmentally sound African agricultural development, with special emphasis on small farms and the women farmers who have previously been neglected by aid programs.

6. In cooperation with African governments that are moving to increase productivity, the United Stated should launch a major and sustained campaign in research and training to create the human and technical building blocks needed for a "Green Revolution" in Africa.

7. The United States should work with the International Planned Parenthood Federation and the United Nations Fund for Population Activities to institute major population programs in each African country that has a bilateral U.S. aid program.

8. The United States should help Africa unleash the creativity of its own private sector through technical help, improved procurement practices, and trade reform.

9. The United States should make a full contribution of $1.33 billion a year over the next three years to the eighth replenishment of the International

Development Association (IDA), the "soft loan" window of the World Bank, to assure more adequate long-term multilateral financing for African development.

10. Congress should amalgamate security and development aid monies for Africa into a single account clearly designated for development purposes to demonstrate that U.S. assistance is geared to African development performance.

To support the U.S. commitment to the Compact for African Development, we propose:

11. Repayments from past U.S. foreign aid loans should be used to help finance new initiatives for Africa.

12. The United States should triple the long-term U.S. finance going to Africa through a combination of bilateral and multilateral programs to reach a new level of $3 billion per year.

We urge private groups to search for ways to be of help both in using their own resources and in advocating a greater public response. We also urge Congress and the Executive Branch to act with foresight to reflect our country's long-term interests in an Africa that can both survive short-term crises and assume its place as a full participant in the world economy.

COMPACT FOR AFRICAN DEVELOPMENT

Africa is suffering from an extraordinary crisis. Its proportions are mythic, its severity almost impossible for the rest of the world to imagine or comprehend.

Even though the worst of the recent famine is over, Africans will be struggling to survive for decades to come. Tens of millions of African children, if they live beyond their first year, may never know a decent, secure existence. Entire communities may perish while African and outside governments stand by helplessly. Unless new measures are adopted, some independent African countries may be doomed to live in a state of perpetual chaos, aggravated by combination of natural disasters, political upheaval, human failings, and financial ruin. Their governments will survive only by depending on others.

The causes of the crisis in Sub-Saharan Africa[1] are many and varied: some were visited upon the continent by outside forces, and some by Africans themselves. It is important to examine and understand those causes, but merely finding and identifying past errors will not guarantee a better future. Something more must be done urgently unless the cycle of catastrophe is to be repeated over and over again, with the bulk of African and outside energies spent on staving off disaster rather than building for the future.

Africa's situation is not hopeless. The continent can emerge from its current dire circumstances. First of all, Africa must help itself, but the international community must also take bold, dramatic steps to help Africa help itself.

The task will be difficult. It will require new approaches, drawing upon the lessons and mistakes of the past but avoiding dogma and narrow ideologies. Cooperative efforts must be undertaken among African states, among developed states, and between Africa and the developed world. Clear, long-term goals must be agreed upon and mutual obligations undertaken. Meaningful progress will require nothing less than a compact—a reciprocal commitment to make sacrifices and work toward lasting change.

Neither a formal covenant nor a legal agreement, the compact would be a mutual undertaking between the United States and other Western donors and African states that wish to take part. We foresee no new institution, but rather regular consultations between donors and African states about what needs to be done to sustain development.

On the African side, the compact calls for strong leadership to build productivity and accountability. From Western donors it will require consistent and selective support for effective African performance. Because U.S. initiatives can be successful only if they are paired with intensive African efforts, the mutuality expressed in the compact is indispensable to both maintaining U.S. commitment and ensuring that it results in self-reliant African development.

As the leader of international relief efforts, the United States has played a crucial, catalytic role in the recent crisis. But American and other Western donors must change their approach to Africa or they risk exacerbating the already serious situation. As a political, economic and technological world power, and as a nation with a history of deep commitments to helping those who help themselves, the United States has a unique potential and responsibility to work with the people and governments of Africa.

In formulating a compact for African development, we must look beyond the current emergency—to focus the attention of international leaders and the world public on the long-term problems of Africa and to help Africans and those that help them face up to their past mistakes. One basis for hope lies in the exceptions to Africa's overall picture of decline. Some African countries show remarkable survival powers amidst the crisis. These countries, relatively more market-oriented than others, tend to enjoy greater political stability. They have lessons to offer their fellow Africans.

In fact, the crisis itself has created an opportunity that must not be lost. Africans see this clearly, as evidenced by the Lagos Plan of Action drawn up in 1980, by the resolutions on development agreed to at the Organization of African Unity's summit in July 1985, and most emphatically in a declaration issued by their planning ministers last April: "What our governments are seeking is a complete restructuring of the African economies so that progress is based on the use of the region's own resources and potential." Western donors realize this too. And increasingly, the World Bank, in its reports on Africa, is stressing longer-term economic reform as a crucial element in African reconstruction efforts. This unique and timely conjuncture makes the compact all the more necessary and appropriate.

The need now is to move from analysis to action.

THE DEPTH OF AFRICA'S CRISIS

What has happened to Africa in the past two decades can be compared to the effects of a world war. Its crisis is different from anything found anywhere else in the world: no other continent is suffering such acute famine and environmental loss, and nowhere else do institutions and skills lag so far behind problems.

No other region of the developed or developing world finds itself in such a steep and steady decline as Africa. Economic growth rates in Africa have been consistently lower than those of other developing areas. The most optimistic current projection from the World Bank is that per capita income in Africa will decline slightly in the next ten years. But if interest rates are high and the industrial countries undergo another recession, African income will slip by at least another 5 per cent.

In Asia and Latin America, per capita food production is increasing and population growth rates are decreasing, while in Africa exactly the reverse is true; per capita food production is declining while population growth rates are soaring. Elsewhere, health improvements are taking place rapidly, but in Africa the famine had led to a dramatic deterioration in the health of its people, particularly its children and its elderly. Even these broad trends do not convey the debilitating effects of endemic diseases, especially malaria and diarrheal disease and widespread malnutrition, all of which exact a heavy toll on the quality of life and the productivity of huge numbers of Africans.

It sometimes seems meaningless to ask when things will begin to improve in Africa; a more basic question is when they will stop getting worse at such a rapid rate. As a matter of fact, Africa is fighting to hold on to what it has. Roads, educational systems, communications networks, and buildings are deteriorating rapidly, and enormous resources are needed just to maintain and preserve these past investments.

By 1985, the existence of some 150 million Africans—more than one in three people in Sub-Saharan Africa—depended partially or totally on imported food. But even with all this imported food, according to World Bank estimates, perhaps 60 per cent of the people who live in Africa consume fewer calories each day than are thought to be necessary for normal life. This helps to explain why five million children die in Africa every year and another five million are permanently crippled by malnutrition and hunger.

Africa's dramatic drought of the early 1970s, which took one hundred thousand lives, looks modest in comparison to recent events. The far more severe drought of the early 1980s, covering a much wider area, has taken an enormous—still uncounted—human toll. At least twenty-four African countries experienced catastrophic food shortages in 1984-85.

More than twenty of the world's thirty-four poorest countries are located in Africa. Their poverty has dimensions that are staggering:

- African agricultural growth has been based on opening up unused land. Now, as growing populations crowd available land, overuse is depleting the natural wealth of Africa's soils. Without new methods of cultivation, Africa will experience absolute declines in agricultural productivity. Also inhibiting output is the spread of livestock diseases. Some of the richest forests have been stripped of wood for fuel. As dryness has prevented the normal growth of plants and trees in recent years, ground water has evaporated more rapidly and soil erosion has become more severe. The specter of spreading desertification haunts Africa.

- Africa's population is growing faster than anywhere else in the world, and even the most optimistic projections of improvements in food production offer little hope of catching up. More than 400 million people live in Sub-Saharan Africa today; at an estimated overall population growth rate of 3.2 per cent a year, the figure could quadruple by the year 2025.

- Africans, because of poverty and adverse environmental factors, are more vulnerable to infectious diseases and other serious illnesses than any other people in the world. Poor sanitation severely limits ability to deal with these health problems. Despite significant improvements, infant mortality rates remain extraordinarily high and average life spans pathetically short.

- Africa is host to about half of the world's estimated 10 million refugees largely as a result of famines and wars, yet refugees in other areas have commanded greater international attention. Despite the hospitality of African governments that spend scarce resources to shelter them, African refugees live close to the margin of existence and often contribute to political instability in their host countries.

- Africa faces a critical shortage of professionals, technicians, and managers. Perhaps even more worrisome is the dearth of people educated to improve agriculture. Africa's shortage of health personnel, the most severe in the world, has been aggravated by a "brain drain" of young people who have been trained abroad. Many talented Africans who might contribute to development are unable to do so because of political differences or repression.

- Africa's urbanization is more rapid than that of any other region: many African cities are growing at a rate of 7-10 per cent a year; the figure may be as high as 13 per cent for Nairobi, the capital of Kenya. As a result, vast shantytowns have sprung up, where hunger, poor health, unemployment, and crime fester, as inadequate urban facilities are increasingly overtaxed.

- Africa's international debt is not as large as that of Latin America, but it is an enormous burden for countries that are living so close to the margin of survival. By the end of 1986, the payments required to cover the interest on Africa's debts will be equal to two-thirds of all the money the continent receives in aid, leaving very little for new development efforts. The continent's balance of trade is bleak; the deficit was up to $7.9 billion in 1984 and is getting worse all the time.

WHAT HAS GONE WRONG IN AFRICA

While generalizations about Sub-Saharan Africa's forty-six countries mask real differences in their development, no one doubts that things have gone awry in Africa. The continent has taken severe external blows and also wasted precious resources. What makes the continent's circumstances particularly disheartening to its friends, and even more intolerable to its own peoples, is the vast gap between the often unrealistic expectations that flourished at the time of independence and the somber reality that prevails today.

The period of decolonization was an especially heady time in Africa. The new regimes were expected, and tried, to provide a vast array of services to their people. They also embarked on the construction of state edifices and industries that would give dramatic, demonstrable reality to their political sovereignty. As long as the relatively favorable economic conditions of the 1960s lasted, all this seemed to be possible. During the early years of independence, plenty of rain and high commodity prices helped Africa sustain stable, if modest, growth. It was Asia that struggled with famine at that time, while Africa raised its nutritional levels.

The "oil shock" of 1973 was the first of a series of crises which introduced Africans to a harsh new reality. The same international economic trends that buffeted the developed countries and the rest of the Third World in the 1970s and early 1980s hit Africa with devastating force, reducing income from exports and raising the price of imports at the same time. Despite efforts of the Organization of Petroleum Exporting Countries (OPEC) to provide special concessional aid, the average loss of income in Africa as a result of skyrocketing energy costs was 10 per cent, and in some countries it was as high as 25 per cent. The purchasing power of African exports declined 30 per cent.

Opportunities for a better life faded with astonishing speed for the first generation of independent Africans. With harvests stunted by drought and overseas markets for crops severely reduced, livelihoods began to evaporate. Inflation caused the buying power of salaries to plunge; the deterioration of national economies caused many jobs to disappear altogether. Roads, lacking proper maintenance, broke up, and travel to the interior of some countries became more difficult. Vehicles rusted out and were often abandoned alongside deteriorating roads. In a number of countries, even the infrastructure inherited from the colonial era became unusable.

To design the remedial steps to be taken, analysis of what has gone wrong is essential. The easiest course—and it has been taken by many angry Africans—is to suggest that Africa is simply the unwitting and helpless victim of colonialism and of external factors such as the oil shocks and the adverse cycles of world economic conditions during the 1970s and 1980s. In fact, these are part of the problem. Africa inherited internal geographic boundaries and political dividing lines that once delineated European spheres of influence; they are now an economic liability.

At independence, colonial powers left African economies for the most part dependent upon a few commodity exports. New African regimes started out with few workable political institutions and had little training to run them. In the short period since independence they have struggled to build political and economic systems simultaneously.

These are the facts of Africa's life, and no programs for development can go forward without taking account of them. At the same time it is important to recognize the serious mistakes that Africans themselves have made in the past quarter-century:

- Agriculture has been severely neglected. Even now, when many countries are newly emphasizing agriculture, that emphasis is not always reflected in the allocation of resources. African states spend an average of only 5 per cent of their budgets on agriculture, whereas in Southeast Asia, the nations that lead in agriculture spend two or three times as much, with impressive results. Much of what is invested in agriculture overlooks the largest and most efficient group of African producers, the small-scale farmers (a very large proportion of whom are women) who grow some 70 per cent of the continent's food.

- The majority of African governments embarked on unwise and economically unfeasible industrial programs. State-controlled corporations were created to manage vast areas of economic activity, frequently with a high degree of centralization and costly government subsidies, and almost always without the skilled personnel that would give them a chance to work successfully. Many of these corporations regarded their main purpose as employment-creation, and burgeoning state payrolls only drained resources further.

- Poor governmental economic policies, particularly controlled prices, often restricted the creativity of Africans, weakening incentives for production and reducing efficiency. While keeping food cheap in the cities, these policies shortchanged the rural areas.

- Corruption has often distorted and sometimes replaced economic management. Governmental and private-sector elites have drained off a substantial percentage of national resources as well as outside aid.

- Many African governments have undertaken wasteful prestige projects—such as the construction of extravagant government office buildings, conference centers, and luxury hotels—that cannot be justified in terms of development priorities.

In many states, these mistakes have both contributed to and been accentuated by political instability. Africa's coup-per-country rate is the highest in the world. Indeed, only twelve African nations have survived since independence without undergoing a single coup, and today at least half of Africa's people live under military rule. Most African countries have failed to develop strong institutions that will help promote a reliable system of political succession. Too often this had led to the repression of opposition. Moreover, through the Organization of African Unity and other international forums Africans have projected an image of indifference to African abuses of human rights and civil liberties. All of this adversely influences the reputation of Africa in the world community, diminishing the believability of African rhetoric and potentially constraining the willingness of others to help Africans solve their problems.

But Africans alone are not to blame for their dismal situation. Usually well-intentioned outsiders have also contributed to the problems:

- Donor aid has often been short-term and uncoordinated. African governments have sometimes been induced to undertake projects simply because aid is available for them from certain countries. Frequently these projects end up interfering with priorities that should have been maintained.

- Some donors have encouraged Africans to undertake obvious white elephants—boondoggles that have less to do with generosity or with genuine development assistance than with domestic political and economic considerations in the country providing the money.

- Outside funds are often available only for purchases of new equipment—for example trucks—from donors. But the real need is for spare parts to maintain items already contributed by someone else or bought with precious foreign exchange, as well as training of Africans to repair existing equipment. The result of this mismatch is the creation of graveyards of unrepaired vehicles while new vehicles continue to be imported.

- Projects are often financed that support a donor's narrow political priorities—including competition between the superpowers and their recruitment of friends in the Third World—and this, too, skews the development priorities of recipient nations. Indeed, the donors' security concerns are occasionally disguised as development imperatives.

- In the heady days of recycling petro-dollars, commercial banks abandoned some of their usual caution and made funds available at bargain rates and in amounts that looked prudent. Some of these loans financed projects whose economic viability was highly questionable. Later, when real interest rates rose and commodity prices fell, these loans became unsupportable.

- Most donors, including international institutions, have jumped from one fad to another to justify development expenditures—from the support of infrastructure development, to a concern with basic human needs, to the most recent heavy focus on agriculture and encouragement of the private sector. In reality, a properly executed, long-term development process probably requires a balance of all these approaches and others.

On both sides, then, there have been ill-conceived policies, haphazard administration, and self-interested motives, but it is the African people who have suffered the consequences.

Outside donors, for all the money that they have poured into Africa since independence, have often made contradictory demands or imposed conflicting conditions on the beneficiaries of their largesse. Meanwhile, proliferating and overlapping projects have drained the administrative energies of African officials and left the continent's landscape strewn with rusted-out bright ideas.

Annual per-capita aid levels in recent years have been higher in Africa than in other regions of the Third World—reaching $20 per person per year by 1982—but the returns on capital investment have generally declined. Africa's ability to use its available resources productively increasingly has been called into question. African governments have lived beyond their means, postponing the day of reckoning to a moment that seemed unforeseeable but that is now upon us.

THE OPPORTUNITY IN AFRICA

The most recent drought and famine, tragic as they have been, have given both Africa and its donor friends an opportunity to start afresh, to correct some of the most grievous errors of the past, and to build a new, more secure future.

No one is more convinced of the need to change course on development than Africans are today. There is a new mood of realism in Africa—a willingness to enter into a tough analysis of past mistakes and present confusion, a sobriety that verges on humiliation. Africans are looking, frequently Westward, for new ideas. In some cases this is already leading to successful innovation.

Throughout Africa, more and more people are recognizing: the necessity of cutting back the role of the state in the economy, the urgency of emphasizing food production, and the gravity of the population problem.

With all its grave weaknesses, the African record so far also shows some striking strengths:

- Ten years have been added to average lifespans during the past three decades.

- Adult literacy has almost tripled, from 16 per cent in 1960 to 43 per cent in 1980, through the addition of thousands of schools and the doubling of primary school and quadrupling of secondary school enrollments in the past twenty years.

- Communication networks have been established, bringing some rural areas into much greater contact with African capitals and governments.

Thousands of miles of new roads and railroads were constructed, and energy consumption more than doubled.

• An impressive degree of nation-building has taken place, despite artificial boundaries and other inherited disadvantages, and despite the pressure created by unrelenting political turmoil.

• A few countries, for example, Malawi, Zimbabwe, and Ivory Coast have made significant strides in agricultural development while others, including Botswana and Cameroon, have shown excellent financial management, keeping imports within the limits imposed by export revenues. Others have begun to remove obstacles to productivity by raising farm prices, trimming state bureaucracies, lowering subsidies, and adjusting exchange rates.

• African people have made great personal sacrifices, willingly spending large proportions of their minimal incomes to educate their children, and often sharing what little they have with others who are more needy. They have, among other things, been uncommonly tolerant of refugee influxes.

Most important is the new attitude among Africans—among government officials, military officers, and the small but influential middle class—that the economic and political management of their nations must improve, that accountability must increase and corruption must decline, and that hard realities must be faced while greater outside interest and help are available. The key task is to take the necessary actions that flow from this frankness and self-criticism before this unique opportunity fades.

Although the economic trends give no grounds for optimism, determination and ingenuity can be combined to attack Africa's fundamental problems.

WHY AMERICANS MUST PLAY A ROLE

The hungry people of Africa are very far away from America in both miles and circumstances: even after seeing graphic films of their plight on television, few of us can imagine the conditions in which most Africans live. But there are strong moral and practical reasons why Americans cannot ignore Africa.

The song is right when it says, "We are the world." The United States and other wealthy societies share the planet with hundreds of millions of people who lack the most basic necessities of a decent existence. According to the tenets of all religions and most political philosophies, it is a fundamental responsibility of the rich to help the poor. It is also in the best American secular tradition to act boldly in such an emergency, to show humanitarian concern without being unduly preoccupied with geopolitical or strategic considerations. Vast numbers of people in Africa are not merely poor, but facing starvation and death; and their circumstances invoke that responsibility with particular urgency. The wealth of the United States and the poverty of Africa is shown in a few statistics: An average African's income is less than one thirtieth of an average American's income. If one adds up the gross national products of all forty-six Sub-Saharan African states, the total is less than 6 per cent of the U.S. gross national product. Africa must support 400 million people on an economy producing only as much as the state of Illinois.

The fact that millions of Americans responded as generously as they did in 1984 and 1985, with at least $170 million in donations to ease African misery, symbolizes the readiness of Americans to respond to human pain. And the fact that much of that money went to Ethiopia, now ruled by a harsh Marxist military regime bitterly critical of the United States, shows that principle can triumph over politics.

Apart from humanitarian considerations, there are compelling reasons for U.S. involvement in helping Africa today. America's economic interests on the continent, for example, go far beyond the concern about strategic minerals in South Africa and Zaire, or with oil in Nigeria. An Africa that is stable and develops in an orderly fashion may eventually be the source of other raw materials and an expanding market for industrial and other finished goods—a continent where normal trade can be conducted in a businesslike fashion to the benefit of both sides.

Indeed, there is an unprecedented opportunity to mobilize African enterprise to play a role in the continent's recovery. The stage can be set for an active African role in international commerce and investment, in which the United States can and should become involved.

Africa matters politically as well. If the United States genuinely cares about advancing the cause of freedom in the world, then Africa, with its dozens of separate, independent countries, certainly merits attention. In international forums, Africans are in a position to advance or impede peace-keeping efforts in the Middle East and other parts of the world. There are also realistic considerations of Western security that come into play in Africa. Turmoil arising from persistent economic chaos might be exploited by those interested in advancing narrow political, ideological, or military interests. In the unlikely event that much of Africa were to fall under the control of forces hostile to the West, the implications would be grave.

Moreover, gaps between rich and poor countries in the world continue to widen—with most of Africa at one extreme and the wealthy countries, especially the United States, at the other. Resentment of American indifference could be exploited, particularly by anti-Western fundamentalist movements whose use of terrorist force may seriously threaten future world order. U.S. commitment now to Africa's growth can help break down divisions that will only grow more rigid if allowed to persist.

International divisions may also cause division in this country. Hostility or desperation in Africa can affect racial feelings in the United States. African turmoil may find echoes here. In an interdependent world, it is important for the United States and for everyone else that Africa develop those human and physical resources that will promote the interests and the well-being of humankind. The world cannot truly advance as long as one of its parts—a huge continent—lags far behind.

Finally, the U.S. experience can help Africa. In the 1930s, America faced a depression in its Western and Southern farm belts similar to what we see in Africa now. That economic and environmental crisis was ended by years of long-term concessional finance, work programs, large-scale soil and water conservation projects, and extension services to help farmers cope with new challenges. U.S. expertise in solving a wide range of problems is probably the best available. Africa can use U.S. scientific capability in agricultural research, medicine, and information. Our Peace Corps, international business, consultants, and voluntary agency staffs offer a large bank of experience to draw upon.

CARRYING OUT THE COMPACT

Africans and those who would help them must act quickly, not only to alleviate the current crisis, but also to chart a long-term course for Africa's recovery and further development. These tasks go hand in hand. At the individual family level, it is clear that those who are starving need food, that they need to be able to regain useful productive lives, and that they then need to be able to improve their well-being through better technology and investment of additional resources. African nations face this same set of challenges. Coherent actions are needed to meet the emergency, rehabilitation, and growth requirements of the sub-continent.

In response to these needs, we are proposing a compact that is, above all, a mutual undertaking. Both Africans and those who want to help them are being asked to evaluate their past performance and make important philosophical and practical changes. The United States and other donor countries and agencies have many of the human, technical, and economic resources that can alleviate Africa's problems, but that alone is not the answer. The task cannot simply be performed or imposed by outsiders. Rather, Africa must be helped to help itself. This is the agenda:

I. MEET THE IMMEDIATE FOOD NEEDS OF HUNGRY PEOPLE WHILE FOSTERING DEVELOPMENT

The American record in providing food aid to Africa over the years has been outstanding. In the recent crisis, U.S. assistance, public and private, has provided half of the emergency famine relief. Indeed, the performance of the entire international community, particularly of the United Nations, in responding to Africa's anguish has been highly commendable; there has been a level and an intensity of involvement that far transcends anything done before. At the same time, the disappearance of prominent, daily news coverage of famine and drought should not allow us to overlook the fact that a crisis is still at hand—and that the long-term problems remain to be dealt with.

It will be necessary over the course of the next few years to maintain significant emergency levels of food aid to Africa. Food aid also will be needed over the longer run. The World Bank estimates that even if by 1988 Africa again benefits from normal rains—the right amounts in the right places at the right times—the continent will still need, as a result of population growth, the same amount of imported food that it received in the 1985 emergency. Given the poor prospects for earning enough foreign exchange to finance growing food import needs, donors and African states should anticipate large food aid programs to Africa for several more years. The question is how to structure this aid to ensure that it helps as much as possible to foster the only long-term solution that is viable: African self-sufficiency in food. Ways must be found to use food aid to promote development rather than dependency.

1. *Using food from the United States and other donors, African states should initiate food-for-work and other food programs to foster agricultural development and increase productivity.*

American food aid can be used to pay for development work. This has been done extensively in Asia, but not in Africa. It will require more oversight, but with American encouragement, African governments should use food aid to pay in cash or kind for rural labor to rehabilitate roads, earthworks, dams, and rural water supplies necessary for agricultural production and distribution as well as health. Other food-for-work programs should focus on soil conservation and reforestation. This will put income into the hands of farmers, enabling millions who have lived at the margin of relief to support themselves again, while giving a boost to those who are struggling to pay for the tools, seeds, and fertilizer needed to maintain or expand output. It will also emphasize the connection between food supplies and maintenance of the environment, establishing the need to prevent further erosion of Africa's productive land as a means of guarding against future famine.

The United States would, in effect, be working both sides of the supply-and-demand equation: reducing the demand by channeling food to the impoverished, while increasing the supply by channeling the local currencies generated by food aid to rural development and agricultural production activities. Local roads and communications will be improved in the process, and people will be given a more direct stake in their own development. To make these efforts effective, the U.S. government should rely more heavily on the private voluntary organizations working in Africa and switch some of its oversight of aid programs from capital cities to rural areas.

2. *The United States and other donors should negotiate longer-term food aid arrangements in Africa, covering up to five years at a time and guaranteeing support in the event of shortfalls during that period for governments that are working vigorously to reform policy and increase investment for higher agricultural productivity.*

In addition to the short-term relief required by African countries, there is a longer-term structural need for financial help to continue importing food to cover the shortfalls from production. Africa now imports 20 per cent of its food supply on a regular basis, and this is apt to increase until the time when the continent becomes significantly more capable of raising its own food supplies.

While this recommendation carries certain burdens for the American public purse, it would also have clear advantages: there would be fewer last-minute dashes to Congress for supplemental appropriations to meet unanticipated needs and a more assured market for U.S. farmers; further, the U.S. government could buy the food it is going to use for aid in a more orderly manner, probably at lower cost. African governments, knowing they could depend on American assistance, would have added incentives to undertake reforms that often involve political risks. No one wants to foster dependency on food aid. Therefore this transitional aid must be structured to achieve steady progress toward local food security for African peoples.

II. STOP THE DETERIORATION OF AFRICA'S ECONOMIES

Before Africa can truly make progress toward self-sufficiency, some of the terms of its current dependency must be altered and greater generosity and patience will be required on the part of those who are already helping.

Africa's debt problem is due not merely to a bad cash flow, but to deep-rooted poverty and insolvency. Until recently, the international community tended to ignore the debt because it apparently did not present a threat to the world financial system. At about $100 billion today, African debt still accounts for only 10 per cent of the world total for developing countries and less than 5 per cent of the debt owed to commercial banks.

But for Africa, the debt burden is staggering. On the average, more than half of all export earnings are now required to service foreign loans; for some countries, debt service actually exceeds export earnings. In 1983, Africa paid $300 million more to private banks than it received from them. As a consequence of this and other factors, the foreign-exchange reserves of most African countries have declined precipitously. At the end of 1984, reserves covered only 27 days' worth of imports, compared with 93 days' worth for Asian countries and 113 days for those of Latin America. Africa is unable to repay its debt and have any margin for progress. Now several African countries are in arrears to the International Monetary Fund. The inability of some to repay or even service their debt has serious implications for the international financial system.

After the 1973 oil price shock, the IMF set up special arrangements to help the poorer countries maintain their energy imports. But after the 1979 oil shock, African borrowing—encouraged by commercial banks and the IMF—led to vast increases in African debts bunched for repayment in the 1985-87 period. A large number of African states simply cannot meet their debt payments. There are two choices: African debts can be stretched out substantially, or huge new amounts of aid can be pumped in just to help pay the debt. Otherwise, Africa literally must take funds that are needed for food and fuel imports and use them to pay off the banks, the IMF, and other official lenders.

The cost to Africa of this debt problem goes far beyond money; it drains valuable human energies that could be devoted to more productive tasks. One of the poorest nations on the continent complains that it took the key people in its government six months just to negotiate a twelve-month extension of debt payments.

Economic stabilization programs of the kind frequently recommended by the IMF can be useful in eliminating wasteful practices. However, when pursued in a short-term manner, compressed reforms are liable to erode further the capacity for recovery in Africa. Drastic cuts in expenditures have high political and social costs in such poor countries, and changing the structure of production takes a long time and requires additional resources. More systematic solutions must be found; in the meantime, intermediate steps can be taken.

3. In exchange for the reaffirmation by African states of ultimate responsibility for their debt, the United States government should re-program, or stretch out over an extended period of time, its share of most African debt.

Until now, Americans have lagged behind the Europeans in offering relief from official debt to Africa. The United States must, by law, suspend all aid to any country, whatever its circumstances, that is more than six months overdue on repaying official U.S. loans; the entire U.S. aid program to Tanzania was jettisoned over this very point.

The cost of making such a concession to all African countries that are in debt to the United States government is relatively small—approximately $20 million a year—but such a move would demonstrate American flexibility in an important area. In return, the African countries involved should reaffirm ultimate responsibility for their debt and should commit themselves to reforms that will increase their productivity and, therefore, their ability to pay.

Another option is for the U.S. government to accept repayments of African debt in local currency using the repayments for financing development programs.

Beyond changing repayment terms, new finance must be found during the next few years to help keep African economies afloat. This will require some $5-6 billion per year. Because new commercial lending and investment are unlikely for some time, the only possibility to meet this need is through a combination of debt refinancing and new aid.

The United States took an important step regarding debt refinancing at the October 1985 IMF/World Bank meetings in Seoul, Korea, when it advocated the use of funds being repaid to the IMF Trust Fund (largely from other countries) to refinance IMF lending to Africa on longer terms. This action should enable the most hard pressed African states to remain current with the IMF and thereby preserve the possibility of debt financing from others. In advocating a resumption of Trust Fund operations, the United States was using its position as the largest shareholder in the IMF to assert real leadership on an issue that threatened to undermine a great many IMF operations.

It also expressed a willingness to explore additional development finance for Africa. This kind of leadership is needed at the World Bank, where the United States is also the largest shareholder.

The debt issue facing Africa needs more than stop-gap measures and the rejuggling of funds and agreements. It requires enough additional capital to enable Africa to grow its way out of debt. This issue can be faced now at some cost or later at considerably greater cost.

Thus we wish to emphasize the need for significant amounts of new money to help meet a fair share of the internal finance gap facing Africa. We believe this should involve tripling the long-term U.S. assistance going to Africa through a combination of bilateral and multilateral programs to reach a new level of $3 billion per year.

4. *The United States should pledge $250 million to the World Bank's Special Facility for Sub-Saharan Africa.*

Contributions of more than $1 billion have been committed by other nations, including several close U.S. allies, to the key international effort organized to address Africa's need for financing imports of critical goods and services. For the first time, the United States has not been in the lead on such a multilateral finance effort—indeed, this is the first time that others have gone ahead without Washington's participation. A contribution from the United States would greatly strengthen this important international initiative to help African nations restart their economies.

The United States should continue the Economic Policy Initiative launched last year with a five year program, averaging $100 million/year, to reward policy reform in Africa with extra assistance. This is a useful effort. But the needs require a greater U.S. response. We also need a channel where larger sums of money are combined for more effective coordination of aid and policy signals to African states during these critical times. Improvements in aid coordination are imperative and can best be accomplished by multilateral institutions in concert with African governments.

An American contribution to the new World Bank effort will underscore the utility of multilateral assistance that is not tied to specific projects, as well as show Africans that Americans understand the depth of their crisis and are willing to be flexible.

III. INITIATE STRATEGIES AND ACTIONS FOR THE
LONGER TERM

Sub-Saharan Africa is now suffering an economic depression. Drought and debt have enforced an austerity that has profound consequences for daily life: massive unemployment; less food and less nourishment; the deterioration of roads, bridges, farms, and industry; declining health services; and, in schools, crowded classrooms, poorly paid and trained teachers, and a few books. In some countries, it is only Africa's strong cultural tradition of communal support that has allowed large numbers of people to survive.

Where should donors place their priorities in trying to help Africans increase productivity and achieve long-term development? It seems clear now that except in the few favored African countries that can count on substantial income from the export of oil, agriculture must serve as the base for all forms of economic progress. With populations increasing dramatically, the central challenge for African countries is to feed themselves. They must be helped to do so and encouraged to emphasize small, efficient farms over large, inefficient ones; to explore new marketing alternatives that avoid excessive centralization; and to improve technical higher education that might help bring Africa its own "Green Revolution."

5. *The United States should lead a drive for increased investment in environmentally sound African agricultural development, with special emphasis on small farms and the women farmers who have previously been neglected by aid programs.*

U.S. policy should reinforce the growing conviction of African governments and multilateral institutions, including the World Bank, that Africa must succeed in the agricultural domain before it can move on to other areas. A hopeful sign was the commitment of Africa's heads of state at their July 1985 summit to increase gradually the share of agriculture in national public investment to 20–25 per cent by 1989. Agriculture is the engine of non-agricultural growth, and more and more Africans are coming to recognize and act on this economic fact. Moreover, the potential for agriculture is great throughout almost all of Africa. But it will often be politically risky for African governments to turn their emphasis away from the cities and industry. The United States should strongly support those governments that are willing to face up to these risks in the long-term interest of their economies.

Addressing the rural political economy also involves challenges. Without question, large-scale progress in African agriculture will only come about when programs focus on small farms, which are the source of subsistence for the vast majority of African families and which produce most of Africa's food. And the majority of the food producers are women. Technologies, services, and resources must be structured to serve the real producers of food in Africa. Fostering agricultural development also requires improving collection, storage, processing, transport to market, and distribution—all of which hold promise for more involvement by the growing local private sectors. All these changes will require a reorientation of programs.

If rural development is to be self-sustaining, maintaining and restoring Africa's natural resource base will be necessary. Technologies and methods suited to the local environment are essential. Africa's Green Revolution will not be like Asia's, where a few breakthroughs had widespread applications. Africa's complex environment requires a broad variety of approaches.

Dealing with environmental problems will require integrating soil, water, and forest management issues into all agricultural sector planning. Only within the past few years have African leaders begun to acknowledge the importance of maintaining their land resources; for many years, conservation had been deemed an alien or "colonial" cause. As with population, U.S. officials need to reiterate the central importance of the environment in general discussions with African officials. The United States should also contribute use of its unique satellite capabilities to help set up climate research and early-warning systems for drought. It should also support mass communications efforts to educate farmers on cost-effective ways to safeguard their natural resource base.

There are no panaceas for restoring the natural resource base in Africa. The best way to get better results than in the past will be seriously to rethink approaches, to recruit staff combining social and environmental expertise, and to involve local peoples and institutions in essentially local activities.

American private voluntary organizations have a special role to play at the village level in Africa, by working directly with agricultural producers as individuals and in community groups. At the same time, American universities and the U.S. private sector can contribute meaningfully to this effort, by applying their talents in agricultural research and management and helping Africans make further progress themselves.

One effective international organization that can help with this effort is the International Fund for Agricultural Development (IFAD), a specialized multilateral bank to which the United States belongs and which has pioneered many approaches to helping the small farmer in the Third World. IFAD has helped the World Bank and other major groups recognize the value of working directly with small farmers: higher productivity, better repayment records, and greater social impact than can be expected from programs that deal exclusively with large-scale agriculture. The United States should work to assure funds so that IFAD can continue and greatly expand its role in African agriculture.

Turning to human resources, it is clear that progress in African development requires far more trained managers and decision makers. Training in administration should be part of the professional preparation of Africans in a wide variety of disciplines. At the same time, the relationship of human resource development and agricultural production in Africa must be a special concern.

6. In cooperation with African governments that are moving to increase productivity, the United States should launch a major and sustained campaign in research and training to create the human and technical building blocks needed for a "Green Revolution" in Africa.

Most African countries lack the in-country research capabilities that are necessary for any breakthrough in agriculture comparable to the ones realized by India during the early 1970s. They also lack productive agricultural training facilities to keep a stream of talent going into research, extension services and agricultural management.

Although women account for 70 per cent of the food production in Africa, to date, research has largely neglected the food crops most commonly grown by African women—tubers, sorghum, and millet, which provide the staple diet for more than half of Africa's people—and it has failed to develop technologies for simplifying food processing. Indeed, the United States, other Western donors, and the World Bank have invested only meager amounts of money in education and training for agriculture.

It may take twenty-five years to see sustained results in this area, but the investment would be worthwhile. What is required is a long-term partnership in which African and American institutions work together, for example, to apply the new lessons of biological, genetic research. U.S. institutions must be willing to provide incentives to encourage good researchers to make time commitments for Africa's needs. African governments also will have to be willing to make commitments to research efforts that may take many years to pay off. In some smaller countries, it may be necessary to sacrifice national prestige and rely upon regional research centers.

7. The United States should work with the International Planned Parenthood Federation and the United Nations Fund for Population Activities to institute major population programs in each African country that has a bilateral U.S. aid program.

African states, fearing that the continent's population, according to some projections, could approach 1 billion by the year 2000, have come to recognize the problem—in some cases, belatedly—and have recently made clear that rapidly increasing population is now a priority concern. This has taken political courage in a setting of great sensitivity. But leaders now recognize that Africa has a far better chance to feed itself at some point in the foreseeable future if it reduces its population growth rates.

At the same time, the United States, acting in response to domestic political considerations, has cut back its important support to the two organizations that have the best outreach in Africa and are in the best position to tailor population programs to particular economic, cultural, and social needs. These cutbacks must be reversed. New programs should be started, with these organizations and others established in the field working with country leaders. Otherwise, the prospects for an effective approach to one of Africa's most serious problems will be imperiled.

A related concern is the health of Africa's people. Here there is room for optimism. A decade ago, the World Health Organization succeeded in eliminating smallpox not just in Africa, but in the entire world. Very low-cost changes in health care being promoted by UNICEF could save millions of infants and young children.

Vaccination, if universal in Africa, would also make a vast difference. Inoculating an African child against measles, diphtheria, whooping cough, tetanus, tuberculosis, and polio would cost only $1.20 per child (exclusive of salaries and transport for medical personnel who would administer the programs). All of Africa's children could thus be vaccinated and millions of young lives saved at a cost of $120 million for vaccine.

New medical discoveries will soon make it possible to vaccinate against the deadliest forms of malaria. Additional health breakthroughs also should be fostered. The United States should pool the medical knowledge developed by its private and public sectors that is of special relevance to Africa and make it available at little or no cost.

American firms doing research on vaccines and treatment methods often come across findings that would be of use to Africa, but they do not develop them because Africa is deemed to be too poor a market. Similarly, federal agencies like the U.S. Public Health Service interpret their mandates narrowly and often fail to direct their efforts toward health problems that plague Africa. Greater public- and private-sector cooperation to help Africa in the health field would be useful and could make an enormous difference. For example, the Public Health Service could become a repository of health knowledge of relevance to Africa developed in the private sector and a focal point for scientific cooperation. The United Nations has had success with simply packaged health innovations, and there is no reason why the United States cannot do the same.

For Africans, health breakthroughs may come faster than population breakthroughs. But health programs can support population policies by providing family planning services within health programs, as well as by actively promoting maternal and child health care, thereby increasing confidence of parents that more of their children will survive.

An improvement in African health services would not only alleviate the miserable lives that so many people on the continent endure, but would also contribute to solving several other problems. It would, for example, bring the welfare of rural areas more into line with that of the cities. Progress on Africa's main health problems could bring major opportunities. Vast areas of cultivable land would open up that remain unsettled because of severe health problems. Assuring clean water supplies can reduce debilitating chronic diseases and thereby increase labor productivity.

But technology alone will not do the job. In many countries, it will be necessary to reorient health-service delivery to reach the majority rather than just urban elites.

8. *The United States should help Africa unleash the creativity of its own private sector through technical help, improved procurement practices, and trade reforms.*

From rural marketplaces to businesses that are national in scope, Africans demonstrate their interest and ability in private enterprise. Now their governments must create conditions that will give internal and external parties confidence that they can invest and trade with the knowledge that payments will be made, agreements will be honored, and legal mechanisms will be available to enforce contracts if necessary. U.S. technical assistance could be helpful in proposing reforms that reflect the realities of the marketplace.

The United States and other donors can also stimulate local private markets by making a special effort to buy local goods and services in carrying out aid programs.

Americans can help to foster trade on the buying side. The United States should review the trade barriers that affect African products, with a view toward lowering them. Admittedly, some particularly sensitive areas are involved, but they warrant exploration. African states tend not to be strong enough politically or well enough organized to request tariff relief from the U.S. government, but this is a field in which the Executive Branch could take initiatives that would have a real impact on African economies.

Trade cooperation within Africa is also desirable. African governments should be encouraged to take advantage of every opening for regional cooperation. Such fundamental areas as easing the convertibility of currencies and lowering trade barriers offer opportunities. The United States cannot get out in front of Africans on these matters, but it should be ready to reinforce whatever progress is made through technical help and political support of regional linkages.

9. *The United States should make a full contribution of $1.33 billion a year over the next three years to the eighth replenishment of the International Development Association (IDA), the "soft loan" window of the World Bank, to assure more adequate long-term multilateral finance for African development.*

Assured World Bank finance for Africa is a critical part of any reasonable approach to Africa's future growth. The Bank is in the lead in discussions concerning strategy and donor coordination, two topics of pervasive relevance to future development. IDA, the part of the World Bank intended to help the poorest countries through long-term concessional loans, requires new funding, and discussions are under way for its eighth three-year replenishment. For the sixth replenishment, the agreed level was $12 billion. The Bank asked for $16 billion for the seventh replenishment, but the United States insisted that the level be $9 billion. It was this inadequate funding that forced the Bank to organize a special program for Africa (see Recommendation 4) to meet current needs. For the next replenishment, a level of $16 billion would be in order, of which 25 per cent would go to Africa. The U.S. share would be about $1.33 billion annually for the next three years. This kind of contribution would create helpful leverage to obtain three times this amount from many other countries and would underline the leading role of the World Bank in the reforms and growth strategies necessary for Africa's future development.

10. *Congress should amalgamate security and development aid for Africa into a single account clearly designated for development purposes in order to demonstrate that our assistance is geared to African development performance.*

Currently, half of U.S. economic aid for Africa comes from Development Assistance funds, which are allocated on the basis of need and tests of economic, social, technical, environmental, and financial feasibility. The other half is in the form of Economic Support Fund activities, formerly known as Security Assistance; this money is allocated more along political lines—in effect as a reward for a country's friendship with the United States. Whereas the first category invokes a rigorous test of development performance, the second can be used more loosely, to finance struggling nations' balance of payments and other kinds of non-project needs that are vital during this period of African rehabilitation. One problem is that economic support funds can be redirected to other parts of the world to meet short-term political needs; thus African countries cannot always count on getting the money they were expecting.

With some African countries getting half of their U.S. aid from each of these programs, it is often unclear whether the central goal of U.S. assistance is development performance or whether it is political support regardless of development needs and performance. It would be useful to clarify this issue by creating a combined fund for Africa to be administered for development purposes. The creation of such a fund, while denying some flexibility to the State Department, would stress the point that the security problems in Africa that overshadow all others are problems of *economic* security.

This step would protect against raids on money designated for Africa, provide the flexibility to meet rehabilitation needs now and development needs later, and reinforce those who wish to operate American assistance programs on more professional and less political lines. For Africa, it would be a clear signal that the real condition for American aid is development performance. Programs that are based on political attachments would not be ruled out, but the recipients would know that something more than rhetoric or a U.N. vote is expected in return.

IV. FINANCIAL AND POLITICAL IMPLICATIONS

The bulk of Africa's development inevitably will be paid for by Africans through improved productivity and through the development of their own resources. But the program presented in this report has clear financial implications for donors, particularly for the United States. The cost to the United States of the steps we recommend would be some $2 billion a year over and above the $1 billion of official U.S. funds already devoted to Africa's long-term development. In addition, there are significant opportunities for the American private sector, including the non-profit sector, to contribute to Africa's long-term development.

The threefold increase of support recommended for the public sector may seem large, but it adds up to approximately $7.50 per African—or less than 1 per cent of the per-capita aid level that the United States currently extends to a single country, Israel, which receives $1000 for every one of its citizens, and just over 12 per cent of the current aid to Egypt, which receives $60 per capita.

Not all of this increase need come from new money. Reallocations within the current $15-billion aid program are possible, and use of past foreign aid loan repayments should be mandated.

11. *Repayments from past U.S. foreign aid loans should be used to help finance new initiatives for Africa.*

Added stability of funding for African development could be obtained by channeling repayments from past aid loans directly to the African development account rather than to the Treasury, as in current practice. Until about a decade ago, repayments from past foreign aid were earmarked for new aid programs. Under the arrangement proposed here, Congress would have to compensate Treasury for the payments, but funding for African development would gain in stability. The amount of such repayments from 11 economic programs is about $500 million per year and rising.

A major benefit of this recommendation is that it would permit the United States to demonstrate to Africans that it seriously contemplates a long-term commitment of funding for African reform and development.

12. The United States should triple the long-term U.S. finance going to Africa, through a combination of bilateral and multilateral programs, to reach a new level of $3 billion per year.

Commitment to establish larger and firmer aid programs for Africa also should be sought from other major donors. In this regard, it should be noted that the European states, in their recent Lomé III agreement with African, Pacific, and Caribbean nations, entered into a five-year commitment on aid, trade, and commodity prices, but without increasing aid levels. There is a great deal more that Europeans can do to provide additional support for African development. Japan has pledged to increase its total foreign aid to $40 billion over the next seven years. As part of a shift of its aid to more developmental purposes, Japan should significantly increase its aid program to Africa. While U.S. support along the lines suggested in this report will be essential to help Africa, it should be part of a program of help in which other major industrial countries do their share, too.

At the same time, the compact proposed here will require a willingness on the part of African countries to institute the kinds of changes that they have already agreed—among themselves and with donors—are necessary. African leaders must recognize that failure to follow agreed-upon policies will undermine, and perhaps make impossible, a significant and coordinated program of long-term assistance.

CONCLUSION

In calling for the Compact, we are suggesting that substantial new funds—some $3 billion per year, a tripling of the current level—be committed to long-term development in Africa. This will be seen as a difficult, if not impossible, feat for the United States at a time of budget stringency. It would be easier to settle for the current program of assistance, which is limited in scope and effect, whose sale to Congress and to the American public already presents a great challenge. But such is the magnitude of Africa's crisis that a much more ambitious and imaginative effort must be mounted. The problems facing Africa will only become more expensive later if they are not realistically addressed soon. It is far easier to rescue economies from further decline than it is to rebuild them from scratch.

America has an opportunity to use publicly supported bilateral and multilateral programs, together with its universities, foundations, corporations, and private voluntary organizations, to help Africa in a coherent, lasting way. We urge private groups to marshal their own resources and to advocate a greater public response. We urge Congress and the Executive Branch to act with forsight to express our country's long-term interests in an Africa that can both survive short-term crises and assume its place as a full participant in the world economy.

COMMENTS BY COMMITTEE MEMBERS

ELLIOT BERG:

The report properly stresses the desperate economic circumstances prevailing in much of Africa, but it paints an excessively bleak picture.

The report does not take adequate account of the fact that policy reform has been a major feature of donor policy for three years at least.

Africa needs plenty of aid money, especially in the next few years, but the report should say more about what it is to be used for. Food-for-work programs cannot absorb much. Agriculture can, but mostly in big dam projects, some of which are of dubious priority. Americans should be willing to spend more money on African aid, but they will want some indication that it will be spent productively, and not repeat the errors of past aid flows.

The report is far too negative about IMF stabilization programs, many of which have positive supply-side effects.

The report contrasts too sharply the "development" impacts of Development Assistance versus the Economic Support Fund. The argument that the aid relationship should be non-political is unrealistic, and if adopted would be counterproductive. Development performance should be one condition, but if it is to be given heavy weight, then why any aid to most African countries? The consequence would not only be a reallocation within the region, but probably less aid to Africa as well.

ROBERT S. BROWNE:

Recommendation 3: The implications of Africa's external debt, both for itself and for its creditors, are currently being examined in various fora. There are, however, clear indications that—even under the most optimistic of assumptions—the economies of several of the African countries may never be able to retire their international debt, and that the consequences of being obliged to attempt to do so may merely destroy these societies without reimbursing the creditors. Some European countries have already chosen to forgive a portion of their African debt, and the United States may well find it in its interest to follow suit. In any case, recommendation 3, by failing to recognize that non-payment is a possible option, is overly restrictive and could prove to be highly unrealistic as well. (Goler T. Butcher and Donald B. Easum wish to be associated with this comment.)

Recommendation 8: The thrust of the recommendation is commendable. Inasmuch as this is the only recommendation that mentions trade, however, it seems the appropriate place for a clear expression of disapproval of protectionism. The text that accompanies the recommendation is entirely too weak and implicitly accedes to a continuation of trade barriers in the very areas of major interest to some African countries. (Goler T. Butcher wishes to be associated with this comment.)

Recommendation 9: Although I vigorously support recommendation 9, I feel that Africa's regional development bank, The African Development Bank/African Development Fund (ADB/ADF), merits an equal measure of attention and support for its important work. The ADB/ADF is currently operating a $1-billion annual development program that is highly appreciated on the continent. Its work deserves to be better known in the donor community. Recommendation 9 should be amended to call for substantially enhanced funding for the forthcoming ADF replenishment. (Goler T. Butcher wishes to be associated with this comment.)

GOLER T. BUTCHER:

Recommendation 5: Regarding this recommendation, I believe that all aided projects in the agricultural sector should be oriented to help small farmers, particularly women.

FRANK C. CARLUCCI:

I agree with the need for substantially increased resources but believe that the precise amount can only be determined by more detailed analysis, including weighing African imperatives against other national priorities—a task which was obviously beyond the scope and capacity of the Committee.

SENATOR JOHN C. DANFORTH:

Recommendation 7: Although this recommendation does not imply support for abortion programs, I wish to be unambiguously clear that I could not support any association of U.S. funding for such activities in Africa or elsewhere.

CAROL LANCASTER:

It may be difficult for the United States to provide decisive support for African development alone. The U.S should actively explore ways to involve other donors as the Compact for African Development evolves.

NOTE

1. The Committee has not addressed the extremely complex questions involved in South Africa in this report. In its first twenty-five years of independence, Africa has been concerned with decolonization and development. Decolonization is all but complete, except in Namibia.

In South Africa, the internal disparities dictated by *apartheid*, the rigid and abhorrent system of racial separation, and the likelihood of continuing unrest and upheaval threaten to undo economic progress for all races, guaranteeing political and social chaos.

Both Namibian independence and *apartheid* remain major concerns of African countries on their merits. These unresolved issues directly affect the economic development of the other countries of southern Africa that sometimes host South Africans opposed to *apartheid*. South Africa's continuing destabilization of its neighbors and the presence of large refugee populations have led to a diversion of resources and to some destruction of already meager infrastructure.

Notes on Contributors

ROBERT J. BERG is co-director, Committee on African Development Strategies, and Senior Fellow, Overseas Development Council.

DAVID COURT is Regional Representative, The Rockefeller Foundation, Nairobi.

CARL K. EICHER is Professor of Argicultural Economics, Michigan State University.

JANE I. GUYER is Associate Professor of Anthropology, Harvard University.

BENJAMIN H. HARDY is Vice President, Equator Holdings Limited.

CHANDRA S. HARDY is Senior Economist, Eastern and Southern Africa Programs, The World Bank.

A.M. HAWKINS is Dean of the Faculty of Commerce and Law, University of Zimbabwe.

NILES E. HELMBOLDT is President and Chief Executive Officer, Equator Holdings Limited.

GORAN HYDEN is Visiting Fellow, Department of Government, Dartmouth College.

BRUCE F. JOHNSTON is Professor of Agricultural Economics, Food Research Institute, Stanford University.

KENNETH KING is Senior Fellow, Centre of African Studies, Edinburgh University.

KABIRU KINYANJUI is Director, Institute of Development Studies, Nairobi University.

DAVID K. LEONARD is Associate Professor of Public Administration, University of California, Berkeley.

STEPHEN R. LEWIS, JR., is Chairman, Department of Economics, Williams College.

CARL LIEDHOLM is Professor of Economics, Michigan State University.

DONALD C. MEAD is Professor of Agricultural Economics, Michigan State University.

BENNO J. NDULU is Professor of Economics, University of Dar es Salaam.

FRED T. SAI, M.D., is Senior Population Adviser, The World Bank.

DUNSTAN S.C. SPENCER is Principal Economist, International Crops Research Institute for the Semi-Arid Tropics, Sahelian Center, Niger.

LLOYD TIMBERLAKE is Editorial Director, Earthscan, International Institute for Environment and Development, London.

TINA WEST is consultant to Equator Holdings Limited.

JENNIFER SEYMOUR WHITAKER is co-director, Committee on African Development Strategies, and Senior Fellow, Council on Foreign Relations.

CRAWFORD YOUNG is Chairman, Department of Political Science, University of Wisconsin.

Index

Compositor:	The Seven Graphic Arts, New York
Printer:	Vail-Ballou Press
Binder:	Vail-Ballou Press
Display:	Palatino
Text:	10/13 Palatino